Selected Writings

New Riverside Editions—American Literature

General Editor for the American Volumes
Paul Lauter

CHARLES W. CHESNUTT, *Selected Writings*
Edited by SallyAnn H. Ferguson

STEPHEN CRANE, *The Red Badge of Courage, Maggie: A Girl of the Streets, and Other Selected Writings*
Edited by Phyllis Frus and Stanley Corkin

RALPH WALDO EMERSON and MARGARET FULLER, *Selected Works*
Edited by John Carlos Rowe

OLAUDAH EQUIANO, MARY ROWLANDSON, AND OTHERS, *American Captivity Narratives*
Edited by Gordon M. Sayre

NATHANIEL HAWTHORNE, *The Scarlet Letter*
Edited by Rita K. Gollin

HENRY JAMES, *The Portrait of a Lady*
Edited by Jan Cohn

HENRY DAVID THOREAU, *Walden and Civil Disobedience*
Edited by Paul Lauter

MARK TWAIN, *Adventures of Huckleberry Finn*
Edited by Susan K. Harris

EDITH WHARTON, *The Age of Innocence*
Edited by Carol J. Singley

New Riverside Editions—British Literature

General Editor for the British Volumes
Alan Richardson

JANE AUSTEN, *Sense and Sensibility*
Edited by Beth Lau

EMILY BRONTE, *Wuthering Heights*
Edited by Diane Long Hoeveler

Three Oriental Tales: FRANCES SHERIDAN, *Nourjahad;* WILLIAM BECKFORD, *Vathek;* LORD BYRON, *The Giaour*
Edited by Alan Richardson

WILLIAM WORDSWORTH and SAMUEL TAYLOR COLERIDGE, *Lyrical Ballads*
Edited by William Richey and Daniel Robinson

NEW RIVERSIDE EDITIONS

General Editor for the American Volumes
Paul Lauter, Trinity College

Charles W. Chesnutt
Selected Writings

Complete Texts with Introduction
Historical Contexts • Critical Essays

edited by

SallyAnn H. Ferguson
The University of North Carolina at Greensboro

HOUGHTON MIFFLIN COMPANY
Boston • New York

For Jimmy, James Alvin, Justin, and John

Senior Sponsoring Editor: Suzanne Phelps Weir
Sponsoring Editor: Michael Gillespie
Development Editor: Janet Young
Editorial Associate: Bruce Cantley
Associate Project Editor: Elisabeth Kehrer
Associate Production/Design Coordinator: Lisa Jelly
Senior Cover Design Coordinator: Deborah Azerrad Savona
Manufacturing Manager: Florence Cadran
Senior Marketing Manager: Nancy Lyman

Cover Photo: Hulton Getty

Printed in the U.S.A.

Library of Congress Catalog Number: 00-110416

ISBN: 0-618-10733-9

23456789-QF-09 08 07

As part of Houghton Mifflin's ongoing commitment to the environment, this text has been printed on recycled paper.

Contents

Part Three: SELECTED CRITICAL PERSPECTIVES   341

About This Series

Paul Lauter

The Riverside name dates back well over a century. Readers of this book may have seen—indeed, may own—Riverside Editions of works by the best-known nineteenth-century American writers, such as Emerson, Thoreau, Lowell, Longfellow, and Hawthorne. Houghton Mifflin and its predecessor, Ticknor & Fields, were the primary publishers of the New England authors who constituted much of the undisputed canon of American literature until well into the twentieth century. The Riverside Editions of works by these writers, and of some later writers such as Amy Lowell, became benchmarks for distinguished and useful editions of standard American authors for home, library, and classroom.

In the 1950s and 1960s, the Riverside name was used for another series of texts, primarily for the college classroom, of well-known American and British literary works. These paperback volumes, edited by distinguished critics of that generation, were among the most widely used and appreciated of their day. They provided carefully edited texts in a handsome and readable format, with insightful critical introductions. They were books one kept beyond the exam, the class, or even the college experience.

In the last quarter century, however, ideas about the American literary canon have changed. Many scholars want to see a canon that reflects a broader American heritage, including significant literary works by previously marginalized writers, many of them women or men of color. These changes began to be institutionalized in curricula as well as in textbooks such as *The Heath Anthology of American Literature,* which Houghton Mifflin started publishing in 1998. The older Riverside series, excellent in its day, ran the risk of appearing outdated; the editors were long retired or deceased, and the authors were viewed by some as too exclusive.

Yet the name Riverside and the ideas behind it continued to have appeal. The name stood for distinction and worth in the publication of

America's literary heritage. Houghton Mifflin's New Riverside Series, initiated in the year 2000, is designed to uphold the Riverside reputation for excellence while offering a more inclusive range of authors. The Series also provides today's reader with books that contain, in addition to notable literary works, introductions by influential critics, as well as a variety of stimulating materials that bring alive the debates, the conversations, and the social and cultural movements within which America's literary classics were formed.

Thus emerged the book you have in hand. Each volume of the New Riverside Editions will contain the basic elements that we think today's readers find interesting and useful: important literary works by significant authors, incisive introductions, and a variety of contextual materials to make the literary text fully engaging. These books will be useful in many kinds of classrooms, but they are also designed to offer the casual reader the enjoyment of a good read in a fresh and accessible format. Among the first group of New Riverside Editions are familiar titles, such as Henry David Thoreau's *Walden* and Mark Twain's *Adventures of Huckleberry Finn*. There are also works in fresh new combinations, such as the collection of early captivity narratives and the volume that pairs texts by Ralph Waldo Emerson and Margaret Fuller. And there are well-known works in distinctively interesting formats, such as the volume containing Edith Wharton's *The Age of Innocence* and the volume of writings by Stephen Crane. Future books will include classics as well as works drawing renewed attention.

The New Riverside Editions will provide discriminating readers with a wide range of important literary works, contextual materials that vividly illuminate those works, and the best of recent critical commentary and analysis. And because we have not confined our editors to a single monotonous format, we think our readers will find that each volume in this new series has a character appropriate to the literary work it presents.

We expect the New Riverside Editions to bring to the twenty-first century the same literary publishing distinction of its nineteenth- and twentieth-century predecessors.

Introduction

CHARLES W. CHESNUTT:
AN AMERICAN SIGNIFIER

SallyAnn H. Ferguson

To understand the African-American literary tradition, one must re- member its paradoxical beginnings within a morally conflicted, racist society and its development in a modern world still trying at once to retain and eliminate a steadily diminishing white privilege based on black dis- crimination institutionalized during America's slavery regime. African- American literature remains entwined with, yet distinct from, a mainstream Euro-American culture that enjoyed grand success and horrific failure in reaching for a variety of high-minded economic, religious, social, political, and moral dreams. When America's democratic slavocracy eventually pro- duced late-nineteenth- and early-twentieth-century short story writer, bi- ographer, novelist, essayist, stenographer, and lawyer Charles Waddell Chesnutt, he—like writers of every American generation—inherited the deep penalties as well as the rewards of the forefathers.

Early in Chesnutt's career, this legacy produced a moralist determined to write for a "high, holy purpose" (*Journals* 21, in this volume) that os- tensibly would convert white bigots and elevate socially, politically, and financially oppressed blacks without "a fierce indiscriminate onslaught" on the country's racist garrison. He would pursue this goal clandestinely, by literary means, and mainly by what might be called genetic theorizing.[1]

---

[1] All quotations are drawn from Richard H. Brodhead, ed., *The Journals of Charles W. Chesnutt*. Page references in text are to selections included in this volume. Chesnutt's

Charles Waddell Chesnutt at age seventy.

At the same time he hoped, indeed expected, to become a self-made man in the obsessively materialistic society of postbellum, "gilded age" America. Throughout his lifetime, Chesnutt never strayed far from these basic literary and personal principles, trying to rationalize their inherent contradictions through an African-American realism he often veiled in Euro-American romanticism.

Born in Cleveland, Ohio, on June 20, 1858, brought up in Fayetteville, North Carolina, Euro-American in physical appearance but raised within

---

controversial theory of racial amalgamation is definitively developed in his three-article "Future American" series, the first of which is included in this volume.

an extended black community, Chesnutt developed his most prominent psychological feature, an African-American double consciousness.[2] Its internal divisions and contradictions made him perhaps the best African-American literary signifier of his day as well as an author with powerfully ambivalent relationships to his audience and himself. In this role, he was also a precursor to such later literary tricksters as Ralph Ellison, whose "heroic intellectualism"[3] in *Invisible Man* (1952) and other writings also champions nonviolent (to some, passive), judicious (to some, cowardly) blacks seeking to prosper materially without preying on their fellow human beings in a predatory, racialized society. But while periodically "passing" across racial lines to seek both stenographic business and intellectual diversity from white bigots, Chesnutt encountered enough racist affronts to render inadequate the little psychological games won over white folks in the pages of books and magazines—the terrain of his work. He required, indeed, an elusive program that both responded to and challenged the institutionalized racism characteristic of the historic moment. In time, his texts as well as his withdrawal from an active literary career came to anticipate works that specifically capture the angst, frustration, and emotional paralysis of the middle-class African-American male.[4]

Yet Chesnutt clearly reveals in many of his writings a profound dismay, outrage, and even desperation about white prejudice against anyone having one drop of black blood during a period characterized by historian

---

[2] In *The Souls of Black Folk* (1903), W. E. B. DuBois defines double consciousness as a "sense of always looking at one's self through the eyes of others. . . . [: T]his twoness, —an American, a Negro; two souls, two thoughts, two unreconciled strivings; two warring ideals in one dark body, whose dogged strength alone keeps it from being torn asunder" (16–17).

[3] For an examination of the strengths and weaknesses of this technique, see Watts.

[4] In a March 7, 1882, journal entry, an upwardly mobile Chesnutt drops his accommodationist mask and confides: "I hear colored men speak of their 'white friends.' I have no white friends. I could not degrade the sacred name of 'Friendship' by associating it with any man who feels himself too good to sit at table with me, or sleep at the same hotel. True friendship can only exist between . . . equals in something . . . and where there is respect as well as admiration" (*Journals* 172). Ironically, in writings such as "A Multitude of Counselors," Chesnutt unwittingly reveals his own class prejudice even as he decries the nationwide racism all blacks face, while accentuating "the strength and extent of which *none but cultivated, self-respecting colored people* [my emphasis] can rightly apprehend" (4). Some postintegration examinations of a similar black middle-class dissatisfaction and ambivalence have come from journalist Ellis Cose, novelist Jake Lamar, sociologist Orlando Patterson, and the special issue of the *Nation* entitled "Whatever Happened to Integration?"

Rayford Logan as the "nadir" of American racial relations.[5] In "The Disfranchisement of the Negro," he declares: "What colored men of the South can do to secure their citizenship today, or in the immediate future, is not very clear. Their utterances on political questions, unless they be to concede away the political rights of their race, or to soothe the consciences of white men by suggesting that the problem is insoluble except by some slow remedial process . . . are received with scant respect . . . and must be cautiously made, lest they meet an actively hostile reception" (119).[6] Accommodating rather than directly confronting this world, Chesnutt never became a civil rights activist, intellectual, or "race" man equal to such contemporaries as Frederick Douglass and W. E. B. DuBois, James Weldon Johnson, and Walter White of the NAACP.[7] Because he also regards black-skinned people as the "only hard problem in connection with the future American race,"[8] Chesnutt concedes instead that white racism is too intractable to be conquered realistically by his passive strategies. As a result, he qualifies his literary campaign and almost exclusively focuses on the concerns of color-line blacks—those like himself who culturally and, more importantly, genetically could straddle America's racial divide.[9] Chesnutt

---

[5] See Logan, *The Betrayal of the Negro: From Rutherford B. Hayes to Woodrow Wilson,* originally published as *The Negro in American Life and Thought: The Nadir, 1877–1901.*

[6] Chesnutt expresses similar sentiments in "Peonage, or the New Slavery."

[7] Earlier in their careers, novelist/civil rights activist George Washington Cable tried to get Chesnutt to serve as secretary to the Open Letter Club, but Chesnutt refused, claiming the club did not pay enough to support his family. He also refused to support Albion Tourgée's "National Citizen" civil rights magazine project, which he thought white people would not read and which would, therefore, be a poor financial investment. See Helen Chesnutt 43–47, 71–72.

[8] "The Future American," 50 in this volume. He repeats these views in such writings as "Obliterating the Color Line" (4). See my extended discussion of this subject in "Genuine Blacks and Future Americans," reprinted in this volume.

[9] On July 3, 1928 (just four years before his death), Chesnutt accepted the Spingarn Medal from the NAACP and remarked that "My physical makeup was such that I knew the psychology of mixed blood in so far as it differed from that of other people, and most of my writings ran along the color line. . . . This was perfectly natural and I have no apologies to make for it" (98 in this volume). Although she tried to edit out unflattering sides to her father in her biography, his daughter Helen nonetheless chooses a title that shows a clear understanding of Chesnutt's main literary focus. In fact, most claims that Chesnutt crusaded equally for blacks of all colors come from others. Joseph R. McElrath, Jr., for example, labels as "anguished" scholars who refuse to ignore Chesnutt's ambivalent treatment of dark-skinned blacks and, like Charles Duncan in *The Absent Man: The Narrative Craft of Charles W. Chesnutt,* attempts to portray the writer as an equal opportunity mocker (20–21). Such critics simply ignore the fallacy central to this

steers a literary course that gives him and his white-looking compatriots a chance, albeit a discriminatory one, at achieving the American economic and social dream. Indeed, his stories are full of slaves, tricksters, conjurers, African Americans who can—and sometimes do—pass for white, but hardly ever an ordinary, turn-of-the-century, free, dark-skinned human being.

In *Deep Down in the Jungle* (1964), folklorist Roger D. Abrahams's definition of signifying overemphasizes the juvenile character of this activity, but its varieties of indirection and masking comport well with Chesnutt's method for a literary "mining" of America's racist garrison:

> The term "signifying" seems to be characteristically Negro in use if not in origin. It can mean any of a number of things; in the case of . . . [a] toast, it certainly refers to the monkey's ability to talk with great innuendo, to carp, cajole, needle and lie. It can mean in other instances the propensity to talk around a subject, never quite coming to the point. It can mean "making fun" of a person or situation. Also it can denote speaking with hands and eyes, and in this respect encompasses a whole complex of expressions and gestures. Thus it is "signifying" to stir up a fight between neighbors by telling stories; it is signifying to make fun of the police by parodying his motions behind his back; it is signifying to ask for a piece of cake by saying, "My brother needs a piece of that cake" (54).[10]

Like the speaker in the poem "We Wear the Mask," written by contemporary Paul Laurence Dunbar, Chesnutt also grins and lies throughout his canon, knowing whites believed too deeply in their stereotypes of blacks—those testaments to their ignorance of and distance from African-American reality—to recognize his truth until he, like his character Uncle Julius, had successfully accomplished some coup.[11] He also knew that

---

writer's either/or literary theory and method—that generally brands whites as immoral and needing Chesnutt to write them into goodness and, concomitantly, presumes blacks are America's archetypal suffering servants. These critics also ignore the complex intraracial empathy and bias between Chesnutt's blue-veined world and the darker-skinned masses. Above all, attempts to define Chesnutt's specific brand of racial realism by redefining African-American culture as monolithic—with Chesnutt, as McElrath predicts, "standing within and speaking for *the* [my emphasis] African American community" (21) rather than for that part of it the author knows best—only distracts from Chesnutt's often frightening vision of a morally ambivalent and violent United States.

[10] See also a more complex, full-length study of African-American "signifyin (g)" in Gates.

[11] Chesnutt's conjure stories and the color-line short stories "The Passing of Grandison" and "Baxter's Procrustes"—all included in this volume—especially exemplify the degree to which powerless African Americans traditionally found signifying to be their primary, if not their only, physical and intellectual self-defense. Perhaps a measure of the whites'

blacks, desperate to have their stories told by one of their own, would be less critical of ambivalent and even skewed portrayals of themselves.

But while Dunbar employs the ironic candor of a narrator who, precisely because he knows whites will not believe him, daringly admits to masking and just as quickly declares the immorality and necessity of doing so ("This debt we pay to human guile" [167]), Chesnutt augments Dunbar's strategy with the Euro-American religious ideal of blood sacrifice, which grants salvation to sinful people through the crucifixion of Jesus Christ.[12] Assuming his "high, holy [artistic] purpose," Chesnutt makes whites the "object[s] of my writing," and "not so much for the elevation of the colored people as the elevation of the whites" (*Journals* 21). In so doing, he dons a disguise of morality that relies on Christian theology more to redeem than actually to convert immoral whites. White deliverance comes not through their willingness to confess and stop their mean behavior but—as Ralph Ellison eloquently explains in "Change the Joke and Slip the Yoke"—"at the expense of American folklore['s] . . . negative sign[s]." These "negative signs" are archetypal black scapegoats whom, ironically enough, the white both ridicules and fears.[13] In fact, Chesnutt's plots and the morality they underwrite come to depend on whites' possessing "the unjust spirit of caste which is so insidious as to pervade a whole nation, and so powerful as to subject a whole race and all connected

---

knowledge and rejection of this signifying is their development and institutionalization of the stereotype of African-American intellectual inferiority.

[12] See Ferguson, "Christian Violence and the Slave Narrative," where I discuss how slave narrators coped with the concept of white salvation through their sacrifice. Chesnutt certainly was familiar with the power of Christianity to justify evil, having based his Beacon biography *Frederick Douglass* on narratives in which Douglass distinguishes between "the pure, peaceable, and impartial Christianity of Christ" and "the corrupt, slaveholding, women-whipping, cradle-plundering, partial and hypocritical Christianity of this land." Douglass adds, "We have men-stealers for ministers, women-whippers for missionaries, and cradle-plunderers for church members. The man who wields the blood-clotted cowskin during the week fills the pulpit on Sunday, and claims to be a minister of the meek and lowly Jesus. The man who robs me of my earnings at the end of each week meets me as a class-leader on Sunday morning, to show me the way of life and the path of salvation. He who sells my sister, for the purposes of prostitution, stands forth as the pious advocate of purity. He who proclaims it a religious duty to read the Bible denies me the right of learning to read the name of the God who made me" (120–21).

[13] Ellison 45–59. Additionally, in her seminal essay on American literature, *Playing in the Dark: Whiteness and the Literary Imagination*, novelist Toni Morrison notes that romantic forms have traditionally enabled the American writer to explore "understandably human fears" and that "this black population was available for meditations on terror—the terror of European outcast, their dread of failure, powerlessness, Nature without limits, natal loneliness, internal aggression, evil, sin, greed" (37–38).

with it to scorn and ostracism" (*Journals* 21). In much of his fiction, this author repeatedly exploits the Christian promise to save devils at the expense of angels and creates dark-skinned, Jesus-like innocents who lead, or at least try to lead, reprobate whites to truth and goodness.

In the novel *The House Behind the Cedars* (1900), this theme means that Chesnutt prevents romance and marriage between two blacks—Rena, who could pass for white, and her devoted but dark-skinned friend Frank Fowler—and even arranges her death when she rejects a presumably redeemed white racist suitor named George Tryon. In the short story "Dave's Neckliss," the cruel slavemaster Mars Dugal comes to regret that he wrongly accused and punished Dave after this slave commits suicide by stringing himself up and literally "curing" his sinless self like a smoked ham. In *The Marrow of Tradition* (1901), whites murder Josh Green for heroically but futilely defending his black community, kill the black Millers' child, and burn down his hospital—all leading to the hope that the white Carterets' young sickly son will survive and embrace more humane values. In "The Sheriff's Children," a white father regrets his parental negligence when his rejected mulatto son conveniently kills himself. Chesnutt less dramatically sacrifices darker- for lighter-skinned blacks in "A Matter of Principle," in which his elaborate, protest-too-much ridicule of the racist Claytons simply does not justify the wrong perpetrated in these characters' elaborate scheme to prevent their white-looking daughter from meeting the unsuspecting Senator H. M. Brown because his last name describes his skin color. In "The Wife of His Youth," considered Chesnutt's best short story during his day, his mostly white readers are reassured about black family survival after slavery because a successful mulatto "husband" sacrifices his own happiness by rejecting what Chesnutt calls a "much more fitting ['young, educated, attractive'] mate for him"[14] to embrace his unnamed, postmenopausal, coal-black, unloved but forever loyal and loving ex-slave "wife."

The consistency of such plot lines suggests that Chesnutt's ultimate "holy" literary goal was not to destroy the materialistic world the whites had wrought by first trafficking in human flesh and then creating separate and altogether unequal social and economic institutions. Rather, his primary objective remained to open that world to as many people light-skinned enough to survive within it. While many scholars and critics assume Chesnutt writes primarily to prevent the American mainstream from further mistreating their traditional black prey, the author, in fact, remains

---

[14] See Max Bennett Thrasher's "Mr. Chesnutt at Work: A Talk with an Author on His Methods," 343 in this volume.

theoretically consistent and *does not* overtly attack this racist stronghold. He thereby leaves in place white privilege maintained through dark-skinned subservience and subjugation but extends some of this power to color-line blacks.

Indeed, a great deal of Chesnutt's work promotes his futuristic vision of a nonthreatening, miscegenated American citizen who, as his first "Future American" essay states, will look "predominantly white," call himself white, and be "moulded by the same culture and dominated by the same ideals" (49). Although writing into existence this new racial and cultural amalgam renders black humanity virtually invisible, Chesnutt's Christian mask—his vivid and compelling portraits of cruel whites and morally superior African-American victims—shields his bold argument from the criticism of both groups, with the former assuming he helps remove the moral stain of slavery and the latter assuming he helps deliver them from centuries-long white torment. In the final analysis, however, Chesnutt's literary exercise in Christian signifying largely obscures the hidden charges African-Americans pay for having this author tell black truth—the sacrifice of Renas, Franks, Daves, Josh Greens, unnamed sheriffs' children, and found slave "wives." While his branding whites as evil also exacts a price, they nevertheless inherit the American earth. Meanwhile, blacks become the author's unheralded symbols of mortal suffering whose rewards await them after death, just as the slavemasters and their beneficiaries always claimed. This stipulation in Chesnutt's race theory—that black skin color effectively disappear from the United States—produces intriguing paradoxes throughout his canon.[15]

Because Chesnutt himself best sets the historical context for his own writing, Part One of this *New Riverside Edition* includes generous selections from his journals and published and unpublished essays, which document the racial, literary, social, and economic milieu he inhabited. Journal excerpts show an idealistic, hardworking teenager and young man who virtually taught himself the mainstream culture in order to prepare for future recognition there. In an entry dated May 8, 1880, Professor Chesnutt of Howard School (now Fayetteville State University in Fayetteville, North Carolina) also demonstrates how he accommodated racist challenges to his ambition:

> On Friday before last, at night, I attended a Republican convention at the Market House, and like a fool accepted a nomination for town commissioner [a position once held by Chesnutt's father, Andrew], after once de-

---

[15] Socken was among the first to note this issue in Chesnutt's nonfiction. Harris, Webb, and Ferguson (1982, 1985) also examine these paradoxes.

clining. The next day my [white] friends remonstrated; Mr. [George] H[aigh] spoke of my indiscretion; and Capt. [J. D.] Williams, [E. P.] Powers, and several others contrived to put so "many fleas in my ear" that I sent in my formal withdrawal to the Ch'm'n of the committee, and backed off as gracefully as possible (135–36).

Chesnutt's essays especially suggest that after degrading incidents like these, he—as so many African Americans have and continue to do—often silently tried to regain his dignity and self-esteem by signifying before white or integrated audiences. This behavior remains in sharp contrast to his practice of communicating directly when inclined to do so. For instance, when Chesnutt delivered the paper entitled "Self-Made Men" on March 10, 1882, before the predominantly black Normal Literary Society in Fayetteville, he straightforwardly asserted that his listeners should follow the examples of Frederick Douglass and Horace Greeley to become American economic and social successes. He has a similar purpose to inform and inspire in later essays such as "The Negro in Cleveland," considered by some sociologists as the best study of this community for its time.

The speech "Some Requisites of a Law Reporter," however, read at the 1891 convention of the predominantly white Ohio Stenographers' Association, is an exercise in the indirect art of signifying—a satiric attempt to convince his audience to become linguists, lawyers, physicians, geologists, surveyors, civil engineers, and astronomers in order to be excellent stenographers. When he found himself unmasked by respondent H. K. Sauder, who recognized that it was impossible to master all these disciplines in one lifetime and called Chesnutt's performance "elaborate sarcasm," Chesnutt apparently assumed that the humor of his act would not be lost on the audience. But amidst the laughter, he gained the tacit satisfaction of outwitting Sauder and others who foolishly assumed that blacks see whites as whites see themselves and do not suspect that the author's hyperbole mocks the idea of merit in an America that requires blacks like himself to be overqualified for jobs secured by rather mediocre whites. As a young principal at the Howard School in Fayetteville, the author learned early to hide his pain and anger after having his ambition thwarted, but like the Brer Rabbits of his black ancestors, he did so only until he could play his own game later, from a safer briar patch.

Similarly, Chesnutt's first major and most popular fiction, the conjure stories of Part Two (the seven stories published in *The Conjure Woman* plus "Dave's Neckliss"), is dominated by the wily Uncle Julius, who was inspired by Joel Chandler Harris's Uncle Remus, a fictional storyteller of original folktales Harris gleaned from southern plantation slaves. Chesnutt's double narrative frame, however, enables him to tell a white and

black version of the same story, thus portraying realistically the white privilege and arrogance that both cause and result from African-American suffering in the throes of American slavery. In addition, Julius's signifying
tales and personal agendas greatly mature Harris's childlike, fairytale Remus, even as Julius himself does little to alter the racial balance of power
in his relationship with John, the white male narrator. Part Two also includes all the color-line stories from *The Wife of His Youth* (1899) as well
as "Baxter's Procrustes," a well-crafted tale of white intellectual disingen-
uousness among a book-buying club.[16] With their variety of themes, characters, and styles, all these stories serve to promote Chesnutt's controversial racial and literary theories, and they complement well his full-length
novels, nonfiction, letters, and poetry.

The critical essays in Part Three feature some of the most original
scholarship written on Chesnutt's work by critics who are courageous and
sophisticated enough to venture into this author's complex signifying
world and deal with it on its own terms. With few exceptions, such as the
"Charles Chesnutt's Cakewalk" chapter from Eric Sundquist's *To Wake
the Nations* (1993)—which imaginatively turns an African-American
dance into a metaphor for theorizing about Chesnutt's writing—this criticism was published during the 1970s and 1980s in academic journals
such as the *CLA Journal* and the *Southern Literary Journal*. Like Sundquist's analysis, Chesnutt's own texts and the culture that bred them form
the basis for this scholarship rather than largely irrelevant theories that
have been gratuitously imposed upon his unique experience.[17] The volume
concludes with recommendations for further Chesnutt study, including
websites.

To understand the works of Charles W. Chesnutt, readers should always remember that he was, above all, a realist who, as a sensible and creative young man, examined his racist democracy and determined that he
could achieve the American Dream of literary, personal, and financial success by following Franklinesque values of education and hard work and by

---

[16] Sylvia Lyons Render published Chesnutt's previously uncollected short writings in *The
Short Fiction of Charles W. Chesnutt*.

[17] An example of the latter approach, Susan Gillman's "Micheaux's Chesnutt," "speculates" that Oscar Micheaux's *Within Our Gates* (1919–20) is a film version of Chesnutt's
The Marrow of Tradition. Gillman makes the "coulda happened" argument that "*Even
without any evidence* [emphasis added] of a Micheaux-Chesnutt deal on *Marrow* [as is
the case overwhelmingly with the Micheaux/Chesnutt movie deal for *The House Behind
the Cedars*], Micheaux's *Gates* and Chesnutt's novel [as well as several others, for that
matter] make a remarkably resonant pair" (1,080).

avoiding America's "subtle almost indefinable feeling of repulsion toward the negro" (*Journals* 21). From his extensive reading of the slave narratives—in which narrators repeatedly damn hypocritical slave owners who used Christian violence to justify their regime—Chesnutt apparently discovered a literary mask that allowed him to manipulate—often in plain sight—myriad literary and cultural forms. Speaking to a targeted audience long accustomed to America's legacy of Christian hypocrisy and black suffering, he became a moralist—branding whites infidels and blacks, comparatively, saints—and set about surreptitiously to effect a partial remedy that would mainly allow white-looking blacks entry into "their midst before they [whites could] think" (*Journals* 21). To unmask this signifier, we must enter his specific African-American briar patch—the place where Chesnutt invites the Harriet Beecher Stowes, Joel Chandler Harrises, and Albion Tourgées to visit, but where he lives.

A Note on the Texts

Since most of the works included in this volume were previously published, there were no serious problems with the texts except for minor errors of spelling and punctuation that have been corrected. *The Conjure Woman* (1899) and *The Wife of His Youth and Other Stories of the Color Line* (1899) are reproduced from their original editions.

PART ONE

Historical, Social, and Literary Perspectives

Journal Entries

April 23 — 1879. . . . I wish just now, to remember the date of my interview with Professor Ladd (J. J.)[1] at the Fayetteville hotel last fall, but cannot. The conversation I remember well. It was like discharging the matter from an old sore. I had a sympathetic ear; a man of Northern birth and education. I told him of my acquirements and my aims, and he was astonished. I read a selection from Virgil, in order that he might criticise my Latin pronunciation. To my surprise and delight it was perfect, and my labor had not been in vain. He declared that he had never met a youth who, at my age and with my limited opportunities for instruction, had made such marked and rapid progress in learning. He encouraged me to continue my studies, and tendered me a job of reporting when I should have mastered Phonography. I read some of my poetical productions, and he admired them very much, declaring that I had poetical taste and talent. From that time I have worked with increased ardor, and with a greater confidence in my own powers.

But I do not place too high a value upon the Professor's opinions. I hope to pass examination at a bar of a higher tribunal, that of the public; but before that can take place there must come long years of hard work, and patient plodding. But I am not at all discouraged. A few weeks ago I sent a

---

Richard H. Brodhead, ed., *The Journals of Charles W. Chesnutt.*

[1] When the State Colored Normal School was founded at Fayetteville, the state government simultaneously created a normal school for the training of white teachers within the University of North Carolina. The Vermont-born John J. Ladd, a graduate of Brown University and formerly the superintendent of schools at Staunton, Virginia, became the chief instructor in this program—and an arbiter, therefore, of Chesnutt's achievements as they would have been measured had his race not excluded him from that school. [Richard Brodhead's note.]

The Howard School, Fayetteville, North Carolina (now Fayetteville State University), where Chesnutt served as principal and teacher from November 1880 to June 1883.

letter and some bits of verse to the Christian Union.[2] I have never heard from them, and as I requested the Editor to consign them to the waste-basket (which he would have done anyway) if they were not worth publishing, I presume he did so; but as they were puerile productions, and sent to a paper of high literary character they were not fit for it. The editor of our Gazette offered to publish them, but my object was not to see them in print, but to find out whether they were worth printing or not.

—I had the pleasure of a long conversation with Dr. Haigh, when he was waiting for the advent of my little Ethel into this "sinful world."[3] He thinks I can succeed in the North, for there are more opportunities, and less prejudice. What they want there is ability[,] and this qualification,

[2] A liberal Congregationalist journal edited by Lyman Abbott after the Civil War.
[3] Chesnutt's first child was born in late April 1879. He had married Susan Perry, a fellow teacher at the Howard School, on June 6, 1878. Dr. T. D. Haigh (1829–1908), a white physician and member of a prominent Fayetteville family, attended Chesnutt's wife during the delivery of Ethel. He served as chairman of the Board of Managers of the State Colored Normal School when Chesnutt was the school's principal. [Richard Brodhead's note.]

with energy and perseverance will carry a man through. I told him that my object was to obtain my proper standing in society, (and that to be judged according to my merit) and he only expressed the same belief that I have had for some time—that when a young man starts out in life with a purpose, and works *for* that purpose he is more than apt to accomplish it.

I will go to the Metropolis, or some other large city, and like Franklin[,] Greely and many others,[4] there will I stick. I will live somehow, but live I will, and work. I can get employment in some literary avocation, or something leading in that direction. I depend principally upon my knowledge of stenography, which I hope will enable me to secure a position on the staff of some good newspaper, and then—work, work, work! I will trust in God and work. I will test the social problem. I will see if it's possible for talent, wealth, genius to acquire social standing and distinction.

This work I shall undertake not for myself alone, but for my children, for the people with whom I am connected—for humanity!

He who would master others should first learn to master himself. *So will Ich strebe zu thun, mitt Gottes Hilfe.*[5]

Mar 16th [1880]. Judge Tourgée has sold the "Fool's Errand," I understand, for $20,000.[6] I suppose he had already received a large royalty on the sale of the first few editions. The work has gained an astonishing degree of popularity, and is to be translated into the French.

Now, Judge Tourgée's book is about the south—the manners, customs, modes of thought, etc., which are prevalent in this section of the country.

---

[4] Benjamin Franklin (1706–1790) and the journalist and political leader Horace Greeley (1811–1872) were major figures in the mythology of the self-made man. The story of Greeley's setting out from obscure origins to make a name for himself in the city had been extensively publicized during his unsuccessful presidential campaign in 1872. [Richard Brodhead's note.]

[5] "So shall I strive to do, with God's help." [Richard Brodhead's note.]

[6] After the Civil War Ohioan Albion W. Tourgée settled in North Carolina, where he became the leader of a political faction advocating Negro suffrage and the rights of lower-class whites *and* blacks against wealth and privilege. With the rise during Radical Reconstruction of a North Carolina Republican party supported by black votes, Tourgée became a superior court judge. After the defeat of Radical Reconstruction Tourgée came to see his struggle to establish an egalitarian society in North Carolina as hopeless. In 1879 he returned to Ohio and wrote his insider's history of Reconstruction in fictional form. His novel *A Fool's Errand* remained a best-seller throughout the 1880s. [Richard Brodhead's note.]

Judge Tourgée is a Northern man, who has lived at the South since the war,
until recently. He knows a great deal about the politics, history, and laws of
the South. He is a close observer of men and things, and has exercised this
faculty of observation upon the character of the Southern people. Nearly
all his stories are more or less about colored people, and this very feature
is one source of their popularity. There is something romantic, to the
Northern mind, about the southern negro, as commonplace and vulgar as
he seems to us who come in contact with him every day. And there is a romantic side to the history of this people. Men are always more ready to extend their sympathy to those at a distance, than to the suffering ones in
their midst. And the north, their eyes not blinded by the dirt and the hazy
moral and social atmosphere which surrounds the average negro in the
south, their interest not blunted by familiarity with the state of affairs in
the south, or prejudiced by a love of "our institutions"—sees the south as
it is; or is ever eager for something which will show it in a correct light.
They see in the Colored people a race, but recently emancipated from a
cruel bondage; struggling for education, for a higher social and moral life,
against wealth, intelligence, and race prejudice, which are all united to
keep them down. And they hear the cry of the oppressed and struggling
ones, and extend a hand to help them; they lend a willing ear to all that is
spoken or written concerning their character, habits, etc. And if Judge
Tourgée, with his necessarily limited intercourse with colored people, and
with his limited stay in the South, can write such interesting descriptions,
such vivid pictures of Southern life and character as to make himself rich
and famous, why could not a colored man, who has lived among colored
people all his life; who is familiar with their habits, their ruling passions,
their prejudices; their whole moral and social condition; their public and
private ambitions; their religious tendencies and habits;—why could not a
colored man who knew all this, and who, besides, had possessed such opportunities for observation and conversation with the better class of white
men in the south as to understand their modes of thinking; who was familiar with the political history of the country, and especially with all the
phases of the slavery question;—why could not such a man, if he possessed
the same ability, write a far better book about the South than Judge
Tourgée or Mrs. Stowe has written? Answer who can! But the man is yet
to make his appearance; and if I can't be the man I shall be the first to re-
joice at his *début* and give God speed! to his work.

I intend to record my impressions of men and things, and such incidents or conversations which take place within my knowledge, with a view
to future use in literary work. I shall not record stale negro minstrel jokes,
or worn out newspaper squibs on the "man and brother." I shall leave the
realm of fiction, where most of this stuff is manufactured, and come down

to hard facts. There are many things about the Colored people which are peculiar, to some extent, to them, and which are interesting to any thoughtful observer, and would be doubly interesting to people who know little about them.

May 29, 1880 . . . I think I must write a book. I am almost afraid to undertake a book so early and with so little experience in composition. But it has been my cherished dream, and I feel an influence that I cannot resist calling me to the task. Besides, I do not know but I am as well prepared as some other successful writers. A fair knowledge of the classics, a speaking acquaintance with the modern languages, an intimate friendship with literature, etc.; seven years experience in the school room, two years of married life, and a habit of studying character have I think, left me not entirely unprepared to write even a book. Fifteen years of life in the South, in one of the most eventful eras of its history; among a people whose life is rich in the elements of romance; under conditions calculated to stir one's soul to the very depths—I think there is here a fund of experience, a supply of material, which a skillful pers[on] could work up with tremendous effect. Besides, If I do write, I shall write for a purpose, a high, holy purpose, and this will inspire me to greater effort. The object of my writings would be not so much the elevation of the colored people as the elevation of the whites—for I consider the unjust spirit of caste which is so insidious as to pervade a whole nation, and so powerful as to subject a whole race and all connected with it to scorn and social ostracism—I consider this a barrier to the moral progress of the American people; and I would be one of the first to head a determined, organized crusade against it. Not a fierce indiscriminate onslaught; not an appeal to force, for this is something that force can but slightly affect; but a moral revolution which must be brought about in a different manner. The Abolition[ist]s stirred up public opinion in behalf of the slave, by appealing in trumpet tones to those principles of justice and humanity which were only lying dormant in the northern heart. The iron hand of power set the slave free from personal bondage, and by admitting him to all the rights of citizenship—the ballot, education— is fast freeing him from the greater bondage of ignorance. But the subtle almost indefinable feeling of repulsion toward the negro, which is common to most Americans—and easily enough accounted for—cannot be stormed and taken by assault; the garrison will not capitulate: so their position must be mined, and we will find ourselves in their midst before they think it.

This work is of a twofold character. The negro's part is to prepare himself for social recognition and equality; and it is the province of literature to open the way for him to get it—to accustom the public mind to the idea; and by while amusing them to ~~familiarize~~ lead them on imperceptibly,

unconsciously step by step to the desired state of feeling. If I can do anything to further this work, and can see any likelihood of obtaining success
in it, I would gladly devote my life to the work.

   Jan 21st [1881]. I had a conversation with Robert Hill[7] last night,
about Southern affairs. He is a very intelligent man, uses good English, and
understands what he talks about. He was once a slave, and was badly
treated. His argument to the white man who tried to coax him to come
over to the Dem. party, and 'let them darn Yankees alone,' was, "Take
away all the laws in our favor that 'them darn Yankees' have made, and
what would be left?" He believes that the local affairs of the South will be
best administered by the property owners, but he is "stalwart Republican"
in all national affairs—in all of which we agree.

   He related a conversation he had with Jno. McLaughlin—a poor
white man, and a clerk in Williams's store.

   "Bob," said McLaughlin, "what kind of fellow is this Chesnutt[?"]

   "Well, sir, he's a ~~nigger~~ perfect gentleman in every respect; I don't
know his superior."

   "Why! he's a nigger, ain't he?"

   "He's classed with the colored people, but—["]

   "Well, what kind of an education has he?"

   "He's not a college bred man, but he has been a hard student all his
life. You can't ask him a question he cannot answer."

   "He's this short-hand writer," musingly.

   "Yes, sir."

   "Does he think he's as good as a white man[?]"

   "Every bit of it, sir"; and he might have added, if he had known my
opinions, that I would think very meanly of myself if I didn't consider myself better than most of the white men I have met in this vale of tears.

   Hill then went to argue about the equality of intelligence and so on,
but McL. wound up with this declaration, which embodies the opinion of
the South on the "Negro Question".

   "Well he's a nigger; and with me a nigger is a nigger, and nothing in
the world can make him anything else but a nigger." Which reminds me of
the sentiment expressed by an old poor white beggar, who was at the time
eating scraps in a colored man's kitchen[:] "Well, for his part, let other
people think as they please, he always did like niggers as long as they kept
in their place, and he wasn't ashamed to say so either."

----

[7] Robert Hill is listed as a thirty-four-year-old black drayman in the 1880 census. [Rich-
ard Brodhead's note.]

I got some new light on the Union League.[8] It seems that the League once suspected the whites of a plot to blow up the lodge where the league met, and a keg of powder was found concealed there. They immediately resolved to defend themselves, and the white folks were given to understand that if they had the firearms, the nigger had the torch—a significant ~~threat~~ hint which had the effect desired.

March 17, Thursday [1881]. I have skimmed "The Negro in the Rebellion," by Dr. Brown, and it only strengthens me in my opinion, that the Negro is yet to become known who can write a good book. Dr. Brown's books are mere compilations, and, as Thos. Jefferson says of Phillis Wheatley[']s poems, "beneath the dignity of criticism."[9] If they were not written by a colored man, they would not sell enough to pay for the printing. I read them merely for facts, but I could appreciate the facts better if they were well presented. The book reminds me of a gentleman ~~clothed~~ in ~~rags~~ a dirty shirt. You are rather apt to doubt his gentility under such circumstances. I am sometimes doubtful of the facts for the same reason—they make but a shabby appearance. I am reading Molière's "Le Mari Confondu" or "the Cuckold". It is amusing.

---

[8] Union League Clubs were first formed in the North in 1863 to help with soldier relief and the recruiting of volunteers. After the war the Union League developed into a Republican political organization in the South strongly linked to the black vote and black political rights. [Richard Brodhead's note.]

[9] *The Negro in the American Rebellion; His Heroism and His Fidelity*, by William Wells Brown, author of the *Narrative of William W. Brown, a Fugitive Slave* and the novel *Clotel*, was published in 1867 and republished in 1880. In *Notes on the State of Virginia* (1787) Thomas Jefferson had said of the African-born poet Phillis Wheatley, author of *Poems on Various Subjects, Religious and Moral:* "Never yet could I find that a Black had uttered a thought above the level of plain narration; never see even an elementary trait of painting or sculpture. . . . Religion indeed has produced a Phyllis Whately [*sic*]; but it could not produce a poet. . . . The compositions published under her name are below the dignity of criticism. The heroes of the Dunciad are to her, as Hercules to the author of that poem." [Richard Brodhead's note.]

Essays

WHAT IS A WHITE MAN?

The fiat having gone forth from the wise men of the South that the "all-pervading, all-conquering Anglo-Saxon race" must continue forever to exercise exclusive control and direction of the government of this so-called Republic, it becomes important to every citizen who values his birthright to know who are included in this grandiloquent term. It is of course perfectly obvious that the writer or speaker who used this expression—perhaps Mr. Grady of Georgia—did not say what he meant. It is not probable that he meant to exclude from full citizenship the Celts and Teutons and Gauls and Slavs who make up so large a proportion of our population; he hardly meant to exclude the Jews, for even the most ardent fire-eater would hardly venture to advocate the disfranchisement of the thrifty race whose mortgages cover so large a portion of Southern soil. What the eloquent gentleman really meant by this high-sounding phrase was simply the white race; and the substance of the argument of that school of Southern writers to which he belongs, is simply that for the good of the country the Negro should have no voice in directing the government or public policy of the Southern States or of the nation.[1]

But it is evident that where the intermingling of the races has made such progress as it has in this country, the line which separates the races must in many instances have been practically obliterated. And there has arisen in the United States a very large class of the population who are certainly not Negroes in an ethnological sense, and whose children will be no nearer

---

The Independent [New York], May 30, 1889.

[1] Henry Woodfin Grady (1850–1889). From 1880 until his death on December 23, 1889, Grady was an editor of the *Atlanta Constitution* and the most visible and eloquent spokesman for the idea of a "new," reconstructed South. He defined the movement in a speech entitled "The New South," presented in New York on December 22, 1886, at the annual dinner of the New England Society. A history of this era and Grady's role in it is discussed by Logan; also see Nixon and Davis.

Negroes than themselves. In view, therefore, of the very positive ground taken by the white leaders of the South, where most of these people reside, it becomes in the highest degree important to them to know what race they belong to. It ought to be also a matter of serious concern to the Southern white people; for if their zeal for good government is so great that they contemplate the practical overthrow of the Constitution and laws of the United States to secure it, they ought at least to be sure that no man entitled to it by their own argument, is robbed of a right so precious as that of free citizenship; the "all-pervading, all conquering Anglo-Saxon" ought to set as high a value on American citizenship as the all-conquering Roman placed upon the franchise of his State two thousand years ago. This discussion would of course be of little interest to the genuine Negro, who is entirely outside of the charmed circle, and must content himself with the acquisition of wealth, the pursuit of learning and such other privileges as his "best friends" may find it consistent with the welfare of the nation to allow him; but to every other good citizen the inquiry ought to be a momentous one, What is a white man?

In spite of the virulence and universality of race prejudice in the United States, the human intellect long ago revolted at the manifest absurdity of classifying men fifteen-sixteenths white as black men; and hence there grew up a number of laws in different states of the Union defining the limit which separated the white and colored races, which was, when these laws took their rise and is now to a large extent, the line which separated freedom and opportunity from slavery or hopeless degradation. Some of these laws are of legislative origin; others are judge-made laws, brought out by the exigencies of special cases which came before the courts for determination. Some day they will, perhaps, become mere curiosities of jurisprudence: the "black laws" will be bracketed with the "blue laws," and will be at best but landmarks by which to measure the progress of the nation.[2] But today these laws are in active operation, and they are, therefore, worthy of attention; for every good citizen ought to know the law, and, if possible, to respect it: and if not worthy of respect, it should be changed by

---

[2] The black codes were legal restrictions enacted to control African Americans politically, socially, and economically in Georgia, Alabama, South Carolina, North Carolina, Virginia, Florida, Louisiana, Tennessee, and several northern states. With these statutes, insecure whites sought to regain power lost over black-skinned people after Emancipation and the Civil War. For a survey of black codes by state, see DuBois; for a survey of statutes that specifically restrict interracial cohabitation, see Reuter, Berger, and Bardolph. Chesnutt's prediction that black codes would go the way of the blue laws, or Sunday-closing ordinances that since colonial days limited certain business activities on the Sabbath, came true. By 1984, at least twelve states had repealed them (see Laband and Heinbunch).

the authority which enacted it. Whether any of the laws referred to here have been in any manner changed by very recent legislation the writer cannot say, but they are certainly embodied in the latest editions of the revised statutes of the states referred to.

The colored people were divided, in most of the Southern States, into two classes, designated by law as Negroes and mulattoes respectively. The term Negro was used in its ethnological sense, and needed no definition; but the term "mulatto" was held by legislative enactment to embrace all persons of color not Negroes. The words "quadroon" and "mestizo" are employed in some of the law books, tho not defined; but the term "octoroon," as indicating a person having one-eighth Negro blood, is not used at all, so far as the writer has been able to observe.

The states vary slightly in regard to what constitutes a mulatto or person of color, and as to what proportion of white blood should be sufficient to remove the disability of color. As a general rule, less than one-fourth of Negro blood left the individual white—in theory; race questions being, however, regulated very differently in practice. In Missouri, by the code of 1855, still in operation, so far as not inconsistent with the Federal Constitution and laws, "any person other than a Negro, any one of whose grandmothers or grandfathers is or shall have been a Negro, tho all of his or her progenitors except those descended from the Negro may have been white persons, shall be deemed a mulatto." [3] Thus the color-line is drawn at one-fourth of Negro blood, and persons with only one-eighth are white.

By the Mississippi code of 1880, the color-line is drawn at one-fourth of Negro blood, all persons having less being theoretically white. [4]

---

[3] The exact code reads: "Every person other than a Negro, any one of whose grandfathers or grandmothers is, or shall have been a Negro, although all his or her other progenitors, except those descending from the Negro, may have been white persons, shall be deemed a mulatto; and every such person, who shall have one-fourth or more Negro blood, shall in like manner, be deemed a mulatto" (*Revised Statutes of the State of Missouri*, 2:1093–94).

[4] *The Revised Code of the Statute Laws of the State of Mississippi* states: "The marriage of a white person and a Negro or mulatto or person who shall have one-fourth or more of Negro blood, shall be unlawful, and such marriage shall be incestuous and void; and any party thereto, on conviction, shall be punished as for a marriage . . . and any attempt to evade this section by marrying out of this state, and returning to it shall be held to be within it." *The Annotated Code of the General Statute Laws of the State of Mississippi* is even more rigid: "The marriage of a white person and a Negro or mulatto or person who shall have one-eighth or more of Negro blood, or with a Mongolian or a person who shall have one-eighth or more Mongolian blood, shall be unlawful, and such marriage shall be unlawful and void . . ." (677).

Under the *code noir* of Louisiana, the descendant of a white and a quadroon is white, thus drawing the line at one-eighth of Negro blood. The code of 1876 abolished all distinctions of color; as to whether they have been re-enacted since the Republican Party went out of power in that state the writer is not informed.[5]

Jumping to the extreme North, persons are white within the meaning of the Constitution of Michigan who have less than one-fourth of Negro blood.[6]

In Ohio the rule, as established by numerous decisions of the Supreme Court, was that a preponderance of white blood constituted a person a white man in the eye of the law, and entitled him to the exercise of all the civil rights of a white man. By a retrogressive step the color-line was extended in 1861 in the case of marriage, which by statute was forbidden between a person of pure white blood and one having a visible admixture of African blood. But by act of legislature, passed in the spring of 1887, all laws establishing or permitting distinctions of color were repealed. In many parts of the state these laws were always ignored, and they would doubtless have been repealed long ago but for the sentiment of the southern counties, separated only by the width of the Ohio River from a former slaveholding state.[7] There was a bill introduced in the legislature during the last

---

[5] *Code noir* ("black code") derives from the "Edict Concerning the Negro Slaves in Louisiana," issued in March 1724 by Louis XV and enacted in Louisiana on September 10, 1724, by Governor Jean Baptiste Le Moyne Sieur de Bienville. The code consisted of fifty-four articles fixing the legal status of slaves and imposing specific obligations and prohibitions on slave owners. Its essential provisions were eventually integrated into the American black codes (*Dictionary of American History* 2:9). The 1876 code reads: "The said right of making private or religious marriages legal, valid and binding, as aforesaid, shall apply to marriages of all persons of whatever race or color, as well as to marriages formerly prohibited by article ninety-five of the Civil Code of Louisiana, or by any other article of said Code, or by any law of the State" (*Revised Statute Laws of the State of Louisiana,* 575).

[6] *The General Statutes of the State of Michigan* states: "All marriages heretofore contracted between white persons and those wholly or in part of African descent are hereby declared valid and effectual in law for all purposes, and the issue of such marriages shall be deemed and taken legitimate as to such issue and as to both of the parents" (1619).

[7] Bishop Benjamin Arnett's bill to repeal school segregation and anti-marriage laws, the last of Ohio's black codes, passed the Ohio Senate February 16, 1887. Because black Arnett had promised his mostly white constituents that he would take no initiative on such legislation, he was soon turned out of office. For further study of Arnett, see Meier 57, Gerber especially 242–43 and 350–69, and Lewis 152–54. The Revised Ohio Statutes also repealed Section 6987 of the January 31, 1861, act that read: "A person of pure white blood, who intermarries with any Negro, or person having a distinct and visible

session to re-enact the "black laws," but it was hopelessly defeated; the
member who introduced it evidently mistook his latitude; he ought to be
a member of the Georgia legislature.

But the state which, for several reasons, one might expect to have the
strictest laws in regard to the relations of the races, has really the loosest.
Two extracts from decisions of the Supreme Court of South Carolina will
make clear the law of that state in regard to the color line.

> The definition of the term mulatto, as understood in this state, seems to be
> vague, signifying generally a person of mixed white or European and Ne-
> gro parentage, in whatever proportions the blood of the two races may be
> mingled in the individual. But it is not invariably applicable to every ad-
> mixture of African blood with the European, nor is one having all the fea-
> tures of a white to be ranked with the degraded class designated by the
> laws of this state as persons of color, because of some remote taint of the
> Negro race. The line of distinction, however, is not ascertained by any
> rule of law. . . . Juries would probably be justified in holding a person to
> be white in whom the admixture of African blood did not exceed the pro-
> portion of one-eighth. But it is in all cases a question for the jury, to be
> determined by them upon the evidence of features and complexion af-
> forded by inspection, the evidence of reputation as to parentage, and the
> evidence of the rank and station in society occupied by the party. The
> only rule which can be laid down by the courts is that where there is a
> distinct and visible admixture of Negro blood, the individual is to be de-
> nominated a mulatto or person of color.

In a later case the court held:

> The question whether persons are colored or white, where color or fea-
> ture are doubtful, is for the jury to decide by reputation, by reception into
> society, and by their exercise of the privileges of the white man, as well as
> by admixture of blood.[8]

---

admixture of African blood, and any Negro, or person having a distinct and visible admixture of African blood, who intermarries with any person of pure white blood, shall
be fined not more than $100, or imprisoned not more than three months, or both"
(quoted in Quillin 93).

[8] *State v. Thomas B. Davis; Same v. William Dana.* These were indictments under the
bastardy act of 1795, tried before Justice Evans during the fall term held in Columbia,
December 1831 (*Report of Cases Argued and Determined in The Supreme Court of
South Carolina . . . Book 8* 257–59). This decision was upheld in 1835 in the case of
State v. Vinson J. Cantey and several other later decisions (*Reports of Cases Argued and
Determined in The Supreme Court of South Carolina . . . Book 9* 334–35).

It is an interesting question why such should have been, and should still be, for that matter, the law of South Carolina, and why there should exist in that state a condition of public opinion which would accept such a law. Perhaps it may be attributed to the fact that the colored population of South Carolina always outnumbered the white population, and the eagerness of the latter to recruit their ranks was sufficient to overcome in some measure their prejudice against the Negro blood. It is certainly true that the color-line is, in practice as in law, more loosely drawn in South Carolina than in any other Southern State, and that no inconsiderable element of the population of that state consists of these legal white persons, who were either born in the state, or, attracted thither by this feature of the laws, have come in from surrounding states, and, forsaking home and kindred, have taken their social position as white people. A reasonable degree of reticence in regard to one's antecedents is, however, usual in such cases.

Before the [Civil] War the color-line, as fixed by law, regulated in theory the civil and political status of persons of color. What that status was, was expressed in the Dred Scott decision.[9] But since the War, or rather since the enfranchisement of the colored people, these laws have been mainly confined—in theory, be it always remembered—to the regulation of the intercourse of the races in schools and in the marriage relation. The extension of the color-line to places of public entertainment and resort, to inns and public highways, is in most states entirely a matter of custom. A colored man can sue in the courts of any Southern State for the violation of his common-law rights, and recover damages of say fifty cents without costs. A colored minister who sued a Baltimore steamboat company a few weeks ago for refusing him first-class accommodation, he having paid first-class fare, did not even meet with that measure of success: the learned judge, a Federal judge by the way, held that the plaintiff's rights had been invaded, and that he had suffered humiliation at the hands of the defendant company, but that "the humiliation was not sufficient to entitle him to damages." And the learned judge dismissed the action without costs to either party.

Having thus ascertained what constitutes a white man, the good citizen may be curious to know what steps have been taken to preserve the purity of the white race, Nature, by some unaccountable oversight having to

---

[9] In 1857, a majority of the Supreme Court decided that Dred Scott, a Missouri slave whose owner had taken him to live in the free state of Illinois and subsequently to a fort in the northern part of the Louisiana Purchase, was not a citizen and therefore could not sue in court. Speaking for the Court, Chief Justice Roger B. Taney held that slavemasters could retain ownership of their slaves even if the latter had lived in a slave free territory (Franklin 202–203).

some extent neglected a matter so important to the future prosperity and progress of mankind. The marriage laws referred to here are in active operation, and cases under them are by no means infrequent. Indeed, instead of being behind the age, the marriage laws in the Southern States are in advance of public opinion; for very rarely will a Southern community stop to figure on the pedigree of the contracting parties to a marriage where one is white and the other is known to have any strain of Negro blood.

In Virginia, under the title "Offenses against Morality," the law provides that "any white person who shall intermarry with a Negro shall be confined in jail not more than one year and fined not exceeding one hundred dollars." In a marginal note on the statute-book, attention is called to the fact that "a similar penalty is not imposed on the Negro"—a stretch of magnanimity to which the laws of other states are strangers. A person who performs the ceremony of marriage in such a case is fined two hundred dollars, one-half of which goes to the informer.

In Maryland, a minister who performs the ceremony of marriage between a Negro and a white person is liable to a fine of one hundred dollars.

In Mississippi, code of 1880, it is provided that "the marriage of a white person to a Negro or mulatto or person who shall have one-fourth or more of Negro blood, shall be unlawful"; and as this prohibition does not seem sufficiently emphatic, it is further declared to be "incestuous and void," and is punished by the same penalty prescribed for marriage within the forbidden degrees of consanguinity.

But it is Georgia, the *alma genetrix* of the chain-gang, which merits the questionable distinction of having the harshest set of color laws. By the law of Georgia the term "person of color" is defined to mean "all such as have an admixture of Negro blood; and the term 'Negro,' includes mulattoes." This definition is perhaps restricted somewhat by another provision, by which "all Negroes, mestizoes, and their descendants, having one-eighth of Negro or mulatto blood in their veins, shall be known in this State as persons of color." A colored minister is permitted to perform the ceremony of marriage between colored persons only, tho white ministers are not forbidden to join persons of color in wedlock. It is further provided that "the marriage relation between white persons and persons of African descent is forever prohibited, and such marriages shall be null and void." This is a very sweeping provision; it will be noticed that the term "persons of color," previously defined, is not employed, the expression "persons of African descent" being used instead. A court which was so inclined would find no difficulty in extending this provision of the law to the remotest strain of African blood. The marriage relation is forever prohibited. Forever is a long time. There is a colored woman in Georgia said to be worth $300,000—

an immense fortune in the poverty stricken South.[10] With a few hundred such women in that state, possessing a fair degree of good looks, the color-line would shrivel up like a scroll in the heat of competition for their hands in marriage. The penalty for the violation of the law against intermarriage is the same sought to be imposed by the defunct Glenn Bill for violation of its provisions: *i.e.,* a fine not to exceed one thousand dollars, and imprisonment not to exceed six months, or twelve months in the chain-gang.[11]

Whatever the wisdom or justice of these laws, there is one objection to them which is not given sufficient prominence in the consideration of the subject, even where it is discussed at all; they make mixed blood a *prima-facie* proof of illegitimacy. It is a fact that at present, in the United States, a colored man or woman whose complexion is white or nearly white is presumed, in the absence of any knowledge of his or her antecedents, to be the offspring of a union not sanctified by law. And by a curious but not uncommon process, such persons are not held in the same low estimation as white people in the same position. The sins of their fathers are not visited upon the children, in that regard at least; and their mothers' lapses from virtue are regarded either as misfortunes or as faults excusable under the circumstances. But in spite of all this, illegitimacy is not a desirable distinction, and is likely to become less so as these people of mixed blood advance in wealth and social standing. This presumption of illegitimacy was once, perhaps, true of the majority of such persons; but the times have changed. More than half of the colored people of the United States are of mixed blood; they marry and are given in marriage, and they beget children of complexions similar to their own. Whether or not, therefore, laws which stamp these children as illegitimate, and which by indirection establish a lower standard of morality for a large part of the population than

---

[10] In its October 23, 1886, weekly Saturday column about African-American life entitled "The Colored Race," the *Cleveland Gazette* named Amanda (Mandy) Eubanks of Rome, Georgia, whose white father left her $400,000 in his will, the richest African-American woman in the South (1). A June 26, 1886, issue of the paper had listed Eubanks as still living in Alabama (1).

[11] On July 11, 1887, Representative W. C. Glenn of Dalton introduced a bill in the state legislature to cut off $8,000 allocated annually to Atlanta University as part of the Morrill Act of 1882. Glenn mainly sought to punish white faculty who refused to stop sending their children to, and thus integrating, the school. The Glenn Bill passed both the House and the Senate August 2, 1887, and was signed by Governor John B. Gordon. It became moot after the state established the State College of Industry for Colored Youth in Savannah in October 1891 and transferred the funds to it. See Bacote 86–101 for a discussion and survey of responses to the bill; also see Harold E. Davis 140–41.

the remaining part is judged by, are wise laws; and whether or not the purity of the white race could not be as well preserved by the exercise of virtue, and the operation of those natural laws which are so often quoted by
Southern writers as the justification of all sorts of Southern "policies"—
are questions which the good citizen may at least turn over in his mind occasionally, pending the settlement of other complications which have
grown out of the presence of the Negro on this continent.

A MULTITUDE OF COUNSELORS

The colored people of this country are just now passing through a trying period in their history, a history full of trying situations—a dark and
gloomy record, with only here and there a flash of light. Even now they are
scarcely in the twilight of their liberties. All over the country they are the
victims of a cruel race prejudice, the strength and extent of which none but
cultivated, self-respecting colored people can rightly apprehend.[1] It pervades every department of life—politics, the schools, the churches, business, society—everywhere, tho not always in the same degree. There is
actually no single locality in the United States where a man avowedly connected by blood with the Negro race can hold up his head and feel that he
is the recognized equal of other men (in the broad sense of the term), or
where he is not taught to feel every day of his life that he is regarded as
something inferior to those who were fortunate enough to be born entirely
white. Colored people who think have long since recognized that in the

---

The Independent [New York], April 2, 1891, as part of the "Condition of the
Negro" series.

[1] Chesnutt is apparently referring to the numerous accounts of racial discrimination directed against African Americans in public accommodations and other incidents of brutality, especially lynching, about which he read in the local media. On January 25, 1890,
the *Cleveland Gazette,* for example, reprinted under "Southern Outrages" a letter written by J. W. Thompson, editor of the *People's Journal* of Jacksonville, Florida, to J. B.
Gordon, governor of Georgia, in which Thompson lists such atrocities as four African-
American women being made to strip naked and then being whipped nearly to death (4).
In a February 22, 1890, front-page story, this same newspaper reported that white Con-
gressman Thomas J. Grimes of Georgia left the Riggs House in Washington, D.C., be-
cause ex-Consul to San Domingo, black H. C. Astwood, was eating there with Nathaniel
McKay, a white friend from New York. In "Barnwell and Jessup Deaths," a *Cleveland
Gazette* editor gives detailed descriptions of massacres of African Americans in Barnwell,
South Carolina, and Jessup, Georgia (4 January 1890:2).

more intimate and personal relations of men, society can have but one opinion, and that the Negro is under the ban of society. They feel that as long as any considerable part of the United States denies them any right or any privilege, something will be lacking to the completeness of their citizenship everywhere else in the United States.

But it is a far cry from slavery—from the Dred Scott decision—to the time when the ghost of negrophobia will be laid. Sufficient unto the day is the evil thereof: and the crying evil of today is the outrageous manner in which the colored people of the South are deprived of the elementary rights of citizenship—the right to the protection of life and limb, the right to trial when accused of crime, the right to assist in the choice of their rulers and the making of their laws, and the right to equal treatment on railroads and in places provided for the accommodation of the traveling public. These are not social privileges; they are public rights, to which these people are entitled under the law. There are other rights of which they are deprived, but which they have not chosen to assert; but the manifest disposition on their part to claim and exercise the rights enumerated, has stirred the Negro-hating spirit of the South to the dregs, and given occasion for a series of outrages within the last month which is without a parallel in number or malignity since the downfall of the Ku Klux [Klan] organization, if the disbanding of that organization after complete sucess [sic] in the object sought by it can be called a downfall.

Mr. George W. Cable advises the colored people to unite and by every peaceable means—by word, by voice, by pen, to forward their own cause.[2] One writer advises the colored people to emigrate to Mexico or South America, another tells them not to yield their tardily acknowledged birthright, but to work out their salvation in the United States. A writer prominently identified with the cause of the colored people advises them to forget the fact that they are Negroes, and to endeavor to feel that they are simply men and citizens. One counselor advises them to emigrate largely

---

[2] In "What Shall the Negro Do," first delivered before an African-American audience in Boston on April 13, 1888, and originally published in *The Forum*, Cable encourages African Americans to seek "the friendly countenance and active co-operation of white men well known in their communities for intelligence and integrity" and cites the goal to form biracial civil rights "New South Clubs"—which eventually were renamed the "Open Letter Club"—"to foster and promote, by every lawful use of the pen, the press, the mails, the laws, and the courts, by public assemblage and petition . . . the legal and the conventional recognition, establishment, and protection of all men in the common rights of humanity . . . " (632). Cable asked Charles Chesnutt to serve as secretary of the Club, but in a May 3, 1889, letter Chesnutt turned down the offer for a better-paying venture (Helen Chesnutt 46–47). Cable's essay has been collected in Turner, ed., 170–184.

from the South, and thus relieve that section of the strain caused by the
fear of Negro majorities. Another advises them to stay in the South and retain their majorities, on the theory that a bird in hand (even if the hand is
shackled) is worth two in the bush. One friend finds a specific for every
race trouble in the division of the colored vote; another, many others in
fact, see no hope for the Negro except in the supremacy of the Republican
Party; they believe, in the language of Frederick Douglass, that to the Negro "the Republican Party is the ship; all else is the ocean." [3] Judge Tourgée
openly predicts a guerilla warfare of races, and can only advise the colored
people to defend themselves in an uneven and hopeless conflict. [4]

When the colored man has read with hopeful eagerness the conflicting advice which his friends have given him, he is apt to reach the conclusion that his counselors are as much in the dark as to what is best for him to
do, or as to what will be the outcome of his presence in the United States,
as he himself is.

From one point of view scarcely any of the courses proposed are [sic]
practicable for the ten million colored people in the United States, or any
considerable proportion of them, to follow. Take, for instance, a wholesale
emigration of the colored people to South America, or Mexico. It is questionable whether they would be welcomed in any such mass. The expense
of transportation, the loss of time, the withdrawal of so many laborers,
would cost the country as much as the late War, and would be infinitely
more injurious to the South than they at one time imagined the loss of their
slaves to be. No such movement has been known in history: the exodus of
the Hebrews from Egypt, the expulsion of the Moors from Spain, the flight
of the Tartar tribe which De Quincey has immortalized, would be mere

---

[3] On April 13, 1872, at the first National Convention of the Colored People held at the
Mechanics Institute in New Orleans, Douglass said: "For colored men the Republican
party is the deck, all outside is the sea" (Blassingame and McKivigan, eds. 298). The
speech was also published in the *New National Era* on May 2, 1872, the *New Orleans
Bee* on April 14, 1872, and the *New Orleans Republican* on April 14, 1872.

[4] In an article supporting a proposed convention for organizing African-American men
with the broad goal of promoting the interests of black people, Judge Tourgée says: "As
soon as the 'bull-dozer' sees that the colored man is in earnest in his determination to
enjoy the rights the Nation has granted him, another epoch of bloodshed is about as certain to be inaugurated as the sun is to shine" (*Cleveland Gazette*, 23 November 1889:1).
He then asks "whether the colored race in America has yet developed martyrs enough
of that sort to make such a movement effective. . . . Such men will not die in vain. Those
who come after them will dip their garments in their blood and press forward all the
more steadily. There is nothing like the blood of martyrs to establish a good cause" (1).

preparatory sketches for such a gigantic movement of population.[5] When it is considered that it has taken four hundred years of immigration and a century of unparalleled national growth, to give the United States a population of sixty millions, the preposterousness of colonizing the whole colored population of the United States is apparent, even supposing no other obstacle than mere numbers in the way of it. A wholesale emigration to any State or Territory is open to similar objections, and to the still stronger one that no State or Territory capable of supporting a large population would be left to the exclusive occupation of the colored people. The lesson of Oklahoma is recent enough to demonstrate this. It is not at all likely that even Africa will be left to the Negro; it is not, indeed, desirable that it should be left entirely to him.[6] But supposing every obstacle to such an emigration removed, the Southern whites would not let the colored people go. This modern Pharaoh, "the white South," is quite as obdurate as his Egyptian prototype. The Negro problem seems to worry the people of Georgia more than those of any other State; and yet the laws of Georgia, to say nothing of public opinion, are such as to render it absolutely impossible for any organized movement for emigration to be successfully carried out. Cheap, abundant and easily managed, white labor is not so readily procured that the Southern white planters would take their chances of getting along without colored labor. The Negroes must, as a mass, remain in the South. A more practicable emigration, that of the Southern whites, who are more able to go, strange to say, does not seem to meet with much favor in their eyes, and yet, if, as they are so fond of asserting, it is impossible for the two races to live together on terms of equality, this is more likely to be the ultimate outcome.

The division of the colored vote is equally impracticable. The whites do not, at present, desire it on such terms as they could get it, that is, the

---

[5] Thomas De Quincey's "The Revolt of the Tartars; or Flight of the Kalmuck Khan and His People from the Russian Territories to the Frontiers of China" appeared in *Blackwood's Edinburgh Magazine* 42 (July 1837): 89–137.
[6] Chesnutt apparently believes the accusations that white-oriented newspapers directed against Edward McCabe, an agent of the Topeka, Kansas–based Oklahoma Immigration Association that actively recruited African Americans for relocation in Oklahoma after the territory was officially opened up for settlement on April 22, 1889. Fearful of African-American political aspirations, these newspapers accused McCabe of setting up all-black towns. But as Kenneth Marvin Hamilton notes, "His [McCabe's] behavior suggested not that he endorsed a separate state but that he recognized that predominantly black-populated towns might better allow blacks to achieve both personal and racial advancement" (102).

recognition of the Negroes' rights under the law. It could be easily effected
on that basis; but that any considerable number of colored people in the
face of the torrent of vilification and abuse, to say nothing of physical outrage, to which they are subjected, should support the party which at the
South justifies and at the North excuses such a course toward them, it is
difficult to see: they do not do it, and will not do it. A colored editor in
New Orleans, who turned Democrat, for the reason, as he asserts, that he
thought the condition of his race would be improved by such changes of
politics, and another in Ohio who forsook his party for similar reasons,
have both returned recently to the Republican Party; even patriotism, or
venality, or whatever their motive may have been, could not resist the arguments of the past month. They have declared that the lives and liberties
of their people are above every other consideration, and that there is neither prospect nor hope for the preservation of either in the Democratic
Party.[7] It is joined to its idols, the bigotry and lawlessness of the Bourbon
Democracy of the South.[8]

---

[7] Pinckney Benton Stewart Pinchback (1837–1921), the grandfather of writer Jean
Toomer and founder and editor of the *New Orleans Weekly Louisianian* from 1870 to
1882, seeking revenge against a Republican party that failed to support his senatorial efforts, led the charge against the party in a crucial gubernatorial vote in Louisiana that
affected the outcome of the November 1876 election, in which Republican Rutherford B.
Hayes won over Democrat Samuel J. Tilden (see Dann, ed. 28 and James Haskins
228–47). As August Meier notes, Mississippi Senator Blanche K. Bruce in 1876 criticized the Republican party for excluding Pinchback from the Senate, and he and Pinchback advised blacks to divide their vote to obtain better political advantage. Both, however, soon became loyal Republicans again. Cincinnati Republican Peter Humphries
Clark joined the Democratic party in 1882 but left after becoming disillusioned by the
"doctrinaire tendencies within the party, which he claimed 'tried to hold members down
to a rigid pattern of ideas.'" He also felt a sense of loyalty to African Americans who had
supported him when local politicians tried to remove him from the principalship of the
local African-American high school. But he returned to the Democrats and gained more
influence with the legislature than any other African-American Democrat as well as becoming editor of the *Cincinnati Afro-American,* the publishing organ for black Ohio
Democrats. When Clark was abandoned by political allies after their mistreatment of African Americans and their interests, including mass arrests of these voters in 1884, he lost
his Democratic political clout and ended up pleading guilty to bribing a key witness in
a conspiracy cover-up of activities by those involved in the 1884 arrests. He then lost his
principalship after the Democrats were defeated in 1886 (Gerber 233–43).
[8] Bourbons, or Redeemers, were white southern politicians who gained control of their
state legislatures at the end of Reconstruction in the 1870s, on the pretense of redeeming these governments from Republican and African-American control. Detractors nick-
named them Bourbons with the implication that they mimicked behavior of French ruling monarchs unable to divest themselves of past ideas and practices. Most were

That the colored people will ever inaugurate anything that could be
seriously called a race war, is not likely. They have the experience of the
past to warn them. Never but once in history have they come out victori-
ous in such a struggle, and the conditions under which they were successful in San Domingo are not apt to be repeated.[9] Even supposing them
equal in numbers and intelligence to the Southern whites, they know from
painful experience that the spirit of slavery is not dead at the North, but
that in the event of any widespread conflict, Southern whites would be re-
enforced by their sympathizers at the North. The people who are characterized as "ignorant, degraded and brutal," know quite enough to appreciate the lessons of the draft riots in New York, the Cincinnati riots, and
the active Copperheadism of the War period.[10]

That the colored people can improve their condition by a general organization, like that of the Irish National League for instance, is hardly

conservative Democrats—joined by some former Whigs—who favored less government,
reduced taxes, and severely limited state services. Most of all, they were commercial-
minded men who aligned themselves with similar interests in the North in order to exploit the natural resources of the South for personal gain. The Populist movement of the
1890s was an unsuccessful attempt to overthrow Bourbon rule (*Dictionary of American
History* 1:354). See also Hicks, *Atlantic Monthly*, and Woodward.

[9] Chesnutt refers to the only successful slave insurrection in the Western hemisphere, led
by Toussaint L'Ouverture (1743–1803) at San Domingo, the colonial name of Haiti.
The French Revolution precipitated the incident because it led France to grant freedom
to all in its domain. But the French, Spanish, and British colonial powers refused to acknowledge this freedom at San Domingo. The more privileged mulattoes fought a civil
war with the colonial powers and were eventually joined by 400,000 black slaves. Together, they forced all whites out of Haiti in 1791.

[10] New York draft riots rested chiefly on the provision that allowed money payments in
lieu of service in the military, thus distinguishing rich men's money from the blood of
poor men. Shortly after the drawing of lots on July 13, 1863, at the Ninth Congressional
District draft headquarters, a mob of mostly immigrant laborers stormed the building;
overpowered attendants, police, firemen, and militia; and attacked residences, other
draft district headquarters, saloons, hotels, restaurants, and even railway tracks. The
riot lasted four days, with 1,000 casualties and $1.5 million in property losses. On July
15, militia regiments from Gettysburg began to restore order (*Dictionary of American
History* 2:368). Riots occurred in both Toledo and Cincinnati when largely immigrant
Irishmen dock workers in 1862 feared African Americans migrating north from the
South would depress wages and lashed out violently. African-American workers were
beaten and their property was destroyed by the rioters (Gerber 29). Copperheads were
originally followers of Andrew Beaumont in Luzerne County, Pennsylvania, who opposed
a Democratic faction led by Hendrick B. Wright. During the Civil War, they opposed the
war policy of President Abraham Lincoln. Sometimes called Butternuts or Peace Democrats, Copperheads sought restoration of the Union through negotiation rather than war,
denounced military arrests, conscription, emancipation, and other war measures. They

possible.[11] The recent troubles in Mississippi grew out of an attempt to organize a colored Farmers' Alliance. If a peaceful organization for industrial protection is discouraged in so emphatic a way—by the estimated murder of at least a hundred colored people, among them the leaders of the organization—what kind of reception would a similar political organization meet?

The advice that colored people should have nothing to say in the prevailing discussion is doubtless intended in the best possible spirit. The writer who gave it is evidently friendly to those whom she would advise. But it is asking too much of poor human nature.[12] Perhaps white people, with centuries of culture behind them, have reached that point of self-control where they could endure in silence such indignities and wrongs as are heaped upon the Negro—tho no such fact is apparent from the study of their history. Indeed, the fact that they have always loved liberty, have spoken and fought to maintain it, is the noblest characteristic of the English-speaking race. The colored people were denied the right to fight for their freedom until the rebellion was substantially over, but that they should now be denied the right to speak for themselves, that they should continue to be the passive bone of contention between North and South, is asking them to be false to Nature, false to humanity, false to every tradition of human liberty.

But since the colored people can do none of these things, what can they do? Perhaps, after all, these conflicting and impracticable opinions can be reconciled in such a manner as to avoid confusion, and thus, after all, to lead to safety.

For instance, if the colored people cannot emigrate *en masse*, they can gradually spread over the country. The advantages of such dispersion are

---

were strongest in Indiana, Illinois, and Ohio, the home state of their leader C. L. Vallandigham, who was eventually arrested (see Benton). The Copperheads were discredited with the successful end to the Civil War.

[11] The Irish National Land League was founded in Dublin on October 21, 1879, as a reaction to the worsening conditions of tenant farmers during the agricultural depression of the 1870s. One of their primary goals was the abolition of landlordism and the establishment of peasant proprietorship. This group eventually united farmers, townspeople, clergy, and laborers, who all suffered from the power of landlords (Hickey and Doherty 291–92). Racial differences most likely would have prevented such a coalition in the American South.

[12] In a front-page story entitled "A Word to Colored People," published in the September 12, 1889, issue of *The Independent,* writer Rebecca Harding Davis "urge[s] them to remain cool and passive during the present vehement discussion of the 'Negro Question,' or the 'Coming Race War.'" She then calls for "Patience, patience, friends! You will not prove to the world that you deserve its best chances by showing that you can be vindictive and virulent."

obvious. It would hasten the ultimate assimilation of the two races, which would be quickest where race prejudice is weakest. It would keep the colored people in touch with their friends, who are most numerous at the North where colored people are fewest—not, indeed, as the Southern whites assert, because they know least about the Negro, but because slavery and proscriptive laws and the supposed exigencies of partisan politics have not benumbed their consciences, or warped their love of liberty. The descendants of the Puritans, who direct the public sentiment of the North and West, would, if confronted with such a condition, find some other method than assassination and disfranchisement to counteract the alleged dangers of Negro ascendancy. There is already a large movement of colored people toward the North. But unfortunately for those who remain, it is a movement of the younger and more aspiring element, who can find in the North larger opportunities for development. For in spite of the assertious Southern white people and their apologists, race prejudice at the North does not entirely prevent colored people from climbing up into the higher walks of life. The writer of this article lives in a city where there are about five thousand colored people—about one in fifty of the population. And he is not guessing when he says there is no colored man in the city qualified to follow any special pursuit requiring special knowledge, who cannot, by reason of race prejudice, find employment at it; and with few exceptions, no pursuit which he cannot, for that reason, qualify himself to follow. With such a state of public opinion, which is true of a large part of the North, it is not strange that young colored people should leave the South. Their departure will better their own condition, and, after all, the progress of any race is dependent on the advancement of individuals. One Vanderbilt, one Stewart, one [U.S. Senator Chauncey] Depew, one [Thomas Alva] Edison, one leader in any department of human endeavor, would do more to enlarge the opportunities of colored people than double the same aggregate of wealth, or talent, or labor, scattered among a hundred or a thousand of them.

If they cannot combine all over the South for the purpose of securing their rights they can in certain localities. They can at the North. By a proper organization of their voting strength, which in many localities and in half a dozen States constitutes the balance of power, they can compel the local recognition of such rights as are still denied them, and force upon the attention of Congress and the Administration the condition of their brethren at the South. The whole machinery of the Government was once put in motion to procure the return of fugitive slaves; it is strange that the combined wisdom of Congress cannot devise some plan whereby the Constitution will be a shield rather than a sword to these struggling millions.

The colored people will instigate no race war. But when they are attacked, they should defend themselves. When the Southern Negro reaches that high conception of liberty that would make him rather die than submit to the lash, when he will meet force with force, there will be an end of Southern outrages. The man who will offer a personal indignity to another who has not injured him, is a tyrant and a coward, and will not continue a conflict with no odds in his favor. History is full of inspiration, and of illustrious example, for the defenders of liberty. The memory of those who die for liberty is cherished; the names of tyrants become the synonyms for all that is basest in human nature.

The colored people can speak out for themselves, and ought to whenever they can safely do so. The right of free speech is as sacred to a freeman as any other right, for through it he sets in motion the agencies which secure his liberty. Whether or not he can exercise his rights is not to the point; he should nevertheless assert them. The Declaration of Independence was not the cool utterance of a nation secure in its position; it was the indignant remonstrance of an outraged, disorganized people; and coming from the heart it went to the heart, and not only inspired Americans to heroic effort, but enlisted the sympathy and admiration of lovers of liberty the world over. Rash and intemperate expression on the part of colored people, where the consequences can easily be foreseen, is to be deplored. But a just self-respect requires that they should let the world know that they are not "dumb, driven cattle," but that they know, and know better than any one else can, the extent to which they are oppressed and outraged. If the colored people of the South could voice in one cry all the agony of their twenty-five years of so-called freedom, the whole world would listen, and give back such an indignant protest as would startle this boasted land of the free into seeing itself, for a moment at least, as others see it—as a country where prejudice has usurped the domain of law, where justice is no longer impartial, and where the citizen deprived of his rights has no redress.

SOME REQUISITES OF A LAW REPORTER

The requisites of a law reporter, in my opinion, may be broadly classified as natural and acquired.

The natural qualifications requisite for a successful law reporter are easily disposed of. Quickness of apprehension—the ability to "catch-on"

Proceedings of the Eighth and Ninth Annual Conventions of the Ohio Stenographers' Association, 1891.

quickly—is one; a reporter must understand, superficially at least, what is going on, and he has no time to study it out. Good hearing is another. When one is listening merely to understand, one word or sentence explains another; but when listening to record, each word, at least each sentence, must explain itself, and therefore must be heard distinctly. Quickness of movement is equally essential; the reporter who takes down correctly a rapid cross-examination has not a second to loose [sic]. His work must be even. The regularity of the piston stroke of an engine would hardly be sufficient to characterize it; it must be rather the steady flow of a stream of water, which pauses only when the initial pressure is interrupted.

A cool head, an even temper, as much modesty as is consistent with a proper self-respect, are other requisites which may be classed as natural, though they may be more or less influenced by education.

The things I have mentioned are requisite in order to write shorthand, after having learned it. In order to learn it, even in the abstract, with no reference to any special application, two things are necessary—patience and perseverance. Perhaps the first generation of law reporters, who acquired the art painfully and without other instruction than the text books afforded, needed more patience in unravelling difficulties than the generation who are receiving instruction in well conducted schools. But perseverence is necessary in any case. One cannot acquire, in a few brief weeks, the ability to record accurately in unaccustomed and abbreviated signs the language which it has taken 20 years to learn to speak and write in longhand with average correctness. Any instance cited to the contrary is a phenomenon.

The acquired requisites of a law reporter are more numerous. We must bear in mind the duties of a law reporter; that he is expected to take down correctly and write out intelligibly whatever takes place in a court of justice. The proceedings of a court in one year, in the present age of commercial and scientific activity, are likely to embrace, in one of our great cities, a large part of the field of human knowledge. To be thoroughly at home in this work, to do it easily and well, a reporter should know everything. Perhaps my claim may seem too broad and I ought to specify. For instance:

I. *A good law reporter should be an accomplished linguist.* Not only should he be thoroughly acquainted with the principal languages of Europe, but with their chief dialects, for he does not know at what moment he may be called upon to report the testimony of a German, a Frenchman, a Pole, a Dutchman, a Russian, or a Spaniard. Perchance the witness will testify in what he intends for English, which will be plentifully interlarded with words and phrases of his mother tongue. If he disclaims a knowledge of English an interpreter is needed, and it is convenient for the reporter to act in that capacity. It adds to the dignity and importance of the profession.

Languages are sometimes very much modified by a new environment. Take the following gem for an example of what German, for instance, may become in the United States: "John Miller, welcher de best gekhnownter Citizen von seine Ward ist, un seit de bloody fourth mit Intschein 33 geronnt hat, ist gestern nacht beinah auf de spout naufgagangen, because er die light extinguishen wollt bei de gas ausblasen. Wenn er seinen Kopf level gehalten hatte, konnte so etwas nicht happen. Glucklicherweise war Dr. Schnabenheiser an die Hand und mit einer Elektrisir Maschine ist Mr. Miller fur seine fellow-citizens gesaved worden. In die zuckerhaftige nach-und-nach sollte Mr. Miller carefuller sein und nicht mit die ward bummers die Districkt roth painten wollen und somit nicht geluscht nach Haus kommen zu Hahnekrah." [1]

The reporter who could struggle successfully with this specimen of transplanted German would certainly have to be a linguist of remarkable powers. I fear that mixed languages would affect the reporter unaccustomed to them somewhat as mixed drinks are popularly supposed to affect the uninitiated. I heard a few years ago of a Chautauqua phonographer who could report foreign languages with no previous acquaintance with them, so marvelous a mastery had he obtained of his art. I have not heard of him lately. I suppose he is dead; in fact, I hardly see how he could expect to live long.[2]

II. The successful law reporter should be thoroughly versed in medical science. Large numbers of law suits are concerned with personal injuries and their resulting complications. In order to report such cases a re-

---

[1] Joachim Baer, retired professor and chairperson of the Department of German at the University of North Carolina at Greensboro, Greensboro, NC, translates this pidgin German as follows: "John Miller, best known citizen in his ward, and who since the 'bloody fourth' ran with 'Intschein 33' (initiation 33?—the 33rd degree of Free Masonic Lodge?), last night almost went up the 'spout' because he wanted to extinguish the light from the gas flames. Had he kept a clear head, this could not have happened. Fortunately, Dr. Schnabenheiser was close by and with his 'electrifying' machine was able to preserve Mr. Miller's life for his fellow citizens. In future, Mr. Miller should be more careful and should not attempt to paint his district red together with the ward bums, and furthermore, should not come home like a 'lush' (inebriated) in the early morning hours when the cocks start crowing." Professor Baer concludes that "Mr. Miller did something wrong, perhaps climbing up a lantern post to extinguish a light while inebriated, and then fell down, and a witness is probably trying to explain what Mr. Miller had done. The statement is a mixture of German words and American slang, with German grammar superimposed on English words."

[2] According to Helen Chesnutt's biography, her father "reported testimony in court for leading corporation and admiralty lawyers, and no matter how scientific or technical the testimony was, his background in education, law, newspaper reporting, and literature enabled him to understand it and reproduce it with absolute accuracy" (183).

porter should be familiar with anatomy, physiology, hygiene, *materia medica* and therapeutics. I would suggest a three years' course in medicine as an excellent and almost indispensable preparation for law reporting. No stenographer could take down the following paragraph, taken at random from a medical work, without some previous knowledge of the subject. It is a description of the course of the facial nerve, which gives expression to the countenance:

"The nerve passes forwards and outwards upon the crus cerebelli, and enters the internal auditory meatus with the auditory nerve. At the bottom of the meatus it enters the aquaeductus Falliopii, and follows the serpentine course of that canal through the petrous portion of the temporal bone from its commencement at the internal meatus to its termination at the stylo-mastoid foramen. It is at first directed outwards towards the hiatus Falliopii, and divides behind the ramus of the inferior maxillary into the tempero-facial and cervico-facial branches. As it emerges from the stylo-mastoid, it sends a twig to the pneumo-gastric, another to the glosso-pharyngeal nerve, and communicates with the carotid-plexus of the sympathetic with the great auricular branch of the cervical plexus and with the auroculo-temporal branch of the inferior maxillary nerve in the parotid gland." Or this simple passage:

"The great or deep cardiac plexus (*plexus magnus profundus*) is situated in front of the trachea at its bifurcation. It is formed by the cardiac nerves derived from the cervical ganglia of the sympathetic, and the cardiac branches of the recurrent laryngeal and pneumo-gastric."

Let the reporter who thinks he knows everything struggle with a few pages of similar matter, and his opinion of his powers may be slightly modified.

III.   The successful law reporter should be a thorough scientist. He should be proficient in electricity, chemistry, mechanics and civil engineering. He should know the difference between a chlorate and a chloride. When an electrical expert casually remarks that "the conductivity of an electrolyte is proportional to the sum of the oppositely directed velocities of the anion and cation," or that "there is a remarkable relation between the migration constants and the conductivities of extremely dilute solutions containing electro chemically equivalent amounts of haloid or oxygen salts," the competent reporter should have the words at his fingers' ends, and be sufficiently well informed on the subject, to know, when he reads it, whether he has it right or not.

IV.   *A successful law reporter should know how to spell.* Those who think this statement an anti-climax should pause and reflect that the man who knows how to spell must know all the rest, and that good spelling is the last accomplishment of the cultivated. A good speller, in a scholarly sense, should know how to spell not only the words he is familiar with, but those he has never heard; he should be thoroughly acquainted with the principles which govern the derivation and formation of technical and scientific terminology.

V. *A good law reporter should be a lawyer.* A majority of the leading reporters of the country, perhaps, have read law. Others, by long experience, are fairly good theoretical lawyers, without any systematic course of reading. In the reporting of charges or opinions, a sufficient knowledge of law to be able to get citations correctly, and to know when a proposition of law is correctly stated, is almost absolutely necessary to an accurate law reporter.

VI. A knowledge of English grammar is essential to a successful law reporter. If a distinguished lawyer or a learned judge uses such an expression as this, for instance: "If the witness had of saw the defendant"—and it is not an uncommon thing for distinguished counsel and venerable judges to make mistakes of that kind—the reporter should be able to write what the judge meant to say. A knowledge of grammar is of vastly more importance to the reporter than to the judge or the lawyer. They deal with ideas, or ought to; the reporter is chiefly concerned with words.

I might go on, perhaps, at great length to tell what a successful law reporter should be. I might say that he should be a gentleman, for he must expect to get most of his employment from among gentlemen, who, very naturally, will prefer to deal with gentlemen. It is not necessary to define the meaning of the word "gentleman" to this audience. A successful reporter must have tact. He must be a good collector. He should know how to take care of money when he gets it. I think that it would add very much to happiness and length of life if every professional reporter had some fad or hobby outside of his profession. The reporter's work does not call into play to any great extent the higher faculties of the mind. Memory and exactness are his main intellectual tools, even if he should acquire every branch of knowledge which has been suggested for his equipment. It is true that a certain grade of reporters have to draw on their imagination, have even to exercise their judgment at times, in deciding what is the best thing with which to fill up a *hiatus* in a report; but this exercise is denied to the skilled reporter, who gets what is said.

An avocation of some kind—music, art, literature, something which calls into play a different set of faculties than his daily work demands—will preserve his mental balance and virility and keep him from falling into a rut from which he cannot extricate himself. A Chicago stenographer is a distinguished amateur astronomer. Several stenographers of my acquaintance are of an inventive turn of mind. There are certain kinds of "fads" which, however, it is well to avoid. It does not help a reporter any to be a

valiant trencher-man or an expert at poker, or to have a too wide an acquaintance with the various liquids which are prepared and sold for the refreshment of the thirsty.

One qualification which I was about to overlook, but which some
members of the profession might deem important, though, perhaps, a secondary consideration, is the ability to write shorthand rapidly and correctly, and to read it back readily. Indeed, upon second thoughts, I suspect
this is the first requisite of a successful law reporter. All the learning of the
ages—the linguistic accomplishments of a Cardinal [Giuseppe] Mezzofanti or an Elihu Burritt; the scientific attainments of a [Charles] Darwin,
a [Michael] Farraday, an Edison;[3] the legal learning of a [Sir William]
Blackstone or a [Joseph] Story; even the wisdom of Solomon, the genius
of a Raphael or a Shakespeare—will not avail you to report a case if you
do not know how.

Perhaps some one may think I have set too high a standard for the law
reporter, higher than there is any reasonable probability of his reaching. If
so, I think it is better to err on the safe side; better to know too much than
too little; better not to attempt what you cannot do well. "Hitch your
wagon to a star," said Emerson, and let me add, if you never reach the star,
you can at least keep your wagon tongue up out of the mud.[4]

"I think it is about time for me to make another speech. If I understand my friend, there is a vast amount of work awaiting the young man or
woman who has an ambition to become a court stenographer. Assuming
that he is a man of fair intelligence and training at the age of 21, and that
he has so far mastered the art of shorthand as to be able to write ordinary
English at the rate of 150 words per minute and read it afterwards, he has
only begun the training that is necessary to fit him for his work. In the first
place, he must become an accomplished linguist, and he must be a very
brilliant man if he can perform the task in the succeeding three years, and
by that time he will be 24. Then he must become a lawyer, and, of course,
he ought to be a good lawyer. That under ordinary circumstances, would
require three years more of study, and then he is 27. He must then qualify
himself as a physician, and, as no half training will answer the purpose, it

---

[3] Italian Cardinal Giuseppe Caspar Mezzofanti (1774–1849) became a professor of Ara-
bic, Asian languages, and Greek. Chesnutt is perhaps impressed with the cardinal's reputation for having "considerable fluency, and in some cases even with attention to dialectic
peculiarities, [in] some fifty or sixty languages of most widely separated families, besides
having a less perfect acquaintance with many others." Elihu Burritt (1810–1879), nick-
named "the learned blacksmith," was an American crusader for peace and a code of international law. He wrote Olive Leaves and had learned fifty languages by age thirty.
[4] A Mr. Sauder immediately responds to Chesnutt:

will take three more years of his time to become an expert in that profession, and by that time he will have reached an even thirty years. Still persisting in the pursuit of knowledge essential to the faithful performance of his duties in his chosen profession, he undertakes to become an expert chemist, and spends three years in learning the mysteries of that profession, when he finds himself 33 years old. By this time he feels encouraged in the thought that he is making some degree of progress, and starts out cheerfully to master the laws of natural philosophy, and spends three years more in becoming an expert physicist, at the end of which time he will be 36 years old. Not content with his limited acquirements, he becomes an expert geologist at the age of 39. He wouldn't dream of calling his education complete without becoming an expert surveyor and civil engineer, and that brings him up to 42. And so he keeps on with a fixed determination that he will never stop until he is thoroughly competent to meet any and every expert who may appear upon the witness stand, and report him with unfailing accuracy and perfect ease. I have been thinking it over and trying to figure it out, and have come to the conclusion that if a man desires to be a competent law stenographer, with the utmost diligence he will find himself about 80 years old before he will reach his goal; and I am not married yet. For there is no limit to the things that he ought to know, and which are necessary for him to know in order to intelligently do his work. Among other things, he must be an expert astronomer. For, if you are going to 'hitch your wagon to a star,' you must be able to find your star, and that will take you at least three years. I asked Mr. Chesnutt how a man could hitch his wagon to a star if he never reached the star, and he said he should lasso it. So he must go out to the wild west and take lessons in throwing the lasso from the cowboys of the plains in order to be able to hitch his wagon to a star after he has located the star. All these things will take time and demand a vast amount of industry, but he must go through it all in order to become a competent court stenographer.

Speaking seriously, there is some truth in the elaborate sarcasm that my friend has presented. There is none of us who has had any considerable experience who has not at times wished that he had the accumulated knowledge of the age, and felt that he might have use for it all in his daily employment. The most discouraging feature of it all is that his patrons do not recognize the necessity of his knowing anything more than simply how to make the little marks that are so mysterious to the uninitiated. It doesn't take a stenographer long to find out how grievous an error that is; but if he undertakes to convince his patrons that it is a mistake he will need another life time in which to do it."

THE FUTURE AMERICAN
What the Race Is Likely to Become in the Process of Time

A Perfect Type Supposably to Be Evolved—
Some Old Theories of Race that Are Exploded—
The Ethnic Elements on Which the Fusion Must Be Based

The future American race is a popular theme for essayists, and has been much discussed. Most expressions upon the subject, however, have been characterized by a conscious or unconscious evasion of some of the main elements of the problem involved in the formation of a future American race, or, to put it perhaps more correctly, a future ethnic type that shall inhabit the northen part of the western continent. Some of these obvious omissions will be touched upon in these articles; and if the writer has any preconceived opinions that would affect his judgment, they are at least not the hackneyed prejudices of the past—if they lead to false conclusions, they at least furnish a new point of view, from which, taken with other widely differing views, the judicious reader may establish a parallax that will enable him to approximate the truth.

The popular theory is that the future American race will consist of a harmonious fusion of the various European elements which now make up our heterogeneous population. The result is to be something infinitely superior to the best of the component elements. This perfection of type—for no good American could for a moment doubt that it will be as perfect as everything else American—is to be brought about by a combination of all the best characteristics of the different European races, and the elimination, by some strange alchemy, of all their undesirable traits—for even a good American will admit that European races, now and then, have some undesirable traits when they first come over. It is a beautiful, a hopeful, and to the eye of faith, a thrilling prospect. The defect of the argument, however, lies in the incompleteness of the premises, and its obliviousness of certain facts of human nature and human history.

Before putting forward any theory upon the subject, it may be well enough to remark that recent scientific research has swept away many hoary anthropological fallacies. It has been demonstrated that the shape or size of the head has little or nothing to do with the civilization or average intelligence of a race; that language, so recently lauded as an infallible test of racial origin is of absolutely no value in this connection, its distribution

Boston Evening Transcript, August 18, 1900.

being dependent upon other conditions than race. Even color, upon which the social structure of the United States is so largely based, has been proved no test of race. The conception of a pure Aryan, Indo-European race has been abandoned in scientific circles, and the secret of the progress of Europe has been found in racial heterogeneity, rather than in racial purity. The theory that the Jews are a pure race has been exploded, and their peculiar type explained upon a different and much more satisfactory hypothesis. To illustrate the change of opinion and the growth of liberality in scientific circles, imagine the reception which would have been accorded to this proposition, if laid down by an American writer fifty or sixty years ago:

"The European races, as a whole, show signs of a secondary or derived origin; certain characteristics, especially the texture of the hair, lead us to class them as intermediate between the extreme primary types of the Asiatic and Negro races respectively." (Professor [William Z.] Ripley's "Races of Europe:[A Sociological Study]," page 457; New York, 1899.)[1] This is put forward by the author, not as a mere hypothesis, but as a proposition fairly susceptible of proof, and is supported by an elaborate argument based upon microscopical comparisons, to which numerous authorities are cited. If this fact be borne in mind it will simplify in some degree our conception of a future American ethnic type.

By modern research the unity of the human race has been proved (if it needed any proof to the careful or fair-minded observer), and the differentiation of races by selection and environment has been so stated as to prove itself. Greater emphasis has been placed upon environment as a factor in ethnic development, and what has been called "the vulgar theory of race," as accounting for progress and culture, has been relegated to the limbo of exploded dogmas. One of the most perspicuous and forceful presentations of these modern conclusions of anthropology is found in the volume above quoted, a book which owes its origin to a Boston scholar.

Proceeding then upon the firm basis laid down by science and the historic parallel, it ought to be quite clear that the future American race—the future American ethnic type—will be formed of a mingling, in a yet to be ascertained proportion, of the various racial varieties which make up the present population of the United States; or, to extend the area a little farther, of the various peoples of the northern hemisphere of the western con-

---

[1] An 1899 first edition of *The Races of Europe: A Sociological Study* by William Z. Ripley was published in New York by D. Appleton Company and a 1900 limited edition in London by Kegan Paul, Trench, Trubner & Co. Ripley also ridicules the belief that longheaded, tall blonds were the first Aryans or the prototype for all humans (453–56). Chesnutt's support for Ripley's views shows forward and mostly accurate thinking in light of recent DNA discoveries and the successful mappings of the human genome.

tinent; for, if certain recent tendencies are an index of the future, it is not safe to fix the boundaries of the future United States anywhere short of the Arctic Ocean on the north and the Isthmus of Panama on the south.[2] But, even with the continuance of the present political divisions, conditions of trade and ease of travel are likely to gradually assimilate to one type all the countries of the hemisphere. Assuming that the country is so well settled that no great disturbance of ratios is likely to result from immigration, or any serious conflict of races, we may safely build our theory of a future American race upon the present population of the country. I use the word "race" here in its popular sense—that of a people who look substantially alike, and are moulded by the same culture and dominated by the same ideals.

By the eleventh census, the ratios of which will probably not be changed materially by the census now under way, the total population of the United States was about 65,000,000, of which about seven million were black and colored, and something over 200,000 were of Indian blood. It is then in the three broad types—white, black and Indian—that the future American race will find the material for its formation. Any dream of a pure white race, of the Anglo-Saxon type, for the United States, may as well be abandoned as impossible, even if desirable. That such future race will be predominately white may well be granted—unless climate in the course of time should modify existing types; that it will call itself white is reasonably sure; that it will conform closely to the white type is likely; but that it will have absorbed and assimilated the blood of the other two races mentioned is as certain as the operation of any law well can be that deals with so uncertain a quantity as the human race.

There are no natural obstacles to such an amalgamation. The unity of the race is not only conceded but demonstrated by actual crossing. Any theory of sterility due to race crossing may as well be abandoned; it is founded mainly on prejudice and cannot be proved by the facts. If it come from Northern or European sources, it is likely to be weakened by lack of knowledge; if from Southern sources, it is sure to be colored by prejudice. My own observation is that in a majority of cases people of mixed blood are very

---

[2] Under the concept of manifest destiny, the United States assumed it had divine sanction for territorial expansion. The phrase was first coined in an 1845 issue of *United States Magazine and Democratic Review* edited by John L. O'Sullivan (*The New Lexicon Webster's Dictionary of the English Language* 606). Chesnutt was apparently noting its recent applications since the Spanish American War.

prolific and very long-lived. The admixture of races in the United States has never taken place under conditions likely to produce the best results; but there have nevertheless been enough conspicuous instances to the contrary in this country, to say nothing of a long and honorable list in other lands, to disprove the theory that people of mixed blood, other things being equal, are less virile, prolific or able than those of purer strains. But whether this be true or not is apart from this argument. Admitting that races may mix, and that they are thrown together under conditions which permit their admixture, the controlling motive will be not abstract considerations with regard to a remote posterity, but present interest and inclination.

The Indian element in the United States proper is so small proportionally—about one in three hundred—and the conditions for its amalgamation so favorable, that it would of itself require scarcely any consideration in this argument. There is no prejudice against the Indian blood, in solution. A half or quarter-breed, removed from the tribal environment, is freely received among white people. After the second or third remove he may even boast of his Indian descent; it gives him a sort of distinction, and involves no social disability. The distribution of the Indian race, however, tends to make the question largely a local one, and the survival of tribal relation may postpone the results for some little time. It will be, however, the fault of the United States Indian himself if he be not speedily amalgamated with the white population.

The Indian element, however, looms up larger when we include Mexico and Central America in our fields of discussion. By the census of Mexico just completed, over eighty per cent of the population is composed of mixed and Indian races. The remainder is presumably of pure Spanish, or European blood, with a dash of Negro along the coast. The population is something over twelve millions, thus adding nine millions of Indians and Mestizos to be taken into account. Add several millions of similar descent in Central America, a million in Porto Rico, who are said to have an aboriginal strain, and it may safely be figured that the Indian element will be quite considerable in the future American race. Its amalgamation will involve no great difficulty, however; it has been going on peacefully in the countries south of us for several centuries, and is likely to continue along similar lines. The peculiar disposition of the American to overlook mixed blood in a foreigner will simplify the gradual absorption of these Southern races.

The real problem, then, the only hard problem in connection with the future American race, lies in the Negro element of our population. As I have said before, I believe it is destined to play its part in the formation of this new type. The process by which this will take place will be no sudden and wholesale amalgamation—a thing certainly not to be expected, and hardly to be desired. If it were held desirable, and one could imagine a government sufficiently autocratic to enforce its behests, it would be no great task to mix the races mechanically, leaving to time merely the fixing of the resultant type.

Let us for curiosity outline the process. To start with, the Negroes are already considerably mixed—many of them in large proportion, and most of them in some degree—and the white people, as I shall endeavor to show later on, are many of them slightly mixed with the Negro. But we will assume, for the sake of the argument, that the two races are absolutely pure. We will assume, too, that the laws of the whole country were as favorable to this amalgamation as the laws of most Southern States are at present against it; i.e., that it were made a misdemeanor for two white or two colored persons to marry, so long as it was possible to obtain a mate of the other race—this would be even more favorable than the Southern rule, which makes no such exception. Taking the population as one-eighth Negro, this eighth, married to an equal number of whites, would give in the next generation a population of which one-fourth would be mulattoes. Mating these in turn with white persons, the next generation would be composed one-half of quadroons, or persons one-fourth Negro. In the third generation, applying the same rule, the entire population would be composed of octoroons, or persons only one-eighth Negro, who would probably call themselves white, if by this time there remained any particular advantage in being so considered. Thus in three generations the pure whites would be entirely eliminated, and there would be no perceptible trace of the blacks left.

The mechanical mixture would be complete; as it would probably be put, the white race would have absorbed the black. There would be no inferior race to domineer over; there would be no superior race to oppress those who differed from them in racial externals. The inevitable social struggle, which in one form or another, seems to be one of the conditions of progress, would proceed along other lines than those of race. If now and then, for a few generations, an occasional trace of the black ancestor should crop out, no one would care, for all would be tarred with the same stick. This is already the case in South America, parts of Mexico and to a large extent in the West Indies. From a negroid nation, which ours is already, we would have become a composite and homogeneous people, and the elements of racial discord which have troubled our civil life so gravely and still threaten our free institutions, would have been entirely eliminated.

But this will never happen. The same result will be brought about slowly and obscurely, and, if the processes of nature are not too violently interrupted by the hand of man, in such a manner as to produce the best results with the least disturbance of natural laws. In another article I shall endeavor to show that this process has been taking place with greater rapidity than is generally supposed, and that the results have been such as to encourage the belief that the formation of a uniform type out of our present racial elements will take place within a measurably near period.

THE WHITE AND THE BLACK

After attending the Negro conference at Tuskegee, which has been fully described in your columns, I paid a visit to Atlanta University, of which institution I was the guest for several days.[1] The contrast, in some respects, between Tuskegee and Atlanta was very striking. In the one, the busy note of industry was predominant; in the other, an air of scholastic quiet pervaded the grounds and the halls. Perhaps the weather, which was unusually cold for Atlanta, had some effect in restraining the natural exuberance of youth. The difference, it seemed to me, however, lay deeper. Atlanta avowedly stands for the higher education. If it be granted that the majority of the Negroes must work with their hands, like the majority of all other races, and that manual training will best prepare them to work effectively, it is none the less true that, abandoned as they are by the Southern whites, in church, in school and in social life, they need leaders along these lines—picked men and women, in whose training special stress has been laid upon the highest ideals of manhood and womanhood, upon culture of mind, character and manners. This school, which is under the charge of New England people, has, in its externals, a completeness of detail

---

Boston Evening Transcript, March 20, 1901.

[1] In "A Visit to Tuskegee," published March 31, 1901, in the *Cleveland Leader,* Chesnutt wrote about attending a conference held at Booker T. Washington's Tuskegee Institute in Tuskegee, Alabama, before he visited Atlanta University and hearing African-American farmers relate economic success stories. Atlanta University was founded in 1865 by benevolent northern organizations, especially the American Missionary Association. See Adams and Bacote.

which is not apparent in some other Southern schools. While there is nothing fine about it, nothing superfluous, there is [sic] a neatness and an attention to little things that makes bareness seem mere simplicity. The teaching force, which is mainly white, has been supplemented by the addition of several colored teachers, men and women of high culture, who do not lower the average. The most conspicuous of these is Dr. W. E. B. Dubois, whose studies in sociology have won him a wide reputation. The group of schools at Atlanta devoted to the education of colored youth have been a powerful lever for the elevation of this neglected race, and it is sincerely to be hoped that no zeal for other forms of training will lead them to suffer. The Negroes of the South need all sorts of training; the South is not able to give it unaided, even if those in power were willing to do so, and they are not over-enthusiastic. The North has a twofold interest: it insisted upon keeping the South in the Union: it has, therefore, a family interest. Another consideration is that under prevailing conditions in the South, many people of color will, in time, prefer to live at the North, and the better prepared they are for citizenship, the less difficulty will the North have in their assimilation. For instance, from the town of Wilmington, N. C., since the "revolution," as the white people call it, or the "massacre," according to the Negroes—it was really both—over fifteen hundred of the best colored citizens have left the town. Most of these have sought homes farther North. It is a curious revival of ante-bellum conditions. The Negroes in the South are not yet free, and social odium at the North is deemed, by many, preferable to the same thing at the South, with oppressive and degrading legal enactments superadded.

I have said that the Southern Negro is not free. The same may be said of the Southern white man, for the laws which seek the separation of the races apply to him as well—but with a very material difference. Society is divided into horizontal strata, with the white man on top. One can endure, with considerable equanimity, restrictions which make him superior, whether he will or no. The brunt of the separation falls upon the Negro, but the white man does not escape.

For instance, on leaving Washington, D.C., the capital of a nation, by the constitution of which all men are equal before the law one is confronted in the Southern Railway Depot with signs in the cars labelled respectively "White" and "Colored." The passenger is supposed to take his seat according to his complexion. If he does not he is sure to be called to order in a short time. The law, however, does not really become effective until the train has crossed the river into Virginia, the old-time mother of presidents and breeder of slaves. She has lost her first preeminence; the existence of these laws shows with what tenacity she clings to the other. But, nevertheless, the American citizen, white or black, who has travelled all over the North and West, with only the private consciousness that his color affected his citizenship, is met at this gate to the Sunny South with a classification which puts a legal stamp upon the one as superior, upon the other as inferior. A white man is never allowed to forget that he is white: lest he forget, a large sign is fastened at either end of the car, keeping him constantly in mind of the fact. A colored man is not permitted to cherish any illusions as to equality; if he should endeavor for a moment, in his temporary isolation, to forget this fact and all it implies, that sign in large white letters keeps him sternly admonished of the fact that between him and mankind not of his own color, or some variety of it, there is a great gulf.

I could almost write a book about these laws, their variations, their applications and curious stories that one hears continually concerning them. When first adopted there was some pretence made of furnishing equal accommodations for the different classes of passengers; but as soon as the Supreme Court of the United States had affirmed the validity of this class of legislation, the pretence of equality was practically dropped.[2] It could not be otherwise. With society thus divided, horizontally, the two classes of travellers were not equal in numbers, in appearance, in means or in any other way. Most of the colored travellers are poor, many of them uncouth and passively submissive to the inevitable. That they should be treated with equal courtesy or be given equal comfort and consideration would be contrary to human nature. The Negro coach is invariably the less comfortable of the two and the less ornate. It is always in the least desirable portion of the train. A colored passenger often does not know where he must sit. He is shifted around from compartment to compartment to suit the convenience of the traffic. The conductor of a train has the power of an autocrat. He nods his Jove-like head, corrugates his high Caucasian brow and the Negro seldom argues, because there is no use in doing so.

"How long," I asked a Virginia conductor, "has this Jim Crow car system been in operation?"

"Since last July," he answered.

---

[2] Homer Plessey was the plaintiff in the precedent-establishing, "separate but equal" case of *Plessey v. Ferguson* (163 U.S. 537). The case challenged the Jim Crow statute that required separate seating based on race on trains in interstate commerce throughout Louisiana.

"Does it work all right?"

"Oh, yes."

"Do the colored people object to it?"

"No, they don't mind it. Some of them kicked a little at first—a nigger likes to show off, you know, put on a little airs; but I told 'em it was the law, and they would have to submit, as I had to. Personally I don't mean to take any chances; I've been hauled up in court once, or threatened with it, for not enforcing the law. I'd put a white man out of the colored car as quick as I'd put a nigger out of this one."

"Do you ever," I asked, "have any difficulty about classifying people who are very near the line?"

"Oh, yes, often."

"What do you do in a case of that kind?"

"I give the passenger the benefit of the doubt."

"That is, you treat him as a white man?"

"Certainly."

"But suppose you should find in the colored car a man who had a white face, but insisted that his descent entitled him to ride in that car; what would you do then?"

"I'd let him stay there," replied the conductor, with unconcealed disgust, which seemed almost to include the questioner who could suppose such a case. "Anyone that is fool enough to rather be a nigger than a white man may have his choice. He could stay there till h—ll froze over for all I'd care."

This reminds me of an incident which happened recently, down in North Carolina, where the conductor had no doubt, but afterward wished he had. On passing through the white car he saw a dark woman sitting there, whom he promptly spotted as colored, and upon whom he pounced with the zeal of a newly promoted man.

"You will have," he said abruptly, "to go into the other car."

"Why so?"

"This car is for white people only."

"I am white."

The conductor smiled incredulously. He knew a Negro when he saw one. "Come on," he said; "my time is valuable. I'll have the porter bring your valise."

The woman submitted. At her destination her son, a palpably and aggressively white man, was at the station to meet her. Upon seeing his mother alight from the Negro car, assisted by a colored porter—conductors in the South, on railroad or street cars, seldom or never assist colored women—the son demanded an explanation, which, when forthcoming, elicted [sic] from him a flood of language not suitable for newspaper publication. The next day suit was brought against the railroad company for $25,000 damages. It is to be hoped that judgment may be recovered. The more expensive this odious class legislation, so inconsistent with free institutions, can be made, the sooner it will be ended.

The same system prevails everywhere. There are separate waiting-rooms at the railway stations. If there is any choice of location the Negro always gets the worst room, and it is seldom so well lighted or clean. The signs usually read: "Waiting Room for White People," "Waiting Room for Colored People." In a certain town in North Carolina they read: "Ladies' Waiting Room," "General Waiting Room." No people of color are admitted to the ladies' waiting room. A colored lady, if she enter the station at all, must wait in the general waiting room, where white men and colored men smoke freely. In Atlanta the signs read: "Colored Waiting Room," "Waiting Room for Ladies and Gentlemen." It must be borne in mind that in the South the terms "gentleman" and "lady" are reserved, so far [as] public use of them is concerned, exclusively for white people. As a rule, only a white woman who is entirely beneath consideration is ever referred to as a "woman." The amount of ingenuity which a Southern newspaper will exercise to speak well of a colored man—they often speak well of individuals—without calling him "Mr." is very curious to study. He is cheerfully dubbed "Bishop," or "Dr.," or "Rev.," or "Professor," but the little prefix "Mr." is reserved exclusively for gentlemen—i.e., white men. It is the stamp of Vere de Vere.[3]

The separate system extends by law to schools, and by social custom to everything else. Two races who must live side by side are taught from infancy that they are essentially different and must not meet in any relation but that of master and servant, or superior and inferior. If the facts conformed always to the theory, the situation might be tolerable. But they are not even distinct races; the colored people certainly are not a distinct race. Many of the latter are persons of education and refinement, who have travelled at the north and in Europe, and who resent bitterly this attempt to degrade them permanently, by law, into a hopelessly inferior caste. That they are often silent proves nothing; they must live, or think they must, and the Negro who talks too much holds his life by uncertain tenure in the Southern States. Then, too, their self-respect prevents them from saying a

---

[3] Chesnutt alludes to Alfred Lord Tennyson's poem "Lady Clara Vere de Vere," which focuses on caste differences.

great deal to outsiders. A man of color who is treated in the North as a citizen, in Europe as a gentleman, does not like to tell strangers that at home he is a pariah and an outcast.

Of the expense to society this system entails, I will not speak; it is easily imaginable. Of the loss to the colored people, who are thus thrown back upon themselves and Northern philanthropists for that leadership which would naturally, under healthful conditions, come in large part from the white people of the community, there is no room to speak. Of the jealousy, the distrust, the deep-seated hatred which such conditions inevitably tend to promote, the less said, perhaps, the better.

There are other things in the South, of which we read in the newspapers, which do not tend to promote good citizenship. There are many good men in that section who will tell you, with a glance over the shoulder to see that no one else is within hearing, that they quite agree with you that the lynchings and burnings and discriminating franchise laws are all wrong, and that the best people do not approve of them. But the best people are evidently not in control, and make no public expression of their disapproval. Let us hope that they may some time pluck up courage to do the right, and assume the leadership to which by character and culture they are entitled. It will be better for the South and for the Negro, who is a large part and perhaps the most distinctive part of the South, when the white man of the South has obtained his freedom.

I cannot close this article without some reflections suggested by a book recently published, "The American Negro," by William Hannibal Thomas of Everett, Mass. Mr. Thomas has lived in Ohio, in Georgia, in South Carolina, and elsewhere.[4] I have recently been in all these States, and find a universal disposition everywhere to let Massachusetts claim him; she is, perhaps, better able to bear the burden than any other State. This book, being in large degree unquotable, and, consisting, as it does, of five or six hundred pages of defamation of a race with which he admits close kinship, it is difficult to pick out particular passages. Suffice it to say that it denies

------

[4] William Hannibal Thomas of Everett, Massachusetts, was of mixed ancestry but usually passed for white. He enlisted in the Ohio infantry during the Civil War, lived in Georgia, practiced law, served in the South Carolina legislature, and later became a colonel in the National Guard (Harlan, ed., 4:328). Chesnutt's review, "A Defamer of His Race," published in April 1901 in the *Critic* (350–51) denounces Thomas's racist book, *The American Negro: What He Was, What He Is. And What He May Become* (1901).

the Negro intellect, character, and capacity for advancement. With my own eyes I have seen, upon revisiting places which I knew eighteen or twenty years ago, that the colored people are acquiring property, in large amounts. Most of it, so far, is in the shape of farms, homes and churches; too much of it, perhaps, is tied up in churches, where a smaller number of those would suffice, for, thrown back largely upon the churches for social life, there are too many splits and dissentions [sic]. By the same token, some of the preachers might be better employed. But that many of them are earnest, God-fearing men, working zealously for the uplifting of their people, and serving them with profit to their moral and religious life, I can give personal testimony. I can say frankly that I was agreeably surprised to find the progress that was apparent on every hand—in culture, in character, in the accumulation of property, and in the power of organization. The recent reaction against the Negro is traceable to this very fact. At each forward step the Negro comes in contact or competition with the white man at some new point. The result is a new friction, with a consequent ebullition of race prejudice.

Mr. Thomas's statements concerning the womanhood and the youth of his race confute themselves by overstatement. I can truthfully say that during a month spent in the South, mainly among colored people, I found no evidence to support his views. The value of his book lies entirely in the character of the writer, his truthfulness, his judgment, and his means of observation; for it is backed up by no statistics.

SUPERSTITIONS AND FOLKLORE OF THE SOUTH

During a recent visit to North Carolina, after a long absence, I took occasion to inquire into the latter-day prevalence of the old-time belief in what was known as "conjuration" or "goopher," my childish recollection of which I have elsewhere embodied into a number of stories. The derivation of the word "goopher" I do not know, nor whether any other writer than myself has recognized its existence, though it is in frequent use in cer-

Modern Culture 13 (May 1901).

tain parts of the South. The origin of this curious superstition itself is perhaps more easily traceable. It probably grew, in the first place, out of African fetichism, which was brought over from the dark continent along with the dark people. Certain features, too, suggest a distant affinity with Voodooism, or snake worship, a cult which seems to have been indigenous to tropical America. These beliefs, which in the place of their origin had all the sanctions of religion and social custom, became, in the shadow of the white man's civilization, a pale reflection of their former selves. In time, too, they were mingled and confused with the witchcraft and ghost lore of the white man, and the tricks and delusions of the Indian conjurer. In the old plantation days they flourished vigorously, though discouraged by the "great house," and their potency was well established among the blacks and the poorer whites. Education, however, has thrown the ban of disrepute upon witchcraft and conjuration. The stern frown of the preacher, who looks upon superstition as the ally of the Evil One; the scornful sneer of the teacher, who sees in it a part of the livery of bondage, have driven this quaint combination of ancestral traditions to the remote chimney corners of old black aunties, from which it is difficult for the stranger to unearth them. Mr. [Joel Chandler] Harris, in his Uncle Remus stories, has, with fine literary discrimination, collected and put into pleasing and enduring form, the plantation stories which dealt with animal lore,[1] but so little attention has been paid to those dealing with so-called conjuration, that they seem in a fair way to disappear, without leaving a trace behind. The loss may not be very great, but these vanishing traditions might furnish valuable data for the sociologist, in the future study of racial development. In writing, a few years ago, the volume entitled "The Conjure Woman" [1899], I suspect that I was more influenced by the literary value of the material than by its sociological bearing, and therefore took, or thought I did, considerable liberty with my subject. Imagination, however, can only act upon data—one must have somewhere in his consciousness the ideas which he puts together to form a connected whole. Creative talent, of whatever grade, is, in the last analysis, only the power of rearrangement—there is nothing new under the sun. I was the more firmly

---

[1] *Uncle Remus: His Songs and His Sayings* (1881). Although Harris's Uncle Remus inspired Chesnutt's Uncle Julius, the author also strongly suggests in the interview with Max Bennett Thrasher included in this volume ("Mr. Chesnutt at Work: A Talk with an Author on His Methods") that the prototype for Uncle Julius is Uncle Henry, the gardener at the Fayetteville, North Carolina, home of Edwin Perry, Chesnutt's father-in-law. Uncle Henry first told Chesnutt the story of the goophered grapevine.

impressed with this thought after I had interviewed half a dozen old women, and a genuine "conjure doctor;" for I discovered that the brilliant touches, due, I had thought, to my own imagination, were after all but dormant ideas, lodged in my childish mind by old Aunt This and old Uncle That, and awaiting only the spur of imagination to bring them again to the surface. For instance, in the story, "Hot-foot Hannibal," there figures a conjure doll with pepper feet. Those pepper feet I regarded as peculiarly my own, a purely original creation. I heard, only the other day, in North Carolina, of the consternation struck to the heart of a certain dark individual, upon finding upon his door-step a rabbit's foot—a good omen in itself perhaps—to which a malign influence had been imparted by tying to one end of it, in the form of a cross, two small pods of red pepper!

Most of the delusions connected with this belief in conjuration grow out of mere lack of enlightenment. As primeval men saw a personality behind every natural phenomenon, and found a god or a devil in wind, rain, and hail, in lightning, and in storm, so the untaught man or woman who is assailed by an unusual ache or pain, some strenuous symptom of serious physical disorder, is prompt to accept the suggestion, which tradition approves, that some evil influence is behind his discomfort; and what more natural than to conclude that some rival in business or in love has set this force in motion?

Relics of ancestral barbarism are found among all peoples, but advanced civilization has at least shaken off the more obvious absurdities of superstition. We no longer attribute insanity to demoniac possession, nor suppose that a king's touch can cure scrofula. To many old people in the South, however, any unusual ache or pain is quite as likely to have been caused by some external evil influence as by natural causes. Tumors, sudden swellings due to inflammatory rheumatism or the bites of insects, are especially open to suspicion. Paralysis is proof positive of conjuration. If there is any doubt, the "conjure doctor" invariably removes it. The credulity of ignorance is his chief stock in trade—there is no question, when he is summoned, but that the patient has been tricked.

The means of conjuration are as simple as the indications. It is a condition of all witch stories that there must in some way be contact, either with the person, or with some object or image intended to represent the person to be affected; or, if not actual contact, at least close proximity. The charm is placed under the door-sill, or buried under the hearth, or hidden in the mattress of the person to be conjured. It may be a crude attempt to imitate the body of the victim, or it may consist merely of a bottle, or a gourd, or a little bag, containing a few rusty nails, crooked pins, or horsehairs. It may be a mysterious mixture thrown surreptitiously upon the person to be injured, or merely a line drawn across a road or path, which line it is fatal for a certain man or woman to cross. I heard of a case of a laboring man who went two miles out of his way, every morning and evening, while going to and from his work, to avoid such a line drawn for him by a certain powerful enemy.

Some of the more gruesome phases of the belief in conjuration suggest possible poisoning, a knowledge of which baleful art was once supposed to be widespread among the imported Negroes of the olden time. The blood or venom of snakes, spiders, and lizards is supposed to be employed for this purpose. The results of its administration are so peculiar, however, and so entirely improbable, that one is supposed to doubt even the initial use of poison, and figure it in as part of the same general delusion. For instance, a certain man "swelled up all over" and became "pieded," that is, pied or spotted. A white physician who was summoned thought that the man thus singularly afflicted was poisoned, but did not recognize the poison nor know the antidote. A conjure doctor, subsequently called in, was more prompt in his diagnosis. The man, he said, was poisoned with a lizard, which at that very moment was lodged somewhere in the patient's anatomy. The lizards and snakes in these stories, by the way, are not confined to the usual ducts and cavities of the human body, but seem to have freedom of movement throughout the whole structure. This lizard, according to the "doctor," would start from the man's shoulder, descend to his hand, return to the shoulder, and pass down the side of the body to the leg. When it reached the calf of the leg the lizard's head would appear right under the skin. After it had been perceptible for three days the lizard was to be cut out with a razor, or the man would die. Sure enough, the lizard manifested its presence in the appointed place at the appointed time; but the patient would not permit the surgery, and at the end of three days paid with death the penalty of his obstinacy. Old Aunt Harriet told me, with solemn earnestness, that she herself had taken a snake from her own arm, in sections, after a similar experience. Old Harriet may have been lying, but was, I imagine, merely self-deluded. Witches, prior to being burned, have often confessed their commerce with the Evil One. Why should Harriet hesitate to relate a simple personal experience which involved her in no blame whatever?

Old Uncle Jim, a shrewd, hard old sinner, and a palpable fraud, who did not, I imagine, believe in himself to any great extent, gave me some private points as to the manner in which these reptiles were thus transferred to the human system. If a snake or a lizard be killed, and a few drops of its blood be dried upon a plate or in a gourd, the person next eating or drinking from the contaminated vessel will soon become the unwilling landlord of a reptilian tenant. There are other avenues, too, by which the reptile may gain admittance; but when expelled by the conjure doctor's arts or medicines, it always leaves at the point where it entered. This belief may have originally derived its existence from the fact that certain tropical insects sometimes lay their eggs beneath the skins of animals, or even of men, from which it is difficult to expel them until the larvae are hatched. The *chico* or "jigger" of the West Indies and the Spanish Main is the most obvious example.

Old Aunt Harriet—last name uncertain, since she had borne those of her master, her mother, her putative father, and half a dozen husbands in succession, no one of which seemed to take undisputed precedence—related some very remarkable experiences. She at first manifested some reluctance to speak of conjuration, in the lore of which she was said to be well versed; but by listening patiently to her religious experiences—she was a dreamer of dreams and a seer of visions—I was able now and then to draw a little upon her reserves of superstition, if indeed her religion itself was much more than superstition.

"W'en I wuz a gal 'bout eighteen er nineteen," she confided, "de w'ite folks use' ter sen' me ter town ter fetch vegetables. One day I met a' ole conjuh man named Jerry Macdonal', an' he said some rough, ugly things ter me. I says, says I, 'You mus' be a fool.' He did n' say nothin', but jes' looked at me wid 'is evil eye. W'en I come 'long back, date ole man wuz stan'in' in de road in front er his house, an' w'en he seed me he stoop' down an' tech' de groun', jes' lack he wuz pickin' up somethin', an' den went 'long back in 'is ya'd. De ve'y minute I step' on de spot he tech', I felt a sha'p pain shoot thoo my right foot, it tu'n't under me, an' I fell down in de road. I pick' myself up' an' by de time I got home, my foot wuz swoll' up twice its nachul size. I cried an' cried an' went on, fer I knowed I'd be'n trick' by dat ole man. Dat night in my sleep a voice spoke ter me an' says: 'Go an' git a plug er terbacker. Steep it in a skillet er wa'm water. Strip it lengthways, an' bin' it ter de bottom er yo' foot'. I never didn' use terbacker, an' I laid dere, an' says I ter myse'f, 'My Lawd, w'at is dat, w'at is dat!' Soon ez my foot got kind er easy, dat voice up an' speaks ag'in.' 'Go an' git a plug er terbacker. Steep it in a skillet er wa'm water, an' bin' it ter de bottom er yo' foot.' I scramble' ter my feet, got de money out er my pocket, woke up de two little boys sleepin' on de flo', an' tol' 'em ter go ter de sto' an' git me a plug er terbacker. Dey didn' want ter go, said de sto' wuz shet, an' de sto' keeper gone ter bed. But I chased 'em fo'th, an' dey found' de sto' keeper an' fetch' de terbacker—dey sho' did. I soaked it in de skillet, an' stripped it 'long by degrees, till I got ter de een', w'en I boun' it under my foot an' roun' my ankle. Den I kneel' down an' prayed, an' next mawnin' de swelin' wuz all gone! Dat voice wus de Spirit er de Lawd talkin' ter me, it sho' wuz! De Lawd have mussy upon us, praise his Holy Name!"

Very obviously Harriet had sprained her ankle while looking at the old man instead of watching the path, and the hot fomentation had reduced the swelling. She is not the first person to hear spirit voices in his or her own vagrant imaginings.

On another occasion, Aunt Harriet's finger swelled up "as big as a corn-cob." She at first supposed the swelling to be due to a felon. She went to old Uncle Julius Lutterloh, who told her that some one had tricked her. "My Lawd!" she exclaimed, "how did they fix my finger?" He explained that it was done while in the act of shaking hands. "Doctor" Julius opened the finger with a sharp knife and showed Harriet two seeds at the bottom of the incision. He instructed her to put a poultice of red onions on the wound over night, and in the morning the seeds would come out. She was then to put the two seeds in a skillet, on the right hand side of the fireplace, in a pint of water, and let them simmer nine mornings, and on the ninth morning she was to let all the water simmer out, and when the last drop should have gone, the one that put the seeds in her hand was to go out of this world! Harriet, however, did not pursue the treatment to the bitter end. The seeds, once extracted, she put into a small phial, which she corked up tightly and put carefully away in her bureau drawer. One morning she went to look at them, and one of them was gone. Shortly afterwards the other disappeared. Aunt Harriet has a theory that she had been tricked by a woman of whom her husband of that time was unduly fond, and that the faithless husband had returned the seeds to their original owner. A part of the scheme of conjuration is that the conjure doctor can remove the spell and put it back upon the one who laid it. I was unable to learn, however, of any instance where this extreme penalty had been insisted upon.

It is seldom that any of these old Negroes will admit that he or she possesses the power to conjure, though those who can remove spells are very willing to make their accomplishment known, and to exercise it for a consideration. The only professional conjure doctor whom I met was old Uncle Jim Davis, with whom I arranged a personal interview. He came to see me one evening, but almost immediately upon his arrival a minister called. The powers of light prevailed over those of darkness, and Jim was dismissed until a later time, with a commission to prepare for me a conjure "hand" or good luck charm of which, he informed some of the children about the house, who were much interested in the proceedings, I was very much in need. I subsequently secured the charm, for which, considering its potency, the small sum of silver it cost me was no extravagant outlay. It is a very small bag of roots and herbs, and, if used according to directions, is guaranteed to insure me good luck and "keep me from losing my job." The directions require it to be wet with spirits nine mornings in succession, to be carried on the person, in a pocket on the right hand side, care being taken that it does not come in contact with any tobacco. When I add that I procured, from an equally trustworthy source, a genuine grave-yard rabbit's foot, I would seem to be reasonably well protected against casual misfortune. I shall not, however, presume upon this immunity, and shall omit no reasonable precaution which the condition of my health or my affairs may render prudent.

An interesting conjure story which I heard, involves the fate of a lost voice. A certain woman's lover was enticed away by another woman, who sang very sweetly, and who, the jilted one suspected, had told lies about her. Having decided upon the method of punishment for this wickedness, the injured woman watched the other closely, in order to find a suitable opportunity for carrying out her purpose; but in vain, for the fortunate one, knowing of her enmity, would never speak to her or remain near her. One day the jilted woman plucked a red rose from her garden, and hid herself in the bushes near her rival's cabin. Very soon an old woman came by, who was accosted by the woman in hiding, and requested to hand the red rose to the woman of the house. The old woman, suspecting no evil, took the rose and approached the house, the other woman following her closely, but keeping herself always out of sight. When the old woman, having reached the door and called out the mistress of the house, delivered the rose as requested, the recipient thanked the giver in a loud voice, knowing the old woman to be somewhat deaf. At the moment she spoke, the woman in hiding reached up and caught her rival's voice, and clasping it tightly in her right hand, escaped, unseen, to her own cabin. At the same instant the afflicted woman missed her voice, and felt a sharp pain shoot through her left arm, just below the elbow. She at first suspected the old woman of having tricked her through the medium of the red rose, but was subsequently informed by a conjure doctor that her voice had been stolen, and that the old woman was innocent. For the pain he gave her a bottle of medicine, of which nine drops were to be applied three times a day, and rubbed in with the first two fingers of the right hand, care being taken not to let any other part of the hand touch the arm, as this would render the medicine useless. By the aid of a mirror, in which he called up her image, the conjure doctor ascertained who was the guilty person. He sought her out and charged her with the crime which she promptly denied. Being pressed, however, she admitted her guilt. The doctor insisted upon immediate restitution. She expressed her willingness, and at the same time her inability to comply—she had taken the voice, but did not possess the power to restore it. The conjure doctor was obdurate and at once placed a spell upon her which is to remain until the lost voice is restored. The case is still pending, I understand; I shall sometime take steps to find out how it terminates.

How far a story like this is original, and how far a mere reflection of familiar wonder stories, is purely a matter of speculation. When the old mammies would tell the tales of Brer Rabbit and Brer Fox to the master's children, these in turn would no doubt repeat the fairy tales which they had read in books or heard from their parents' lips. The magic mirror is as old as literature. The inability to restore the stolen voice is foreshadowed in the Arabian Nights, when the "Open Sesame" is forgotten. The act of catching the voice has a simplicity which stamps it as original, the only analogy of which I can at present think being the story of later date, of the words which were frozen silent during the extreme cold of an Arctic winter, and became audible again the following summer when they had thawed out.

THE DISFRANCHISEMENT OF THE NEGRO

The right of American citizens of African descent, commonly called Negroes, to vote upon the same terms as other citizens of the United States, is plainly declared and firmly fixed by the Constitution. No such person is called upon to present reasons why he should possess this right: that question is foreclosed by the Constitution. The object of the elective franchise is to give representation. So long as the Constitution retains its present form, any State Constitution, or statute, which seeks, by juggling the ballot, to deny the colored race fair representation, is a clear violation of the fundamental law of the land, and a corresponding injustice to those thus deprived of this right.

For thirty-five years this has been the law. As long as it was measurably respected, the colored people made rapid strides in education, wealth, character and self-respect. This the census proves, all statements to the contrary notwithstanding. A generation has grown to manhood and womanhood under the great, inspiring freedom conferred by the Constitution and protected by the right of suffrage—protected in large degree by the

---

The Negro Problem: A Series of Articles by Representative American Negroes of To-day, 1903.

mere naked right, even when its exercise was hindered or denied by un-lawful means. They have developed, in every Southern community, good citizens, who, if sustained and encouraged by just laws and liberal institu-tions, would greatly augment their number with the passing years, and soon wipe out the reproach of ignorance, unthrift, low morals and social in-efficiency, thrown at them indiscriminately and therefore unjustly, and made the excuse for the equally undiscriminating contempt of their per-sons and their rights. They have reduced their illiteracy nearly 50 per cent. Excluded from the institutions of higher learning in their own States, their young men hold their own, and occasionally carry away honors, in the uni-versities of the North. They have accumulated three hundred million dol-lars worth of real and personal property. Individuals among them have ac-quired substantial wealth, and several have attained to something like national distinction in art, letters and educational leadership. They are nu-merously represented in the learned professions. Heavily handicapped, they have made such rapid progress that the suspicion is justified that their advancement, rather than any stagnation or retrogression, is the true secret of the virulent Southern hostility to their rights, which has so influenced Northern opinion that it stands mute, and leaves the colored people, upon whom the North conferred liberty, to the tender mercies of those who have always denied their fitness for it.

It may be said, in passing, that the word "Negro," where used in this paper, is used solely for convenience. By the census of 1890 there were 1,000,000 colored people in the country who were half, or more than half, white, and logically there must be, as in fact there are, so many who share the white blood in some degree, as to justify the assertion that the race problem in the United States concerns the welfare and the status of a mixed race. Their rights are not one whit the more sacred because of this fact; but in an argument where injustice is sought to be excused because of funda-mental differences of race, it is well enough to bear in mind that the race whose rights and liberties are endangered all over this country by disfran-chisement at the South, are the colored people who live in the United States to-day, and not the low-browed, man-eating savage whom the Southern white likes to set upon a block and contrast with Shakespeare and New-ton and Washington and Lincoln.

Despite and in defiance of the Federal Constitution, to-day in the six Southern States of Mississippi, Louisiana, Alabama, North Carolina, South Carolina and Virginia, containing an aggregate colored population of about 6,000,000, these have been, to all intents and purposes, denied, so far as the States can effect it, the right to vote. This disfranchisement is accomplished by various methods, devised with much transparent ingenu-ity, the effort being in each instance to violate the spirit of the Federal Constitution by disfranchising the Negro, while seeming to respect its letter by avoiding the mention of race or color.

These restrictions fall into three groups. The first comprises a property qualification—the ownership of $300 worth or more of real or personal property (Alabama, Louisiana, Virginia and South Carolina); the payment of a poll tax (Mississippi, North Carolina, Virginia); an educational qualification—the ability to read and write (Alabama, Louisiana, North Carolina). Thus far, those who believe in a restricted suffrage everywhere, could perhaps find no reasonable fault with any one of these qualifications, applied either separately or together.

But the Negro has made such progress that these restrictions alone would perhaps not deprive him of effective representation. Hence the second group. This comprises an "understanding" clause—the applicant must be able "to read, or understand when read to him, any clause in the Constitution" (Mississippi), or to read and explain, or to understand and explain when read to him, any section of the Constitution (Virginia); an employment qualification—the voter must be regularly employed in some lawful occupation (Alabama); a character qualification—the voter must be a person of good character and who "understands the duties and obligations of citizens under a republican (!) form of government" (Alabama). The qualifications under the first group it will be seen, are capable of exact demonstration; those under the second group are left to the discretion and judgment of the registering officer—for in most instances these are all requirements for registration, which must precede voting.

But the first group, by its own force, and the second group, under imaginable conditions, might exclude not only the Negro vote, but a large part of the white vote. Hence, the third group, which comprises: a military service qualification—any man who went to war, willingly or unwillingly, in a good cause or a bad, is entitled to register (Ala., Va.); a prescriptive qualification, under which are included all male persons who were entitled to vote on January 1, 1867, at which date the Negro had not yet been given the right to vote; a hereditary qualification, (the so-called "grandfather" clause), whereby any son (Va.), or descendant (Ala.), of a soldier, and (N.C.) the descendant of any person who had the right to vote on January 1, 1867, inherits that right. If the voter wish to take advantage of these last provisions, which are in the nature of exceptions to a general rule, he must register within a stated time, whereupon he becomes a member of a privileged class of permanently enrolled voters not subject to any of the other restrictions.

It will be seen that these restrictions are variously combined in the different States, and it is apparent that if combined to their declared end, practically every Negro may, under color of law, be denied the right to vote, and practically every white man accorded that right. The effectiveness of these provisions to exclude the Negro vote is proved by the Alabama registration under the new State Constitution. Out of a total, by the census of 1900, of 181,471 Negro "males of voting age," less than 3,000 are registered; in Montgomery county alone, the seat of the State capital, where there are 7,000 Negro males of voting age, only 47 have been allowed to register, while in several counties not one single Negro is permitted to exercise the franchise.

These methods of disfranchisement have stood such tests as the United States Courts, including the Supreme Court, have thus far seen fit to apply, in such cases as have been before them for adjudication. These include a case based upon the "understanding" clause of the Mississippi Constitution, in which the Supreme Court held, in effect, that since there was no ambiguity in the language employed and the Negro was not directly named, the Court would not go behind the wording of the Constitution to find a meaning which discriminated against the colored voter; and the recent case of Jackson vs. Giles, brought by a colored citizen of Montgomery, Alabama, in which the Supreme Court confesses itself impotent to provide a remedy for what, by inference, it acknowledges *may* be a "great political wrong," carefully avoiding, however, to state that it is a wrong, although the vital prayer of the petition was for a decision upon this very point.[1]

Now, what is the effect of this wholesale disfranchisement of colored men, upon their citizenship? The value of food to the human organism is not measured by the pains of an occasional surfeit, but by the effect of its entire deprivation. Whether a class of citizens should vote, even if not always wisely—what class does?—may best be determined by considering their condition when they are without the right to vote.

The colored people are left, in the States where they have been disfranchised, absolutely without representation, direct or indirect, in any

---

[1] Harlan writes: "Some of the blacks denied [voter] registration formed the Colored Men's Suffrage Association of Alabama, centered in Montgomery, and its president Jackson W. Giles became the plaintiff in two Alabama suffrage cases, [not *Jackson v. Giles*—as Chesnutt indicates—but *Giles v. Harris* (189 U.S. 475) in 1903 and *Giles v. Teasley* (193 U.S. 146) in 1904, both of which reached the Supreme Court]. . . . Not even Giles and the other members of his association apparently knew that Wilford H. Smith, the lawyer they employed and paid a pittance, was actually paid by Washington to litigate these cases" (245– 46). To hide his involvement, Booker T. Washington had his assistant Emmett Scott handle all the correspondence with Smith, even to the point of assigning Smith the code name "Filipino." In his telegrams to Scott, Smith adopted the code name "McAdoo," the last name of his secretary (246). Both cases were eventually thrown out of the U.S. Supreme Court on technicalities and Smith lacked the will to continue them (247).

law-making body, in any court of justice, in any branch of government—
for the feeble remnant of voters left by law is so inconsiderable as to be
without a shadow of power. Constituting one-eighth of the population of
the whole country, two-fifths of the whole Southern people, and a majority in several States, they are not able, because disfranchised where most
numerous, to send one representative to the Congress, which, by the decision in the Alabama case, is held by the Supreme Court to be the only
body, outside of the State itself, competent to give relief from a great political wrong. By former decisions of the same tribunal, even Congress is
impotent to protect their civil rights, the Fourteenth Amendment having
long since, by the consent of the same Court, been in many respects as
completely nullified as the Fifteenth Amendment is now sought to be. They
have no direct representation in any Southern legislature, and no voice in
determining the choice of white men who might be friendly to their rights.
Nor are they able to influence the election of judges or other public
officials, to whom are entrusted the protection of their lives, their liberties
and their property. No judge is rendered careful, no sheriff diligent, for
fear that he may offend a black constituency; the contrary is most lamentably true; day after day the catalogue of lynchings and anti-Negro riots
upon every imaginable pretext, grows longer and more appalling. The
country stands face to face with the revival of slavery; at the moment of
this writing a federal grand jury in Alabama is uncovering a system of peonage established under cover of law.

Under the Southern program it is sought to exclude colored men from
every grade of the public service; not only from the higher administrative
functions, to which few of them would in any event, for a long time aspire,
but from the lowest as well. A Negro may not be a constable or a policeman.
He is subjected by law to many degrading discriminations. He is required
to be separated from white people on railroads and street cars, and, by custom, debarred from inns and places of public entertainment. His equal
right to a free public education is constantly threatened and is nowhere eq-
uitably recognized. In Georgia, as has been shown by Dr. [William E. B.]
DuBois, where the law provides for a pro rata distribution of the public
school fund between the races, and where the colored school population is
48 per cent. of the total, the amount of the fund devoted to their schools
is only 20 per cent. In New Orleans, with an immense colored population,
many of whom are persons of means and culture, all colored public schools
above the fifth grade have been abolished.

The Negro is subjected to taxation without representation, which the
forefathers of this Republic made the basis of a bloody revolution.

Flushed with their local success, and encouraged by the timidity of the
Courts and the indifference of public opinion, the Southern whites have

carried their campaign into the national government, with an ominous degree of success. If they shall have their way, no Negro can fill any federal office, or occupy, in the public service, any position that is not menial. This is not an inference, but the openly, passionately avowed sentiment of the white South. The right to employment in the public service is an exceedingly valuable one, for which white men have struggled and fought. A vast army of men are employed in the administration of public affairs. Many avenues of employment are closed to colored men by popular prejudice. If their right to public employment is recognized, and the way to it open through the civil service, or the appointing power, or the suffrages of the people, it will prove, as it has already, a strong incentive to effort and a powerful lever for advancement. Its value to the Negro, like that of the right to vote, may be judged by the eagerness of the whites to deprive him of it.

Not only is the Negro taxed without representation in the States referred to, but he pays, through the tariff and internal revenue, a tax to a National government whose supreme judicial tribunal declares that it cannot, through the executive arm, enforce its own decrees, and, therefore, refuses to pass upon a question, squarely before it, involving a basic right of citizenship. For the decision of the Supreme Court in the Giles case, if it foreshadows the attitude which the Court will take upon other cases to the same general end which will soon come before it, is scarcely less than a reaffirmation of the Dred Scott decision; it certainly amounts to this—that in spite of the Fifteenth Amendment, colored men in the United States have no political rights which the States are bound to respect. To say this much is to say that all privileges and immunities which Negroes henceforth enjoy, must be by favor of the whites; they are not *rights*. The whites have so declared; they proclaim that the country is theirs, that the Negro should be thankful that he has so much, when so much more might be withheld from him. He stands upon a lower footing than any alien; he has no government to which he may look for protection.

Moreover, the white South sends to Congress, on a basis including the Negro population, a delegation nearly twice as large as it is justly entitled to, and one which may always safely be relied upon to oppose in Congress every measure which seeks to protect the equality, or to enlarge the rights of colored citizens. The grossness of this injustice is all the more apparent since the Supreme Court, in the Alabama case referred to, has declared the legislative and political department of the government to be the only power which can right a political wrong. Under this decision still further attacks upon the liberties of the citizen may be confidently expected. Armed with the Negro's sole weapon of defense, the white South stands ready to smite down his rights. The ballot was first given to the Negro to defend him against this very thing. He needs it now far more than then, and for even stronger reasons. The 9,000,000 free colored people of to-day have vastly more to defend than the 3,000,000 hapless blacks who had just emerged from slavery. If there be those who maintain that it was a mistake to give the Negro the ballot at the time and in the manner in which it was given, let them take to heart this reflection: that to deprive him of it to-day, or to so restrict it as to leave him utterly defenseless against the present relentless attitude of the South toward his rights, will prove to be a mistake so much greater than the first, as to be no less than a crime, from which not alone the Southern Negro must suffer, but for which the nation will as surely pay the penalty as it paid for the crime of slavery. Contempt for law is death to a republic, and this one has developed alarming symptoms of the disease.

And now, having thus robbed the Negro of every political and civil *right,* the white South, in palliation of its course, makes a great show of magnanimity in leaving him, as the sole remnant of what he acquired through the Civil War, a very inadequate public school education, which, by the present program, is to be directed mainly towards making him a better agricultural laborer. Even this is put forward as a favor, although the Negro's property is taxed to pay for it, and his labor as well. For it is a well settled principle of political economy, that land and machinery of themselves produce nothing, and that labor indirectly pays its fair proportion of the tax upon the public's wealth. The white South seems to stand to the Negro at present as one, who, having been reluctantly compelled to release another from bondage, sees him stumbling forward and upward, neglected by his friends and scarcely yet conscious of his own strength; seizes him, binds him, and having bereft him of speech, of sight and of manhood, "yokes him with the mule" and exclaims, with a show of virtue which ought to deceive no one: "Behold how good a friend I am of yours! Have I not left you a stomach and a pair of arms, and will I not generously permit you to work for me with the one, that you may thereby gain enough to fill the other? A brain you do not need. We will relieve you of any responsibility that might seem to demand such an organ."

The argument of peace-loving Northern white men and Negro opportunists that the political power of the Negro having long ago been suppressed by unlawful means, his right to vote is a mere paper right, of no real value, and therefore to be lightly yielded for the sake of a hypothetical harmony, is fatally short-sighted. It is precisely the attitude and essentially the argument which would have surrendered to the South in the sixties, and would have left this country to rot in slavery for another generation. White men do not thus argue concerning their own rights. They know too well the value of ideals. Southern white men see too clearly the latent power of these unexercised rights. If the political power of the Negro was

a nullity because of his ignorance and lack of leadership, why were they
not content to leave it so, with the pleasing assurance that if it ever became
effective, it would be because the Negroes had grown fit for its exercise?
On the contrary, they have not rested until the possibility of its revival was
apparently headed off by new State Constitutions. Nor are they satisfied
with this. There is no doubt that an effort will be made to secure the repeal of the Fifteenth Amendment, and thus forestall the development of the
wealthy and educated Negro, whom the South seems to anticipate as a
greater menace than the ignorant ex-slave. However improbable this repeal may seem, it is not a subject to be lightly dismissed; for it is within the
power of the white people of the nation to do whatever they wish in the
premises—they did it once; they can do it again. The Negro and his friends
should see to it that the white majority shall never wish to do anything to
his hurt. There still stands, before the Negro-hating whites of the South,
the specter of a Supreme Court which will interpret the Constitution to
mean what it says, and what those who enacted it meant, and what the nation, which ratified it, understood, and which will find power, in a nation
which goes beyond seas to administer the affairs of distant peoples, to enforce its own fundamental laws; the specter, too, of an aroused public
opinion which will compel Congress and the Courts to preserve the liberties of the Republic, which are the liberties of the people. To wilfully neglect the suffrage, to hold it lightly, is to tamper with a sacred right; to yield
it for anything else whatever is simply suicidal. Dropping the element of
race, disfranchisement is no more than to say to the poor and poorly taught,
that they must relinquish the right to defend themselves against oppression
until they shall have become rich and learned, in competition with those
already thus favored and possessing the ballot in addition. This is not the
philosophy of history. The growth of liberty has been the constant struggle
of the poor against the privileged classes; and the goal of that struggle has
ever been the equality of all men before the law. The Negro who would
yield this right, deserves to be a slave; he has the servile spirit. The rich and
the educated can, by virtue of their influence, command many votes; can
find other means of protection; the poor man has but one; he should guard
it as a sacred treasure. Long ago, by fair treatment, the white leaders of the
South might have bound the Negro to themselves with hoops of steel. They
have not chosen to take this course, but by assuming from the beginning
an attitude hostile to his rights, have never gained his confidence, and now
seek by foul means to destroy where they have never sought by fair means
to control.

I have spoken of the effect of disfranchisement upon the colored race;
it is to the race as a whole, that the argument of the problem is generally
directed. But the unit of society in a republic is the individual, and not the

race, the failure to recognize this fact being the fundamental error which has beclouded the whole discussion. The effect of disfranchisement upon the individual is scarcely less disastrous. I do not speak of the moral effect of injustice upon those who suffer from it; I refer rather to the practical consequences which may be appreciated by any mind. No country is free in which the way upward is not open for every man to try, and for every properly qualified man to attain whatever of good the community life may offer. Such a condition does not exist, at the South, even in theory, for any man of color. In no career can such a man compete with white men upon equal terms. He must not only meet the prejudice of the individual, not only the united prejudice of the white community; but lest some one should wish to treat him fairly, he is met at every turn with some legal prohibition which says, "Thou shalt not," or "Thus far shalt thou go and no farther." But the Negro race is viable; it adapts itself readily to circumstances; and being thus adaptable, there is always the temptation to

"Crook the pregnant hinges of the knee,
Where thrift may follow fawning."

He who can most skilfully balance himself upon the advancing or receding wave of white opinion concerning his race, is surest of such measure of prosperity as is permitted to men of dark skins. There are Negro teachers in the South—the privilege of teaching in their own schools is the one respectable branch of the public service still left open to them—who, for a grudging appropriation from a Southern legislature, will decry their own race, approve their own degradation, and laud their oppressors. Deprived of the right to vote, and, therefore, of any power to demand what is their due, they feel impelled to buy the tolerance of the whites at any sacrifice. If to live is the first duty of man, as perhaps it is the first instinct, then those who thus stoop to conquer may be right. But is it needful to stoop so low, and if so, where lies the ultimate responsibility for this abasement?

I shall say nothing about the moral effect of disfranchisement upon the white people, or upon the State itself. What slavery made of the Southern whites is a matter of history. The abolition of slavery gave the South an opportunity to emerge from barbarism. Present conditions indicate that the spirit which dominated slavery still curses the fair section over which that institution spread its blight.

And now, is the situation remediless? If not so, where lies the remedy? First let us take up those remedies suggested by the men who approve of disfranchisement, though they may sometimes deplore the method, or regret the necessity.

Time, we are told, heals all diseases, rights all wrongs, and is the only cure for this one. It is a cowardly argument. These people are entitled to their rights to-day, while they are yet alive to enjoy them; and it is poor statesmanship and worse morals to nurse a present evil and thrust it forward upon a future generation for correction. The nation can no more honestly do this than it could thrust back upon a past generation the responsibility for slavery. It had to meet that responsibility; it ought to meet this one.

Education has been put forward as the great corrective—preferably industrial education. The intellect of the whites is to be educated to the point where they will so appreciate the blessings of liberty and equality, as of their own motion to enlarge and defend the Negro's rights. The Negroes, on the other hand, are to be so trained as to make them, not equal with the whites in any way—God save the mark! this would be unthinkable!—but so useful to the community that the whites will protect them rather than to lose their valuable services. Some few enthusiasts go so far as to maintain that by virtue of education the Negro will, in time, become strong enough to protect himself against any aggression of the whites; this, it may be said, is a strictly Northern view.

It is not quite clearly apparent how education alone, in the ordinary meaning of the word, is to solve, in any appreciable time, the problem of the relations of Southern white and black people. The need of education of all kinds for both races is wofully apparent. But men and nations have been free without being learned, and there have been educated slaves. Liberty has been known to languish where culture had reached a very high development. Nations do not first become rich and learned and then free, but the lesson of history has been that they first become free and then rich and learned, and oftentimes fall back into slavery again because of too great wealth, and the resulting luxury and carelessness of civic virtues. The process of education has been going on rapidly in the Southern States since the Civil War, and yet, if we take superficial indications, the rights of the Negroes are at a lower ebb than at any time during the thirty-five years of their freedom, and the race prejudice more intense and uncompromising. It is not apparent that educated Southerners are less rancorous than others in their speech concerning the Negro, or less hostile in their attitude toward his rights. It is their voice alone that we have heard in this discussion; and if, as they state, they are liberal in their views as compared with the more ignorant whites, then God save the Negro!

I was told, in so many words, two years ago, by the Superintendent of Public Schools of a Southern city that "there was no place in the modern world for the Negro, except under the ground." If gentlemen holding such opinions are to instruct the white youth of the South, would it be at all surprising if these, later on, should devote a portion of their leisure to the improvement of civilization by putting under the ground as many of this superfluous race as possible?

The sole excuse made in the South for the prevalent injustice to the Negro is the difference in race, and the inequalities and antipathies resulting therefrom. It has nowhere been declared as a part of the Southern program that the Negro, when educated, is to be given a fair representation in government or an equal opportunity in life; the contrary has been strenuously asserted; education can never make of him anything but a Negro, and, therefore, essentially inferior, and not to be safely trusted with any degree of power. A system of education which would tend to soften the asperities and lessen the inequalities between the races would be of inestimable value. An education which by a rigid separation of the races from the kindergarten to the university, fosters this racial antipathy, and is directed toward emphasizing the superiority of one class and the inferiority of another, might easily have disastrous, rather than beneficial results. It would render the oppressing class more powerful to injure, the oppressed quicker to perceive and keener to resent the injury, without proportionate power of defense. The same assimilative education which is given at the North to all children alike, whereby native and foreign, black and white, are taught side by side in every grade of instruction, and are compelled by the exigencies of discipline to keep their prejudices in abeyance, and are given the opportunity to learn and appreciate one another's good qualities, and to establish friendly relations which may exist throughout life, is absent from the Southern system of education, both of the past and as proposed for the future. Education is in a broad sense a remedy for all social ills; but the disease we have to deal with now is not only constitutional but acute. A wise physician does not simply give a tonic for a diseased limb, or a high fever; the patient might be dead before the constitutional remedy could become effective. The evils of slavery, its injury to whites and blacks, and to the body politic, was clearly perceived and acknowledged by the educated leaders of the South as far back as the Revolutionary War and the Constitutional Convention, and yet they made no effort to abolish it. Their remedy was the same—time, education, social and economic development—and yet a bloody war was necessary to destroy slavery and put its spirit temporarily to sleep. When the South and its friends are ready to propose a system of education which will recognize and teach the equality of all men before the law, the potency of education alone to settle the race problem will be more clearly apparent.

At present even good Northern men, who wish to educate the Negroes, feel impelled to buy this privilege from the none too eager white South, by conceding away the civil and political rights of those whom they would benefit. They have, indeed, gone farther than the Southerners themselves in approving the disfranchisement of the colored race. Most Southern men, now that they have carried their point and disfranchised the Negro, are willing to admit, in the language of a recent number of the *Charleston Evening Post*, that "the attitude of the Southern white man toward the Negro is incompatible with the fundamental ideas of the republic." It remained for our Clevelands and Abbotts and Parkhursts to assure them that their unlawful course was right and justifiable, and for the most distinguished Negro leader to declare that "every revised Constitution throughout the Southern States has put a premium upon intelligence, ownership of property, thrift and character." So does every penitentiary sentence put a premium upon good conduct; but it is poor consolation to the one unjustly condemned, to be told that he may shorten his sentence somewhat by good behavior. Dr. Booker T. Washington, whose language is quoted above, has, by his eminent services in the cause of education, won deserved renown. If he has seemed, at times, to those jealous of the best things for their race, to decry the higher education, it can easily be borne in mind that his career is bound up in the success of an industrial school; hence any undue stress which he may put upon that branch of education may safely be ascribed to the natural zeal of the promoter, without detracting in any degree from the essential value of his teachings in favor of manual training, thrift and character-building. But Mr. Washington's prominence as an educational leader, among a race whose prominent leaders are so few, has at times forced him, perhaps reluctantly, to express himself in regard to the political condition of his people, and here his utterances have not always been so wise nor so happy. He has declared himself in favor of a restricted suffrage, which at present means, for his own people, nothing less than complete loss of representation—indeed it is only in that connection that the question has been seriously mooted; and he has advised them to go slow in seeking to enforce their civil and political rights, which, in effect, means silent submission to injustice. Southern white men may applaud this advice as wise, because it fits in with their purposes; but Senator [Samuel D.] McEnery of Louisiana, in a recent article in the *Independent*, voices the Southern white opinion of such acquiescence when he says: "What other race would have submitted so many years to slavery without complaint? *What other race would have submitted so quietly to disfranchisement?* These facts stamp his (the Negro's) inferiority to the white race."[2] The

---

[2] Louisiana's Senator Samuel D. McEnery's "Race Problem in the South," *Independent* 55 (February 1903): 424–30.

time to philosophize about the good there is in evil, is not while its correction is still possible, but, if at all, after all hope of correction is past. Until then it calls for nothing but rigorous condemnation. To try to read any good thing into these fraudulent Southern constitutions, or to accept them as an accomplished fact, is to condone a crime against one's race. Those who commit crime should bear the odium. It is not a pleasing spectacle to see the robbed applaud the robber. Silence were better.

It has become fashionable to question the wisdom of the Fifteenth Amendment. I believe it to have been an act of the highest statesmanship, based upon the fundamental idea of this Republic, entirely justified by conditions; experimental in its nature, perhaps, as every new thing must be, but just in principle; a choice between methods, of which it seemed to the great statesmen of that epoch the wisest and the best, and essentially the most just, bearing in mind the interests of the freedmen and the Nation, as well as the feelings of the Southern whites; never fairly tried, and therefore, not yet to be justly condemned. Not one of those who condemn it, has been able, even in the light of subsequent events, to suggest a better method by which the liberty and civil rights of the freedmen and their descendants could have been protected. Its abandonment, as I have shown, leaves this liberty and these rights frankly without any guaranteed protection. All the education which philanthropy or the State could offer as a *substitute* for equality of rights, would be a poor exchange; there is no defensible reason why they should not go hand in hand, each encouraging and strengthening the other. The education which one can demand as a right is likely to do more good than the education for which one must sue as a favor.

The chief argument against Negro suffrage, the insistently proclaimed argument, worn threadbare in Congress, on the platform, in the pulpit, in the press, in poetry, in fiction, in impassioned rhetoric, is the reconstruction period. And yet the evils of that period were due far more to the venality and indifference of white men than to the incapacity of black voters. The revised Southern Constitutions adopted under reconstruction reveal a higher statesmanship than any which preceded or have followed them, and prove that the freed voters could as easily have been led into the paths of civic righteousness as into those of misgovernment. Certain it is that under reconstruction the civil and political rights of all men were more secure in those States than they have ever been since. We will hear less of the evils of reconstruction; now that the bugaboo has served its purpose by disfranchising the Negro, it will be laid aside for a time while the nation discusses the political corruption of great cities; the scandalous conditions in Rhode Island; the evils attending reconstruction in the Philippines, and the scandals in the postoffice department—for none of which, by the way, is the Negro charged with any responsibility, and for none of which is the restriction of the suffrage a remedy seriously proposed. Rhode Island is indeed the only Northern State which has a property qualification for the franchise!

There are three tribunals to which the colored people may justly appeal for the protection of their rights: the United States Courts, Congress and public opinion. At present all three seem mainly indifferent to any question of human rights under the Constitution. Indeed, Congress and the Courts merely follow public opinion, seldom lead it. Congress never enacts a measure which is believed to oppose public opinion—your Congressman keeps his ear to the ground. The high, serene atmosphere of the Courts is not impervious to its voice; they rarely enforce a law contrary to public opinion, even the Supreme Court being able, as Charles Sumner once put it, to find a reason for every decision it may wish to render; or, as experience has shown, a method to evade any question which it cannot decently decide in accordance with public opinion. The art of straddling is not confined to the political arena. The Southern situation has been well described by a colored editor in Richmond: "When we seek relief at the hands of Congress, we are informed that our plea involves a legal question, and we are referred to the Courts. When we appeal to the Courts, we are gravely told that the question is a political one, and that we must go to Congress. When Congress enacts remedial legislation, our enemies take it to the Supreme Court, which promptly declares it unconstitutional." [3] The Negro might chase his rights round and round this circle until the end of time, without finding any relief.

Yet the Constitution is clear and unequivocal in its terms, and no Supreme Court can indefinitely continue to construe it as meaning anything but what it says. This Court should be bombarded with suits until it makes some definite pronouncement, one way or the other, on the broad question of the constitutionality of the disfranchising Constitutions of the Southern States. The Negro and his friends will then have a clean-cut issue to take to the forum of public opinion, and a distinct ground upon which to demand legislation for the enforcement of the Federal Constitution. The case from Alabama was carried to the Supreme Court expressly to determine the constitutionality of the Alabama Constitution. The Court declared itself without jurisdiction, and in the same breath went into the merits of the case far enough to deny relief, without passing upon the real issue. Had it said, as it might with absolute justice and perfect propriety, that the Ala-

---

[3] John R. Mitchell's (1863–1929) "Another Decision," *Richmond* [Virginia] *Planet*, 2 May 1903:4.

bama Constitution is a bold and impudent violation of the Fifteenth Amendment, the purpose of the lawsuit would have been accomplished and a righteous cause vastly strengthened.

But public opinion cannot remain permanently indifferent to so vital a question. The agitation is already on. It is at present largely academic, but is slowly and resistlessly, forcing itself into politics, which is the medium through which republics settle such questions. It cannot much longer be contemptuously or indifferently elbowed aside. The South itself seems bent upon forcing the question to an issue, as, by its arrogant assumptions, it brought on the Civil War. From that section, too, there come now and then, side by side with tales of Southern outrage, excusing voices, which at the same time are accusing voices; which admit that the white South is dealing with the Negro unjustly and unwisely; that the Golden Rule has been forgotten; that the interests of white men alone have been taken into account, and that their true interests as well are being sacrificed. There is a silent white South, uneasy in conscience, darkened in counsel, groping for the light, and willing to do the right. They are as yet a feeble folk, their voices scarcely audible above the clamor of the mob. May their convictions ripen into wisdom, and may their numbers and their courage increase! If the class of Southern white men of whom Judge Jones of Alabama, is so noble a representative, are supported and encouraged by a righteous public opinion at the North, they may, in time, become the dominant white South, and we may then look for wisdom and justice in the place where, so far as the Negro is concerned, they now seem well-nigh strangers. But even these gentlemen will do well to bear in mind that so long as they discriminate in any way against the Negro's equality of right, so long do they set class against class and open the door to every sort of discrimination. There can be no middle ground between justice and injustice, between the citizen and the serf.

It is not likely that the North, upon the sober second thought, will permit the dearly-bought results of the Civil War to be nullified by any change in the Constitution. As long as the Fifteenth Amendment stands, the *rights* of colored citizens are ultimately secure. There were would-be despots in England after the granting of Magna Charta; but it outlived them all, and the liberties of the English people are secure. There was slavery in this land after the Declaration of Independence, yet the faces of those who love liberty have ever turned to that immortal document. So will the Constitution and its principles outlive the prejudices which would seek to overthrow it.

What colored men of the South can do to secure their citizenship today, or in the immediate future, is not very clear. Their utterances on political questions, unless they be to concede away the political rights of their race, or to soothe the consciences of white men by suggesting that the problem is insoluble except by some slow remedial process which will become effectual only in the distant future, are received with scant respect— could scarcely, indeed, be otherwise received, without a voting constituency to back them up—and must be cautiously made, lest they meet an actively hostile reception. But there are many colored men at the North, where their civil and political rights in the main are respected. There every honest man has a vote, which he may freely cast, and which is reasonably sure to be fairly counted. When this race develops a sufficient power of combination, under adequate leadership—and there are signs already that this time is near at hand—the Northern vote can be wielded irresistibly for the defense of the rights of their Southern brethren.

In the meantime the Northern colored men have the right of free speech, and they should never cease to demand their rights, to clamor for them, to guard them jealously, and insistently to invoke law and public sentiment to maintain them. He who would be free must learn to protect his freedom. Eternal vigilance is the price of liberty. He who would be respected must respect himself. The best friend of the Negro is he who would rather see, within the borders of this republic one million free citizens of that race, equal before the law, than ten million cringing serfs existing by a contemptuous sufferance. A race that is willing to survive upon any other terms is scarcely worthy of consideration.

The direct remedy for the disfranchisement of the Negro lies through political action. One scarcely sees the philosophy of distinguishing between a civil and a political right. But the Supreme Court has recognized this distinction and has designated Congress as the power to right a political wrong. The Fifteenth Amendment gives Congress power to enforce its provisions. The power would seem to be inherent in government itself; but anticipating that the enforcement of the Amendment might involve difficulty, they made the supererogatory declaration. Moreover, they went further, and passed laws by which they provided for such enforcement. These the Supreme Court has so far declared insufficient. It is for Congress to make more laws. It is for colored men and for white men who are not content to see the blood-bought results of the Civil War nullified, to urge and direct public opinion to the point where it will demand stringent legislation to enforce the Fourteenth and Fifteenth Amendments. This demand will rest in law, in morals and in true statesmanship; no difficulties attending it could be worse than the present ignoble attitude of the Nation toward its own laws and its own ideals—without courage to enforce them, without conscience to change them, the United States presents the spectacle of a Nation drifting aimlessly, so far as this vital, National problem is concerned, upon the sea of irresolution, toward the maelstrom of anarchy.

The right of Congress, under the Fourteenth Amendment, to reduce Southern representation can hardly be disputed. But Congress has a simpler and more direct method to accomplish the same end. It is the sole judge of the qualifications of its own members, and the sole judge of whether any member presenting his credentials has met those qualifications. It can refuse to seat any member who comes from a district where voters have been disfranchised; it can judge for itself whether this has been done, and there is no appeal from its decision.

If, when it has passed a law, any Court shall refuse to obey its behests, it can impeach the judges. If any president refuse to lend the executive arm of the government to the enforcement of the law, it can impeach the president. No such extreme measures are likely to be necessary for the enforcement of the Fourteenth and Fifteenth Amendments—and the Thirteenth, which is also threatened—but they are mentioned as showing that Congress is supreme; and Congress proceeds, the House directly, the Senate indirectly, from the people and is governed by public opinion. If the reduction of Southern representation were to be regarded in the light of a bargain by which the Fifteenth Amendment was surrendered, then it might prove fatal to liberty. If it be inflicted as a punishment and a warning, to be followed by more drastic measures if not sufficient, it would serve a useful purpose. The Fifteenth Amendment declares that the right to vote *shall not* be denied or abridged on account of color; and any measure adopted by Congress should look to that end. Only as the power to injure the Negro in Congress is reduced thereby, would a reduction of representation protect the Negro; without other measures it would still leave him in the hands of the Southern whites, who could safely be trusted to make him pay for their humiliation.

Finally, there is, somewhere in the Universe a "Power that works for righteousness," and that leads men to do justice to one another. To this power, working upon the hearts and consciences of men, the Negro can always appeal. He has the right upon his side, and in the end the right will prevail. The Negro will, in time, attain to full manhood and citizenship throughout the United States. No better guaranty of this is needed than a comparison of his present with his past. Toward this he must do his part, as lies within his power and his opportunity. But it will be, after all, largely a white man's conflict, fought out in the forum of the public conscience. The Negro, though eager enough when opportunity offered, had comparatively little to do with the abolition of slavery, which was a vastly more formidable task than will be the enforcement of the Fifteenth Amendment.

PEONAGE, OR THE NEW SLAVERY

Something more than a year ago the country was startled by the announcement that numerous indictments had been made in the Federal Court for the District of Alabama, for the crime of peonage. The dictionary failed to disclose the exact nature of this novel offense, but the facts stated in the news despatches, made it clear that human slavery, with its most revolting features, was openly practiced, under color of local law, and in violation of a Federal statute, in certain remote districts of the South. The machinery of the crime was simple. By conspiracy between the officers of the law—justices and constables, mostly white men of the baser sort—and heartless employers, all white men—ignorant and friendless Negroes were arrested on trumped up charges, fined to the full limit of harsh laws, sold at hard labor, worked under armed guards, cruelly flogged, and kept in this worse form of slavery long after the fine and costs imposed upon them had been worked out.

By the efforts of the Department of Justice, at the suggestion of Federal Judge [Thomas G.] Jones of Alabama, one of President [Theodore] Roosevelt's appointees, and at the personal instance of the President himself, it was ascertained and made known that this iniquitous system of involuntary servitude was flourishing widely and had been practiced for years in the "black belt" of Alabama and adjoining States, and was spreading to the upland counties. Convictions followed the indictments; many of the guilty were punished, and warning was given that the Federal Government would no longer tolerate this state of things. The State press acknowledged the existence of the evil, and declared that owing to local conditions and feeling upon the race question, the Federal Government alone was competent to deal adequately with it. So general was the condemnation of this new slavery that not even the morbid and diseased politics of the Southern States could find in it a political issue. There are still some indictments pending, but the crime, as far as can be seen at present, is no longer safe.

Now, why was this evil permitted to grow up? It was due, in the first place, to perfectly natural causes, and would have happened almost anywhere under like conditions. Nothing is slower than social movements. A form of government may be radically changed and laws easily enacted without modifying for a long period thereafter the social customs, the habits of thought, the feelings, in other words the genius, of a people. The labor sys-

---

Voice of the Negro, September 1904.

tem of the South had grown upon a basis of slavery, under which the black laborer worked for the benefit of the white masters, receiving as his hire merely the simplest necessaries of life; this not only by law but with the warrant of Scripture. Had not St. Paul written, "Servants, obey your masters"?[1] That a people who still retained to their former slaves the relation of employers, should immediately and cheerfully pay them a fair wage for their labor, was highly improbable. That there were just men who paid the market price is true enough, but the market price was inadequate. Fifteen dollars a month for a farm laborer who has to "find" himself, is not a liberal wage. This is far more than the average Negro laborer receives.

Under the renting system, the crop mortgage laws leave the laborer but little more than a slave to the soil, while at its worst the Southern labor system presents peonage, or the new slavery. The old habit of making the Negroes work for the white people for their board and clothes has in large measure survived. Enough Negroes have risen above this level to present a remarkable average of industrial progress, but the majority are still subject in one way or another to the old rule.

This continuity of social custom is sufficient in part to account for the survival of slavery in some modified form. When to this is added the temptation of greed and cunning to take advantage of poverty and ignorance, it is not strange that peonage should exist. Taking into account the artificial solidarity of the white South on all questions relating to the rights of the Negro and in all matters between white and black, it is easily seen why the State Courts were inadequate to cope with the evil. The individuals who bribe constables and justices to arrest ignorant and friendless Negroes and sentence them to servitude, are the same men who, in a more Northern latitude, would exploit imported foreign workmen in factories and sweatshops, or immature white children in the cotton mills, and bribe legislatures and city councils to betray the rights of the people and grind the faces of the poor in the interest of their own selfish greed.

The only sure preventive of the recurrence of slavery in some other form is the development of the Negro. No one will seek to rob those whom [sic] he knows are abundantly able to defend themselves. But pending this slow development which is to result from greater learning and growing thrift and larger liberty, just laws impartially administered can curb the greed of evil men. If this impartial enforcement of law does not come from within it must be sought without. The time is not far distant when there

---

[1] Colossians 3:22 reads: "Servants, obey in all things your masters according to the flesh. . . ."

will exist among Southern white men a body of thought which will demand justice for Southern black men. They will not all agree as to what that justice shall consist of, and their views on the subject will enlarge as the years go by, but they will demand, first and unanimously fair play in the courts and just treatment of the labor upon which the prosperity of the South depends. When this influence is strong enough, the South may safely be left to wash its own dirty linen; but in the meantime it is in the hands of unfriendly white men, and it has been left to the Federal Government, under the administration of President Roosevelt, to expose this peonage iniquity and stretch out the long arm of the Nation to punish and prevent it. There is such a thing as national citizenship, and there should be lodged in the power of the government the right to protect it. This question of peonage, involving as it does the simplest and most fundamental elements of citizenship, has an important bearing on the attitude of colored voters in the presidential campaign. The Democratic party has nominated for President an able candidate, upon a platform in some respects admirable. There is no reason to believe that Judge [Alton B.] Parker would personally be anything but friendly to the colored race and just in his dealings with colored men.[2] The National Republican party has of late done little to protect the rights of the Negro, and its platforms and policies, given over to a rampant commercialism and dreams of empire, no longer ring true to its old ideals. No colored voter owes the present Republican party anything. But he does owe to Theodore Roosevelt who stands for the open door of opportunity his unqualified support. When a Negro votes in the coming presidential election, it should be with an eye single to the future welfare of his race. This ought to be synonymous with the welfare of the Republic; if it is not so in every particular, it is surely not the Negro's fault. He is quite willing to ignore questions of race, in politics and elsewhere, whenever the white people see fit to do so.

The Negro cannot trust the Democratic party on the vital questions of his rights. The Southern Democracy, where lies the main strength of the party, is frankly hostile to his rights and would if possible limit them still more. Thinking colored men can only view with apprehension the prospect of a cabinet dominated by the Gormans, Tillmans, Vardamans, or others of their kind. With all its shortcomings the Republican party, by virtue of its traditions, and in view of the large Northern colored vote, cannot afford to be actively unfriendly to the Negro. It might be still more indifferent and still be the lesser of two evils.

---

[2] Judge Alton Brooks Parker (1852–1926), the Southern Democratic candidate, lost the presidency to Theodore Roosevelt in 1904.

But the chief reason why colored men who vote will support the Republican ticket in the coming campaign lies in the personality of the candidates. President Roosevelt and his appointees in the Federal Courts have made a strong effort to break up the new slavery ere it became firmly established, and in many other ways the President has endeavored to stem the tide of prejudice, which, sweeping up from the South, has sought to overwhelm the Negro everywhere; and he has made it clear that he regards himself as the representative of all the people. The influence of the executive is greater in the nation than ever before. The opponents of President Roosevelt criticise him as impulsive; his impulses are friendly toward the colored race. He is said to be impolitic in his attitude upon the race question; his impolicy in that regard has been in the line of justice and generosity. We have nothing to hope for from the national Democratic party; its success in the present campaign would be a menace to our liberty. With four more years of a courageous and friendly executive, the South will have time for a sober second thought on its attitude towards the Negro, the Southern party friendly to human rights will have time to grow, and the colored race will be stronger to resist oppression, and to press its claim for justice at the hands of the party it supports.

RACE PREJUDICE: ITS CAUSES AND ITS CURE

The prejudice against the Negro, in which is involved the race problem of the United States, grew out of the accumulation of differences between the two sharply defined types of mankind which the institution of slavery brought together. They differed physically, the one being black and the other white. The one had constituted for poets and sculptors the ideal of beauty and grace; the other was rude and unpolished in form and feature. The one possessed the arts of civilization and the learning of the schools, the other, at most, the simple speech and rude handicrafts of his native tribe, and no written language at all. The one was Christian, the other heathen. The one was master of the soil; the other frankly alien and himself the object of ownership. This accumulation of superficial differences brought into play an antagonism measured by the sum of that due

---

Alexander's Magazine, July 15, 1905.

to each. There was the contempt of the instructed for the ignorant, of the fair and comely for the black and homely, of the master for the slave, of the Christian for the heathen, of the native for the foreigner, of the citizen for the alien, of one who spoke a language fluently for one who spoke it brokenly or not at all. Such was the combination of differences with their resulting antagonism which the Negro had to face in the long struggle for equality stretching through the centuries in front of him.

These were the causes of race antagonism. Where lies the remedy? It lies in the removal of the antagonisms by the removal of the causes which gave rise to them. The instinct of antagonism will disappear as the characteristics that called it into play are modified; in other words, as the structure was built up beam by beam, stone by stone, so it must be torn down stone by stone, beam by beam. There is no magic wand which can be waved to make it vanish.

If this doctrine be correct, it should be borne out by a retrospect of history. Passing over 250 years of colonial and national development, to what extent had these differences been modified at the period just before the civil war? In language the Negroes were one with the whites, and there was no longer any barrier of alien speech between them. The heathen religions had disappeared, the relation of master and slave was still the rule, although there were many free people of color. The one was citizen and the other, if not alien, was still not a citizen, and had no rights which the other held himself bound to respect. The physical characteristics had been greatly though not uniformly modified. A constant infusion of white blood, permitted by the customs of slavery, had left its impress upon the black race. The two races had thus been brought closer together at many points, and the antagonism was essentially less than at any earlier period.

The civil war removed others of these differences; all men were now alike free; all were voters, and therefore theoretically equal citizens. Thus radically were swept away several of the barriers which separated these two peoples. But the whites were still relatively rich and instructed, the black poor and ignorant. The control of the social organism, the habit of command, the pride of race and of authority still remained with the whites.

What further modification of these differences has taken place in the 40 years since the civil war? A political reaction in the south has temporarily denied the equality of the citizen; but this is temporary, and will in due time pass away, for the principle is embodied in the constitution, and is as vital to the liberties of white men as to those of black. The destruction of slavery and the marriage laws of the south have checked in some degree the admixture of the races, but the strain of white blood has been more generally diffused within the Negro race, thus bringing about a gradual change of type, and the customs of slavery have not entirely disappeared. For other reasons the physical type of the colored people has improved. They have been better fed and better clad; with better opportunities and larger liberty there has been a gradual softening of crudities and refinement of type. They have made a great advance in education and general enlightenment. There are 27,000 colored teachers. They conduct in the English language several hundred newspapers, including several monthly magazines, and there is a small and increasing number of their writers who have a respectful hearing beyond the limits of their own race. Several thousand of them have been graduated from higher institutions of learning. They have accumulated property estimated at three to four hundred millions. Their style of living and standards of culture have improved in even greater proportion, for many of them live better than white people of similar station would consider themselves able to afford. In Virginia, for instance, they have acquired 1-20 of the acreage of the state. The Negro church societies include 300,000 members, own $40,000,000 of church property, and send missionaries to Africa and the British West Indies.

Thus our savage has become civilized, our heathen Christian, our foreigner a native, our slave a citizen, our Negro a man of mixed blood, our pauper a land owner. The prejudice against him has decreased. With many individuals it has disappeared entirely. It varies in strength with locality. When left to natural laws it decreases relatively with the differences, but throughout the most of our southern states it has been deliberately and designedly stimulated for political purposes, and hence may seem to have become greater instead of less within the past generation. Another reason which retards the decline of prejudice is the inertia of preconceived opinion. Notice the strain with which a team of horses start a wagon and the ease with which they draw it over a good road. Forty years have been barely sufficient to start our wagon.

What can we do to still further modify these differences and reduce this prejudice; what remains to be done to complete our adjustment to our environment? Where do we stand in comparison with the white race, who constitute the main feature of our environment and with whom we must live in harmony and unity in order to live wholesomely and happily? Language and religion, as elements of antagonism, have disappeared, though some of us might use the language better and might have more religion without being at all too good for this world. The relation of master and slave no longer exists, though that of employer and servant is still very imperfectly adjusted and the customs of slavery die hard.

Of the differences which remain to be adjusted a vital one is education, or rather the social efficiency which grows out of training. So important and fundamental is this question that it has for the moment overshadowed every other element of the race problem, and it is immensely significant and hopeful that in the discussion of this problem all good men, whatever their color, and however they may differ in other ways, are agreed that education, training in the arts of life, is a primary element of any attempted or possible solution. The matter of education, too, is important to us as a means as well as an end, since the temporary closing of other avenues of activity has directed toward it much of the best thought of our ablest men and given their talents a healthy outlet and a worthy career. Much progress has been made, upon which we may justly congratulate ourselves. But let us not deceive ourselves. Much more remains to be done. The census shows that we have reduced our illiteracy over 50 percent. But what does that mean? By the census definition it merely means that 52 percent of the Colored people have stated to the census enumerator that they can read and write. By the census 88 percent of the southern white people are returned as literate. But does that mean that the 52 percent of the Colored are as well educated as the 88 percent of the whites? I think we would not claim it. There are 15,528 Colored clergymen as compared with 94,437 whites. What is their relative degree of education, morality and zeal for the cure of souls? This, and not their number, is the real test of their influence. By the census we have a large number of business men, but in the census statistics, the grocer with a $200 stock counts as much as the grocer with a $200,000 stock. The census figures show so many white children and so many Colored children in attendance at the public schools, and it is easy to stop upon these figures and overlook the fact that in some places the white schools are open ten months and the Colored but ten weeks. To close this gap so as to compete with the whites in social efficiency or value to the community, the Colored people must be relatively as well educated, their teachers of relatively as high a grade, their schools open as many days in the year, their grocers have relatively as large stocks, their banks relatively as large capital and volume of transactions. The mere raising of percentages in quantity without a corresponding advance in quality does not by any means eliminate the difference. Whatever can be done by organization or by individual effort to dignify labor, to make it more efficient and thereby to increase its rewards is an advantage to our people, and whoever helps this cause forward is their benefactor. We should not permit ourselves in our impatience of results, in our resentment of well known wrongs to forget the philanthropy which has given so fully and freely both of money and lives toward the education of the Negro in the South.

The standing controversy with reference to the kind of education which the colored people in their present condition need most, recalls to one's mind the old story of the shield which hung across the roadway in front of a castle which two knights in armor were approaching from different directions. One maintained that it was gold and the other that it was silver. After the fashion of their age they set their lances and fought for their opinions until they were both unhorsed, and when they were carried into the castle to have their wounds dressed they discovered that both were right— one side of the shield was gold and the other silver. Our old ideals of education were based purely upon intellectual training, with a dash of morality and religion. But in this modern day the definition of education has been enlarged to take in a wider training for social usefulness. The great mass of men have always earned, must always earn their living by the labor of their hands, and that these hands should be trained in schools is a vital necessity for any people who hope to register progress; and especially necessary to a people who by the decline of the apprenticeship system, the selfishness of labor unions and a prejudice which limits their opportunities, are compelled to compete with those possessing greater advantages. Will any one pretend to say that this necessity among our people has been fully met or more than merely begun upon? An institution like Hampton or Tuskegee in every southern state for another generation would not meet the need of the Negro for training in the practical arts of life.

But the need of the higher education is equally important, not for so many perhaps, but certainly for a great many more than have enjoyed it. There are living and have died in the United States since the civil war at least 15,000,000 Colored people. They have had about 2,500 liberally educated Colored men and women as leaders, one to six thousand. There are towns in the United States where there is one saloon to every 30 or 40 people. Were there no color line, there are trained white men in every southern community who could furnish leadership for the Colored people. But there is a color line, deep and dark and wide, and our southern brethren are thrown back upon themselves for all sorts of leadership. To supply this need they want all the higher education that can be supplied by southern colleges and by the free northern universities. A Fisk [University, Nashville, Tennessee] or an Atlanta [University, Atlanta, Georgia] in every southern state, and a hundred Colored graduates from every great northern college for a generatios [sic] to come would be none too many to supply the demand for trained teachers and preachers, engineers and architects and professional and business men required for the healthy and diversified development of a people who are likely a generation hence to number 30,000,000—a population as large as that of the whole country at the outbreak of the civil war. The state has assumed the burden of primary education, but owing to the poverty of the south, is but imperfectly performing this duty for either whites or blacks. The state has also undertaken in some degree to provide for the higher education, but the separate school system of the south has excluded the Negro from the state institutions, and private philanthropy has in some measure supplied the need. It is a question whether the nation ought not to take up the matter of southern education. Well might not we ask whether we have a duty to perform at home before we spend the nation's money in carrying the blessings of civilization to distant and alien peoples. By what color of reason do we spend the nation's money in teaching science to the Filipinos, when a great portion of our own population, white and Colored, cannot read or write?

Poverty is still a characteristic of the Negro, which must cease to be a race trait before the prejudice is eliminated. Statistics show that Colored men own in whole or in part 186,000 farms out of a total of 5,739,657 farms in the United States, or one farm in 31. If we stop there, this would not be a bad showing, but pursuing our investigation we find that these Negro farms contain but 15,827,000 acres out of a total farm acreage of 841,201,000, or only one acre in 53, and that the value of these farms owned by them is reported at $177,915,000 out of a total farm value in the United States of $20,439,906,000, or $1.00 in $133. To bring the Colored farmer to economic equality with the white farmer he must own one farm in every eight, instead of one in every 31. These farms must contain one acre in every eight instead of one in 53, and these farms must be worth one-eighth of the entire farm valuation of the country instead of 1-133. We are loosely credited with property to the value of three to four hundred million dollars. It is a very respectable sum, and would make half a dozen white men fairly well to do; it would make one white man very rich. There are several families in New York who could buy out the whole Colored race and have money to spare. The aggregate wealth of the nation in 1900 was given by the bureau of statistics as $94,300,000,000. We have the $300,000,000; they have the $94,000,000,000; dividing it up, we are worth an average of $3 apiece; they are worth an average of $1,446 apiece. I need not argue that before the Negro shall have attained financial equality with the white, he must possess one dollar in every eight instead of one in every three hundred.

The disparity of civil and political rights must be removed; our constitution must be respected and our laws made to conform to it. I believe in manhood suffrage, that in some way—and what other way is possible except by the ballot?—every sane man, not in prison, who contributes by his labor to the wealth of the community, should have a voice in the selection of those who make and administer the laws. But if there is any restriction upon the suffrage, it should apply to all men alike. I have sometimes thought, however, that some qualification of character or education might be, not unwisely, required for holding office. The progressive debasement of state and municipal legislatures suggests that in some way a higher standard must be sought.

But wherever men's rights are fixed by law, those laws should apply equally. Entrance and promotion into every branch of the public service should be governed by merit alone. Discriminating laws which classify men and fix their rights and opportunities by race or color are utterly abhorrent to the spirit of liberty.

The last and most difficult of these differences which holds us apart from our fellow citizens is the still strongly marked difference in physical characteristics—in other words, in color or race, as we usually term it. I have shown how this difference has been modified. Should it disappear entirely race prejudice and the race problem would no longer exist. Problems there might be, but they would not be those of race. Do we wish to perpetuate this difference? We have had preached to us of late a new doctrine, that of race integrity. We are told that we must glory in our color and zealously guard it as a priceless heritage. Frankly, I take no stock in this doctrine. It seems to me a modern invention of the white people to perpetuate the color line. It is they who preach it, and it is their racial integrity which they wish to preserve; they have never been unduly careful of the purity of the black race. I can scarcely restrain a smile when I hear a mulatto talking of race integrity or a quadroon dwelling upon race pride. What they mean is a very fine thing, and a very desirable thing, but it is not at all what they say. Why should a man be proud any more than he should be ashamed of a thing for which he is not at all responsible? Manly self-respect, based upon one's humanity, a self-respect which claims nothing for color and yields nothing to color, every man should cherish. But the Negro in the United States has suffered too much from the race pride of other people to justify him in cultivating something equally offensive for himself. Of what should we be proud? Of any inherent superiority? Why deny it in others, proclaiming the equality of men. Of any great achievement? We are still in the infancy of achievement, and the showing we can make is not by comparison with others, but with our own less fortunate past. We complain because others judge us by our worst, and yet we ourselves are too prone to compare ourselves with ourselves, to look down rather than up, backward rather than forward. What we have done merely marks the inevitable advance of a people surrounded by many things which stimulate to advancement, and while some of us have been cruelly hampered by lack of opportunity, I think we will all admit, here in the privacy of our own family circle, that the masses of us have not taken the fullest advantage of the opportunities we have had.

Why should we wish to perpetuate this disastrous difference between us and our fellow citizens? Every other people who come to this country seek to lose their separate identity as soon as possible, and to become Americans with no distinguishing mark. For a generation they have their ghettoes,

their residence quarters, their churches, their social clubs. For another generation they may still retain a sentimental interest in these things. In the
third generation they are all Americans, seldom speak of their foreign descent and often modify their names so that they will not suggest it. They
enter fully and completely, if they are capable and worthy, into the life of
this republic. Are we to help the white people to build up walls between
themselves and us to fence in a gloomy back yard for our descendants to
play in? This nation, with the war amendments, threw that theory over-
board when it established the equality of all men before the law. The northern states have long since repudiated it, when they abolished discriminating laws and threw open the public schools to all alike, and if it still lingers
among us it is due to that inertia of which I have spoken, which makes it
difficult to change deep-rooted social questions. The southern states in attempting to perpetuate the color line, are trying to do the impossible, and
I for one do not wish to encourage them for one moment by accepting their
views any further than they can compel their acceptance by force. Race
prejudice will not perhaps entirely disappear until the difference of color
shall have disappeared, or at least until all of us, white and Colored, shall
have resolutely shut our eyes to those differences and shall have learned to
judge men by other standards. I ask you to dismiss from your mind any
theory, however cherished, that there can be built up in a free country, under equal laws, two separate sorts of civilization, two standards of human
development. I not only believe that the mixture of races will in time become an accomplished fact, but that it will be a good thing for all concerned. It is already well forward and events seem to be paving the way to
embrace the Negro in the general process by which all the races of mankind are being fused together here into one people. Millions of foreigners,
much nearer the Negro in some respects than our native whites, are pouring into the country. Perhaps in the economy of divine Providence, they
may help to solve our problems by furnishing a bridge with which to span
the race chasm. This is not a matter with which we of this generation need
greatly concern ourselves, except for the principle involved. It is not left for
us to say whether it shall take place or not, and it is not likely to affect any
of us. But that in the long run it will come to pass, is, I think, the lesson of
history and the conclusion of sound logic. I hope the prejudice may disappear long before that distant period, but I am quite sure it will disappear
when there is no longer anything for it to feed upon. I wish I had time to
quote in this connection some recent utterances on this subject, from the
pen of a former governor of the island of Jamaica, who has lived for 20 years
in that community, where the black population has outnumbered the
whites by 40 to one, and where the doctrine of the equality of all men before the law has been faithfully and consistently worked out to form a con-

tented, happy and progressive community. I quote a few words: "The color line is not a rational line, the logic neither of words nor of facts will uphold it. If adopted it infallibly aggravates the virus of the color problem. The more it is ignored and forgotten, the more is that virus attenuated." [1] The Negro in Jamaica has thus far been raised, and a freedom of civic mixture between the races has been made tolerable by the continuous application of the doctrine of humanity and equality, and equal claim of the black with the white to share, according to personal capacity and development, in all the inheritances of humanity. My comparison of conditions in the Republic and in the West Indies has brought me to the conviction that no solution of color difficulties can be found except by resolutely turning the back to the color line and race differentiation theory.

And now to close, may I venture a prophecy? There are many who see the world through smoked glasses, and who view this problem of race solely from the pessimistic point of view. I think for my own part that it is in a healthy process of solution, which by sticking closely to correct principles and by acting upon them when the opportunity offers, we can help to further. Looking down the vista of time I see an epoch in our nation's history, not in my time or yours, but in the not distant future, when there shall be in the United States but one people, moulded by the same culture, swayed by the same patriotic ideals, holding their citizenship in such high esteem that for another to share it is of itself to entitle him to fraternal regard; when men will be esteemed and honored for their character and talents. When hand in hand and heart with heart all the people of this nation will join to preserve to all and to each of them for all future time that ideal of human liberty which the fathers of the republic set out in the Declaration of Independence which declared that all men are created equal, the ideal for which [William] Garrison and [Wendell] Phillips and [Charles] Sumner lived and worked; the ideal for which Lincoln died, the ideal embodied in the words of the Book which the slave mother learned by stealth to read, with slow-moving finger and faltering speech, and which I fear

---

[1] Sydney H. Olivier's "White Man's Burden at Home," from which Chesnutt quotes significantly in the longer version of "Race Prejudices." In this longer version, Chesnutt combines race theory with several economic, social, and political views already addressed in other essays. Because the two versions show the impact of audience on Chesnutt's texts, they should be read alongside each other. The editors of *Alexander's Magazine* apparently required this high-profile black writer to focus primarily on those ideas that could have the greatest impact on their mostly African-American readers, especially Chesnutt's controversial miscegenation theory—which most blacks and whites did not support—and his anointing the beneficiaries of ex-slavemasters as ideals of high physical and cultural breeding and civilization.

that some of us with our freedom and our culture have forgotten to read at all—the Book which declares that "God is no respecter of persons, and that of one blood hath He made all the nations of the earth."

REMARKS OF CHARLES WADDELL CHESNUTT, OF CLEVELAND, IN ACCEPTING THE SPINGARN MEDAL AT LOS ANGELES, JULY 3, 1928.

Madam Chairman, Lieutenant Governor [Buron R.] Fitts, Officers of the National Headquarters [of the National Association for the Advancement of Colored People], Honored Delegates, Ladies and Gentlemen—and any others, if any there be, who managed to slip by the doorkeepers or climb in the windows, and may therefore happen to be here:

I imagine that the proper response from a literary man upon an occasion of this kind would be an ornate and scholarly oration exemplifying the literary style and quality of his writings. But even if this be so, you have had so much eloquent and uplifting oratory during the week and during the evening that I am going to breach the custom, to use a legal expression, and put my sentiments into simple and almost colloquial form.

In expressing my sincere thanks for, and my profound appreciation of the signal honor which has been publicly conferred upon me here, I shall outline a few of the reasons why I value this medal and what it signifies. I shall state these reasons, not in the order of their importance, but as they occur to me.

First, the intrinsic value of the medal. It is made of gold, the king of metals, ever since the dawn of history the medium of exchange and the symbol of wealth and power and splendor, with which the perfervid imagination of the Hebrew sacred poets paved the streets of Heaven, and of which the Negro singers have made the slippers in which to walk those streets. How comfortable golden slippers would be I don't know, but they would certainly look fine!

Again, I value this medal because it is an exquisitely beautiful work of art, worthy of a place in any collector's cabinet. On its shining face stands

Charles W. Chesnutt Collection. Fisk University Library, Nashville, Tennessee.

the serene and majestic figure of Justice, the scales in one hand, the sword in the other, and on the obverse side an appropriate inscription.

Another reason is that this medal originated in the great heart of its founder, Joel E. Spingarn, distinguished scholar, teacher, author, publisher, and friend and supporter of all good causes, who has done so much from its inception to make the National Association for the Advancement of Colored People [NAACP] the success it is today.

Still another reason that I value this medal is the personnel of the Committee of Award, all of them men of distinction and all but two of whom I have known personally for many years, and whose wisdom and good judgment, as evidenced by their selection of the winner of the medal from year to year, and especially this year, I am in no position to question. I should not have chosen myself, but I bow to their decision and feel honored by their confidence, which has added my name to the roll of able and distinguished men and women who have been selected to receive this reward of merit, which I value also because of the company in which it places me.

Then, again, this medal is particularly valuable to me because the award is made, through the hands of your distinguished Lieutenant Governor, by the National Association for the Advancement of Colored People, the first successful and worthwhile organization for the protection of the rights and the promotion and advancement of all worthy interests of the Negroid group which we designate as the colored people or as the American Negro. For nineteen years, led by a band of noble and devoted men and women, it has conducted a vigorous and increasingly effective campaign against racial intolerance. The result you all know. It has been reported in detail throughout the week of this Conference. The Association is the spokesman of the race and its approval is the highest of honors. This medal is a service medal, given me by the people I have sought to serve, and honor from one's own people in one's own country is worth more than from all the rest of the world combined. It is an earnest of the love and respect and confidence of a great group which is growing in numbers, in wisdom, and in social efficiency—in all the respects which make for good citizenship. I am proud to be numbered among them and to be found worthy of their esteem.

Another reason that I value this honor is that it has enabled me to spend a whole week with my good friends of the National Office of the Association and by this intimate daily intercourse to exchange views upon many weighty subjects and still further strengthen and cement the ties of friendship which bind us.

These might seem to be sufficient reasons for my appreciation of this honor, but there is one more, and that not the least important, though it is only a collateral reason, and that is that it gave one the opportunity to revisit your beautiful city. Some years ago, before the Great War and before the big boom which put Los Angeles on the map, I was here for a day or two. I came to see the country and was n't particularly interested in the people. I had no acquaintance in the city, I stopped in a downtown hotel, and except for the colored servants and an occasional well dressed man or woman on the street, I would n't have known that there were any Negroes in the city.

When my distinguished friend Mr. [James Weldon] Johnson, the National Secretary, advised me of my selection as the recipient of the Spingarn medal for this year, he said in his letter that if it were not convenient for me to be present at Los Angeles the medal could be delivered to a proxy, and a subsequent ceremony take place in Ohio. Mrs. [Susan Perry] Chesnutt—some of you have met her and others of you may have seen this quiet, unassuming little woman who leads me around and looks me up when I get lost—as I have been several times in this land of the wide open spaces—who tells me what to do, and when and how to do it—when she had opened and read my letter, she handed it to me and said, "Of course you are going to Los Angeles. It would be beneath our dignity to receive this medal by proxy." "Well," I replied, "I was never very strong on dignity; as [Octavus Roy Cohen's characters] Florian Slappey or Lawyer Evans Chew would say, 'It's sump'n I've got eve'ything e'se but.' However, a second ceremony would be a little tame, like eating hash or getting married to the same woman the second time."

Then she went on and told me that another reason why I was going to Los Angeles—note the language, not why I *should* go but why I *was going*—was that she had never been to the Pacific Coast, and that it had been the dream of her life to go there, and that this was her golden opportunity. So, as a result of these various inducements, I found myself able, in due course of time, to say, like the American soldiers at Lafayette's tomb, "Los Angeles, we are here. What have you?"

Well, I began immediately to find out what you have. I found your city grown to be the metropolis of Southern California, with a population which your citizens modestly claim is larger than that of Cleveland, though I suspect the census takers made a mistake or have a grudge against your city and have not given you proper credit for your numbers. Instead of a few Negroes, here and there, I have found a large and progressive body of colored people, with many outstanding representatives in the professions and in business. I am stopping at a hotel owned and managed by colored people, which for its size and cost is as beautiful and as well managed as any hotel I have ever seen. I have found your people well represented in the schools and in the public service. And your hospitality—well, *superb* is none too strong a word for it.

One of your number, a young architect whose talent is almost genius, took my party and me for a little afternoon spin of 150 miles, in the course of which we visited several handsome homes which he had built. I have ridden over a thousand miles in automobiles and have only paid two or three small taxi fares.

Since I have been here I have gained much useful information and had some illusions shattered. On some of these drives I learned, among other things, that this is a land not only of wide open spaces but of wide open statements. If I asked my host about the size of a park for instance, or an oil refinery, or the citrus fruit crop, and he did n't know the correct answer he would say so, but would add that it was the biggest in the world, and after I had checked up on a few of these statements, I reached the conclusion that they were probably true.

I came here with the preconceived notion that this was a dry country. I found it dry enough, in the present-day use of the word, to reasonably satisfy even Mr. Volstead,[1] if that were possible, but my thought had been with reference to the aridity of the climate. But one of the gentlemen, if I remember correctly, informed me that it required thirty-five barrels of water for every pound of produce grown in Los Angeles County. When I recalled the mountains of vegetables and fruits and nuts I had seen in your great markets, and the thousands of acres of them I had seen growing, this seemed incredible, but my informant was a man whose name is a synonym of veracity—it is generally admitted that he could no more tell a lie than the infant George Washington—and I was forced to revise my opinion about the dryness of the climate. If the statement were true—and I could not doubt it, in view of my friend's reputation for truthfulness—you must have almost as much water here as there is in the Pacific Ocean.

Since I have been here I have met many former friends and fellow townsmen, and some pupils of mine in the dim and distant past when I taught school, and they have all vied with one another to make our stay among you pleasant. One of them, an old friend of my young manhood, has devoted almost his entire time to our entertainment. So I thank the Spingarn Medal Award Committee and Mrs. Chesnutt for having induced me to come to Los Angeles.

It was suggested to me by Mr. Johnson that it is customary for the winners of the Spingarn medal to say something, in accepting it, about how they happened to do the things which entitled them to this reward,

---

[1] Chesnutt jokingly refers to the Volstead Act, a law passed in 1919 by the United States Congress defining alcoholic beverages, which led to the enforcement of Prohibition. The law is named after Andrew Joseph Volstead (1860–1947) who promoted it.

and what they had in mind when they did them, and since my writings are my chief title to recognition, I shall follow that custom.

I was always an omnivorous reader. Indeed I cannot remember when I did not read. My maternal grandmother once remarked in my hearing that had she not been present at my delivery she could have believed that I was born with a book in my hand. And I observed, as soon as I was capable of intelligent observation, that the Negro in fiction had become standardized, and that there were very few kinds of Negroes. There was the bad Negro, as most of them were, who either broke the laws or made himself obnoxious to the white people by demanding his rights or protesting against his wrongs; the good Negro who loved old "Massa" and preserved the same attitude toward his children as they had taken to him, that of a simple and childlike deference and respect—the good old Uncle and Mammy types; and the modern "white man's nigger," as we call him, who, as teacher or preacher or politician or whatever you will,

"Crooks the pregnant hinges of the knee,
Where thrift may follow fawning."

Then there was the wastrel type, who squandered his substance in riotous living, and the minstrel type, who tried to keep the white folks in a good humor by his capers and antics.

Now, I knew very well that while these types were true enough so far as they went, they were by no means all the types of Negroes. I knew there were among them many thrifty, progressive and serious-minded people, with a sincere respect for their own type, with high aspirations for themselves and their children, whose ideals of character and citizenship were of the best, with no more respect or deference for white people than their attitude toward the Negro entitled them to, and a keen resentment of race prejudice and social intolerance.

When I began to write serious books, after the usual apprenticeship aspiring authors must go through, I thought I saw the literary and artistic value of different types of Negroes than these, and I set out to depict them in my books. I did n't write my stories as Negro propaganda—propaganda is apt to be deadly to art—but I used the better types, confident that the truth would prove the most valuable propaganda; that it is infinitely more effective in a novel to have a character do a fine and noble deed, and thus let him speak for himself and his people, than merely to say he was a fine and noble fellow and a credit to his race.

While I was born in the North, my father, who had left the South and gone North in the late fifties of the last century and had served four years in the Union Army, returned along with the carpet-baggers to North Carolina, where he was born, and where he had some ancestral property. I was brought up in North Carolina as one of the colored people, and have ever since remained one of them, so that I knew whereof I spoke when I sought to depict their lives, their sufferings and disappointments, their hopes and fears, their successes and failures. I tried to write of them not primarily as a Negro writing about Negroes, but as a human being writing about other human beings, and whenever I let my feelings get the better of me and become dogmatic and argumentative in a book, I found that its artistic quality suffered, and its success accordingly. My physical makeup was such that I knew the psychology of people of mixed blood in so far as it differed from that of other people, and most of my writings ran along the color line, the vaguely defined line where the two major races of the country meet. It has more dramatic possibilities than life within clearly defined and widely differentiated groups. This was perfectly natural and I have no apologies to make for it, for we are all one people, and the suffering and triumphs the failures and successes of one of us are those of all of us.

My books were written, from one point of view, a generation too soon. There was no such demand then as there is now for books by and about colored people. And I was writing against the trend of public opinion on the race question at that particular time. And I had to sell my books chiefly to white readers. There were few colored book buyers. At that time the Negro was inarticulate; I think I was the first man in the United States who shared his blood, to write serious fiction about the Negro. But in this later and happier, though yet far from perfect age, there are a number of colored men who write books, and a still larger number of white men and women who write books about the Negro, who, if they do not write the Negro up at least seek to tell the truth about the conditions in which he lives, and the truth is in the Negro's favor.

The great pioneer work of fiction about the Negro, Uncle Tom's Cabin, wasted no long pages in anti-slavery argument. It has been some time since I last read it, but I recall few, if any, diatribes against slavery. It was its description of the institution as affecting the lives of its victims, white, black and those of mixed blood, that stirred the heart and conscience of the nation and was perhaps the most powerful influence in the abolition of slavery.

My books had their day and I hope that, as my good friends, the Spingarn Medal Committee, have decided, they contributed somewhat to the advancement of colored people, as I meant them to do. I am writing another novel, dealing with present day conditions, and, when it is published, as I confidently expect it will be, those of you who, for whatever reason, have read none of my other books, will have an opportunity to get acquainted with my work, and those of you who survived reading my other writings will have the opportunity to renew our acquaintance.

Again I thank you, sir, and the committee and the association, for this splendid testimonial. It will be a strong incentive to further effort along the same line and help me to prove still further that your confidence and esteem are not misplaced.

POST-BELLUM—PRE-HARLEM

My first book, *The Conjure Woman,* was published by the Houghton Mifflin Company in 1899. It was not, strictly speaking, a novel, though it has been so called, but a collection of short stories in Negro dialect, put in the mouth of an old Negro gardener, and related by him in each instance to the same audience, which consisted of the Northern lady and gentleman who employed him. They are naive and simple stories, dealing with alleged incidents of chattel slavery, as the old man had known it and as I had heard of it, and centering around the professional activities of old Aunt Peggy, the plantation conjure woman, and others of that ilk.

In every instance Julius had an axe to grind, for himself or his church, or some member of his family, or a white friend. The introductions to the stories, which were written in the best English I could command, developed the characters of Julius's employers and his own, and the wind-up of each story reveals the old man's ulterior purpose, which, as a general thing, is accomplished.

Most of the stories in *The Conjure Woman* had appeared in the *Atlantic Monthly* from time to time, the first story, *The Goophered Grapevine,* in the issue of August, 1887, and one of them, *The Conjurer's Revenge,* in the *Overland Monthly.* Two of them were first printed in the bound volume.

After the book had been accepted for publication, a friend of mine, the late Judge Madison W. Beacom, of Cleveland, a charter member of the Rowfant Club, suggested to the publishers a limited edition, which appeared in advance of the trade edition in an issue of one hundred and fifty numbered copies and was subscribed for almost entirely by members of the Rowfant Club and of the Cleveland bar. It was printed by the Riverside

---

The Colophon: A Book Collectors Quarterly, Part 5, 1931.

Charles W. Chesnutt, "Post-Bellum—Pre-Harlem" is reprinted with the permission of Simon and Schuster from *Breaking Into Print* by Elmer Adler. Copyright © by Simon and Schuster.

Press on large hand-made linen paper, bound in yellow buckram, with the name on the back in black letters on a white label, a very handsome and dignified volume. The trade edition was bound in brown cloth and on the front was a picture of a white-haired old Negro, flanked on either side by a long-eared rabbit. The dust-jacket bore the same illustration.

The name of the story teller, "Uncle" Julius, and the locale of the stories, as well as the cover design, were suggestive of Mr. [Joel Chandler] Harris's *Uncle Remus*, but the tales are entirely different. They are sometimes referred to as folk tales, but while they employ much of the universal machinery of wonder stories, especially the metamorphosis, with one exception, that of the first story, *The Goophered Grapevine*, of which the norm was a folk tale, the stories are the fruit of my own imagination, in which respect they differ from the *Uncle Remus* stories which are avowedly folk tales.

Several subsequent editions of *The Conjure Woman* were brought out; just how many copies were sold altogether I have never informed myself, but not enough for the royalties to make me unduly rich, and in 1929, just thirty years after the first appearance of the book, a new edition was issued by Houghton Mifflin Company. It was printed from the original plates, with the very handsome title page of the limited edition, an attractive new cover in black and red, and a very flattering foreword by Colonel Joel Spingarn.

Most of my books are out of print, but I have been told that it is quite unusual for a volume of short stories which is not one of the accepted modern classics to remain on sale for so long a time.

At the time when I first broke into print seriously, no American colored writer had ever secured critical recognition except Paul Laurence Dunbar, who had won his laurels as a poet. Phillis Wheatley, a Colonial poet, had gained recognition largely because she was a slave and born in Africa, but the short story, or the novel of life and manners, had not been attempted by any one of that group.

There had been many novels dealing with slavery and the Negro. Harriet Beecher Stowe, especially in *Uncle Tom's Cabin,* had covered practically the whole subject of slavery and race admixture. George W. Cable had dwelt upon the romantic and some of the tragic features of racial contacts in Louisiana, and Judge Albion W. Tourgée, in what was one of the best sellers of his day, *A Fool's Errand,* and in his *Bricks Without Straw,* had dealt with the problems of reconstruction.

Thomas Dixon was writing the Negro down industriously and with marked popular success. Thomas Nelson Page was disguising the harshness of slavery under the mask of sentiment. The trend of public sentiment at the moment was distinctly away from the Negro. He had not developed any real political or business standing; socially he was outcast. His musical and stage successes were still for the most part unmade, and on the whole he was a small frog in a large pond, and there was a feeling of pessimism in regard to his future.

Publishers are human, and of course influenced by the opinions of their public. The firm of Houghton Mifflin, however, was unique in some respects. One of the active members of the firm was Francis J. Garrison, son of William Lloyd Garrison, from whom he had inherited his father's hatred of slavery and friendliness to the Negro. His partner, George H. Mifflin, was a liberal and generous gentleman trained in the best New England tradition. They were both friendly to my literary aspirations and became my personal friends.

But the member of their staff who was of most assistance to me in publishing my first book was Walter Hines Page, later ambassador to England under President Wilson, and at that time editor of the *Atlantic Monthly,* as well as literary adviser for the publishing house, himself a liberalized Southerner, who derived from the same part of the South where the stories in *The Conjure Woman* are located, and where I passed my adolescent years. He was a graduate of Macon College, a fellow of Johns Hopkins University, had been attached to the staff of the *Forum* and the *New York Evening Post,* and was as broad-minded a Southerner as it was ever my good fortune to meet.

Three of the *Atlantic* editors wrote novels dealing with race problems—William Dean Howells in *An Imperative Duty,* Bliss Perry in *The Plated City,* and Mr. Page in *The Autobiography of Nicholas Worth.*

The first of my conjure stories had been accepted for the *Atlantic* by Thomas Bailey Aldrich, the genial auburn-haired poet who at that time presided over the editorial desk. My relations with him, for the short time they lasted, were most cordial and friendly.

Later on I submitted to Mr. Page several stories of post-war life among the colored people which the *Atlantic* published, and still later the manuscript of a novel. The novel was rejected, and was subsequently rewritten and published by Houghton Mifflin under the title of *The House Behind the Cedars* [1900]. Mr. Page, who had read the manuscript, softened its rejection by the suggestion that perhaps a collection of the conjure stories might be undertaken by the firm with a better prospect of success. I was in the hands of my friends, and submitted the collection. After some omissions and additions, all at the advice of Mr. Page, the book was accepted and announced as *The Conjure Woman,* in 1899, and I enjoyed all the delights of proof-reading and the other pleasant emotions attending the publication of a first book. Mr. Page, Mr. Garrison and Mr. Mifflin vied with each other in helping to make our joint venture a literary and financial success.

The book was favorably reviewed by literary critics. If I may be pardoned one quotation, William Dean Howells, always the friend of the aspiring author, in an article published in the *Atlantic Monthly* for May, 1900, wrote:

"The stories of *The Conjure Woman* have a wild, indigenous poetry, the creation of sincere and original imagination, which is imparted with a tender humorousness and a very artistic reticence. As far as his race is concerned, or his sixteenth part of a race, it does not greatly matter whether Mr. Chesnutt invented their motives, or found them, as he feigns, among his distant cousins of the Southern cabins. In either case the wonder of their beauty is the same, and whatever is primitive and sylvan or campestral in the reader's heart is touched by the spells thrown on the simple black lives in these enchanting tales. Character, the most precious thing in fiction, is faithfully portrayed." [1]

Imagine the thrill with which a new author would read such an encomium from such a source!

From the publisher's standpoint, the book proved a modest success. This was by no means a foregone conclusion, even assuming its literary merit and the publisher's imprint, for reasons which I shall try to make clear.

I have been referred to as the "first Negro novelist," meaning, of course, in the United States; Pushkin in Russia and the two Dumas in France had produced a large body of popular fiction. At that time a literary work by an American of acknowledged color was a doubtful experiment, both for the writer and for the publisher, entirely apart from its intrinsic merit. Indeed, my race was never mentioned by the publishers in announcing or advertising the book. From my own viewpoint it was a personal matter. It never occurred to me to claim any merit because of it, and I have always resented the denial of anything on account of it. My colored friends, however, with a very natural and laudable zeal for the race, with which I found no fault, saw to it that the fact was not overlooked, and I have before me a copy of a letter written by one of them to the editor of the *Atlanta Constitution,* which had published a favorable review of the book, accompanied by my portrait, chiding him because the reviewer had not referred to my color.

---

[1] "Mr. Charles W. Chesnutt's Stories," *Atlantic Monthly* 85 (May 1900): 699–701.

A woman critic of Jackson, Mississippi, questioning what she called
the rumor as to my race, added, "Some people claim that Alexander Dumas, author of *The Count of Monte Cristo* and *The Three Musketeers*,
was a colored man. This is obviously untrue, because no Negro could possibly have written these books"—a pontifical announcement which would
seem to settle the question definitely, despite the historical evidence to the
contrary.

While *The Conjure Woman* was in the press, the *Atlantic* published a
short story of mine called *The Wife of His Youth* which attracted wide attention. James McArthur, at that time connected with the *Critic*, later with
Harper's, in talking one day with Mr. Page, learned of my race and requested leave to mention it as a matter of interest to the literary public.
Mr. Page demurred at first on the ground that such an announcement might
be harmful to the success of my forthcoming book, but finally consented,
and Mr. McArthur mentioned the fact in the *Critic*, referring to me as a
"mulatto."

As a matter of fact, substantially all of my writings, with the exception of *The Conjure Woman*, have dealt with the problems of people of
mixed blood, which, while in the main the same as those of the true Negro, are in some instances and in some respects much more complex and
difficult of treatment, in fiction as in life.

I have lived to see, after twenty years or more, a marked change in the attitude of publishers and the reading public in regard to the Negro in
fiction. The development of Harlem, with its large colored population in
all shades, from ivory to ebony, of all degrees of culture, from doctors of
philosophy to the lowest grade of illiteracy; its various origins, North
American, South American, West Indian and African; its morals ranging
from the highest to the most debased; with the vivid life of its cabarets,
dance halls, and theatres; with its ambitious business and professional
men, its actors, singers, novelists and poets, its aspirations and demands
for equality—without which any people would merit only contempt—presented a new field for literary exploration which of recent years has been
cultivated assiduously.

One of the first of the New York writers to appreciate the possibilities
of Harlem for literary purposes was Carl Van Vechten, whose novel *Nigger
Heaven* was rather severely criticized by some of the colored intellectuals
as a libel on the race, while others of them praised it highly. I was prejudiced

in its favor for reasons which those who have read the book will understand. I found it a vivid and interesting story which presented some new
and better types of Negroes and treated them sympathetically.

The Negro novel, whether written by white or colored authors, has
gone so much farther now in the respects in which it was criticized that *Nigger Heaven,* in comparison with some of these later productions, would be
almost as mild as a Sunday School tract compared to *The Adventures of
Fanny Hill.* Several of these novels, by white and colored authors alike, reveal such an intimate and meticulous familiarity with the baser aspects of
Negro life, North and South, that one is inclined to wonder how and from
what social sub-sewers they gathered their information. With the exception of one or two of the earlier ones, the heroine of the novel is never
chaste, though for the matter of that few post-Victorian heroines are, and
most of the male characters are likewise weaklings or worse.

I have in mind a recent novel, brilliantly written by a gifted black author, in which, to my memory, there is not a single decent character, male
or female.[2] These books are written primarily for white readers, as it is extremely doubtful whether a novel, however good, could succeed financially
on its sales to colored readers alone. But it seems to me that a body of
twelve million people, struggling upward slowly but surely from a lowly
estate, must present all along the line of its advancement many situations
full of dramatic interest, ranging from farce to tragedy, with many admirable types worthy of delineation.

Caste, a principal motive of fiction from [Samuel] Richardson down
through the Victorian epoch, has pretty well vanished among white Americans. Between the whites and the Negroes it is acute, and is bound to develop an increasingly difficult complexity, while among the colored people
themselves it is just beginning to appear.

Negro writers no longer have any difficulty in finding publishers.
Their race is no longer a detriment but a good selling point, and publishers are seeking their books, sometimes, I am inclined to think, with less regard for quality than in the case of white writers. To date, colored writers
have felt restricted for subjects to their own particular group, but there is
every reason to hope that in the future, with proper encouragement, they
will make an increasingly valuable contribution to literature, and perhaps
produce chronicles of life comparable to those of Dostoievsky, Dumas,
Dickens or Balzac.

---

[2] Probably *Home to Harlem* (1928), by Claude McKay, whose novelistic skills Chesnutt
repeatedly praises but whose themes he labels immoral.

THE NEGRO IN CLEVELAND

There are in Cleveland, according to the best available information, about 75,000 persons of African descent, classed as Negroes, though they vary in blood from one thirty-second to full Negro, and in color from ivory or pale pink to ebony.

They reside, for the most part, in the district lying between 14th Street on the west and 105th Street on the east, and between Cedar and Woodland Avenues, with some extension to the south, from Woodland, and to the east from 105th, and quite a number out Kinsman way, in what is known as Mt. Pleasant. In these districts they can purchase or rent and occupy property without objection, and many of them own their own homes. Other residential districts are resistant to their advent, sometimes by intimidation or violence, but there are quite a few scattered in the district between Superior Avenue and the lake, in the vicinity of East 105th Street.

Forbidden Ground

The whole Heights development is practically closed to them, though a few families not obviously Negroid have secured a foothold. It is about as difficult for a Negro to buy property on the Heights, except in one village, as it is for the traditional camel to pass through the eye of the traditional needle. This exclusiveness is maintained by care in sales, and by restrictive clauses in deeds, the legality of which is doubtful and has never been thoroughly tested.[1] The objection to their proximity does not include servants, so that Negroes in fact live all over the city.

Negroes as a class live on a low economic plane. Most of them are poor, some of them very poor; many of their children go to school undernourished and insufficiently clad. They have no rich men, measuring wealth by a very low standard, although their aggregate possessions would reach a very respectable figure. Of the upper tenth, a few own handsome, well-furnished homes with many evidences of taste and culture. The majority live in drab, middle or low class houses, none too well kept up, or in the moderate priced apartment houses which are found in their neighbor-

---

The Clevelander 5, November 1930.

[1] While Cleveland's population during the 1920s increased only 11 percent, exclusive and mostly white neighborhoods encircling the inner city grew at the following rates: Cleveland Heights by 234 percent, Garfield Heights by 511 percent, and the ultra-exclusive Shaker Heights by a whopping 1,000 percent (Kusmer 165–66).

hoods; while the poor live in dilapidated rack-rented shacks, sometimes a whole family in one or two rooms, as a rule paying higher rents than white tenants for the same space.

The first and fundamental concern of all men is the supply of their physical needs—food, clothing and shelter. To meet these simplest wants on the lowest plane demands money, and to get money one has to find work. Much of the Negro labor is common labor. The restriction of immigration, by lessening competition has helped the Negro in this field, though the multiplication of machines has been a strong counter-agent. Odd jobs are the least dependable form of employment, and many colored people have no other source of income. Domestic service, skilled or unskilled, supports many others.

When such numbers of them came North during and after the war, many were employed in the mills and factories at high wages, but the return of the white soldiers and, later, the financial slump, reduced this employment materially. There are many colored men in the building trades, especially in the rougher and harder work. They are received in most of the building trades unions, the notable exceptions being the electrical workers, the plumbers and the structural iron workers. But in the distribution of work through the unions, they are generally the last to be considered.

In spite of liberal resolutions passed from time to time by the American Federation of Labor, many unions, including most of the railroad unions, exclude Negroes from membership.

The waiters', waitresses' and cooks' unions do not admit colored members.

Due to the disappearance of the old-time system of apprenticeship, it is hard for a colored youth to learn a trade, and the trade schools conducted by the Board of Education are so tied up by rules and regulations, largely dictated by the labor unions, that it is difficult for a Negro boy to acquire a trade in them. He cannot study unless he secures in advance the promise of a job where he can do practical work on part time during his studies, or where he will be permanently employed at the end of his course. The difficulty in placing them has caused the officials to discourage the attendance of Negro students. A colored youth can take elementary training in the East Technical High School, but practical training in many trades can only be acquired in factories which discourage or limit the number of apprentices and especially Negro apprentices. The advantage of labor unions to the Negro lies chiefly in the advance in wages secured by the unions, which is reflected in the wages paid for common and non-union labor.

Gaining a Foothold

The thousands of places as clerks and salesmen in the great department and chain stores are closed to them with very few exceptions. Recently one of the chain store companies has had a store in a colored neighborhood with an entire Negro personnel.

There are no Negro conductors or motormen on the Cleveland Street Railway. In Detroit, where the street railways are city owned and operated, there are about one hundred. The East Ohio Gas Company, the Ohio Bell Telephone Company, indeed none of the great public utilities, employ colored people in anything but the humblest positions. In many of the industrial plants they are employed for the harder kinds of labor but have suffered disproportionately by the recent industrial decline, being generally the first to be let out when the force is reduced.

The development of business among Negroes in Cleveland has been backward, for obvious reasons—the lack of capital, experience and inherited business aptitude. Nevertheless, there are many kinds of business owned and operated by them. There are ten undertaking establishments, many small groceries, drug stores, restaurants, barber shops and pressing shops, and at least two small factories which manufacture brass specialties and metal grinding materials. There are few partnerships and no commercial corporations. They operate a number of gasoline service stations, including a chain of seven. There are colored photographers, caterers, music and furniture dealers; they conduct several hotels and various other business enterprises.

The number of Negro newspapers varies from time to time. At present there are two. They publish news of special interest to their group, including in every issue a list of lynchings and other outrages, as well as a chronicle of successes.[2]

The Negroes of Cleveland are well represented numerically in the learned professions.

There are about thirty-five colored lawyers practicing in the courts of the city and county, mostly in the Municipal and Police Courts. They have little commercial business, because most of their clients are of their own people, who have no large commercial or manufacturing business, for which reason a Negro lawyer is never appointed receiver or referee in an important case, though they are often appointed by the judges to defend criminals, the county paying their fees. Several of them have been recom-

---

[2] The *Cleveland Gazette,* the city's oldest "race" newspaper, founded in 1883, merged with the *Call and Post* around the end of the 1930s (Kusmer 194–95).

mended and others declared qualified by the Citizens' League and the Bar Associations when they run for office, and are well spoken of by the white lawyers and judges.

In the medical profession the Negro fares even better. There are fifty Negro doctors practicing in Cleveland. Six are attached to the staff of Lakeside Hospital, the main teaching unit of Western Reserve University, which has been very generous toward the Negro physician. One of them, who has been in the Department of Pediatrics for nine years, was sent to Harvard last year by the Department of Surgery for special study under a famous specialist. There is one in the Ophthalmological Department and one in the Department of Neurology.

Charity Hospital, a Catholic institution, has a Negro physician in the roentgenological department. The Salvation Army maternity home and hospital for colored women has an all-Negro staff, with the exception of a white chief-of-staff, and for years there has been a colored physician on the courtesy staff of Charity Hospital in minor surgery and medicine.

A Luxury

There are several dentists, but dentistry is one of the decorative arts and does not thrive among poor people in hard times, although in the boom years following the war the amount of gold used by Negro dentists must have seriously depleted the gold reserve of the nation.

There is a widely varying attitude toward the Negro in the social service agencies, embracing in the term those supported in whole or in part by the Community Fund.

The Y.M.C.A. and the Y.W.C.A. do not admit colored members, though colored students are received in the Y School of Technology and the Y.M.C.A. branch at Cedar Avenue and 77th Street is open to all young people without discrimination. The executive secretary in charge of the branch was captain in a colored regiment of the A.E.F.[3] The Phillis Wheatley Association for colored working girls, probably the most widely known of the Negro welfare agencies, occupies a large and commodious building, erected by popular subscription, at 40th Street and Cedar Avenue, where

---

[3] After a prolonged controversy beginning in 1906, when *Cleveland Journal* editor Nahum Daniel Brascher proposed a separate African-American branch of the YMCA, it was founded in 1921 and moved to Cedar Avenue/77th Street in 1923. Charles E. Frye served in the American Expeditionary Forces (A.E.F.) during the war before becoming secretary, manager, and finally executive director of the Cedar Avenue Branch. See Gerber 455–57, Kusmer 265–66, and McElrath, ed. 543.

it furnishes rooms for young women and conducts an employment agency and a restaurant which is open to the public. It conducts training classes in domestic service and home economics, presents pageants and plays, and has an auditorium which can be rented for meetings. It also has a branch on East 105th Street.

The Neighborhood Settlement, on 38th Street, long known as the "Play House," serves colored and white children on equal terms, and has long been doing a great cultural service for the Negro. Its very capable dramatic club, the Gilpin Players, has a small theater on Central Avenue, and it has also presented plays in the Little Theater at Public Hall.[4]

For the Race

The Negro Welfare Association is performing a very useful service in opening up new fields of employment for Negroes, in probation and Big Brother work and other welfare activities. The local branch of the National Association for the Advancement of Colored People concerns itself with racial discrimination of all sorts.

No colored children are received at any Cleveland Orphan Asylum, though Negro orphans are looked after very thoroughly by the Cleveland Humane Society. None of the "old folks' homes," male or female, are [sic] open to Negroes, except the Cleveland Home for Aged Colored Persons on Cedar Avenue, near 40th Street. This institution was founded and is managed by colored people and has places for sixteen inmates, all of which are taken.

The Salvation Army conducts a rescue home for colored women on Kinsman Avenue. Its other ministrations seem to be extended to the colored poor impartially, though it does not furnish lodging to the Negro "down-and-out."

The place where colored people get the best break is the public service. The reason is obvious—in Cleveland they vote, and they are learning, under an increasingly efficient leadership, to use their vote effectively. In certain districts the Negro vote is controlling, due to residence segregation, whether voluntary or forced. There are a colored Representative in the State Legislature, three members of the City Council, a member of the City Civil Service Commission and an Examiner in its office, and a mem-

---

[4]The Gilpin Players, an amateur Cleveland theater group, was formed in 1920 by six young African Americans inspired by the great African-American actor Charles Gilpin. For further discussion of this group, including its beginnings as the Dumas Club, see Selby 43–48 and Kusmer 217–18.

ber of the City Planning Commission. The Garbage Collection Department is entirely manned by Negroes, including the superintendency.

There are colored patrolmen and detectives, but no Negro firemen— perhaps for social reasons, since the firemen live in the stations. They are called for jury duty just as other citizens, though not accepted on juries quite as often. They have at least one clerk or deputy in each of the county offices, and have put forward candidates for the office of judge, so far without success. The supply of judgeships is so small and the demand and salaries so large that a colored lawyer has small chance of election to one of them. There are several colored probation officers in the Juvenile and Municipal Courts.

In the Federal Post Office, where places are under the Civil Service, they hold many of the low salaried positions, as office clerks, postal clerks and mail carriers. Several of them are or have been employed as government meat inspectors in stockyards and abattoirs.

There has never been racial segregation in the public schools. A colored woman is a member of the Board of Education, elected thereto by popular vote, the majority of which was white. The office pays no salary and there is little opportunity for graft.

There are nearly a hundred colored teachers in the public high and grade schools, and colored teachers are trained in the Normal School. They sometimes claim they are discriminated against in admission to the Normal School, but perhaps they are unduly sensitive. The requirements for registration are very rigid, as to education, health and "personality," and many of the white applicants do not qualify.

The Quincy Avenue branch of the Cleveland Public Library employs one colored young woman, and the Sterling Branch Library has two, one being a library school attendant and working in the library on part time. Another, a college graduate, is working full time and attending Cleveland College. The library has five colored pages. The total number of professional librarians in the whole system is between three hundred and fifty and four hundred, besides others who work part time, so that the Negro is not over-represented.

There is a Negro underworld and there are many Negro criminals. But crime, under the 18th Amendment and the Volstead Law, has become a major industry, and Negroes do not conduct major industries.

Only Petty Crime

There are small bootleggers and drug peddlers among them, a great deal of policy and "numbers" gambling, an occasional gas-station or grocery holdup, with perhaps an incidental murder, but colored men as a whole have neither the money nor the organization to carry on big boot-legging and racketeering enterprises, nor the reckless daring which marks the bank burglaries and payroll hold-ups which fill so much space in our police records. They have small opportunity for embezzlement or official graft. The most conspicuous instance of alleged criminality in Cleveland along this line among Cleveland Negroes involved only two hundred dollars. Other racial groups have taken precedence over the Negro in the field of crime, in which he might cheerfully admit his inferiority.

Socially, in the narrow sense of the word, colored people in Cleveland are strictly segregated. There are a few, close to the color line, who exchange social visits with a few white people. I do not know more than one place down town where I could take for luncheon a dark-colored man. A few years ago the Chamber of Commerce had for its speaking guest a very prominent and very dark Negro. It secured accommodation for him at a leading hotel, after another hotel had refused to entertain the Chamber's guest except upon condition that his meals be served in his room.

With the exception of the City Club, which has several colored members, I know of only three clubs in Cleveland with club houses which have any colored members, and they have only two in the aggregate, both members of the same family and superficially white. I do not refer, of course, to colored clubs, of which there are two that own their club houses, but they do not conduct restaurants.

There is a civil service law which forbids discrimination in public places, but it is difficult and expensive to enforce. One does not care to have to bring a lawsuit or swear out a warrant every time one wants a sandwich or a cup of coffee. A dark face may occasionally be seen at a hotel dining table, at some dinner given by a professional or civic organization of which he is a member, but almost never otherwise.

The church, in modern times, has become largely a social institution. There are a few colored members of white churches, but most of the Negroes belong to their own churches, of which there are more than they need, or can properly support. Some of them have pastors with a high sense of civic duty who are capable and earnest leaders.

The reaction to the barrier of segregation which confronts the Negro almost everywhere has resulted, in Cleveland as elsewhere, in the effort to supply among his own people many of the opportunities which he is denied. A few days ago an insurance agent called on me to solicit automobile insurance. He stated proudly, as what he considered a fine selling point, that his company wrote no insurance for colored people or for anyone living between Cedar and Woodland Avenues.

Insurance and Banking

To meet such discrimination, which is general all over the country, Negroes have organized their own insurance companies, of which nine have agencies or branch offices in Cleveland, all of which carry substantial amounts of insurance. They have no banks with checking accounts, but have three mortgage and loan companies, of which one expects shortly to meet all the requirements of the State Banking Department necessary to make it a regular bank. These institutions furnish employment for a number of young colored men and women, giving them the opportunity to learn by experience, sometimes, as elsewhere, at the expense of their stockholders, how to conduct financial operations safely and profitably. Several of the large banks in Cleveland have more capital, deposits and surplus than all the Negro banks in the United States. The Negro financial enterprises are small things, but as an index are not to be despised, and so far they have had no such catastrophes as have ingloriously terminated the career of so many of the much larger mortgage and loan companies of Cleveland. Fortunately, they have no stockbrokers.

The Negro has almost lost several of his ancestral occupations. The Italians and Greeks, perhaps because they are better business men, have almost entirely taken over the shoeshining parlors, though Negroes are generally employed to do the work.

The jobs as hotel help had practically vanished until the recent walkout of the union workers resulted in the employment of several hundred Negro cooks and waiters who had formerly been crowded out by the unions.

The increase of white barber shops has almost put the Negro barber out of business, so far as white patronage is concerned, and the Barbers' Union, in which no Negro is admitted to membership, has been trying to complete their ruin by proposing a state barber's licensing law requiring examination and acceptance by a committee dominated by the union.

The denial to the Negro of membership in beneficial and fraternal societies has resulted in the formation among their own group of a similar organization for practically every such order, often with the same name, to the amusement of the social cynic, and often to the exasperation of the white orders. There have always been Negro Masons, but now there are Negro Elks, Moose, Knights of Pythias, Odd Fellows, Eagles, etc., *ad infinitum*. Why, asks the white Moose, indignantly or plaintively, do they not originate something of their own? They answer that what is good enough for the white people is good enough for them, and, moreover, that the white orders have used up all the worthy names in the fauna and flora, leaving only the skunk, the snake, the buzzard and the jimson weed for the Negro to choose from.

There is a Negro lawyers' club, though colored lawyers are freely admitted to the two other local bar associations, and there is a Negro Medical Association, though there are several colored members of the local Academy of Medicine.

There is a race problem in Cleveland, but it is not acute. From the Negroes' side it is mainly concerned with a fair living, a decent place to live, making his way in the world on equal terms with others, and living at peace with his neighbors. With these things, or any of them, denied to any material extent, that the problem might become acute is evidenced by the race riots which a few years ago convulsed Chicago, Detroit and St. Louis. With fair play, the Negro makes a very good citizen. He vastly enjoys his small successes and considers himself a regular fellow. Abuse him and he becomes in his own eyes a martyr, and the martyr complex is not conducive to good citizenship. It might, conceivably, make the colored people a fertile soil for socialist or communist propaganda; for whatever the weaknesses of communism, it teaches human equality, which makes an irresistible appeal to those who are denied it.

The greatest handicap which the Negro in Cleveland, as elsewhere, has to meet is his color, which he cannot change, and the consequences of which he cannot escape. Plausibly good reasons are given for any discrimination of which the Negro is a victim, but on analysis it all fines down to his color, which makes generalization in his case easy and exposes him to all the inherited prejudgments which have grown up about him. A white man can live down the lowest origin. The Negro's color is always with him.

The better class of white people in Cleveland are in some ways very generous toward the Negro, and can generally be relied upon to respond liberally, financially, to any call on their part for money for any worthy purpose. But they could render them a better service by cultivating fraternal or, if that be too much, at least friendly relations with them, not so much by way of condescension, as from man to man, thereby making their advancement easier along all lines. For they still have a long and hard road to travel to reach that democratic equality upon the theory of which our government and our social system are founded, not to desire and seek which would make them unworthy of contempt.

PART TWO

Conjure Stories
and Color-Line Stories

THE CONJURE
WOMAN

Charles W. Chesnutt

Cover from *The Conjure Woman,* Houghton Mifflin and Company, 1899.

The Conjure Woman

THE GOOPHERED GRAPEVINE

Some years ago my wife was in poor health, and our family doctor, in whose skill and honesty I had implicit confidence, advised a change of climate. I shared, from an unprofessional standpoint, his opinion that the raw winds, the chill rains, and the violent changes of temperature that characterized the winters in the region of the Great Lakes tended to aggravate my wife's difficulty, and would undoubtedly shorten her life if she remained exposed to them. The doctor's advice was that we seek, not a temporary place of sojourn, but a permanent residence, in a warmer and more equable climate. I was engaged at the time in grape-culture in northern Ohio, and, as I liked the business and had given it much study, I decided to look for some other locality suitable for carrying it on. I thought of sunny France, of sleepy Spain, of Southern California, but there were objections to them all. It occurred to me that I might find what I wanted in some one of our own Southern States. It was a sufficient time after the war for conditions in the South to have become somewhat settled; and I was enough of a pioneer to start a new industry, if I could not find a place where grape-culture had been tried. I wrote to a cousin who had gone into the turpentine business in central North Carolina. He assured me, in response to my inquiries, that no better place could be found in the South than the State and neighborhood where he lived; the climate was perfect for health, and, in conjunction with the soil, ideal for grape-culture; labor was cheap, and land could be bought for a mere song. He gave us a cordial invitation to come and visit him while we looked into the matter. We accepted the invitation, and after several days of leisurely travel, the last hundred miles of which were up a river on a sidewheel steamer, we reached our destination, a quaint old town, which I shall call Patesville, because, for one reason, that is not its

Boston: Houghton Mifflin Company, 1899. London: Gay & Bird, 1899.

name. There was a red brick market-house in the public square, with a tall tower, which held a four-faced clock that struck the hours, and from which there pealed out a curfew at nine o'clock. There were two or three hotels, a court-house, a jail, stores, offices, and all the appurtenances of a county seat and a commercial emporium; for while Patesville numbered only four or five thousand inhabitants, of all shades of complexion, it was one of the principal towns in North Carolina, and had a considerable trade in cotton and naval stores. This business activity was not immediately apparent to my unaccustomed eyes. Indeed, when I first saw the town, there brooded over it a calm that seemed almost sabbatic in its restfulness, though I learned later on that underneath its somnolent exterior the deeper currents of life—love and hatred, joy and despair, ambition and avarice, faith and friendship—flowed not less steadily than in livelier latitudes.

We found the weather delightful at that season, the end of summer, and were hospitably entertained. Our host was a man of means and evidently regarded our visit as a pleasure, and we were therefore correspondingly at our ease, and in a position to act with the coolness of judgment desirable in making so radical a change in our lives. My cousin placed a horse and buggy at our disposal, and himself acted as our guide until I became somewhat familiar with the country.

I found that grape-culture, while it had never been carried on to any great extent, was not entirely unknown in the neighborhood. Several planters thereabouts had attempted it on a commercial scale, in former years, with greater or less success; but like most Southern industries, it had felt the blight of war and had fallen into desuetude.

I went several times to look at a place that I thought might suit me. It was a plantation of considerable extent, that had formerly belonged to a wealthy man by the name of McAdoo. The estate had been for years involved in litigation between disputing heirs, during which period shiftless cultivation had well-nigh exhausted the soil. There had been a vineyard of some extent on the place, but it had not been attended to since the war, and had lapsed into utter neglect. The vines—here partly supported by decayed and broken-down trellises, there twining themselves among the branches of the slender saplings which had sprung up among them—grew in wild and unpruned luxuriance, and the few scattered grapes they bore were the undisputed prey of the first comer. The site was admirably adapted to grape-raising; the soil, with a little attention, could not have been better; and with the native grape, the luscious scuppernong, as my main reliance in the beginning, I felt sure that I could introduce and cultivate successfully a number of other varieties.

One day I went over with my wife to show her the place. We drove out of the town over a long wooden bridge that spanned a spreading mill-pond, passed the long whitewashed fence surrounding the county fair-ground, and struck into a road so sandy that the horse's feet sank to the fetlocks. Our route lay partly up hill and partly down, for we were in the sand-hill county; we drove past cultivated farms, and then by abandoned fields grown up in scrub-oak and short-leaved pine, and once or twice through the solemn aisles of the virgin forest, where the tall pines, well-nigh meeting over the narrow road, shut out the sun, and wrapped us in cloistral solitude. Once, at a cross-roads, I was in doubt as to the turn to take, and we sat there waiting ten minutes—we had already caught some of the native infection of restfulness—for some human being to come along, who could direct us on our way. At length a little negro girl appeared, walking straight as an arrow, with a piggin full of water on her head. After a little patient investigation, necessary to overcome the child's shyness, we learned what we wished to know, and at the end of about five miles from the town reached our destination.

We drove between a pair of decayed gateposts—the gate itself had long since disappeared—and up a straight sandy lane, between two lines of rotting rail fence, partly concealed by jimson-weeds and briers, to the open space where a dwelling-house had once stood, evidently a spacious mansion, if we might judge from the ruined chimneys that were still standing, and the brick pillars on which the sills rested. The house itself, we had been informed, had fallen a victim to the fortunes of war.

We alighted from the buggy, walked about the yard for a while, and then wandered off into the adjoining vineyard. Upon Annie's complaining of weariness I led the way back to the yard, where a pine log, lying under a spreading elm, afforded a shady though somewhat hard seat. One end of the log was already occupied by a venerable-looking colored man. He held on his knees a hat full of grapes, over which he was smacking his lips with great gusto, and a pile of grapeskins near him indicated that the performance was no new thing. We approached him at an angle from the rear, and were close to him before he perceived us. He respectfully rose as we drew near, and was moving away, when I begged him to keep his seat.

"Don't let us disturb you," I said. "There is plenty of room for us all."

He resumed his seat with somewhat of embarrassment. While he had been standing, I had observed that he was a tall man, and, though slightly bowed by the weight of years, apparently quite vigorous. He was not entirely black, and this fact, together with the quality of his hair, which was about six inches long and very bushy, except on the top of his head, where he was quite bald, suggested a slight strain of other than negro blood. There was a shrewdness in his eyes, too, which was not altogether African, and which, as we afterwards learned from experience, was indicative of a corresponding shrewdness in his character. He went on eating the grapes, but

did not seem to enjoy himself quite so well as he had apparently done before he became aware of our presence.

"Do you live around here?" I asked, anxious to put him at his ease.

"Yas, suh. I lives des ober yander, behine de nex' san'-hill, on de Lumberton plank-road."

"Do you know anything about the time when this vineyard was
cultivated?"

"Lawd bless you, suh, I knows all about it. Dey ain' na'er a man in dis
settlement w'at won' tell you ole Julius McAdoo 'uz bawn en raise' on dis
yer same plantation. Is you de Norv'n gemman w'at's gwine ter buy de ole
vimya'd?"

"I am looking at it," I replied; "but I don't know that I shall care to
buy unless I can be reasonably sure of making something out of it."

"Well, suh, you is a stranger ter me, en I is a stranger ter you, en we
is bofe strangers ter one anudder, but 'f I 'uz in yo' place, I would n' buy
dis vimya'd."

"Why not?" I asked.

"Well, I dunno whe'r you b'lieves in cunj'in' er not—some er de w'ite
folks don't, er says dey don't—but de truf er de matter is dat dis yer ole
vimya'd is goophered."

"Is what?" I asked, not grasping the meaning of this unfamiliar word.

"Is goophered—cunju'd, bewitch'."

He imparted this information with such solemn earnestness, and with
such an air of confidential mystery, that I felt somewhat interested, while
Annie was evidently much impressed, and drew closer to me.

"How do you know it is bewitched?" I asked.

"I would n' spec' fer you ter b'lieve me 'less you know all 'bout de fac's.
But ef you en young miss dere doan' min' lis'nin' ter a ole nigger run on a
minute er two w'ile you er restin', I kin 'splain to you how it all happen'."

We assured him that we would be glad to hear how it all happened,
and he began to tell us. At first the current of his memory—or imagination—seemed somewhat sluggish; but as his embarrassment wore off, his
language flowed more freely, and the story acquired perspective and co-
herence. As he became more and more absorbed in the narrative, his eyes
assumed a dreamy expression, and he seemed to lose sight of his auditors,
and to be living over again in monologue his life on the old plantation.

"Ole Mars Dugal' McAdoo," he began, "bought dis place long many
years befo' de wah, en I 'member well w'en he sot out all dis yer part er de
plantation in scuppernon's. De vimes growed monst'us fas', en Mars Dugal'
made a thousan' gallon er scuppernon' wine eve'y year.

"Now, ef dey's an'thing a nigger lub, nex' ter 'possum, en chick'n, en
watermillyuns, it's scuppernon's. Dey ain' nuffin dat kin stan' up side'n de

scuppernon' fer sweetness; sugar ain't a suckumstance ter scuppernon'. W'en de season is nigh 'bout ober, en de grapes begin ter swivel up des a little wid de wrinkles er ole age—w'en de skin git sof' en brown—den de scuppernon' make you smack yo' lip en roll yo' eye en wush fer mo'; so I reckon it ain' very 'stonishin' dat niggers lub scuppernon'.

"Dey wuz a sight er niggers in de naberhood er de vimya'd. Dere wuz ole Mars Henry Brayboy's niggers, en ole Mars Jeems McLean's niggers, en Mars Dugal's own niggers; den dey wuz a settlement er free niggers en po' buckrahs down by de Wim'l'ton Road, en Mars Dugal' had de only vimya'd in de naberhood. I reckon it ain' so much so nowadays, but befo' de wah, in slab'ry times, a nigger did n' mine goin' fi' er ten mile in a night, w'en dey wuz sump'n good ter eat at de yuther een'.

"So atter a w'ile Mars Dugal' begin ter miss his scuppernon's. Co'se he 'cuse' de niggers er it, but dey all 'nied it ter de las'. Mars Dugal' sot spring guns en steel traps, en he en de oberseah sot up nights once't er twice't, tel one night Mars Dugal'—he 'uz a monst'us keerless man—got his leg shot full er cow-peas. But somehow er nudder dey could n' nebber ketch none er de niggers. I dunner how it happen, but it happen des like I tell you, en de grapes kep' on a-goin' des de same.

"But bimeby ole Mars Dugal' fix' up a plan ter stop it. Dey wuz a cun-juh 'oman livin' down 'mongs' de free niggers on de Wim'l'ton Road, en all de darkies fum Rockfish ter Beaver Crick wuz feared er her. She could wuk de mos' powerfulles' kin' er goopher—could make people hab fits, er rheu-matiz, er make 'em des dwinel away en die; en dey say she went out ridin' de niggers at night, fer she wuz a witch 'sides bein' a cunjuh 'oman. Mars Dugal' hearn 'bout Aun' Peggy's doin's, en begun ter 'flect whe'r er no he could n' git her ter he'p him keep de niggers off'n de grapevimes. One day in de spring er de year, ole miss pack' up a basket er chick'n en poun'-cake, en a bottle er scuppernon' wine, en Mars Dugal' tuk it in his buggy en driv ober ter Aun' Peggy's cabin. He tuk de basket in, en had a long talk wid Aun' Peggy.

"De nex' day Aun' Peggy come up ter de vimya'd. De niggers seed her slippin' 'roun', en dey soon foun' out what she 'uz doin' dere. Mars Dugal' had hi'ed her ter goopher de grapevimes. She sa'ntered 'roun' 'mongs' de vimes, en tuk a leaf fum dis one, en a grape-hull fum dat one, en a grape-seed fum anudder one; en den a little twig fum here, en a little pinch er dirt fum dere—en put it all in a big black bottle, wid a snake's toof en a speckle' hen's gall en some ha'rs fum a black cat's tail, en den fill' de bottle wid scuppernon' wine. W'en she got de goopher all ready en fix', she tuk 'n went out in de woods en buried it under de root uv a red oak tree, en den come back en tole one er de niggers she done goopher de grapevimes, en a'er a nigger w'at eat dem grapes 'ud be sho ter die inside'n twel' mont's.

"Atter dat de niggers let de scuppernon's 'lone, en Mars Dugal' did n' hab no 'casion ter fine no mo' fault; en de season wuz mos' gone, w'en a strange gemman stop at de plantation one night ter see Mars Dugal' on some business; en his coachman, seein' de scuppernon's growin' so nice en sweet, slip 'roun' behine de smoke-house, en et all de scuppernon's he could hole. Nobody did n' notice it at de time, but dat night, on de way home, de gemman's hoss runned away en kill' de coachman. W'en we hearn de noos, Aun' Lucy, de cook, she up 'n say she seed de strange nigger eat'n' er de scuppernon's behine de smoke-house; en den we knowed de goopher had b'en er wukkin'. Den one er de nigger chilluns runned away fum de quarters one day, en got in de scuppernon's, en died de nex' week. W'ite folks say he die' er de fevuh, but de niggers knowed it wuz de goopher. So you k'n be sho de darkies did n' hab much ter do wid dem scuppernon' vimes.

"W'en de scuppernon' season 'uz ober fer dat year, Mars Dugal' foun' he had made fifteen hund'ed gallon er wine; en one er de niggers hearn him laffin' wid de oberseah fit ter kill, en sayin' dem fifteen hund'ed gallon er wine wuz monst'us good intrus' on de ten dollars he laid out on de vimya'd. So I 'low ez he paid Aun' Peggy ten dollars fer to goopher de grapevimes.

"De goopher did n' wuk no mo' tel de nex' summer, w'en 'long to'ds de middle er de season one er de fiel' han's died; en ez dat lef' Mars Dugal' sho't er han's, he went off ter town ter ter buy anudder. He fotch de noo nigger home wid 'im. He wuz er ole nigger, er de color er a gingy-cake, en ball ez a hoss-apple on de top er his head. He wuz a peart ole nigger, do', en could do a big day's wuk.

"Now it happen dat one er de niggers on de nex' plantation, one er ole Mars Henry Brayboy's niggers, had runned away de day befo', en tuk ter de swamp, en ole Mars Dugal' en some er de yuther nabor w'ite folks had gone out wid dere guns en dere dogs fer ter he'p 'em hunt fer de nigger; en de han's on our own plantation wuz all so flusterated dat we fuhgot ter tell de noo han' 'bout de goopher on de scuppernon' vimes. Co'se he smell de grapes en see de vimes, an atter dahk de fus' thing he done wuz ter slip off ter de grapevimes 'dout sayin' nuffin ter nobody. Nex' mawnin' he tole some er de niggers 'bout de fine bait er scuppernon' he et de night befo'.

"W'en dey tole 'im 'bout de goopher on de grapevimes, he 'uz dat tarrified dat he turn pale, en look des like he gwine ter die right in his tracks. De oberseah come up en axed w'at 'uz de matter; en w'en dey tole 'im Henry be'n eatin' er de scuppernon's, en got de goopher on 'im, he gin Henry a big drink er w'iskey, en 'low dat de nex' rainy day he take 'im ober ter Aun' Peggy's, en see ef she would n' take de goopher off'n him, seein' ez he did n' know nuffin erbout it tel he done et de grapes.

"Sho nuff, it rain de nex' day, en de oberseah went ober ter Aun' Peggy's wid Henry. En Aun' Peggy say dat bein' ez Henry did n' know 'bout

de goopher, en et de grapes in ign'ance er de conseq'ences, she reckon she
mought be able fer ter take de goopher off'n him. So she fotch out er bottle
wid some cunjuh medicine in it, en po'd some out in a go'd fer Henry ter
drink. He manage ter git it down; he say it tas'e like whiskey wid sump'n
bitter in it. She 'lowed dat 'ud keep de goopher off'n him tel de spring; but
w'en de sap begin ter rise in de grapevimes he ha' ter come en see her ag'in,
en she tell him w'at e's ter do.

"Nex' spring, w'en de sap commence' ter rise in de scuppernon' vime,
Henry tuk a ham one night. Whar 'd he git de ham? *I* doan know; dey
wa'n't no hams on de plantation 'cep'n' w'at 'uz in de smoke-house, but *I*
never see Henry 'bout de smoke-house. But ez I wuz a-sayin', he tuk de ham
ober ter Aun' Peggy's; en Aun' Peggy tole 'im dat w'en Mars Dugal' begin
ter prune de grapevimes, he mus' go en take 'n scrape off de sap whar it ooze
out'n de cut een's er de vimes, en 'n'int his ball head wid it; en ef he do dat
once't a year de goopher would n' wuk agin 'im long ez he done it. En bein'
ez he fotch her de ham, she fix' it so he kin eat all de scuppernon' he want.

"So Henry 'n'int his head wid de sap out'n de big grapevime des ha'f
way 'twix' de quarters en de big house, en de goopher nebber wuk agin
him dat summer. But de beatenes' thing you eber see happen ter Henry. Up
ter dat time he wuz ez ball ez a sweeten' 'tater, but des ez soon ez de young
leaves begun ter come out on de grapevimes, de ha'r begun ter grow out
on Henry's head, en by de middle er de summer he had de bigges' head er
ha'r on de plantation. Befo' dat, Henry had tol'able good ha'r 'roun' de
aidges, but soon ez de young grapes begun ter come, Henry's ha'r begun to
quirl all up in little balls, des like dis yer reg'lar grapy ha'r, en by de time de
grapes got ripe his head look des like a bunch er grapes. Combin' it did n'
do no good; he wuk at it ha'f de night wid er Jim Crow,[1] en think he git it
straighten' out, but in de mawnin' de grapes 'ud be dere des de same. So
he gin it up, en tried ter keep de grapes down by havin' his ha'r cut sho't.

"But dat wa'n't de quares' thing 'bout de goopher. When Henry come
ter de plantation, he wuz gittin' a little ole an stiff in de j'ints. But dat summer he got des ez spry en libely ez any young nigger on de plantation; fac',
he got so biggity dat Mars Jackson, de oberseah, ha' ter th'eaten ter whip
'im, ef he did n' stop cuttin' up his didos en behave hisse'f. But de mos'
cur'ouses' thing happen' in de fall, when de sap begin ter go down in de
grapevimes. Fus', when de grapes 'uz gethered, de knots begun ter
straighten out'n Henry's ha'r; en w'en de leaves begin ter fall, Henry's ha'r
'mence' ter drap out; en when de vimes 'uz bar', Henry's head wuz baller

---

[1] A small card, resembling a currycomb in construction, and used by negroes in the rural
districts instead of a comb. [Original publisher's note.]

'n it wuz in de spring, en he begin ter git ole en stiff in de j'ints ag'in, en paid no mo' 'tention ter de gals dyoin' er de whole winter. En nex' spring, w'en he rub de sap on ag'in, he got young ag'in, en so soopl en libely dat none er de young niggers on de plantation could n' jump, ner dance, ner hoe ez much cotton ez Henry. But in de fall er de year his grapes 'mence' ter straighten out, en his j'ints ter git stiff, en his ha'r drap off, en de rheumatiz begin ter wrastle wid 'im.

"Now, ef you 'd 'a' knowed ole Mars Dugal' McAdoo, you 'd 'a' knowed dat it ha' ter be a mighty rainy day when he could n' fine sump'n fer his niggers ter do, en it ha' ter be a mighty little hole he could n' crawl thoo, en ha' ter be a monst'us cloudy night when a dollar git by him in de dahkness; en w'en he see how Henry git young in de spring en ole in de fall, he 'lowed ter hisse'f ez how he could make mo' money out'n Henry dan by wukkin' him in de cotton-fiel'. 'Long de nex' spring, atter de sap 'mence' ter rise, en Henry 'n'int 'is head en sta'ted fer ter git young en soopl, Mars Dugal' up 'n tuk Henry ter town, en sole 'im fer fifteen hunder' dollars. Co'se de man w'at bought Henry did n' know nuffin 'bout de goopher, en Mars Dugal' did n' see no 'casion fer ter tell 'im. Long to'ds de fall, w'en de sap went down, Henry begin ter git ole ag'in same ez yuzhal, en his noo marster begin ter git skeered les'n he gwine ter lose his fifteen-hunder'-dollar nigger. He sent fer a mighty fine doctor, but de med'cine did n' 'pear ter do no good; de goopher had a good holt. Henry tole de doctor 'bout de goopher, but de doctor des laff at 'im.

"One day in de winter Mars Dugal' went ter town, en wuz santerin' 'long de Main Street, when who should he meet but Henry's noo marster. Dey said 'Hoddy,' en Mars Dugal' ax 'im ter hab a seegyar; en atter dey run on awhile 'bout de craps en de weather, Mars Dugal' ax 'im, sorter keerless, like ez ef he des thought of it—

"'How you like de nigger I sole you las' spring?'

"Henry's marster shuck his head en knock de ashes off'n his seegyar.

"'Spec' I made a bad bahgin when I bought dat nigger. Henry done good wuk all de summer, but sence de fall set in he 'pears ter be sorter pinin' away. Dey ain' nuffin pertickler de matter wid 'im—leastways de doctor say so—'cep'n' a tech er de rheumatiz; but his ha'r is all fell out, en ef he don't pick up his strenk mighty soon, I spec' I'm gwine ter lose 'im.'

"Dey smoked on awhile, en bimeby ole mars say, 'Well, a bahgin 's a bahgin, but you en me is good fren's, en I doan wan' ter see you lose all de money you paid fer dat nigger; en ef w'at you say is so, en I ain't 'sputin' it, he ain't wuf much now. I 'spec's you wukked him too ha'd dis summer, er e'se de swamps down here don't agree wid de san'-hill nigger. So you des lemme know, en ef he gits any wusser I 'll be willin' ter gib yer five hund'ed dollars fer 'im, en take my chances on his livin'.'

"Sho 'nuff, when Henry begun ter draw up wid de rheumatiz en it look like he gwine ter die fer sho, his noo marster sen' fer Mars Dugal', en Mars Dugal' gin him what he promus, en brung Henry home ag'in. He tuk good keer uv 'im dyoin' er de winter—give 'im w'iskey ter rub his rheumatiz, en terbacker ter smoke, en all he want ter eat—'caze a nigger w'at he could make a thousan' dollars a year off'n did n' grow on eve'y huckleberry bush.

"Nex' spring, w'en de sap ris en Henry's ha'r commence' ter sprout, Mars Dugal' sole 'im ag'in, down in Robeson County dis time; en he kep' dat sellin' business up fer five year er mo'. Henry nebber say nuffin 'bout de goopher ter his noo marsters, 'caze he know he gwine ter be tuk good keer uv de nex' winter, w'en Mars Dugal' buy him back. En Mars Dugal' made 'nuff money off'n Henry ter buy anudder plantation ober on Beaver Crick.

"But 'long 'bout de een' er dat five year dey come a stranger ter stop at de plantation. De fus' day he 'uz dere he went out wid Mars Dugal' en spent all de mawnin' lookin' ober de vimya'd, en atter dinner dey spent all de evenin' playin' kya'ds. De niggers soon 'skiver' dat he wuz a Yankee, en dat he come down ter Norf C'lina fer ter l'arn de w'ite folks how to raise grapes en make wine. He promus Mars Dugal' he c'd make de grapevimes b'ar twice't ez many grapes, en dat de noo winepress he wuz a-sellin' would make mo' d'n twice't ez many gallons er wine. En ole Mars Dugal' des drunk it all in, des 'peared ter be bewitch' wid dat Yankee. W'en de darkies see dat Yankee runnin' 'roun' de vimya'd en diggin' under de grape-vimes, dey shuk dere heads, en 'lowed dat dey feared Mars Dugal' losin' his min'. Mars Dugal' had all de dirt dug away fum under de roots er all de scuppernon' vimes, an' let 'em stan' dat away fer a week er mo'. Den dat Yankee made de niggers fix up a mixtry er lime en ashes en manyo, en po' it 'roun' de roots er de grapevimes. Den he 'vise Mars Dugal' fer ter trim de vimes close't, en Mars Dugal' tuck 'n done eve'ything de Yankee tole him ter do. Dyoin' all er dis time, mind yer, dis yer Yankee wuz libbin' off'n de fat er de lan', at de big house, en playin' kya'ds wid Mars Dugal' eve'y night; en dey say Mars Dugal' los' mo'n a thousan' dollars dyoin' er de week dat Yankee wuz a-ruinin' de grapevimes.

"W'en de sap ris nex' spring, ole Henry 'n'inted his head ez yuzhal, en his ha'r 'mence' ter grow des de same ez it done eve'y year. De scuppernon' vimes growed monst's fas', en de leaves wuz greener en thicker dan dey eber be'n dyoin' my rememb'ance; en Henry's ha'r growed out thicker dan eber, en he 'peared ter git younger 'n younger, en soopler 'n soopler; en seein' ez he wuz sho't er han's dat spring, havin' tuk in consid'able noo groun', Mars Dugal' 'cluded he would n' sell Henry 'tel he git de crap in en de cotton chop'. So he kep' Henry on de plantation.

"But 'long 'bout time fer de grapes ter come on de scuppernon' vimes, dey 'peared ter come a change ober 'em; de leaves withered en swivel' up,

en de young grapes turn' yaller, en bimeby eve'ybody on de plantation could
see dat de whole vimya'd wuz dyin'. Mars Dugal' tuk 'n water de vimes en
done all he could, but 't wa'n' no use: dat Yankee had done bus' de water-
millyum. One time de vimes picked up a bit, en Mars Dugal' 'lowed dey
wuz gwine ter come out ag'in; but dat Yankee done dug too close under de
roots, en prune de branches too close ter de vime, en all dat lime en ashes
done burn' de life out'n de vimes, en dey des kep' a-with'in' en a-swivelin'.

"All dis time de goopher wuz a-wukkin'. When de vimes sta'ted ter
wither, Henry 'mence' ter complain er his rheumatiz; en when de leaves begin ter dry up, his ha'r 'mence' ter drap out. When de vimes fresh' up a bit,
Henry 'd git peart ag'in, en when de vimes wither' ag'in, Henry 'd git ole
ag'in, en des kep' gittin' mo' en mo' fitten fer nuffin; he des pined away, en
pined away, en fine'ly tuk ter his cabin; en when de big vime whar he got
de sap ter 'n'int his head withered en turned yaller en died, Henry died
too—des went out sorter like a cannel. Dey did n't 'pear ter be nuffin de
matter wid 'im, 'cep'n' de rheumatiz, but his strenk des dwinel' away 'tel
he did n' hab ernuff lef' ter draw his bref. De goopher had got de under
holt, en th'owed Henry dat time fer good en all.

"Mars Dugal' tuk on might'ly 'bout losin' his vimes en his nigger in
de same year; en he swo' dat ef he could git holt er dat Yankee he 'd wear
'im ter a frazzle, en den chaw up de frazzle; en he 'd done it, too, for Mars
Dugal' 'uz a monst'us brash man w'en he once git started. He sot de
vimya'd out ober ag'in, but it wuz th'ee er fo' year befo' de vimes got ter
b'arin' any scuppernon's.

"W'en de wah broke out, Mars Dugal' raise' a comp'ny, en went off ter
fight de Yankees. He say he wuz mighty glad dat wah come, en he des want
ter kill a Yankee fer eve'y dollar he los' 'long er dat grape-raisin' Yankee. En
I 'spec' he would 'a' done it, too, ef de Yankees had n' s'picioned sump'n, en
killed him fus'. Atter de s'render ole miss move' ter town, de niggers all scattered 'way fum de plantation, en de vimya'd ain' be'n cultervated sence."

"Is that story true?" asked Annie doubtfully, but seriously, as the old
man concluded his narrative.

"It's des ez true ez I 'm a-settin' here, miss. Dey 's a easy way ter prove
it: I kin lead de way right ter Henry's grave ober yander in de plantation
buryin'-groun'. En I tell yer w'at, marster, I would n' 'vise you to buy dis
yer ole vimya'd, 'caze de goopher 's on it yit, en dey ain' no tellin' w'en it 's
gwine ter crap out."

"But I thought you said all the old vines died."

"Dey did 'pear ter die, but a few un 'em come out ag'in, en is mixed
in 'mongs' de yuthers. I ain' skeered ter eat de grapes, 'caze I knows de old
vimes fum de noo ones; but wid strangers dey ain' no tellin' w'at mought
happen. I would n' 'vise yer ter buy dis vimya'd."

I bought the vineyard, nevertheless, and it has been for a long time in a thriving condition, and is often referred to by the local press as a striking illustration of the opportunities open to Northern capital in the development of Southern industries. The luscious scuppernong holds first rank among our grapes, though we cultivate a great many other varieties, and our income from grapes packed and shipped to the Northern markets is quite considerable. I have not noticed any developments of the goopher in the vineyard, although I have a mild suspicion that our colored assistants do not suffer from want of grapes during the season.

I found, when I bought the vineyard, that Uncle Julius had occupied a cabin on the place for many years, and derived a respectable revenue from the product of the neglected grapevines. This, doubtless, accounted for his advice to me not to buy the vineyard, though whether it inspired the goopher story I am unable to state. I believe, however, that the wages I paid him for his services as coachman, for I gave him employment in that capacity, were more than an equivalent for anything he lost by the sale of the vineyard.

PO' SANDY

On the northeast corner of my vineyard in central North Carolina, and fronting on the Lumberton plank-road, there stood a small frame house, of the simplest construction. It was built of pine lumber, and contained but one room, to which one window gave light and one door admission. Its weather-beaten sides revealed a virgin innocence of paint. Against one end of the house, and occupying half its width, there stood a huge brick chimney: the crumbling mortar had left large cracks between the bricks; the bricks themselves had begun to scale off in large flakes, leaving the chimney sprinkled with unsightly blotches. These evidences of decay were but partially concealed by a creeping vine, which extended its slender branches hither and thither in an ambitious but futile attempt to cover the whole chimney. The wooden shutter, which had once protected the unglazed window, had fallen from its hinges, and lay rotting in the rank grass and jimson-weeds beneath. This building, I learned when I bought the place, had been used as a schoolhouse for several years prior to the breaking out of the war, since which time it had remained unoccupied, save when some stray cow or vagrant hog had sought shelter within its walls from the chill rains and nipping winds of winter.

One day my wife requested me to build her a new kitchen. The house erected by us, when we first came to live upon the vineyard, contained a very conveniently arranged kitchen; but for some occult reason my wife wanted a kitchen in the back yard, apart from the dwelling-house, after the usual Southern fashion. Of course I had to build it.

To save expense, I decided to tear down the old schoolhouse, and use the lumber, which was in a good state of preservation, in the construction of the new kitchen. Before demolishing the old house, however, I made an estimate of the amount of material contained in it, and found that I would have to buy several hundred feet of lumber additional, in order to build the new kitchen according to my wife's plan.

One morning old Julius McAdoo, our colored coachman, harnessed the gray mare to the rockaway, and drove my wife and me over to the saw-mill from which I meant to order the new lumber. We drove down the long lane which led from our house to the plank-road; following the plank-road for about a mile, we turned into a road running through the forest and across the swamp to the sawmill beyond. Our carriage jolted over the half-rotted corduroy road which traversed the swamp, and then climbed the long hill leading to the sawmill. When we reached the mill, the foreman had gone over to a neighboring farmhouse, probably to smoke or gossip, and we were compelled to await his return before we could transact our business. We remained seated in the carriage, a few rods from the mill, and watched the leisurely movements of the mill-hands. We had not waited long before a huge pine log was placed in position, the machinery of the mill was set in motion, and the circular saw began to eat its way through the log, with a loud whir which resounded throughout the vicinity of the mill. The sound rose and fell in a sort of rhythmic cadence, which, heard from where we sat, was not unpleasing, and not loud enough to prevent conversation. When the saw started on its second journey through the log, Julius observed, in a lugubrious tone, and with a perceptible shudder:

"Ugh! but dat des do cuddle my blood!"

"What 's the matter, Uncle Julius?" inquired my wife, who is of a very sympathetic turn of mind. "Does the noise affect your nerves?"

"No, Mis' Annie," replied the old man, with emotion, "I ain' narvous; but dat saw, a-cuttin' en grindin' thoo dat stick er timber, en moanin', en groanin', en sweekin', kyars my 'memb'ance back ter ole times, en 'min's me er po' Sandy." The pathetic intonation with which he lengthened out the "po' Sandy" touched a responsive chord in our own hearts.

"And who was poor Sandy?" asked my wife, who takes a deep interest in the stories of plantation life which she hears from the lips of the older colored people. Some of these stories are quaintly humorous; others wildly extravagant, revealing the Oriental cast of the negro's imagination; while others, poured freely into the sympathetic ear of a Northern-bred woman, disclose many a tragic incident of the darker side of slavery.

"Sandy," said Julius, in reply to my wife's question, "was a nigger w'at useter b'long ter ole Mars Marrabo McSwayne. Mars Marrabo's place wuz on de yuther side'n de swamp, right nex' ter yo' place. Sandy wuz a monst'us good nigger, en could do so many things erbout a plantation, en al-luz 'ten' ter his wuk so well, dat w'en Mars Marrabo's chilluns growed up en married off, dey all un 'em wanted dey daddy fer ter gin 'em Sandy fer a weddin' present. But Mars Marrabo knowed de res' would n' be satisfied ef he gin Sandy ter a'er one un 'em; so w'en dey wuz all done married, he fix it by 'lowin' one er his chilluns ter take Sandy fer a mont' er so, en den ernudder for a mont' er so, en so on dat erway tel dey had all had 'im de same lenk er time; en den dey would all take him roun' ag'in, 'cep'n' oncet in a w'ile w'en Mars Marrabo would len' 'im ter some er his yuther kinfolks 'roun' de country, w'en dey wuz short er han's; tel bimeby it go so Sandy did n' hardly knowed whar he wuz gwine ter stay fum one week's een' ter de yuther.

"One time w'en Sandy wuz lent out ez yushal, a spekilater come er-long wid a lot er niggers, en Mars Marrabo swap' Sandy's wife off fer a noo 'oman. W'en Sandy come back, Mars Marrabo gin 'im a dollar, en 'lowed he wuz monst'us sorry fer ter break up de fambly, but de spekilater had gin 'im big boot, en times wuz hard en money skase, en so he wuz bleedst ter make de trade. Sandy tuk on some 'bout losin' his wife, but he soon seed dey want no use cryin' ober spilt merlasses; en bein' ez he lacked de looks er de noo 'oman, he tuk up wid her atter she'd be'n on de plantation a mont' er so.

"Sandy en his noo wife got on mighty well tergedder, en de niggers all 'mence' ter talk about how lovin' dey wuz. W'en Tenie wuz tuk sick oncet, Sandy useter set up all night wid 'er, en den go ter wuk in de mawnin' des lack he had his reg'lar sleep; en Tenie would 'a' done anythin' in de worl' for her Sandy.

"Sandy en Tenie had n' be'n libbin' tergedder fer mo' d'n two mont's befo' Mars Marrabo's old uncle, w'at libbed down in Robeson County, sent up ter fin' out ef Mars Marrabo could n' len' 'im er hire 'im a good han' fer a mont' er so. Sandy's marster wuz one er dese yer easy-gwine folks w'at wanter please eve'ybody, en he says yas, he could len' 'im Sandy. En Mars Marrabo tol' Sandy fer ter git ready ter go down ter Robeson nex' day, fer ter stay a mont' er so.

"It wuz monst'us hard on Sandy fer ter take 'im 'way fum Tenie. It wuz so fur down ter Robeson dat he did n' hab no chance er comin' back ter see her tel de time wuz up; he would n' 'a' mine comin' ten er fifteen mile at night ter see Tenie, but Mars Marrabo's uncle's plantation wuz mo' d'n forty mile off. Sandy wuz mighty sad en cas' down atter w'at Mars Marrabo tol' 'im, en he says ter Tenie, sezee:

"'I 'm gittin' monst'us ti'ed er dish yer gwine roun' so much. Here I is lent ter Mars Jeems dis mont', en I got ter do so-en-so; en ter Mars Archie de nex' mont', en I got ter do so-en-so; den I got ter go ter Miss Jinnie's: en hit 's Sandy dis en Sandy dat, en Sandy yer en Sandy dere, tel it 'pears ter me I ain' got no home, ner no marster, ner no mistiss, ner no nuffin. I can't eben keep a wife: my yuther ole 'oman wuz sol' away widout my gittin' a chance fer ter tell her good-by; en now I got ter go off en leab you, Tenie, en I dunno whe'r I 'm eber gwine ter see you ag'in er no. I wisht I wuz a tree, er a stump, er a rock, er sump'n w'at could stay on de plantation fer a w'ile.'

"Atter Sandy got thoo talkin', Tenie did n' say naer word, but des sot dere by de fier, studyin' en studyin'. Bimeby she up'n' says:

"'Sandy, is I eber tol' you I wuz a cunjuh 'oman?'

"Co'se Sandy had n' nebber dremp' er nuffin lack dat, en he made a great 'miration w'en he hear w'at Tenie say. Bimeby Tenie went on:

"'I ain' goophered nobody, ner done no cunjuh wuk, fer fifteen year er mo'; en w'en I got religion I made up my mine I would n' wuk no mo' goopher. But dey is some things I doan b'lieve it 's no sin fer ter do; en ef you doan wanter be sent roun' fum pillar ter pos', en ef you doan wanter go down ter Robeson, I kin fix things so you won't haf ter. Ef you 'll des say de word, I kin turn you ter w'ateber you wanter be, en you kin stay right whar you wanter, ez long ez you mineter.'

"Sandy say he doan keer; he's willin' fer ter do anythin' fer ter stay close ter Tenie. Den Tenie ax 'im ef he doan wanter be turnt inter a rabbit.

"Sandy say, 'No, de dogs mought git atter me.'

"'Shill I turn you ter a wolf?' sez Tenie.

"'No, eve'ybody's skeered er a wolf, en I doan want nobody ter be skeered er me.'

"'Shill I turn you ter a mawkin'-bird?'

"'No, a hawk mought ketch me. I wanter be turnt inter sump'n w'at 'll stay in one place.'

"'I kin turn you ter a tree,' sez Tenie. 'You won't hab no mouf ner years, but I kin turn you back oncet in a w'ile, so you kin git sump'n ter eat, en hear w'at 's gwine on.'

"Well, Sandy say dat 'll do. En so Tenie tuk 'im down by de aidge er de swamp, not fur fum de quarters, en turnt 'im inter a big pine-tree, en sot 'im out 'mongs' some yuther trees. En de nex' mawnin', ez some er de fiel' han's wuz gwine long dere, dey seed a tree w'at dey did n' 'member er habbin' seed befo'; it wuz monst'us quare, en dey wuz bleedst ter 'low dat dey had n' 'membered right, er e'se one er de saplin's had be'n growin' monst'us fas'.

"W'en Mars Marrabo 'skiver' dat Sandy wuz gone, he 'lowed Sandy had runned away. He got de dogs out, but de las' place dey could track Sandy ter wuz de foot er dat pine-tree. En dere de dogs stood en barked, en bayed, en pawed at de tree, en tried ter climb up on it; en w'en dey wuz tuk roun' thoo de swamp ter look fer de scent, dey broke loose en made fer dat tree ag'in. It wuz de beatenis' thing de w'ite folks eber hearn of, en Mars Marrabo 'lowed dat Sandy must 'a' clim' up on de tree en jump' off on a mule er sump'n, en rid fur ernuff fer ter spile de scent. Mars Marrabo wanted ter 'cuse some er de yuther niggers er heppin' Sandy off, but dey all 'nied it ter de las'; en eve'ybody knowed Tenie sot too much sto' by Sandy fer ter he'p 'im run away whar she could n' nebber see 'im no mo'.

"W'en Sandy had be'n gone long ernuff fer folks ter think he done got clean away, Tenie useter go down ter de woods at night en turn 'im back, en den dey 'd slip up ter de cabin en set by de fire en talk. But dey ha' ter be monst'us keerful, er e'se somebody would 'a' seed 'em, en dat would 'a' spile' de whole thing; so Tenie alluz turnt Sandy back in de mawnin' early, befo' anybody wuz a-stirrin'.

"But Sandy did n' git erlong widout his trials en tribberlations. One day a woodpecker come erlong en 'mence' ter peck at de tree; en de nex' time Sandy wuz turnt back he had a little roun' hole in his arm, des lack a sharp stick be'n stuck in it. Atter dat Tenie sot a sparrer-hawk fer ter watch de tree; en w'en de woodpecker come erlong nex' mawnin' fer ter finish his nes', he got gobble' up mos' 'fo' he stuck his bill in de bark.

"Nudder time, Mars Marrabo sent a nigger out in de woods fer ter chop tuppentime boxes. De man chop a box in dish yer tree, en hack' de bark up two er th'ee feet, fer ter let de tuppentime run. De nex' time Sandy wuz turnt back he had a big skyar on his lef' leg, des lack it be'n skunt; en it tuk Tenie nigh 'bout all night fer ter fix a mixtry ter kyo it up. Atter dat, Tenie sot a hawnet fer ter watch de tree; en w'en de nigger come back ag'in fer ter cut ernudder box on de yuther side'n de tree, de hawnet stung 'im so hard dat de ax slip en cut his foot nigh 'bout off.

"W'en Tenie see so many things happenin' ter de tree, she 'cluded she 'd ha' ter turn Sandy ter sump'n e'se; en atter studyin' de matter ober, en talkin' wid Sandy one ebenin', she made up her mine fer ter fix up a goo-pher mixtry w'at would turn herse'f en Sandy ter foxes, er sump'n, so dey could run away en go some'rs whar dey could be free en lib lack w'ite folks.

"But dey ain' no tellin' w'at 's gwine ter happen in dis worl'. Tenie had got de night sot fer her en Sandy ter run away, w'en dat ve'y day one er Mars Marrabo's sons rid up ter de big house in his buggy, en say his wife wuz monst'us sick, en he want his mammy ter len' 'im a 'oman fer ter nuss his wife. Tenie's mistiss say sen' Tenie; she wuz a good nuss. Young mars wuz in a tarrible hurry fer ter git back home. Tenie wuz washin' at de big house dat day, en her mistiss say she should go right 'long wid her young marster. Tenie tried ter make some 'scuse fer ter git away en hide 'tel night, w'en she would have eve'ything fix' up fer her en Sandy; she say she wanter go ter her cabin fer ter git her bonnet. Her mistiss say it doan matter 'bout de bonnet; her head-hankcher wuz good ernuff. Den Tenie say she wanter git her bes' frock; her mistiss say no, she doan need no mo' frock, en w'en dat one got dirty she could git a clean one whar she wuz gwine. So Tenie had ter git in de buggy en go 'long wid young Mars Dunkin ter his plantation, w'ich wuz mo' d'n twenty mile away; en dey wa'n't no chance er her seein' Sandy no mo' 'tel she come back home. De po' gal felt monst'us bad 'bout de way things wuz gwine on, en she knowed Sandy mus' be a wond'rin' why she did n' come en turn 'im back no mo'.

"W'iles Tenie wuz away nussin' young Mars Dunkin's wife, Mars Marrabo tuk a notion fer ter buil' 'im a noo kitchen; en bein' ez he had lots er timber on his place, he begun ter look 'roun' fer a tree ter hab de lumber sawed out'n. En I dunno how it come to be so, but he happen fer ter hit on de ve'y tree w'at Sandy wuz turnt inter. Tenie wuz gone, en dey wa'n't nobody ner nuffin fer ter watch de tree.

"De two men w'at cut de tree down say dey nebber had sech a time wid a tree befo': dey axes would glansh off, en did n' 'pear ter make no prōgress thoo de wood; en of all de creakin', en shakin', en wobblin' you eber see, dat tree done it w'en it commence' ter fall. It wuz de beatenis' thing!

"W'en dey got de tree all trim' up, dey chain it up ter a timber waggin, en start fer de sawmill. But dey had a hard time gittin' de log dere: fus' dey got stuck in de mud w'en dey wuz gwine crosst de swamp, en it wuz two er th'ee hours befo' dey could git out. W'en dey start' on ag'in, de chain kep' a-comin' loose, en dey had ter keep a-stoppin' en a-stoppin' fer ter hitch de log up ag'in. W'en dey commence' ter climb de hill ter de sawmill, de log broke loose, en roll down de hill en in 'mongs' de trees, en hit tuk nigh 'bout half a day mo' ter git it haul' up ter de sawmill.

"De nex' mawnin' atter de day de tree wuz haul' ter de sawmill, Tenie come home. W'en she got back ter her cabin, de fus' thing she done wuz ter run down ter de woods en see how Sandy wuz gittin' on. W'en she seed de stump standin' dere, wid de sap runnin' out'n it, en de limbs layin' scattered roun', she nigh 'bout went out'n her min'. She run ter her cabin, en got her goopher mixtry, en den follered de track er de timber waggin ter de sawmill. She knowed Sandy could n' lib mo' d'n a minute er so ef she turnt him back, fer he wuz all chop' up so he 'd 'a' be'n bleedst ter die. But she wanted ter turn 'im back long ernuff fer ter 'splain ter 'im dat she had n' went off a-purpose, en lef' 'im ter be chop' down en sawed up. She did n' want Sandy ter die wid no hard feelin's to'ds her.

"De han's at de sawmill had des got de big log on de kerridge, en wuz startin' up de saw, w'en dey seed a 'oman runnin' up de hill, all out er bref, cryin' en gwine on des lack she wuz plumb 'stracted. It wuz Tenie; she come right inter de mill, en th'owed herse'f on de log, right in front er de saw, a-hollerin' en cryin' ter her Sandy ter fergib her, en not ter think hard er her, fer it wa'n't no fault er hern. Den Tenie 'membered de tree did n' hab no years, en she wuz gittin' ready fer ter wuk her goopher mixtry so ez ter turn Sandy back, w'en de mill-hands kotch holt er her en tied her arms wid a rope, en fasten' her to one er de posts in de sawmill; en den dey started de saw up ag'in, en cut de log up inter bo'ds en scantlin's right befo' her eyes. But it wuz mighty hard wuk; fer of all de sweekin', en moanin', en groanin', dat log done it w'iles de saw wuz a-cuttin' thoo it. De saw wuz one er dese yer ole-timey, up-en-down saws, en hit tuk longer dem days ter saw a log 'en it do now. Dey greased de saw, but dat did n' stop de fuss; hit kep' right on, tel fin'ly dey got de log all sawed up.

"W'en de oberseah w'at run de sawmill come fum breakfas', de han's up en tell him 'bout de crazy 'oman—ez dey s'posed she wuz—w'at had come runnin' in de sawmill, a-hollerin' en gwine on, en tried ter th'ow herse'f befo' de saw. En de oberseah sent two er th'ee er de han's fer ter take Tenie back ter her marster's plantation.

"Tenie 'peared ter be out'n her min' fer a long time, en her marster ha' ter lock her up in de smoke-'ouse 'tel she got ober her spells. Mars Marrabo wuz monst'us mad, en hit would 'a' made yo' flesh crawl fer ter hear him cuss, 'caze he say de spekilater w'at he got Tenie fum had fooled 'im by wukkin' a crazy 'oman off on him. W'iles Tenie wuz lock up in de smoke-'ouse, Mars Marrabo tuk 'n' haul de lumber fum de sawmill, en put up his noo kitchen.

"W'en Tenie got quiet' down, so she could be 'lowed ter go 'roun' de plantation, she up'n' tole her marster all erbout Sandy en de pine-tree; en w'en Mars Marrabo hearn it, he 'lowed she wuz de wuss 'stracted nigger he eber hearn of. He did n' know w'at ter do wid Tenie: fus' he thought he 'd put her in de po'-house; but fin'ly, seein' ez she did n' do no harm ter nobody ner nuffin, but des went 'roun' moanin', en groanin', en shakin' her head, he 'cluded ter let her stay on de plantation en nuss de little nigger chilluns w'en dey mammies wuz ter wuk in de cotton-fiel'.

"De noo kitchen Mars Marrabo buil' wuz n' much use, fer it had n' be'n put up long befo' de niggers 'mence' ter notice quare things erbout it. Dey could hear sump'n moanin' en groanin' 'bout de kitchen in de night-time, en w'en de win' would blow dey could hear sump'n a-hollerin' en sweekin' lack it wuz in great pain en sufferin'. En it got so atter a w'ile dat it wuz all Mars Marrabo's wife could do ter git a 'oman ter stay in de kitchen in de daytime long ernuff ter do de cookin'; en dey wa'n't naer nigger on de plantation w'at would n' rudder take forty dan ter go 'bout dat kitchen atter dark—dat is, 'cep'n' Tenie; she did n' 'pear ter min' de ha'nts. She useter slip 'roun' at night, en set on de kitchen steps, en lean up agin de do'-jamb, en run on ter herse'f wid some kine er foolishness w'at nobody could n' make out; fer Mars Marrabo had th'eaten' ter sen' her off'n de plantation ef she say anything ter any er de yuther niggers 'bout de pine-tree. But somehow er 'nudder de niggers foun' out all erbout it, en dey all knowed de kitchen wuz ha'nted by Sandy's sperrit. En bimeby hit got so Mars Marrabo's wife herse'f wuz skeered ter go out in de yard atter dark.

"W'en it come ter dat, Mars Marrabo tuk en to' de kitchen down, en use' de lumber fer ter buil' dat ole school'ouse w'at you er talkin' 'bout pullin' down. De school'ouse wuz n' use' 'cep'n' in de daytime, en on dark nights folks gwine 'long de road would hear quare soun's en see quare things. Po' ole Tenie useter go down dere at night, en wander 'roun' de school'ouse; en de niggers all 'lowed she went fer ter talk wid Sandy's sperrit. En one winter mawnin', w'en one er de boys went ter school early fer ter start de fire, w'at should he fin' but po' ole Tenie, layin' on de flo', stiff, en col', en dead. Dere did n' 'pear ter be nuffin pertickler de matter wid her—she had des grieve' herse'f ter def fer her Sandy. Mars Marrabo did n' shed no tears. He thought Tenie wuz crazy, en dey wa'n't no tellin' w'at she mought do nex'; en dey ain' much room in dis worl' fer crazy w'ite folks, let 'lone a crazy nigger.

"Hit wa'n't long atter dat befo' Mars Marrabo sol' a piece er his track er lan' ter Mars Dugal' McAdoo—my ole marster—en dat 's how de ole school'ouse happen to be on yo' place. W'en de wah broke out, de school stop', en de ole school'ouse be'n stannin' empty ever sence—dat is, 'cep'n' fer de ha'nts. En folks sez dat de ole school'ouse, er any yuther house w'at got any er dat lumber in it w'at wuz sawed out'n de tree w'at Sandy wuz turnt inter, is gwine ter be ha'nted tel de las' piece er plank is rotted en crumble' inter dus'."

Annie had listened to this gruesome narrative with strained attention. "What a system it was," she exclaimed, when Julius had finished, "under which such things were possible!"

"What things?" I asked, in amazement. "Are you seriously considering the possibility of a man's being turned into a tree?"

"Oh, no," she replied quickly, "not that;" and then she murmured absently, and with a dim look in her fine eyes, "Poor Tenie!"

We ordered the lumber, and returned home. That night, after we had gone to bed, and my wife had to all appearances been sound asleep for half an hour, she startled me out of an incipient doze by exclaiming suddenly

"John, I don't believe I want my new kitchen built out of the lumber in that old schoolhouse."

"You would n't for a moment allow yourself," I replied, with some asperity, "to be influenced by that absurdly impossible yarn which Julius was spinning today?"

"I know the story is absurd," she replied dreamily, "and I am not so silly as to believe it. But I don't think I should ever be able to take any pleasure in that kitchen if it were built out of that lumber. Besides, I think the kitchen would look better and last longer if the lumber were all new."

Of course she had her way. I bought the new lumber, though not without grumbling. A week or two later I was called away from home on business. On my return, after an absence of several days, my wife remarked to me

"John, there has been a split in the Sandy Run Colored Baptist Church, on the temperance question. About half the members have come out from the main body, and set up for themselves. Uncle Julius is one of the seceders, and he came to me yesterday and asked if they might not hold their meetings in the old schoolhouse for the present."

"I hope you did n't let the old rascal have it," I returned, with some warmth. I had just received a bill for the new lumber I had bought.

"Well," she replied, "I could n't refuse him the use of the house for so good a purpose."

"And I 'll venture to say," I continued, "that you subscribed something toward the support of the new church?"

She did not attempt to deny it.

"What are they going to do about the ghost?" I asked, somewhat curious to know how Julius would get around this obstacle.

"Oh," replied Annie, "Uncle Julius says that ghosts never disturb religious worship, but that if Sandy's spirit *should* happen to stray into meeting by mistake, no doubt the preaching would do it good."

MARS JEEMS'S NIGHTMARE

We found old Julius very useful when we moved to our new residence. He had a thorough knowledge of the neighborhood, was familiar with the roads and the watercourses, knew the qualities of the various soils and what they would produce, and where the best hunting and fishing were to be had. He was a marvelous hand in the management of horses and dogs, with whose mental processes he manifested a greater familiarity than mere use would seem to account for, though it was doubtless due to the simplicity of a life that had kept him close to nature. Toward my tract of land and the things that were on it—the creeks, the swamps, the hills, the meadows, the stones, the trees—he maintained a peculiar personal attitude, that might be called predial rather than proprietary. He had been accustomed, until long after middle life, to look upon himself as the property of another. When this relation was no longer possible, owing to the war, and to his master's death and the dispersion of the family, he had been unable to break off entirely the mental habits of a lifetime, but had attached himself to the old plantation, of which he seemed to consider himself an appurtenance. We found him useful in many ways and entertaining in others, and my wife and I took quite a fancy to him.

Shortly after we became established in our home on the sand-hills, Julius brought up to the house one day a colored boy of about seventeen, whom he introduced as his grandson, and for whom he solicited employment. I was not favorably impressed by the youth's appearance—quite the contrary, in fact; but mainly to please the old man I hired Tom—his name was Tom—to help about the stables, weed the garden, cut wood and bring water, and in general to make himself useful about the outdoor work of the household.

My first impression of Tom proved to be correct. He turned out to be very trifling, and I was much annoyed by his laziness, his carelessness, and his apparent lack of any sense of responsibility. I kept him longer than I should, on Julius's account, hoping that he might improve; but he seemed to grow worse instead of better, and when I finally reached the limit of my patience, I discharged him.

"I am sorry, Julius," I said to the old man; "I should have liked to oblige you by keeping him; but I can't stand Tom any longer. He is absolutely untrustworthy."

"Yas, suh," replied Julius, with a deep sigh and a long shake of the head, "I knows he ain' much account, en dey ain' much 'pen'ence ter be put on 'im. But I wuz hopin' dat you mought make some 'lowance fuh a' ign'ant young nigger, suh, en gib 'im one mo' chance."

But I had hardened my heart. I had always been too easily imposed upon, and had suffered too much from this weakness. I determined to be firm as a rock in this instance.

"No, Julius," I rejoined decidedly, "it is impossible. I gave him more than a fair trial, and he simply won't do."

When my wife and I set out for our drive in the cool of the evening— afternoon is "evening" in Southern parlance—one of the servants put into the rockaway two large earthenware jugs. Our drive was to be down through the swamp to the mineral spring at the foot of the sand-hills beyond. The water of this spring was strongly impregnated with sulphur and iron, and, while not particularly agreeable of smell or taste, was used by us, in moderation, for sanitary reasons.

When we reached the spring, we found a man engaged in cleaning it out. In answer to an inquiry he said that if we would wait five or ten minutes, his task would be finished and the spring in such condition that we could fill our jugs. We might have driven on, and come back by way of the spring, but there was a bad stretch of road beyond, and we concluded to remain where we were until the spring should be ready. We were in a cool and shady place. It was often necessary to wait awhile in North Carolina; and our Northern energy had not been entirely proof against the influences of climate and local custom.

While we sat there, a man came suddenly around a turn of the road ahead of us. I recognized in him a neighbor with whom I had exchanged formal calls. He was driving a horse, apparently a high-spirited creature, possessing, so far as I could see at a glance, the marks of good temper and good breeding; the gentleman, I had heard it suggested, was slightly deficient in both. The horse was rearing and plunging, and the man was beating him furiously with a buggy-whip. When he saw us, he flushed a fiery red, and, as he passed, held the reins with one hand, at some risk to his safety, lifted his hat, and bowed somewhat constrainedly as the horse darted by us, still panting and snorting with fear.

"He looks as though he were ashamed of himself," I observed.

"I 'm sure he ought to be," exclaimed my wife indignantly. "I think there is no worse sin and no more disgraceful thing than cruelty."

"I quite agree with you," I assented.

"A man w'at 'buses his hoss is gwine ter be ha'd on de folks w'at wuks fer 'im," remarked Julius. "Ef young Mistah McLean doan min', he 'll hab a bad dream one er dese days, des lack 'is grandaddy had way back yander, long yeahs befo' de wah."

"What was it about Mr. McLean's dream, Julius?" I asked. The man had not yet finished cleaning the spring, and we might as well put in time listening to Julius as in any other way. We had found some of his plantation tales quite interesting.

"Mars Jeems McLean," said Julius, "wuz de grandaddy er dis yer gent'eman w'at is des gone by us beatin' his hoss. He had a big plantation en a heap er niggers. Mars Jeems wuz a ha'd man, en monst'us stric' wid his han's. Eber sence he growed up he nebber 'peared ter hab no feelin' fer nobody. W'en his daddy, ole Mars John McLean, died, de plantation en all de niggers fell ter young Mars Jeems. He had be'n bad 'nuff befo', but it wa'n't long atterwa'ds 'tel he got so dey wuz no use in libbin' at all ef you ha' ter lib roun' Mars Jeems. His niggers wuz bleedzd ter slabe fum daylight ter da'k, w'iles yuther folks's did n' hafter wuk 'cep'n' fum sun ter sun; en dey did n' git no mo' ter eat dan dey oughter, en dat de coa'ses' kin'. Dey wa'n't 'lowed ter sing, ner dance, ner play de banjo w'en Mars Jeems wuz roun' de place; fer Mars Jeems say he would n' hab no sech gwines-on— said he bought his han's ter wuk, en not ter play, en w'en night come dey mus' sleep en res', so dey 'd be ready ter git up soon in de mawnin' en go ter dey wuk fresh en strong.

"Mars Jeems did n' 'low no co'tin' er juneseyin' roun' his plantation— said he wanted his niggers ter put dey min's on dey wuk, en not be wastin' dey time wid no sech foolis'ness. En he would n' let his han's git married— said he wuz n' raisin' niggers, but wuz raisin' cotton. En w'eneber any er de boys en gals 'ud 'mence ter git sweet on one ernudder, he 'd sell one er de yuther un 'em, er sen' 'em way down in Robeson County ter his yuther plantation, whar dey could n' nebber see one ernudder.

"Ef any er de niggers eber complained, dey got fo'ty; so co'se dey did n' many un 'em complain. But dey did n' lack it, des de same, en nobody could n' blame 'em, fer dey had a ha'd time. Mars Jeems did n' make no 'lowance fer nachul bawn laz'ness, ner sickness, ner trouble in de min', ner nuffin; he wuz des gwine ter git so much wuk outer eve'y han', er know de reason w'y.

"Dey wuz one time de niggers 'lowed, fer a spell, dat Mars Jeems mought git bettah. He tuk a lackin' ter Mars Marrabo McSwayne's oldes' gal, Miss Libbie, en useter go ober dere eve'y day er eve'y ebenin', en folks said dey wuz gwine ter git married sho'. But it 'pears dat Miss Libbie heared 'bout de gwines-on on Mars Jeems's plantation, en she des 'lowed she could n' trus' herse'f wid no sech a man; dat he mought git so useter 'busin' his niggers dat he 'd 'mence ter 'buse his wife atter he got useter habbin' her roun' de house. So she 'clared she wuz n' gwine ter hab nuffin mo' ter do wid young Mars Jeems.

"De niggers wuz all monst'us sorry w'en de match wuz bust' up, fer now Mars Jeems got wusser 'n he wuz befo' he sta'ted sweethea'tin'. De time he useter spen' co'tin' Miss Libbie he put in findin' fault wid de nig- gers, en all his bad feelin's 'ca'se Miss Libbie th'owed 'im ober he 'peared ter try ter wuk off on de po' niggers.

"W'iles Mars Jeems wuz co'tin' Miss Libbie, two er de han's on de plantation had got ter settin' a heap er sto' by one ernudder. One un 'em wuz name' Solomon, en de yuther wuz a 'oman w'at wukked in de fiel' 'long er 'im—I fe'git dat 'oman's name, but it doan 'mount ter much in de tale no- how. Now, whuther 'ca'se Mars Jeems wuz so tuk up wid his own junesey dat he did n' paid no 'tention fer a w'ile ter w'at wuz gwine on 'twix' Solo- mon en his junesey, er whuther his own co'tin' made 'im kin' er easy on de co'tin' in de qua'ters, dey ain' no tellin'. But dey's one thing sho', dat w'en Miss Libbie th'owed 'im ober, he foun' out 'bout Solomon en de gal monst'us quick, en gun Solomon fo'ty, en sont de gal down ter de Robeson County plantation, en tol' all de niggers ef he ketch 'em at any mo' sech foolishness, he wuz gwine ter skin 'em alibe en tan dey hides befo' dey ve'y eyes. Co'se he would n' 'a' done it, but he mought 'a' made things wusser 'n dey wuz. So you kin 'magine dey wa'n't much lub-makin' in de qua'ters fer a long time.

"Mars Jeems useter go down ter de yuther plantation sometimes fer a week er mo', en so he had ter hab a oberseah ter look atter his wuk w'iles he 'uz gone. Mars Jeems's oberseah wuz a po' w'ite man name' Nick Johnson—de niggers called 'im Mars Johnson ter his face, but behin' his back dey useter call 'im Ole Nick, en de name suited 'im ter a T. He wuz wusser 'n Mars Jeems ever da'ed ter be. Co'se de darkies did n' lack de way Mars Jeems used 'em, but he wuz de marster, en had a right ter do ez he please'; but dis yer Ole Nick wa'n't nuffin but a po' buckrah, en all de niggers 'spised 'im ez much ez dey hated 'im, fer he did n' own nobody, en wa'n't no bettah 'n a nigger, fer in dem days any 'spectable pusson would ruther be a nigger dan a po' w'ite man.

"Now, atter Solomon's gal had be'n sont away, he kep' feelin' mo' en mo' bad erbout it, 'tel fin'lly he 'lowed he wuz gwine ter see ef dey could n' be sump'n done fer ter git 'er back, en ter make Mars Jeems treat de darkies bettah. So he tuk a peck er co'n out'n de ba'n one night, en went ober ter see ole Aun' Peggy, de free-nigger cunjuh 'oman down by de Wim'l'ton Road.

"Aun' Peggy listen' ter 'is tale, en ax' him some queshtuns, en den tol' 'im she 'd wuk her roots, en see w'at dey 'd say 'bout it, en ter-morrer night he sh'd come back ag'in en fetch ernudder peck er co'n, en den she 'd hab sump'n fer ter tell 'im.

"So Solomon went back de nex' night, en sho' 'nuff, Aun' Peggy tol' 'im w'at ter do. She gun 'im some stuff w'at look' lack it be'n made by poundin' up some roots en yarbs wid a pestle in a mo'tar.

"'Dis yer stuff,' sez she, 'is monst'us pow'ful kin' er goopher. You take dis home, en gin it ter de cook, ef you kin trus' her, en tell her fer ter put it in yo' marster's soup de fus' cloudy day he hab okra soup fer dinnah. Min' you follers de d'rections.'

"'It ain' gwineter p'isen 'im, is it?' ax' Solomon, gittin' kin' er skeered; fer Solomon wuz a good man, en did n' want ter do nobody no rale ha'm.

"'Oh, no,' sez ole Aun' Peggy, 'it 's gwine ter do 'im good, but he'll hab a monst'us bad dream fus'. A mont' fum now you come down heah en lemme know how de goopher is wukkin'. Fer I ain' done much er dis kin' er cunj'in' er late yeahs, en I has ter kinder keep track un it ter see dat it

doan 'complish no mo' d'n I 'lows fer it ter do. En I has ter be kinder keerful 'bout cunj'in' w'ite folks; so be sho' en lemme know, w'ateber you do,
des w'at is gwine on roun' de plantation.'

"So Solomon say all right, en tuk de goopher mixtry up ter de big house
en gun it ter de cook, en tol' her fer ter put it in Mars Jeems's soup de fus'
cloudy day she hab okra soup fer dinnah. It happen' dat de ve'y nex' day
wuz a cloudy day, en so de cook made okra soup fer Mars Jeems's dinnah,
en put de powder Solomon gun her inter de soup, en made de soup rale
good, so Mars Jeems eat a whole lot of it en 'peared ter enjoy it.

"De nex' mawnin' Mars Jeems tol' de oberseah he wuz gwine 'way on
some bizness, en den he wuz gwine ter his yuther plantation, down in
Robeson County, en he did n' 'spec' he 'd be back fer a mont' er so.

" 'But,' sezee, 'I wants you ter run dis yer plantation fer all it's wuth.
Dese yer niggers is gittin' monst'us triflin' en lazy en keerless, en dey ain' no
'pen'ence ter be put in 'em. I wants dat stop', en w'iles I'm gone erway I
wants de 'spenses cut 'way down en a heap mo' wuk done. Fac', I wants dis
yer plantation ter make a reco'd dat 'll show w'at kinder oberseah you is.'

"Ole Nick did n' said nuffin but 'Yas, suh,' but de way he kinder grin'
ter hisse'f en show' his big yaller teef, en snap' de rawhide he useter kyar
roun' wid 'im, made col' chills run up and down de backbone er dem niggers w'at heared Mars Jeems a-talkin'. En dat night dey wuz mo'nin' en
groanin' down in de qua'ters, fer de niggers all knowed w'at wuz comin'.

"So, sho' 'nuff, Mars Jeems went erway nex' mawnin', en de trouble
begun. Mars Johnson sta'ted off de ve'y fus' day fer ter see w'at he could
hab ter show Mars Jeems w'en he come back. He made de tasks bigger en
de rashuns littler, en w'en de niggers had wukked all day, he 'd fin' sump'n
fer 'em ter do roun' de ba'n er som'ers atter da'k, fer ter keep 'em busy a'
hour er so befo' dey went ter sleep.

"About th'ee er fo' days atter Mars Jeems went erway, young Mars
Dunkin McSwayne rode up ter de big house one day wid a nigger settin' be-
hin' 'im in de buggy, tied ter de seat, en ax' ef Mars Jeems wuz home. Mars
Johnson wuz at de house, and he say no.

" 'Well,' sez Mars Dunkin, sezee, 'I fotch dis nigger ober ter Mistah
McLean fer ter pay a bet I made wid 'im las' week w'en we wuz playin'
kya'ds te'gedder. I bet 'im a nigger man, en heah 's one I reckon 'll fill de bill.
He wuz tuk up de yuther day fer a stray nigger, en he could n' gib no 'count
er hisse'f, en so he wuz sol' at oction, en I bought 'im. He's kinder brash,
but I knows yo' powers, Mistah Johnson, en I reckon ef anybody kin make
'im toe de ma'k, you is de man.'

"Mars Johnson grin' one er dem grins w'at show' all his snaggle teef,
en make de niggers 'low he look lack de ole debbil, en sezee ter Mars
Dunkin:

"'I reckon you kin trus' me, Mistah Dunkin, fer ter tame any nigger wuz eber bawn. De nigger doan lib w'at I can't take down in 'bout fo' days.'

"Well, Ole Nick had 'is han's full long er dat noo nigger; en w'iles de res' er de darkies wuz sorry fer de po' man, dey 'lowed he kep' Mars Johnson so busy dat dey got along better 'n dey 'd 'a' done ef de noo nigger had nebber come.

"De fus' thing dat happen', Mars Johnson sez ter dis yer noo man:

"'W'at 's yo' name, Sambo?'

"'My name ain' Sambo,' 'spon' de noo nigger.

"'Did I ax you w'at yo' name wa'n't?' sez Mars Johnson. 'You wants ter be pa'tic'lar how you talks ter me. Now, w'at is yo' name, en whar did you come fum?'

"'I dunno my name,' sez de nigger, 'en I doan 'member whar I come fum. My head is all kin' er mix' up.'

"'Yas,' sez Mars Johnson, 'I reckon I 'll ha' ter gib you sump'n fer ter cl'ar yo' head. At de same time, it 'll l'arn you some manners, en atter dis mebbe you 'll say "suh" w'en you speaks ter me.'

"Well, Mars Johnson haul' off wid his rawhide en hit de noo nigger once. De noo man look' at Mars Johnson fer a minute ez ef he did n' know w'at ter make er dis yer kin' er l'arnin'. But w'en de oberseah raise' his w'ip ter hit him ag'in, de noo nigger des haul' off en made fer Mars Johnson, en ef some er de yuther niggers had n' stop' 'im, it 'peared ez ef he mought 'a' made it wa'm fer Ole Nick dere fer a w'ile. But de oberseah made de yuther niggers he'p tie de noo nigger up, en den gun 'im fo'ty, wid a dozen er so th'owed in fer good measure, fer Ole Nick wuz nebber stingy wid dem kin' er rashuns. De nigger went on at a tarrable rate, des lack a wil' man, but co'se he wuz bleedzd ter take his med'cine, fer he wuz tied up en could n' he'p hisse'f.

"Mars Johnson lock' de noo nigger up in de ba'n, en did n' gib 'im nuffin ter eat fer a day er so, 'tel he got 'im kin'er quiet' down, en den he tu'nt 'im loose en put 'im ter wuk. De nigger 'lowed he wa'n't useter wukkin', en would n' wuk, en Mars Johnson gun 'im anudder fo'ty fer laziness en impidence, en let 'im fas' a day er so mo', en den put 'im ter wuk ag'in. De nigger went ter wuk, but did n' 'pear ter know how ter han'le a hoe. It tuk des 'bout half de oberseah's time lookin' atter 'im, en dat po' nigger got mo' lashin's en cussin's en cuffin's dan any fo' yuthers on de plantation. He did n' mix' wid ner talk much ter de res' er de niggers, en could n' 'pear ter git it th'oo his min' dat he wuz a slabe en had ter wuk en min' de w'ite folks, spite er de fac' dat Ole Nick gun 'im a lesson eve'y day. En fin'lly Mars Johnson 'lowed dat he could n' do nuffin wid 'im; dat ef he wuz his nigger, he 'd break his sperrit er break 'is neck, one er de yuther. But co'se he wuz only sont ober on trial, en ez he did n' gib sat'sfaction, en he had n' heared fum

Mars Jeems 'bout w'en he wuz comin' back; en ez he wuz feared he 'd git mad some time er 'nuther en kill de nigger befo' he knowed it, he 'lowed he 'd better sen' 'im back whar he come fum. So he tied 'im up en sont 'im back ter Mars Dunkin.

"Now, Mars Dunkin McSwayne wuz one er dese yer easy-gwine gent'emen w'at did n' lack ter hab no trouble wid niggers er nobody e'se, en he knowed ef Mars Ole Nick could n' git 'long wid dis nigger, nobody could. So he tuk de nigger ter town dat same day, en sol' 'im ter a trader w'at wuz gittin' up a gang er lackly niggers fer ter ship off on de steamboat ter go down de ribber ter Wim'l'ton en fum dere ter Noo Orleans.

"De nex' day atter de noo man had be'n sont away, Solomon wuz wukkin' in de cotton-fiel', en w'en he got ter de fence nex' ter de woods, at de een' er de row, who sh'd he see on de yuther side but ole Aun' Peggy. She beckon' ter 'im—de oberseah wuz down on de yuther side er de fiel'—en sez she:

" 'W'y ain' you done come en 'po'ted ter me lack I tol' you?'

" 'W'y, law! Aun' Peggy,' sez Solomon, 'dey ain' nuffin ter 'po't. Mars Jeems went away de day atter we gun 'im de goopher mixtry, en we ain' seed hide ner hair un 'im sence, en co'se we doan know nuffin 'bout w'at 'fec' it had on 'im.'

" 'I doan keer nuffin 'bout yo' Mars Jeems now; w'at I wants ter know is w'at is be'n gwine on 'mongs' de niggers. Has you be'n gittin' 'long any better on de plantation?'

" 'No, Aun' Peggy, we be'n gittin' 'long wusser. Mars Johnson is stric'er 'n he eber wuz befo', en de po' niggers doan ha'dly git time ter draw dey bref, en dey 'lows dey mought des ez well be dead ez alibe.'

" 'Uh huh!' sez Aun' Peggy, sez she, 'I tol' you dat 'uz monst'us pow'ful goopher, en its wuk doan 'pear all at once.'

" 'Long ez we had dat noo nigger heah,' Solomon went on, 'he kep' Mars Johnson busy pa't er de time; but now he 's gone erway, I s'pose de res' un us 'll ketch it wusser 'n eber.'

" 'W'at 's gone wid de noo nigger?' sez Aun' Peggy, rale quick, battin' her eyes en straight'nin' up.

" 'Ole Nick done sont 'im back ter Mars Dunkin, who had fotch 'im heah fer ter pay a gamblin' debt ter Mars Jeems,' sez Solomon, 'en I heahs Mars Dunkin has sol' 'im ter a nigger-trader up in Patesville, w'at 's gwine ter ship 'im off wid a gang ter-morrer.'

"Ole Aun' Peggy 'peared ter git rale stirred up w'en Solomon tol' 'er dat, en sez she, shakin' her stick at 'im:

" 'W'y did n' you come en tell me 'bout dis noo nigger hein' sol' erway? Did n' you promus me, ef I 'd gib you dat goopher, you 'd come en 'po't ter me 'bout all w'at wuz gwine on on dis plantation? Co'se I could 'a'

foun' out fer myse'f, but I 'pended on yo' tellin' me, en now by not doin'
it I 's feared you gwine spile my cunj'in'. You come down ter my house ter-
night en do w'at I tells you, er I 'll put a spell on you dat 'll make yo' ha'r
fall out so you 'll be bal', en yo' eyes drap out so you can't see, en yo teef
fall out so you can't eat, en yo' years grow up so you can't heah. W'en you
is foolin' wid a cunjuh 'oman lack me, you got ter min' yo' P's en Q's er
dey 'll be trouble sho' 'nuff.'

"So co'se Solomon went down ter Aun' Peggy's dat night, en she gun
'im a roasted sweet'n' 'tater.

"'You take dis yer sweet'n' 'tater,' sez she—'I done goophered it
'speshly fer dat noo nigger, so you better not eat it yo'se'f er you 'll wush
you had n'—en slip off ter town, en fin' dat strange man, en gib 'im dis yer
sweet'n' 'tater. He mus' eat it befo' mawnin', sho', ef he doan wanter be
sol' erway ter Noo Orleans.'

"'But s'posen de patteroles ketch me, Aun' Peggy, w'at I gwine ter do?'
sez Solomon.

"'De patteroles ain' gwine tech you, but ef you doan fin' dat nigger,
I'm gwine git you, en you 'll fin' me wusser 'n de patteroles. Des hol' on a
minute, en I 'll sprinkle you wid some er dis mixtry out'n dis yer bottle, so
de patteroles can't see you, en you kin rub yo' feet wid some er dis yer
grease out'n dis go'd, so you kin run fas', en rub some un it on yo' eyes so
you kin see in de da'k; en den you mus' fin' dat noo nigger en gib 'im dis
yer 'tater, er you gwine ter hab mo' trouble on yo' han's 'n you eber had
befo' in yo' life er eber will hab sence.'

"So Solomon tuk de sweet'n' 'tater en sta'ted up de road fas' ez he
could go, en befo' long he retch' town. He went right 'long by de patteroles,
en dey did n' 'pear ter notice 'im, en bimeby he foun' whar de strange nigger was kep', en he walked right pas' de gyard at de do' en foun' 'im. De
nigger could n' see 'im, ob co'se, en he could n' 'a' seed de nigger in de da'k,
ef it had n' be'n fer de stuff Aun' Peggy gun 'im ter rub on 'is eyes. De nigger
wuz layin' in a co'nder, 'sleep, en Solomon des slip' up ter 'im, en hilt dat
sweet'n' 'tater 'fo' de nigger's nose, en he des nach'ly retch' up wid his han',
en tuk de 'tater en eat it in his sleep, widout knowin' it. W'en Solomon seed
he 'd done eat de 'tater, he went back en tol' Aun' Peggy, en den went home
ter his cabin ter sleep, 'way 'long 'bout two o'clock in de mawnin'.

"De nex' day wuz Sunday, en so de niggers had a little time ter deyse'ves. Solomon wuz kinder 'sturb' in his min' thinkin' 'bout his junesey
w'at 'uz gone away, en wond'rin' w'at Aun' Peggy had ter do wid dat noo
nigger; en he had sa'ntered up in de woods so 's ter be by hisse'f a little, en
at de same time ter look atter a rabbit-trap he 'd sot down in de aidge er
de swamp, w'en who sh'd he see stan'in' unner a tree but a w'ite man.

"Solomon did n' knowed de w'ite man at fus', 'tel de w'ite man spoke up ter 'im.

" 'Is dat you, Solomon?' sezee.

"Den Solomon reco'nized de voice.

" 'Fer de Lawd's sake, Mars Jeems! is dat you?'

" 'Yas, Solomon,' sez his marster, 'dis is me, er w'at 's lef' er me.'

"It wa'n't no wonder Solomon had n' knowed Mars Jeems at fus', fer he wuz dress' lack a po' w'ite man, en wuz barefooted, en look' monst'us pale en peaked, ez ef he 'd des come th'oo a ha'd spell er sickness.

" 'You er lookin' kinder po'ly, Mars Jeems,' sez Solomon. 'Is you be'n sick, suh?'

" 'No, Solomon,' sez Mars Jeems, shakin' his head, en speakin' sorter slow en sad, 'I ain' be'n sick, but I 's had a monst'us bad dream—fac', a reg'lar, nach'ul nightmare. But tell me how things has be'n gwine on up ter de plantation sence I be'n gone, Solomon.'

"So Solomon up en tol' 'im 'bout de craps, en 'bout de hosses en de mules, en 'bout de cows en de hawgs. En w'en he 'mence' ter tell 'bout de noo nigger, Mars Jeems prick' up 'is yeahs en listen', en eve'y now en den he 'd say, 'Uh huh! uh huh!' en nod 'is head. En bimeby, w'en he 'd ax' Solomon some mo' queshtuns, he sez, sezee:

" 'Now, Solomon, I doan want you ter say a wo'd ter nobody 'bout meetin' me heah, but I wants you ter slip up ter de house, en fetch me some clo's en some shoes—I fergot ter tell you dat a man rob' me back yander on de road en swap' clo's wid me widout axin' me whuther er no—but you neenter say nuffin 'bout dat, nuther. You go en fetch me some clo's heah, so nobody won't see you, en keep yo' mouf shet, en I 'll gib you a dollah.'

"Solomon wuz so 'stonish' he lack ter fell ober in his tracks, w'en Mars Jeems promus' ter gib 'im a dollah. Dey su't'nly wuz a change come ober Mars Jeems, w'en he offer' one er his niggers dat much money. Solomon 'mence' ter 'spec' dat Aun' Peggy's cunj'ation had be'n wukkin' monst'us strong.

"Solomon fotch Mars Jeems some clo's en shoes, en dat same eb'nin' Mars Jeems 'peared at de house, en let on lack he des dat minute got home fum Robeson County. Mars Johnson was all ready ter talk ter 'im, but Mars Jeems sont 'im wo'd he wa'n't feelin' ve'y well dat night, en he 'd see 'im ter-morrer.

"So nex' mawnin' atter breakfus' Mars Jeems sont fer de oberseah, en ax' 'im fer ter gib 'count er his styoa'dship. Ole Nick tol' Mars Jeems how much wuk be'n done, en got de books en showed 'im how much money be'n save'. Den Mars Jeems ax' 'im how de darkies be'n behabin', en Mars Johnson say dey be'n behabin' good, most un 'em, en dem w'at did n' behabe good at fus' change dey conduc' atter he got holt un 'em a time er two.

"'All,' sezee, ''cep'n' de noo nigger Mistah Dunkin fotch ober heah en lef' on trial, w'iles you wuz gone.'

"'Oh, yas,' 'lows Mars Jeems, 'tell me all 'bout dat noo nigger. I heared a little 'bout dat quare noo nigger las' night, en it wuz des too redik'lus. Tell me all 'bout dat noo nigger.'

"So seein' Mars Jeems so good-nachu'd 'bout it, Mars Johnson up en tol' 'im how he tied up de noo han' de fus' day en gun 'im fo'ty 'ca'se he would n' tell 'im 'is name.

"'Ha, ha, ha!' sez Mars Jeems, laffin' fit ter kill, 'but dat is too funny fer any use. Tell me some mo' 'bout dat noo nigger.'

"So Mars Johnson went on en tol' 'im how he had ter starbe de noo nigger 'fo' he could make 'im take holt er a hoe.

"'Dat wuz de beatinis' notion fer a nigger,' sez Mars Jeems, 'puttin' on airs, des lack he wuz a w'ite man! En I reckon you did n' do nuffin ter 'im?'

"'Oh, no, suh,' sez de oberseah, grinnin' lack a chessy-cat, 'I did n' do nuffin but take de hide off'n 'im.'

"Mars Jeems lafft en lafft, 'tel it 'peared lack he wuz des gwine ter bu'st. '*Tell* me some mo' 'bout dat noo nigger, oh, *tell* me some mo'. Dat noo nigger int'rusts me, he do, en dat is a fac'.'

"Mars Johnson did n' quite un'erstan' w'y Mars Jeems sh'd make sich a great 'miration 'bout de noo nigger, but co'se he want' ter please de gent'eman w'at hi'ed 'im, en so he 'splain' all 'bout how many times he had ter cowhide de noo nigger, en how he made 'im do tasks twicet ez big ez some er de yuther han's, en how he'd chain 'im up in de ba'n at night en feed 'im on co'n-bread en water.

"'Oh! but you is a monst'us good oberseah; you is de bes' oberseah in dis county, Mistah Johnson,' sez Mars Jeems, w'en de oberseah got th'oo wid his tale; 'en dey ain' nebber be'n no nigger-breaker lack you roun' heah befo'. En you desarbes great credit fer sendin' dat nigger 'way befo' you sp'ilt 'im fer de market. Fac', you is sech a monst'us good oberseah, en you is got dis yer plantation in sech fine shape, dat I reckon I doan need you no mo'. You is got dese yer darkies so well train' dat I 'spec' I kin run 'em my-se'f fum dis time on. But I does wush you had 'a' hilt on ter dat noo nigger 'tel I got home, fer I'd 'a' lack ter 'a' seed 'im, I su't'nly should.'

"De oberseah wuz so 'stonish' he did n' ha'dly know w'at ter say, but fin'lly he ax' Mars Jeems ef he would n' gib 'im a riccommen' fer ter git ernudder place.

"'No, suh,' sez Mars Jeems, 'somehow er'nuther I doan lack yo' looks sence I come back dis time, en I'd much ruther you would n' stay roun' heah. Fac', I's feared ef I'd meet you alone in de woods some time, I mought wan-ter ha'm you. But layin' dat aside, I be'n lookin' ober dese yer books er yo'n w'at you kep' w'iles I wuz 'way, en fer a yeah er so back, en dere's some figgers w'at ain' des cl'ar ter me. I ain' got no time fer ter talk 'bout 'em now, but I 'spec' befo' I settles wid you fer dis las' mont', you better come up heah ter-morrer, atter I's look' de books en 'counts ober some mo', en den we 'll straighten ou' business all up.'

"Mars Jeems 'lowed atterwa'ds dat he wuz des shootin' in de da'k w'en he said dat 'bout de books, but howsomeber, Mars Nick Johnson lef' dat naberhood 'twix' de nex' two suns, en nobody roun' dere nebber seed hide ner hair un 'im sence. En all de darkies t'ank de Lawd, en 'lowed it wuz a good riddance er bad rubbage.

"But all dem things I done tol' you ain' nuffin 'side'n de change w'at come ober Mars Jeems fum dat time on. Aun' Peggy's goopher had made a noo man un 'im enti'ely. De nex' day atter he come back, he tol' de han's dey neenter wuk on'y fum sun ter sun, en he cut dey tasks down so dey did n' nobody hab ter stan' ober 'em wid a rawhide er a hick'ry. En he 'lowed ef de niggers want ter hab a dance in de big ba'n any Sad'day night, dey mought hab it. En bimeby, w'en Solomon seed how good Mars Jeems wuz, he ax' 'im ef he would n' please sen' down ter de yuther plantation fer his junesey. Mars Jeems say su't'nly, en gun Solomon a pass en a note ter de oberseah on de yuther plantation, en sont Solomon down ter Robeson County wid a hoss en buggy fer ter fetch his junesey back. W'en de niggers see how fine Mars Jeems gwine treat 'em, dey all tuk ter sweethea'tin' en juneseyin' en singin' en dancin', en eight er ten couples got married, en bimeby eve'ybody 'mence' ter say Mars Jeems McLean got a finer plantation, en slicker-lookin' niggers, en dat he 'uz makin' mo' cotton en co'n, dan any yuther gent'eman in de county. En Mars Jeems's own junesey, Miss Libbie, heared 'bout de noo gwines-on on Mars Jeems's plantation, en she change' her min' 'bout Mars Jeems en tuk 'im back ag'in, en 'fo' long dey had a fine weddin', en all de darkies had a big feas', en dey wuz fiddlin' en dancin' en funnin' en frolic'in' fum sundown 'tel mawnin'."

"And they all lived happy ever after," I said, as the old man reached a full stop.

"Yas, suh," he said, interpreting my remarks as a question, "dey did. Solomon useter say," he added, "dat Aun' Peggy's goopher had turnt Mars Jeems ter a nigger, en dat dat noo han' wuz Mars Jeems hisse'f. But co'se Solomon did n' das' ter let on 'bout w'at he 'spicioned, en ole Aun' Peggy would 'a' 'nied ef she had be'n ax', fer she 'd 'a' got in trouble sho', ef it 'uz knowed she'd be'n cunj'in' de w'ite folks.

"Dis yer tale goes ter show," concluded Julius sententiously, as the man came up and announced that the spring was ready for us to get water, "dat w'ite folks w'at is so ha'd en stric', en doan make no 'lowance fer po' ign'ant niggers w'at ain' had no chanst ter l'arn, is li'ble ter hab bad dreams, ter say de leas', en dat dem w'at is kin' en good ter po' people is sho' ter prosper en git 'long in de worl'."

"That is a very strange story, Uncle Julius," observed my wife, smiling, "and Solomon's explanation is quite improbable."

"Yes, Julius," said I, "that was powerful goopher. I am glad, too, that you told us the moral of the story; it might have escaped us otherwise. By the way, did you make that up all by yourself?"

The old man's face assumed an injured look, expressive more of sorrow than of anger, and shaking his head he replied:

"No, suh, I heared dat tale befo' you er Mis' Annie dere wuz bawn, suh. My mammy tol' me dat tale w'en I wa'n't mo' d'n knee-high ter a hoppergrass."

I drove to town next morning, on some business, and did not return until noon; and after dinner I had to visit a neighbor, and did not get back until supper-time. I was smoking a cigar on the back piazza in the early evening, when I saw a familiar figure carrying a bucket of water to the barn. I called my wife.

"My dear," I said severely, "what is that rascal doing here? I thought I discharged him yesterday for good and all."

"Oh, yes," she answered, "I forgot to tell you. He was hanging round the place all the morning, and looking so down in the mouth, that I told him that if he would try to do better, we would give him one more chance. He seems so grateful, and so really in earnest in his promises of amendment, that I'm sure you'll not regret taking him back."

I was seriously enough annoyed to let my cigar go out. I did not share my wife's rose-colored hopes in regard to Tom; but as I did not wish the servants to think there was any conflict of authority in the household, I let the boy stay.

THE CONJURER'S REVENGE

Sunday was sometimes a rather dull day at our place. In the morning, when the weather was pleasant, my wife and I would drive to town, a distance of about five miles, to attend the church of our choice. The afternoons we spent at home, for the most part, occupying ourselves with the newspapers and magazines, and the contents of a fairly good library. We had a piano in the house, on which my wife played with skill and feeling. I possessed a passable baritone voice, and could accompany myself indifferently well when my wife was not by to assist me. When these resources failed us, we were apt to find it a little dull.

One Sunday afternoon in early spring—the balmy spring of North Carolina, when the air is in that ideal balance between heat and cold where one wishes it could always remain—my wife and I were seated on the front piazza, she wearily but conscientiously ploughing through a missionary report, while I followed the impossible career of the blonde heroine of a rudimentary novel. I had thrown the book aside in disgust, when I saw Julius coming through the yard, under the spreading elms, which were already in full leaf. He wore his Sunday clothes, and advanced with a dignity of movement quite different from his week-day slouch.

"Have a seat, Julius," I said, pointing to an empty rocking-chair.

"No, thanky, boss, I'll des set here on de top step."

"Oh, no, Uncle Julius," exclaimed Annie, "take this chair. You will find it much more comfortable."

The old man grinned in appreciation of her solicitude, and seated himself somewhat awkwardly.

"Julius," I remarked, "I am thinking of setting out scuppernong vines on that sand hill where the three persimmon trees are; and while I'm working there, I think I'll plant watermelons between the vines, and get a little something to pay for my first year's work. The new railroad will be finished by the middle of summer, and I can ship the melons North, and get a good price for them."

"Ef you er gwine ter hab any mo' ploughin' ter do," replied Julius, "I 'spec' you'll ha' ter buy ernudder creetur, 'ca'se hit's much ez dem hosses kin do ter 'ten' ter de wuk dey got now."

"Yes, I had thought of that. I think I'll get a mule; a mule can do more work, and does n't require as much attention as a horse."

"I would n' 'vise you ter buy no mule," remarked Julius, with a shake of his head.

"Why not?"

"Well, you may 'low hit's all foolis'ness, but ef I wuz in yo' place, I would n' buy no mule."

"But that isn't a reason; what objection have you to a mule?"

"Fac' is," continued the old man, in a serious tone, "I doan lack ter dribe a mule. I's alluz afeared I mought be imposin' on some human creetur; eve'y time I cuts a mule wid a hick'ry, 'pears ter me mos' lackly I's cuttin' some er my own relations, er somebody e'se w'at can't he'p deyse'ves."

"What put such an absurd idea into your head?" I asked.

My question was followed by a short silence, during which Julius seemed engaged in a mental struggle.

"I dunno ez hit's wuf w'ile ter tell you dis," he said, at length. "I doan ha'dly 'spec' fer you ter b'lieve it. Does you 'member dat club-footed man w'at hilt de hoss fer you de yuther day w'en you was gittin' out'n de rock-away down ter Mars Archie McMillan's sto'?"

"Yes, I believe I do remember seeing a club-footed man there."

"Did you eber see a club-footed nigger befo' er sence?"

"No, I can't remember that I ever saw a club-footed colored man," I replied, after a moment's reflection.

"You en Mis' Annie would n' wanter b'lieve me, ef I wuz ter 'low dat dat man was oncet a mule?"

"No," I replied, "I don't think it very likely that you could make us believe it."

"Why, Uncle Julius!" said Annie severely, "what ridiculous nonsense!"

This reception of the old man's statement reduced him to silence, and it required some diplomacy on my part to induce him to vouchsafe an explanation. The prospect of a long, dull afternoon was not alluring, and I was glad to have the monotony of Sabbath quiet relieved by a plantation legend.

"W'en I wuz a young man," began Julius, when I had finally prevailed upon him to tell us the story, "dat club-footed nigger—his name is Primus—use' ter b'long ter ole Mars Jim McGee ober on de Lumbe'ton plank-road. I use' ter go ober dere ter see a 'oman w'at libbed on de plantation; dat's how I come ter know all erbout it. Dis yer Primus wuz de livelies' han' on de place, alluz a-dancin', en drinkin', en runnin' roun', en singin', en pickin' de banjo; 'cep'n' once in a w'ile, w'en he'd 'low he wa'n't treated right 'bout sump'n ernudder, he'd git so sulky en stubborn dat de w'ite folks could n' ha'dly do nuffin wid 'im.

"It wuz 'gin' de rules fer any er de han's ter go 'way fum de plantation at night; but Primus did n' min' de rules, en went w'en he felt lack it; en de w'ite folks purten' lack dey did n' know it, fer Primus was dange'ous w'en he got in dem stubborn spells, en dey'd ruther not fool wid 'im.

"One night in de spring er de year, Primus slip' off fum de plantation, en went down on de Wim'l'ton Road ter a dance gun by some er de free niggers down dere. Dey wuz a fiddle, en a banjo, en a jug gwine roun' on de outside, en Primus sung en dance' 'tel 'long 'bout two o'clock in de mawnin', w'en he start' fer home. Ez he come erlong back, he tuk a nigh-cut 'cross de cotton-fiel's en 'long by de aidge er de Min'al Spring Swamp, so ez ter git shet er de patteroles w'at rid up en down de big road fer ter keep de dark-ies fum runnin' roun' nights. Primus was sa'nt'rin' 'long, studyin' 'bout de good time he 'd had wid de gals, w'en, ez he wuz gwine by a fence co'nder, w'at sh'd he heah but sump'n grunt. He stopped a minute ter listen, en he heared sump'n grunt ag'in. Den he went ober ter de fence whar he heard de fuss, en dere, layin' in de fence co'nder, on a pile er pine straw, he seed a fine, fat shote.

"Primus look' ha'd at de shote, en den sta'ted home. But somehow er 'nudder he could n' git away fum dat shote; w'en he tuk one step for'ards wid one foot, de yuther foot 'peared ter take two steps back'ards, en so he kep' nachly gittin' closeter en closeter ter de shote. It was de beatin'es' thing! De shote des 'peared ter cha'm Primus, en fus' thing you know Primus foun' hisse'f 'way up de road wid de shote on his back.

"Ef Primus had 'a' knowed whose shote dat wuz, he 'd 'a' manage' ter git pas' it somehow er 'nudder. Ez it happen', de shote b'long ter a cunjuh man w'at libbed down in de free-nigger sett'ement. Co'se de cunjuh man did n' hab ter wuk his roots but a little w'ile 'fo' he foun' out who tuk his shote, en den de trouble begun. One mawnin', a day er so later, en befo' he got de shote eat up, Primus did n' go ter wuk w'en de hawn blow, en w'en de oberseah wen' ter look fer him, dey wa' no trace er Primus ter be 'skivered nowhar. W'en he did n' come back in a day er so mo', eve'ybody on de plantation 'lowed he had runned erway. His marster a'vertise' him in de papers, en offered a big reward fer 'im. De nigger-ketchers fotch out dey dogs, en track' 'im down ter de aidge er de swamp, en den de scent gin out; en dat was de las' anybody seed er Primus fer a long, long time.

"Two er th'ee wecks atter Primus disappear', his marster went ter town one Sad'day. Mars Jim was stan'in' in front er Sandy Campbell's bar-room, up by de ole wagon-ya'd, w'en a po' w'ite man fum down on de Wim'l'ton Road come up ter 'im en ax' 'im, kinder keerless lack, ef he did n' wanter buy a mule.

"'I dunno,' says Mars Jim; 'it 'pen's on de mule, en on de price. Whar is de mule?'

"'Des 'roun' heah back er ole Tom McAllister's sto',' says de po' w'ite man.

"'I reckon I'll hab a look at de mule,' says Mars Jim, 'en ef he suit me, I dunno but w'at I mought buy 'im.'

"So de po' w'ite man tuk Mars Jim 'roun' back er de sto', en dere stood a monst'us fine mule. W'en de mule see Mars Jim, he gun a whinny, des lack he knowed him befo'. Mars Jim look' at de mule, en de mule 'peared ter be soun' en strong. Mars Jim 'lowed dey 'peared ter be sump'n fermilyus 'bout de mule's face, 'spesh'ly his eyes; but he had n' los' naer mule, en did n' hab no recommemb'ance er habin' seed de mule befo'. He ax' de po' buckrah whar he got de mule, en de po' buckrah say his brer raise' de mule down on Rockfish Creek. Mars Jim was a little s'picious er seein' a po' w'ite man wid sech a fine creetur, but he fin'lly 'greed ter gib de man fifty dollars fer de mule—'bout ha'f w'at a good mule was wuf dem days.

"He tied de mule behin' de buggy w'en he went home, en put 'im ter ploughin' cotton de nex' day. De mule done mighty well fer th'ee er fo' days, en den de niggers 'mence' ter notice some quare things erbout him. Dey wuz a medder on de plantation whar dey use' ter put de hosses en mules ter pastur'. Hit was fence' off fum de cornfiel' on one side, but on de yuther side'n de pastur' was a terbacker-patch w'at wa'n't fence' off, 'ca'se de beastisses doan none un 'em eat terbacker. Dey doan know w'at 's good! Terbacker is lack religion, de good Lawd made it fer people, en dey ain' no yuther creetur w'at kin 'preciate it. De darkies notice' dat de fus' thing de new mule done, w'en he was turnt inter de pastur', wuz ter make fer de terbacker-patch. Co'se dey did n' think nuffin un it, but nex' mawnin', w'en dey went ter ketch 'im, dey 'skivered dat he had eat up two whole rows er terbacker plants. Atter dat dey had ter put a halter on 'im, en tie 'im ter a stake, er e'se dey would n' 'a' been naer leaf er terbacker lef' in de patch.

"Ernudder day one er de han's, name' 'Dolphus, hitch' de mule up, en dribe up here ter dis yer vimya'd—dat wuz w'en ole Mars Dugal' own' dis place. Mars Dugal' had kilt a yearlin', en de naber w'ite folks all sont ober fer ter git some fraish beef, en Mars Jim had sont 'Dolphus fer some too. Dey wuz a winepress in de ya'd whar 'Dolphus lef' de mule a-stan'in', en right in front er de press dey wuz a tub er grape-juice, des pressed out, en a little ter one side a bairl erbout half full er wine w'at had be'n stan'in' two er th'ee days, en had begun ter git sorter sha'p ter de tas'e. Dey wuz a couple er bo'ds on top er dis yer bairl, wid a rock laid on 'em ter hol' 'em down. Ez I wuz a-sayin', 'Dolphus lef' de mule stan'in' in de ya'd, en went inter de smoke-house fer ter git de beef. Bimeby, w'en he come out, he seed de mule a-stagg'rin' 'bout de ya'd; en 'fo' 'Dolphus could git dere ter fin' out w'at wuz de matter, de mule fell right ober on his side, en laid dere des' lack he was dead.

"All de niggers 'bout de house run out dere fer ter see w'at wuz de matter. Some say de mule had de colic; some say one thing en some ernudder; 'tel bimeby one er de han's seed de top wuz off'n de bairl, en run en looked in.

" 'Fo' de Lawd!' he say, 'dat mule drunk! he be'n drinkin' de wine.' En sho' 'nuff, de mule had pas' right by de tub er fraish grape-juice en push' de kiver off'n de bairl, en drunk two er th'ee gallon er de wine w'at had been stan'in' long ernough fer ter begin ter git sha'p.

"De darkies all made a great 'miration 'bout de mule gittin' drunk. Dey never had n' seed nuffin lack it in dey bawn days. Dey po'd water ober de mule, en tried ter sober 'im up; but it wa'n't no use, en 'Dolphus had ter take de beef home on his back, en leabe de mule dere, 'tel he slep' off 'is spree.

"I doan 'member whe'r I tol' you er no, but w'en Primus disappear' fum de plantation, he lef' a wife behin' 'im—a monst'us good-lookin' yaller gal, name' Sally. W'en Primus had be'n gone a mont' er so, Sally 'mence' fer ter git lonesome, en tuk up wid ernudder young man name' Dan, w'at b'long' on de same plantation. One day dis yer Dan tuk de noo mule out in de cotton-fiel' fer ter plough, en w'en dey wuz gwine 'long de tu'n-row, who sh'd he meet but dis yer Sally. Dan look' 'roun' en he did n' see de oberseah nowhar, so he stop' a minute fer ter run on wid Sally.

"'Hoddy, honey,' sezee. 'How you feelin' dis mawnin'?'

"'Fus' rate,' 'spon' Sally.

"Dey wuz lookin' at one ernudder, en dey did n' naer one un 'em pay no 'tention ter de mule, who had turnt 'is head 'roun' en wuz lookin' at Sally ez ha'd ez he could, en stretchin' 'is neck en raisin' 'is years, en whin-nyin' kinder sof' ter hisse'f.

"'Yas, honey,' 'lows Dan, 'en you gwine ter feel fus' rate long ez you sticks ter me. Fer I's a better man dan dat low-down runaway nigger Primus dat you be'n wastin' yo' time wid.'

"Dan had let go de plough-handle, en had put his arm 'roun' Sally, en wuz des gwine ter kiss her, w'en sump'n ketch' 'im by de scruff er de neck en flung 'im 'way ober in de cotton-patch. W'en he pick' 'isse'f up, Sally had gone kitin' down de tu'n-row, en de mule wuz stan'in' dere lookin' ez ca'm en peaceful ez a Sunday mawnin'.

"Fus' Dan had 'lowed it wuz de oberseah w'at had cotch' 'im wastin' 'is time. But dey wa'n't no oberseah in sight, so he 'cluded it must 'a' be'n de mule. So he pitch' inter de mule en lammed 'im ez ha'd ez he could. De mule tuk it all, en 'peared ter be ez 'umble ez a mule could be; but w'en dey wuz makin' de turn at de een' er de row, one er de plough-lines got under de mule's hin' leg. Dan retch' down ter git de line out, sorter keerless like, w'en de mule haul' off en kick him clean ober de fence inter a brier-patch on de yuther side.

"Dan wuz mighty so' fum 'is woun's en scratches, en wuz laid up fer two er th'ee days. One night de noo mule got out'n de pastur', en went down to de quarters. Dan wuz layin' dere on his pallet, w'en he heard sump'n bangin' erway at de side er his cabin. He raise' up on one shoulder en look' roun', w'en w'at should he see but de noo mule's head stickin' in de winder, wid his lips drawed back over his toofs, grinnin' en snappin' at Dan des' lack he wanter eat 'im up. Den de mule went roun' ter de do', en kick' er-way lack he wanter break de do' down, 'tel bimeby somebody come 'long en driv him back ter de pastur'. W'en Sally come in a little later fum de big house, whar she'd be'n waitin' on de w'ite folks, she foun' po' Dan nigh 'bout dead, he wuz so skeered. She 'lowed Dan had had de nightmare; but w'en dey look' at de do', dey seed de marks er de mule's huffs, so dey could n' be no mistake 'bout w'at had happen'.

"Co'se de niggers tol' dey marster 'bout de mule's gwines-on. Fust he did n' pay no 'tention ter it, but atter a w'ile he tol' 'em ef dey did n' stop dey foolis'ness, he gwine tie some un 'em up. So atter dat dey did n' say nuffin mo' ter dey marster, but dey kep' on noticin' de mule's quare ways des de same.

"'Long 'bout de middle er de summer dey wuz a big camp-meetin' broke out down on de Wim'l'ton Road, en nigh 'bout all de po' w'ite folks en free niggers in de settlement got 'ligion, en lo en behol'! 'mongs' 'em wuz de cunjuh man w'at own' de shote w'at cha'med Primus.

"Dis cunjuh man wuz a Guinea nigger, en befo' he wuz sot free had use' ter b'long ter a gent'eman down in Sampson County. De cunjuh man say his daddy wuz a king, er a guv'ner, er some sorter w'at-you-may-call-'em 'way ober yander in Affiky whar de niggers come fum, befo' he was stoled erway en sol' ter de spekilaters. De cunjuh man had he'ped his marster out'n some trouble ernudder wid his goopher, en his marster had sot him free, en bought him a trac' er land down on de Wim'l'ton Road. He purten' ter be a cow-doctor, but eve'ybody knowed w'at he r'al'y wuz.

"De cunjuh man had n' mo' d'n come th'oo good, befo' he wuz tuk sick wid a col' w'at he kotch kneelin' on de groun' so long at de mou'ners' bench. He kep' gittin' wusser en wusser, en bimeby de rheumatiz tuk holt er 'im, en drawed him all up, 'tel one day he sont word up ter Mars Jim McGee's plantation, en ax' Pete, de nigger w'at tuk keer er de mules, fer ter come down dere dat night en fetch dat mule w'at his marster had bought fum de po' w'ite man dyoin' er de summer.

"Pete did n' know w'at de cunjuh man wuz dribin' at, but he did n' daster stay way; en so dat night, w'en he'd done eat his bacon en his hoe-cake, en drunk his 'lasses-en-water, he put a bridle on de mule, en rid 'im down ter de cunjuh man's cabin. W'en he got ter de do', he lit en hitch' de mule, en den knock' at de do'. He felt mighty jubous 'bout gwine in, but he was bleedst ter do it; he knowed he could n' he'p 'isse'f.

"'Pull de string,' sez a weak voice, en w'en Pete lif' de latch en went in, de cunjuh man was layin' on de bed, lookin' pale en weak, lack he did n' hab much longer fer ter lib.

"'Is you fotch' de mule?' sezee.

"Pete say yas, en de cunjuh man kep' on.

"'Brer Pete,' sezee, 'I's be'n a monst'us sinner man, en I's done a power er wickedness endyoin' er my days; but de good Lawd is wash' my sins erway, en I feels now dat I's boun' fer de kingdom. En I feels, too, dat I ain' gwine ter git up fum dis bed no mo' in dis worl', en I wants ter ondo some er de harm I done. En dat's de reason, Brer Pete, I sont fer you ter fetch dat mule down here. You 'member dat shote I was up ter yo' plantation inquirin' 'bout las' June?'

"'Yas,' says Brer Pete, 'I 'member yo' axin' 'bout a shote you had los'.'

"'I dunno whe'r you eber l'arnt it er no,' says de cunjuh man, 'but I done knowed yo' marster's Primus had tuk de shote, en I wuz boun' ter git eben wid 'im. So one night I cotch' 'im down by de swamp on his way ter a candy-pullin', en I th'owed a goopher mixtry on 'im, en turnt 'im ter a mule, en got a po' w'ite man ter sell de mule, en we 'vided de money. But I doan want ter die 'tel I turn Brer Primus back ag'in.'

"Den de cunjuh man ax' Pete ter take down one er two go'ds off'n a she'f in de corner, en one er two bottles wid some kin' er mixtry in 'em, en set 'em on a stool by de bed; en den he ax' 'im ter fetch de mule in.

"W'en de mule come in de do', he gin a snort, en started fer de bed, des lack he was gwine ter jump on it.

"'Hol' on dere, Brer Primus!' de cunjuh man hollered. 'I's monst'us weak, en ef you 'mence on me, you won't nebber hab no chance fer ter git turn' back no mo'.'

"De mule seed de sense er dat, en stood still. Den de cunjuh man tuk de go'ds en bottles, en 'mence' ter wuk de roots en yarbs, en de mule 'mence' ter turn back ter a man—fust his years, den de res' er his head, den his shoulders en arms. All de time de cunjuh man kep' on wukkin' his roots; en Pete en Primus could see he wuz gittin' weaker en weaker all de time.

"'Brer Pete,' sezee, bimeby, 'gimme a drink er dem bitters out'n dat green bottle on de she'f yander. I's gwine fas', en it'll gimme strenk fer ter finish dis wuk.'

"Brer Pete look' up on de mantel-piece, en he seed a bottle in de corner. It was so da'k in de cabin he could n' tell whe'r it wuz a green bottle er no. But he hilt de bottle ter de cunjuh man's mouf, en he tuk a big mouff'l. He had n' mo' d'n swallowed it befo' he 'mence' ter holler.

"'You gimme de wrong bottle, Brer Pete; dis yer bottle 's got pizen in it, en I's done fer dis time, sho'. Hol' me up, fer de Lawd's sake! 'tel I git th'oo turnin' Brer Primus back.'

"So Pete hilt him up, en he kep' on wukkin' de roots, 'tel he got de goopher all tuk off'n Brer Primus 'cep'n' one foot. He had n' got dis foot mo' d'n half turnt back befo' his strenk gun out enti'ely, en he drap' de roots en fell back on de bed.

"'I can't do no mo' fer you, Brer Primus,' sezee, 'but I hopes you will fergib me fer w'at harm I done you. I knows de good Lawd done fergib me, en I hope ter meet you bofe in glory. I sees de good angels waitin' fer me up yander, wid a long w'ite robe en a starry crown, en I'm on my way ter jine 'em.' En so de cunjuh man died, en Pete en Primus went back ter de plantation.

"De darkies all made a great 'miration w'en Primus come back. Mars Jim let on lack he did n' b'lieve de tale de two niggers tol'; he sez Primus had runned erway, en stay' 'tel he got ti'ed er de swamps, en den come back on him ter be fed. He tried ter 'count fer de shape er Primus' foot by sayin' Primus got his foot smash', er snake-bit, er sump'n, w'iles he wuz erway, en den stayed out in de woods whar he could n' git it kyoed up straight, 'stidder comin' long home whar a doctor could 'a' 'tended ter it. But de niggers all notice' dey marster did n' tie Primus up, ner take on much 'ca'se de mule wuz gone. So dey 'lowed dey marster must 'a' had his s'picions 'bout dat cunjuh man."

My wife had listened to Julius's recital with only a mild interest. When the old man had finished it she remarked:

"That story does not appeal to me, Uncle Julius, and is not up to your usual mark. It is n't pathetic, it has no moral that I can discover, and I can't see why you should tell it. In fact, it seems to me like nonsense."

The old man looked puzzled as well as pained. He had not pleased the lady, and he did not seem to understand why.

"I'm sorry, ma'm," he said reproachfully, "ef you doan lack dat tale. I can't make out w'at you means by some er dem wo'ds you uses, but I'm tellin' nuffin but de truf. Co'se I did n' see de cunjuh man tu'n 'im back, fer I wuz n' dere; but I be'n hearin' de tale fer twenty-five yeahs, en I ain' got no 'casion fer ter 'spute it. Dey's so many things a body knows is lies, dat dey ain' no use gwine roun' findin' fault wid tales dat mought des ez well be so ez not. F' instance, dey's a young nigger gwine ter school in town, en he come out heah de yuther day en 'lowed dat de sun stood still en de yeath turnt roun' eve'y day on a kinder axletree. I tol' dat young nigger ef he did n' take hisse'f 'way wid dem lies, I'd take a buggy-trace ter 'im; fer I sees de yeath stan'in' still all de time, en I sees de sun gwine roun' it, en ef a man can't b'lieve w'at 'e sees, I can't see no use in libbin'—mought's well die en be whar we can't see nuffin. En ernudder thing w'at proves de tale 'bout dis ole Primus is de way he goes on ef anybody ax' him how he come by dat club-foot. I axed 'im one day, mighty perlite en civil, en he call' me a' ole fool, en got so mad he ain' spoke ter me sence. Hit's monst'us quare. But dis is a quare worl', anyway yer kin fix it," concluded the old man, with a weary sigh.

"Ef you makes up yo' min' not ter buy dat mule, suh," he added, as he rose to go, "I knows a man w'at's got a good hoss he wants ter sell—leas'ways dat's w'at I heared. I'm gwine ter pra'rmeetin' ter-night, en I'm gwine right by de man's house, en ef you'd lack ter look at de hoss, I'll ax 'im ter fetch him roun'."

"Oh, yes," I said, "you can ask him to stop in, if he is passing. There will be no harm in looking at the horse, though I rather think I shall buy a mule."

Early next morning the man brought the horse up to the vineyard. At that time I was not a very good judge of horse-flesh. The horse appeared sound and gentle, and, as the owner assured me, had no bad habits. The man wanted a large price for the horse, but finally agreed to accept a much smaller sum, upon payment of which I became possessed of a very fine-looking animal. But alas for the deceitfulness of appearances! I soon ascertained that the horse was blind in one eye, and that the sight of the other was very defective; and not a month elapsed before my purchase developed most of the diseases that horse-flesh is heir to, and a more worthless, broken-winded, spavined quadruped never disgraced the noble name of horse. After worrying through two or three months of life, he expired one night in a fit of the colic. I replaced him with a mule, and Julius henceforth had to take his chances of driving some metamorphosed unfortunate.

Circumstances that afterwards came to my knowledge created in my mind a strong suspicion that Julius may have played a more than unconscious part in this transaction. Among other significant facts was his appearance, the Sunday following the purchase of the horse, in a new suit of store clothes, which I had seen displayed in the window of Mr. Solomon Cohen's store on my last visit to town, and had remarked on account of their striking originality of cut and pattern. As I had not recently paid Julius any money, and as he had no property to mortgage, I was driven to conjecture to account for his possession of the means to buy the clothes. Of course I would not charge him with duplicity unless I could prove it, at least to a moral certainty, but for a long time afterwards I took his advice only in small doses and with great discrimination.

SIS' BECKY'S PICKANINNY

We had not lived in North Carolina very long before I was able to note a marked improvement in my wife's health. The ozone-laden air of the surrounding piney woods, the mild and equable climate, the peaceful leisure of country life, had brought about in hopeful measure the cure we had anticipated. Toward the end of our second year, however, her ailment took an unexpected turn for the worse. She became the victim of a settled melancholy, attended with vague forebodings of impending misfortune.

"You must keep up her spirits," said our physician, the best in the neighboring town. "This melancholy lowers her tone too much, tends to lessen her strength, and, if it continue too long, may be fraught with grave consequences."

I tried various expedients to cheer her up. I read novels to her. I had the hands on the place come up in the evening and serenade her with plantation songs. Friends came in sometimes and talked, and frequent letters from the North kept her in touch with her former home. But nothing seemed to rouse her from the depression into which she had fallen.

One pleasant afternoon in spring, I placed an armchair in a shaded portion of the front piazza, and filling it with pillows led my wife out of the house and seated her where she would have the pleasantest view of a somewhat monotonous scenery. She was scarcely placed when old Julius came through the yard, and, taking off his tattered straw hat, inquired, somewhat anxiously:

"How is you feelin' dis afternoon, ma'm?"

"She is not very cheerful, Julius," I said. My wife was apparently without energy enough to speak for herself.

The old man did not seem inclined to go away, so I asked him to sit down. I had noticed, as he came up, that he held some small object in his hand. When he had taken his seat on the top step, he kept fingering this object—what it was I could not quite make out.

"What is that you have there, Julius?" I asked, with mild curiosity.

"Dis is my rabbit foot, suh."

This was at a time before this curious superstition had attained its present jocular popularity among white people, and while I had heard of it before, it had not yet outgrown the charm of novelty.

"What do you do with it?"

"I kyars it wid me fer luck, suh."

"Julius," I observed, half to him and half to my wife, "your people will never rise in the world until they throw off these childish superstitions and learn to live by the light of reason and common sense. How absurd to imagine that the fore-foot of a poor dead rabbit, with which he timorously felt his way along through a life surrounded by snares and pitfalls, beset by enemies on every hand, can promote happiness or success, or ward off failure or misfortune!"

"It is ridiculous," assented my wife, with faint interest.

"Dat's w'at I tells dese niggers roun' heah," said Julius. "De fo'-foot ain' got no power. It has ter be de hin'-foot, suh—de lef' hin'-foot er a grabeya'd rabbit, killt by a cross-eyed nigger on a da'k night in de full er de moon."

"They must be very rare and valuable," I said.

"Dey is kinder ska'ce, suh, en dey ain' no 'mount er money could buy mine, suh. I mought len' it ter anybody I sot sto' by, but I would n' sell it, no indeed, suh, I would n'."

"How do you know it brings good luck?" I asked.

"'Ca'se I ain' had no bad luck sence I had it, suh, en I's had dis rabbit foot fer fo'ty yeahs. I had a good marster befo' de wah, en I wa'n't sol' er-way, en I wuz sot free; en dat 'uz all good luck."

"But that does n't prove anything," I rejoined. "Many other people have gone through a similar experience, and probably more than one of them had no rabbit's foot."

"Law, suh! you doan hafter prove 'bout de rabbit foot! Eve'ybody knows dat; leas'ways eve'ybody roun' heah knows it. But ef it has ter be prove' ter folks w'at wa'n't bawn en raise' in dis naberhood, dey is a' easy way ter prove it. Is I eber tol' you de tale er Sis' Becky en her pickaninny?"

"No," I said, "let us hear it." I thought perhaps the story might inter-est my wife as much as or more than the novel I had meant to read from.

"Dis yer Becky," Julius began, "useter b'long ter ole Kunnel Pen'leton, who owned a plantation down on de Wim'l'ton Road, 'bout ten miles fum heah, des befo' you gits ter Black Swamp. Dis yer Becky wuz a fiel'-han', en a monst'us good 'un. She had a husban' oncet, a nigger w'at b'longed on de nex' plantation, but de man w'at owned her husban' died, en his lan' en his niggers had ter be sol' fer ter pay his debts. Kunnel Pen'leton 'lowed he'd 'a' bought dis nigger, but he had be'n bettin' on hoss races, en did n' hab no money, en so Becky's husban' wuz sol' erway ter Fuhginny.

"Co'se Becky went on some 'bout losin' her man, but she could n' he'p herse'f; en 'sides dat, she had her pickaninny fer ter comfo't her. Dis yer little Mose wuz de cutes', blackes', shiny-eyedes' little nigger you eber laid eyes on, en he wuz ez fon' er his mammy ez his mammy wuz er him. Co'se Becky had ter wuk en did n' hab much time ter was'e wid her baby. Ole Aun' Nancy, de plantation nuss down at de qua'ters, useter take keer er little Mose in de daytime, en atter de niggers come in fum de cotton-fiel' Becky 'ud git her chile en kiss 'im en nuss 'im, en keep 'im 'tel mawnin'; en on Sun-days she'd hab 'im in her cabin wid her all day long.

"Sis' Becky had got sorter useter gittin' 'long widout her husban', w'en one day Kunnel Pen'leton went ter de races. Co'se w'en he went ter de races, he tuk his hosses, en co'se he bet on 'is own hosses, en co'se he los' his money; fer Kunnel Pen'leton did n' nebber hab no luck wid his hosses, ef he did keep hisse'f po' projeckin' wid 'em. But dis time dey wuz a hoss name' Lightnin' Bug, w'at b'longed ter ernudder man, en dis hoss won de sweep-stakes; en Kunnel Pen'leton tuk a lackin' ter dat hoss, en ax' his owner w'at he wuz willin' ter take fer 'im.

"'I'll take a thousan' dollahs fer dat hoss,' sez dis yer man, who had a big plantation down to'ds Wim'l'ton, whar he raise' hosses fer ter race en ter sell.

"Well, Kunnel Pen'leton scratch' 'is head, en wonder whar he wuz gwine ter raise a thousan' dollahs; en he did n' see des how he could do it, fer he owed ez much ez he could borry a'ready on de skyo'ity he could gib. But he wuz des boun' ter hab dat hoss, so sezee:

"'I'll gib you my note fer 'leven hund'ed dollahs fer dat hoss.'

"De yuther man shuck 'is head, en sezee:

"'Yo' note, suh, is better'n gol', I doan doubt; but I is made it a rule in my bizness not ter take no notes fum nobody. Howsomeber, suh, ef you is kinder sho't er fun's, mos' lackly we kin make some kin' er bahg'in. En w'iles we is talkin', I mought's well say dat I needs ernudder good nigger down on my place. Ef you is got a good one ter spar', I mought trade wid you.'

"Now, Kunnel Pen'leton did n' r'ally hab no niggers fer ter spar', but he 'lowed ter hisse'f he wuz des bleedzd ter hab dat hoss, en so he sez, sezee:

"'Well, I doan lack ter, but I reckon I'll haf ter. You come out ter my plantation ter-morrer en look ober my niggers, en pick out de one you wants.'

"So sho' 'nuff nex' day dis yer man come out ter Kunnel Pen'leton's place en rid roun' de plantation en glanshed at de niggers, en who sh'd he pick out fum 'em all but Sis' Becky.

"'I needs a noo nigger 'oman down ter my place,' sezee, 'fer ter cook en wash, en so on; en dat young 'oman 'll des fill de bill. You gimme her, en you kin hab Lightnin' Bug.'"

"Now, Kunnel Pen'leton did n' lack ter trade Sis' Becky, 'ca'se she wuz nigh 'bout de bes' fiel'-han' he had; en 'sides, Mars Dugal' did n' keer ter take de mammies 'way fum dey chillun w'iles de chillun wuz little. But dis man say he want Becky, er e'se Kunnel Pen'leton could n' hab de race hoss.

"'Well,' sez de kunnel, 'you kin hab de 'oman. But I doan lack ter sen' her 'way fum her baby. W'at 'll you gimme fer dat nigger baby?'

"'I doan want de baby,' sez de yuther man. 'I ain' got no use fer de baby.'

"'I tell yer w'at I'll do,' 'lows Kunnel Pen'leton, 'I'll th'ow dat picka-ninny in fer good measure.'

"But de yuther man shuck his head. 'No,' sezee, 'I's much erbleedzd, but I doan raise niggers; I raises hosses, en I doan wanter be both'rin' wid no nigger babies. Nemmine de baby. I'll keep dat 'oman so busy she'll fer-git de baby; fer niggers is made ter wuk, en dey ain' got no time fer no sich foolis'ness ez babies.'

"Kunnel Pen'leton did n' wanter hu't Becky's feelin's—fer Kunnel Pen'leton wuz a kin'-hea'ted man, en nebber lack' ter make no trouble fer nobody—en so he tol' Becky he wuz gwine sen' her down ter Robeson County fer a day er so, ter he'p out his son-in-law in his wuk; en bein' ez dis yuther man wuz gwine dat way, he had ax' 'im ter take her 'long in his buggy.

"'Kin I kyar little Mose wid me, marster?' ax' Sis' Becky.

"'N-o,' sez de kunnel, ez ef he wuz studyin' whuther ter let her take 'im er no; 'I reckon you better let Aun' Nancy look atter yo' baby fer de day er two you'll be gone, en she'll see dat he gits ernuff ter eat 'tel you gits back.'

"So Sis' Becky hug' en kiss' little Mose, en tol' 'im ter be a good little pickaninny, en take keer er hisse'f, en not fergit his mammy w'iles she wuz gone. En little Mose put his arms roun' his mammy en lafft en crowed des lack it wuz monst'us fine fun fer his mammy ter go 'way en leabe 'im.

"Well, dis yer hoss trader sta'ted out wid Becky, en bimeby, atter dey'd gone down de Lumbe'ton Road fer a few miles er so, dis man tu'nt roun' in a diffe'nt d'rection, en kep' goin' dat erway, 'tel bimeby Sis' Becky up 'n ax' 'im ef he wuz gwine ter Robeson County by a noo road.

"'No, nigger,' sezee, 'I ain' gwine ter Robeson County at all. I's gwine ter Bladen County, whar my plantation is, en whar I raises all my hosses.'

"'But how is I gwine ter git ter Mis' Laura's plantation down in Robeson County?' sez Becky, wid her hea't in her mouf, fer she 'mence' ter git skeered all er a sudden.

"'You ain' gwine ter git dere at all,' sez de man. 'You b'longs ter me now, fer I done traded my bes' race hoss fer you, wid yo' ole marster. Ef you is a good gal, I'll treat you right, en ef you doan behabe yo'se'f—w'y, w'at e'se happens 'll be yo' own fault.'

"Co'se Sis' Becky cried en went on 'bout her pickaninny, but co'se it did n' do no good, en bimeby dey got down ter dis yer man's place, en he put Sis' Becky ter wuk, en fergot all 'bout her habin' a pickaninny.

"Meanw'iles, w'en ebenin' come, de day Sis' Becky wuz tuk 'way, little Mose 'mence' ter git res'less, en bimeby, w'en his mammy did n' come, he sta'ted ter cry fer 'er. Aun' Nancy fed 'im en rocked 'im en rocked 'im, en fin'lly he des cried en cried 'tel he cried hisse'f ter sleep.

"De nex' day he did n' 'pear ter be as peart ez yushal, en w'en night come he fretted en went on wuss 'n he did de night befo'. De nex' day his little eyes 'mence' ter lose dey shine, en he would n' eat nuffin, en he 'mence' ter look so peaked dat Aun' Nancy tuk 'n kyared 'im up ter de big house, en showed 'im ter her ole missis, en her ole missis gun her some med'cine fer 'im, en 'lowed ef he did n' git no better she sh'd fetch 'im up ter de big house ag'in, en dey 'd hab a doctor, en nuss little Mose up dere. Fer Aun' Nancy's ole missis 'lowed he wuz a lackly little nigger en wu'th raisin'.

"But Aun' Nancy had l'arn' ter lack little Mose, en she did n' wanter hab 'im tuk up ter de big house. En so w'en he did n' git no better, she gethered a mess er green peas, and tuk de peas en de baby, en went ter see ole Aun' Peggy, de cunjuh 'oman down by de Wim'l'ton Road. She gun Aun' Peggy de mess er peas, en tol' her all 'bout Sis' Becky en little Mose.

"'Dat is a monst'us small mess er peas you is fotch' me,' sez Aun' Peggy, sez she.

" 'Yas, I knows,' 'lowed Aun' Nancy, 'but dis yere is a monst'us small pickaninny.'

" 'You'll hafter fetch me sump'n mo',' sez Aun' Peggy, 'fer you can't 'spec' me ter was'e my time diggin' roots en wukkin' cunj'ation fer nuffin.'

" 'All right,' sez Aun' Nancy, 'I'll fetch you sump'n mo' nex' time.'

" 'You bettah,' sez Aun' Peggy, 'er e'se dey'll be trouble. W'at dis yer little pickaninny needs is ter see his mammy. You leabe 'im heah 'tel ebenin' en I'll show 'im his mammy.'

"So w'en Aun' Nancy had gone 'way, Aun' Peggy tuk'n wukked her roots, en tu'nt little Mose ter a hummin'-bird, en sont 'im off fer ter fin' his mammy.

"So little Mose flewed, en flewed, en flewed away, 'tel bimeby he got ter de place whar Sis' Becky b'longed. He seed his mammy wukkin' roun' de ya'd, en he could tell fum lookin' at her dat she wuz trouble' in her min' 'bout sump'n, en feelin' kin' er po'ly. Sis' Becky heared sump'n hummin' roun' en roun' her, sweet en low. Fus' she 'lowed it wuz a hummin'-bird; den she thought it sounded lack her little Mose croonin' on her breas' way back yander on de ole plantation. En she des 'magine' it wuz her little Mose, en it made her feel bettah, en she went on 'bout her wuk pearter 'n she'd done sence she'd be'n down dere. Little Mose stayed roun' 'tel late in de ebenin', en den flewed back ez hard ez he could ter Aun' Peggy. Ez fer Sis' Becky, she dremp all dat night dat she wuz holdin' her pickaninny in her arms, en kissin' him, en nussin' him, des lack she useter do back on de ole plantation whar he wuz bawn. En fer th'ee er fo' days Sis' Becky went 'bout her wuk wid mo' sperrit dan she'd showed sence she'd be'n down dere ter dis man's plantation.

"De nex' day atter he come back, little Mose wuz mo' pearter en better 'n he had be'n fer a long time. But to'ds de een' er de week he 'mence' ter git res'less ag'in, en stop' eatin', en Aun' Nancy kyared 'im down ter Aun' Peggy once mo', en she tu'nt 'im ter a mawkin'-bird dis time, en sont 'im off ter see his mammy ag'in.

"It did n' take him long fer ter git dere, en w'en he did, he seed his mammy standin' in de kitchen, lookin' back in de d'rection little Mose wuz comin' fum. En dey wuz tears in her eyes, en she look' mo' po'ly en peaked 'n she had w'en he wuz down dere befo'. So little Mose sot on a tree in de ya'd en sung, en sung, en sung, des fittin' ter split his th'oat. Fus' Sis' Becky did n' notice 'im much, but dis mawkin'-bird kep' stayin' roun' de house all day, en bimeby Sis' Becky des 'magine' dat mawkin'-bird wuz her little Mose crowin' en crowin', des lack he useter do w'en his mammy would come home at night fum de cotton-fiel'. De mawkin'-bird stayed roun' dere 'mos' all day, en w'en Sis' Becky went out in de ya'd one time, dis yer mawkin'-bird lit on her shoulder en peck' at de piece er bread she wuz eatin', en fluttered his wings so dey rub' up agin de side er her head. En w'en he flewed away 'long late in de ebenin', des 'fo' sundown, Sis' Becky felt mo' better 'n she had sence she had heared dat hummin'-bird a week er so pas'. En dat night she dremp 'bout ole times ag'in, des lack she did befo'.

"But dis yer totin' little Mose down ter ole Aun' Peggy, en dis yer gittin' things fer ter pay de cunjuh 'oman, use' up a lot er Aun' Nancy's time, en she begun ter git kinder ti'ed. 'Sides dat, w'en Sis' Becky had be'n on de plantation, she had useter he'p Aun' Nancy wid de young uns ebenin's en Sundays; en Aun' Nancy 'mence' ter miss 'er monst'us, 'speshly sence she got a tech er de rheumatiz herse'f, en so she 'lows ter ole Aun' Peggy one day:

"'Aun' Peggy, ain' dey no way you kin fetch Sis' Becky back home?'

"'Huh!' sez Aun' Peggy, 'I dunno 'bout dat. I'll hafter wuk my roots en fin' out whuther I kin er no. But it'll take a monst'us heap er wuk, en I can't was'e my time fer nuffin. Ef you'll fetch me sump'n ter pay me fer my trouble, I reckon we kin fix it.'

"So nex' day Aun' Nancy went down ter see Aun' Peggy ag'in.

"'Aun' Peggy,' sez she, 'I is fotch' you my bes' Sunday head-hankercher. Will dat do?'

"Aun' Peggy look' at de head-hankercher, en run her han' ober it, en sez she:

"'Yas, dat 'll do fus'-rate. I's be'n wukkin' my roots sence you be'n gone, en I 'lows mos' lackly I kin git Sis' Becky back, but it 's gwine take fig'rin' en studyin' ez well ez cunj'in'. De fus' thing ter do 'll be ter stop fetchin' dat pickaninny down heah, en not sen' 'im ter see his mammy no mo'. Ef he gits too po'ly, you lemme know, en I'll gib you some kin' er mixtry fer ter make 'im fergit Sis' Becky fer a week er so. So 'less'n you comes fer dat, you neenter come back ter see me no mo' 'tel I sen's fer you.'

"So Aun' Peggy sont Aun' Nancy erway, en de fus' thing she done wuz ter call a hawnet fum a nes' unner her eaves.

"'You go up ter Kunnel Pen'leton's stable, hawnet,' sez she, 'en sting de knees er de race hoss name' Lightnin' Bug. Be sho' en git de right one.'

"So de hawnet flewed up ter Kunnel Pen'leton's stable en stung Lightnin' Bug roun' de laigs, en de nex' mawnin' Lightnin' Bug's knees wuz all swoll' up, twice't ez big ez dey oughter be. W'en Kunnel Pen'leton went out ter de stable en see de hoss's laigs, hit would 'a' des made you trimble lack a leaf fer ter heah him cuss dat hoss trader. Howsomeber, he cool' off bimeby en tol' de stable boy fer ter rub Lightnin' Bug's laigs wid some linimum. De boy done ez his marster tol' 'im, en by de nex' day de swellin' had gone down consid'able. Aun' Peggy had sont a sparrer, w'at had a nes' in one er de trees close ter her cabin, fer ter watch w'at wuz gwine on 'roun' de big house, en w'en dis yer sparrer tol' 'er de hoss wuz gittin' ober de

swellin', she sont de hawnet back fer ter sting 'is knees some mo', en de
nex' mawnin' Lightnin' Bug's laigs wuz swoll' up wuss 'n befo'.

"Well, dis time Kunnel Pen'leton wuz mad th'oo en th'oo, en all de
way 'roun', en he cusst dat hoss trader up en down, fum *A* ter *Izzard*. He
cusst so ha'd dat de stable boy got mos' skeered ter def, en went off en hid
hisse'f in de hay.

"Ez fer Kunnel Pen'leton, he went right up ter de house en got out his
pen en ink, en tuk off his coat en roll' up his sleeves, en writ a letter ter dis
yer hoss trader, en sezee:

" 'You is sol' me a hoss w'at is got a ringbone er a spavin er sump'n, en
w'at I paid you fer wuz a soun' hoss. I wants you ter sen' my nigger 'oman
back en take yo' ole hoss, er e'se I'll sue you, sho 's you bawn.'

"But dis yer man wa'n't skeered a bit, en he writ back ter Kunnel
Pen'leton dat a bahg'in wuz a bahg'in; dat Lightnin' Bug wuz soun' w'en
he sol' 'im, en ef Kunnel Pen'leton did n' knowed ernuff 'bout hosses ter
take keer er a fine racer, dat wuz his own fune'al. En he say Kunnel Pen'leton kin sue en be cusst fer all he keer, but he ain' gwine ter gib up de nigger he bought en paid fer.

"W'en Kunnel Pen'leton got dis letter he wuz madder 'n he wuz befo',
'speshly 'ca'se dis man 'lowed he did n' know how ter take keer er fine
hosses. But he could n' do nuffin but fetch a lawsuit, en he knowed, by his
own 'spe'ience, dat lawsuits wuz slow ez de seben-yeah eetch and cos' mo'
d'n dey come ter, en he 'lowed he better go slow en wait awhile.

"Aun' Peggy knowed w'at wuz gwine on all dis time, en she fix' up a
little bag wid some roots en one thing en ernudder in it, en gun it ter dis
sparrer er her'n, en tol' 'im ter take it 'way down yander whar Sis' Becky
wuz, en drap it right befo' de do' er her cabin, so she'd be sho' en fin' it de
fus' time she come out'n de do'.

"One night Sis' Becky dremp' her pickaninny wuz dead, en de nex'
day she wuz mo'nin' en groanin' all day. She dremp' de same dream th'ee
nights runnin', en den, de nex' mawnin' atter de las' night, she foun' dis yer
little bag de sparrer had drap' in front her do'; en she 'lowed she'd be'n
cunju'd, en wuz gwine ter die, en ez long ez her pickaninny wuz dead dey
wa'n't no use tryin' ter do nuffin nohow. En so she tuk 'n went ter bed, en
tol' her marster she'd be'n cunju'd en wuz gwine ter die.

"Her marster lafft at her, en argyed wid her, en tried ter 'suade her
out'n dis yer fool notion, ez he called it—fer he wuz one er dese yer w'ite
folks w'at purten' dey doan b'liebe in cunj'in'—but hit wa'n't no use. Sis'
Becky kep' gittin' wusser en wusser, 'tel fin'lly dis yer man 'lowed Sis' Becky
wuz gwine ter die, sho' 'nuff. En ez he knowed dey had n' be'n nuffin de matter wid Lightnin' Bug w'en he traded 'im, he 'lowed mebbe he could kyo'
'im en fetch 'im roun' all right, leas'ways good 'nuff ter sell ag'in. En any-

how, a lame hoss wuz better 'n a dead nigger. So he sot down en writ Kunnel Pen'leton a letter.

"'My conscience,' sezee, 'has be'n troublin' me 'bout dat ringbone' hoss I sol' you. Some folks 'lows a hoss trader ain' got no conscience, but dey doan know me, fer dat is my weak spot, en de reason I ain' made no mo' money hoss tradin'. Fac' is,' sezee, 'I is got so I can't sleep nights fum studyin' 'bout dat spavin' hoss; en I is made up my min' dat, w'iles a bahg'in is a bahg'in, en you seed Lightnin' Bug befo' you traded fer 'im, principle is wuth mo' d'n money er hosses er niggers. So ef you'll sen' Lightnin' Bug down heah, I'll sen' yo' nigger 'oman back, en we 'll call de trade off, en be ez good frien's ez we eber wuz, en no ha'd feelin's.'

"So sho' 'nuff, Kunnel Pen'leton sont de hoss back. En w'en de man w'at come ter bring Lightnin' Bug tol' Sis' Becky her pickaninny wa'n't dead, Sis' Becky wuz so glad dat she 'lowed she wuz gwine ter try ter lib 'tel she got back whar she could see little Mose once mo'. En w'en she retch' de ole plantation en seed her baby kickin' en crowin' en holdin' out his little arms to'ds her, she wush' she wuz n' cunju'd en did n' hafter die. En w'en Aun' Nancy tol' 'er all 'bout Aun' Peggy, Sis' Becky went down ter see de cunjuh 'oman, en Aun' Peggy tol' her she had cunju'd her. En den Aun' Peggy tuk de goopher off'n her, en she got well, en stayed on de plantation, en raise' her pickaninny. En w'en little Mose growed up, he could sing en whistle des lack a mawkin'-bird, so dat de w'ite folks useter hab 'im come up ter de big house at night, en whistle en sing fer 'em, en dey useter gib 'im money en vittles en one thing er ernudder, w'ich he alluz tuk home ter his mammy; fer he knowed all 'bout w'at she had gone th'oo. He tu'nt out ter be a sma't man, en l'arnt de blacksmif trade; en Kunnel Pen'leton let 'im hire his time. En bimeby he bought his mammy en sot her free, en den he bought hisse'f, en tuk keer er Sis' Becky ez long ez dey bofe libbed."

My wife had listened to this story with greater interest than she had manifested in any subject for several days. I had watched her furtively from time to time during the recital, and had observed the play of her countenance. It had expressed in turn sympathy, indignation, pity, and at the end lively satisfaction.

"That is a very ingenious fairy tale, Julius," I said, "and we are much obliged to you."

"Why, John!" said my wife severely, "the story bears the stamp of truth, if ever a story did."

"Yes," I replied, "especially the humming-bird episode, and the mocking-bird digression, to say nothing of the doings of the hornet and the sparrow."

"Oh, well, I don't care," she rejoined, with delightful animation; "those are mere ornamental details and not at all essential. The story is true to nature, and might have happened half a hundred times, and no doubt did happen, in those horrid days before the war."

"By the way, Julius," I remarked, "your story does n't establish what you started out to prove—that a rabbit's foot brings good luck."

"Hit's plain 'nuff ter me, suh," replied Julius. "I bet young missis dere kin 'splain it herse'f."

"I rather suspect," replied my wife promptly, "that Sis' Becky had no rabbit's foot."

"You is hit de bull's-eye de fus' fire, ma'm," assented Julius. "Ef Sis' Becky had had a rabbit foot, she nebber would 'a' went th'oo all dis trouble."

I went into the house for some purpose, and left Julius talking to my wife. When I came back a moment later, he was gone.

My wife's condition took a turn for the better from this very day, and she was soon on the way to ultimate recovery. Several weeks later, after she had resumed her afternoon drives, which had been interrupted by her illness, Julius brought the rockaway round to the front door one day, and I assisted my wife into the carriage.

"John," she said, before I had taken my seat, "I wish you would look in my room, and bring me my handkerchief. You will find it in the pocket of my blue dress."

I went to execute the commission. When I pulled the handkerchief out of her pocket, something else came with it and fell on the floor. I picked up the object and looked at it. It was Julius's rabbit's foot.

THE GRAY WOLF'S HA'NT

It was a rainy day at the vineyard. The morning had dawned bright and clear. But the sky had soon clouded, and by nine o'clock there was a light shower, followed by others at brief intervals. By noon the rain had settled into a dull, steady downpour. The clouds hung low, and seemed to grow denser instead of lighter as they discharged their watery burden, and there was now and then a muttering of distant thunder. Outdoor work was suspended, and I spent most of the day at the house, looking over my accounts and bringing up some arrears of correspondence.

Towards four o'clock I went out on the piazza, which was broad and dry, and less gloomy than the interior of the house, and composed myself for a quiet smoke. I had lit my cigar and opened the volume I was reading at that time, when my wife, whom I had left dozing on a lounge, came out and took a rocking-chair near me.

"I wish you would talk to me, or read to me—or something," she exclaimed petulantly. "It's awfully dull here today."

"I'll read to you with pleasure," I replied, and began at the point where I had found my bookmark:

" 'The difficulty of dealing with transformations so many-sided as those which all existences have undergone, or are undergoing, is such as to make a complete and deductive interpretation almost hopeless. So to grasp the total process of redistribution of matter and motion as to see simultaneously its several necessary results in their actual interdependence is scarcely possible. There is, however, a mode of rendering the process as a whole tolerably comprehensible. Though the genesis of the rearrangement of every evolving aggregate is in itself one, it presents to our intelligence' "—

"John," interrupted my wife, "I wish you would stop reading that nonsense and see who that is coming up the lane."

I closed my book with a sigh. I had never been able to interest my wife in the study of philosophy, even when presented in the simplest and most lucid form.

Some one was coming up the lane; at least, a huge faded cotton umbrella was making progress toward the house, and beneath it a pair of nether extremities in trousers was discernible. Any doubt in my mind as to whose they were was soon resolved when Julius reached the steps and, putting the umbrella down, got a good dash of the rain as he stepped up on the porch.

"Why in the world, Julius," I asked, "did n't you keep the umbrella up until you got under cover?"

"It's bad luck, suh, ter raise a' umbrella in de house, en w'iles I dunno whuther it's bad luck ter kyar one inter de piazzer er no, I 'lows it's alluz bes' ter be on de safe side. I did n' s'pose you en young missis 'u'd be gwine on yo' dribe ter-day, but bein' ez it's my pa't ter take you ef you does, I 'lowed I'd repo't fer dooty, en let you say whuther er no you wants ter go."

"I'm glad you came, Julius," I responded. "We don't want to go driving, of course, in the rain, but I should like to consult you about another matter. I'm thinking of taking in a piece of new ground. What do you imagine it would cost to have that neck of woods down by the swamp cleared up?"

The old man's countenance assumed an expression of unwonted seriousness, and he shook his head doubtfully.

"I dunno 'bout dat, suh. It mought cos' mo', en it mought cos' less, ez fuh ez money is consarned. I ain' denyin' you could cl'ar up dat trac' er lan' fer a hund'ed er a couple er hund'ed dollahs—ef you wants ter cl'ar it up. But ef dat 'uz my trac' er lan', I would n' 'sturb it, no, suh, I would n'; sho 's you bawn, I would n'."

"But why not?" I asked.

"It ain' fittin' fer grapes, fer noo groun' nebber is."

"I know it, but"—

"It ain' no yeathly good fer cotton, 'ca'se it's too low."

"Perhaps so; but it will raise splendid corn."

"I dunno," rejoined Julius deprecatorily. "It's so nigh de swamp dat de 'coons 'll eat up all de cawn."

"I think I'll risk it," I answered.

"Well, suh," said Julius, "I wushes you much joy er yo' job. Ef you has bad luck er sickness er trouble er any kin', doan blame *me*. You can't say ole Julius did n' wa'n you."

"Warn him of what, Uncle Julius?" asked my wife.

"Er de bad luck w'at follers folks w'at 'sturbs dat trac' er lan'. Dey is snakes en sco'pions in dem woods. En ef you manages ter 'scape de p'isen animals, you is des boun' ter hab a ha'nt ter settle wid—ef you doan hab two."

"Whose haunt?" my wife demanded, with growing interest.

"De gray wolf's ha'nt, some folks calls it—but I knows better."

"Tell us about it, Uncle Julius," said my wife. "A story will be a god-send to-day."

It was not difficult to induce the old man to tell a story, if he were in a reminiscent mood. Of tales of the old slavery days he seemed indeed to possess an exhaustless store—some weirdly grotesque, some broadly humorous; some bearing the stamp of truth, faint, perhaps, but still discernible; others palpable inventions, whether his own or not we never knew, though his fancy doubtless embellished them. But even the wildest was not without an element of pathos—the tragedy, it might be, of the story itself; the shadow, never absent, of slavery and of ignorance; the sadness, always, of life as seen by the fading light of an old man's memory.

"Way back yander befo' de wah," began Julius, "ole Mars Dugal' McAdoo useter own a nigger name' Dan. Dan wuz big en strong en hearty en peaceable en good-nachu'd most er de time, but dange'ous ter agger-vate. He alluz done his task, en nebber had no trouble wid de w'ite folks, but woe be unter de nigger w'at 'lowed he c'd fool wid Dan, fer he wuz mos' sho' ter git a good lammin'. Soon ez eve'ybody foun' Dan out, dey did n' many un 'em 'temp' ter 'sturb 'im. De one dat did would 'a' wush' he had n', ef he could 'a' libbed long ernuff ter do any wushin'.

"It all happen' dis erway. Dey wuz a cunjuh man w'at libbed ober t' other side er de Lumbe'ton Road. He had be'n de only cunjuh doctor in de naberhood fer lo ! dese many yeahs, 'tel ole Aun' Peggy sot up in de bizness down by de Wim'l'ton Road. Dis cunjuh man had a son w'at libbed wid 'im, en it wuz dis yer son w'at got mix' up wid Dan—en all 'bout a 'oman. "Dey wuz a gal on de plantation name' Mahaly. She wuz a monst'us lackly gal—tall en soopl', wid big eyes, en a small foot, en a lively tongue, en w'en Dan tuk ter gwine wid 'er eve'ybody 'lowed dey wuz well match', en none er de yuther nigger men on de plantation das' ter go nigh her, fer dey wuz all feared er Dan.

"Now, it happen' dat dis yer cunjuh man's son wuz gwine 'long de road one day, w'en who sh'd come pas' but Mahaly. En de minute dis man sot eyes on Mahaly, he 'lowed he wuz gwine ter hab her fer hisse'f. He come up side er her en 'mence' ter talk ter her; but she did n' paid no 'tention ter 'im, fer she wuz studyin' 'bout Dan, en she did n' lack dis nigger's looks nohow. So w'en she got ter whar she wuz gwine, dis yer man wa'n't no fu'ther 'long dan he wuz w'en he sta'ted.

"Co'se, atter he had made up his min' fer ter git Mahaly, he 'mence' ter 'quire 'roun', en soon foun' out all 'bout Dan, en w'at a dange'ous nigger he wuz. But dis man 'lowed his daddy wuz a cunjuh man, en so he'd come out all right in de een'; en he kep' right on atter Mahaly. Meanw'iles Dan's marster had said dey could git married ef dey wanter, en so Dan en Mahaly had tuk up wid one ernudder, en wuz libbin' in a cabin by deyse'ves, en wuz des wrop' up in one ernudder.

"But dis yer cunjuh man's son did n' 'pear ter min' Dan's takin' up wid Mahaly, en he kep' on hangin' 'roun' des de same, 'tel fin'lly one day Mahaly sez ter Dan, sez she:

"'I wush you'd do sump'n ter stop dat free nigger man fum follerin' me 'roun'. I doan lack him nohow, en I ain' got no time fer ter was'e wid no man but you.'

"Co'se Dan got mad w'en he heared 'bout dis man pest'rin' Mahaly, en de nex' night, w'en he seed dis nigger comin' 'long de road, he up en ax' 'im w'at he mean by hangin' 'roun' his 'oman. De man did n' 'spon' ter suit Dan, en one wo'd led ter ernudder, 'tel bimeby dis cunjuh man's son pull' out a knife en sta'ted ter stick it in Dan; but befo' he could git it drawed good, Dan haul' off en hit 'im in de head so ha'd dat he nebber got up. Dan 'lowed he'd come to atter a w'ile en go 'long 'bout his bizness, so he went off en lef' 'im layin' dere on de groun'.

"De nex' mawnin' de man wuz foun' dead. Dey wuz a great 'miration made 'bout it, but Dan did n' say nuffin, en none er de yuther niggers had n' seed de fight, so dey wa'n't no way ter tell who done de killin'. En bein' ez it wuz a free nigger, en dey wa'n't no w'ite folks 'speshly int'rusted, dey wa'n't nuffin done 'bout it, en de cunjuh man come en tuk his son en kyared 'im 'way en buried 'im.

"Now, Dan had n' meant ter kill dis nigger, en w'iles he knowed de man had n' got no mo' d'n he desarved, Dan 'mence' ter worry mo' er less. Fer he knowed dis man's daddy would wuk his roots en prob'ly fin' out who had killt 'is son, en make all de trouble fer 'im he could. En Dan kep' on studyin' 'bout dis 'tel he got so he did n' ha'dly das' ter eat er drink fer fear dis cunjuh man had p'isen' de vittles er de water. Fin'lly he 'lowed he'd go ter see Aun' Peggy, de noo cunjuh 'oman w'at had moved down by de Wim'l'ton Road, en ax her fer ter do sump'n ter pertec' 'im fum dis cunjuh man. So he tuk a peck er 'taters en went down ter her cabin one night.

"Aun' Peggy heared his tale, en den sez she:

"'Dat cunjuh man is mo' d'n twice't ez ole ez I is, en he kin make monst'us powe'ful goopher. W'at you needs is a life-cha'm, en I'll make you one ter-morrer; it's de on'y thing w'at 'll do you any good. You leabe me a couple er ha'rs fum yo' head, en fetch me a pig ter-morrer night fer ter roas', en w'en you come I'll hab de cha'm all ready fer you.'

"So Dan went down ter Aun' Peggy de nex' night—wid a young shote—en Aun' Peggy gun 'im de cha'm. She had tuk de ha'rs Dan had lef' wid 'er, en a piece er red flannin, en some roots en yarbs, en had put 'em in a little bag made out'n 'coon-skin.

"'You take dis cha'm,' sez she, 'en put it in a bottle er a tin box, en bury it deep unner de root er a live-oak tree, en ez long ez it stays dere safe en soun', dey ain' no p'isen kin p'isen you, dey ain' no rattlesnake kin bite you, dey ain' no sco'pion kin sting you. Dis yere cunjuh man mought do one thing er 'nudder ter you, but he can't kill you. So you neenter be at all skeered, but go 'long 'bout yo' bizness en doan bother yo' min'.'

"So Dan went down by de ribber, en 'way up on de bank he buried de cha'm deep unner de root er a live-oak tree, en kivered it up en stomp' de dirt down en scattered leaves ober de spot, en den went home wid his min' easy.

"Sho' 'nuff, dis yer cunjuh man wukked his roots, des ez Dan had 'spected he would, en soon l'arn' who killt his son. En co'se he made up his min' fer ter git eben wid Dan. So he sont a rattlesnake fer ter sting 'im, but de rattlesnake say de nigger's heel wuz so ha'd he could n' git his sting in. Den he sont his jay-bird fer ter put p'isen in Dan's vittles, but de p'isen did n' wuk. Den de cunjuh man 'low' he'd double Dan all up wid de rheumatiz, so he could n' git 'is han' ter his mouf ter eat, en would hafter sta've ter def; but Dan went ter Aun' Peggy, en she gun 'im a' 'intment ter kyo de rheumatiz. Den de cunjuh man 'lowed he'd bu'n Dan up wid a fever, but Aun' Peggy tol' 'im how ter make some yarb tea fer dat. Nuffin dis man tried would kill Dan, so fin'lly de cunjuh man 'lowed Dan mus' hab a life-cha'm.

"Now, dis yer jay-bird de cunjuh man had wuz a monst'us sma't creeter—fac', de niggers 'lowed he wuz de ole Debbil hisse'f, des settin' roun' waitin' ter kyar dis ole man erway w'en he'd retch' de een' er his rope. De cunjuh man sont dis jay-bird fer ter watch Dan en fin' out whar he kep' his cha'm. De jay-bird hung roun' Dan fer a week er so, en one day he seed Dan go down by de ribber en look at a live-oak tree; en den de jay-bird went back ter his marster, en tol' 'im he 'spec' de nigger kep' his life-cha'm under dat tree.

"De cunjuh man lafft en lafft, en he put on his bigges' pot, en fill' it wid his stronges' roots, en b'iled it en b'iled it, 'tel bimeby de win' blowed en blowed, 'tel it blowed down de live-oak tree. Den he stirred some more roots in de pot, en it rained en rained 'tel de water run down de ribber bank en wash' Dan's life-cha'm inter de ribber, en de bottle went bobbin' down de current des ez onconsarned ez ef it wa'n't takin' po' Dan's chances all 'long wid it. En den de cunjuh man lafft some mo', en 'lowed ter hisse'f dat he wuz gwine ter fix Dan now, sho' 'nuff; he wa'n't gwine ter kill 'im des yet, fer he could do sump'n ter 'im w'at would hu't wusser 'n killin'.

"So dis cunjuh man 'mence' by gwine up ter Dan's cabin eve'y night, en takin' Dan out in his sleep en ridin' 'im roun' de roads en fiel's ober de rough groun'. In de mawnin' Dan would be ez ti'ed ez ef he had n' be'n ter sleep. Dis kin' er thing kep' up fer a week er so, en Dan had des 'bout made up his min' fer ter go en see Aun' Peggy ag'in, w'en who sh'd he come across, gwine 'long de road one day, to'ds sundown, but dis yer cunjuh man. Dan felt kinder skeered at fus'; but den he 'membered 'bout his life-cha'm, w'ich he had n' be'n ter see fer a week er so, en 'lowed wuz safe en soun' unner de live-oak tree, en so he hilt up 'is head en walk' 'long, des lack he did n' keer nuffin 'bout dis man no mo' d'n any yuther nigger. W'en he got close ter de cunjuh man, dis cunjuh man sez, sezee:

"'Hoddy, Brer Dan? I hopes you er well?'

"W'en Dan seed de cunjuh man wuz in a good humor en did n' 'pear ter bear no malice, Dan 'lowed mebbe de cunjuh man had n' foun' out who killt his son, en so he 'termine' fer ter let on lack he did n' know nuffin, en so sezee:

"'Hoddy, Unk' Jube?'—dis ole cunjuh man's name wuz Jube. 'I's p'utty well, I thank you. How is you feelin' dis mawnin'?'

"'I's feelin' ez well ez a' ole nigger could feel w'at had los' his only son, en his main 'pen'ence in 'is ole age.

"'But den my son wuz a bad boy,' sezee, 'en I could n' 'spec' nuffin e'se. I tried ter l'arn him de arrer er his ways en make him go ter chu'ch en pra'r meetin'; but it wa'n't no use. I dunno who killt 'im, en I doan wanter know, fer I'd be mos' sho' ter fin' out dat my boy had sta'ted de fuss. Ef I'd 'a' had a son lack you, Brer Dan, I'd 'a' be'n a proud nigger; oh, yas, I would, sho's you bawn. But you ain' lookin' ez well ez you oughter, Brer Dan. Dey's sump'n de matter wid you, en w'at 's mo', I 'spec' you dunno w'at it is.'

"Now, dis yer kin' er talk nach'ly th'owed Dan off'n his gya'd, en fus' thing he knowed he wuz talkin' ter dis ole cunjuh man des lack he wuz one er his bes' frien's. He tol' 'im all 'bout not feelin' well in de mawnin', en ax' 'im ef he could tell w'at wuz de matter wid 'im.

"'Yas,' sez de cunjuh man. 'Dey is a witch be'n ridin' you right 'long. I kin see de marks er de bridle on yo' mouf. En I'll des bet yo' back is raw whar she's be'n beatin' you.'

"'Yas,' 'spon' Dan, 'so it is.' He had n' notice it befo', but now he felt des lack de hide had be'n tuk off'n 'im.

"'En yo' thighs is des raw whar de spurrers has be'n driv' in you,' sez de cunjuh man. 'You can't see de raw spots, but you kin feel 'em.'

"'Oh, yas,' 'lows Dan, 'dey does hu't pow'ful bad.'

"'En w'at's mo',' sez de cunjuh man, comin' up close ter Dan en whusp'in' in his yeah, 'I knows who it is be'n ridin' you.'

"'Who is it?' ax' Dan. 'Tell me who it is.'

"'It's a' ole nigger 'oman down by Rockfish Crick. She had a pet rabbit, en you cotch' 'im one day, en she's been squarin' up wid you eber sence. But you better stop her, er e'se you'll be rid ter def in a mont' er so.'

"'No,' sez Dan, 'she can't kill me, sho'.'

"'I dunno how dat is,' said de cunjuh man, 'but she kin make yo' life mighty mis'able. Ef I wuz in yo' place, I'd stop her right off.'

"'But how is I gwine ter stop her?' ax' Dan. 'I dunno nuffin 'bout stoppin' witches.'

"'Look a heah, Dan,' sez de yuther; 'you is a good young man. I lacks you monst'us well. Fac', I feels lack some er dese days I mought buy you fum yo' marster, ef I could eber make money ernuff at my bizness dese hard times, en 'dop' you fer my son. I lacks you so well dat I'm gwine ter he'p you git rid er dis yer witch fer good en all; fer des ez long ez she libs, you is sho' ter hab trouble, en trouble, en mo' trouble.'

"'You is de bes' frien' I got, Unk' Jube,' sez Dan, 'en I'll 'member yo' kin'ness ter my dyin' day. Tell me how I kin git rid er dis yer ole witch w'at 's be'n ridin' me so ha'd.'

"'In de fus' place,' sez de cunjuh man, 'dis ole witch nebber comes in her own shape, but eve'y night, at ten o'clock, she tu'ns herse'f inter a black cat, en runs down ter yo' cabin en bridles you, en mounts you, en dribes you out th'oo de chimbly, en rides you ober de roughes' places she kin fin'. All you got ter do is ter set fer her in de bushes 'side er yo' cabin, en hit her in de head wid a rock er a lighterd-knot w'en she goes pas'.'

"'But,' sez Dan, 'how kin I see her in de da'k? En s'posen I hits at her en misses her? Er s'posen I des woun's her, en she gits erway—w'at she gwine do ter me den?'

"'I is done studied 'bout all dem things,' sez de cunjuh man, 'en it 'pears ter me de bes' plan fer you ter foller is ter lemme tu'n you ter some creetur w'at kin see in de da'k, en w'at kin run des ez fas' ez a cat, en w'at kin bite, en bite fer ter kill; en den you won't hafter hab no trouble atter de job is done. I dunno whuther you'd lack dat er no, but dat is de sho'es' way.'

"'I doan keer,' 'spon' Dan. 'I'd des ez lief be anything fer a'hour er so, ef I kin kill dat ole witch. You kin do des w'at you er mineter.'

"'All right, den,' sez de cunjuh man, 'you come down ter my cabin at half-past nine o'clock ter-night, en I'll fix you up.'

"Now, dis cunjuh man, w'en he had got th'oo talkin' wid Dan, kep' on down de road 'long de side er de plantation, 'tel he met Mahaly comin' home fum wuk des atter sundown.

"'Hoddy do, ma'm,' sezee; 'is yo' name Sis' Mahaly, w'at b'longs ter Mars Dugal' McAdoo?'

"'Yas,' 'spon' Mahaly, 'dat's my name, en I b'longs ter Mars Dugal'.'

"'Well,' sezee, 'yo' husban' Dan wuz down by my cabin dis ebenin', en he got bit by a spider er sump'n, en his foot is swoll' up so he can't walk. En he ax' me fer ter fin' you en fetch you down dere ter he'p 'im home.'

"Co'se Mahaly wanter see w'at had happen' ter Dan, en so she sta'ted down de road wid de cunjuh man. Ez soon ez he got her inter his cabin, he shet de do', en sprinkle' some goopher mixtry on her, en tu'nt her ter a black cat. Den he tuk'n put her in a bairl, en put a bo'd on de bairl, en a rock on de bo'd, en lef' her dere 'tel he got good en ready fer ter use her.

"'Long 'bout half-pas' nine o'clock Dan come down ter de cunjuh man's cabin. It wuz a wa'm night, en de do' wuz stan'in' open. De cunjuh man 'vited Dan ter come in, en pass' de time er day wid 'im. Ez soon ez Dan 'mence' talkin', he heared a cat miauin' en scratchin' en gwine on at a tarrable rate.

"'W'at 's all dat fuss 'bout?' ax' Dan.

"'Oh, dat ain' nuffin but my ole gray tomcat,' sez de cunjuh man. 'I has ter shet 'im up sometimes fer ter keep 'im in nights, en co'se he doan lack it.

"'Now,' 'lows de cunjuh man, 'lemme tell you des w'at you is got ter do. W'en you ketches dis witch, you mus' take her right by de th'oat en bite her right th'oo de neck. Be sho' yo' teef goes th'oo at de fus' bite, en den you won't nebber be bothe'd no mo' by dat witch. En w'en you git done, come back heah en I'll tu'n you ter yo'se'f ag'in, so you kin go home en git yo' night's res'.'

"Den de cunjuh man gun Dan sump'n nice en sweet ter drink out'n a new go'd, en in 'bout a minute Dan foun' hisse'f tu'nt ter a gray wolf; en soon ez he felt all fo' er his noo feet on de groun', he sta'ted off fas' ez he could fer his own cabin, so he could be sho' en be dere time ernuff ter ketch de witch, en put a' een' ter her kyarin's-on.

"Ez soon ez Dan wuz gone good, de cunjuh man tuk de rock off'n de bo'd, en de bo'd off'n de bairl, en out le'p' Mahaly en sta'ted fer ter go home, des lack a cat er a 'oman er anybody e'se would w'at wuz in trouble; en it wa'n't many minutes befo' she wuz gwine up de path ter her own do'.

"Meanw'iles, w'en Dan had retch' de cabin, he had hid hisse'f in a bunch er jimson weeds in de ya'd. He had n' wait' long befo' he seed a black cat run up de path to'ds de do'. Des ez soon ez she got close ter 'im, he le'p' out en ketch' her by de th'oat, en got a grip on her, des lack de cunjuh man had tol' 'im ter do. En lo en behol'! no sooner had de blood 'mence' ter flow dan de black cat tu'nt back ter Mahaly, en Dan seed dat he had killt his own wife. En w'iles her bref wuz gwine she call' out:

"'O Dan! O my husban'! come en he'p me! come en sabe me fum dis wolf w'at 's killin' me!'

"W'en po' Dan sta'ted to'ds her, ez any man nach'ly would, it des made her holler wuss en wuss; fer she did n' knowed dis yer wolf wuz her Dan. En Dan des had ter hide in de weeds, en grit his teef en hol' hisse'f in, 'tel she passed out'n her mis'ry, callin' fer Dan ter de las', en wond'rin' w'y he did n' come en he'p her. En Dan 'lowed ter hisse'f he'd ruther 'a' be'n killt a dozen times 'n ter 'a' done w'at he had ter Mahaly.

"Dan wuz mighty nigh 'stracted, but w'en Mahaly wuz dead en he got his min' straighten' out a little, it did n' take 'im mo' d'n a minute er so fer ter see th'oo all de cunjuh man's lies, en how de cunjuh man had fooled 'im en made 'im kill Mahaly, fer ter git eben wid 'im fer killin' er his son. He kep' gittin' madder en madder, en Mahaly had n' much mo' d'n drawed her' las bref befo' he sta'ted back ter de cunjuh man's cabin ha'd ez he could run.

"W'en he got dere, de do' wuz stan'in' open; a lighterd-knot wuz flick-'rin' on de h'a'th, en de ole cunjuh man wuz settin' dere noddin' in de cor-ner. Dan le'p' in de do' en jump' fer dis man's th'oat, en got de same grip on 'im w'at de cunjuh man had tol' 'im 'bout half a' hour befo'. It wuz ha'd wuk dis time, fer de ole man's neck wuz monst'us tough en stringy, but Dan hilt on long ernuff ter be sho' his job wuz done right. En eben den he did n' hol' on long ernuff; fer w'en he tu'nt de cunjuh man loose en he fell ober on de flo', de cunjuh man rollt his eyes at Dan, en sezee:

"'I's eben wid you, Brer Dan, en you er eben wid me; you killt my son en I killt yo' 'oman. En ez I doan want no mo' d'n w'at 's fair 'bout dis thing, ef you'll retch up wid yo' paw en take down dat go'd hangin' on dat peg ober de chimbly, en take a sip er dat mixtry, it'll tu'n you back ter a nigger ag'in, en I kin die mo' sad'sfied 'n ef I lef' you lack you is.'

"Dan nebber 'lowed fer a minute dat a man would lie wid his las' bref, en co'se he seed de sense er gittin' tu'nt back befo' de cunjuh man died; so he clumb on a chair en retch' fer de go'd, en tuk a sip er de mixtry. En ez soon ez he'd done dat de cunjuh man lafft his las' laf, en gapsed out wid 'is las' gaps:

"'Uh huh! I reckon I's square wid you now fer killin' me, too; fer dat goopher on you is done fix' en sot now fer good, en all de cunj'in' in de worl' won't nebber take it off.

'Wolf you is en wolf you stays,
All de rest er yo' bawn days.'

"Co'se Brer Dan could n' do nuffin. He knowed it wa'n't no use, but he clumb up on de chimbly en got down de go'ds en bottles en yuther cunjuh fixin's, en tried 'em all on hisse'f, but dey did n' do no good. Den he run down ter ole Aun' Peggy, but she did n' know de wolf langwidge, en could n't 'a' tuk off dis yuther goopher nohow, eben ef she 'd 'a' unnerstood w'at Dan wuz sayin'. So po' Dan wuz bleedgd ter be a wolf all de rest er his bawn days.

"Dey foun' Mahaly down by her own cabin nex' mawnin', en eve'y body made a great 'miration 'bout how she 'd be'n killt. De niggers 'lowed a wolf had bit her. De w'ite folks say no, dey ain' be'n no wolves 'roun' dere fer ten yeahs er mo'; en dey did n' know w'at ter make out'n it. En w'en dey could n' fin' Dan nowhar, dey 'lowed he 'd quo'lled wid Mahaly en killt her, en run erway; en dey did n' know w'at ter make er dat, fer Dan en Mahaly wuz de mos' lovin' couple on de plantation. Dey put de dawgs on Dan's scent, en track' 'im down ter ole Unk' Jube's cabin, en foun' de ole man dead, en dey did n' know w'at ter make er dat; en den Dan's scent gun out, en dey did n' know w'at ter make er dat. Mars Dugal' tuk on a heap 'bout losin' two er his bes' han's in one day, en ole missis 'lowed it wuz a jedgment on 'im fer sump'n he 'd done. But dat fall de craps wuz monst'us big, so Mars Dugal' say de Lawd had temper' de win' ter de sho'n ram, en make up ter 'im fer w'at he had los'.

"Dey buried Mahaly down in dat piece er low groun' you er talkin' 'bout cl'arin' up. Ez fer po' Dan, he did n' hab nowhar e'se ter go, so he des stayed 'roun' Mahaly's grabe, w'en he wa'n't out in de yuther woods gittin' sump'n ter eat. En sometimes, w'en night would come, de niggers useter heah him howlin' en howlin' down dere, des fittin' ter break his hea't. En den some mo' un 'em said dey seed Mahaly's ha'nt dere 'bun'ance er times, colloguin' wid dis gray wolf. En eben now, fifty yeahs sence, long atter ole Dan has died en dried up in de woods, his ha'nt en Mahaly's hangs 'roun' dat piece er low groun', en eve'body w'at goes 'bout dere has some bad luck er 'nuther; fer ha'nts doan lack ter be 'sturb' on dey own stompin'-groun'."

The air had darkened while the old man related this harrowing tale. The rising wind whistled around the eaves, slammed the loose window-shutters, and, still increasing, drove the rain in fiercer gusts into the piazza. As Julius finished his story and we rose to seek shelter within doors, the blast caught the angle of some chimney or gable in the rear of the house, and bore to our ears a long, wailing note, an epitome, as it were, of re-morse and hopelessness.

"Dat's des lack po' ole Dan useter howl," observed Julius, as he reached for his umbrella, "en w'at I be'n tellin' you is de reason I doan lack ter see dat neck er woods cl'ared up. Co'se it b'longs ter you, en a man kin do ez he choose' wid 'is own. But ef you gits rheumatiz er fever en agur, er ef you er snake-bit er p'isen' wid some yarb er 'nuther, er ef a tree falls on you, er a ha'nt runs you en makes you git 'stracted in yo' min', lack some folks I knows w'at went foolin' 'roun' dat piece er lan', you can't say I neber wa'ned you, suh, en tol' you w'at you mought look fer en be sho' ter fin'."

When I cleared up the land in question, which was not until the fol-lowing year, I recalled the story Julius had told us, and looked in vain for a sunken grave or perhaps a few weather-bleached bones of some denizen of the forest. I cannot say, of course, that some one had not been buried there; but if so, the hand of time had long since removed any evidence of the fact. If some lone wolf, the last of his pack, had once made his den there, his bones had long since crumbled into dust and gone to fertilize the rank vegetation that formed the undergrowth of this wild spot. I did find, however, a bee-tree in the woods, with an ample cavity in its trunk, and an opening through which convenient access could be had to the stores of honey within. I have reason to believe that ever since I had bought the place, and for many years before, Julius had been getting honey from this tree. The gray wolf's haunt had doubtless proved useful in keeping off too inquisitive people, who might have interfered with his monopoly.

HOT-FOOT HANNIBAL

"I hate you and despise you! I wish never to see you or speak to you again!"

"Very well; I will take care that henceforth you have no opportunity to do either."

These words—the first in the passionately vibrant tones of my sister-in-law, and the latter in the deeper and more restrained accents of an angry man—startled me from my nap. I had been dozing in my hammock on the front piazza, behind the honeysuckle vine. I had been faintly aware of a buzz of conversation in the parlor, but had not at all awakened to its import until these sentences fell, or, I might rather say, were hurled upon my ear. I presume the young people had either not seen me lying there—the Venetian blinds opening from the parlor windows upon the piazza were partly closed on account of the heat—or else in their excitement they had forgotten my proximity.

I felt somewhat concerned. The young man, I had remarked, was proud, firm, jealous of the point of honor, and, from my observation of him, quite likely to resent to the bitter end what he deemed a slight or an injustice. The girl, I knew, was quite as high-spirited as young Murchison. I feared she was not so just, and hoped she would prove more yielding. I knew that her affections were strong and enduring, but that her temperament was capricious, and her sunniest moods easily overcast by some small cloud of jealousy or pique. I had never imagined, however, that she was capable of such intensity as was revealed by these few words of hers. As I say, I felt concerned. I had learned to like Malcolm Murchison, and had heartily consented to his marriage with my ward; for it was in that capacity that I had stood for a year or two to my wife's younger sister, Mabel. The match thus rudely broken off had promised to be another link binding me to the kindly Southern people among whom I had not long before taken up my residence.

Young Murchison came out of the door, cleared the piazza in two strides without seeming aware of my presence, and went off down the lane at a furious pace. A few moments later Mabel began playing the piano loudly, with a touch that indicated anger and pride and independence and a dash of exultation, as though she were really glad that she had driven away forever the young man whom the day before she had loved with all the ardor of a first passion.

I hoped that time might heal the breach and bring the two young people together again. I told my wife what I had overheard. In return she gave me Mabel's version of the affair.

"I do not see how it can ever be settled," my wife said. "It is something more than a mere lovers' quarrel. It began, it is true, because she found fault with him for going to church with that hateful Branson girl. But before it ended there were things said that no woman of any spirit could stand. I am afraid it is all over between them."

I was sorry to hear this. In spite of the very firm attitude taken by my wife and her sister, I still hoped that the quarrel would be made up within a day or two. Nevertheless, when a week had passed with no word from young Murchison, and with no sign of relenting on Mabel's part, I began to think myself mistaken.

One pleasant afternoon, about ten days after the rupture, old Julius drove the rockaway up to the piazza, and my wife, Mabel, and I took our seats for a drive to a neighbor's vineyard, over on the Lumberton plank-road.

"Which way shall we go," I asked, "the short road or the long one?"

"I guess we had better take the short road," answered my wife. "We will get there sooner."

"It's a mighty fine dribe roun' by de big road, Mis' Annie," observed Julius, "en it doan take much longer to git dere."

"No," said my wife, "I think we will go by the short road. There is a bay-tree in blossom near the mineral spring, and I wish to get some of the flowers."

"I 'spec's you'd fin' some bay-trees 'long de big road, ma'm," suggested Julius.

"But I know about the flowers on the short road, and they are the ones I want."

We drove down the lane to the highway, and soon struck into the short road leading past the mineral spring. Our route lay partly through a swamp, and on each side the dark, umbrageous foliage, unbroken by any clearing, lent to the road solemnity, and to the air a refreshing coolness. About half a mile from the house, and about half-way to the mineral spring, we stopped at the tree of which my wife had spoken, and reaching up to the low-hanging boughs, I gathered a dozen of the fragrant white flowers. When I resumed my seat in the rockaway, Julius started the mare. She went on for a few rods, until we had reached the edge of a branch crossing the road, when she stopped short.

"Why did you stop, Julius?" I asked.

"I did n', suh," he replied. " 'T wuz de mare stop'. G' 'long dere, Lucy! W'at you mean by dis foolis'ness?"

Julius jerked the reins and applied the whip lightly, but the mare did not stir.

"Perhaps you had better get down and lead her," I suggested. "If you get her started, you can cross on the log and keep your feet dry."

Julius alighted, took hold of the bridle, and vainly essayed to make the mare move. She planted her feet with even more evident obstinacy.

"I don't know what to make of this," I said. "I have never known her to balk before. Have you, Julius?"

"No, suh," replied the old man, "I neber has. It's a cu'ous thing ter me, suh."

"What's the best way to make her go?"

"I 'spec's, suh, dat ef I'd tu'n her 'roun', she'd go de udder way."

"But we want her to go this way."

"Well, suh, I 'low ef we des set heah fo' er fibe minutes, she'll sta't up by herse'f."

"All right," I rejoined; "it is cooler here than any place I have struck today. We'll let her stand for a while, and see what she does."

We had sat in silence for a few minutes, when Julius suddenly ejaculated, "Uh huh! I knows w'y dis mare doan go. It des flash' 'cross my recommemb'ance."

"Why is it, Julius?" I inquired.

" 'Ca'se she sees Chloe."

"Where is Chloe?" I demanded.

"Chloe's done be'n dead dese fo'ty years er mo'," the old man returned. "Her ha'nt is settin' ober yander on de udder side er de branch, unner dat willer-tree, dis blessed minute."

"Why, Julius!" said my wife, "do you see the haunt?"

"No 'm," he answered, shaking his head, "I doan see 'er, but de mare sees 'er."

"How do you know?" I inquired.

"Well, suh, dis yer is a gray hoss, en dis yer is a Friday; en a gray hoss kin alluz see a ha'nt w'at walks on Friday."

"Who was Chloe?" said Mabel.

"And why does Chloe's haunt walk?" asked my wife.

"It 's all in de tale, ma'm," Julius replied, with a deep sigh. "It 's all in de tale."

"Tell us the tale," I said. "Perhaps, by the time you get through, the haunt will go away and the mare will cross."

I was willing to humor the old man's fancy. He had not told us a story for some time; and the dark and solemn swamp around us; the amber-colored stream flowing silently and sluggishly at our feet, like the waters of Lethe; the heavy, aromatic scent of the bays, faintly suggestive of funeral wreaths—all made the place an ideal one for a ghost story.

"Chloe," Julius began in a subdued tone, "use' ter b'long ter ole Mars' Dugal' McAdoo—my ole marster. She wuz a lackly gal en a smart gal, en ole mis' tuk her up ter de big house, en l'arnt her ter wait on de w'ite folks, 'tel bimeby she come ter be mis's own maid, en 'peared ter 'low she run de house herse'f, ter heah her talk erbout it. I wuz a young boy den, en use' ter wuk 'bout de stables, so I knowed eve'ythin' dat wuz gwine on 'roun' de plantation.

"Well, one time Mars' Dugal' wanted a house boy, en sont down ter de qua'ters fer ter hab Jeff en Hannibal come up ter de big house nex' mawnin'. Ole marster en ole mis' look' de two boys ober, en 'sco'sed wid deyse'ves fer a little w'ile, en den Mars' Dugal' sez, sezee:

"'We lacks Hannibal de bes', en we gwine ter keep him. Heah, Hannibal, you'll wuk at de house fum now on. En ef you er a good nigger en min's yo' bizness, I'll gib you Chloe fer a wife nex' spring. You other nigger, you Jeff, you kin go back ter de qua'ters. We ain' gwine ter need you.'

"Now Chloe had be'n stan'in' dere behin' ole mis' dyoin' all er dis yer talk, en Chloe made up her min' fum de ve'y fus' minute she sot eyes on dem two dat she did n' lack dat nigger Hannibal, en wa'n't neber gwine keer fer 'im, en she wuz des ez sho' dat she lack' Jeff, en wuz gwine ter set sto' by 'im, whuther Mars' Dugal' tuk 'im in de big house er no; en so co'se Chloe wuz monst'us sorry w'en ole Mars' Dugal' tuk Hannibal en sont Jeff back. So she slip' roun' de house en waylaid Jeff on de way back ter de qua'ters, en tol' 'im not ter be down-hea'ted, fer she wuz gwine ter see ef she could n' fin' some way er 'nuther ter git rid er dat nigger Hannibal, en git Jeff up ter de house in his place.

"De noo house boy kotch' on monst'us fas', en it wa'n't no time ha'dly befo' Mars' Dugal' en ole mis' bofe 'mence' ter 'low Hannibal wuz de bes' house boy dey eber had. He wuz peart en soopl', quick ez lightnin', en sha'p ez a razor. But Chloe did n' lack his ways. He wuz so sho' he wuz gwine ter git 'er in de spring, dat he did n' 'pear ter 'low he had ter do any co'tin', en w'en he 'd run 'cross Chloe 'bout de house, he 'd swell roun' 'er in a biggity way en say:

"'Come heah en kiss me, honey. You gwine ter be mine in de spring. You doan 'pear ter be ez fon' er me ez you oughter be.'

"Chloe did n' keer nuffin fer Hannibal, en had n' keered nuffin fer 'im, en she sot des ez much sto' by Jeff ez she did de day she fus' laid eyes on 'im. En de mo' fermilyus dis yer Hannibal got, de mo' Chloe let her min' run on Jeff, en one ebenin' she went down ter de qua'ters en watch', 'tel she got a chance fer ter talk wid 'im by hisse'f. En she tol' Jeff fer ter go down en see ole Aun' Peggy, de cunjuh 'oman down by de Wim'l'ton Road, en ax her ter gib 'im sump'n ter he'p git Hannibal out'n de big house, so de w'ite folks 'u'd sen' fer Jeff ag'in. En bein' ez Jeff did n' hab nuffin ter gib Aun' Peggy, Chloe gun 'im a silber dollah en a silk han'kercher fer ter pay her wid, fer Aun' Peggy neber lack ter wuk fer nobody fer nuffin.

"So Jeff slip' off down ter Aun' Peggy's one night, en gun 'er de present he brung, en tol' 'er all 'bout 'im en Chloe en Hannibal, en ax' 'er ter he'p 'im out. Aun' Peggy tol' 'im she 'd wuk 'er roots, en fer 'im ter come back de nex' night, en she 'd tell 'im w'at she c'd do fer 'im.

"So de nex' night Jeff went back, en Aun' Peggy gun 'im a baby doll, wid a body made out'n a piece er co'n-stalk, en wid splinters fer a'ms en laigs, en a head made out'n elderberry peth, en two little red peppers fer feet.

"'Dis yer baby doll,' sez she, 'is Hannibal. Dis yer peth head is Hannibal's head, en dese yer pepper feet is Hannibal's feet. You take dis en hide it unner de house, on de sill unner de do', whar Hannibal 'll hafter walk ober it eve'y day. En ez long ez Hannibal comes anywhar nigh dis baby doll, he 'll be des lack it is—light-headed en hot-footed; en ef dem two things doan git 'im inter trouble mighty soon, den I 'm no cunjuh 'oman. But w'en you git Hannibal out'n de house, en git all th'oo wid dis baby doll, you mus' fetch it back ter me, fer it 's monst'us powerful goopher, en is liable ter make mo' trouble ef you leabe it layin' roun'.'

"Well, Jeff tuk de baby doll, en slip' up ter de big house, en whistle' ter Chloe, en w'en she come out he tol' 'er w'at ole Aun' Peggy had said. En Chloe showed 'im how ter git unner de house, en w'en he had put de cunjuh doll on de sill, he went 'long back ter de qua'ters—en des waited.

"Nex' day, sho' 'nuff, de goopher 'mence' ter wuk. Hannibal sta'ted in de house soon in de mawnin' wid a armful er wood ter make a fire, en he had n' mo' d'n got 'cross de do'-sill befo' his feet begun ter bu'n so dat he drap' de armful er wood on de flo' en woke ole mis' up a' hour sooner 'n yushal, en co'se ole mis' did n' lack dat, en spoke sha'p erbout it.

"W'en dinner-time come, en Hannibal wuz help'n' de cook kyar de dinner f'm de kitchen inter de big house, en wuz gittin' close ter de do' whar he had ter go in, his feet sta'ted ter bu'n en his head begun ter swim, en he let de big dish er chicken en dumplin's fall right down in de dirt, in de middle er de ya'd, en de w'ite folks had ter make dey dinner dat day off'n col' ham en sweet'n' 'taters.

"De nex' mawnin' he overslep' hisse'f, en got inter mo' trouble. Atter breakfus', Mars' Dugal' sont 'im ober ter Mars' Marrabo Utley's fer ter borry a monkey wrench. He oughter be'n back in ha'f a' hour, but he come pokin' home 'bout dinner-time wid a screw-driver stidder a monkey wrench. Mars' Dugal' sont ernudder nigger back wid de screw-driver, en Hannibal did n' git no dinner. 'Long in de atternoon, ole mis' sot Hannibal ter weedin' de flowers in de front gya'den, en Hannibal dug up all de bulbs ole mis' had sont erway fer, en paid a lot er money fer, en tuk 'em down ter de hawg-pen by de ba'nya'd, en fed 'em ter de hawgs. W'en ole mis' come out in de cool er de ebenin', en seed w'at Hannibal had done, she wuz mos' crazy, en she wrote a note en sont Hannibal down ter de oberseah wid it.

"But w'at Hannibal got fum de oberseah did n' 'pear ter do no good. Eve'y now en den 'is feet 'd 'mence ter torment 'im, en 'is min' 'u'd git all mix' up, en his conduc' kep' gittin' wusser en wusser, 'tel fin'lly de w'ite folks could n' stan' it no longer, en Mars' Dugal' tuk Hannibal back down ter de qua'ters.

"'Mr. Smif,' sez Mars' Dugal' ter de oberseah, 'dis yer nigger has done got so triflin' yer lately dat we can't keep 'im at de house no mo', en I 's fotch' 'im ter you ter be straighten' up. You 's had 'casion ter deal wid 'im once, so he knows w'at ter expec'. You des take 'im in han', en lemme know how he tu'ns out. En w'en de han's comes in fum de fiel' dis ebenin' you kin sen' dat yaller nigger Jeff up ter de house. I'll try 'im, en see ef he 's any better 'n Hannibal.'

"So Jeff went up ter de big house, en pleas' Mars' Dugal' en ole mis' en de res' er de fambly so well dat dey all got ter lackin' 'im fus'rate; en dey 'd 'a' fergot all 'bout Hannibal, ef it had n' be'n fer de bad repo'ts w'at come up fum de qua'ters 'bout 'im fer a mont' er so. Fac' is, dat Chloe en Jeff wuz so int'rusted in one ernudder sence Jeff be'n up ter de house, dat dey fer-got all 'bout takin' de baby doll back ter Aun' Peggy, en it kep' wukkin' fer a w'ile, en makin' Hannibal's feet bu'n mo' er less, 'tel all de folks on de plantation got ter callin' 'im Hot-Foot Hannibal. He kep' gittin' mo' en mo' triflin', 'tel he got de name er bein' de mos' no 'countes' nigger on de plantation, en Mars' Dugal' had ter th'eaten ter sell 'im in de spring, w'en bimeby de goopher quit wukkin', en Hannibal 'mence' ter pick up some en make folks set a little mo' sto' by 'im.

"Now, dis yer Hannibal was a monst'us sma't nigger, en w'en he got rid er dem so' feet, his min' kep' runnin' on 'is udder troubles. Heah th'ee er fo' weeks befo' he'd had a' easy job, waitin' on de w'ite folks, libbin' off'n de fat er de lan', en promus' de fines' gal on de plantation fer a wife in de spring, en now heah he wuz back in de co'n-fiel', wid de oberseah a-cussin' en a-r'arin' ef he did n' get a ha'd tas' done; wid nuffin but co'n bread en bacon en merlasses ter eat; en all de fiel'-han's makin' rema'ks, en pokin' fun at 'im 'ca'se he'd be'n sont back fum de big house ter de fiel'. En de mo' Hannibal studied 'bout it de mo' madder he got, 'tel he fin'lly swo' he wuz gwine ter git eben wid Jeff en Chloe, ef it wuz de las' ac'.

"So Hannibal slipped 'way fum de qua'ters one Sunday en hid in de co'n up close ter de big house, 'tel he see Chloe gwine down de road. He waylaid her, en sezee:

"'Hoddy; Chloe?'

"'I ain' got no time fer ter fool wid fiel'-han's,' sez Chloe, tossin' her head; 'w'at you want wid me, Hot-Foot?'

"'I wants ter know how you en Jeff is gittin' 'long.'

"'I 'lows dat's none er yo' bizness, nigger. I doan see w'at 'casion any common fiel'-han' has got ter mix in wid de 'fairs er folks w'at libs in de big house. But ef it 'll do you any good ter know, I mought say dat me en Jeff is gittin' 'long mighty well, en we gwine ter git married in de spring, en you ain' gwine ter be 'vited ter de weddin' nuther.'

"'No, no!' sezee, 'I would n' 'spec' ter be 'vited ter de weddin'—a common, low-down fiel'-han' lack I is. But I's glad ter heah you en Jeff is gittin' 'long so well. I did n' knowed but w'at he had 'mence' ter be a little ti'ed.'

"'Ti'ed er me? Dat's rediklus!' sez Chloe. 'W'y, dat nigger lubs me so I b'liebe he 'd go th'oo fire en water fer me. Dat nigger is des wrop' up in me.'

"'Uh huh,' sez Hannibal, 'den I reckon it mus' be some udder nigger w'at meets a 'oman down by de crick in de swamp eve'y Sunday ebenin', ter say nuffin 'bout two er th'ee times a week.'

"'Yas, hit is ernudder nigger, en you is a liah w'en you say it wuz Jeff.'

"'Mebbe I is a liah, en mebbe I ain' got good eyes. But 'less'n I is a liah, en 'less'n I ain' got good eyes, Jeff is gwine ter meet dat 'oman dis ebenin' 'long 'bout eight o'clock right down dere by de crick in de swamp 'bout half-way betwix' dis plantation en Mars' Marrabo Utley's.'

"Well, Chloe tol' Hannibal she did n' b'liebe a wo'd he said, en call' 'im a low-down nigger, who wuz tryin' ter slander Jeff 'ca'se he wuz mo' luckier 'n he wuz. But all de same, she could n' keep her min' fum runnin' on w'at Hannibal had said. She 'membered she 'd heared one er de niggers say dey wuz a gal ober at Mars' Marrabo Utley's plantation w'at Jeff use' ter go wid some befo' he got 'quainted wid Chloe. Den she 'mence' ter figger back, en sho' 'nuff, dey wuz two er th'ee times in de las' week w'en she 'd be'n he'pin' de ladies wid dey dressin' en udder fixin's in de ebenin', en Jeff mought 'a' gone down ter de swamp widout her knowin' 'bout it at all. En den she 'mence' ter 'member little things w'at she had n' tuk no notice of befo', en w'at 'u'd make it 'pear lack Jeff had sump'n on his min'.

"Chloe set a monst'us heap er sto' by Jeff, en would 'a' done mos' anythin' fer 'im, so long ez he stuck ter her. But Chloe wuz a mighty jealous 'oman, en w'iles she did n' b'liebe w'at Hannibal said, she seed how it could 'a' be'n so, en she 'termine' fer ter fin' out fer herse'f whuther it wuz so er no.

"Now, Chloe had n' seed Jeff all day, fer Mars' Dugal' had sont Jeff ober ter his daughter's house, young Mis' Ma'g'ret's, w'at libbed 'bout fo' miles fum Mars' Dugal's, en Jeff wuz n' 'spected home 'tel ebenin'. But des atter supper wuz ober, en w'iles de ladies wuz settin' out on de piazzer, Chloe slip' off fum de house en run down de road—dis yer same road we come; en w'en she got mos' ter de crick—dis yer same crick right befo' us— she kin' er kep' in de bushes at de side er de road, 'tel fin'lly she seed Jeff settin' on de bank on de udder side er de crick—right unner dat ole willer-tree droopin' ober de water yander. En eve'y now en den he 'd git up en look up de road to'ds Mars' Marrabo's on de udder side er de swamp.

"Fus' Chloe felt lack she 'd go right ober de crick en gib Jeff a piece er her min'. Den she 'lowed she better be sho' befo' she done anythin'. So she helt herse'f in de bes' she could, gittin' madder en madder eve'y minute, 'tel bimeby she seed a'oman comin' down de road on de udder side fum to'ds Mars' Marrabo Utley's plantation. En w'en she seed Jeff jump up en run to'ds dat 'oman, en th'ow his a'ms roun' her neck, po' Chloe did n' stop ter see no mo', but des tu'nt roun' en run up ter de house, en rush' up on de piazzer, en up en tol' Mars' Dugal' en ole mis' all 'bout de baby doll, en all 'bout Jeff gittin' de goopher fum Aun' Peggy, en 'bout w'at de goopher had done ter Hannibal.

"Mars' Dugal' wuz monst'us mad. He did n' let on at fus' lack he b'liebed Chloe, but w'en she tuk en showed 'im whar ter fin' de baby doll, Mars' Dugal' tu'nt w'ite ez chalk.

"'W'at debil's wuk is dis?' sezee. 'No wonder de po' nigger's feet eetched. Sump'n got ter be done ter l'arn dat ole witch ter keep her han's off'n my niggers. En ez fer dis yer Jeff, I'm gwine ter do des w'at I promus', so de darkies on dis plantation 'll know I means w'at I sez.'

"Fer Mars' Dugal' had warned de han's befo' 'bout foolin' wid cunju'ation; fac', he had los' one er two niggers hisse'f fum dey bein' goophered, en he would 'a' had ole Aun' Peggy whip' long ago, on'y Aun' Peggy wuz a free 'oman, en he wuz 'feard she 'd cunjuh him. En w'iles Mars' Dugal' say he did n' b'liebe in cunj'in' en sich, he 'peared ter 'low it wuz bes' ter be on de safe side, en let Aun' Peggy alone.

"So Mars' Dugal' done des ez he say. Ef ole mis' had ple'd fer Jeff, he mought 'a' kep' 'im. But ole mis' had n' got ober losin' dem bulbs yit, en she neber said a wo'd. Mars' Dugal' tuk Jeff ter town nex' day en' sol' 'im ter a spekilater, who sta'ted down de ribber wid 'im nex' mawnin' on a steamboat, fer ter take 'im ter Alabama.

"Now, w'en Chloe tol' ole Mars' Dugal' 'bout dis yer baby doll en dis udder goopher, she had n' ha'dly 'lowed Mars' Dugal' would sell Jeff down Souf. Howsomeber, she wuz so mad wid Jeff dat she 'suaded herse'f she did n' keer; en so she hilt her head up en went roun' lookin' lack she wuz rale glad 'bout it. But one day she wuz walkin' down de road, w'en who sh'd come 'long but dis yer Hannibal.

"W'en Hannibal seed 'er, he bus' out laffin' fittin' fer ter kill: 'Yah, yah, yah! ho, ho, ho! ha, ha, ha! Oh, hol' me, honey, hol' me, er I 'll laf myse'f ter def. I ain' nebber laf' so much sence I be'n bawn.'

"'W'at you laffin' at, Hot-Foot?'

"'Yah, yah, yah! W'at I laffin' at? W'y, I's laffin' at myse'f, tooby sho'— laffin' ter think w'at a fine 'oman I made.'

"Chloe tu'nt pale, en her hea't come up in her mouf.

"'W'at you mean, nigger?' sez she, ketchin' holt er a bush by de road fer ter stiddy herse'f. 'W'at you mean by de kin' er 'oman you made?'

"'W'at do I mean? I means dat I got squared up wid you fer treatin' me de way you done, en I got eben wid dat yaller nigger Jeff fer cuttin' me out. Now, he 's gwine ter know w'at it is ter eat co'n bread en merlasses once mo', en wuk fum daylight ter da'k, en ter hab a oberseah dribin' 'im fum one day's een' ter de udder. I means dat I sont wo'd ter Jeff dat Sunday dat you wuz gwine ter be ober ter Mars' Marrabo's visitin' dat ebenin', en you want 'im ter meet you down by de crick on de way home en go de rest er de road wid you. En den I put on a frock en a sun-bonnet, en fix' myse'f up ter look lack a 'oman; en w'en Jeff seed me comin', he run ter meet me, en you seed 'im—fer I 'd be'n watchin' in de bushes befo' en 'skivered you comin' down de road. En now I reckon you en Jeff bofe knows w'at it means ter mess wid a nigger lack me.'

"Po' Chloe had n' heared mo' d'n half er de las' part er w'at Hannibal said, but she had heared 'nuff to l'arn dat dis nigger had fooled her en Jeff, en dat po' Jeff had n' done nuffin, en dat fer lovin' her too much en goin' ter meet her she had cause' 'im ter be sol' erway whar she 'd neber, neber see 'im no mo'. De sun mought shine by day, de moon by night, de flowers mought bloom, en de mawkin'-birds mought sing, but po' Jeff wuz done los' ter her fereber en fereber.

"Hannibal had n' mo' d'n finish' w'at he had ter say, w'en Chloe's knees gun 'way unner her, en she fell down in de road, en lay dere half a' hour er so befo' she come to. W'en she did, she crep' up ter de house des ez pale ez a ghos'. En fer a mont' er so she crawled roun' de house, en 'peared ter be so po'ly dat Mars' Dugal' sont fer a doctor; en de doctor kep' on axin' her questions 'tel he foun' she wuz des pinin' erway fer Jeff.

"W'en he tol' Mars' Dugal', Mars' Dugal' lafft, en said he 'd fix dat. She could hab de noo house boy fer a husban'. But ole mis' say, no, Chloe ain' dat kin'er gal, en dat Mars' Dugal' sh'd buy Jeff back.

"So Mars' Dugal' writ a letter ter dis yer spekilater down ter Wim'l'ton, en tol' ef he ain' done sol' dat nigger Souf w'at he bought fum 'im, he 'd lack ter buy 'im back ag'in. Chloe 'mence' ter pick up a little w'en ole mis' tol' her 'bout dis letter. Howsomeber, bimeby Mars' Dugal' got a' answer fum de spekilater, who said he wuz monst'us sorry, but Jeff had fell ove'boa'd er jumped off'n de steamboat on de way ter Wim'l'ton, en got drownded, en co'se he could n' sell 'im back, much ez he 'd lack ter 'bleedge Mars' Dugal'.

"Well, atter Chloe heared dis, she wa'n't much mo' use ter nobody. She pu'tended ter do her wuk, en ole mis' put up wid her, en had de doctor gib her medicine, en let 'er go ter de circus, en all so'ts er things fer ter take her min' off'n her troubles. But dey did n' none un 'em do no good. Chloe got ter slippin' down here in de ebenin' des lack she 'uz comin' ter meet Jeff, en she 'd set dere unner dat willer-tree on de udder side, en wait fer 'im, night

atter night. Bimeby she got so bad de w'ite folks sont her ober ter young
Mis' Ma'g'ret's fer ter gib her a change; but she runned erway de fus' night,
en w'en dey looked fer 'er nex' mawnin', dey foun' her co'pse layin' in de
branch yander, right 'cross fum whar we 're settin' now.

"Eber sence den," said Julius in conclusion, "Chloe's ha'nt comes eve'y
ebenin' en sets down unner dat willer-tree en waits fer Jeff, er e'se walks up
en down de road yander, lookin' en lookin', en waitin' en waitin', fer her
sweethea't w'at ain' neber, neber come back ter her no mo'."

There was silence when the old man had finished, and I am sure I saw
a tear in my wife's eye, and more than one in Mabel's.

"I think, Julius," said my wife, after a moment, "that you may turn
the mare around and go by the long road."

The old man obeyed with alacrity, and I noticed no reluctance on the
mare's part.

"You are not afraid of Chloe's haunt, are you?" I asked jocularly.

My mood was not responded to, and neither of the ladies smiled.

"Oh, no," said Annie, "but I've changed my mind. I prefer the other
route."

When we had reached the main road and had proceeded along it for
a short distance, we met a cart driven by a young negro, and on the cart
were a trunk and a valise. We recognized the man as Malcolm Murchison's
servant, and drew up a moment to speak to him.

"Who's going away, Marshall?" I inquired.

"Young Mistah Ma'colm gwine 'way on de boat ter Noo Yo'k dis
ebenin', suh, en I 'm takin' his things down ter de wharf, suh."

This was news to me, and I heard it with regret. My wife looked sorry,
too, and I could see that Mabel was trying hard to hide her concern.

"He 's comin' 'long behin', suh, en I 'spec's you 'll meet 'im up de road
a piece. He 's gwine ter walk down ez fur ez Mistah Jim Williams's, en take
de buggy fum dere ter town. He 'spec's ter be gone a long time, suh, en say
prob'ly he ain' neber comin' back."

The man drove on. There were a few words exchanged in an undertone between my wife and Mabel, which I did not catch. Then Annie said:
"Julius, you may stop the rockaway a moment. There are some trumpet-
flowers by the road there that I want. Will you get them for me, John?"

I sprang into the underbrush, and soon returned with a great bunch
of scarlet blossoms.

"Where is Mabel?" I asked, noting her absence.

"She has walked on ahead. We shall overtake her in a few minutes."

The carriage had gone only a short distance when my wife discovered
that she had dropped her fan.

"I had it where we were stopping. Julius, will you go back and get it for me?"

Julius got down and went back for the fan. He was an unconscionably long time finding it. After we got started again we had gone only a little way, when we saw Mabel and young Murchison coming toward us. They were walking arm in arm, and their faces were aglow with the light of love.

I do not know whether or not Julius had a previous understanding with Malcolm Murchison by which he was to drive us round by the long road that day, nor do I know exactly what motive influenced the old man's exertions in the matter. He was fond of Mabel, but I was old enough, and knew Julius well enough, to be skeptical of his motives. It is certain that a most excellent understanding existed between him and Murchison after the reconciliation, and that when the young people set up housekeeping over at the old Murchison place, Julius had an opportunity to enter their service. For some reason or other, however, he preferred to remain with us. The mare, I might add, was never known to balk again.

Another Conjure Story

DAVE'S NECKLISS

"Have some dinner, Uncle Julius?" said my wife.

It was a Sunday afternoon in early autumn. Our two women-servants had gone to a camp-meeting some miles away, and would not return until evening. My wife had served the dinner, and we were just rising from the table, when Julius came up the lane, and, taking off his hat, seated himself on the piazza.

The old man glanced through the open door at the dinner-table, and his eyes rested lovingly upon a large sugar-cured ham, from which several slices had been cut, exposing a rich pink expanse that would have appealed strongly to the appetite of any hungry Christian.

"Thanky, Miss Annie," he said, after a momentary hesitation, "I dunno ez I keers ef I does tas'e a piece er dat ham, ef yer 'll cut me off a slice un it."

"No," said Annie, "I won't. Just sit down to the table and help yourself; eat all you want, and don't be bashful."

Julius drew a chair up to the table, while my wife and I went out on the piazza. Julius was in my employment; he took his meals with his own family, but when he happened to be about our house at meal-times, my wife never let him go away hungry.

I threw myself into a hammock, from which I could see Julius through an open window. He ate with evident relish, devoting his attention chiefly to the ham, slice after slice of which disappeared in the spacious cavity of his mouth. At first the old man ate rapidly, but after the edge of his appetite had been taken off he proceeded in a more leisurely manner. When he had cut the sixth slice of ham (I kept count of them from a lazy curiosity to see how much he *could* eat) I saw him lay it on his plate; as he adjusted the knife and fork to cut it into smaller pieces, he paused, as if struck by a sud-

Atlantic Monthly 64 (October 1889).

den thought, and a tear rolled down his rugged cheek and fell upon the slice of ham before him. But the emotion, whatever the thought that caused it, was transitory, and in a moment he continued his dinner. When he was through eating, he came out on the porch, and resumed his seat with the satisfied expression of countenance that usually follows a good dinner.

"Julius," I said, "you seemed to be affected by something, a moment ago. Was the mustard so strong that it moved you to tears?"

"No, suh, it wa'n't de mustard; I wuz studyin' 'bout Dave."

"Who was Dave, and what about him?" I asked.

The conditions were all favorable to story-telling. There was an autumnal languor in the air, and a dreamy haze softened the dark green of the distant pines and the deep blue of the Southern sky. The generous meal he had made had put the old man in a very good humor. He was not always so, for his curiously undeveloped nature was subject to moods which were almost childish in their variableness. It was only now and then that we were able to study, through the medium of his recollection, the simple but intensely human inner life of slavery. His way of looking at the past seemed very strange to us; his view of certain sides of life was essentially different from ours. He never indulged in any regrets for the Arcadian joyousness and irresponsibility which was a somewhat popular conception of slavery; his had not been the lot of the petted house-servant, but that of the toiling field-hand. While he mentioned with a warm appreciation the acts of kindness which those in authority had shown to him and his people, he would speak of a cruel deed, not with the indignation of one accustomed to quick feeling and spontaneous expression, but with a furtive disapproval which suggested to us a doubt in his own mind as to whether he had a right to think or to feel, and presented to us the curious psychological spectacle of a mind enslaved long after the shackles had been struck off from the limbs of its possessor. Whether the sacred name of liberty ever set his soul aglow with a generous fire; whether he had more than the most elementary ideas of love, friendship, patriotism, religion—things which are half, and the better half, of life to us; whether he even realized, except in a vague, uncertain way, his own degradation, I do not know. I fear not; and if not, then centuries of repression had borne their legitimate fruit. But in the simple human feeling, and still more in the undertone of sadness, which pervaded his stories, I thought I could see a spark which, fanned by favoring breezes and fed by the memories of the past, might become in his children's children a glowing flame of sensibility, alive to every thrill of human happiness or human woe.

"Dave use' ter b'long ter my ole marster," said Julius; "he wuz raise' on dis yer plantation, en I kin 'member all erbout 'im, fer I wuz ole 'nuff

ter chop cotton w'en it all happen'. Dave wuz a tall man, en monst'us
strong: he could do mo' wuk in a day dan any yuther two niggers on de
plantation. He wuz one er dese yer solemn kine er men, en nebber run on
wid much foolishness, like de yuther darkies. He use' ter go out in de
woods en pray; en w'en he hear de han's on de plantation cussin' en gwine
on wid dere dancin' en foolishness, he use' ter tell 'em 'bout religion en
jedgmen'-day, w'en dey would haf ter gin account fer eve'y idle word en all
dey yuther sinful kyarin's-on.

"Dave had l'arn' how ter read de Bible. Dey wuz a free nigger boy in
de settlement w'at wuz monst'us smart, en could write en cipher, en wuz
alluz readin' books er papers. En Dave had hi'ed dis free boy fer ter l'arn
'im how ter read. Hit wuz 'g'in' de law, but co'se none er de niggers did n'
say nuffin ter de w'ite folks 'bout it. Howsomedever, one day Mars
Walker—he wuz de oberseah—foun' out Dave could read. Mars Walker
wa'n't nuffin but a po' bockrah, en folks said he could n' read ner write
hisse'f, en co'se he did n' lack ter see a nigger w'at knowed mo' d'n he did;
so he went en tole Mars Dugal'. Mars Dugal' sont fer Dave, en ax' 'im
'bout it.

"Dave did n't hardly knowed w'at ter do; but he could n' tell no lie,
so he 'fessed he could read de Bible a little by spellin' out de words. Mars
Dugal' look' mighty solemn.

"'Dis yer is a se'ious matter,' sezee; 'it's 'g'in' de law ter l'arn niggers
how ter read, er 'low 'em ter hab books. But w'at yer l'arn out'n dat Bible,
Dave?'

"Dave wa'n't no fool, ef he wuz a nigger, en sezee:

"'Marster, I l'arns dat it 's a sin fer ter steal, er ter lie, er fer ter want
w'at doan b'long ter yer; en I l'arns fer ter love de Lawd en ter 'bey my
marster.'

"Mars Dugal' sorter smile' en laf' ter hisse'f, like he 'uz might'ly
tickle' 'bout sump'n, en sezee:

"'Doan 'pear ter me lack readin' de Bible done yer much harm, Dave.
Dat 's w'at I wants all my niggers fer ter know. Yer keep right on readin',
en tell de yuther han's w'at yer be'n tellin' me. How would yer lack fer ter
preach ter de niggers on Sunday?'

"Dave say he 'd be glad fer ter do w'at he could. So Mars Dugal' tole
de oberseah fer ter let Dave preach ter de niggers, en tell 'em w'at wuz in
de Bible, en it would he'p ter keep 'em fum stealin' er runnin' erway.

"So Dave 'mence' ter preach, en done de han's on de plantation a heap
er good, en most un 'em lef' off dey wicked ways, en 'mence' ter love ter
hear 'bout God, en religion, en de Bible; en dey done dey wuk better, en
did n' gib de oberseah but mighty little trouble fer ter manage 'em.

"Dave wuz one er dese yer men w'at did n' keer much fer de gals—leastways he did n' 'tel Dilsey come ter de plantation. Dilsey wuz a mon-st'us peart, good-lookin', gingybread-colored gal—one er dese yer high-steppin' gals w'at hol's dey heads up, en won' stan' no foolishness fum no man. She had b'long' ter a gemman over on Rockfish, w'at died, en whose 'state ha' ter be sol' fer ter pay his debts. En Mars Dugal' had be'n ter de oction, en w'en he seed dis gal a-cryin' en gwine on 'bout bein' sol' erway fum her ole mammy, Aun' Mahaly, Mars Dugal' bid 'em bofe in, en fotch 'em ober ter our plantation.

"De young nigger men on de plantation wuz des wil' atter Dilsey, but it did n' do no good, en none un 'em could n' git Dilsey fer dey junesey,[1] tel Dave 'mence' fer ter go roun' Aun' Mahaly's cabin. Dey wuz a fine-lookin' couple, Dave en Dilsey wuz, bofe tall, en well-shape', en soopl'. En dey sot a heap by one ernudder. Mars Dugal' seed 'em tergedder one Sun-day, en de nex' time he seed Dave atter dat, sezee:

" 'Dave, w'en yer en Dilsey gits ready fer ter git married, I ain' got no rejections. Dey's a poun' er so er chawin'-terbacker up at de house, en I reckon yo' mist'iss kin fine a frock en a ribbin er two fer Dilsey. Youer bofe good niggers, en yer neenter be feared er bein' sol' 'way fum one ernudder long ez I owns dis plantation; en I 'spec's ter own it fer a long time yit.'

"But dere wuz one man on de plantation w'at did n' lack ter see Dave en Dilsey tergedder ez much ez ole marster did. W'en Mars Dugal' went ter de sale whar he got Dilsey en Mahaly, he bought ernudder han', by de name er Wiley. Wiley wuz one er dese yer shiny-eyed, double-headed little niggers, sha'p ez a steel trap, en sly ez de fox w'at keep out'n it. Dis yer Wiley had be'n pesterin' Dilsey 'fo' she come ter our plantation, en had nigh 'bout worried de life out'n her. She did n' keer nuffin fer 'im, but he pestered her so she ha' ter th'eaten ter tell her marster fer ter make Wiley let her 'lone. W'en he come ober to our place it wuz des ez bad, 'tel bimeby Wiley seed dat Dilsey had got ter thinkin' a heap 'bout Dave, en den he sorter hilt off aw'ile, en purten' lack he gin Dilsey up. But he wuz one er dese yer 'ceitful niggers, en w'ile he wuz laffin' en jokin' wid de yuther han's 'bout Dave en Dilsey, he wuz settin' a trap fer ter ketch Dave en git Dilsey back fer hisse'f.

"Dave en Dilsey made up dere min's fer ter git married long 'bout Christmas time, w'en dey 'd hab mo' time fer a weddin'. But 'long 'bout two weeks befo' dat time ole mars 'mence' ter lose a heap er bacon. Eve'y night er so somebody 'ud steal a side er bacon, er a ham, er a shoulder, er

---

[1] Sweetheart. [Original publisher's note.]

sump'n, fum one er de smoke-'ouses. De smoke-'ouses wuz lock', but somebody had a key, en manage' ter git in some way er 'nudder. Dey 's mo' ways 'n one ter skin a cat, en dey 's mo' d'n one way ter git in a smoke-'ouse—leastways dat 's w'at I hearn say. Folks w'at had bacon fer ter sell did n' hab no trouble 'bout gittin' rid un it. Hit wuz 'g'in' de law fer ter buy things fum slabes; but Lawd! dat law did n' 'mount ter a hill er peas. Eve'y week er so one er dese yer big covered waggins would come 'long de road, peddlin' terbacker en w'iskey. Dey wuz a sight er room in one er dem big waggins, en it wuz monst'us easy fer ter swop off bacon fer sump'n ter chaw er ter wa'm yer up in de winter-time. I s'pose de peddlers did n' knowed dey wuz breakin' de law, caze de niggers alluz went at night, en stayed on de dark side er de waggin; en it wuz mighty hard fer ter tell *w'at* kine er folks dey wuz.

"Atter two er th'ee hund'ed er meat had be'n stole', Mars Walker call all de niggers up one ebenin', en tol' 'em dat de fus' nigger he cot stealin' bacon on dat plantation would git sump'n fer ter 'member it by long ez he lib'. En he say he 'd gin fi' dollars ter de nigger w'at 'skiver' de rogue. Mars Walker say he s'picion' one er two er de niggers, but he could n' tell fer sho, en co'se dey all 'nied it w'en he 'cuse em un it.

"Dey wa'n't no bacon stole' fer a week er so, 'tel one dark night w'en somebody tuk a ham fum one er de smoke-'ouses. Mars Walker des cusst awful w'en he foun' out de ham wuz gone, en say he gwine ter sarch all de niggers' cabins; w'en dis yer Wiley I wuz tellin' yer 'bout up'n say he s'picion' who tuk de ham, fer he seed Dave comin' 'cross de plantation fum to'ds de smoke-'ouse de night befo'. W'en Mars Walker hearn dis fum Wiley, he went en sarch' Dave's cabin, en foun' de ham hid under de flo'.

"Eve'ybody wuz 'stonish'; but dere wuz de ham. Co'se Dave 'nied it ter de las', but dere wuz de ham. Mars Walker say it wuz des ez he 'spected: he did n' b'lieve in dese yer readin' en prayin' niggers; it wuz all 'pocrisy, en sarve' Mars Dugal' right fer 'lowin' Dave ter be readin' books w'en it wuz 'g'in' de law.

"W'en Mars Dugal' hearn 'bout de ham, he say he wuz might'ly 'ceived en disapp'inted in Dave. He say he would n' nebber hab no mo' conferdence in no nigger, en Mars Walker could do des ez he wuz a mineter wid Dave er any er de res' er de niggers. So Mars Walker tuk'n tied Dave up en gin 'im forty; en den he got some er dis yer wire clof w'at dey uses fer ter make sifters out'n, en tuk'n wrap' it roun' de ham en fasten it tergedder at de little een'. Den he tuk Dave down ter de blacksmif-shop, en had Unker Silas, de plantation blacksmif, fasten a chain ter de ham, en den fasten de yuther een' er de chain roun' Dave's neck. En den he says ter Dave, sezee:

" 'Now, suh, yer 'll wear dat neckliss fer de nex' six mont's; en I 'spec's
yer ner none er de yuther niggers on dis plantation won' steal no mo' bacon dyoin' er dat time.'

"Well, it des 'peared ez if fum dat time Dave did n' hab nuffin but
trouble. De niggers all turnt ag'in' 'im, caze he be'n de 'casion er Mars Dugal' turnin' 'em all ober ter Mars Walker. Mars Dugal' wa'n't a bad
marster hisse'f, but Mars Walker wuz hard ez a rock. Dave kep' on sayin'
he did n' take de ham, but none un 'em did n' b'lieve 'im.

"Dilsey wa'n't on de plantation w'en Dave wuz 'cused er stealin' de
bacon. Ole mist'iss had sont her ter town fer a week er so fer ter wait on
one er her darters w'at had a young baby, en she did n' fine out nuffin 'bout
Dave's trouble 'tel she got back ter de plantation. Dave had patien'ly endy-
oed de finger er scawn, en all de hard words w'at de niggers pile' on 'im,
caze he wuz sho' Dilsey would stan' by 'im, en would n' b'lieve he wuz a
rogue, ner none er de yuther tales de darkies wuz tellin' 'bout 'im.

"W'en Dilsey come back fum town, en got down fum behine de buggy
whar she b'en ridin' wid ole mars, de fus' nigger 'ooman she met says
ter her—

" 'Is yer seed Dave, Dilsey?'

" 'No, I ain' seed Dave,' says Dilsey.

" 'Yer des oughter look at dat nigger; reckon yer would n' want 'im fer
yo' junesey no mo'. Mars Walker cotch 'im stealin' bacon, en gone en fasten' a ham roun' his neck, so he can't git it off'n hisse'f. He sut'nly do look
quare.' En den de 'ooman bus' out laffin' fit ter kill herse'f. W'en she got
thoo laffin' she up'n tole Dilsey all 'bout de ham, en all de yuther lies w'at
de niggers be'n tellin' on Dave.

"W'en Dilsey started down ter de quarters, who should she meet but
Dave, comin' in fum de cotton-fiel'. She turnt her head ter one side, en
purten' lack she did n' seed Dave.

" 'Dilsey!' sezee.

"Dilsey walk' right on, en did n' notice 'im.

" '*Oh*, Dilsey!'

"Dilsey did n' paid no 'tention ter 'im, en den Dave knowed some er
de niggers be'n tellin' her 'bout de ham. He felt monst'us bad, but he 'lowed
ef he could des git Dilsey fer ter listen ter 'im fer a minute er so, he could
make her b'lieve he did n' stole de bacon. It wuz a week er two befo' he
could git a chance ter speak ter her ag'in; but fine'ly he cotch her down by
de spring one day, en sezee:

" 'Dilsey, w'at fer yer won' speak ter me, en purten' lack yer doan see
me? Dilsey, yer knows me too well fer ter b'lieve I 'd steal, er do dis yuther
wick'ness de niggers is all layin' ter me—yer *knows* I would n' do dat,
Dilsey. Yer ain' gwine back on yo' Dave, is yer?'

"But w'at Dave say did n' hab no 'fec' on Dilsey. Dem lies folks b'en tellin' her had p'isen' her min' 'g'in' Dave.

"'I doan wanter talk ter no nigger,' says she, 'w'at be'n whip' fer stealin', en w'at gwine roun' wid sich a lookin' thing ez dat hung roun' his neck. I 's a 'spectable gal, I is. W'at yer call dat, Dave? Is dat a cha'm fer ter keep off witches, er is it a noo kine er neckliss yer got?'

"Po' Dave did n' knowed w'at ter do. De las' one he had 'pended on fer ter stan' by 'im had gone back on 'im, en dey did n' 'pear ter be nuffin mo' wuf libbin' fer. He could n' hol' no mo' pra'r-meetin's, fer Mars Walker would n' 'low 'im ter preach, en de darkies would n' 'a' listen' ter 'im ef he had preach'. He did n' eben hab his Bible fer ter comfort hisse'f wid, fer Mars Walker had tuk it erway fum 'im en burnt it up, en say ef he ketch any mo' niggers wid Bibles on de plantation he 'd do 'em wuss'n he done Dave.

"En ter make it still harder fer Dave, Dilsey tuk up wid Wiley. Dave could see him gwine up ter Aun' Mahaly's cabin, en settin' out on de bench in de moonlight wid Dilsey, en singin' sinful songs en playin' de banjer. Dave use' ter scrouch down behine de bushes, en wonder w'at de Lawd sen' 'im all dem tribberlations fer.

"But all er Dave's yuther troubles wa'n't nuffin side er dat ham. He had wrap' de chain roun' wid a rag, so it did n' hurt his neck; but w'eneber he went ter wuk, dat ham would be in his way; he had ter do his task, how-somedever, des de same ez ef he did n' hab de ham. W'eneber he went ter lay down, dat ham would be in de way. Ef he turn ober in his sleep, dat ham would be tuggin' at his neck. It wuz de las' thing he seed at night, en de fus' thing he seed in de mawnin'. W'eneber he met a stranger, de ham would be de fus' thing de stranger would see. Most un 'em would 'mence' ter laf, en whareber Dave went he could see folks p'intin' at him, en year 'em sayin':

"'W'at kine er collar dat nigger got roun' his neck?' er, ef dey knowed 'im, 'Is yer stole any mo' hams lately?' er 'W'at yer take fer yo' neckliss, Dave?' er some joke er 'nuther 'bout dat ham.

"Fus' Dave did n' mine it so much, caze he knowed he had n' done nuffin. But bimeby he got so he could n' stan' it no longer, en he 'd hide hisse'f in de bushes w'eneber he seed anybody comin', en alluz kep' hisse'f shet up in his cabin atter he come in fum wuk.

"It wuz monst'us hard on Dave, en bimeby, w'at wid dat ham eber-lastin' en etarnally draggin' roun' his neck, he 'mence' fer ter do en say quare things, en make de niggers wonder ef he wa'n't gittin' out'n his mine. He got ter gwine roun' talkin' ter hisse'f, en singin' cornshuckin' songs, en laffin' fit ter kill 'bout nuffin. En one day he tole one er de niggers he had 'skivered a noo way fer ter raise hams—gwine ter pick 'em off'n trees, en save de expense er smoke-'ouses by kyoin' 'em in de sun. En one day he

up'n tole Mars Walker he got sump'n pertickler fer ter say ter 'im; en he tuk
Mars Walker off ter one side, en tole 'im he wuz gwine ter show 'im a place
in de swamp whar dey wuz a whole trac' er lan' covered wid hamtrees.

"W'en Mars Walker hearn Dave talkin' dis kine er fool-talk, en w'en
he seed how Dave wuz 'mencin' ter git behine in his wuk, en w'en he ax'
de niggers en dey tole 'im how Dave be'n gwine on, he 'lowed he reckon'
he 'd punish' Dave ernuff, en it mou't do mo' harm dan good fer ter keep
de ham on his neck any longer. So he sont Dave down ter de blacksmif-
shop en had de ham tuk off. Dey wa'n't much er de ham lef' by dat time,
fer de sun had melt all de fat, en de lean had all swivel' up, so dey wa'n't
but th'ee er fo' poun's lef'.

"W'en de ham had be'n tuk off'n Dave, folks kinder stopped talkin'
'bout 'im so much. But de ham had be'n on his neck so long dat Dave had
sorter got use' ter it. He look des lack he 'd los' sump'n fer a day er so atter de ham wuz tuk off, en did n' 'pear ter know w'at ter do wid hisse'f; en
fine'ly he up'n tuk'n tied a lighterd-knot ter a string, en hid it under de flo'
er his cabin, en w'en nobody wuz n' lookin' he 'd take it out en hang it
roun' his neck, en go off in de woods en holler en sing; en he allus tied it
roun' his neck w'en he went ter sleep. Fac', it 'peared lack Dave done gone
clean out'n his mine. En atter a w'ile he got one er de quarest notions you
eber hearn tell un. It wuz 'bout dat time dat I come back ter de plantation
fer ter wuk—I had be'n out ter Mars Dugal's yuther place on Beaver Crick
for a mont' er so. I had hearn 'bout Dave en de bacon, en 'bout w'at wuz
gwine on on de plantation; but I did n' b'lieve w'at dey all say 'bout Dave,
fer I knowed Dave wa'n't dat kine er man. One day atter I come back, me'n
Dave wuz choppin' cotton tergedder, w'en Dave lean' on his hoe, en motion' fer me ter come ober close ter 'im; en den he retch' ober en w'ispered
ter me.

" 'Julius,' sezee, 'did yer knowed yer wuz wukkin' long yer wid a ham?'

"I could n' 'magine w'at he meant. 'G'way fum yer, Dave,' says I. 'Yer
ain' wearin' no ham no mo'; try en fergit 'bout dat; 't ain' gwine ter do yer
no good fer ter 'member it.'

" 'Look a-yer, Julius,' sezee, 'kin yer keep a secret?'

" 'Co'se I kin, Dave,' says I. 'I doan go roun' tellin' people w'at yuther
folks says ter me.'

" 'Kin I trus' yer, Julius? Will yer cross yo' heart?'

"I cross' my heart. 'Wush I may die ef I tells a soul,' says I.

"Dave look' at me des lack he wuz lookin' thoo me en 'way on de
yuther side er me, en sezee:

" 'Did yer knowed I wuz turnin' ter a ham, Julius?'

"I tried ter 'suade Dave dat dat wuz all foolishness, en dat he ought
n't ter be talkin' dat-a-way—hit wa'n't right. En I tole 'im ef he 'd des be

patien', de time would sho'ly come w'en eve'ything would be straighten'
out, en folks would fine out who de rale rogue wuz w'at stole de bacon.
Dave 'peared ter listen ter w'at I say, en promise' ter do better, en stop
gwine on dat-a-way; en it seem lack he pick' up a bit w'en he seed dey wuz
one pusson did n' b'lieve dem tales 'bout 'im.

"Hit wa'n't long atter dat befo' Mars Archie McIntyre, ober on de
Wimbleton road, 'mence' ter complain 'bout somebody stealin' chickens
fum his hen-'ouse. De chickens kep' on gwine, en at las' Mars Archie tole
de han's on his plantation dat he gwine ter shoot de fus' man he ketch in
his hen-'ouse. In less'n a week atter he gin dis warnin', he cotch a nigger in
de hen-'ouse, en fill' 'im full er squir'l-shot. W'en he got a light, he
'skivered it wuz a strange nigger; en w'en he call' one er his own sarven's,
de nigger tole 'im it wuz our Wiley. W'en Mars Archie foun' dat out, he
sont ober ter our plantation fer ter tell Mars Dugal' he had shot one er his
niggers, en dat he could sen' ober dere en git w'at wuz lef' un 'im.

"Mars Dugal' wuz mad at fus'; but w'en he got ober dere en hearn
how it all happen', he did n' hab much ter say. Wiley wuz shot so bad he
wuz sho' he wuz gwine ter die, so he up'n says ter ole marster:

"'Mars Dugal',' sezee, 'I knows I's be'n a monst'us bad nigger, but
befo' I go I wanter git sump'n off'n my mine. Dave did n' steal dat bacon
w'at wuz tuk out'n de smoke-'ouse. *I* stole it all, en I hid de ham under
Dave's cabin fer ter th'ow de blame on him—en may de good Lawd fergib
me fer it.'

"Mars Dugal' had Wiley tuk back ter de plantation, en sont fer a doctor fer ter pick de shot out'n 'im. En de ve'y nex' mawnin' Mars Dugal'
sont fer Dave ter come up ter de big house; he felt kinder sorry fer de way
Dave had be'n treated. Co'se it wa'n't no fault er Mars Dugal's, but he wuz
gwine ter do w'at he could fer ter make up fer it. So he sont word down
ter de quarters fer Dave en all de yuther han's ter 'semble up in de yard
befo' de big house at sun-up nex' mawnin'.

"Yearly in de mawnin' de niggers all swarm' up in de yard. Mars Dugal' wuz feelin' so kine dat he had brung up a bairl er cider, en tole de niggers all fer ter he'p deyselves.

"All de han's on de plantation come but Dave; en bimeby, w'en it seem
lack he wa'n't comin', Mars Dugal' sont a nigger down ter de quarters ter
look fer 'im. De sun wuz gittin' up, en dey wuz a heap er wuk ter be done,
en Mars Dugal' sorter got ti'ed waitin'; so he up'n says:

"'Well, boys en gals, I sont fer yer all up yer fer ter tell yer dat all dat
'bout Dave's stealin' er de bacon wuz a mistake, ez I s'pose yer all done
hearn befo' now, en I 's mighty sorry it happen'. I wants ter treat all my
niggers right, en I wants yer all ter know dat I sets a heap by all er my han's
w'at is hones' en smart. En I want yer all ter treat Dave des lack yer did

befo' dis thing happen', en mine w'at he preach ter yer; fer Dave is a good
nigger, en has had a hard row ter hoe. En de fus' one I ketch sayin' anythin' 'g'in' Dave, I 'll tell Mister Walker ter gin 'im forty. Now take ernudder drink er cider all roun', en den git at dat cotton, fer I wanter git dat
Persimmon Hill trac' all pick' ober ter-day.'

"W'en de niggers wuz gwine 'way, Mars Dugal' tole me fer ter go en
hunt up Dave, en bring 'im up ter de house. I went down ter Dave's cabin,
but could n' fine 'im dere. Den I look' roun' de plantation, en in de aidge
er de woods, en 'long de road; but I could n' fine no sign er Dave. I wuz
'bout ter gin up de sarch, w'en I happen' fer ter run 'cross a foot-track w'at
look' lack Dave's. I had wukked 'long wid Dave so much dat I knowed his
tracks: he had a monst'us long foot, wid a holler instep, w'ich wuz sump'n
skase 'mongs' black folks. So I follered dat track 'cross de fiel' fum de
quarters 'tel I got ter de smoke-'ouse. De fus' thing I notice' wuz smoke
comin' out'n de cracks: it wuz cu'ous, caze dey had n' be'n no hogs kill' on
de plantation fer six mont' er so, en all de bacon in de smoke-'ouse wuz
done kyoed. I could n' 'magine fer ter sabe my life w'at Dave wuz doin' in
dat smoke-'ouse. I went up ter de do' en hollered:

" 'Dave!'

"Dey did n' nobody answer. I did n' wanter open de do', fer w'ite folks
is monst'us pertickler 'bout dey smoke-'ouses; en ef de oberseah had a-
come up en cotch me in dere, he mou't not wanter b'lieve I wuz des lookin'
fer Dave. So I sorter knock at de do' en call' out ag'in:

" 'O Dave, hit 's me—Julius! Doan be skeered. Mars Dugal' wants yer
ter come up ter de big house—he done 'skivered who stole de ham.'

"But Dave did n' answer. En w'en I look' roun' ag'in en did n' seed
none er his tracks gwine way fum de smoke-'ouse, I knowed he wuz in dere
yit, en I wuz 'termine' fer ter fetch 'im out; so I push de do' open en look in.

"Dey wuz a pile er bark burnin' in de middle er de flo', en right ober
de fier, hangin' fum one er de rafters, wuz Dave; dey wuz a rope roun' his
neck, en I did n' haf ter look at his face mo' d'n once fer ter see he wuz dead.

"Den I knowed how it all happen'. Dave had kep' on gittin' wusser en
wusser in his mine, 'tel he des got ter b'lievin' he wuz all done turnt ter a
ham; en den he had gone en built a fier, en tied a rope roun' his neck, des
lack de hams wuz tied, en had hung hisse'f up in de smoke-'ouse fer ter kyo.

"Dave wuz buried down by de swamp, in de plantation buryin'-groun'.
Wiley did n' died fum de woun' he got in Mars McIntyre's hen-'ouse; he
got well atter a w'ile, but Dilsey would n' hab nuffin mo' ter do wid 'im,
en 't wa'n't long 'fo' Mars Dugal' sol' 'im ter a spekilater on his way souf—
he say he did n' want no sich a nigger on de plantation, ner in de county,
ef he could he'p it. En w'en de een' er de year come, Mars Dugal' turnt
Mars Walker off, en run de plantation hisse'f atter dat.

"Eber sence den," said Julius in conclusion, "w'eneber I eats ham, it min's me er Dave. I lacks ham, but I nebber kin eat mo' d'n two er th'ee poun's befo' I gits ter studyin' 'bout Dave, en den I has ter stop en leab de res' fer ernudder time."

There was a short silence after the old man had finished his story, and then my wife began to talk to him about the weather, on which subject he was an authority. I went into the house. When I came out, half an hour later, I saw Julius disappearing down the lane, with a basket on his arm.

At breakfast, next morning, it occurred to me that I should like a slice of ham. I said as much to my wife.

"Oh, no, John," she responded, "you should n't eat anything so heavy for breakfast."

I insisted.

"The fact is," she said, pensively, "I could n't have eaten any more of that ham, and so I gave it to Julius."

The Wife of His Youth and Other Stories of the Color Line

THE WIFE OF HIS YOUTH

I

Mr. Ryder was going to give a ball. There were several reasons why this was an opportune time for such an event.

Mr. Ryder might aptly be called the dean of the Blue Veins. The original Blue Veins were a little society of colored persons organized in a certain Northern city shortly after the war. Its purpose was to establish and maintain correct social standards among a people whose social condition presented almost unlimited room for improvement. By accident, combined perhaps with some natural affinity, the society consisted of individuals who were, generally speaking, more white than black. Some envious outsider made the suggestion that no one was eligible for membership who was not white enough to show blue veins. The suggestion was readily adopted by those who were not of the favored few, and since that time the society, though possessing a longer and more pretentious name, had been known far and wide as the "Blue Vein Society," and its members as the "Blue Veins."

The Blue Veins did not allow that any such requirement existed for admission to their circle, but, on the contrary, declared that character and culture were the only things considered; and that if most of their members were light-colored, it was because such persons, as a rule, had had better opportunities to qualify themselves for membership. Opinions differed, too, as to the usefulness of the society. There were those who had been

Boston: Houghton Mifflin Company, 1899.

known to assail it violently as a glaring example of the very prejudice from
which the colored race had suffered most; and later, when such critics had
succeeded in getting on the inside, they had been heard to maintain with
zeal and earnestness that the society was a lifeboat, an anchor, a bulwark
and a shield—a pillar of cloud by day and of fire by night, to guide their
people through the social wilderness. Another alleged prerequisite for Blue
Vein membership was that of free birth; and while there was really no such
requirement, it is doubtless true that very few of the members would have
been unable to meet it if there had been. If there were one or two of the
older members who had come up from the South and from slavery, their
history presented enough romantic circumstances to rob their servile origin of its grosser aspects.

While there were no such tests of eligibility, it is true that the Blue
Veins had their notions on these subjects, and that not all of them were
equally liberal in regard to the things they collectively disclaimed. Mr. Ryder was one of the most conservative. Though he had not been among the
founders of the society, but had come in some years later, his genius for social leadership was such that he had speedily become its recognized adviser
and head, the custodian of its standards, and the preserver of its traditions.
He shaped its social policy, was active in providing for its entertainment,
and when the interest fell off, as it sometimes did, he fanned the embers
until they burst again into a cheerful flame.

There were still other reasons for his popularity. While he was not as
white as some of the Blue Veins, his appearance was such as to confer distinction upon them. His features were of a refined type, his hair was almost
straight; he was always neatly dressed; his manners were irreproachable,
and his morals above suspicion. He had come to Groveland a young man,
and obtaining employment in the office of a railroad company as messenger had in time worked himself up to the position of stationery clerk, having charge of the distribution of the office supplies for the whole company.
Although the lack of early training had hindered the orderly development
of a naturally fine mind, it had not prevented him from doing a great deal
of reading or from forming decidedly literary tastes. Poetry was his passion. He could repeat whole pages of the great English poets; and if his
pronunciation was sometimes faulty, his eye, his voice, his gestures, would
respond to the changing sentiment with a precision that revealed a poetic
soul and disarmed criticism. He was economical, and had saved money; he
owned and occupied a very comfortable house on a respectable street. His
residence was handsomely furnished, containing among other things a
good library, especially rich in poetry, a piano, and some choice engravings. He generally shared his house with some young couple, who looked
after his wants and were company for him; for Mr. Ryder was a single

man. In the early days of his connection with the Blue Veins he had been regarded as quite a catch, and young ladies and their mothers had manoeuvred with much ingenuity to capture him. Not, however, until Mrs. Molly Dixon visited Groveland had any woman ever made him wish to change his condition to that of a married man.

Mrs. Dixon had come to Groveland from Washington in the spring, and before the summer was over she had won Mr. Ryder's heart. She possessed many attractive qualities. She was much younger than he; in fact, he was old enough to have been her father, though no one knew exactly how old he was. She was whiter than he, and better educated. She had moved in the best colored society of the country, at Washington, and had taught in the schools of that city. Such a superior person had been eagerly welcomed to the Blue Vein Society, and had taken a leading part in its activities. Mr. Ryder had at first been attracted by her charms of person, for she was very good looking and not over twenty-five; then by her refined manners and the vivacity of her wit. Her husband had been a government clerk, and at his death had left a considerable life insurance. She was visiting friends in Groveland, and, finding the town and the people to her liking, had prolonged her stay indefinitely. She had not seemed displeased at Mr. Ryder's attentions, but on the contrary had given him every proper encouragement; indeed, a younger and less cautious man would long since have spoken. But he had made up his mind, and had only to determine the time when he would ask her to be his wife. He decided to give a ball in her honor, and at some time during the evening of the ball to offer her his heart and hand. He had no special fears about the outcome, but, with a little touch of romance, he wanted the surroundings to be in harmony with his own feelings when he should have received the answer he expected.

Mr. Ryder resolved that this ball should mark an epoch in the social history of Groveland. He knew, of course—no one could know better— the entertainments that had taken place in past years, and what must be done to surpass them. His ball must be worthy of the lady in whose honor it was to be given, and must, by the quality of its guests, set an example for the future. He had observed of late a growing liberality, almost a laxity, in social matters, even among members of his own set, and had several times been forced to meet in a social way persons whose complexions and callings in life were hardly up to the standard which he considered proper for the society to maintain. He had a theory of his own.

"I have no race prejudice," he would say, "but we people of mixed blood are ground between the upper and the nether millstone. Our fate lies between absorption by the white race and extinction in the black. The one does n't want us yet, but may take us in time. The other would welcome us, but it would be for us a backward step. 'With malice towards none, with charity for all,' we must do the best we can for ourselves and those who are to follow us. Self-preservation is the first law of nature."

His ball would serve by its exclusiveness to counteract leveling tendencies, and his marriage with Mrs. Dixon would help to further the upward process of absorption he had been wishing and waiting for.

II

The ball was to take place on Friday night. The house had been put in order, the carpets covered with canvas, the halls and stairs decorated with palms and potted plants; and in the afternoon Mr. Ryder sat on his front porch, which the shade of a vine running up over a wire netting made a cool and pleasant lounging place. He expected to respond to the toast "The Ladies" at the supper, and from a volume of Tennyson—his favorite poet—was fortifying himself with apt quotations. The volume was open at "A Dream of Fair Women." His eyes fell on these lines, and he read them aloud to judge better of their effect:

> "At length I saw a lady within call,
>   Stiller than chisell'd marble, standing there;
> A daughter of the gods, divinely tall,
>   And most divinely fair."

He marked the verse, and turning the page read the stanza beginning,

> "O sweet pale Margaret,
>   O rare pale Margaret."

He weighed the passage a moment, and decided that it would not do. Mrs. Dixon was the palest lady he expected at the ball, and she was of a rather ruddy complexion, and of lively disposition and buxom build. So he ran over the leaves until his eye rested on the description of Queen Guinevere:

> "She seem'd a part of joyous Spring:
> A gown of grass-green silk she wore,
> Buckled with golden clasps before;

A light-green tuft of plumes she bore
5 Closed in a golden ring.

.   .   .   .   .   .

"She look'd so lovely, as she sway'd
The rein with dainty finger-tips,
A man had given all other bliss,
And all his worldly worth for this,
10 To waste his whole heart in one kiss
Upon her perfect lips."

As Mr. Ryder murmured these words audibly, with an appreciative thrill, he heard the latch of his gate click, and a light footfall sounding on the steps. He turned his head, and saw a woman standing before his door.

She was a little woman, not five feet tall, and proportioned to her height. Although she stood erect, and looked around her with very bright and restless eyes, she seemed quite old; for her face was crossed and re-crossed with a hundred wrinkles, and around the edges of her bonnet could be seen protruding here and there a tuft of short gray wool. She wore a blue calico gown of ancient cut, a little red shawl fastened around her shoulders with an old-fashioned brass brooch, and a large bonnet pro-fusely ornamented with faded red and yellow artificial flowers. And she was very black—so black that her toothless gums, revealed when she opened her mouth to speak, were not red, but blue. She looked like a bit of the old plantation life, summoned up from the past by the wave of a ma-gician's wand, as the poet's fancy had called into being the gracious shapes of which Mr. Ryder had just been reading.

He rose from his chair and came over to where she stood.

"Good-afternoon, madam," he said.

"Good-evenin', suh," she answered, ducking suddenly with a quaint curtsy. Her voice was shrill and piping, but softened somewhat by age. "Is dis yere whar Mistuh Ryduh lib, suh?" she asked, looking around her doubtfully, and glancing into the open windows, through which some of the preparations for the evening were visible.

"Yes," he replied, with an air of kindly patronage, unconsciously flat-tered by her manner, "I am Mr. Ryder. Did you want to see me?"

"Yas, suh, ef I ain't 'sturbin' of you too much."

"Not at all. Have a seat over here behind the vine, where it is cool. What can I do for you?"

"'Scuse me, suh," she continued, when she had sat down on the edge of a chair, "'scuse me, suh, I's lookin' for my husban'. I heerd you wuz a big man an' had libbed heah a long time, an' I 'lowed you would n't min' ef I'd come roun' an' ax you ef you'd ever heerd of a merlatter man by de name er Sam Taylor 'quirin' roun' in de chu'ches ermongs' de people fer his wife 'Liza Jane?"

Mr. Ryder seemed to think for a moment.

"There used to be many such cases right after the war," he said, "but it has been so long that I have forgotten them. There are very few now. But tell me your story, and it may refresh my memory."

She sat back farther in her chair so as to be more comfortable, and folded her withered hands in her lap.

"My name's 'Liza," she began, "'Liza Jane. W'en I wuz young I us'ter b'long ter Marse Bob Smif, down in ole Missoura. I wuz bawn down dere. W'en I wuz a gal I wuz married ter a man named Jim. But Jim died, an' after dat I married a merlatter man named Sam Taylor. Sam wuz free-bawn, but his mammy and daddy died, an' de w'ite folks 'prenticed him ter my marster fer ter work fer 'im 'tel he wuz growed up. Sam worked in de fiel', an' I wuz de cook. One day Ma'y Ann, ole miss's maid, came rushin' out ter de kitchen, an' says she, ''Liza Jane, ole marse gwine sell yo' Sam down de ribber.'

"'Go way f'm yere,' says I; 'my husban' 's free!'

"'Don' make no diff'ence. I heerd ole marse tell ole miss he wuz gwine take yo' Sam 'way wid 'im ter-morrow, fer he needed money, an' he knowed whar he could git a t'ousan' dollars fer Sam an' no questions axed.'

"W'en Sam come home f'm de fiel' dat night, I tole him 'bout ole marse gwine steal 'im, an' Sam run erway. His time wuz mos' up, an' he swo' dat w'en he wuz twenty-one he would come back an' he'p me run erway, er else save up de money ter buy my freedom. An' I know he'd 'a' done it, fer he thought a heap er me, Sam did. But w'en he come back he did n' fin' me, fer I wuz n' dere. Ole marse had heerd dat I warned Sam, so he had me whip' an' sol' down de ribber.

"Den de wah broke out, an' w'en it wuz ober de cullud folks wuz scattered. I went back ter de ole home; but Sam wuz n' dere, an' I could n' l'arn nuffin' 'bout 'im. But I knowed he'd be'n dere to look fer me an' had n' foun' me, an' had gone erway ter hunt fer me.

"I's be'n lookin' fer 'im eber sence," she added simply, as though twenty-five years were but a couple of weeks, "an' I knows he 's be'n lookin' fer me. Fer he sot a heap er sto' by me, Sam did, an' I know he 's be'n huntin' fer me all dese years—'less'n he 's be'n sick er sump'n, so he could n' work, er out'n his head, so he could n' 'member his promise. I went back down de ribber, fer I 'lowed he 'd gone down dere lookin' fer me. I's be'n ter Noo

Orleens, an' Atlanty, an' Charleston, an' Richmon'; an' w'en I'd be'n all ober de Souf I come ter de Norf. Fer I knows I'll fin' 'im some er dese days," she added softly, "er he'll fin' me, an' den we'll bofe be as happy in freedom as we wuz in de ole days befo' de wah." A smile stole over her withered countenance as she paused a moment, and her bright eyes softened into a faraway look.

This was the substance of the old woman's story. She had wandered a little here and there. Mr. Ryder was looking at her curiously when she finished.

"How have you lived all these years?" he asked.

"Cookin', suh. I's a good cook. Does you know anybody w'at needs a good cook, suh? I's stoppin' wid a cullud fam'ly roun' de corner yonder 'tel I kin git a place."

"Do you really expect to find your husband? He may be dead long ago."

She shook her head emphatically. "Oh no, he ain' dead. De signs an' de tokens tells me. I dremp three nights runnin' on'y dis las' week dat I foun' him."

"He may have married another woman. Your slave marriage would not have prevented him, for you never lived with him after the war, and without that your marriage does n't count."

"Would n' make no diff'ence wid Sam. He would n' marry no yuther 'ooman 'tel he foun' out 'bout me. I knows it," she added. "Sump'n 's be'n tellin' me all dese years dat I's gwine fin' Sam 'fo' I dies."

"Perhaps he's outgrown you, and climbed up in the world where he would n't care to have you find him."

"No, indeed, suh," she replied, "Sam ain' dat kin' er man. He wuz good ter me, Sam wuz, but he wuz n' much good ter nobody e'se, fer he wuz one er de triflin'es' han's on de plantation. I 'spec's ter haf ter suppo't 'im w'en I fin' 'im, fer he nebber would work 'less'n he had ter. But den he wuz free, an' he did n' git no pay fer his work, an' I don' blame 'im much. Mebbe he's done better sence he run erway, but I ain' 'spectin' much."

"You may have passed him on the street a hundred times during the twenty-five years, and not have known him; time works great changes."

She smiled incredulously. "I'd know 'im 'mongs' a hund'ed men. Fer dey wuz n' no yuther merlatter man like my man Sam, an' I could n' be mistook. I 's toted his picture roun' wid me twenty-five years."

"May I see it?" asked Mr. Ryder. "It might help me to remember whether I have seen the original."

As she drew a small parcel from her bosom he saw that it was fastened to a string that went around her neck. Removing several wrappers, she brought to light an old-fashioned daguerreotype in a black case. He looked long and intently at the portrait. It was faded with time, but the features were still distinct, and it was easy to see what manner of man it had represented.

He closed the case, and with a slow movement handed it back to her.

"I don't know of any man in town who goes by that name," he said, "nor have I heard of any one making such inquiries. But if you will leave me your address, I will give the matter some attention, and if I find out anything I will let you know."

She gave him the number of a house in the neighborhood, and went away, after thanking him warmly.

He wrote the address on the fly-leaf of the volume of Tennyson, and, when she had gone, rose to his feet and stood looking after her curiously. As she walked down the street with mincing step, he saw several persons whom she passed turn and look back at her with a smile of kindly amusement. When she had turned the corner, he went upstairs to his bedroom, and stood for a long time before the mirror of his dressing-case, gazing thoughtfully at the reflection of his own face.

III

At eight o'clock the ballroom was a blaze of light and the guests had begun to assemble; for there was a literary programme and some routine business of the society to be gone through with before the dancing. A black servant in evening dress waited at the door and directed the guests to the dressing-rooms.

The occasion was long memorable among the colored people of the city; not alone for the dress and display, but for the high average of intelligence and culture that distinguished the gathering as a whole. There were a number of school-teachers, several young doctors, three or four lawyers, some professional singers, an editor, a lieutenant in the United States army spending his furlough in the city, and others in various polite callings; these were colored, though most of them would not have attracted even a casual glance because of any marked difference from white people. Most of the ladies were in evening costume, and dress coats and dancing pumps were the rule among the men. A band of string music, stationed in an alcove behind a row of palms, played popular airs while the guests were gathering.

The dancing began at half past nine. At eleven o'clock supper was served. Mr. Ryder had left the ballroom some little time before the intermission, but reappeared at the supper-table. The spread was worthy of the occasion, and the guests did full justice to it. When the coffee had been served, the toast-master, Mr. Solomon Sadler, rapped for order. He made a brief introductory speech, complimenting host and guests, and then presented in their order the toasts of the evening. They were responded to with a very fair display of after-dinner wit.

"The last toast," said the toast-master, when he reached the end of the list, "is one which must appeal to us all. There is no one of us of the sterner sex who is not at some time dependent upon woman—in infancy for protection, in manhood for companionship, in old age for care and comforting. Our good host has been trying to live alone, but the fair faces I see around me to-night prove that he too is largely dependent upon the gentler sex for most that makes life worth living—the society and love of friends—and rumor is at fault if he does not soon yield entire subjection to one of them. Mr. Ryder will now respond to the toast—The Ladies."

There was a pensive look in Mr. Ryder's eyes as he took the floor and adjusted his eyeglasses. He began by speaking of woman as the gift of Heaven to man, and after some general observations on the relations of the sexes he said: "But perhaps the quality which most distinguishes woman is her fidelity and devotion to those she loves. History is full of examples, but has recorded none more striking than one which only to day came under my notice."

He then related, simply but effectively, the story told by his visitor of the afternoon. He gave it in the same soft dialect, which came readily to his lips, while the company listened attentively and sympathetically. For the story had awakened a responsive thrill in many hearts. There were some present who had seen, and others who had heard their fathers and grandfathers tell, the wrongs and sufferings of this past generation, and all of them still felt, in their darker moments, the shadow hanging over them. Mr. Ryder went on:

"Such devotion and confidence are rare even among women. There are many who would have searched a year, some who would have waited five years, a few who might have hoped ten years; but for twenty-five years this woman has retained her affection for and her faith in a man she has not seen or heard of in all that time.

"She came to me to-day in the hope that I might be able to help her find this long-lost husband. And when she was gone I gave my fancy rein, and imagined a case I will put to you.

"Suppose that this husband, soon after his escape, had learned that his wife had been sold away, and that such inquiries as he could make brought no information of her whereabouts. Suppose that he was young, and she much older than he; that he was light, and she was black; that their marriage was a slave marriage, and legally binding only if they chose to make it so after the war. Suppose, too, that he made his way to the North, as some of us have done, and there, where he had larger opportunities, had improved them, and had in the course of all these years grown to be as different from the ignorant boy who ran away from fear of slavery as the day is from the night. Suppose, even, that he had qualified himself, by industry, by thrift, and by study, to win the friendship and be considered worthy the society of such people as these I see around me to-night, gracing my board and filling my heart with gladness; for I am old enough to remember the day when such a gathering would not have been possible in this land. Suppose, too, that, as the years went by, this man's memory of the past grew more and more indistinct, until at last it was rarely, except in his dreams, that any image of this bygone period rose before his mind. And then suppose that accident should bring to his knowledge the fact that the wife of his youth, the wife he had left behind him—not one who had walked by his side and kept pace with him in his upward struggle, but one upon whom advancing years and a laborious life had set their mark—was alive and seeking him, but that he was absolutely safe from recognition or discovery, unless he chose to reveal himself. My friends, what would the man do? I will presume that he was one who loved honor, and tried to deal justly with all men. I will even carry the case further, and suppose that perhaps he had set his heart upon another, whom he had hoped to call his own. What would he do, or rather what ought he to do, in such a crisis of a lifetime?

"It seemed to me that he might hesitate, and I imagined that I was an old friend, a near friend, and that he had come to me for advice; and I argued the case with him. I tried to discuss it impartially. After we had looked upon the matter from every point of view, I said to him, in words that we all know:

'This above all: to thine own self be true,
And it must follow, as the night the day,
Thou canst not then be false to any man.'

Then, finally, I put the question to him, 'Shall you acknowledge her?'

"And now, ladies and gentlemen, friends and companions, I ask you, what should he have done?"

There was something in Mr. Ryder's voice that stirred the hearts of those who sat around him. It suggested more than mere sympathy with an imaginary situation; it seemed rather in the nature of a personal appeal. It was observed, too, that his look rested more especially upon Mrs. Dixon, with a mingled expression of renunciation and inquiry.

She had listened, with parted lips and streaming eyes. She was the first to speak: "He should have acknowledged her."

"Yes," they all echoed, "he should have acknowledged her."

"My friends and companions," responded Mr. Ryder, "I thank you, one and all. It is the answer I expected, for I knew your hearts."

He turned and walked toward the closed door of an adjoining room, while every eye followed him in wondering curiosity. He came back in a moment, leading by the hand his visitor of the afternoon, who stood startled and trembling at the sudden plunge into this scene of brilliant gayety. She was neatly dressed in gray, and wore the white cap of an elderly woman.

"Ladies and gentlemen," he said, "this is the woman, and I am the man, whose story I have told you. Permit me to introduce to you the wife of my youth."

HER VIRGINIA MAMMY

1

The pianist had struck up a lively two-step, and soon the floor was covered with couples, each turning on its own axis, and all revolving around a common centre, in obedience perhaps to the same law of motion that governs the planetary systems. The dancing-hall was a long room, with a waxed floor that glistened with the reflection of the lights from the chandeliers. The walls were hung in paper of blue and white, above a varnished hard wood wainscoting; the monotony of surface being broken by numerous windows draped with curtains of dotted muslin, and by occasional engravings and colored pictures representing the dances of various nations, judiciously selected. The rows of chairs along the two sides of the room were left unoccupied by the time the music was well under way, for the pianist, a tall colored woman with long fingers and a muscular wrist, played with a verve and a swing that set the feet of the listeners involuntarily in motion.

The dance was sure to occupy the class for a quarter of an hour at least, and the little dancing-mistress took the opportunity to slip away to her own sitting-room, which was on the same floor of the block, for a few minutes of rest. Her day had been a hard one. There had been a matinée at two o'clock, a children's class at four, and at eight o'clock the class now on the floor had assembled.

When she reached the sitting-room she gave a start of pleasure. A young man rose at her entrance, and advanced with both hands extended—a tall, broad-shouldered, fair-haired young man, with a frank and kindly countenance, now lit up with the animation of pleasure. He seemed about twenty-six or twenty-seven years old. His face was of the type one instinctively associates with intellect and character, and it gave the impression, besides, of that intangible something which we call race. He was neatly and carefully dressed, though his clothing was not without indications that he found it necessary or expedient to practice economy.

"Good-evening, Clara," he said, taking her hands in his; "I've been waiting for you five minutes. I supposed you would be in, but if you had been a moment later I was going to the hall to look you up. You seem tired to-night," he added, drawing her nearer to him and scanning her features at short range. "This work is too hard; you are not fitted for it. When are you going to give it up?"

"The season is almost over," she answered, "and then I shall stop for the summer."

He drew her closer still and kissed her lovingly. "Tell me, Clara," he said, looking down into her face—he was at least a foot taller than she— "when I am to have my answer."

"Will you take the answer you can get to-night?" she asked with a wan smile.

"I will take but one answer, Clara. But do not make me wait too long for that. Why, just think of it! I have known you for six months."

"That is an extremely long time," said Clara, as they sat down side by side.

"It has been an age," he rejoined. "For a fortnight of it, too, which seems longer than all the rest, I have been waiting for my answer. I am turning gray under the suspense. Seriously, Clara dear, what shall it be? or rather, when shall it be? for to the other question there is but one answer possible."

He looked into her eyes, which slowly filled with tears. She repulsed him gently as he bent over to kiss them away.

"You know I love you, John, and why I do not say what you wish. You must give me a little more time to make up my mind before I can consent to burden you with a nameless wife, one who does not know who her mother was" —

"She was a good woman, and beautiful, if you are at all like her."

"Or her father"—

"He was a gentleman and a scholar, if you inherited from him your mind or your manners."

"It is good of you to say that, and I try to believe it. But it is a serious matter; it is a dreadful thing to have no name."

"You are known by a worthy one, which was freely given you, and is legally yours."

"I know—and I am grateful for it. After all, though, it is not my real name; and since I have learned that it was not, it seems like a garment—something external, accessory, and not a part of myself. It does not mean what one's own name would signify."

"Take mine, Clara, and make it yours; I lay it at your feet. Some honored men have borne it."

"Ah yes, and that is what makes my position the harder. Your great-grandfather was governor of Connecticut."

"I have heard my mother say so."

"And one of your ancestors came over in the Mayflower."

"In some capacity—I have never been quite clear whether as ship's cook or before the mast."

"Now you are insincere, John; but you cannot deceive me. You never spoke in that way about your ancestors until you learned that I had none. I know you are proud of them, and that the memory of the governor and the judge and the Harvard professor and the Mayflower pilgrim makes you strive to excel, in order to prove yourself worthy of them."

"It did until I met you, Clara. Now the one inspiration of my life is the hope to make you mine."

"And your profession?"

"It will furnish me the means to take you out of this; you are not fit for toil."

"And your book—your treatise that is to make you famous?"

"I have worked twice as hard on it and accomplished twice as much since I have hoped that you might share my success."

"Oh! if I but knew the truth!" she sighed, "or could find it out! I realize that I am absurd, that I ought to be happy. I love my parents—my foster-parents—dearly. I owe them everything. Mother—poor, dear mother!—could not have loved me better or cared for me more faithfully had I been her own child. Yet—I am ashamed to say it—I always felt that I was not like them, that there was a subtle difference between us. They were contented in prosperity, resigned in misfortune; I was ever restless, and filled with vague ambitions. They were good, but dull. They loved me, but they never said so. I feel that there is warmer, richer blood coursing in my veins than the placid stream that crept through theirs."

"There will never be any such people to me as they were," said her lover, "for they took you and brought you up for me."

"Sometimes," she went on dreamily, "I feel sure that I am of good family, and the blood of my ancestors seems to call to me in clear and certain tones. Then again when my mood changes, I am all at sea—I feel that even if I had but simply to turn my hand to learn who I am and whence I came, I should shrink from taking the step, for fear that what I might learn would leave me forever unhappy."

"Dearest," he said, taking her in his arms, while from the hall and down the corridor came the softened strains of music, "put aside these unwholesome fancies. Your past is shrouded in mystery. Take my name, as you have taken my love, and I'll make your future so happy that you won't have time to think of the past. What are a lot of musty, mouldy old grandfathers, compared with life and love and happiness? It's hardly good form to mention one's ancestors nowadays, and what's the use of them at all if one can't boast of them?"

"It's all very well of you to talk that way," she rejoined. "But suppose you should marry me, and when you become famous and rich, and patients flock to your office, and fashionable people to your home, and every one wants to know who you are and whence you came, you'll be obliged to bring out the governor, and the judge, and the rest of them. If you should refrain, in order to forestall embarrassing inquiries about *my* ancestry, I should have deprived you of something you are entitled to, something which has a real social value. And when people found out all about you, as they eventually would from some source, they would want to know—we Americans are a curious people—who your wife was, and you could only say" —

"The best and sweetest woman on earth, whom I love unspeakably."

"You know that is not what I mean. You could only say—a Miss Nobody, from Nowhere."

"A Miss Hohlfelder, from Cincinnati, the only child of worthy German parents, who fled from their own country in '49 to escape political persecution—an ancestry that one surely need not be ashamed of."

"No; but the consciousness that it was not true would be always with me, poisoning my mind, and darkening my life and yours."

"Your views of life are entirely too tragic, Clara," the young man argued soothingly. "We are all worms of the dust, and if we go back far enough, each of us has had millions of ancestors; peasants and serfs, most of them; thieves, murderers, and vagabonds, many of them, no doubt; and therefore the best of us have but little to boast of. Yet we are all made after God's own image, and formed by his hand, for his ends; and therefore not to be lightly despised, even the humblest of us, least of all by ourselves. For the past we can claim no credit, for those who made it died with it. Our destiny lies in the future."

"Yes," she sighed, "I know all that. But I am not like you. A woman is not like a man; she cannot lose herself in theories and generalizations.

And there are tests that even all your philosophy could not endure. Suppose you should marry me, and then some time, by the merest accident, you should learn that my origin was the worst it could be—that I not only had no name, but was not entitled to one."

"I cannot believe it," he said, "and from what we do know of your history it is hardly possible. If I learned it, I should forget it, unless, perchance, it should enhance your value in my eyes, by stamping you as a rare work of nature, an exception to the law of heredity, a triumph of pure beauty and goodness over the grosser limitations of matter. I cannot imagine, now that I know you, anything that could make me love you less. I would marry you just the same—even if you were one of your dancing-class to-night."

"I must go back to them," said Clara, as the music ceased.

"My answer," he urged, "give me my answer!"

"Not to-night, John," she pleaded. "Grant me a little longer time to make up my mind—for your sake."

"Not for my sake, Clara, no."

"Well—for mine." She let him take her in his arms and kiss her again.

"I have a patient yet to see to-night," he said as he went out. "If I am not detained too long, I may come back this way—if I see the lights in the hall still burning. Do not wonder if I ask you again for my answer, for I shall be unhappy until I get it."

II

A stranger entering the hall with Miss Hohlfelder would have seen, at first glance, only a company of well-dressed people, with nothing to specially distinguish them from ordinary humanity in temperate climates. After the eye had rested for a moment and begun to separate the mass into its component parts, one or two dark faces would have arrested its attention; and with the suggestion thus offered, a closer inspection would have revealed that they were nearly all a little less than white. With most of them this fact would not have been noticed, while they were alone or in company with one another, though if a fair white person had gone among them it would perhaps have been more apparent. From the few who were undistinguishable from pure white, the colors ran down the scale by minute gradations to the two or three brown faces at the other extremity.

It was Miss Hohlfelder's first colored class. She had been somewhat startled when first asked to take it. No person of color had ever applied to her for lessons; and while a woman of that race had played the piano for her for several months, she had never thought of colored people as possible pupils. So when she was asked if she would take a class of twenty or thirty, she had hesitated, and begged for time to consider the application. She knew that several of the more fashionable dancing-schools tabooed all pupils, singly or in classes, who labored under social disabilities—and this included the people of at least one other race who were vastly farther along in the world than the colored people of the community where Miss Hohlfelder lived. Personally she had no such prejudice, except perhaps a little shrinking at the thought of personal contact with the dark faces of whom Americans always think when "colored people" are spoken of. Again, a class of forty pupils was not to be despised, for she taught for money, which was equally current and desirable, regardless of its color. She had consulted her foster-parents, and after them her lover. Her foster-parents, who were German-born, and had never become thoroughly Americanized, saw no objection. As for her lover, he was indifferent.

"Do as you please," he said. "It may drive away some other pupils. If it should break up the business entirely, perhaps you might be willing to give me a chance so much the sooner."

She mentioned the matter to one or two other friends, who expressed conflicting opinions. She decided at length to take the class, and take the consequences.

"I don't think it would be either right or kind to refuse them for any such reason, and I don't believe I shall lose anything by it."

She was somewhat surprised, and pleasantly so, when her class came together for their first lesson, at not finding them darker and more un-couth. Her pupils were mostly people whom she would have passed on the street without a second glance, and among them were several whom she had known by sight for years, but had never dreamed of as being colored people. Their manners were good, they dressed quietly and as a rule with good taste, avoiding rather than choosing bright colors and striking com-binations—whether from natural preference, or because of a slightly mor-bid shrinking from criticism, of course she could not say. Among them, the dancing-mistress soon learned, there were lawyers and doctors, teachers, telegraph operators, clerks, milliners and dressmakers, students of the lo-cal college and scientific school, and, somewhat to her awe at the first meeting, even a member of the legislature. They were mostly young, al-though a few light-hearted older people joined the class, as much for com-pany as for the dancing.

"Of course, Miss Hohlfelder," explained Mr. Solomon Sadler, to whom the teacher had paid a compliment on the quality of the class, "the more advanced of us are not numerous enough to make the fine distinc-tions that are possible among white people; and of course as we rise in life we can't get entirely away from our brothers and our sisters and our cousins, who don't always keep abreast of us. We do, however, draw certain lines of character and manners and occupation. You see the sort of people we are. Of course we have no prejudice against color, and we regard all labor as honorable, provided a man does the best he can. But we must have standards that will give our people something to aspire to."

The class was not a difficult one, as many of the members were already fairly good dancers. Indeed the class had been formed as much for pleasure as for instruction. Music and hall rent and a knowledge of the latest dances could be obtained cheaper in this way than in any other. The pupils had made rapid progress, displaying in fact a natural aptitude for rhythmic motion, and a keen susceptibility to musical sounds. As their race had never been criticised for these characteristics, they gave them full play, and soon developed, most of them, into graceful and indefatigable dancers. They were now almost at the end of their course, and this was the evening of the last lesson but one.

Miss Hohlfelder had remarked to her lover more than once that it was a pleasure to teach them. "They enter into the spirit of it so thoroughly, and they seem to enjoy themselves so much."

"One would think," he suggested, "that the whitest of them would find their position painful and more or less pathetic; to be so white and yet to be classed as black—so near and yet so far."

"They don't accept our classification blindly. They do not acknowledge any inferiority; they think they are a great deal better than any but the best white people," replied Miss Hohlfelder. "And since they have been coming here, do you know," she went on, "I hardly think of them as any different from other people. I feel perfectly at home among them."

"It is a great thing to have faith in one's self," he replied. "It is a fine thing, too, to be able to enjoy the passing moment. One of your greatest charms in my eyes, Clara, is that in your lighter moods you have this faculty. You sing because you love to sing. You find pleasure in dancing, even by way of work. You feel the *joi de vivre*—the joy of living. You are not always so, but when you are so I think you most delightful."

Miss Hohlfelder, upon entering the hall, spoke to the pianist and then exchanged a few words with various members of the class. The pianist began to play a dreamy Strauss waltz. When the dance was well under way Miss Hohlfelder left the hall again and stepped into the ladies' dressing-room. There was a woman seated quietly on a couch in a corner, her hands folded on her lap.

"Good-evening, Miss Hohlfelder. You do not seem as bright as usual to-night."

Miss Hohlfelder felt a sudden yearning for sympathy. Perhaps it was the gentle tones of the greeting; perhaps the kindly expression of the soft though faded eyes that were scanning Miss Hohlfelder's features. The woman was of the indefinite age between forty and fifty. There were lines on her face which, if due to years, might have carried her even past the half-century mark, but if caused by trouble or ill health might leave her somewhat below it. She was quietly dressed in black, and wore her slightly wavy hair low over her ears, where it lay naturally in the ripples which some others of her sex so sedulously seek by art. A little woman, of clear olive complexion and regular features, her face was almost a perfect oval, except as time had marred its outline. She had been in the habit of coming to the class with some young women of the family she lived with, part boarder, part seamstress and friend of the family. Sometimes, while waiting for her young charges, the music would jar her nerves, and she would seek the comparative quiet of the dressing-room.

"Oh, I'm all right, Mrs. Harper," replied the dancing-mistress, with a brave attempt at cheerfulness—"just a little tired, after a hard day's work."

She sat down on the couch by the elder woman's side. Mrs. Harper took her hand and stroked it gently, and Clara felt soothed and quieted by her touch.

"There are tears in your eyes and trouble in your face. I know it, for I have shed the one and known the other. Tell me, child, what ails you? I am older than you, and perhaps I have learned some things in the hard school of life that may be of comfort or service to you."

Such a request, coming from a comparative stranger, might very properly have been resented or lightly parried. But Clara was not what would be called self-contained. Her griefs seemed lighter when they were shared with others, even in spirit. There was in her nature a childish strain that craved sympathy and comforting. She had never known—or if so it was only in a dim and dreamlike past—the tender, brooding care that was her conception of a mother's love. Mrs. Hohlfelder had been fond of her in a placid way, and had given her every comfort and luxury her means permitted. Clara's ideal of maternal love had been of another and more romantic type; she had thought of a fond, impulsive mother, to whose bosom she could fly when in trouble or distress, and to whom she could communicate her sorrows and trials; who would dry her tears and soothe her with caresses. Now, when even her kind foster-mother was gone, she felt still more the need of sympathy and companionship with her own sex; and when this little Mrs. Harper spoke to her so gently, she felt her heart respond instinctively.

"Yes, Mrs. Harper," replied Clara with a sigh, "I am in trouble, but it is trouble that you nor any one else can heal."

"You do not know, child. A simple remedy can sometimes cure a very grave complaint. Tell me your trouble, if it is something you are at liberty to tell."

"I have a story," said Clara, "and it is a strange one—a story I have told to but one other person, one very dear to me."

"He must be dear to you indeed, from the tone in which you speak of him. Your very accents breathe love."

"Yes, I love him, and if you saw him—perhaps you have seen him, for he has looked in here once or twice during the dancing-lessons—you would know why I love him. He is handsome, he is learned, he is ambitious, he is brave, he is good; he is poor, but he will not always be so; and he loves me, oh, so much!"

The other woman smiled. "It is not so strange to love, nor yet to be loved. And all lovers are handsome and brave and fond."

"That is not all of my story. He wants to marry me." Clara paused, as if to let this statement impress itself upon the other.

"True lovers always do," said the elder woman.

"But sometimes, you know, there are circumstances which prevent them."

"Ah yes," murmured the other reflectively, and looking at the girl with deeper interest, "circumstances which prevent them. I have known of such a case."

"The circumstance which prevents us from marrying is my story."

"Tell me your story, child, and perhaps, if I cannot help you otherwise, I can tell you one that will make yours seem less sad."

"You know me," said the young woman, "as Miss Hohlfelder; but that is not actually my name. In fact I do not know my real name, for I am not the daughter of Mr. and Mrs. Hohlfelder, but only an adopted child. While Mrs. Hohlfelder lived, I never knew that I was not her child. I knew I was very different from her and father—I mean Mr. Hohlfelder. I knew they were fair and I was dark; they were stout and I was slender; they were slow and I was quick. But of course I never dreamed of the true reason of this difference. When mother—Mrs. Hohlfelder—died, I found among her things one day a little packet, carefully wrapped up, containing a child's slip and some trinkets. The paper wrapper of the packet bore an inscription that awakened my curiosity. I asked father Hohlfelder whose the things had been, and then for the first time I learned my real story.

"I was not their own daughter, he stated, but an adopted child. Twenty-three years ago, when he had lived in St. Louis, a steamboat explosion had occurred up the river, and on a piece of wreckage floating down stream, a girl baby had been found. There was nothing on the child to give a hint of its home or parentage; and no one came to claim it, though the fact that a child had been found was advertised all along the river. It was believed that the infant's parents must have perished in the wreck, and certainly no one of those who were saved could identify the child. There had been a passenger list on board the steamer, but the list, with the officer who kept it, had been lost in the accident. The child was turned over to an orphan asylum, from which within a year it was adopted by the two kind-hearted and childless German people who brought it up as their own. I was that child."

The woman seated by Clara's side had listened with strained attention. "Did you learn the name of the steamboat?" she asked quietly, but quickly, when Clara paused.

"The Pride of St. Louis," answered Clara. She did not look at Mrs. Harper, but was gazing dreamily toward the front, and therefore did not see the expression that sprang into the other's face—a look in which hope struggled with fear, and yearning love with both—nor the strong effort with which Mrs. Harper controlled herself and moved not one muscle while the other went on.

"I was never sought," Clara continued, "and the good people who brought me up gave me every care. Father and mother—I can never train my tongue to call them anything else—were very good to me. When they adopted me they were poor; he was a pharmacist with a small shop. Later on he moved to Cincinnati, where he made and sold a popular 'patent' medicine and amassed a fortune. Then I went to a fashionable school, was taught French, and deportment, and dancing. Father Hohlfelder made some bad investments, and lost most of his money. The patent medicine fell off in popularity. A year or two ago we came to this city to live. Father bought this block and opened the little drug store below. We moved into the rooms upstairs. The business was poor, and I felt that I ought to do something to earn money and help support the family. I could dance; we had this hall, and it was not rented all the time, so I opened a dancing-school."

"Tell me, child," said the other woman, with restrained eagerness, "what were the things found upon you when you were taken from the river?"

"Yes," answered the girl, "I will. But I have not told you all my story, for this is but the prelude. About a year ago a young doctor rented an office in our block. We met each other, at first only now and then, and afterwards oftener; and six months ago he told me that he loved me."

She paused, and sat with half opened lips and dreamy eyes, looking back into the past six months.

"And the things found upon you"—

"Yes, I will show them to you when you have heard all my story. He wanted to marry me, and has asked me every week since. I have told him that I love him, but I have not said I would marry him. I don't think it would be right for me to do so, unless I could clear up this mystery. I believe he is going to be great and rich and famous, and there might come a time when he would be ashamed of me. I don't say that I shall never marry him; for I have hoped—I have a presentiment that in some strange way I shall find out who I am, and who my parents were. It may be mere imagination on my part, but somehow I believe it is more than that."

"Are you sure there was no mark on the things that were found upon you?" said the elder woman.

"Ah yes," sighed Clara, "I am sure, for I have looked at them a hundred times. They tell me nothing, and yet they suggest to me many things. Come," she said, taking the other by the hand, "and I will show them to you."

She led the way along the hall to her sitting-room, and to her bedchamber beyond. It was a small room hung with paper showing a pattern of morning-glories on a light ground, with dotted muslin curtains, a white iron bedstead, a few prints on the wall, a rocking-chair—a very dainty room. She went to the maple dressing-case, and opened one of the drawers.

As they stood for a moment, the mirror reflecting and framing their image, more than one point of resemblance between them was emphasized. There was something of the same oval face, and in Clara's hair a faint suggestion of the wave in the older woman's; and though Clara was fairer of complexion, and her eyes were gray and the other's black, there was visible, under the influence of the momentary excitement, one of those indefinable likenesses which are at times encountered—sometimes marking blood relationship, sometimes the impress of a common training; in one case perhaps a mere earmark of temperament, and in another the index of a type. Except for the difference in color, one might imagine that if the younger woman were twenty years older the resemblance would be still more apparent.

Clara reached her hand into the drawer and drew out a folded packet, which she unwrapped, Mrs. Harper following her movements meanwhile with a suppressed intensity of interest which Clara, had she not been absorbed in her own thoughts, could not have failed to observe.

When the last fold of paper was removed there lay revealed a child's muslin slip. Clara lifted it and shook it gently until it was unfolded before their eyes. The lower half was delicately worked in a lacelike pattern, revealing an immense amount of patient labor.

The elder woman seized the slip with hands which could not disguise their trembling. Scanning the garment carefully, she seemed to be noting the pattern of the needlework, and then, pointing to a certain spot, exclaimed:

"I thought so! I was sure of it! Do you not see the letters—M. S.?"

"Oh, how wonderful!" Clara seized the slip in turn and scanned the monogram. "How strange that you should see that at once and that I should not have discovered it, who have looked at it a hundred times! And here," she added, opening a small package which had been inclosed in the other, "is my coral necklace. Perhaps your keen eyes can find something in that."

It was a simple trinket, at which the older woman gave but a glance— a glance that added to her emotion.

"Listen, child," she said, laying her trembling hand on the other's arm. "It is all very strange and wonderful, for that slip and necklace, and, now that I have seen them, your face and your voice and your ways, all tell me who you are. Your eyes are your father's eyes, your voice is your father's voice. The slip was worked by your mother's hand."

"Oh!" cried Clara, and for a moment the whole world swam before her eyes.

"I was on the Pride of St. Louis, and I knew your father—and your mother."

Clara, pale with excitement, burst into tears, and would have fallen had not the other woman caught her in her arms. Mrs. Harper placed her on the couch, and, seated by her side, supported her head on her shoulder. Her hands seemed to caress the young woman with every touch.

"Tell me, oh, tell me all!" Clara demanded, when the first wave of emotion had subsided. "Who were my father and my mother, and who am I?"

The elder woman restrained her emotion with an effort, and answered as composedly as she could—

"There were several hundred passengers on the Pride of St. Louis when she left Cincinnati on that fateful day, on her regular trip to New Orleans. Your father and mother were on the boat—and I was on the boat. We were going down the river, to take ship at New Orleans for France, a country which your father loved."

"Who was my father?" asked Clara. The woman's words fell upon her ear like water on a thirsty soil.

"Your father was a Virginia gentleman, and belonged to one of the first families, the Staffords, of Melton County."

Clara drew herself up unconsciously, and into her face there came a frank expression of pride which became it wonderfully, setting off a beauty that needed only this to make it all but perfect of its type.

"I knew it must be so," she murmured. "I have often felt it. Blood will always tell. And my mother?"

"Your mother—also belonged to one of the first families of Virginia, and in her veins flowed some of the best blood of the Old Dominion."

"What was her maiden name?"

"Mary Fairfax. As I was saying, your father was a Virginia gentleman. He was as handsome a man as ever lived, and proud, oh, so proud!—and good, and kind. He was a graduate of the University and had studied abroad."

"My mother—was she beautiful?"

"She was much admired, and your father loved her from the moment he first saw her. Your father came back from Europe, upon his father's sudden death, and entered upon his inheritance. But he had been away from Virginia so long, and had read so many books, that he had outgrown his home. He did not believe that slavery was right, and one of the first things he did was to free his slaves. His views were not popular, and he sold out his lands a year before the war, with the intention of moving to Europe."

"In the mean time he had met and loved and married my mother?"

"In the mean time he had met and loved your mother."

"My mother was a Virginia belle, was she not?"

"The Fairfaxes," answered Mrs. Harper, "were the first of the first families, the bluest of the blue-bloods. The Miss Fairfaxes were all beautiful and all social favorites."

"What did my father do then, when he had sold out in Virginia?"

"He went with your mother and you—you were then just a year old—to Cincinnati, to settle up some business connected with his estate. When he had completed his business, he embarked on the Pride of St. Louis with you and your mother and a colored nurse."

"And how did you know about them?" asked Clara.

"I was one of the party. I was" —

"You were the colored nurse?—my 'mammy,' they would have called you in my old Virginia home?"

"Yes, child, I was—your mammy. Upon my bosom you have rested; my breasts once gave you nourishment; my hands once ministered to you; my arms sheltered you, and my heart loved you and mourned you like a mother loves and mourns her firstborn."

"Oh, how strange, how delightful!" exclaimed Clara. "Now I understand why you clasped me so tightly, and were so agitated when I told you my story. It is too good for me to believe. I am of good blood, of an old and aristocratic family. My presentiment has come true. I can marry my lover, and I shall owe all my happiness to you. How can I ever repay you?"

"You can kiss me, child, kiss your mammy."

Their lips met, and they were clasped in each other's arms. One put into the embrace all of her new found joy, the other all the suppressed feeling of the last half hour, which in turn embodied the unsatisfied yearning of many years.

The music had ceased and the pupils had left the hall. Mrs. Harper's charges had supposed her gone, and had left for home without her. But the two women, sitting in Clara's chamber, hand in hand, were oblivious to external things and noticed neither the hour nor the cessation of the music.

"Why, dear mammy," said the young woman musingly, "did you not find me, and restore me to my people?"

"Alas, child! I was not white, and when I was picked up from the water, after floating miles down the river, the man who found me kept me prisoner for a time, and, there being no inquiry for me, pretended not to believe that I was free, and took me down to New Orleans and sold me as a slave. A few years later the war set me free. I went to St. Louis but could find no trace of you. I had hardly dared to hope that a child had been saved, when so many grown men and women had lost their lives. I made such inquiries as I could, but all in vain."

"Did you go to the orphan asylum?"

"The orphan asylum had been burned and with it all the records. The war had scattered the people so that I could find no one who knew about a lost child saved from a river wreck. There were many orphans in those days, and one more or less was not likely to dwell in the public mind."

"Did you tell my people in Virginia?"

"They, too, were scattered by the war. Your uncles lost their lives on the battlefield. The family mansion was burned to the ground. Your father's remaining relatives were reduced to poverty, and moved away from Virginia."

"What of my mother's people?"

"They are all dead. God punished them. They did not love your father, and did not wish him to marry your mother. They helped to drive him to his death."

"I am alone in the world, then, without kith or kin," murmured Clara, "and yet, strange to say, I am happy. If I had known my people and lost them, I should be sad. They are gone, but they have left me their name and their blood. I would weep for my poor father and mother if I were not so glad."

Just then some one struck a chord upon the piano in the hall, and the sudden breaking of the stillness recalled Clara's attention to the lateness of the hour.

"I had forgotten about the class," she exclaimed. "I must go and attend to them."

They walked along the corridor and entered the hall. Dr. Winthrop was seated at the piano, drumming idly on the keys.

"I did not know where you had gone," he said. "I knew you would be around, of course, since the lights were not out, and so I came in here to wait for you."

"Listen, John, I have a wonderful story to tell you."

Then she told him Mrs. Harper's story. He listened attentively and sympathetically, at certain points taking his eyes from Clara's face and glancing keenly at Mrs. Harper, who was listening intently. As he looked from one to the other he noticed the resemblance between them, and something in his expression caused Mrs. Harper's eyes to fall, and then glance up appealingly.

"And now," said Clara, "I am happy. I know my name. I am a Virginia Stafford. I belong to one, yes, to two of what were the first families of Virginia. John, my family is as good as yours. If I remember my history correctly, the Cavaliers looked down upon the Roundheads."

"I admit my inferiority," he replied. "If you are happy I am glad."

"Clara Stafford," mused the girl. "It is a pretty name."

"You will never have to use it," her lover declared, "for now you will take mine."

"Then I shall have nothing left of all that I have found" —

"Except your husband," asserted Dr. Winthrop, putting his arm around her, with an air of assured possession.

Mrs. Harper was looking at them with moistened eyes in which joy and sorrow, love and gratitude, were strangely blended. Clara put out her hand to her impulsively.

"And my mammy," she cried, "my dear Virginia mammy."

THE SHERIFF'S CHILDREN

Branson County, North Carolina, is in a sequestered district of one of the staidest and most conservative States of the Union. Society in Branson County is almost primitive in its simplicity. Most of the white people own the farms they till, and even before the war there were no very wealthy families to force their neighbors, by comparison, into the category of "poor whites."

To Branson County, as to most rural communities in the South, the war is the one historical event that overshadows all others. It is the era from which all local chronicles are dated — births, deaths, marriages, storms, freshets. No description of the life of any Southern community would be perfect that failed to emphasize the all pervading influence of the great conflict.

Yet the fierce tide of war that had rushed through the cities and along the great highways of the country had comparatively speaking but slightly disturbed the sluggish current of life in this region, remote from railroads and navigable streams. To the north in Virginia, to the west in Tennessee, and all along the seaboard the war had raged; but the thunder of its cannon had not disturbed the echoes of Branson County, where the loudest sounds heard were the crack of some hunter's rifle, the baying of some deep-mouthed hound, or the yodel of some tuneful negro on his way through the pine forest. To the east, Sherman's army had passed on its march to the sea; but no straggling band of "bummers" had penetrated the confines of Branson County. The war, it is true, had robbed the county of the flower of its young manhood; but the burden of taxation, the doubt and uncertainty of the conflict, and the sting of ultimate defeat, had been borne by the people with an apathy that robbed misfortune of half its sharpness.

The nearest approach to town life afforded by Branson County is found in the little village of Troy, the county seat, a hamlet with a population of four or five hundred.

Ten years make little difference in the appearance of these remote Southern towns. If a railroad is built through one of them, it infuses some enterprise; the social corpse is galvanized by the fresh blood of civilization that pulses along the farthest ramifications of our great system of commercial highways. At the period of which I write, no railroad had come to Troy. If a traveler, accustomed to the bustling life of cities, could have ridden through Troy on a summer day, he might easily have fancied himself in a deserted village. Around him he would have seen weather-beaten houses, innocent of paint, the shingled roofs in many instances covered with a rich growth of moss. Here and there he would have met a razor-backed hog lazily rooting his way along the principal thoroughfare; and more than once he would probably have had to disturb the slumbers of some yellow dog, dozing away the hours in the ardent sunshine, and reluctantly yielding up his place in the middle of the dusty road.

On Saturdays the village presented a somewhat livelier appearance, and the shade trees around the court house square and along Front Street served as hitching-posts for a goodly number of horses and mules and stunted oxen, belonging to the farmer-folk who had come in to trade at the two or three local stores.

A murder was a rare event in Branson County. Every well-informed citizen could tell the number of homicides committed in the county for fifty years back, and whether the slayer, in any given instance, had escaped, either by flight or acquittal, or had suffered the penalty of the law. So, when it became known in Troy early one Friday morning in summer, about ten years after the war, that old Captain Walker, who had served in Mexico under Scott, and had left an arm on the field of Gettysburg, had been foully murdered during the night, there was intense excitement in the village. Business was practically suspended, and the citizens gathered in little groups to discuss the murder, and speculate upon the identity of the murderer. It transpired from testimony at the coroner's inquest, held during the morning, that a strange mulatto had been seen going in the direction of Captain Walker's house the night before, and had been met going away from Troy early Friday morning, by a farmer on his way to town. Other circumstances seemed to connect the stranger with the crime. The sheriff organized a posse to search for him, and early in the evening, when most of the citizens of Troy were at supper, the suspected man was brought in and lodged in the county jail.

By the following morning the news of the capture had spread to the farthest limits of the county. A much larger number of people than usual came to town that Saturday—bearded men in straw hats and blue homespun shirts, and butternut trousers of great amplitude of material and vagueness of outline; women in homespun frocks and slat-bonnets, with faces as expressionless as the dreary sandhills which gave them a meagre sustenance.

The murder was almost the sole topic of conversation. A steady stream of curious observers visited the house of mourning, and gazed upon the rugged face of the old veteran, now stiff and cold in death; and more than one eye dropped a tear at the remembrance of the cheery smile, and the joke—sometimes superannuated, generally feeble, but always good-natured—with which the captain had been wont to greet his acquaintances. There was a growing sentiment of anger among these stern men, toward the murderer who had thus cut down their friend, and a strong feeling that ordinary justice was too slight a punishment for such a crime.

Toward noon there was an informal gathering of citizens in Dan Tyson's store.

"I hear it 'lowed that Square Kyahtah's too sick ter hol' co'te this evenin'," said one, "an' that the purlim'nary hearin' 'll haf ter go over 'tel nex' week."

A look of disappointment went round the crowd.

"Hit 's the durndes', meanes' murder ever committed in this caounty," said another, with moody emphasis.

"I s'pose the nigger 'lowed the Cap'n had some greenbacks," observed a third speaker.

"The Cap'n," said another, with an air of superior information, "has left two bairls of Confedrit money, which he 'spected 'ud be good some day er nuther."

This statement gave rise to a discussion of the speculative value of Confederate money; but in a little while the conversation returned to the murder.

"Hangin' air too good fer the murderer," said one; "he oughter be burnt, stidier bein' hung."

There was an impressive pause at this point, during which a jug of moonlight whiskey went the round of the crowd.

"Well," said a round-shouldered farmer, who, in spite of his peaceable expression and faded gray eye, was known to have been one of the most daring followers of a rebel guerrilla chieftain, "what air yer gwine ter do about it? Ef you fellers air gwine ter set down an' let a wuthless nigger kill the bes' white man in Branson, an' not say nuthin' ner do nuthin', *I'll* move outen the caounty."

This speech gave tone and direction to the rest of the conversation. Whether the fear of losing the round-shouldered farmer operated to bring about the result or not is immaterial to this narrative; but, at all events, the crowd decided to lynch the negro. They agreed that this was the least that could be done to avenge the death of their murdered friend, and that it was a becoming way in which to honor his memory. They had some vague notions of the majesty of the law and the rights of the citizen, but in the passion of the moment these sunk into oblivion; a white man had been killed by a negro.

"The Cap'n was an ole sodger," said one of his friends solemnly. "He'll sleep better when he knows that a co'te-martial has be'n hilt an' jestice done."

By agreement the lynchers were to meet at Tyson's store at five o'clock in the afternoon, and proceed thence to the jail, which was situated down the Lumberton Dirt Road (as the old turnpike antedating the plank-road was called), about half a mile south of the court-house. When the preliminaries of the lynching had been arranged, and a committee appointed to manage the affair, the crowd dispersed, some to go to their dinners, and some to secure recruits for the lynching party.

It was twenty minutes to five o'clock, when an excited negro, panting and perspiring, rushed up to the back door of Sheriff Campbell's dwelling, which stood at a little distance from the jail and somewhat farther than the latter building from the court-house. A turbaned colored woman came to the door in response to the negro's knock.

"Hoddy, Sis' Nance."

"Hoddy, Brer Sam."

"Is de shurff in," inquired the negro.

"Yas, Brer Sam, he's eatin' his dinner," was the answer.

"Will yer ax 'im ter step ter de do' a minute, Sis' Nance?"

The woman went into the dining-room, and a moment later the sheriff came to the door. He was a tall, muscular man, of a ruddier complexion than is usual among Southerners. A pair of keen, deep-set gray eyes looked out from under bushy eyebrows, and about his mouth was a masterful expression, which a full beard, once sandy in color, but now profusely sprinkled with gray, could not entirely conceal. The day was hot; the sheriff had discarded his coat and vest, and had his white shirt open at the throat.

"What do you want, Sam?" he inquired of the negro, who stood hat in hand, wiping the moisture from his face with a ragged shirt-sleeve.

"Shurff, dey gwine ter hang de pris'ner w'at's lock' up in de jail. Dey're comin' dis a-way now. I wuz layin' down on a sack er corn down at de sto', behine a pile er flour-bairls, w'en I hearn Doc' Cain en Kunnel Wright talkin' erbout it. I slip' outen de back do', en run here as fas' as I could. I hearn you say down ter de sto' once't dat you would n't let nobody take a pris'ner 'way fum you widout walkin' over yo' dead body, en I thought I'd let you know 'fo' dey come, so yer could pertec' de pris'ner."

The sheriff listened calmly, but his face grew firmer, and a determined gleam lit up his gray eyes. His frame grew more erect, and he unconsciously assumed the attitude of a soldier who momentarily expects to meet the enemy face to face.

"Much obliged, Sam," he answered. "I'll protect the prisoner. Who's coming?"

"I dunno who-all *is* comin'," replied the negro. "Dere's Mistah McSwayne, en Doc' Cain, en Maje' McDonal', en Kunnel Wright, en a heap er yuthers. I wuz so skeered I done furgot mo' d'n half un em. I spec' dey mus' be mos' here by dis time, so I'll git outen de way, fer I don' want nobody fer ter think I wuz mix' up in dis business." The negro glanced nervously down the road toward the town, and made a movement as if to go away.

"Won't you have some dinner first?" asked the sheriff.

The negro looked longingly in at the open door, and sniffed the appetizing odor of boiled pork and collards.

"I ain't got no time fer ter tarry, Shurff," he said, "but Sis' Nance mought gin me sump'n I could kyar in my han' en eat on de way."

A moment later Nancy brought him a huge sandwich of split corn-pone, with a thick slice of fat bacon inserted between the halves, and a couple of baked yams. The negro hastily replaced his ragged hat on his head, dropped the yams in the pocket of his capacious trousers, and, taking the sandwich in his hand, hurried across the road and disappeared in the woods beyond.

The sheriff reëntered the house, and put on his coat and hat. He then took down a double-barreled shotgun and loaded it with buckshot. Filling the chambers of a revolver with fresh cartridges, he slipped it into the pocket of the sack-coat which he wore.

A comely young woman in a calico dress watched these proceedings with anxious surprise.

"Where are you going, father?" she asked. She had not heard the conversation with the negro.

"I am goin' over to the jail," responded the sheriff. "There's a mob comin' this way to lynch the nigger we've got locked up. But they won't do it," he added, with emphasis.

"Oh, father! don't go!" pleaded the girl, clinging to his arm; "they'll shoot you if you don't give him up."

"You never mind me, Polly," said her father reassuringly, as he gently unclasped her hands from his arm. "I'll take care of myself and the prisoner, too. There ain't a man in Branson County that would shoot me. Besides, I have faced fire too often to be scared away from my duty. You keep close in the house," he continued, "and if any one disturbs you just use the old horse-pistol in the top bureau drawer. It's a little old-fashioned, but it did good work a few years ago."

The young girl shuddered at this sanguinary allusion, but made no further objection to her father's departure.

The sheriff of Branson was a man far above the average of the community in wealth, education, and social position. His had been one of the few families in the county that before the war had owned large estates and numerous slaves. He had graduated at the State University at Chapel Hill, and had kept up some acquaintance with current literature and advanced thought. He had traveled some in his youth, and was looked up to in the county as an authority on all subjects connected with the outer world. At first an ardent supporter of the Union, he had opposed the secession movement in his native State as long as opposition availed to stem the tide of public opinion. Yielding at last to the force of circumstances, he had entered the Confederate service rather late in the war, and served with distinction through several campaigns, rising in time to the rank of colonel. After the war he had taken the oath of allegiance, and had been chosen by the people as the most available candidate for the office of sheriff, to which he had been elected without opposition. He had filled the office for several terms, and was universally popular with his constituents.

Colonel or Sheriff Campbell, as he was indifferently called, as the military or civil title happened to be most important in the opinion of the person addressing him, had a high sense of the responsibility attaching to his office. He had sworn to do his duty faithfully, and he knew what his duty was, as sheriff, perhaps more clearly than he had apprehended it in other passages of his life. It was, therefore, with no uncertainty in regard to his course that he prepared his weapons and went over to the jail. He had no fears for Polly's safety.

The sheriff had just locked the heavy front door of the jail behind him when a half dozen horsemen, followed by a crowd of men on foot, came round a bend in the road and drew near the jail. They halted in front of the picket fence that surrounded the building, while several of the committee of arrangements rode on a few rods farther to the sheriff's house. One of them dismounted and rapped on the door with his riding-whip.

"Is the sheriff at home?" he inquired.

"No, he has just gone out," replied Polly, who had come to the door.

"We want the jail keys," he continued.

"They are not here," said Polly. "The sheriff has them himself." Then she added, with assumed indifference, "He is at the jail now."

The man turned away, and Polly went into the front room, from which she peered anxiously between the slats of the green blinds of a window that looked toward the jail. Meanwhile the messenger returned to his companions and announced his discovery. It looked as though the sheriff had learned of their design and was preparing to resist it.

One of them stepped forward and rapped on the jail door.

"Well, what is it?" said the sheriff, from within.

"We want to talk to you, Sheriff," replied the spokesman.

There was a little wicket in the door; this the sheriff opened, and answered through it.

"All right, boys, talk away. You are all strangers to me, and I don't know what business you can have." The sheriff did not think it necessary to recognize anybody in particular on such an occasion; the question of identity sometimes comes up in the investigation of these extra-judicial executions.

"We're a committee of citizens and we want to get into the jail."

"What for? It ain't much trouble to get into jail. Most people want to keep out."

The mob was in no humor to appreciate a joke, and the sheriff's witticism fell dead upon an unresponsive audience.

"We want to have a talk with the nigger that killed Cap'n Walker."

"You can talk to that nigger in the courthouse, when he's brought out for trial. Court will be in session here next week. I know what you fellows want, but you can't get my prisoner to-day. Do you want to take the bread out of a poor man's mouth? I get seventy-five cents a day for keeping this prisoner, and he's the only one in jail. I can't have my family suffer just to please you fellows."

One or two young men in the crowd laughed at the idea of Sheriff Campbell's suffering for want of seventy-five cents a day; but they were frowned into silence by those who stood near them.

"Ef yer don't let us in," cried a voice, "we'll bu's' the do' open."

"Bust away," answered the sheriff, raising his voice so that all could hear. "But I give you fair warning. The first man that tries it will be filled with buckshot. I'm sheriff of this county; I know my duty, and I mean to do it."

"What's the use of kicking, Sheriff?" argued one of the leaders of the mob. "The nigger is sure to hang anyhow; he richly deserves it; and we've got to do something to teach the niggers their places, or white people won't be able to live in the county."

"There's no use talking, boys," responded the sheriff. "I'm a white man outside, but in this jail I'm sheriff; and if this nigger's to be hung in this county, I propose to do the hanging. So you fellows might as well right-about-face, and march back to Troy. You've had a pleasant trip, and the exercise will be good for you. You know *me*. I've got powder and ball, and I've faced fire before now, with nothing between me and the enemy, and I don't mean to surrender this jail while I'm able to shoot." Having thus announced his determination, the sheriff closed and fastened the wicket, and looked around for the best position from which to defend the building.

The crowd drew off a little, and the leaders conversed together in low tones.

The Branson County jail was a small, two-story brick building, strongly constructed, with no attempt at architectural ornamentation. Each story was divided into two large cells by a passage running from front to rear. A grated iron door gave entrance from the passage to each of the four cells. The jail seldom had many prisoners in it, and the lower windows had been boarded up. When the sheriff had closed the wicket, he ascended the steep wooden stairs to the upper floor. There was no window at the front of the upper passage, and the most available position from which to watch the movements of the crowd below was the front window of the cell occupied by the solitary prisoner.

The sheriff unlocked the door and entered the cell. The prisoner was crouched in a corner, his yellow face, blanched with terror, looking ghastly in the semi-darkness of the room. A cold perspiration had gathered on his forehead, and his teeth were chattering with affright.

"For God's sake, Sheriff," he murmured hoarsely, "don't let 'em lynch me; I did n't kill the old man."

The sheriff glanced at the cowering wretch with a look of mingled contempt and loathing.

"Get up," he said sharply. "You will probably be hung sooner or later, but it shall not be to-day, if I can help it. I'll unlock your fetters, and if I can't hold the jail, you'll have to make the best fight you can. If I'm shot, I'll consider my responsibility at an end."

There were iron fetters on the prisoner's ankles, and handcuffs on his wrists. These the sheriff unlocked, and they fell clanking to the floor.

"Keep back from the window," said the sheriff. "They might shoot if they saw you."

The sheriff drew toward the window a pine bench which formed a part of the scanty furniture of the cell, and laid his revolver upon it. Then he took his gun in hand, and took his stand at the side of the window where he could with least exposure of himself watch the movements of the crowd below.

The lynchers had not anticipated any determined resistance. Of course they had looked for a formal protest, and perhaps a sufficient show of opposition to excuse the sheriff in the eye of any stickler for legal formalities. They had not however come prepared to fight a battle, and no one of them seemed willing to lead an attack upon the jail. The leaders of the party conferred together with a good deal of animated gesticulation, which was visible to the sheriff from his outlook, though the distance was too great for him to hear what was said. At length one of them broke away from the group, and rode back to the main body of the lynchers, who were restlessly awaiting orders.

"Well, boys," said the messenger, "we'll have to let it go for the present. The sheriff says he'll shoot, and he's got the drop on us this time. There ain't any of us that want to follow Cap'n Walker jest yet. Besides, the sheriff is a good fellow, and we don't want to hurt 'im. But," he added, as if to reassure the crowd, which began to show signs of disappointment, "the nigger might as well say his prayers, for he ain't got long to live."

There was a murmur of dissent from the mob, and several voices insisted that an attack be made on the jail. But pacific counsels finally prevailed, and the mob sullenly withdrew.

The sheriff stood at the window until they had disappeared around the bend in the road. He did not relax his watchfulness when the last one was out of sight. Their withdrawal might be a mere feint, to be followed by a further attempt. So closely, indeed, was his attention drawn to the outside, that he neither saw nor heard the prisoner creep stealthily across the floor, reach out his hand and secure the revolver which lay on the bench behind the sheriff, and creep as noiselessly back to his place in the corner of the room.

A moment after the last of the lynching party had disappeared there was a shot fired from the woods across the road; a bullet whistled by the window and buried itself in the wooden casing a few inches from where the sheriff was standing. Quick as thought, with the instinct born of a semi-guerrilla army experience, he raised his gun and fired twice at the point from which a faint puff of smoke showed the hostile bullet to have been sent. He stood a moment watching, and then rested his gun against the window, and reached behind him mechanically for the other weapon. It was not on the bench. As the sheriff realized this fact, he turned his head and looked into the muzzle of the revolver.

"Stay where you are, Sheriff," said the prisoner, his eyes glistening, his face almost ruddy with excitement.

The sheriff mentally cursed his own carelessness for allowing him to be caught in such a predicament. He had not expected anything of the kind. He had relied on the negro's cowardice and subordination in the presence of an armed white man as a matter of course. The sheriff was a brave man, but realized that the prisoner had him at an immense disadvantage. The two men stood thus for a moment, fighting a harmless duel with their eyes.

"Well, what do you mean to do?" asked the sheriff with apparent calmness.

"To get away, of course," said the prisoner, in a tone which caused the sheriff to look at him more closely, and with an involuntary feeling of apprehension; if the man was not mad, he was in a state of mind akin to madness, and quite as dangerous. The sheriff felt that he must speak the prisoner fair, and watch for a chance to turn the tables on him. The keen-eyed, desperate man before him was a different being altogether from the groveling wretch who had begged so piteously for life a few minutes before.

At length the sheriff spoke:

"Is this your gratitude to me for saving your life at the risk of my own? If I had not done so, you would now be swinging from the limb of some neighboring tree."

"True," said the prisoner, "you saved my life, but for how long? When you came in, you said Court would sit next week. When the crowd went away they said I had not long to live. It is merely a choice of two ropes."

"While there's life there's hope," replied the sheriff. He uttered this commonplace mechanically, while his brain was busy in trying to think out some way of escape. "If you are innocent you can prove it."

The mulatto kept his eye upon the sheriff. "I did n't kill the old man," he replied; "but I shall never be able to clear myself. I was at his house at nine o'clock. I stole from it the coat that was on my back when I was taken. I would be convicted, even with a fair trial, unless the real murderer were discovered beforehand."

The sheriff knew this only too well. While he was thinking what argument next to use, the prisoner continued:

"Throw me the keys—no, unlock the door."

The sheriff stood a moment irresolute. The mulatto's eye glittered ominously. The sheriff crossed the room and unlocked the door leading into the passage.

"Now go down and unlock the outside door."

The heart of the sheriff leaped within him. Perhaps he might make a dash for liberty, and gain the outside. He descended the narrow stairs, the prisoner keeping close behind him.

The sheriff inserted the huge iron key into the lock. The rusty bolt yielded slowly. It still remained for him to pull the door open.

"Stop!" thundered the mulatto, who seemed to divine the sheriff's purpose. "Move a muscle, and I'll blow your brains out."

The sheriff obeyed; he realized that his chance had not yet come.

"Now keep on that side of the passage, and go back upstairs."

Keeping the sheriff under cover of the revolver, the mulatto followed him up the stairs. The sheriff expected the prisoner to lock him into the cell and make his own escape. He had about come to the conclusion that the best thing he could do under the circumstances was to submit quietly, and take his chances of recapturing the prisoner after the alarm had been given. The sheriff had faced death more than once upon the battlefield. A few minutes before, well armed, and with a brick wall between him and them he had dared a hundred men to fight; but he felt instinctively that the desperate man confronting him was not to be trifled with, and he was too prudent a man to risk his life against such heavy odds. He had Polly to look after, and there was a limit beyond which devotion to duty would be quixotic and even foolish.

"I want to get away," said the prisoner, "and I don't want to be captured; for if I am I know I will be hung on the spot. I am afraid," he added somewhat reflectively, "that in order to save myself I shall have to kill you."

"Good God!" exclaimed the sheriff in involuntary terror; "you would not kill the man to whom you owe your own life."

"You speak more truly than you know," replied the mulatto. "I indeed owe my life to you."

The sheriff started. He was capable of surprise, even in that moment of extreme peril. "Who are you?" he asked in amazement.

"Tom, Cicely's son," returned the other. He had closed the door and stood talking to the sheriff through the grated opening. "Don't you remember Cicely—Cicely whom you sold, with her child, to the speculator on his way to Alabama?"

The sheriff did remember. He had been sorry for it many a time since. It had been the old story of debts, mortgages, and bad crops. He had quarreled with the mother. The price offered for her and her child had been

unusually large, and he had yielded to the combination of anger and pe-
cuniary stress.

"Good God!" he gasped, "you would not murder your own father?"

"My father?" replied the mulatto. "It were well enough for me to
claim the relationship, but it comes with poor grace from you to ask anything by reason of it. What father's duty have you ever performed for me?
Did you give me your name, or even your protection? Other white men
gave their colored sons freedom and money, and sent them to the free States.
You sold me to the rice swamps."

"I at least gave you the life you cling to," murmured the sheriff.

"Life?" said the prisoner, with a sarcastic laugh. "What kind of a life?
You gave me your own blood, your own features—no man need look at us
together twice to see that—and you gave me a black mother. Poor wretch!
She died under the lash, because she had enough womanhood to call her
soul her own. You gave me a white man's spirit, and you made me a slave,
and crushed it out."

"But you are free now," said the sheriff. He had not doubted, could
not doubt, the mulatto's word. He knew whose passions coursed beneath
that swarthy skin and burned in the black eyes opposite his own. He saw
in this mulatto what he himself might have become had not the safeguards
of parental restraint and public opinion been thrown around him.

"Free to do what?" replied the mulatto. "Free in name, but despised
and scorned and set aside by the people to whose race I belong far more
than to my mother's."

"There are schools," said the sheriff. "You have been to school." He
had noticed that the mulatto spoke more eloquently and used better language than most Branson County people.

"I have been to school, and dreamed when I went that it would work
some marvelous change in my condition. But what did I learn? I learned to
feel that no degree of learning or wisdom will change the color of my skin
and that I shall always wear what in my own country is a badge of degradation. When I think about it seriously I do not care particularly for such
a life. It is the animal in me, not the man, that flees the gallows. I owe you
nothing," he went on, "and expect nothing of you; and it would be no
more than justice if I should avenge upon you my mother's wrongs and my
own. But still I hate to shoot you; I have never yet taken human life—for
I did not kill the old captain. Will you promise to give no alarm and make
no attempt to capture me until morning, if I do not shoot?"

So absorbed were the two men in their colloquy and their own tu-
multuous thoughts that neither of them had heard the door below move
upon its hinges. Neither of them had heard a light step come stealthily up

the stairs, nor seen a slender form creep along the darkening passage toward the mulatto.

The sheriff hesitated. The struggle between his love of life and his sense
of duty was a terrific one. It may seem strange that a man who could sell
his own child into slavery should hesitate at such a moment, when his life
was trembling in the balance. But the baleful influence of human slavery
poisoned the very fountains of life, and created new standards of right. The
sheriff was conscientious; his conscience had merely been warped by his
environment. Let no one ask what his answer would have been; he was
spared the necessity of a decision.

"Stop," said the mulatto, "you need not promise. I could not trust you
if you did. It is your life for mine; there is but one safe way for me; you
must die."

He raised his arm to fire, when there was a flash—a report from the
passage behind him. His arm fell heavily at his side, and the pistol dropped
at his feet.

The sheriff recovered first from his surprise, and throwing open the
door secured the fallen weapon. Then seizing the prisoner he thrust him
into the cell and locked the door upon him; after which he turned to Polly,
who leaned half-fainting against the wall, her hands clasped over her
heart.

"Oh, father, I was just in time!" she cried hysterically, and, wildly sobbing, threw herself into her father's arms.

"I watched until they all went away," she said. "I heard the shot from
the woods and I saw you shoot. Then when you did not come out I feared
something had happened, that perhaps you had been wounded. I got out
the other pistol and ran over here. When I found the door open, I knew
something was wrong, and when I heard voices I crept upstairs, and
reached the top just in time to hear him say he would kill you. Oh, it was
a narrow escape!"

When she had grown somewhat calmer, the sheriff left her standing
there and went back into the cell. The prisoner's arm was bleeding from a
flesh wound. His bravado had given place to a stony apathy. There was no
sign in his face of fear or disappointment or feeling of any kind. The sheriff sent Polly to the house for cloth, and bound up the prisoner's wound
with a rude skill acquired during his army life.

"I'll have a doctor come and dress the wound in the morning," he said
to the prisoner. "It will do very well until then, if you will keep quiet. If the
doctor asks you how the wound was caused, you can say that you were
struck by the bullet fired from the woods. It would do you no good to have
it known that you were shot while attempting to escape."

The prisoner uttered no word of thanks or apology, but sat in sullen silence. When the wounded arm had been bandaged, Polly and her father returned to the house.

The sheriff was in an unusually thoughtful mood that evening. He put salt in his coffee at supper, and poured vinegar over his pancakes. To many of Polly's questions he returned random answers. When he had gone to bed he lay awake for several hours.

In the silent watches of the night, when he was alone with God, there came into his mind a flood of unaccustomed thoughts. An hour or two before, standing face to face with death, he had experienced a sensation similar to that which drowning men are said to feel—a kind of clarifying of the moral faculty, in which the veil of the flesh, with its obscuring passions and prejudices, is pushed aside for a moment, and all the acts of one's life stand out, in the clear light of truth, in their correct proportions and relations—a state of mind in which one sees himself as God may be supposed to see him. In the reaction following his rescue, this feeling had given place for a time to far different emotions. But now, in the silence of midnight, something of this clearness of spirit returned to the sheriff. He saw that he had owed some duty to this son of his—that neither law nor custom could destroy a responsibility inherent in the nature of mankind. He could not thus, in the eyes of God at least, shake off the consequences of his sin. Had he never sinned, this wayward spirit would never have come back from the vanished past to haunt him. As these thoughts came, his anger against the mulatto died away, and in its place there sprang up a great pity. The hand of parental authority might have restrained the passions he had seen burning in the prisoner's eyes when the desperate man spoke the words which had seemed to doom his father to death. The sheriff felt that he might have saved this fiery spirit from the slough of slavery; that he might have sent him to the free North, and given him there, or in some other land, an opportunity to turn to usefulness and honorable pursuits the talents that had run to crime, perhaps to madness; he might, still less, have given this son of his the poor simulacrum of liberty which men of his caste could possess in a slave-holding community; or least of all, but still something, he might have kept the boy on the plantation, where the burdens of slavery would have fallen lightly upon him.

The sheriff recalled his own youth. He had inherited an honored name to keep untarnished; he had had a future to make; the picture of a fair young bride had beckoned him on to happiness. The poor wretch now stretched upon a pallet of straw between the brick walls of the jail had had none of these things—no name, no father, no mother—in the true meaning of motherhood—and until the past few years no possible future, and then one vague and shadowy in its outline, and dependent for form and substance upon the slow solution of a problem in which there were many unknown quantities.

From what he might have done to what he might yet do was an easy transition for the awakened conscience of the sheriff. It occurred to him, purely as a hypothesis, that he might permit his prisoner to escape; but his oath of office, his duty as sheriff, stood in the way of such a course, and the sheriff dismissed the idea from his mind. He could, however, investigate the circumstances of the murder, and move Heaven and earth to discover the real criminal, for he no longer doubted the prisoner's innocence; he could employ counsel for the accused, and perhaps influence public opinion in his favor. An acquittal once secured, some plan could be devised by which the sheriff might in some degree atone for his crime against this son of his—against society—against God.

When the sheriff had reached this conclusion he fell into an unquiet slumber, from which he awoke late the next morning.

He went over to the jail before breakfast and found the prisoner lying on his pallet, his face turned to the wall; he did not move when the sheriff rattled the door.

"Good-morning," said the latter, in a tone intended to waken the prisoner.

There was no response. The sheriff looked more keenly at the recumbent figure; there was an unnatural rigidity about its attitude.

He hastily unlocked the door and, entering the cell, bent over the prostrate form. There was no sound of breathing; he turned the body over—it was cold and stiff. The prisoner had torn the bandage from his wound and bled to death during the night. He had evidently been dead several hours.

A MATTER OF PRINCIPLE

I

"What our country needs most in its treatment of the race problem," observed Mr. Cicero Clayton at one of the monthly meetings of the Blue Vein Society, of which he was a prominent member, "is a clearer conception of the brotherhood of man."

The same sentiment in much the same words had often fallen from Mr. Clayton's lips—so often, in fact, that the younger members of the society sometimes spoke of him—among themselves of course—as

"Brotherhood Clayton." The sobriquet derived its point from the application he made of the principle involved in this oft-repeated proposition.

The fundamental article of Mr. Clayton's social creed was that he himself was not a negro.

"I know," he would say, "that the white people lump us all together as negroes, and condemn us all to the same social ostracism. But I don't accept this classification, for my part, and I imagine that, as the chief party in interest, I have a right to my opinion. People who belong by half or more of their blood to the most virile and progressive race of modern times have as much right to call themselves white as others have to call them negroes."

Mr. Clayton spoke warmly, for he was well informed, and had thought much upon the subject; too much, indeed, for he had not been able to escape entirely the tendency of too much concentration upon one subject to make even the clearest minds morbid.

"Of course we can't enforce our claims, or protect ourselves from being robbed of our birthright; but we can at least have principles, and try to live up to them the best we can. If we are not accepted as white, we can at any rate make it clear that we object to being called black. Our protest cannot fail in time to impress itself upon the better class of white people; for the Anglo-Saxon race loves justice, and will eventually do it, where it does not conflict with their own interests."

Whether or not the fact that Mr. Clayton meant no sarcasm, and was conscious of no inconsistency in this eulogy, tended to establish the racial identity he claimed may safely be left to the discerning reader.

In living up to his creed Mr. Clayton declined to associate to any considerable extent with black people. This was sometimes a little inconvenient, and occasionally involved a sacrifice of some pleasure for himself and his family, because they would not attend entertainments where many black people were likely to be present. But they had a social refuge in a little society of people like themselves; they attended, too, a church, of which nearly all the members were white, and they were connected with a number of the religious and benevolent associations open to all good citizens, where they came into contact with the better class of white people, and were treated, in their capacity of members, with a courtesy and consideration scarcely different from that accorded to other citizens.

Mr. Clayton's racial theory was not only logical enough, but was in his own case backed up by substantial arguments. He had begun life with a small patrimony, and had invested his money in a restaurant, which by careful and judicious attention had grown from a cheap eating-house into the most popular and successful confectionery and catering establishment in Groveland. His business occupied a double store on Oakwood Avenue. He owned houses and lots, and stocks and bonds, had good credit at the banks, and lived in a style befitting his income and business standing. In person he was of olive complexion, with slightly curly hair. His features approached the Cuban or Latin-American type rather than the familiar broad characteristics of the mulatto, this suggestion of something foreign being heightened by a Vandyke beard and a carefully waxed and pointed mustache. When he walked to church on Sunday mornings with his daughter Alice, they were a couple of such striking appearance as surely to attract attention.

Miss Alice Clayton was queen of her social set. She was young, she was handsome. She was nearly white; she frankly confessed her sorrow that she was not entirely so. She was accomplished and amiable, dressed in good taste, and had for her father by all odds the richest colored man—the term is used with apologies to Mr. Clayton, explaining that it does not necessarily mean a negro—in Groveland. So pronounced was her superiority that really she had but one social rival worthy of the name—Miss Lura Watkins, whose father kept a prosperous livery stable and lived in almost as good style as the Claytons. Miss Watkins, while good-looking enough, was not so young nor quite so white as Miss Clayton. She was popular, however, among their mutual acquaintances, and there was a good-natured race between the two as to which should make the first and best marriage.

Marriages among Miss Clayton's set were serious affairs. Of course marriage is always a serious matter, whether it be a success or a failure, and there are those who believe that any marriage is better than no marriage. But among Miss Clayton's friends and associates matrimony took on an added seriousness because of the very narrow limits within which it could take place. Miss Clayton and her friends, by reason of their assumed superiority to black people, or perhaps as much by reason of a somewhat morbid shrinking from the curiosity manifested toward married people of strongly contrasting colors, would not marry black men, and except in rare instances white men would not marry them. They were therefore restricted for a choice to the young men of their own complexion. But these, unfortunately for the girls, had a wider choice. In any State where the laws permit freedom of the marriage contract, a man, by virtue of his sex, can find a wife of whatever complexion he prefers; of course he must not always ask too much in other respects, for most women like to better their social position when they marry. To the number thus lost by "going on the other side," as the phrase went, add the worthless contingent whom no self-respecting woman would marry, and the choice was still further restricted; so that it had become fashionable, when the supply of eligible men ran short, for those of Miss Clayton's set who could afford it to go traveling, ostensibly for pleasure, but with the serious hope that they might meet their fate away from home.

Miss Clayton had perhaps a larger option than any of her associates. Among such men as there were she could have taken her choice. Her beauty, her position, her accomplishments, her father's wealth, all made her eminently desirable. But, on the other hand, the same things rendered her more difficult to reach, and harder to please. To get access to her heart, too, it was necessary to run the gauntlet of her parents, which, until she had reached the age of twenty-three, no one had succeeded in doing safely. Many had called, but none had been chosen.

There was, however, one spot left unguarded, and through it Cupid, a veteran sharpshooter, sent a dart. Mr. Clayton had taken into his service and into his household a poor relation, a sort of cousin several times removed. This boy—his name was Jack—had gone into Mr. Clayton's service at a very youthful age—twelve or thirteen. He had helped about the housework, washed the dishes, swept the floors, taken care of the lawn and the stable for three or four years, while he attended school. His cousin had then taken him into the store, where he had swept the floor, washed the windows, and done a class of work that kept fully impressed upon him the fact that he was a poor dependent. Nevertheless he was a cheerful lad, who took what he could get and was properly grateful, but always meant to get more. By sheer force of industry and affability and shrewdness, he forced his employer to promote him in time to a position of recognized authority in the establishment. Any one outside of the family would have perceived in him a very suitable husband for Miss Clayton; he was of about the same age, or a year or two older, was as fair of complexion as she, when she was not powdered, and was passably good-looking, with a bearing of which the natural manliness had been no more warped than his training and racial status had rendered inevitable; for he had early learned the law of growth, that to bend is better than to break. He was sometimes sent to accompany Miss Clayton to places in the evening, when she had no other escort, and it is quite likely that she discovered his good points before her parents did. That they should in time perceive them was inevitable. But even then, so accustomed were they to looking down upon the object of their former bounty, that they only spoke of the matter jocularly.

"Well, Alice," her father would say in his bluff way, "you'll not be absolutely obliged to die an old maid. If we can't find anything better for you, there's always Jack. As long as he does n't take to some other girl, you can fall back on him as a last chance. He'd be glad to take you to get into the business."

Miss Alice had considered the joke a very poor one when first made, but by occasional repetition she became somewhat familiar with it. In time it got around to Jack himself, to whom it seemed no joke at all. He had long considered it a consummation devoutly to be wished, and when he became aware that the possibility of such a match had occurred to the other parties in interest, he made up his mind that the idea should in due course of time become an accomplished fact. He had even suggested as much to Alice, in a casual way, to feel his ground; and while she had treated the matter lightly, he was not without hope that she had been impressed by the suggestion. Before he had had time, however, to follow up this lead, Miss Clayton, in the spring of 187–, went away on a visit to Washington.

The occasion of her visit was a presidential inauguration. The new President owed his nomination mainly to the votes of the Southern delegates in the convention, and was believed to be correspondingly well disposed to the race from which the Southern delegates were for the most part recruited. Friends of rival and unsuccessful candidates for the nomination had more than hinted that the Southern delegates were very substantially rewarded for their support at the time when it was given; whether this was true or not the parties concerned know best. At any rate the colored politicians did not see it in that light, for they were gathered from near and far to press their claims for recognition and patronage. On the evening following the White House inaugural ball, the colored people of Washington gave an "inaugural" ball at a large public hall. It was under the management of their leading citizens, among them several high officials holding over from the last administration, and a number of professional and business men. This ball was the most noteworthy social event that colored circles up to that time had ever known. There were many visitors from various parts of the country. Miss Clayton attended the ball, the honors of which she carried away easily. She danced with several partners, and was introduced to innumerable people whom she had never seen before, and whom she hardly expected ever to meet again. She went away from the ball, at four o'clock in the morning, in a glow of triumph, and with a confused impression of senators and representatives and lawyers and doctors of all shades, who had sought an introduction, led her through the dance, and overwhelmed her with compliments. She returned home the next day but one, after the most delightful week of her life.

II

One afternoon, about three weeks after her return from Washington, Alice received a letter through the mail. The envelope bore the words "House of Representatives" printed in one corner, and in the opposite corner, in a bold running hand, a Congressman's frank "Hamilton M. Brown, M.C." The letter read as follows:

House of Representatives,
Washington, D.C., March 30, 187–.
Miss Alice Clayton, Groveland.

Dear Friend (if I may be permitted to call you so after so
brief an acquaintance)—I remember with sincerest pleasure our
recent meeting at the inaugural ball, and the sensation created
by your beauty, your amiable manners, and your graceful dancing. Time has so strengthened the impression I then received, that
I should have felt inconsolable had I thought it impossible ever
to again behold the charms which had brightened the occasion
of our meeting and eclipsed by their brilliancy the leading belles
of the capital. I had hoped, however, to have the pleasure of
meeting you again, and circumstances have fortunately placed it
in my power to do so at an early date. You have doubtless learned
that the contest over the election in the Sixth Congressional District of South Carolina has been decided in my favor, and that I
now have the honor of representing my native State at the national capital. I have just been appointed a member of a special
committee to visit and inspect the Sault River and the Straits of
Mackinac, with reference to the needs of lake navigation. I have
made arrangements to start a week ahead of the other members
of the committee, whom I am to meet in Detroit on the 20th. I
shall leave here on the 2d, and will arrive in Groveland on the 3d,
by the 7:30 evening express. I shall remain in Groveland several
days, in the course of which I shall be pleased to call, and renew
the acquaintance so auspiciously begun in Washington, which it
is my fondest hope may ripen into a warmer friendship.

If you do not regard my visit as presumptuous, and do not
write me in the mean while forbidding it, I shall do myself the
pleasure of waiting on you the morning after my arrival in
Groveland.

With renewed expressions of my sincere admiration and profound esteem, I remain,

Sincerely yours,
Hamilton M. Brown, M.C.

To Alice, and especially to her mother, this bold and flowery letter had
very nearly the force of a formal declaration. They read it over again and
again, and spent most of the afternoon discussing it. There were few young
men in Groveland eligible as husbands for so superior a person as Alice
Clayton, and an addition to the number would be very acceptable. But the

mere fact of his being a Congressman was not sufficient to qualify him; there were other considerations.

"I've never heard of this Honorable Hamilton M. Brown," said Mr. Clayton. The letter had been laid before him at the supper-table. "It's strange, Alice, that you have n't said anything about him before. You must have met lots of swell folks not to recollect a Congressman."

"But he was n't a Congressman then," answered Alice; "he was only a claimant. I remember Senator Bruce, and Mr. Douglass; but there were so many doctors and lawyers and politicians that I could n't keep track of them all. Still I have a faint impression of a Mr. Brown who danced with me."

She went into the parlor and brought out the dancing programme she had used at the Washington ball. She had decorated it with a bow of blue ribbon and preserved it as a souvenir of her visit.

"Yes," she said, after examining it, "I must have danced with him. Here are the initials—'H. M. B.'"

"What color is he?" asked Mr. Clayton, as he plied his knife and fork.

"I have a notion that he was rather dark—darker than any one I had ever danced with before."

"Why did you dance with him?" asked her father. "You were n't obliged to go back on your principles because you were away from home."

"Well, father, 'when you're in Rome'—you know the rest. Mrs. Clearweather introduced me to several dark men, to him among others. They were her friends, and common decency required me to be courteous."

"If this man is black, we don't want to encourage him. If he's the right sort, we'll invite him to the house."

"And make him feel at home," added Mrs. Clayton, on hospitable thoughts intent.

"We must ask Sadler about him to-morrow," said Mr. Clayton, when he had drunk his coffee and lighted his cigar. "If he's the right man he shall have cause to remember his visit to Groveland. We'll show him that Washington is not the only town on earth."

The uncertainty of the family with regard to Mr. Brown was soon removed. Mr. Solomon Sadler, who was supposed to know everything worth knowing concerning the colored race, and everybody of importance connected with it, dropped in after supper to make an evening call. Sadler was familiar with the history of every man of negro ancestry who had distinguished himself in any walk of life. He could give the pedigree of Alexander Pushkin, the titles of scores of Dumas's novels (even Sadler had not time to learn them all), and could recite the whole of Wendell Phillips's lecture on Toussaint l'Ouverture. He claimed a personal acquaintance with Mr. Frederick Douglass, and had been often in Washington, where he was well known and well received in good colored society.

"Let me see," he said reflectively, when asked for information about the Honorable Hamilton M. Brown. "Yes, I think I know him. He studied at Oberlin just after the war. He was about leaving there when I entered. There were two H. M. Browns there—a Hamilton M. Brown and a Henry M. Brown. One was stout and dark and the other was slim and quite light; you could scarcely tell him from a dark white man. They used to call them 'light Brown' and 'dark Brown.' I did n't know either of them except by sight, for they were there only a few weeks after I went in. As I remember them, Hamilton was the fair one—a very good-looking, gentlemanly fellow, and, as I heard, a good student and a fine speaker."

"Do you remember what kind of hair he had?" asked Mr. Clayton.

"Very good indeed; straight, as I remember it. He looked something like a Spaniard or a Portuguese."

"Now that you describe him," said Alice, "I remember quite well dancing with such a gentleman; and I'm wrong about my 'H. M. B.' The dark man must have been some one else; there are two others on my card that I can't remember distinctly, and he was probably one of those."

"I guess he's all right, Alice," said her father when Sadler had gone away. "He evidently means business, and we must treat him white. Of course he must stay with us; there are no hotels in Groveland while he is here. Let's see—he'll be here in three days. That is n't very long, but I guess we can get ready. I'll write a letter this afternoon—or you write it, and invite him to the house, and say I'll meet him at the depot. And you may have *carte blanche* for making the preparations."

"We must have some people to meet him."

"Certainly; a reception is the proper thing. Sit down immediately and write the letter and I'll mail it first thing in the morning, so he'll get it before he has time to make other arrangements. And you and your mother put your heads together and make out a list of guests, and I'll have the invitations printed to-morrow. We will show the darkeys of Groveland how to entertain a Congressman."

It will be noted that in moments of abstraction or excitement Mr. Clayton sometimes relapsed into forms of speech not entirely consistent with his principles. But some allowance must be made for his atmosphere; he could no more escape from it than the leopard can change his spots, or the— In deference to Mr. Clayton's feelings the quotation will be left incomplete.

Alice wrote the letter on the spot and it was duly mailed, and sped on its winged way to Washington.

The preparations for the reception were made as thoroughly and elaborately as possible on so short a notice. The invitations were issued; the house was cleaned from attic to cellar; an orchestra was engaged for the evening; elaborate floral decorations were planned and the flowers ordered.

Even the refreshments, which ordinarily, in the household of a caterer, would be mere matter of familiar detail, became a subject of serious consultation and study.

The approaching event was a matter of very much interest to the fortunate ones who were honored with invitations, and this for several reasons. They were anxious to meet this sole representative of their race in the —th Congress, and as he was not one of the old-line colored leaders, but a new star risen on the political horizon, there was a special curiosity to see who he was and what he looked like. Moreover, the Claytons did not often entertain a large company, but when they did, it was on a scale commensurate with their means and position, and to be present on such an occasion was a thing to remember and to talk about. And, most important consideration of all, some remarks dropped by members of the Clayton family had given rise to the rumor that the Congressman was seeking a wife. This invested his visit with a romantic interest, and gave the reception a practical value; for there were other marriageable girls besides Miss Clayton, and if one was left another might be taken.

III

On the evening of April 3d, at fifteen minutes of six o'clock, Mr. Clayton, accompanied by Jack, entered the livery carriage waiting at his gate and ordered the coachman to drive to the Union Depot. He had taken Jack along, partly for company, and partly that Jack might relieve the Congressman of any trouble about his baggage, and make himself useful in case of emergency. Jack was willing enough to go, for he had foreseen in the visitor a rival for Alice's hand—indeed he had heard more or less of the subject for several days—and was glad to make a reconnaissance before the enemy arrived upon the field of battle. He had made—at least he had thought so—considerable progress with Alice during the three weeks since her return from Washington, and once or twice Alice had been perilously near the tender stage. This visit had disturbed the situation and threatened to ruin his chances; but he did not mean to give up without a struggle.

Arrived at the main entrance, Mr. Clayton directed the carriage to wait, and entered the station with Jack. The Union Depot at Groveland was an immense oblong structure, covering a dozen parallel tracks and furnishing terminal passenger facilities for half a dozen railroads. The tracks ran east and west, and the depot was entered from the south, at about the middle of the building. On either side of the entrance, the waiting-rooms, refreshment rooms, baggage and express departments, and other administrative offices, extended in a row for the entire length of the building; and beyond them and parallel with them stretched a long open space, separated from the tracks by an iron fence or *grille*. There were two entrance gates in the fence, at which tickets must be shown before access could be had to trains, and two other gates, by which arriving passengers came out.

Mr. Clayton looked at the blackboard on the wall underneath the station clock, and observed that the 7:30 train from Washington was five minutes late. Accompanied by Jack he walked up and down the platform until the train, with the usual accompaniment of panting steam and clanging bell and rumbling trucks, pulled into the station, and drew up on the third or fourth track from the iron railing. Mr. Clayton stationed himself at the gate nearest the rear end of the train, reasoning that the Congressman would ride in a parlor car, and would naturally come out by the gate nearest the point at which he left the train.

"You'd better go and stand by the other gate, Jack," he said to his companion, "and stop him if he goes out that way."

The train was well filled and a stream of passengers poured through. Mr. Clayton scanned the crowd carefully as they approached the gate, and scrutinized each passenger as he came through, without seeing any one that met the description of Congressman Brown, as given by Sadler, or any one that could in his opinion be the gentleman for whom he was looking. When the last one had passed through he was left to the conclusion that his expected guest had gone out by the other gate. Mr. Clayton hastened thither.

"Did n't he come out this way, Jack?" he asked.

"No, sir," replied the young man, "I have n't seen him."

"That's strange," mused Mr. Clayton, somewhat anxiously. "He would hardly fail to come without giving us notice. Surely we must have missed him. We'd better look around a little. You go that way and I'll go this."

Mr. Clayton turned and walked several rods along the platform to the men's waiting-room, and standing near the door glanced around to see if he could find the object of his search. The only colored person in the room was a stout and very black man, wearing a broadcloth suit and a silk hat, and seated a short distance from the door. On the seat by his side stood a couple of valises. On one of them, the one nearest him, on which his arm rested, was written, in white letters, plainly legible—

H.M. BROWN, M.C.
Washington, D.C.

Mr. Clayton's feelings at this discovery can better be imagined than described. He hastily left the waiting-room, before the black gentleman, who was looking the other way, was even aware of his presence, and, walking rapidly up and down the platform, communed with himself upon what course of action the situation demanded. He had invited to his house, had come down to meet, had made elaborate preparations to entertain on the following evening, a light-colored man—a white man by his theory, an acceptable guest, a possible husband for his daughter, an avowed suitor for her hand. If the Congressman had turned out to be brown, even dark brown, with fairly good hair, though he might not have desired him as a son-in-law, yet he could have welcomed him as a guest. But even this softening of the blow was denied him, for the man in the waiting-room was palpably, aggressively black, with pronounced African features and woolly hair, without apparently a single drop of redeeming white blood. Could he, in the face of his well-known principles, his lifelong rule of conduct, take this negro into his home and introduce him to his friends? Could he subject his wife and daughter to the rude shock of such a disappointment? It would be bad enough for them to learn of the ghastly mistake, but to have him in the house would be twisting the arrow in the wound.

Mr. Clayton had the instincts of a gentleman, and realized the delicacy of the situation. But to get out of his difficulty without wounding the feelings of the Congressman required not only diplomacy but dispatch. Whatever he did must be done promptly; for if he waited many minutes the Congressman would probably take a carriage and be driven to Mr. Clayton's residence.

A ray of hope came for a moment to illumine the gloom of the situation. Perhaps the black man was merely sitting there, and not the owner of the valise! For there were two valises, one on each side of the supposed Congressman. For obvious reasons he did not care to make the inquiry himself, so he looked around for his companion, who came up a moment later.

"Jack," he exclaimed excitedly, "I'm afraid we're in the worst kind of a hole, unless there's some mistake! Run down to the men's waiting-room and you'll see a man and a valise, and you'll understand what I mean. Ask that darkey if he is the Honorable Mr. Brown, Congressman from South Carolina. If he says yes, come back right away and let me know, without giving him time to ask any questions, and put your wits to work to help me out of the scrape."

"I wonder what's the matter?" said Jack to himself, but did as he was told. In a moment he came running back.

"Yes, sir," he announced; "he says he's the man."

"Jack," said Mr. Clayton desperately, "if you want to show your appreciation of what I've done for you, you must suggest some way out of this. I'd never dare to take that negro to my house, and yet I'm obliged to treat him like a gentleman."

Jack's eyes had worn a somewhat reflective look since he had gone to make the inquiry. Suddenly his face brightened with intelligence, and then, as a newsboy ran into the station calling his wares, hardened into determination.

"Clarion, special extry 'dition! All about de epidemic er dipt'eria!" clamored the newsboy with shrill childish treble, as he made his way toward the waiting-room. Jack darted after him, and saw the man to whom he had spoken buy a paper. He ran back to his employer, and dragged him over toward the ticket-seller's window.

"I have it, sir!" he exclaimed, seizing a telegraph blank and writing rapidly, and reading aloud as he wrote. "How's this for a way out?"

"*Dear Sir,* I write you this note here in the depot to inform you of an unfortunate event which has interfered with my plans and those of my family for your entertainment while in Groveland. Yesterday my daughter Alice complained of a sore throat, which by this afternoon had developed into a case of malignant diphtheria. In consequence our house has been quarantined; and while I have felt myself obliged to come down to the depot, I do not feel that I ought to expose you to the possibility of infection, and I therefore send you this by another hand. The bearer will conduct you to a carriage which I have ordered placed at your service, and unless you should prefer some other hotel, you will be driven to the Forest Hill House, where I beg you will consider yourself my guest during your stay in the city, and make the fullest use of every convenience it may offer. From present indications I fear no one of our family will be able to see you, which we shall regret beyond expression, as we have made elaborate arrangements for your entertainment. I still hope, however, that you may enjoy your visit, as there are many places of interest in the city, and many friends will doubtless be glad to make your acquaintance.

"With assurances of my profound regret, I am

Sincerely yours,
"*Cicero Clayton.*"

"Splendid!" cried Mr. Clayton. "You've helped me out of a horrible scrape. Now, go and take him to the hotel and see him comfortably located, and tell them to charge the bill to me."

"I suspect, sir," suggested Jack, "that I'd better not go up to the house, and you'll have to stay in yourself for a day or two, to keep up appearances. I'll sleep on the lounge at the store, and we can talk business over the telephone."

"All right, Jack, we'll arrange the details later. But for Heaven's sake get him started, or he'll be calling a hack to drive up to the house. I'll go home on a street car."

"So far so good," sighed Mr. Clayton to himself as he escaped from the station. "Jack is a deuced clever fellow, and I'll have to do something more for him. But the tug-of-war is yet to come. I've got to bribe a doctor, shut up the house for a day or two, and have all the ill-humor of two disappointed women to endure until this negro leaves town. Well, I'm sure my wife and Alice will back me up at any cost. No sacrifice is too great to escape having to entertain him; of course I have no prejudice against his color—he can't help that—but it is the *principle* of the thing. If we received him it would be a concession fatal to all my views and theories. And I am really doing him a kindness, for I'm sure that all the world could not make Alice and her mother treat him with anything but cold politeness. It'll be a great mortification to Alice, but I don't see how else I could have got out of it."

He boarded the first car that left the depot, and soon reached home. The house was lighted up, and through the lace curtains of the parlor windows he could see his wife and daughter, elegantly dressed, waiting to receive their distinguished visitor. He rang the bell impatiently, and a servant opened the door.

"The gentleman did n't come?" asked the maid.

"No," he said as he hung up his hat. This brought the ladies to the door.

"He did n't come?" they exclaimed. "What's the matter?"

"I'll tell you," he said. "Mary," this to the servant, a white girl, who stood in open-eyed curiosity, "we shan't need you any more to-night."

Then he went into the parlor, and, closing the door, told his story. When he reached the point where he had discovered the color of the honorable Mr. Brown, Miss Clayton caught her breath, and was on the verge of collapse.

"That nigger," said Mrs. Clayton indignantly, "can never set foot in this house. But what did you do with him?"

Mr. Clayton quickly unfolded his plan, and described the disposition he had made of the Congressman.

"It's an awful shame," said Mrs. Clayton. "Just think of the trouble and expense we have gone to! And poor Alice'll never get over it, for everybody knows he came to see her and that he's smitten with her. But you've done just right; we never would have been able to hold up our heads again if we had introduced a black man, even a Congressman, to the people that are invited here tomorrow night, as a sweetheart of Alice. Why, she would n't marry him if he was President of the United States and plated with gold an inch thick. The very idea!"

"Well," said Mr. Clayton, "then we've got to act quick. Alice must wrap up her throat—by the way, Alice, how *is* your throat?"

"It's sore," sobbed Alice, who had been in tears almost from her father's return, "and I don't care if I do have diphtheria and die, no, I don't!" and she wept on.

"Wrap up your throat and go to bed, and I'll go over to Doctor Pillsbury's and get a diphtheria card to nail up on the house. In the morning, first thing, we'll have to write notes recalling the invitations for to-morrow evening, and have them delivered by messenger boys. We were fools for not finding out all about this man from some one who knew, before we invited him here. Sadler don't know more than half he thinks he does, anyway. And we'll have to do this thing thoroughly, or our motives will be misconstrued, and people will say we are prejudiced and all that, when it is only a matter of principle with us."

The programme outlined above was carried out to the letter. The invitations were recalled, to the great disappointment of the invited guests. The family physician called several times during the day. Alice remained in bed, and the maid left without notice, in such a hurry that she forgot to take her best clothes.

Mr. Clayton himself remained at home. He had a telephone in the house, and was therefore in easy communication with his office, so that the business did not suffer materially by reason of his absence from the store. About ten o'clock in the morning a note came up from the hotel, expressing Mr. Brown's regrets and sympathy. Toward noon Mr. Clayton picked up the morning paper, which he had not theretofore had time to read, and was glancing over it casually, when his eye fell upon a column headed "A Colored Congressman." He read the article with astonishment that rapidly turned to chagrin and dismay. It was an interview describing the Congressman as a tall and shapely man, about thirty-five years old, with an olive complexion not noticeably darker than many a white man's, straight hair, and eyes as black as sloes.

"The bearing of this son of South Carolina reveals the polished manners of the Southern gentleman, and neither from his appearance nor his conversation would one suspect that the white blood which flows in his veins in such preponderating measure had ever been crossed by that of a darker race," wrote the reporter, who had received instructions at the office that for urgent business considerations the lake shipping interest wanted Representative Brown treated with marked consideration.

There was more of the article, but the introductory portion left Mr. Clayton in such a state of bewilderment that the paper fell from his hand. What was the meaning of it? Had he been mistaken? Obviously so, or else the reporter was wrong, which was manifestly improbable. When he had recovered himself somewhat, he picked up the newspaper and began reading where he had left off.

"Representative Brown traveled to Groveland in company with Bishop Jones of the African Methodist Jerusalem Church, who is *en route* to attend the general conference of his denomination at Detroit next week. The bishop, who came in while the writer was interviewing Mr. Brown, is a splendid type of the pure negro. He is said to be a man of great power among his people, which may easily be believed after one has looked upon his expressive countenance and heard him discuss the questions which affect the welfare of his church and his race."

Mr. Clayton stared at the paper. "'The bishop,'" he repeated, "'is a splendid type of the pure negro.' I must have mistaken the bishop for the Congressman! But how in the world did Jack get the thing balled up? I'll call up the store and demand an explanation of him.

"Jack," he asked, "what kind of a looking man was the fellow you gave the note to at the depot?"

"He was a very wicked-looking fellow, sir," came back the answer. "He had a bad eye, looked like a gambler, sir. I am not surprised that you did n't want to entertain him, even if he was a Congressman."

"What color was he—that's what I want to know—and what kind of hair did he have?"

"Why, he was about my complexion, sir, and had straight black hair."

The rules of the telephone company did not permit swearing over the line. Mr. Clayton broke the rules.

"Was there any one else with him?" he asked when he had relieved his mind.

"Yes, sir, Bishop Jones of the African Methodist Jerusalem Church was sitting there with him; they had traveled from Washington together. I drove the bishop to his stopping-place after I had left Mr. Brown at the hotel. I did n't suppose you'd mind."

Mr. Clayton fell into a chair, and indulged in thoughts unutterable.

He folded up the paper and slipped it under the family Bible, where it was least likely to be soon discovered.

"I'll hide the paper, anyway," he groaned. "I'll never hear the last of this till my dying day, so I may as well have a few hours' respite. It's too late to go back, and we've got to play the farce out. Alice is really sick with disappointment, and to let her know this now would only make her worse. May be he'll leave town in a day or two, and then she'll be in condition to stand it. Such luck is enough to disgust a man with trying to do right and live up to his principles."

Time hung a little heavy on Mr. Clayton's hands during the day. His wife was busy with the housework. He answered several telephone calls about Alice's health, and called up the store occasionally to ask how the business was getting on. After lunch he lay down on a sofa and took a nap, from which he was aroused by the sound of the door-bell. He went to the door. The evening paper was lying on the porch, and the newsboy, who had not observed the diphtheria sign until after he had rung, was hurrying away as fast as his legs would carry him.

Mr. Clayton opened the paper and looked it through to see if there was any reference to the visiting Congressman. He found what he sought and more. An article on the local page contained a résumé of the information given in the morning paper, with the following additional paragraph:

"A reporter, who called at the Forest Hill this morning to interview Representative Brown, was informed that the Congressman had been invited to spend the remainder of his time in Groveland as the guest of Mr. William Watkins, the proprietor of the popular livery establishment on Main Street. Mr. Brown will remain in the city several days, and a reception will be tendered him at Mr. Watkins's on Wednesday evening."

"That ends it," sighed Mr. Clayton. "The dove of peace will never again rest on my roof-tree."

But why dwell longer on the sufferings of Mr. Clayton, or attempt to describe the feelings or chronicle the remarks of his wife and daughter when they learned the facts in the case?

As to Representative Brown, he was made welcome in the hospitable home of Mr. William Watkins. There was a large and brilliant assemblage at the party on Wednesday evening, at which were displayed the costumes prepared for the Clayton reception. Mr. Brown took a fancy to Miss Lura Watkins, to whom, before the week was over, he became engaged to be married. Meantime poor Alice, the innocent victim of circumstances and principles, lay sick abed with a supposititious case of malignant diphtheria, and a real case of acute disappointment and chagrin.

"Oh, Jack!" exclaimed Alice, a few weeks later, on the way home from evening church in company with the young man, "what a dreadful thing it all was! And to think of that hateful Lura Watkins marrying the Congressman!"

The street was shaded by trees at the point where they were passing, and there was no one in sight. Jack put his arm around her waist, and, leaning over, kissed her.

"Never mind, dear," he said soothingly, "you still have your 'last chance' left, and I'll prove myself a better man than the Congressman."

Occasionally, at social meetings, when the vexed question of the future of the colored race comes up, as it often does, for discussion, Mr. Clayton may still be heard to remark sententiously:

"What the white people of the United States need most, in dealing with this problem, is a higher conception of the brotherhood of man. For of one blood God made all the nations of the earth."

CICELY'S DREAM

I

The old woman stood at the back door of the cabin, shading her eyes with her hand, and looking across the vegetable garden that ran up to the very door. Beyond the garden she saw, bathed in the sunlight, a field of corn, just in the ear, stretching for half a mile, its yellow, pollen-laden tassels overtopping the dark green mass of broad glistening blades; and in the distance, through the faint morning haze of evaporating dew, the line of the woods, of a still darker green, meeting the clear blue of the summer sky. Old Dinah saw, going down the path, a tall, brown girl, in a homespun frock, swinging a slat-bonnet in one hand and a splint basket in the other.

"Oh, Cicely!" she called.

The girl turned and answered in a resonant voice, vibrating with youth and life,

"Yes, granny!"

"Be sho' and pick a good mess er peas, chile, fer yo' gran'daddy 's gwine ter be home ter dinner ter-day."

The old woman stood a moment longer and then turned to go into the house. What she had not seen was that the girl was not only young, but lithe and shapely as a sculptor's model; that her bare feet seemed to spurn the earth as they struck it; that though brown, she was not so brown but that her cheek was darkly red with the blood of another race than that which gave her her name and station in life; and the old woman did not see that Cicely's face was as comely as her figure was superb, and that her eyes were dreamy with vague yearnings.

Cicely climbed the low fence between the garden and the cornfield, and started down one of the long rows leading directly away from the house. Old Needham was a good ploughman, and straight as an arrow ran the furrow between the rows of corn, until it vanished in the distant perspective. The peas were planted beside alternate hills of corn, the corn-stalks serving as supports for the climbing pea-vines. The vines nearest the house had been picked more or less clear of the long green pods, and Cicely walked down the row for a quarter of a mile, to where the peas were more plentiful. And as she walked she thought of her dream of the night before.

She had dreamed a beautiful dream. The fact that it was a beautiful dream, a delightful dream, her memory retained very vividly. She was troubled because she could not remember just what her dream had been about. Of one other fact she was certain, that in her dream she had found something, and that her happiness had been bound up with the thing she had found. As she walked down the corn-row she ran over in her mind the various things with which she had always associated happiness. Had she found a gold ring? No, it was not a gold ring—of that she felt sure. Was it a soft, curly plume for her hat? She had seen town people with them, and had indulged in day-dreams on the subject; but it was not a feather. Was it a bright-colored silk dress? No; as much as she had always wanted one, it was not a silk dress. For an instant, in a dream, she had tasted some great and novel happiness, and when she awoke it was dashed from her lips, and she could not even enjoy the memory of it, except in a vague, indefinite, and tantalizing way.

Cicely was troubled, too, because dreams were serious things. Dreams had certain meanings, most of them, and some dreams went by contraries. If her dream had been a prophecy of some good thing, she had by forgetting it lost the pleasure of anticipation. If her dream had been one of those that go by contraries, the warning would be in vain, because she would not know against what evil to provide. So, with a sigh, Cicely said to herself that it was a troubled world, more or less; and having come to a promising point, began to pick the tenderest pea-pods and throw them into her basket.

By the time she had reached the end of the line the basket was nearly full. Glancing toward the pine woods beyond the rail fence, she saw a brier bush loaded with large, luscious blackberries. Cicely was fond of blackberries, so she set her basket down, climbed the fence, and was soon busily engaged in gathering the fruit, delicious even in its wild state.

She had soon eaten all she cared for. But the berries were still numerous, and it occurred to her that her granddaddy would like a blackberry pudding for dinner. Catching up her apron, and using it as a receptacle for the berries, she had gathered scarcely more than a handful when she heard a groan.

Cicely was not timid, and her curiosity being aroused by the sound, she stood erect, and remained in a listening attitude. In a moment the sound was repeated, and, gauging the point from which it came, she plunged resolutely into the thick underbrush of the forest. She had gone but a few yards when she stopped short with an exclamation of surprise and concern.

Upon the ground, under the shadow of the towering pines, a man lay at full length—a young man, several years under thirty, apparently, so far as his age could be guessed from a face that wore a short soft beard, and was so begrimed with dust and incrusted with blood that little could be seen of the underlying integument. What was visible showed a skin browned by nature or by exposure. His hands were of even a darker brown, almost as dark as Cicely's own. A tangled mass of very curly black hair, matted with burs, dank with dew, and clotted with blood, fell partly over his forehead, on the edge of which, extending back into the hair, an ugly scalp wound was gaping, and, though apparently not just inflicted, was still bleeding slowly, as though reluctant to stop, in spite of the coagulation that had almost closed it.

Cicely with a glance took in all this and more. But, first of all, she saw the man was wounded and bleeding, and the nurse latent in all womankind awoke in her to the requirements of the situation. She knew there was a spring a few rods away, and ran swiftly to it. There was usually a gourd at the spring, but now it was gone. Pouring out the blackberries in a little heap where they could be found again, she took off her apron, dipped one end of it into the spring, and ran back to the wounded man. The apron was clean, and she squeezed a little stream of water from it into the man's mouth. He swallowed it with avidity. Cicely then knelt by his side, and with the wet end of her apron washed the blood from the wound lightly, and the dust from the man's face. Then she looked at her apron a moment, debating whether she should tear it or not.

"I'm feared granny 'll be mad," she said to herself. "I reckon I'll jes' use de whole apron."

So she bound the apron around his head as well as she could, and then sat down a moment on a fallen tree trunk, to think what she should do next. The man already seemed more comfortable; he had ceased moaning, and lay quiet, though breathing heavily.

"What shall I do with that man?" she reflected. "I don' know whether he 's a w'ite man or a black man. Ef he 's a w'ite man, I oughter go an' tell de w'ite folks up at de big house, an' dey 'd take keer of 'im. If he 's a black man, I oughter go tell granny. He don' look lack a black man somehow er nuther, an' yet he don' look lack a w'ite man; he 's too dahk, an' his hair's too curly. But I mus' do somethin' wid 'im. He can't be lef' here ter die in de woods all by hisse'f. Reckon I'll go an' tell granny."

She scaled the fence, caught up the basket of peas from where she had left it, and ran, lightly and swiftly as a deer, toward the house. Her short skirt did not impede her progress, and in a few minutes she had covered the half mile and was at the cabin door, a slight heaving of her full and yet youthful breast being the only sign of any unusual exertion.

Her story was told in a moment. The old woman took down a black bottle from a high shelf, and set out with Cicely across the cornfield, toward the wounded man.

As they went through the corn Cicely recalled part of her dream. She had dreamed that under some strange circumstances—what they had been was still obscure—she had met a young man—a young man whiter than she and yet not all white—and that he had loved her and courted her and married her. Her dream had been all the sweeter because in it she had first tasted the sweetness of love, and she had not recalled it before because only in her dream had she known or thought of love as something supremely desirable.

With the memory of her dream, however, her fears revived. Dreams were solemn things. To Cicely the fabric of a vision was by no means baseless. Her trouble arose from her not being able to recall, though she was well versed in dream-lore, just what event was foreshadowed by a dream of finding a wounded man. If the wounded man were of her own race, her dream would thus far have been realized, and having met the young man, the other joys might be expected to follow. If he should turn out to be a white man, then her dream was clearly one of the kind that go by contraries, and she could expect only sorrow and trouble and pain as the proper sequences of this fateful discovery.

II

The two women reached the fence that separated the cornfield from the pine woods.

"How is I gwine ter git ovuh dat fence, chile?" asked the old woman.

"Wait a minute, granny," said Cicely; "I'll take it down."

It was only an eight-rail fence, and it was a matter of but a few minutes for the girl to lift down and lay to either side the ends of the rails that formed one of the angles. This done, the old woman easily stepped across the remaining two or three rails. It was only a moment before they stood by the wounded man. He was lying still, breathing regularly, and seemingly asleep.

"What is he, granny," asked the girl anxiously, "a w'ite man, or not?"

Old Dinah pushed back the matted hair from the wounded man's brow, and looked at the skin beneath. It was fairer there, but yet of a decided brown. She raised his hand, pushed back the tattered sleeve from his wrist, and then she laid his hand down gently.

"Mos' lackly he's a mulatter man f'om up de country somewhar. He don' look lack dese yer niggers roun' yere, ner yet lack a w'ite man. But de po' boy's in a bad fix, w'ateber he is, an' I 'spec's we bettah do w'at we kin fer 'im, an' w'en he comes to he'll tell us w'at he is—er w'at he calls hisse'f. Hol' 'is head up, chile, an' I'll po' a drop er dis yer liquor down his th'oat; dat'll bring 'im to quicker 'n anything e'se I knows."

Cicely lifted the sick man's head, and Dinah poured a few drops of the whiskey between his teeth. He swallowed it readily enough. In a few minutes he opened his eyes and stared blankly at the two women. Cicely saw that his eyes were large and black, and glistening with fever.

"How you feelin', suh?" asked the old woman.

There was no answer.

"Is you feelin' bettah now?"

The wounded man kept on staring blankly. Suddenly he essayed to put his hand to his head, gave a deep groan, and fell back again unconscious.

"He 's gone ag'in," said Dinah. "I reckon we'll hafter tote 'im up ter de house and take keer er 'im dere. W'ite folks would n't want ter fool wid a nigger man, an' we doan know who his folks is. He's outer his head an' will be fer some time yet, an' we can't tell nuthin' 'bout 'im tel he comes ter his senses."

Cicely lifted the wounded man by the arms and shoulders. She was strong, with the strength of youth and a sturdy race. The man was pitifully emaciated; how much, the two women had not suspected until they raised him. They had no difficulty whatever, except for the awkwardness of such a burden, in lifting him over the fence and carrying him through the cornfield to the cabin.

They laid him on Cicely's bed in the little lean-to shed that formed a room separate from the main apartment of the cabin. The old woman sent Cicely to cook the dinner, while she gave her own attention exclusively to the still unconscious man. She brought water and washed him as though he were a child.

"Po' boy," she said, "he doan feel lack he's be'n eatin' nuff to feed a sparrer. He 'pears ter be mos' starved ter def."

She washed his wound more carefully, made some lint—the art was well known in the sixties—and dressed his wound with a fair degree of skill.

"Somebody must 'a' be'n tryin' ter put yo' light out, chile," she muttered to herself as she adjusted the bandage around his head. "A little higher er a little lower, an' you would n' 'a' be'n yere ter tell de tale. Dem clo's," she argued, lifting the tattered garments she had removed from her patient, "don' b'long 'roun' yere. Dat kinder weavin' come f'om down to'ds Souf Ca'lina. I wish Needham 'u'd come erlong. He kin tell who dis man is, an' all erbout 'im."

She made a bowl of gruel, and fed it, drop by drop, to the sick man. This roused him somewhat from his stupor, but when Dinah thought he had enough of the gruel, and stopped feeding him, he closed his eyes again and relapsed into a heavy sleep that was so closely akin to unconsciousness as to be scarcely distinguishable from it.

When old Needham came home at noon, his wife, who had been anxiously awaiting his return, told him in a few words the story of Cicely's discovery and of the subsequent events.

Needham inspected the stranger with a professional eye. He had been something of a plantation doctor in his day, and was known far and wide for his knowledge of simple remedies. The negroes all around, as well as many of the poorer white people, came to him for the treatment of common ailments.

"He's got a fevuh," he said, after feeling the patient's pulse and laying his hand on his brow, "an' we'll hafter gib 'im some yarb tea an' nuss 'im tel de fevuh w'ars off. I 'spec'," he added, "dat I knows whar dis boy come f'om. He's mos' lackly one er dem bright mulatters, f'om Robeson County— some of 'em call deyse'ves Croatan Injins—w'at's been conscripted an' sent ter wu'k on de fo'tifications down at Wimbleton er some'er's er nuther, an' done 'scaped, and got mos' killed gittin' erway, an' wuz n' none too well fed befo', an' nigh 'bout starved ter def sence. We'll hafter hide dis man, er e'se we is lackly ter git inter trouble ou'se'ves by harb'rin' 'im. Ef dey ketch 'im yere, dey's liable ter take 'im out an' shoot 'im—an' des ez lackly us too."

Cicely was listening with bated breath.

"Oh, gran'daddy," she cried with trembling voice, "don' let 'em ketch 'im! Hide 'im somewhar."

"I reckon we'll leave 'im yere fer a day er so. Ef he had come f'om roun' yere I'd be skeered ter keep 'im, fer de w'ite folks 'u'd prob'ly be lookin' fer 'im. But I knows ev'ybody w'at's be'n conscripted fer ten miles 'roun', an' dis yere boy don' b'long in dis neighborhood. W'en 'e gits so 'e kin he'p 'isse'f we'll put 'im up in de lof' an' hide 'im till de Yankees come. Fer dey're comin', sho'. I dremp' las' night dey wuz close ter han', and I hears de w'ite folks talkin' ter deyse'ves 'bout it. An' de time is comin' w'en de good Lawd gwine ter set his people free, an' it ain' gwine ter be long, nuther."

Needham's prophecy proved true. In less than a week the Confederate garrison evacuated the arsenal in the neighboring town of Patesville, blew up the buildings, destroyed the ordnance and stores, and retreated across the Cape Fear River, burning the river bridge behind them—two acts of war afterwards unjustly attributed to General Sherman's army, which followed close upon the heels of the retreating Confederates.

When there was no longer any fear for the stranger's safety, no more pains were taken to conceal him. His wound had healed rapidly, and in a week he had been able with some help to climb up the ladder into the loft. In all this time, however, though apparently conscious, he had said no word to any one, nor had he seemed to comprehend a word that was spoken to him.

Cicely had been his constant attendant. After the first day, during which her granny had nursed him, she had sat by his bedside, had fanned his fevered brow, had held food and water and medicine to his lips. When it was safe for him to come down from the loft and sit in a chair under a spreading oak, Cicely supported him until he was strong enough to walk about the yard. When his strength had increased sufficiently to permit of greater exertion, she accompanied him on long rambles in the fields and woods.

In spite of his gain in physical strength, the newcomer changed very little in other respects. For a long time he neither spoke nor smiled. To questions put to him he simply gave no reply, but looked at his questioner with the blank unconsciousness of an infant. By and by he began to recognize Cicely, and to smile at her approach. The next step in returning consciousness was but another manifestation of the same sentiment. When Cicely would leave him he would look his regret, and be restless and uneasy until she returned.

The family were at a loss what to call him. To any inquiry as to his name he answered no more than to other questions.

"He come jes' befo' Sherman," said Needham, after a few weeks, "lack John de Baptis' befo' de Lawd. I reckon we bettah call 'im John."

So they called him John. He soon learned the name. As time went on Cicely found that he was quick at learning things. She taught him to speak her own negro English, which he pronounced with absolute fidelity to her intonations; so that barring the quality of his voice, his speech was an echo of Cicely's own.

The summer wore away and the autumn came. John and Cicely wandered in the woods together and gathered walnuts, and chinquapins and wild grapes. When harvest time came, they worked in the fields side by side—plucked the corn, pulled the fodder, and gathered the dried peas from the yellow pea-vines. Cicely was a phenomenal cotton-picker, and John accompanied her to the fields and stayed by her hours at a time, though occasionally he would complain of his head, and sit under a tree and rest part of the day while Cicely worked, the two keeping one another always in sight.

They did not have a great deal of intercourse with other people. Young men came to the cabin sometimes to see Cicely, but when they found her entirely absorbed in the stranger they ceased their visits. For a time Cicely kept him away, as much as possible, from others, because she did not wish them to see that there was anything wrong about him. This was her motive at first, but after a while she kept him to herself simply because she was happier so. He was hers—hers alone. She had found him, as Pharaoh's daughter had found Moses in the bulrushes; she had taught him to speak, to think, to love. She had not taught him to remember; she would not have wished him to; she would have been jealous of any past to which he might have proved bound by other ties. Her dream so far had come true. She had found him; he loved her. The rest of it would as surely follow, and that before long. For dreams were serious things, and time had proved hers to have been not a presage of misfortune, but one of the beneficent visions that are sent, that we may enjoy by anticipation the good things that are in store for us.

III

But a short interval of time elapsed after the passage of the warlike host that swept through North Carolina, until there appeared upon the scene the vanguard of a second army, which came to bring light and the fruits of liberty to a land which slavery and the havoc of war had brought to ruin. It is fashionable to assume that those who undertook the political rehabilitation of the Southern States merely rounded out the ruin that the war had wrought—merely ploughed up the desolate land and sowed it with salt. Perhaps the gentler judgments of the future may recognize that their task was a difficult one, and that wiser and honester men might have failed as egregiously. It may even, in time, be conceded that some good came out of the carpet-bag governments, as, for instance, the establishment of a system of popular education in the former slave States. Where it had been a crime to teach people to read or write, a schoolhouse dotted every hillside, and the State provided education for rich and poor, for white and black alike. Let us lay at least this token upon the grave of the carpet-baggers. The evil they did lives after them, and the statute of limitations does not seem to run against it. It is but just that we should not forget the good.

Long, however, before the work of political reconstruction had begun, a brigade of Yankee schoolmasters and schoolma'ams had invaded Dixie, and one of the latter had opened a Freedman's Bureau School in the town of Patesville, about four miles from Needham Green's cabin on the neighboring sandhills.

It had been quite a surprise to Miss Chandler's Boston friends when she had announced her intention of going South to teach the freedmen. Rich, accomplished, beautiful, and a social favorite, she was giving up the comforts and luxuries of Northern life to go among hostile strangers, where her associates would be mostly ignorant negroes. Perhaps she might meet occasionally an officer of some Federal garrison, or a traveler from the North; but to all intents and purposes her friends considered her as going into voluntary exile. But heroism was not rare in those days, and Martha Chandler was only one of the great multitude whose hearts went out toward an oppressed race, and who freely poured out their talents, their money, their lives—whatever God had given them—in the sublime and not unfruitful effort to transform three millions of slaves into intelligent freemen. Miss Chandler's friends knew, too, that she had met a great sorrow, and more than suspected that out of it had grown her determination to go South.

When Cicely Green heard that a school for colored people had been opened at Patesville she combed her hair, put on her Sunday frock and such bits of finery as she possessed, and set out for town early the next Monday morning.

There were many who came to learn the new gospel of education, which was to be the cure for all the freedmen's ills. The old and gray-haired, the full-grown man and woman, the toddling infant—they came to acquire the new and wonderful learning that was to make them the equals of the white people. It was the teacher's task, by no means an easy one, to select from this incongruous mass the most promising material, and to distribute among them the second-hand books and clothing that were sent, largely by her Boston friends, to aid her in her work; to find out what they knew, to classify them by their intelligence rather than by their knowledge, for they were all lamentably ignorant. Some among them were the children of parents who had been free before the war, and of these some few could read and one or two could write. One paragon, who could repeat the multiplication table, was immediately promoted to the position of pupil teacher.

Miss Chandler took a liking to the tall girl who had come so far to sit under her instruction. There was a fine, free air in her bearing, a lightness in her step, a sparkle in her eye, that spoke of good blood—whether fused by nature in its own alembic, out of material despised and spurned of men, or whether some obscure ancestral strain, the teacher could not tell. The girl proved intelligent and learned rapidly, indeed seemed almost feverishly anxious to learn. She was quiet, and was, though utterly untrained, instinctively polite, and profited from the first day by the example of her teacher's quiet elegance. The teacher dressed in simple black. When Cicely came back to school the second day, she had left off her glass beads and her red ribbon, and had arranged her hair as nearly like the teacher's as her skill and its quality would permit.

The teacher was touched by these efforts at imitation, and by the intense devotion Cicely soon manifested toward her. It was not a sycophantic, troublesome devotion, that made itself a burden to its object. It found expression in little things done rather than in any words the girl said. To the degree that the attraction was mutual, Martha recognized in it a sort of freemasonry of temperament that drew them together in spite of the differences between them. Martha felt sometimes, in the vague way that one speculates about the impossible, that if she were brown, and had been brought up in North Carolina, she would be like Cicely; and that if Cicely's ancestors had come over in the Mayflower, and Cicely had been reared on Beacon Street, in the shadow of the State House dome, Cicely would have been very much like herself.

Miss Chandler was lonely sometimes. Her duties kept her occupied all day. On Sundays she taught a Bible class in the schoolroom. Correspondence with bureau officials and friends at home furnished her with additional occupation. At times, nevertheless, she felt a longing for the company of women of her own race; but the white ladies of the town did not call, even in the most formal way, upon the Yankee school-teacher. Miss Chandler was therefore fain to do the best she could with such companionship as was available. She took Cicely to her home occasionally, and asked her once to stay all night. Thinking, however, that she detected a reluctance on the girl's part to remain away from home, she did not repeat her invitation.

Cicely, indeed, was filling a double rôle. The learning acquired from Miss Chandler she imparted to John at home. Every evening, by the light of the pine-knots blazing on Needham's ample hearth, she taught John to read the simple words she had learned during the day. Why she did not take him to school she had never asked herself; there were several other pupils as old as he seemed to be. Perhaps she still thought it necessary to protect him from curious remark. He worked with Needham by day, and she could see him at night, and all of Saturdays and Sundays. Perhaps it was the jealous selfishness of love. She had found him; he was hers. In the spring, when school was over, her granny had said that she might marry him. Till then her dream would not yet have come true, and she must keep him to herself. And yet she did not wish him to lose this golden key to the avenues of opportunity. She would not take him to school, but she would teach him each day all that she herself had learned. He was not difficult to teach, but learned, indeed, with what seemed to Cicely marvelous ease — always, however, by her lead, and never of his own initiative. For while he could do a man's work, he was in most things but a child, without a child's curiosity. His love for Cicely appeared the only thing for which he needed no suggestion; and even that possessed an element of childish dependence that would have seemed, to minds trained to thoughtful observation, infinitely pathetic.

The spring came and cotton-planting time. The children began to drop out of Miss Chandler's school one by one, as their services were required at home. Cicely was among those who intended to remain in school until the term closed with the "exhibition," in which she was assigned a leading part. She had selected her recitation, or "speech," from among half a dozen poems that her teacher had suggested, and to memorizing it she devoted considerable time and study. The exhibition, as the first of its kind, was sure to be a notable event. The parents and friends of the children were invited to attend, and a colored church, recently erected—the largest available building—was secured as the place where the exercises should take place.

On the morning of the eventful day, uncle Needham, assisted by John, harnessed the mule to the two-wheeled cart, on which a couple of splint-bottomed chairs were fastened to accommodate Dinah and Cicely. John put on his best clothes—an ill-fitting suit of blue jeans—a round wool hat, a pair of coarse brogans, a homespun shirt, and a bright blue necktie. Cicely wore her best frock, a red ribbon at her throat, another in her hair, and carried a bunch of flowers in her hand. Uncle Needham and aunt Dinah were also in holiday array. Needham and John took their seats on opposite sides of the cart frame, with their feet dangling down, and thus the equipage set out leisurely for the town.

Cicely had long looked forward impatiently to this day. She was going to marry John the next week, and then her dream would have come entirely true. But even this anticipated happiness did not overshadow the importance of the present occasion, which would be an epoch in her life, a day of joy and triumph. She knew her speech perfectly, and timidity was not one of her weaknesses. She knew that the red ribbons set off her dark beauty effectively, and that her dress fitted neatly the curves of her shapely figure. She confidently expected to win the first prize, a large morocco-covered Bible, offered by Miss Chandler for the best exercise.

Cicely and her companions soon arrived at Patesville. Their entrance into the church made quite a sensation, for Cicely was not only an acknowledged belle, but a general favorite, and to John there attached a tinge of mystery which inspired a respect not bestowed upon those who had grown up in the neighborhood. Cicely secured a seat in the front part of the church, next to the aisle, in the place reserved for the pupils. As the house was already partly filled by townspeople when the party from the country arrived, Needham and his wife and John were forced to content themselves with places somewhat in the rear of the room, from which they could see and hear what took place on the platform, but where they were not at all conspicuously visible to those at the front of the church.

The schoolmistress had not yet arrived, and order was preserved in the audience by two of the elder pupils, adorned with large rosettes of red, white, and blue, who ushered the most important visitors to the seats reserved for them. A national flag was gracefully draped over the platform, and under it hung a lithograph of the Great Emancipator, for it was thus these people thought of him. He had saved the Union, but the Union had never meant anything good to them. He had proclaimed liberty to the captive, which meant all to them; and to them he was and would ever be the Great Emancipator.

The schoolmistress came in at a rear door and took her seat upon the platform. Martha was dressed in white; for once she had laid aside the sombre garb in which alone she had been seen since her arrival at Patesville. She wore a yellow rose at her throat, a bunch of jasmine in her belt. A sense of responsibility for the success of the exhibition had deepened the habitual seriousness of her face, yet she greeted the audience with a smile.

"Don' Miss Chan'ler look sweet," whispered the little girls to one another, devouring her beauty with sparkling eyes, their lips parted over a wealth of ivory.

"De Lawd will bress dat chile," said one old woman, in soliloquy. "I t'ank de good Marster I's libbed ter see dis day."

Even envy could not hide its noisome head: a pretty quadroon whispered to her neighbor:

"I don't b'liebe she's natch'ly ez white ez dat. I 'spec' she's be'n powd'rin'! An' I know all dat hair can't be her'n; she's got on a switch, sho's you bawn."

"You knows dat ain' so, Ma'y 'Liza Smif," rejoined the other, with a look of stern disapproval; "you *knows* dat ain' so. You'd gib yo' everlastin' soul 'f you wuz ez white ez Miss Chan'ler, en yo' ha'r wuz ez long ez her'n."

"By Jove, Maxwell!" exclaimed a young officer, who belonged to the Federal garrison stationed in the town, "but that girl is a beauty." The speaker and a companion were in fatigue uniform, and had merely dropped in for an hour between garrison duty. The ushers had wished to give them seats on the platform, but they had declined, thinking that perhaps their presence there might embarrass the teacher. They sought rather to avoid observation by sitting behind a pillar in the rear of the room, around which they could see without attracting undue attention.

"To think," the lieutenant went on, "of that Junonian figure, those lustrous orbs, that golden coronal, that flower of Northern civilization, being wasted on these barbarians!" The speaker uttered an exaggerated but suppressed groan.

His companion, a young man of clean-shaven face and serious aspect, nodded assent, but whispered reprovingly—

"'Sh! some one will hear you. The exercises are going to begin."

When Miss Chandler stepped forward to announce the hymn to be sung by the school as the first exercise, every eye in the room was fixed upon her, except John's, which saw only Cicely. When the teacher had uttered a few words, he looked up to her, and from that moment did not take his eyes off Martha's face.

After the singing, a little girl, dressed in white, crossed by ribbons of red and blue, recited with much spirit a patriotic poem.

When Martha announced the third exercise, John's face took on a more than usually animated expression, and there was a perceptible deepening of the troubled look in his eyes, never entirely absent since Cicely had found him in the woods.

A little yellow boy, with long curls, and a frightened air, next ascended the platform.

"Now, Jimmie, be a man, and speak right out," whispered his teacher, tapping his arm reassuringly with her fan as he passed her.

Jimmie essayed to recite the lines so familiar to a past generation of schoolchildren:

> "I knew a widow very poor,
>   Who four small children had;
> The eldest was but six years old,
>   A gentle, modest lad."

He ducked his head hurriedly in a futile attempt at a bow; then, following instructions previously given him, fixed his eyes upon a large cardboard motto hanging on the rear wall of the room, which admonished him in bright red letters to

"ALWAYS SPEAK THE TRUTH,"

and started off with assumed confidence—

> "I knew a widow very poor,
>   Who"—

At this point, drawn by an irresistible impulse, his eyes sought the level of the audience. Ah, fatal blunder! He stammered, but with an effort raised his eyes and began again:

> "I knew a widow very poor,
>   Who four"—

Again his treacherous eyes fell, and his little remaining self-possession utterly forsook him. He made one more despairing effort:

> "I knew a widow very poor,
>   Who four small"—

and then, bursting into tears, turned and fled amid a murmur of sympathy.

Jimmie's inglorious retreat was covered by the singing in chorus of "The Star-spangled Banner," after which Cicely Green came forward to recite her poem.

"By Jove, Maxwell!" whispered the young officer, who was evidently a connoisseur of female beauty, "that is n't bad for a bronze Venus. I'll tell you"—

" 'Sh!" said the other. "Keep still."

When Cicely finished her recitation, the young officers began to applaud, but stopped suddenly in some confusion as they realized that they were the only ones in the audience so engaged. The colored people had either not learned how to express their approval in orthodox fashion, or else their respect for the sacred character of the edifice forbade any such demonstration. Their enthusiasm found vent, however, in a subdued murmur, emphasized by numerous nods and winks and suppressed exclamations. During the singing that followed Cicely's recitation the two officers quietly withdrew, their duties calling them away at this hour.

At the close of the exercises, a committee on prizes met in the vestibule, and unanimously decided that Cicely Green was entitled to the first prize. Proudly erect, with sparkling eyes and cheeks flushed with victory, Cicely advanced to the platform to receive the coveted reward. As she turned away, her eyes, shining with gratified vanity, sought those of her lover.

John sat bent slightly forward in an attitude of strained attention; and Cicely's triumph lost half its value when she saw that it was not at her, but at Miss Chandler, that his look was directed. Though she watched him thenceforward, not one glance did he vouchsafe to his jealous sweetheart, and never for an instant withdrew his eyes from Martha, or relaxed the unnatural intentness of his gaze. The imprisoned mind, stirred to unwonted effort, was struggling for liberty; and from Martha had come the first ray of outer light that had penetrated its dungeon.

Before the audience was dismissed, the teacher rose to bid her school farewell. Her intention was to take a vacation of three months; but what might happen in that time she did not know, and there were duties at home of such apparent urgency as to render her return to North Carolina at least doubtful; so that in her own heart her *au revoir* sounded very much like a farewell.

She spoke to them of the hopeful progress they had made, and praised them for their eager desire to learn. She told them of the serious duties of life, and of the use they should make of their acquirements. With prophetic finger she pointed them to the upward way which they must climb with patient feet to raise themselves out of the depths.

Then, an unusual thing with her, she spoke of herself. Her heart was full; it was with difficulty that she maintained her composure; for the faces that confronted her were kindly faces, and not critical, and some of them she had learned to love right well.

"I am going away from you, my children," she said; "but before I go I want to tell you how I came to be in North Carolina; so that if I have been able to do anything here among you for which you might feel inclined, in your good nature, to thank me, you may thank not me alone, but another who came before me, and whose work I have but taken up where *he* laid it down. I had a friend—a dear friend—why should I be ashamed to say it?—a lover, to whom I was to be married—as I hope all you girls may some day be happily married. His country needed him, and I gave him up. He came to fight for the Union and for Freedom, for he believed that all men are brothers. He did not come back again—he gave up his life for you. Could I do less than he? I came to the land that he sanctified by his death, and I have tried in my weak way to tend the plant he watered with his blood, and which, in the fullness of time, will blossom forth into the perfect flower of liberty."

She could say no more, and as the whole audience thrilled in sympathy with her emotion, there was a hoarse cry from the men's side of the room, and John forced his way to the aisle and rushed forward to the platform.

"Martha! Martha!"

"Arthur! O Arthur!"

Pent-up love burst the flood-gates of despair and oblivion, and caught these two young hearts in its torrent. Captain Arthur Carey, of the 1st Massachusetts, long since reported missing, and mourned as dead, was restored to reason and to his world.

It seemed to him but yesterday that he had escaped from the Confederate prison at Salisbury; that in an encounter with a guard he had received a wound in the head; that he had wandered on in the woods, keeping himself alive by means of wild berries, with now and then a piece of bread or a potato from a friendly negro. It seemed but the night before that he had laid himself down, tortured with fever, weak from loss of blood, and with no hope that he would ever rise again. From that moment his memory of the past was a blank until he recognized Martha on the platform and took up again the thread of his former existence where it had been broken off.

And Cicely? Well, there is often another woman, and Cicely, all unwittingly to Carey or to Martha, had been the other woman. For, after all, her beautiful dream had been one of the kind that go by contraries.

THE PASSING OF GRANDISON

I

When it is said that it was done to please a woman, there ought perhaps to be enough said to explain anything; for what a man will not do to please a woman is yet to be discovered. Nevertheless, it might be well to state a few preliminary facts to make it clear why young Dick Owens tried to run one of his father's negro men off to Canada.

In the early fifties, when the growth of anti-slavery sentiment and the constant drain of fugitive slaves into the North had so alarmed the slaveholders of the border States as to lead to the passage of the Fugitive Slave Law, a young white man from Ohio, moved by compassion for the sufferings of a certain bondman who happened to have a "hard master," essayed to help the slave to freedom. The attempt was discovered and frustrated; the abductor was tried and convicted for slave-stealing, and sentenced to a term of imprisonment in the penitentiary. His death, after the expiration of only a small part of the sentence, from cholera contracted while nursing stricken fellow prisoners, lent to the case a melancholy interest that made it famous in anti-slavery annals.

Dick Owens had attended the trial. He was a youth of about twenty-two, intelligent, handsome, and amiable, but extremely indolent, in a graceful and gentlemanly way; or, as old Judge Fenderson put it more than once, he was lazy as the Devil—a mere figure of speech, of course, and not one that did justice to the Enemy of Mankind. When asked why he never did anything serious, Dick would good-naturedly reply, with a well-modulated drawl, that he did n't have to. His father was rich; there was but one other child, an unmarried daughter, who because of poor health would probably never marry, and Dick was therefore heir presumptive to a large estate. Wealth or social position he did not need to seek, for he was born to both. Charity Lomax had shamed him into studying law, but notwithstanding an hour or so a day spent at old Judge Fenderson's office, he did not make remarkable headway in his legal studies.

"What Dick needs," said the judge, who was fond of tropes, as became a scholar, and of horses, as was befitting a Kentuckian, "is the whip of necessity, or the spur of ambition. If he had either, he would soon need the snaffle to hold him back."

But all Dick required, in fact, to prompt him to the most remarkable thing he accomplished before he was twenty-five, was a mere suggestion from Charity Lomax. The story was never really known to but two persons until after the war, when it came out because it was a good story and there was no particular reason for its concealment.

Young Owens had attended the trial of this slave-stealer, or martyr—either or both—and, when it was over, had gone to call on Charity Lomax, and, while they sat on the veranda after sundown, had told her all about the trial. He was a good talker, as his career in later years disclosed, and described the proceedings very graphically.

"I confess," he admitted, "that while my principles were against the prisoner, my sympathies were on his side. It appeared that he was of good family, and that he had an old father and mother, respectable people, de pendent upon him for support and comfort in their declining years. He had been led into the matter by pity for a negro whose master ought to have been run out of the county long ago for abusing his slaves. If it had been merely a question of old Sam Briggs's negro, nobody would have cared anything about it. But father and the rest of them stood on the principle of the thing, and told the judge so, and the fellow was sentenced to three years in the penitentiary."

Miss Lomax had listened with lively interest.

"I've always hated old Sam Briggs," she said emphatically, "ever since the time he broke a negro's leg with a piece of cordwood. When I hear of a cruel deed it makes the Quaker blood that came from my grandmother assert itself. Personally I wish that all Sam Briggs's negroes would run away. As for the young man, I regard him as a hero. He dared something for humanity. I could love a man who would take such chances for the sake of others."

"Could you love me, Charity, if I did something heroic?"

"You never will, Dick. You're too lazy for any use. You'll never do anything harder than playing cards or fox-hunting."

"Oh, come now, sweetheart! I've been courting you for a year, and it's the hardest work imaginable. Are you never going to love me?" he pleaded.

His hand sought hers, but she drew it back beyond his reach.

"I'll never love you, Dick Owens, until you have done something. When that time comes, I'll think about it."

"But it takes so long to do anything worth mentioning, and I don't want to wait. One must read two years to become a lawyer, and work five more to make a reputation. We shall both be gray by then."

"Oh, I don't know," she rejoined. "It does n't require a lifetime for a man to prove that he is a man. This one did something, or at least tried to."

"Well, I'm willing to attempt as much as any other man. What do you want me to do, sweetheart? Give me a test."

"Oh, dear me!" said Charity, "I don't care what you *do*, so you do *something*. Really, come to think of it, why should I care whether you do anything or not?"

"I'm sure I don't know why you should, Charity," rejoined Dick humbly, "for I'm aware that I'm not worthy of it."

"Except that I do hate," she added, relenting slightly, "to see a really clever man so utterly lazy and good for nothing."

"Thank you, my dear; a word of praise from you has sharpened my wits already. I have an idea! Will you love me if *I* run a negro off to Canada?"

"What nonsense!" said Charity scornfully. "You must be losing your wits. Steal another man's slave, indeed, while your father owns a hundred!"

"Oh, there'll be no trouble about that," responded Dick lightly; "I'll run off one of the old man's; we've got too many anyway. It may not be quite as difficult as the other man found it, but it will be just as unlawful, and will demonstrate what I am capable of."

"Seeing's believing," replied Charity. "Of course, what you are talking about now is merely absurd. I'm going away for three weeks, to visit my aunt in Tennessee. If you're able to tell me, when I return, that you've done something to prove your quality, I'll—well, you may come and tell me about it."

II

Young Owens got up about nine o'clock next morning, and while making his toilet put some questions to his personal attendant, a rather bright looking young mulatto of about his own age.

"Tom," said Dick.

"Yas, Mars Dick," responded the servant.

"I'm going on a trip North. Would you like to go with me?"

Now, if there was anything that Tom would have liked to make, it was a trip North. It was something he had long contemplated in the abstract, but had never been able to muster up sufficient courage to attempt in the concrete. He was prudent enough, however, to dissemble his feelings.

"I would n't min' it, Mars Dick, ez long ez you'd take keer er me an' fetch me home all right."

Tom's eyes belied his words, however, and his young master felt well assured that Tom needed only a good opportunity to make him run away. Having a comfortable home, and a dismal prospect in case of failure, Tom was not likely to take any desperate chances; but young Owens was satis fied that in a free State but little persuasion would be required to lead Tom astray. With a very logical and characteristic desire to gain his end with the least necessary expenditure of effort, he decided to take Tom with him, if his father did not object.

Colonel Owens had left the house when Dick went to breakfast, so Dick did not see his father till luncheon.

"Father," he remarked casually to the colonel, over the fried chicken, "I'm feeling a trifle run down. I imagine my health would be improved somewhat by a little travel and change of scene."

"Why don't you take a trip North?" suggested his father. The colonel added to paternal affection a considerable respect for his son as the heir of a large estate. He himself had been "raised" in comparative poverty, and had laid the foundations of his fortune by hard work; and while he despised the ladder by which he had climbed, he could not entirely forget it, and unconsciously manifested, in his intercourse with his son, some of the poor man's deference toward the wealthy and well-born.

"I think I'll adopt your suggestion, sir," replied the son, "and run up to New York; and after I've been there awhile I may go on to Boston for a week or so. I've never been there, you know."

"There are some matters you can talk over with my factor in New York," rejoined the colonel, "and while you are up there among the Yankees, I hope you'll keep your eyes and ears open to find out what the rascally abolitionists are saying and doing. They're becoming altogether too active for our comfort, and entirely too many ungrateful niggers are running away. I hope the conviction of that fellow yesterday may discourage the rest of the breed. I'd just like to catch any one trying to run off one of my darkeys. He'd get short shrift; I don't think any Court would have a chance to try him."

"They are a pestiferous lot," assented Dick, "and dangerous to our institutions. But say, father, if I go North I shall want to take Tom with me."

Now, the colonel, while a very indulgent father, had pronounced views on the subject of negroes, having studied them, as he often said, for a great many years, and, as he asserted oftener still, understanding them perfectly. It is scarcely worth while to say, either, that he valued more highly than if he had inherited them the slaves he had toiled and schemed for.

"I don't think it safe to take Tom up North," he declared, with promptness and decision. "He's a good enough boy, but too smart to trust among those low-down abolitionists. I strongly suspect him of having learned to read, though I can't imagine how. I saw him with a newspaper the other day, and while he pretended to be looking at a woodcut, I'm almost sure he was reading the paper. I think it by no means safe to take him."

Dick did not insist, because he knew it was useless. The colonel would have obliged his son in any other matter, but his negroes were the outward and visible sign of his wealth and station, and therefore sacred to him.

"Whom do you think it safe to take?" asked Dick. "I suppose I'll have to have a body-servant."

"What's the matter with Grandison?" suggested the colonel. "He's handy enough, and I reckon we can trust him. He's too fond of good eating, to risk losing his regular meals; besides, he's sweet on your mother's maid, Betty, and I've promised to let 'em get married before long. I'll have Grandison up, and we'll talk to him. Here, you boy Jack," called the colonel to a yellow youth in the next room who was catching flies and pulling their wings off to pass the time, "go down to the barn and tell Grandison to come here."

"Grandison," said the colonel, when the negro stood before him, hat in hand.

"Yas, marster."

"Have n't I always treated you right?"

"Yas, marster."

"Have n't you always got all you wanted to eat?"

"Yas, marster."

"And as much whiskey and tobacco as was good for you, Grandison?"

"Y-a-s, marster."

"I should just like to know, Grandison, whether you don't think yourself a great deal better off than those poor free negroes down by the plank road, with no kind master to look after them and no mistress to give them medicine when they're sick and—and"—

"Well, I sh'd jes' reckon I is better off, suh, dan dem low-down free niggers, suh! Ef anybody ax 'em who dey b'long ter, dey has ter say nobody, er e'se lie erbout it. Anybody ax me who I b'longs ter, I ain' got no 'casion ter be shame' ter tell 'em, no, suh, 'deed I ain', suh!"

The colonel was beaming. This was true gratitude, and his feudal heart thrilled at such appreciative homage. What cold-blooded, heartless monsters they were who would break up this blissful relationship of kindly protection on the one hand, of wise subordination and loyal dependence on the other! The colonel always became indignant at the mere thought of such wickedness.

"Grandison," the colonel continued, "your young master Dick is going North for a few weeks, and I am thinking of letting him take you along. I shall send you on this trip, Grandison, in order that you may take care of your young master. He will need some one to wait on him, and no one can ever do it so well as one of the boys brought up with him on the old plantation. I am going to trust him in your hands, and I'm sure you'll do your duty faithfully, and bring him back home safe and sound—to old Kentucky."

Grandison grinned. "Oh yas, marster, I'll take keer er young Mars Dick."

"I want to warn you, though, Grandison," continued the colonel impressively, "against these cussed abolitionists, who try to entice servants from their comfortable homes and their indulgent masters, from the blue skies, the green fields, and the warm sunlight of their southern home, and send them away off yonder to Canada, a dreary country, where the woods are full of wildcats and wolves and bears, where the snow lies up to the eaves of the houses for six months of the year, and the cold is so severe that it freezes your breath and curdles your blood; and where, when runaway niggers get sick and can't work, they are turned out to starve and die, unloved and uncared for. I reckon, Grandison, that you have too much sense to permit yourself to be led astray by any such foolish and wicked people."

"'Deed, suh, I would n' low none er dem cussed, low-down abolitioners ter come nigh me, suh. I'd—I'd—would I be 'lowed ter hit 'em, suh?"

"Certainly, Grandison," replied the colonel, chuckling, "hit 'em as hard as you can. I reckon they'd rather like it. Begad, I believe they would! It would serve 'em right to be hit by a nigger!"

"Er ef I did n't hit 'em, suh," continued Grandison reflectively, "I'd tell Mars Dick, en he 'd fix 'em. He'd smash de face off'n 'em, suh, I jes' knows he would."

"Oh yes, Grandison, your young master will protect you. You need fear no harm while he is near."

"Dey won't try ter steal me, will dey, marster?" asked the negro, with sudden alarm.

"I don't know, Grandison," replied the colonel, lighting a fresh cigar. "They're a desperate set of lunatics, and there's no telling what they may resort to. But if you stick close to your young master, and remember always that he is your best friend, and understands your real needs, and has your true interests at heart, and if you will be careful to avoid strangers who try to talk to you, you'll stand a fair chance of getting back to your home and your friends. And if you please your master Dick, he'll buy you a present, and a string of beads for Betty to wear when you and she get married in the fall."

"Thanky, marster, thanky, suh," replied Grandison, oozing gratitude at every pore; "you is a good marster, to be sho', suh; yas, 'deed you is. You kin jes' bet me and Mars Dick gwine git 'long jes' lack I wuz own boy ter Mars Dick. En it won't be my fault ef he don' want me fer his boy all de time, w'en we come back home ag'in."

"All right, Grandison, you may go now. You need n't work any more to-day, and here's a piece of tobacco for you off my own plug."

"Thanky, marster, thanky, marster! You is de bes' marster any nigger ever had in dis worl'." And Grandison bowed and scraped and disappeared round the corner, his jaws closing around a large section of the colonel's best tobacco.

"You may take Grandison," said the colonel to his son. "I allow he's abolitionist proof."

III

Richard Owens, Esq., and servant, from Kentucky, registered at the fashionable New York hostelry for Southerners in those days, a hotel where an atmosphere congenial to Southern institutions was sedulously maintained. But there were negro waiters in the dining-room, and mulatto bell-boys, and Dick had no doubt that Grandison, with the native gregariousness and garrulousness of his race, would foregather and palaver with them sooner or later, and Dick hoped that they would speedily inoculate him with the virus of freedom. For it was not Dick's intention to say anything to his servant about his plan to free him, for obvious reasons. To mention one of them, if Grandison should go away, and by legal process be recaptured, his young master's part in the matter would doubtless become known, which would be embarrassing to Dick, to say the least. If, on the other hand, he should merely give Grandison sufficient latitude, he had no doubt he would eventually lose him. For while not exactly skeptical about Grandison's perfervid loyalty, Dick had been a somewhat keen observer of human nature, in his own indolent way, and based his expectations upon the force of the example and argument that his servant could scarcely fail to encounter. Grandison should have a fair chance to become free by his own initiative; if it should become necessary to adopt other measures to get rid of him, it would be time enough to act when the necessity arose; and Dick Owens was not the youth to take needless trouble.

The young master renewed some acquaintances and made others, and spent a week or two very pleasantly in the best society of the metropolis, easily accessible to a wealthy, well-bred young Southerner, with proper introductions. Young women smiled on him, and young men of convivial habits pressed their hospitalities; but the memory of Charity's sweet, strong face and clear blue eyes made him proof against the blandishments of the one sex and the persuasions of the other. Meanwhile he kept Grandison supplied with pocket-money, and left him mainly to his own devices. Every night when Dick came in he hoped he might have to wait upon himself, and every morning he looked forward with pleasure to the prospect of making his toilet unaided. His hopes, however, were doomed to disappointment, for every night when he came in Grandison was on hand with a bootjack, and a nightcap mixed for his young master as the colonel had taught him to mix it, and every morning Grandison appeared with his master's boots blacked and his clothes brushed, and laid his linen out for the day.

"Grandison," said Dick one morning, after finishing his toilet, "this is the chance of your life to go around among your own people and see how they live. Have you met any of them?"

"Yas, suh, I's seen some of 'em. But I don' keer nuffin fer 'em, suh. Dey're diffe'nt f'm de niggers down ou' way. Dey 'lows dey're free, but dey ain' got sense 'nuff ter know dey ain' half as well off as dey would be down Souf, whar dey'd be 'preciated."

When two weeks had passed without any apparent effect of evil example upon Grandison, Dick resolved to go on to Boston, where he thought the atmosphere might prove more favorable to his ends. After he had been at the Revere House for a day or two without losing Grandison, he decided upon slightly different tactics.

Having ascertained from a city directory the addresses of several well-known abolitionists, he wrote them each a letter something like this:

Dear Friend and Brother:

A wicked slaveholder from Kentucky, stopping at the Revere House, has dared to insult the liberty-loving people of Boston by bringing his slave into their midst. Shall this be tolerated? Or shall steps be taken in the name of liberty to rescue a fellow-man from bondage? For obvious reasons I can only sign myself,

A Friend of Humanity

That his letter might have an opportunity to prove effective, Dick made it a point to send Grandison away from the hotel on various errands. On one of these occasions Dick watched him for quite a distance down the street. Grandison had scarcely left the hotel when a long-haired, sharp-featured man came out behind him, followed him, soon overtook him, and kept along beside him until they turned the next corner. Dick's hopes were roused by this spectacle, but sank correspondingly when Grandison returned to the hotel. As Grandison said nothing about the encounter, Dick hoped there might be some self-consciousness behind this unexpected reticence, the results of which might develop later on.

But Grandison was on hand again when his master came back to the hotel at night, and was in attendance again in the morning, with hot water, to assist at his master's toilet. Dick sent him on further errands from day to day, and upon one occasion came squarely up to him—inadvertently of course—while Grandison was engaged in conversation with a young white man in clerical garb. When Grandison saw Dick approaching, he edged away from the preacher and hastened toward his master, with a very evident expression of relief upon his countenance.

"Mars Dick," he said, "dese yer abolitioners is jes' pesterin' de life out er me tryin' ter git me ter run away. I don' pay no 'tention ter 'em, but dey riles me so sometimes dat I'm feared I'll hit some of 'em some er dese days, an' dat mought git me inter trouble. I ain' said nuffin' ter you 'bout it, Mars Dick, fer I did n' wanter 'sturb yo' min'; but I don' like it, suh; no, suh, I don'! Is we gwine back home 'fo' long, Mars Dick?"

"We'll be going back soon enough," replied Dick somewhat shortly, while he inwardly cursed the stupidity of a slave who could be free and would not, and registered a secret vow that if he were unable to get rid of Grandison without assassinating him, and were therefore compelled to take him back to Kentucky, he would see that Grandison got a taste of an article of slavery that would make him regret his wasted opportunities. Meanwhile he determined to tempt his servant yet more strongly.

"Grandison," he said next morning, "I'm going away for a day or two, but I shall leave you here. I shall lock up a hundred dollars in this drawer and give you the key. If you need any of it, use it and enjoy yourself—spend it all if you like—for this is probably the last chance you'll have for some time to be in a free State, and you'd better enjoy your liberty while you may."

When he came back a couple of days later and found the faithful Grandison at his post, and the hundred dollars intact, Dick felt seriously annoyed. His vexation was increased by the fact that he could not express his feelings adequately. He did not even scold Grandison; how could he, indeed, find fault with one who so sensibly recognized his true place in the economy of civilization, and kept it with such touching fidelity?

"I can't say a thing to him," groaned Dick. "He deserves a leather medal, made out of his own hide tanned. I reckon I'll write to father and let him know what a model servant he has given me."

He wrote his father a letter which made the colonel swell with pride and pleasure. "I really think," the colonel observed to one of his friends, "that Dick ought to have the nigger interviewed by the Boston papers, so that they may see how contented and happy our darkeys really are."

Dick also wrote a long letter to Charity Lomax, in which he said, among many other things, that if she knew how hard he was working, and under what difficulties, to accomplish something serious for her sake, she would no longer keep him in suspense, but overwhelm him with love and admiration.

Having thus exhausted without result the more obvious methods of getting rid of Grandison, and diplomacy having also proved a failure, Dick was forced to consider more radical measures. Of course he might run away himself, and abandon Grandison, but this would be merely to leave him in the United States, where he was still a slave, and where, with his notions of loyalty, he would speedily be reclaimed. It was necessary, in order to accomplish the purpose of his trip to the North, to leave Grandison permanently in Canada, where he would be legally free.

"I might extend my trip to Canada," he reflected, "but that would be too palpable. I have it! I'll visit Niagara Falls on the way home, and lose him on the Canada side. When he once realizes that he is actually free, I'll warrant that he'll stay."

So the next day saw them westward bound, and in due course of time, by the somewhat slow conveyances of the period, they found themselves at Niagara. Dick walked and drove about the Falls for several days, taking Grandison along with him on most occasions. One morning they stood on the Canadian side, watching the wild whirl of the waters below them.

"Grandison," said Dick, raising his voice above the roar of the cataract, "do you know where you are now?"

"I's wid you, Mars Dick; dat's all I keers."

"You are now in Canada, Grandison, where your people go when they run away from their masters. If you wished, Grandison, you might walk away from me this very minute, and I could not lay my hand upon you to take you back."

Grandison looked around uneasily.

"Let's go back ober de ribber, Mars Dick. I's feared I'll lose you ovuh heah, an' den I won' hab no marster, an' won't nebber be able to git back home no mo'."

Discouraged, but not yet hopeless, Dick said, a few minutes later—

"Grandison, I'm going up the road a bit, to the inn over yonder. You stay here until I return. I'll not be gone a great while."

Grandison's eyes opened wide and he looked somewhat fearful.

"Is dey any er dem dadblasted abolitioners roun' heah, Mars Dick?"

"I don't imagine that there are," replied his master, hoping there might be. "But I'm not afraid of *your* running away, Grandison. I only wish I were," he added to himself.

Dick walked leisurely down the road to where the whitewashed inn, built of stone, with true British solidity, loomed up through the trees by the roadside. Arrived there he ordered a glass of ale and a sandwich, and took a seat at a table by a window, from which he could see Grandison in the distance. For a while he hoped that the seed he had sown might have fallen on fertile ground, and that Grandison, relieved from the restraining power of a master's eye, and finding himself in a free country, might get up and walk away; but the hope was vain, for Grandison remained faithfully at his post, awaiting his master's return. He had seated himself on a broad flat stone, and, turning his eyes away from the grand and awe-inspiring spectacle that lay close at hand, was looking anxiously toward the inn where his master sat cursing his ill-timed fidelity.

By and by a girl came into the room to serve his order, and Dick very naturally glanced at her; and as she was young and pretty and remained in attendance, it was some minutes before he looked for Grandison. When he did so his faithful servant had disappeared.

To pay his reckoning and go away without the change was a matter quickly accomplished. Retracing his footsteps toward the Falls, he saw, to his great disgust, as he approached the spot where he had left Grandison, the familiar form of his servant stretched out on the ground, his face to the sun, his mouth open, sleeping the time away, oblivious alike to the grandeur of the scenery, the thunderous roar of the cataract, or the insidious voice of sentiment.

"Grandison," soliloquized his master, as he stood gazing down at his ebony encumbrance, "I do not deserve to be an American citizen; I ought not to have the advantages I possess over you; and I certainly am not worthy of Charity Lomax, if I am not smart enough to get rid of you. I have an idea! You shall yet be free, and I will be the instrument of your deliverance. Sleep on, faithful and affectionate servitor, and dream of the blue grass and the bright skies of old Kentucky, for it is only in your dreams that you will ever see them again!"

Dick retraced his footsteps towards the inn. The young woman chanced to look out of the window and saw the handsome young gentleman she had waited on a few minutes before, standing in the road a short distance away, apparently engaged in earnest conversation with a colored man employed as hostler for the inn. She thought she saw something pass from the white man to the other, but at that moment her duties called her away from the window, and when she looked out again the young gentleman had disappeared, and the hostler, with two other young men of the neighborhood, one white and one colored, were walking rapidly towards the Falls.

IV

Dick made the journey homeward alone, and as rapidly as the conveyances of the day would permit. As he drew near home his conduct in going back without Grandison took on a more serious aspect than it had borne at any previous time, and although he had prepared the colonel by a letter sent several days ahead, there was still the prospect of a bad quarter of an hour with him; not, indeed, that his father would upbraid him, but he was likely to make searching inquiries. And notwithstanding the vein of quiet recklessness that had carried Dick through his preposterous scheme, he was a very poor liar, having rarely had occasion or inclination to tell anything but the truth. Any reluctance to meet his father was more than offset, however, by a stronger force drawing him homeward, for Charity Lomax must long since have returned from her visit to her aunt in Tennessee.

Dick got off easier than he had expected. He told a straight story, and a truthful one, so far as it went.

The colonel raged at first, but rage soon subsided into anger, and anger moderated into annoyance, and annoyance into a sort of garrulous sense of injury. The colonel thought he had been hardly used; he had trusted this negro, and he had broken faith. Yet, after all, he did not blame Grandison so much as he did the abolitionists, who were undoubtedly at the bottom of it.

As for Charity Lomax, Dick told her, privately of course, that he had run his father's man, Grandison, off to Canada, and left him there.

"Oh, Dick," she had said with shuddering alarm, "what have you done? If they knew it they'd send you to the penitentiary, like they did that Yankee."

"But they don't know it," he had replied seriously; adding, with an injured tone, "you don't seem to appreciate my heroism like you did that of the Yankee; perhaps it's because I was n't caught and sent to the penitentiary. I thought you wanted me to do it."

"Why, Dick Owens!" she exclaimed. "You know I never dreamed of any such outrageous proceeding."

"But I presume I'll have to marry you," she concluded, after some insistence on Dick's part, "if only to take care of you. You are too reckless for anything; and a man who goes chasing all over the North, being entertained by New York and Boston society and having negroes to throw away, needs some one to look after him."

"It's a most remarkable thing," replied Dick fervently, "that your views correspond exactly with my profoundest convictions. It proves beyond question that we were made for one another."

They were married three weeks later. As each of them had just returned from a journey, they spent their honeymoon at home.

A week after the wedding they were seated, one afternoon, on the piazza of the colonel's house, where Dick had taken his bride, when a negro from the yard ran down the lane and threw open the big gate for the colonel's buggy to enter. The colonel was not alone. Beside him, ragged and travel-stained, bowed with weariness, and upon his face a haggard look that told of hardship and privation, sat the lost Grandison.

The colonel alighted at the steps.

"Take the lines, Tom," he said to the man who had opened the gate, "and drive round to the barn. Help Grandison down—poor devil, he's so stiff he can hardly move!—and get a tub of water and wash him and rub him down, and feed him, and give him a big drink of whiskey, and then let him come round and see his young master and his new mistress."

The colonel's face wore an expression compounded of joy and indignation—joy at the restoration of a valuable piece of property; indignation for reasons he proceeded to state.

"It's astounding, the depths of depravity the human heart is capable of! I was coming along the road three miles away, when I heard some one call me from the roadside. I pulled up the mare, and who should come out of the woods but Grandison. The poor nigger could hardly crawl along, with the help of a broken limb. I was never more astonished in my life. You could have knocked me down with a feather. He seemed pretty far gone—he could hardly talk above a whisper—and I had to give him a mouthful of whiskey to brace him up so he could tell his story. It's just as I thought from the beginning, Dick; Grandison had no notion of running away; he knew when he was well off, and where his friends were. All the persuasions of abolition liars and runaway niggers did not move him. But the desperation of those fanatics knew no bounds; their guilty consciences gave them no rest. They got the notion somehow that Grandison belonged to a niggercatcher, and had been brought North as a spy to help capture ungrateful runaway servants. They actually kidnaped him—just think of it!—and gagged him and bound him and threw him rudely into a wagon, and carried him into the gloomy depths of a Canadian forest, and locked him in a lonely hut, and fed him on bread and water for three weeks. One of the scoundrels wanted to kill him, and persuaded the others that it ought to be done; but they got to quarreling about how they should do it, and before they had their minds made up Grandison escaped, and, keeping his back steadily to the North Star, made his way, after suffering incredible hardships, back to the old plantation, back to his master, his friends, and his home. Why, it's as good as one of Scott's novels! Mr. Simms or some other one of our Southern authors ought to write it up."

"Don't you think, sir," suggested Dick, who had calmly smoked his cigar throughout the colonel's animated recital, "that that kidnaping yarn sounds a little improbable? Is n't there some more likely explanation?"

"Nonsense, Dick; it's the gospel truth! Those infernal abolitionists are capable of anything—everything! Just think of their locking the poor, faithful nigger up, beating him, kicking him, depriving him of his liberty, keeping him on bread and water for three long, lonesome weeks, and he all the time pining for the old plantation!"

There were almost tears in the colonel's eyes at the picture of Grandison's sufferings that he conjured up. Dick still professed to be slightly skeptical, and met Charity's severely questioning eye with bland unconsciousness.

The colonel killed the fatted calf for Grandison, and for two or three weeks the returned wanderer's life was a slave's dream of pleasure. His fame spread throughout the county, and the colonel gave him a permanent place among the house servants, where he could always have him conveniently at hand to relate his adventures to admiring visitors.

About three weeks after Grandison's return the colonel's faith in sable humanity was rudely shaken, and its foundations almost broken up. He came near losing his belief in the fidelity of the negro to his master—the servile virtue most highly prized and most sedulously cultivated by the colonel and his kind. One Monday morning Grandison was missing. And not only Grandison, but his wife, Betty the maid; his mother, aunt Eunice; his father, uncle Ike; his brothers, Tom and John, and his little sister Elsie, were likewise absent from the plantation; and a hurried search and inquiry in the neighborhood resulted in no information as to their whereabouts. So much valuable property could not be lost without an effort to recover it, and the wholesale nature of the transaction carried consternation to the hearts of those whose ledgers were chiefly bound in black. Extremely energetic measures were taken by the colonel and his friends. The fugitives were traced, and followed from point to point, on their northward run through Ohio. Several times the hunters were close upon their heels, but the magnitude of the escaping party begot unusual vigilance on the part of those who sympathized with the fugitives, and strangely enough, the underground railroad seemed to have had its tracks cleared and signals set for this particular train. Once, twice, the colonel thought he had them, but they slipped through his fingers.

One last glimpse he caught of his vanishing property, as he stood, accompanied by a United States marshal, on a wharf at a port on the south shore of Lake Erie. On the stern of a small steamboat which was receding rapidly from the wharf, with her nose pointing toward Canada, there stood a group of familiar dark faces, and the look they cast backward was not one of longing for the fleshpots of Egypt. The colonel saw Grandison point him out to one of the crew of the vessel, who waved his hand derisively toward the colonel. The latter shook his fist impotently—and the incident was closed.

UNCLE WELLINGTON'S WIVES

I

Uncle Wellington Braboy was so deeply absorbed in thought as he walked slowly homeward from the weekly meeting of the Union League, that he let his pipe go out, a fact of which he remained oblivious until he had reached the little frame house in the suburbs of Patesville, where he lived with aunt Milly, his wife. On this particular occasion the club had been addressed by a visiting brother from the North, Professor Patterson, a tall, well-formed mulatto, who wore a perfectly fitting suit of broadcloth, a shiny silk hat, and linen of dazzling whiteness—in short, a gentleman of such distinguished appearance that the doors and windows of the offices and stores on Front Street were filled with curious observers as he passed through that thoroughfare in the early part of the day. This polished stranger was a traveling organizer of Masonic lodges, but he also claimed to be a high officer in the Union League, and had been invited to lecture before the local chapter of that organization at Patesville.

The lecture had been largely attended, and uncle Wellington Braboy had occupied a seat just in front of the platform. The subject of the lecture was "The Mental, Moral, Physical, Political, Social, and Financial Improvement of the Negro Race in America," a theme much dwelt upon, with slight variations, by colored orators. For to this struggling people, then as now, the problem of their uncertain present and their doubtful future was the chief concern of life. The period was the hopeful one. The Federal Government retained some vestige of authority in the South, and the newly emancipated race cherished the delusion that under the Constitution, that enduring rock on which our liberties are founded, and under the equal laws it purported to guarantee, they would enter upon the era of freedom and opportunity which their Northern friends had inaugurated with such solemn sanctions. The speaker pictured in eloquent language the state of ideal equality and happiness enjoyed by colored people at the North: how they sent their children to school with the white children; how they sat by white people in the churches and theatres, ate with them in the public restaurants, and buried their dead in the same cemeteries. The professor waxed eloquent with the development of his theme, and, as a finishing touch to an alluring picture, assured the excited audience that the intermarriage of the races was common, and that he himself had espoused a white woman.

Uncle Wellington Braboy was a deeply interested listener. He had heard something of these facts before, but his information had always come in such vague and questionable shape that he had paid little attention to it. He knew that the Yankees had freed the slaves, and that runaway negroes had always gone to the North to seek liberty; any such equality, however, as the visiting brother had depicted, was more than uncle Wellington had ever conceived as actually existing anywhere in the world. At first he felt inclined to doubt the truth of the speaker's statements; but the cut of his clothes, the eloquence of his language, and the flowing length of his whiskers, were so far superior to anything uncle Wellington had ever met among the colored people of his native State, that he felt irresistibly impelled to the conviction that nothing less than the advantages claimed for the North by the visiting brother could have produced such an exquisite flower of civilization. Any lingering doubts uncle Wellington may have felt were entirely dispelled by the courtly bow and cordial grasp of the hand with which the visiting brother acknowledged the congratulations showered upon him by the audience at the close of his address.

The more uncle Wellington's mind dwelt upon the professor's speech, the more attractive seemed the picture of Northern life presented. Uncle Wellington possessed in large measure the imaginative faculty so freely bestowed by nature upon the race from which the darker half of his blood was drawn. He had indulged in occasional day-dreams of an ideal state of social equality, but his wildest flights of fancy had never located it nearer than heaven, and he had felt some misgivings about its practical working even there. Its desirability he had never doubted, and the speech of the evening before had given a local habitation and a name to the forms his imagination had bodied forth. Giving full rein to his fancy, he saw in the North a land flowing with milk and honey—a land peopled by noble men and beautiful women, among whom colored men and women moved with the ease and grace of acknowledged right. Then he placed himself in the foreground of the picture. What a fine figure he would have made in the world if he had been born at the free North! He imagined himself dressed like the professor, and passing the contribution-box in a white church; and most pleasant of his dreams, and the hardest to realize as possible, was that of the gracious white lady he might have called wife. Uncle Wellington was a mulatto, and his features were those of his white father, though tinged with the hue of his mother's race; and as he lifted the kerosene lamp at evening, and took a long look at his image in the little mirror over the mantelpiece, he said to himself that he was a very good-looking man, and could have adorned a much higher sphere in life than that in which the accident of birth had placed him. He fell asleep and dreamed that he lived in a two-story brick house, with a spacious flower garden in front, the whole inclosed by a high iron fence; that he kept a carriage and servants, and never did a stroke of work. This was the highest style of living in Patesville, and he could conceive of nothing finer.

Uncle Wellington slept later than usual the next morning, and the sunlight was pouring in at the open window of the bedroom, when his dreams were interrupted by the voice of his wife, in tones meant to be harsh, but which no ordinary degree of passion could rob of their native unctuousness.

"Git up f'm dere, you lazy, good-fuh-nuffin' nigger! Is you gwine ter sleep all de mawnin'? I's ti'ed er dis yer runnin' 'roun' all night an' den sleepin' all day. You won't git dat tater patch hoed ovuh ter-day 'less'n you git up f'm dere an' git at it."

Uncle Wellington rolled over, yawned cavernously, stretched himself, and with a muttered protest got out of bed and put on his clothes. Aunt Milly had prepared a smoking breakfast of hominy and fried bacon, the odor of which was very grateful to his nostrils.

"Is breakfus' done ready?" he inquired, tentatively, as he came into the kitchen and glanced at the table.

"No, it ain't ready, an' 't ain't gwine ter be ready 'tel you tote dat wood an' water in," replied aunt Milly severely, as she poured two teacups of boiling water on two tablespoonfuls of ground coffee.

Uncle Wellington went down to the spring and got a pail of water, after which he brought in some oak logs for the fireplace and some lightwood for kindling. Then he drew a chair towards the table and started to sit down.

"Wonduh what's de matter wid you dis mawnin' anyhow," remarked aunt Milly. "You must 'a' be'n up ter some devilment las' night, fer yo' recommemb'ance is so po' dat you fus' fergit ter git up, an' den fergit ter wash yo' face an' hands fo' you set down ter de table. I don' 'low nobody ter eat at my table dat a-way."

"I don' see no use 'n washin' 'em so much," replied Wellington wearily. "Dey gits dirty ag'in right off, an' den you got ter wash 'em ovuh ag'in; it's jes' pilin' up wuk what don' fetch in nuffin'. De dirt don' show nohow, 'n' I don' see no advantage in bein' black, ef you got to keep on washin' yo' face 'n' han's jes' lack w'ite folks." He nevertheless performed his ablutions in a perfunctory way, and resumed his seat at the breakfast-table.

"Ole 'oman," he asked, after the edge of his appetite had been taken off, "how would you lack ter live at de Norf?"

"I dunno nuffin' 'bout de Norf," replied aunt Milly. "It's hard 'nuff ter git erlong heah, whar we knows all erbout it."

"De brother what 'dressed de meetin' las' night say dat de wages at de Norf is twicet ez big ez dey is heah."

"You could make a sight mo' wages heah ef you 'd 'ten' ter yo' wuk better," replied aunt Milly.

Uncle Wellington ignored this personality, and continued, "An' he say de cullud folks got all de privileges er de w'ite folks—dat dey chillen goes ter school tergedder, dat dey sets on same seats in chu'ch, an' sarves on jury, 'n' rides on de kyars an' steamboats wid de w'ite folks, an' eats at de fus' table."

"Dat 'u'd suit you," chuckled aunt Milly, "an' you 'd stay dere fer de secon' table, too. How dis man know 'bout all dis yer foolis'ness?" she asked incredulously.

"He come f'm de Norf," said uncle Wellington, "an' he 'speunced it all hisse'f."

"Well, he can't make me b'lieve it," she rejoined, with a shake of her head.

"An' you would n' lack ter go up dere an' 'joy all dese privileges?" asked uncle Wellington, with some degree of earnestness.

The old woman laughed until her sides shook. "Who gwine ter take me up dere?" she inquired.

"You got de money yo'se'f."

"I ain' got no money fer ter was'e," she replied shortly, becoming serious at once; and with that the subject was dropped.

Uncle Wellington pulled a hoe from under the house, and took his way wearily to the potato patch. He did not feel like working, but aunt Milly was the undisputed head of the establishment, and he did not dare to openly neglect his work. In fact, he regarded work at any time as a disagreeable necessity to be avoided as much as possible.

His wife was cast in a different mould. Externally she would have impressed the casual observer as a neat, well-preserved, and good-looking black woman, of middle age, every curve of whose ample figure—and her figure was all curves—was suggestive of repose. So far from being indolent, or even deliberate in her movements, she was the most active and energetic woman in the town. She went through the physical exercises of a prayer-meeting with astonishing vigor. It was exhilarating to see her wash a shirt, and a study to watch her do it up. A quick jerk shook out the dampened garment; one pass of her ample palm spread it over the ironing-board, and a few well-directed strokes with the iron accomplished what would have occupied the ordinary laundress for half an hour.

To this uncommon, and in uncle Wellington's opinion unnecessary and unnatural activity, his own habits were a steady protest. If aunt Milly had been willing to support him in idleness, he would have acquiesced without a murmur in her habits of industry. This she would not do, and, moreover, insisted on his working at least half the time. If she had invested the proceeds of her labor in rich food and fine clothing, he might have endured it better; but to her passion for work was added a most detestable thrift. She absolutely refused to pay for Wellington's clothes, and required him to furnish a certain proportion of the family supplies. Her savings were carefully put by, and with them she had bought and paid for the modest cottage which she and her husband occupied. Under her careful hand it was always neat and clean; in summer the little yard was gay with bright-colored flowers, and woe to the heedless pickaninny who should stray into her yard and pluck a rose or a verbena! In a stout oaken chest under her bed she kept a capacious stocking, into which flowed a steady stream of fractional currency. She carried the key to this chest in her pocket, a proceeding regarded by uncle Wellington with no little disfavor. He was of the opinion—an opinion he would not have dared to assert in her presence—that his wife's earnings were his own property; and he looked upon this stocking as a drunkard's wife might regard the saloon which absorbed her husband's wages.

Uncle Wellington hurried over the potato patch on the morning of the conversation above recorded, and as soon as he saw aunt Milly go away with a basket of clothes on her head, returned to the house, put on his coat, and went uptown.

He directed his steps to a small frame building fronting on the main street of the village, at a point where the street was intersected by one of the several creeks meandering through the town, cooling the air, providing numerous swimming-holes for the amphibious small boy, and furnishing waterpower for grist-mills and saw-mills. The rear of the building rested on long brick pillars, built up from the bottom of the steep bank of the creek, while the front was level with the street. This was the office of Mr. Matthew Wright, the sole representative of the colored race at the bar of Chinquapin County. Mr. Wright came of an "old issue" free colored family, in which, though the negro blood was present in an attenuated strain, a line of free ancestry could be traced beyond the Revolutionary War. He had enjoyed exceptional opportunities, and enjoyed the distinction of being the first, and for a long time the only colored lawyer in North Carolina. His services were frequently called into requisition by impecunious people of his own race; when they had money they went to white lawyers, who, they shrewdly conjectured, would have more influence with judge or jury than a colored lawyer, however able.

Uncle Wellington found Mr. Wright in his office. Having inquired after the health of the lawyer's family and all his relations in detail, uncle Wellington asked for a professional opinion.

"Mistah Wright, ef a man's wife got money, whose money is dat befo' de law—his'n er her'n?"

The lawyer put on his professional air, and replied:

"Under the common law, which in default of special legislative enactment is the law of North Carolina, the personal property of the wife belongs to her husband."

"But dat don' jes' tech de p'int, suh. I wuz axin' 'bout money."

"You see, uncle Wellington, your education has not rendered you familiar with legal phraseology. The term 'personal property' or 'estate' embraces, according to Blackstone, all property other than land, and therefore includes money. Any money a man's wife has is his, constructively, and will be recognized as his actually, as soon as he can secure possession of it."

"Dat is ter say, suh—my eddication don' quite 'low me ter understan' dat—dat is ter say"—

"That is to say, it's yours when you get it. It is n't yours so that the law will help you get it; but on the other hand, when you once lay your hands on it, it is yours so that the law won't take it away from you."

Uncle Wellington nodded to express his full comprehension of the law as expounded by Mr. Wright, but scratched his head in a way that expressed some disappointment. The law seemed to wobble. Instead of enabling him to stand up fearlessly and demand his own, it threw him back upon his own efforts; and the prospect of his being able to overpower or outwit aunt Milly by any ordinary means was very poor.

He did not leave the office, but hung around awhile as though there were something further he wished to speak about. Finally, after some discursive remarks about the crops and politics, he asked, in an offhand, disinterested manner, as though the thought had just occurred to him:

"Mistah Wright, w'ile's we're talkin' 'bout law matters, what do it cos' ter git a defoce?"

"That depends upon circumstances. It is n't altogether a matter of expense. Have you and aunt Milly been having trouble?"

"Oh no, suh; I was jes' a-wond'rin'."

"You see," continued the lawyer, who was fond of talking, and had nothing else to do for the moment, "a divorce is not an easy thing to get in this State under any circumstances. It used to be the law that divorce could be granted only by special act of the legislature; and it is but recently that the subject has been relegated to the jurisdiction of the courts."

Uncle Wellington understood a part of this, but the answer had not been exactly to the point in his mind.

"S'pos'n', den, jes' fer de argyment, me an' my ole 'oman sh'd fall out en wanter separate, how could I git a defoce?"

"That would depend on what you quarreled about. It's pretty hard work to answer general questions in a particular way. If you merely wished to separate, it would n't be necessary to get a divorce; but if you should want to marry again, you would have to be divorced, or else you would be guilty of bigamy, and could be sent to the penitentiary. But, by the way, uncle Wellington, when were you married?"

"I got married 'fo' de wah, when I was livin' down on Rockfish Creek."

"When you were in slavery?"

"Yas, suh."

"Did you have your marriage registered after the surrender?"

"No, suh; never knowed nuffin' 'bout dat."

After the war, in North Carolina and other States, the freed people who had sustained to each other the relation of husband and wife as it existed among slaves, were required by law to register their consent to continue in the marriage relation. By this simple expedient their former marriages of convenience received the sanction of law, and their children the seal of legitimacy. In many cases, however, where the parties lived in districts remote from the larger towns, the ceremony was neglected, or never heard of by the freedmen.

"Well," said the lawyer, "if that is the case, and you and aunt Milly should disagree, it wouldn't be necessary for you to get a divorce, even if you should want to marry again. You were never legally married."

"So Milly ain't my lawful wife, den?"

"She may be your wife in one sense of the word, but not in such a sense as to render you liable to punishment for bigamy if you should marry another woman. But I hope you will never want to do anything of the kind, for you have a very good wife now."

Uncle Wellington went away thoughtfully, but with a feeling of unaccustomed lightness and freedom. He had not felt so free since the memorable day when he had first heard of the Emancipation Proclamation. On leaving the lawyer's office, he called at the workshop of one of his friends, Peter Williams, a shoemaker by trade, who had a brother living in Ohio.

"Is you hearn f'm Sam lately?" uncle Wellington inquired, after the conversation had drifted through the usual generalities.

"His mammy got er letter f'm 'im las' week; he's livin' in de town er Groveland now."

"How's he gittin' on?"

"He says he gittin' on monst'us well. He 'low ez how he make five dollars a day w'itewashin', an' have all he kin do."

The shoemaker related various details of his brother's prosperity, and uncle Wellington returned home in a very thoughtful mood, revolving in his mind a plan of future action. This plan had been vaguely assuming form ever since the professor's lecture, and the events of the morning had brought out the detail in bold relief.

Two days after the conversation with the shoemaker, aunt Milly went, in the afternoon, to visit a sister of hers who lived several miles out in the country. During her absence, which lasted until nightfall, uncle Wellington went uptown and purchased a cheap oilcloth valise from a shrewd son of Israel, who had penetrated to this locality with a stock of notions and cheap clothing. Uncle Wellington had his purchase done up in brown paper, and took the parcel under his arm. Arrived at home he unwrapped the valise, and thrust into its capacious jaws his best suit of clothes, some underwear, and a few other small articles for personal use and adornment. Then he carried the valise out into the yard, and, first looking cautiously around to see if there was any one in sight, concealed it in a clump of bushes in a corner of the yard.

It may be inferred from this proceeding that uncle Wellington was preparing for a step of some consequence. In fact, he had fully made up his mind to go to the North; but he still lacked the most important requisite for traveling with comfort, namely, the money to pay his expenses. The idea of tramping the distance which separated him from the promised land of liberty and equality had never occurred to him. When a slave, he had several times been importuned by fellow servants to join them in the attempt to escape from bondage, but he had never wanted his freedom badly enough to walk a thousand miles for it; if he could have gone to Canada by stage-coach, or by rail, or on horseback, with stops for regular meals, he would probably have undertaken the trip. The funds he now needed for his journey were in aunt Milly's chest. He had thought a great deal about his right to this money. It was his wife's savings, and he had never dared to dispute, openly, her right to exercise exclusive control over what she earned; but the lawyer had assured him of his right to the money, of which he was already constructively in possession, and he had therefore determined to possess himself actually of the coveted stocking. It was impracticable for him to get the key of the chest. Aunt Milly kept it in her pocket by day and under her pillow at night. She was a light sleeper, and, if not awakened by the abstraction of the key, would certainly have been disturbed by the unlocking of the chest. But one alternative remained, and that was to break open the chest in her absence.

There was a revival in progress at the colored Methodist church. Aunt Milly was as energetic in her religion as in other respects, and had not missed a single one of the meetings. She returned at nightfall from her visit to the country and prepared a frugal supper. Uncle Wellington did not eat as heartily as usual. Aunt Milly perceived his want of appetite, and spoke of it. He explained it by saying that he did not feel very well.

"Is you gwine ter chu'ch ter-night?" inquired his wife.

"I reckon I'll stay home an' go ter bed," he replied. "I ain't be'n feelin' well dis evenin', an' I 'spec' I better git a good night's res'."

"Well, you kin stay ef you mineter. Good preachin' 'u'd make you feel better, but ef you ain't gwine, don' fergit ter tote in some wood an' lighterd 'fo' you go ter bed. De moon is shinin' bright, an' you can't have no 'scuse' bout not bein' able ter see."

Uncle Wellington followed her out to the gate, and watched her receding form until it disappeared in the distance. Then he reentered the house with a quick step, and taking a hatchet from a corner of the room, drew the chest from under the bed. As he applied the hatchet to the fastenings, a thought struck him, and by the flickering light of the pine-knot blazing on the hearth, a look of hesitation might have been seen to take the place of the determined expression his face had worn up to that time. He had argued himself into the belief that his present action was lawful and justifiable. Though this conviction had not prevented him from trembling in every limb, as though he were committing a mere vulgar theft, it had still nerved him to the deed. Now even his moral courage began to weaken. The lawyer had told him that his wife's property was his own; in taking it he was therefore only exercising his lawful right. But at the point of breaking open the chest, it occurred to him that he was taking this money in order to get away from aunt Milly, and that he justified his desertion of her by the lawyer's opinion that she was not his lawful wife. If she was not his wife, then he had no right to take the money; if she was his wife, he had no right to desert her, and would certainly have no right to marry another woman. His scheme was about to go to shipwreck on this rock, when another idea occurred to him.

"De lawyer say dat in one sense er de word de ole 'oman is my wife, an' in anudder sense er de word she ain't my wife. Ef I goes ter de Norf an' marry a w'ite 'oman, I ain't commit no brigamy, 'caze in dat sense er de word she ain't my wife; but ef I takes dis money, I ain't stealin' it, 'caze in dat sense er de word she is my wife. Dat 'splains all de trouble away."

Having reached this ingenious conclusion, uncle Wellington applied the hatchet vigorously, soon loosened the fastenings of the chest, and with trembling hands extracted from its depths a capacious blue cotton stocking. He emptied the stocking on the table. His first impulse was to take the whole, but again there arose in his mind a doubt—a very obtrusive, unreasonable doubt, but a doubt, nevertheless—of the absolute rectitude of his conduct; and after a moment's hesitation he hurriedly counted the money—it was in bills of small denominations—and found it to be about two hundred and fifty dollars. He then divided it into two piles of one hundred and twenty-five dollars each. He put one pile into his pocket, returned the remainder to the stocking, and replaced it where he had found it. He then closed the chest and shoved it under the bed. After having arranged the fire so that it could safely be left burning, he took a last look around the room, and went out into the moonlight, locking the door behind him, and hanging the key on a nail in the wall, where his wife would be likely to look for it. He then secured his valise from behind the bushes, and left the yard. As he passed by the wood-pile, he said to himself:

"Well, I declar' ef I ain't done fergot ter tote in dat lighterd; I reckon de ole 'oman, 'll ha' ter fetch it in herse'f dis time."

He hastened through the quiet streets, avoiding the few people who were abroad at that hour, and soon reached the railroad station, from which a North-bound train left at nine o'clock. He went around to the dark side of the train, and climbed into a second-class car, where he shrank into the darkest corner and turned his face away from the dim light of the single dirty lamp. There were no passengers in the car except one or two sleepy negroes, who had got on at some other station, and a white man who had gone into the car to smoke, accompanied by a gigantic bloodhound.

Finally the train crept out of the station. From the window uncle Wellington looked out upon the familiar cabins and turpentine stills, the new barrel factory, the brickyard where he had once worked for some time; and as the train rattled through the outskirts of the town, he saw gleaming in the moonlight the white headstones of the colored cemetery where his only daughter had been buried several years before.

Presently the conductor came around. Uncle Wellington had not bought a ticket, and the conductor collected a cash fare. He was not acquainted with uncle Wellington, but had just had a drink at the saloon near the depot, and felt at peace with all mankind.

"Where are you going, uncle?" he inquired carelessly.

Uncle Wellington's face assumed the ashen hue which does duty for pallor in dusky countenances, and his knees began to tremble. Controlling his voice as well as he could, he replied that he was going up to Jonesboro, the terminus of the railroad, to work for a gentleman at that place. He felt immensely relieved when the conductor pocketed the fare, picked up his lantern, and moved away. It was very unphilosophical and very absurd that a man who was only doing right should feel like a thief, shrink from the sight of other people, and lie instinctively. Fine distinctions were not in uncle Wellington's line, but he was struck by the unreasonableness of his feelings, and still more by the discomfort they caused him. By and by, however, the motion of the train made him drowsy; his thoughts all ran together in confusion; and he fell asleep with his head on his valise, and one hand in his pocket, clasped tightly around the roll of money.

II

The train from Pittsburg drew into the Union Depot at Groveland, Ohio, one morning in the spring of 187–, with bell ringing and engine puffing; and from a smoking-car emerged the form of uncle Wellington Braboy, a little dusty and travel-stained, and with a sleepy look about his eyes. He mingled in the crowd, and, valise in hand, moved toward the main exit from the depot. There were several tracks to be crossed, and more than once a watchman snatched him out of the way of a baggage-truck, or a train backing into the depot. He at length reached the door, beyond which, and as near as the regulations would permit, stood a number of hackmen, vociferously soliciting patronage. One of them, a colored man, soon secured several passengers. As he closed the door after the last one he turned to uncle Wellington, who stood near him on the sidewalk, looking about irresolutely.

"Is you goin' uptown?" asked the hackman, as he prepared to mount the box.

"Yas, suh."

"I'll take you up fo' a quahtah, ef you want ter git up here an' ride on de box wid me."

Uncle Wellington accepted the offer and mounted the box. The hackman whipped up his horses, the carriage climbed the steep hill leading up to the town, and the passengers inside were soon deposited at their hotels.

"Whereabouts do you want to go?" asked the hackman of uncle Wellington, when the carriage was emptied of its last passengers.

"I want ter go ter Brer Sam Williams's," said Wellington.

"What's his street an' number?"

Uncle Wellington did not know the street and number, and the hackman had to explain to him the mystery of numbered houses, to which he was a total stranger.

"Where is he from?" asked the hackman, "and what is his business?"

"He is f'm Norf Ca'lina," replied uncle Wellington, "an' makes his livin' w'itewashin'."

"I reckon I knows de man," said the hackman. "I 'spec' he's changed his name. De man I knows is name' Johnson. He b'longs ter my chu'ch. I'm gwine out dat way ter git a passenger fer de ten o'clock train, an' I'll take you by dere."

They followed one of the least handsome streets of the city for more than a mile, turned into a cross street, and drew up before a small frame house, from the front of which a sign, painted in white upon a black background, announced to the reading public, in letters inclined to each other at various angles, that whitewashing and kalsomining were "dun" there. A knock at the door brought out a slatternly looking colored woman. She had evidently been disturbed at her toilet, for she held a comb in one hand, and the hair on one side of her head stood out loosely, while on the other side it was braided close to her head. She called her husband, who proved to be the Patesville shoemaker's brother. The hackman introduced the traveler, whose name he had learned on the way out, collected his quarter, and drove away.

Mr. Johnson, the shoemaker's brother, welcomed uncle Wellington to Groveland, and listened with eager delight to the news of the old town, from which he himself had run away many years before, and followed the North Star to Groveland. He had changed his name from "Williams" to "Johnson," on account of the Fugitive Slave Law, which, at the time of his escape from bondage, had rendered it advisable for runaway slaves to court obscurity. After the war he had retained the adopted name. Mrs. Johnson prepared breakfast for her guest, who ate it with an appetite sharpened by his journey. After breakfast he went to bed, and slept until late in the afternoon.

After supper Mr. Johnson took uncle Wellington to visit some of the neighbors who had come from North Carolina before the war. They all expressed much pleasure at meeting "Mr. Braboy," a title which at first sounded a little odd to uncle Wellington. At home he had been "Wellin'-ton," "Brer Wellin'ton," or "uncle Wellin'ton"; it was a novel experience to be called "Mister," and he set it down, with secret satisfaction, as one of the first fruits of Northern liberty.

"Would you lack ter look 'roun' de town a little?" asked Mr. Johnson at breakfast next morning. "I ain' got no job dis mawnin', an' I kin show you some er de sights."

Uncle Wellington acquiesced in this arrangement, and they walked up to the corner to the street-car line. In a few moments a car passed. Mr. Johnson jumped on the moving car, and uncle Wellington followed his example, at the risk of life or limb, as it was his first experience of street cars.

There was only one vacant seat in the car and that was between two white women in the forward end. Mr. Johnson motioned to the seat, but Wellington shrank from walking between those two rows of white people, to say nothing of sitting between the two women, so he remained standing in the rear part of the car. A moment later, as the car rounded a short curve, he was pitched sidewise into the lap of a stout woman magnificently attired in a ruffled blue calico gown. The lady colored up, and uncle Wellington, as he struggled to his feet amid the laughter of the passengers, was absolutely helpless with embarrassment, until the conductor came up behind him and pushed him toward the vacant place.

"Sit down, will you," he said; and before uncle Wellington could collect himself, he was seated between the two white women. Everybody in the car seemed to be looking at him. But he came to the conclusion, after he had pulled himself together and reflected a few moments, that he would find this method of locomotion pleasanter when he got used to it, and then he could score one more glorious privilege gained by his change of residence.

They got off at the public square, in the heart of the city, where there were flowers and statues, and fountains playing. Mr. Johnson pointed out the court-house, the post-office, the jail, and other public buildings fronting on the square. They visited the market near by, and from an elevated point, looked down upon the extensive lumber yards and factories that were the chief sources of the city's prosperity. Beyond these they could see the fleet of ships that lined the coal and iron ore docks of the harbor. Mr. Johnson, who was quite a fluent talker, enlarged upon the wealth and prosperity of the city; and Wellington, who had never before been in a town of more than three thousand inhabitants, manifested sufficient interest and wonder to satisfy the most exacting *cicerone*. They called at the office of a colored lawyer and member of the legislature, formerly from North Carolina, who, scenting a new constituent and a possible client, greeted the stranger warmly, and in flowing speech pointed out the superior advantages of life at the North, citing himself as an illustration of the possibilities of life in a country really free. As they wended their way homeward to dinner uncle Wellington, with quickened pulse and rising hopes, felt that this was indeed the promised land, and that it must be flowing with milk and honey.

Uncle Wellington remained at the residence of Mr. Johnson for several weeks before making any effort to find employment. He spent this period in looking about the city. The most commonplace things possessed for him the charm of novelty, and he had come prepared to admire. Shortly after his arrival, he had offered to pay for his board, intimating at the same time that he had plenty of money. Mr. Johnson declined to accept anything from him for board, and expressed himself as being only too proud to have

Mr. Braboy remain in the house on the footing of an honored guest, until
he had settled himself. He lightened in some degree, however, the burden
of obligation under which a prolonged stay on these terms would have
placed his guest, by soliciting from the latter occasional small loans, until
uncle Wellington's roll of money began to lose its plumpness, and with an
empty pocket staring him in the face, he felt the necessity of finding something to do.

During his residence in the city he had met several times his first acquaintance, Mr. Peterson, the hackman, who from time to time inquired
how he was getting along. On one of these occasions Wellington mentioned
his willingness to accept employment. As good luck would have it, Mr. Peterson knew of a vacant situation. He had formerly been coachman for a
wealthy gentleman residing on Oakwood Avenue, but had resigned the situation to go into business for himself. His place had been filled by an Irishman, who had just been discharged for drunkenness, and the gentleman
that very day had sent word to Mr. Peterson, asking him if he could recommend a competent and trustworthy coachman.

"Does you know anything erbout hosses?" asked Mr. Peterson.

"Yas, indeed, I does," said Wellington. "I wuz raise' 'mongs' hosses."

"I tol' my ole boss I'd look out fer a man, an' ef you reckon you kin fill
de 'quirements er de situation, I'll take yo' roun' dere ter-morrer mornin'.
You wants ter put on yo' bes' clothes an' slick up, fer dey're partic'lar
people. Ef you git de place I'll expec' you ter pay me fer de time I lose in
'tendin' ter yo' business, fer time is money in dis country, an' folks don't
do much fer nuthin'."

Next morning Wellington blacked his shoes carefully, put on a clean
collar, and with the aid of Mrs. Johnson tied his cravat in a jaunty bow
which gave him quite a sprightly air and a much younger look than his
years warranted. Mr. Peterson called for him at eight o'clock. After traversing several cross streets they turned into Oakwood Avenue and walked
along the finest part of it for about half a mile. The handsome houses of
this famous avenue, the stately trees, the wide-spreading lawns, dotted with
flower beds, fountains and statuary, made up a picture so far surpassing
anything in Wellington's experience as to fill him with an almost oppressive sense of its beauty.

"Hit looks lack hebben," he said softly.

"It's a pootty fine street," rejoined his companion, with a judicial air,
"but I don't like dem big lawns. It's too much trouble ter keep de grass
down. One er dem lawns is big enough to pasture a couple er cows."

They went down a street running at right angles to the avenue, and
turned into the rear of the corner lot. A large building of pressed brick,
trimmed with stone, loomed up before them.

"Do de gemman lib in dis house?" asked Wellington, gazing with awe at the front of the building.

"No, dat's de barn," said Mr. Peterson with good-natured contempt; and leading the way past a clump of shrubbery to the dwelling-house, he went up the back steps and rang the door-bell.

The ring was answered by a buxom Irishwoman, of a natural freshness of complexion deepened to a fiery red by the heat of a kitchen range. Wellington thought he had seen her before, but his mind had received so many new impressions lately that it was a minute or two before he recognized in her the lady whose lap he had involuntarily occupied for a moment on his first day in Groveland.

"Faith," she exclaimed as she admitted them, "an' it's mighty glad I am to see ye ag'in, Misther Payterson! An' how hev ye be'n, Misther Payterson, sence I see ye lahst?"

"Middlin' well, Mis' Flannigan, middlin' well, 'ceptin' a tech er de rheumatiz. S'pose you be'n doin' well as usual?"

"Oh yis, as well as a dacent woman could do wid a drunken baste about the place like the lahst coachman. O Misther Payterson, it would make yer heart bleed to see the way the spalpeen cut up a-Saturday! But Misther Todd discharged 'im the same avenin', widout a character, bad 'cess to 'im, an' we've had no coachman sence at all, at all. An' it's sorry I am"—

The lady's flow of eloquence was interrupted at this point by the appearance of Mr. Todd himself, who had been informed of the men's arrival. He asked some questions in regard to Wellington's qualifications and former experience, and in view of his recent arrival in the city was willing to accept Mr. Peterson's recommendation instead of a reference. He said a few words about the nature of the work, and stated his willingness to pay Wellington the wages formerly allowed Mr. Peterson, thirty dollars a month and board and lodging.

This handsome offer was eagerly accepted, and it was agreed that Wellington's term of service should begin immediately. Mr. Peterson, being familiar with the work, and financially interested, conducted the new coachman through the stables and showed him what he would have to do. The silver-mounted harness, the variety of carriages, the names of which he learned for the first time, the arrangements for feeding and watering the horses—these appointments of a rich man's stable impressed Wellington very much, and he wondered that so much luxury should be wasted on mere horses. The room assigned to him, in the second story of the barn, was a finer apartment than he had ever slept in; and the salary attached to the situation was greater than the combined monthly earnings of himself and aunt Milly in their Southern home. Surely, he thought, his lines had fallen in pleasant places.

Under the stimulus of new surroundings Wellington applied himself diligently to work, and, with the occasional advice of Mr. Peterson, soon mastered the details of his employment. He found the female servants, with whom he took his meals, very amiable ladies. The cook, Mrs. Katie Flannigan, was a widow. Her husband, a sailor, had been lost at sea. She was a woman of many words, and when she was not lamenting the late Flannigan's loss—according to her story he had been a model of all the virtues—she would turn the batteries of her tongue against the former coachman. This gentleman, as Wellington gathered from frequent remarks dropped by Mrs. Flannigan, had paid her attentions clearly susceptible of a serious construction. These attentions had not borne their legitimate fruit, and she was still a widow unconsoled—hence Mrs. Flannigan's tears. The housemaid was a plump, good-natured German girl, with a pronounced German accent. The presence on washdays of a Bohemian laundress, of recent importation, added another to the variety of ways in which the English tongue was mutilated in Mr. Todd's kitchen. Association with the white women drew out all the native gallantry of the mulatto, and Wellington developed quite a helpful turn. His politeness, his willingness to lend a hand in kitchen or laundry, and the fact that he was the only male servant on the place, combined to make him a prime favorite in the servants' quarters.

It was the general opinion among Wellington's acquaints that he was a single man. He had come to the city alone, had never been heard to speak of a wife, and to personal questions bearing upon the subject of matrimony had always returned evasive answers. Though he had never questioned the correctness of the lawyer's opinion in regard to his slave marriage, his conscience had never been entirely at ease since his departure from the South, and any positive denial of his married condition would have stuck in his throat. The inference naturally drawn from his reticence in regard to the past, coupled with his expressed intention of settling permanently in Groveland, was that he belonged in the ranks of the unmarried, and was therefore legitimate game for any widow or old maid who could bring him down. As such game is bagged easiest at short range, he received numerous invitations to tea-parties, where he feasted on unlimited chicken and pound cake. He used to compare these viands with the plain fare often served by aunt Milly, and the result of the comparison was another item to the credit of the North upon his mental ledger. Several of the colored ladies who smiled upon him were blessed with good looks, and uncle Wellington, naturally of a susceptible temperament, as people of lively imagination are apt to be, would probably have fallen a victim to the charms of some woman of his own race, had it not been for a strong counter-attraction in the person of Mrs. Flannigan. The attentions of the lately discharged coachman had lighted anew the smouldering fires of her widowed heart, and awakened longings which still remained unsatisfied. She was thirty-five years old, and felt the need of some one else to love. She was not a woman of lofty ideals; with her a man was a man—

> "For a' that an' a' that";

and, aside from the accident of color, uncle Wellington was as personable a man as any of her acquaintance. Some people might have objected to his complexion; but then, Mrs. Flannigan argued, he was at least half white; and, this being the case, there was no good reason why he should be regarded as black.

Uncle Wellington was not slow to perceive Mrs. Flannigan's charms of person, and appreciated to the full the skill that prepared the choice tidbits reserved for his plate at dinner. The prospect of securing a white wife had been one of the principal inducements offered by a life at the North; but the awe of white people in which he had been reared was still too strong to permit his taking any active steps toward the object of his secret desire, had not the lady herself come to his assistance with a little of the native coquetry of her race.

"Ah, Misther Braboy," she said one evening when they sat at the supper table alone—it was the second girl's afternoon off, and she had not come home to supper—"it must be an awful lonesome life ye've been afther l'adin', as a single man, wid no one to cook fer ye, or look afther ye."

"It are a kind er lonesome life, Mis' Flannigan, an' dat's a fac'. But sence I had de privilege er eatin' yo' cookin' an' 'joyin' yo' society, I ain' felt a bit lonesome."

"Yer flatthrin' me, Misther Braboy. An' even if ye mane it"—

"I means eve'y word of it, Mis' Flannigan."

"An' even if ye mane it, Misther Braboy, the time is liable to come when things 'll be different; for service is uncertain, Misther Braboy. An' then you'll wish you had some nice, clean woman, 'at knowed how to cook an' wash an' iron, ter look afther ye, an' make yer life comfortable."

Uncle Wellington sighed, and looked at her languishingly.

"It 'u'd all be well ernuff, Mis' Flannigan, ef I had n' met you; but I don' know whar I's ter fin' a colored lady w'at 'll begin ter suit me after habbin' libbed in de same house wid you."

"Colored lady, indade! Why, Misther Braboy, ye don't nade ter demane yerself by marryin' a colored lady—not but they're as good as anybody else, so long as they behave themselves. There's many a white woman 'u'd be glad ter git as fine a lookin' man as ye are."

"Now *you're* flattrin' *me*, Mis' Flannigan," said Wellington. But he felt a sudden and substantial increase in courage when she had spoken, and it was with astonishing ease that he found himself saying:

"Dey ain' but one lady, Mis' Flannigan, dat could injuce me ter want ter change de lonesomeness er my singleness fer de 'sponsibilities er matermony, an' I'm feared she'd say no ef I'd ax her."

"Ye'd better ax her, Misther Braboy, an' not be wastin' time a-wond'rin'. Do I know the lady?"

"You knows 'er better 'n anybody else, Mis' Flannigan. *You* is de only lady I'd be satisfied ter marry after knowin' you. Ef you casts me off I'll spen' de rest er my days in lonesomeness an' mis'ry."

Mrs. Flannigan affected much surprise and embarrassment at this bold declaration.

"Oh, Misther Braboy," she said, covering him with a coy glance, "an' it's rale 'shamed I am to hev b'en talkin' ter ye ez I hev. It looks as though I'd b'en doin' the coortin'. I did n't drame that I'd b'en able ter draw yer affections to mesilf."

"I's loved you ever sence I fell in yo' lap on de street car de fus' day I wuz in Groveland," he said, as he moved his chair up closer to hers.

One evening in the following week they went out after supper to the residence of Rev. Caesar Williams, pastor of the colored Baptist church, and, after the usual preliminaries, were pronounced man and wife.

III

According to all his preconceived notions, this marriage ought to have been the acme of uncle Wellington's felicity. But he soon found that it was not without its drawbacks. On the following morning Mr. Todd was informed of the marriage. He had no special objection to it, or interest in it, except that he was opposed on principle to having husband and wife in his employment at the same time. As a consequence, Mrs. Braboy, whose place could be more easily filled than that of her husband, received notice that her services would not be required after the end of the month. Her husband was retained in his place as coachman.

Upon the loss of her situation Mrs. Braboy decided to exercise the married woman's prerogative of letting her husband support her. She rented the upper floor of a small house in an Irish neighborhood. The newly wedded pair furnished their rooms on the installment plan and began housekeeping.

There was one little circumstance, however, that interfered slightly with their enjoyment of that perfect freedom from care which ought to characterize a honeymoon. The people who owned the house and occupied the lower floor had rented the upper part to Mrs. Braboy in person, it never occurring to them that her husband could be other than a white man. When it became known that he was colored, the landlord, Mr. Dennis O'Flaherty, felt that he had been imposed upon, and, at the end of the first month, served notice upon his tenants to leave the premises. When Mrs. Braboy, with characteristic impetuosity, inquired the meaning of this proceeding, she was informed by Mr. O'Flaherty that he did not care to live in the same house "wid naygurs." Mrs. Braboy resented the epithet with more warmth than dignity, and for a brief space of time the air was green with choice specimens of brogue, the altercation barely ceasing before it had reached the point of blows.

It was quite clear that the Braboys could not longer live comfortably in Mr. O'Flaherty's house, and they soon vacated the premises, first letting the rent get a couple of weeks in arrears as a punishment to the too fastidious landlord. They moved to a small house on Hackman Street, a favorite locality with colored people.

For a while, affairs ran smoothly in the new home. The colored people seemed, at first, well enough disposed toward Mrs. Braboy, and she made quite a large acquaintance among them. It was difficult, however, for Mrs. Braboy to divest herself of the consciousness that she was white, and therefore superior to her neighbors. Occasional words and acts by which she manifested this feeling were noticed and resented by her keen-eyed and sensitive colored neighbors. The result was a slight coolness between them. That her few white neighbors did not visit her, she naturally and no doubt correctly imputed to disapproval of her matrimonial relations.

Under these circumstances, Mrs. Braboy was left a good deal to her own company. Owing to lack of opportunity in early life, she was not a woman of many resources, either mental or moral. It is therefore not strange that, in order to relieve her loneliness, she should occasionally have recourse to a glass of beer, and, as the habit grew upon her, to still stronger stimulants. Uncle Wellington himself was no teetotaler, and did not interpose any objection so long as she kept her potations within reasonable limits, and was apparently none the worse for them; indeed, he sometimes joined her in a glass. On one of these occasions he drank a little too much, and, while driving the ladies of Mr. Todd's family to the opera, ran against a lamp-post and overturned the carriage, to the serious discomposure of the ladies' nerves, and at the cost of his situation.

A coachman discharged under such circumstances is not in the best position for procuring employment at his calling, and uncle Wellington, under the pressure of need, was obliged to seek some other means of livelihood. At the suggestion of his friend Mr. Johnson, he bought a whitewash brush, a peck of lime, a couple of pails, and a handcart, and began work as a whitewasher. His first efforts were very crude, and for a while he lost a customer in every person he worked for. He nevertheless managed to pick up a living during the spring and summer months, and to support his wife and himself in comparative comfort.

The approach of winter put an end to the whitewashing season, and left uncle Wellington dependent for support upon occasional jobs of unskilled labor. The income derived from these was very uncertain, and Mrs. Braboy was at length driven, by stress of circumstances, to the washtub, that last refuge of honest, able-bodied poverty, in all countries where the use of clothing is conventional.

The last state of uncle Wellington was now worse than the first. Under the soft firmness of aunt Milly's rule, he had not been required to do a great deal of work, prompt and cheerful obedience being chiefly what was expected of him. But matters were very different here. He had not only to bring in the coal and water, but to rub the clothes and turn the wringer, and to humiliate himself before the public by emptying the tubs and hanging out the wash in full view of the neighbors; and he had to deliver the clothes when laundered.

At times Wellington found himself wondering if his second marriage had been a wise one. Other circumstances combined to change in some degree his once rose-colored conception of life at the North. He had believed that all men were equal in this favored locality, but he discovered more degrees of inequality than he had ever perceived at the South. A colored man might be as good as a white man in theory, but neither of them was of any special consequence without money, or talent, or position. Uncle Wellington found a great many privileges open to him at the North, but he had not been educated to the point where he could appreciate them or take advantage of them; and the enjoyment of many of them was expensive, and, for that reason alone, as far beyond his reach as they had ever been. When he once began to admit even the possibility of a mistake on his part, these considerations presented themselves to his mind with increasing force. On occasions when Mrs. Braboy would require of him some unusual physical exertion, or when too frequent applications to the bottle had loosened her tongue, uncle Wellington's mind would revert, with a remorseful twinge of conscience, to the *dolce far niente* of his Southern home; a film would come over his eyes and brain, and, instead of the red-faced Irishwoman opposite him, he could see the black but comely disk of aunt Milly's countenance bending over the washtub; the elegant brogue of Mrs. Braboy would deliquesce into the soft dialect of North Carolina; and he would only be aroused from this blissful reverie by a wet shirt or a handful of suds thrown into his face, with which gentle reminder his wife would recall his attention to the duties of the moment.

There came a time, one day in spring, when there was no longer any question about it: uncle Wellington was desperately homesick.

Liberty, equality, privileges—all were but as dust in the balance when weighed against his longing for old scenes and faces. It was the natural reaction in the mind of a middle-aged man who had tried to force the current of a sluggish existence into a new and radically different channel. An active, industrious man, making the change in early life, while there was time to spare for the waste of adaptation, might have found in the new place more favorable conditions than in the old. In Wellington age and temperament combined to prevent the success of the experiment; the spirit of enterprise and ambition into which he had been temporarily galvanized could no longer prevail against the inertia of old habits of life and thought.

One day when he had been sent to deliver clothes he performed his errand quickly, and boarding a passing street car, paid one of his very few five-cent pieces to ride down to the office of the Hon. Mr. Brown, the colored lawyer whom he had visited when he first came to the city, and who was well known to him by sight and reputation.

"Mr. Brown," he said, "I ain' gitt'n' 'long very well wid my ole 'oman."

"What's the trouble?" asked the lawyer, with business-like curtness, for he did not scent much of a fee.

"Well, de main trouble is she doan treat me right. An' den she gits drunk, an' wuss'n dat, she lays vi'lent han's on me. I kyars de marks er dat 'oman on my face now."

He showed the lawyer a long scratch on the neck.

"Why don't you defend yourself?"

"You don' know Mis' Braboy, suh; you don' know dat 'oman," he replied, with a shake of the head. "Some er dese yer w'ite women is monst'us strong in de wris'."

"Well, Mr. Braboy, it's what you might have expected when you turned your back on your own people and married a white woman. You were n't content with being a slave to the white folks once, but you must try it again. Some people never know when they 've got enough. I don't see that there 's any help for you; unless," he added suggestively, "you had a good deal of money."

" 'Pears ter me I heared somebody say sence I be'n up heah, dat it wuz 'gin de law fer w'ite folks an' colored folks ter marry."

"That was once the law, though it has always been a dead letter in Groveland. In fact, it was the law when you got married, and until I introduced a bill in the legislature last fall to repeal it. But even that law did n't hit cases like yours. It was unlawful to make such a marriage, but it was a good marriage when once made."

"I don' jes' git dat th'oo my head," said Wellington, scratching that member as though to make a hole for the idea to enter.

"It 's quite plain, Mr. Braboy. It's unlawful to kill a man, but when he 's killed he 's just as dead as though the law permitted it. I'm afraid you have n't much of a case, but if you 'll go to work and get twenty-five dollars together, I 'll see what I can do for you. We may be able to pull a case through on the ground of extreme cruelty. I might even start the case if you brought in ten dollars."

Wellington went away sorrowfully. The laws of Ohio were very little more satisfactory than those of North Carolina. And as for the ten dollars— the lawyer might as well have told him to bring in the moon, or a deed for the Public Square. He felt very, very low as he hurried back home to supper, which he would have to go without if he were not on hand at the usual supper-time.

But just when his spirits were lowest, and his outlook for the future most hopeless, a measure of relief was at hand. He noticed, when he reached home, that Mrs. Braboy was a little preoccupied, and did not abuse him as vigorously as he expected after so long an absence. He also perceived the smell of strange tobacco in the house, of a better grade than he could afford to use. He thought perhaps some one had come in to see about the washing; but he was too glad of a respite from Mrs. Braboy's rhetoric to imperil it by indiscreet questions.

Next morning she gave him fifty cents.

"Braboy," she said, "ye 've be'n helpin' me nicely wid the washin', an' I'm going ter give ye a holiday. Ye can take yer hook an' line an' go fishin' on the breakwater. I 'll fix ye a lunch, an' ye need n't come back till night. An' there 's half a dollar; ye can buy yerself a pipe er terbacky. But be careful an' don't waste it," she added, for fear she was overdoing the thing.

Uncle Wellington was overjoyed at this change of front on the part of Mrs. Braboy; if she would make it permanent he did not see why they might not live together very comfortably.

The day passed pleasantly down on the breakwater. The weather was agreeable, and the fish bit freely. Towards evening Wellington started home with a bunch of fish that no angler need have been ashamed of. He looked forward to a good warm supper; for even if something should have happened during the day to alter his wife's mood for the worse, any ordinary variation would be more than balanced by the substantial addition of food to their larder. His mouth watered at the thought of the finny beauties sputtering in the frying-pan.

He noted, as he approached the house, that there was no smoke coming from the chimney. This only disturbed him in connection with the matter of supper. When he entered the gate he observed further that the window-shades had been taken down.

"'Spec' de ole 'oman's been house-cleanin'," he said to himself. "I wonder she did n' make me stay an' he'p 'er."

He went round to the rear of the house and tried the kitchen door. It was locked. This was somewhat of a surprise, and disturbed still further his expectations in regard to supper. When he had found the key and opened the door, the gravity of his next discovery drove away for the time being all thoughts of eating.

The kitchen was empty. Stove, table, chairs, wash-tubs, pots and pans, had vanished as if into thin air.

"Fo' de Lawd's sake!" he murmured in open-mouthed astonishment.

He passed into the other room—they had only two—which had served as bedroom and sitting-room. It was as bare as the first, except that in the middle of the floor were piled uncle Wellington's clothes. It was not a large pile, and on the top of it lay a folded piece of yellow wrapping-paper.

Wellington stood for a moment as if petrified. Then he rubbed his eyes and looked around him.

"W'at do dis mean?" he said. "Is I erdreamin', er does I see w'at I 'pears ter see?" He glanced down at the bunch of fish which he still held. "Heah 's de fish; heah 's de house; heah I is; but whar 's de ole 'oman, an' whar 's de fu'niture? I can't figure out w'at dis yer all means."

He picked up the piece of paper and unfolded it. It was written on one side. Here was the obvious solution of the mystery—that is, it would have been obvious if he could have read it; but he could not, and so his fancy continued to play upon the subject. Perhaps the house had been robbed, or the furniture taken back by the seller, for it had not been entirely paid for.

Finally he went across the street and called to a boy in a neighbor's yard.

"Does you read writin', Johnnie?"

"Yes, sir, I'm in the seventh grade."

"Read dis yer paper fuh me."

The youngster took the note, and with much labor read the following:

"*Mr. Braboy:*

"In lavin' ye so suddint I have ter say that my first husban' has turned up unixpected, having been saved onbeknownst ter me from a wathry grave an' all the money wasted I spint fer masses fer ter rist his sole an' I wish I had it back I feel it my dooty ter go an' live wid 'im again. I take the furnacher because I bought

it yer close is yors I leave them and wishin' yer the best of luck
I remane oncet yer wife but now agin

"*Mrs. Katie Flannigan.*

"N. B. I'm lavin town terday so it won't be no use lookin'
fer me."

On inquiry uncle Wellington learned from the boy that shortly after
his departure in the morning a white man had appeared on the scene, followed a little later by a moving-van, into which the furniture had been
loaded and carried away. Mrs. Braboy, clad in her best clothes, had locked
the door, and gone away with the strange white man.

The news was soon noised about the street. Wellington swapped his
fish for supper and a bed at a neighbor's, and during the evening learned
from several sources that the strange white man had been at his house the
afternoon of the day before. His neighbors intimated that they thought
Mrs. Braboy's departure a good riddance of bad rubbish, and Wellington
did not dispute the proposition.

Thus ended the second chapter of Wellington's matrimonial experiences. His wife's departure had been the one thing needful to convince
him, beyond a doubt, that he had been a great fool. Remorse and home-
sickness forced him to the further conclusion that he had been knave as
well as fool, and had treated aunt Milly shamefully. He was not altogether
a bad old man, though very weak and erring, and his better nature now
gained the ascendency. Of course his disappointment had a great deal to
do with his remorse; most people do not perceive the hideousness of sin
until they begin to reap its consequences. Instead of the beautiful Northern life he had dreamed of, he found himself stranded, penniless, in a
strange land, among people whose sympathy he had forfeited, with no one
to lean upon, and no refuge from the storms of life. His outlook was very
dark, and there sprang up within him a wild longing to get back to North
Carolina—back to the little whitewashed cabin, shaded with china and
mulberry trees; back to the wood-pile and the garden; back to the old
cronies with whom he had swapped lies and tobacco for so many years.
He longed to kiss the rod of aunt Milly's domination. He had purchased
his liberty at too great a price.

The next day he disappeared from Groveland. He had announced his
departure only to Mr. Johnson, who sent his love to his relations in
Patesville.

It would be painful to record in detail the return journey of uncle
Wellington—Mr. Braboy no longer—to his native town; how many weary

miles he walked; how many times he risked his life on railroad trucks and between freight cars; how he depended for sustenance on the grudging hand of back-door charity. Nor would it be profitable or delicate to mention any slight deviations from the path of rectitude, as judged by conventional standards, to which he may occasionally have been driven by a too insistent hunger; or to refer in the remotest degree to a compulsory sojourn of thirty days in a city where he had no references, and could show no visible means of support. True charity will let these purely personal matters remain locked in the bosom of him who suffered them.

IV

Just fifteen months after the date when uncle Wellington had left North Carolina, a weather-beaten figure entered the town of Patesville after nightfall, following the railroad track from the north. Few would have recognized in the hungry-looking old brown tramp, clad in dusty rags and limping along with bare feet, the trim-looking middle-aged mulatto who so few months before had taken the train from Patesville for the distant North; so, if he had but known it, there was no necessity for him to avoid the main streets and sneak around by unfrequented paths to reach the old place on the other side of the town. He encountered nobody that he knew, and soon the familiar shape of the little cabin rose before him. It stood distinctly outlined against the sky, and the light streaming from the half-opened shutters showed it to be occupied. As he drew nearer, every familiar detail of the place appealed to his memory and to his affections, and his heart went out to the old home and the old wife. As he came nearer still, the odor of fried chicken floated out upon the air and set his mouth to watering, and awakened unspeakable longings in his half-starved stomach.

At this moment, however, a fearful thought struck him; suppose the old woman had taken legal advice and married again during his absence? Turn about would have been only fair play. He opened the gate softly, and with his heart in his mouth approached the window on tiptoe and looked in.

A cheerful fire was blazing on the hearth, in front of which sat the familiar form of aunt Milly—and another, at the sight of whom uncle Wellington's heart sank within him. He knew the other person very well; he had sat there more than once before uncle Wellington went away. It was the minister of the church to which his wife belonged. The preacher's former visits, however, had signified nothing more than pastoral courtesy, or appreciation of good eating. His presence now was of serious portent; for Wellington recalled, with acute alarm, that the elder's wife had died only a few weeks before his own departure for the North. What was the occasion of his presence this evening? Was it merely a pastoral call? or was he courting? or had aunt Milly taken legal advice and married the elder?

Wellington remembered a crack in the wall, at the back of the house, through which he could see and hear, and quietly stationed himself there.

"Dat chicken smells mighty good, Sis' Milly," the elder was saying; "I can't fer de life er me see why dat low-down husban' er yo'n could ever run away f'm a cook like you. It 's one er de beatenis' things I ever heared. How he could lib wid you an' not 'preciate you I can't understan', no indeed I can't."

Aunt Milly sighed. "De trouble wid Wellin'ton wuz," she replied, "dat he did n' know when he wuz well off. He wuz alluz wishin' fer change, er studyin' 'bout somethin' new."

"Ez fer me," responded the elder earnestly, "I likes things what has be'n prove' an' tried an' has stood de tes', an' I can't 'magine how anybody could spec' ter fin' a better housekeeper er cook dan you is, Sis' Milly. I'm a gittin' mighty lonesome sence my wife died. De Good Book say it is not good fer man ter lib alone, en it 'pears ter me dat you an' me mought git erlong tergether monst'us well."

Wellington's heart stood still, while he listened with strained attention. Aunt Milly sighed.

"I ain't denyin', elder, but what I 've be'n kinder lonesome myse'f fer quite a w'ile, an' I doan doubt dat w'at de Good Book say 'plies ter women as well as ter men."

"You kin be sho' it do," averred the elder, with professional authoritativeness; "yas 'm, you kin be cert'n sho'."

"But, of co'se," aunt Milly went on, "havin' los' my ole man de way I did, it has tuk me some time fer ter git my feelin's straighten' out like dey oughter be."

"I kin 'magine yo' feelin's Sis' Milly," chimed in the elder sympathetically, "w'en you come home dat night an' foun' yo' chist broke open, an' yo' money gone dat you had wukked an' slaved fuh f'm mawnin' 'tel night, year in an' year out, an' w'en you foun' dat no-'count nigger gone wid his clo's an' you lef' all alone in de worl' ter scuffle 'long by yo'self."

"Yas, elder," responded aunt Milly, "I wa'n't used right. An' den w'en I heared 'bout his goin' ter de lawyer ter fin' out 'bout a defoce, an' w'en I heared w'at de lawyer said 'bout my not bein' his wife 'less he wanted me, it made me so mad, I made up my min' dat ef he ever put his foot on my do'-sill ag'in, I'd shet de do' in his face an' tell 'im ter go back whar he come f'm."

To Wellington, on the outside, the cabin had never seemed so comfortable, aunt Milly never so desirable, chicken never so appetizing, as at this moment when they seemed slipping away from his grasp forever.

"Yo' feelin's does you credit, Sis' Milly," said the elder, taking her hand, which for a moment she did not withdraw. "An' de way fer you ter close yo' do' tightes' ag'inst 'im is ter take me in his place. He ain' got no claim on you no mo'. He tuk his ch'ice 'cordin' ter w'at de lawyer tol' 'im, an' 'termine' dat he wa'n't yo' husban'. Ef he wa'n't yo' husban', he had no right ter take yo' money, an' ef he comes back here ag'in you kin hab 'im tuck up an' sent ter de penitenchy fer stealin' it."

Uncle Wellington's knees, already weak from fasting, trembled violently beneath him. The worst that he had feared was now likely to happen. His only hope of safety lay in flight, and yet the scene within so fascinated him that he could not move a step.

"It 'u'd serve him right," exclaimed aunt Milly indignantly, "ef he wuz sent ter de penitenchy fer life! Dey ain't nuthin' too mean ter be done ter 'im. What did I ever do dat he should use me like he did?"

The recital of her wrongs had wrought upon aunt Milly's feelings so that her voice broke, and she wiped her eyes with her apron.

The elder looked serenely confident, and moved his chair nearer hers in order the better to play the rôle of comforter. Wellington, on the outside, felt so mean that the darkness of the night was scarcely sufficient to hide him; it would be no more than right if the earth were to open and swallow him up.

"An' yet aftuh all, elder," said Milly with a sob, "though I knows you is a better man, an' would treat me right, I wuz so use' ter dat ole nigger, an' libbed wid 'im so long, dat ef he 'd open dat do' dis minute an' walk in, I 'm feared I 'd be foolish ernuff an' weak ernuff to forgive 'im an' take 'im back ag'in."

With a bound, uncle Wellington was away from the crack in the wall. As he ran round the house he passed the wood-pile and snatched up an armful of pieces. A moment later he threw open the door.

"Ole 'oman," he exclaimed, "here 's dat wood you tol' me ter fetch in! Why, elder," he said to the preacher, who had started from his seat with surprise, "w'at 's yo' hurry? Won't you stay an' hab some supper wid us?"

THE BOUQUET

Mary Myrover's friends were somewhat surprised when she began to teach a colored school. Miss Myrover's friends are mentioned here, because nowhere more than in a Southern town is public opinion a force which cannot be lightly contravened. Public opinion, however, did not oppose Miss Myrover's teaching colored children; in fact, all the colored public schools in town—and there were several—were taught by white teachers, and had been so taught since the State had undertaken to provide free public instruction for all children within its boundaries. Previous to that time, there had been a Freedman's Bureau school and a Presbyterian missionary school, but these had been withdrawn when the need for them became less pressing. The colored people of the town had been for some time agitating their right to teach their own schools, but as yet the claim had not been conceded.

The reason Miss Myrover's course created some surprise was not, therefore, the fact that a Southern white woman should teach a colored school; it lay in the fact that up to this time no woman of just her quality had taken up such work. Most of the teachers of colored schools were not of those who had constituted the aristocracy of the old régime; they might be said rather to represent the new order of things, in which labor was in time to become honorable, and men were, after a somewhat longer time, to depend, for their place in society, upon themselves rather than upon their ancestors. Mary Myrover belonged to one of the proudest of the old families. Her ancestors had been people of distinction in Virginia before a collateral branch of the main stock had settled in North Carolina. Before the war, they had been able to live up to their pedigree; but the war brought sad changes. Miss Myrover's father—the Colonel Myrover who led a gallant but desperate charge at Vicksburg—had fallen on the battlefield, and his tomb in the white cemetery was a shrine for the family. On the Confederate Memorial Day, no other grave was so profusely decorated with flowers, and, in the oration pronounced, the name of Colonel Myrover was always used to illustrate the highest type of patriotic devotion and self-sacrifice. Miss Myrover's brother, too, had fallen in the conflict; but his bones lay in some unknown trench, with those of a thousand others who had fallen on the same field. Ay, more, her lover, who had hoped to come home in the full tide of victory and claim his bride as a reward for gallantry, had shared the fate of her father and brother. When the war was over, the remnant of the family found itself involved in the common ruin— more deeply involved, indeed, than some others; for Colonel Myrover had believed in the ultimate triumph of his cause, and had invested most of his wealth in Confederate bonds, which were now only so much waste paper.

There had been a little left. Mrs. Myrover was thrifty, and had laid by a few hundred dollars, which she kept in the house to meet unforeseen contingencies. There remained, too, their home, with an ample garden and a well-stocked orchard, besides a considerable tract of country land, partly cleared, but productive of very little revenue.

With their shrunken resources, Miss Myrover and her mother were able to hold up their heads without embarrassment for some years after the close of the war. But when things were adjusted to the changed conditions, and the stream of life began to flow more vigorously in the new channels, they saw themselves in danger of dropping behind, unless in some way they could add to their meagre income. Miss Myrover looked over the field of employment, never very wide for women in the South, and found it occupied. The only available position she could be supposed prepared to fill, and which she could take without distinct loss of caste, was that of a teacher, and there was no vacancy except in one of the colored schools. Even teaching was a doubtful experiment; it was not what she would have preferred, but it was the best that could be done.

"I don't like it, Mary," said her mother. "It's a long step from owning such people to teaching them. What do they need with education? It will only make them unfit for work."

"They 're free now, mother, and perhaps they 'll work better if they 're taught something. Besides, it 's only a business arrangement, and does n't involve any closer contact than we have with our servants."

"Well, I should say not!" sniffed the old lady. "Not one of them will ever dare to presume on your position to take any liberties with us. I 'll see to that."

Miss Myrover began her work as a teacher in the autumn, at the opening of the school year. It was a novel experience at first. Though there had always been negro servants in the house, and though on the streets colored people were more numerous than those of her own race, and though she was so familiar with their dialect that she might almost be said to speak it, barring certain characteristic grammatical inaccuracies, she had never been brought in personal contact with so many of them at once as when she confronted the fifty or sixty faces—of colors ranging from a white almost as clear as her own to the darkest livery of the sun—which were gathered in the schoolroom on the morning when she began her duties. Some of the inherited prejudice of her caste, too, made itself felt, though she tried to repress any outward sign of it; and she could perceive that the children were not altogether responsive; they, likewise, were not entirely free from antagonism. The work was unfamiliar to her. She was not physically very strong, and at the close of the first day went home with a splitting headache. If she could have resigned then and there without causing comment or annoyance to others, she would have felt it a privilege to do so. But a night's rest banished her headache and improved her spirits, and the next morning she went to her work with renewed vigor, fortified by the experience of the first day.

Miss Myrover's second day was more satisfactory. She had some natural talent for organization, though hitherto unaware of it, and in the course of the day she got her classes formed and lessons under way. In a week or two she began to classify her pupils in her own mind, as bright or stupid, mischievous or well behaved, lazy or industrious, as the case might be, and to regulate her discipline accordingly. That she had come of a long line of ancestors who had exercised authority and mastership was perhaps not without its effect upon her character, and enabled her more readily to maintain good order in the school. When she was fairly broken in, she found the work rather to her liking, and derived much pleasure from such success as she achieved as a teacher.

It was natural that she should be more attracted to some of her pupils than to others. Perhaps her favorite—or, rather, the one she liked best, for she was too fair and just for conscious favoritism—was Sophy Tucker. Just the ground for the teacher's liking for Sophy might not at first be apparent. The girl was far from the whitest of Miss Myrover's pupils; in fact, she was one of the darker ones. She was not the brightest in intellect, though she always tried to learn her lessons. She was not the best dressed, for her mother was a poor widow, who went out washing and scrubbing for a living. Perhaps the real tie between them was Sophy's intense devotion to the teacher. It had manifested itself almost from the first day of the school, in the rapt look of admiration Miss Myrover always saw on the little black face turned toward her. In it there was nothing of envy, nothing of regret; nothing but worship for the beautiful white lady—she was not especially handsome, but to Sophy her beauty was almost divine—who had come to teach her. If Miss Myrover dropped a book, Sophy was the first to spring and pick it up; if she wished a chair moved, Sophy seemed to anticipate her wish; and so of all the numberless little services that can be rendered in a schoolroom.

Miss Myrover was fond of flowers, and liked to have them about her. The children soon learned of this taste of hers, and kept the vases on her desk filled with blossoms during their season. Sophy was perhaps the most active in providing them. If she could not get garden flowers, she would make excursions to the woods in the early morning, and bring in great dew-laden bunches of bay, or jasmine, or some other fragrant forest flower which she knew the teacher loved.

"When I die, Sophy," Miss Myrover said to the child one day, "I want to be covered with roses. And when they bury me, I'm sure I shall rest better if my grave is banked with flowers, and roses are planted at my head and at my feet."

Miss Myrover was at first amused at Sophy's devotion; but when she grew more accustomed to it, she found it rather to her liking. It had a sort of flavor of the old régime, and she felt, when she bestowed her kindly notice upon her little black attendant, some of the feudal condescension of the mistress toward the slave. She was kind to Sophy, and permitted her to play the rôle she had assumed, which caused sometimes a little jealousy among the other girls. Once she gave Sophy a yellow ribbon which she took from her own hair. The child carried it home, and cherished it as a priceless treasure, to be worn only on the greatest occasions.

Sophy had a rival in her attachment to the teacher, but the rivalry was altogether friendly. Miss Myrover had a little dog, a white spaniel, answering to the name of Prince. Prince was a dog of high degree, and would have very little to do with the children of the school; he made an exception, however, in the case of Sophy, whose devotion for his mistress he seemed to comprehend. He was a clever dog, and could fetch and carry, sit up on his haunches, extend his paw to shake hands, and possessed several other canine accomplishments. He was very fond of his mistress, and always, unless shut up at home, accompanied her to school, where he spent most of his time lying under the teacher's desk, or, in cold weather, by the stove, except when he would go out now and then and chase an imaginary rabbit round the yard, presumably for exercise.

At school Sophy and Prince vied with each other in their attentions to Miss Myrover. But when school was over, Prince went away with her, and Sophy stayed behind; for Miss Myrover was white and Sophy was black, which they both understood perfectly well. Miss Myrover taught the colored children, but she could not be seen with them in public. If they occasionally met her on the street, they did not expect her to speak to them, unless she happened to be alone and no other white person was in sight. If any of the children felt slighted, she was not aware of it, for she intended no slight; she had not been brought up to speak to negroes on the street, and she could not act differently from other people. And though she was a woman of sentiment and capable of deep feeling, her training had been such that she hardly expected to find in those of darker hue than herself the same susceptibility—varying in degree, perhaps, but yet the same in kind—that gave to her own life the alternations of feeling that made it most worth living.

Once Miss Myrover wished to carry home a parcel of books. She had the bundle in her hand when Sophy came up.

"Lemme tote yo' bundle fer yer, Miss Ma'y?" she asked eagerly. "I 'm gwine yo' way."

"Thank you, Sophy," was the reply. "I 'll be glad if you will."

Sophy followed the teacher at a respectful distance. When they reached Miss Myrover's home, Sophy carried the bundle to the doorstep, where Miss Myrover took it and thanked her.

Mrs. Myrover came out on the piazza as Sophy was moving away. She said, in the child's hearing, and perhaps with the intention that she should hear: "Mary, I wish you would n't let those little darkeys follow you to the house. I don't want them in the yard. I should think you 'd have enough of them all day."

"Very well, mother," replied her daughter. "I won't bring any more of them. The child was only doing me a favor."

Mrs. Myrover was an invalid, and opposition or irritation of any kind brought on nervous paroxysms that made her miserable, and made life a burden to the rest of the household, so that Mary seldom crossed her whims. She did not bring Sophy to the house again, nor did Sophy again offer her services as porter.

One day in spring Sophy brought her teacher a bouquet of yellow roses.

"Dey come off'n my own bush, Miss Ma'y," she said proudly, "an' I did n' let nobody e'se pull 'em, but saved 'em all fer you, 'cause I know you likes roses so much. I 'm gwine bring 'em all ter you as long as dey las'."

"Thank you, Sophy," said the teacher; "you are a very good girl."

For another year Mary Myrover taught the colored school, and did excellent service. The children made rapid progress under her tuition, and learned to love her well; for they saw and appreciated, as well as children could, her fidelity to a trust that she might have slighted, as some others did, without much fear of criticism. Toward the end of her second year she sickened, and after a brief illness died.

Old Mrs. Myrover was inconsolable. She ascribed her daughter's death to her labors as teacher of negro children. Just how the color of the pupils had produced the fatal effects she did not stop to explain. But she was too old, and had suffered too deeply from the war, in body and mind and estate, ever to reconcile herself to the changed order of things following the return of peace; and, with an unsound yet perfectly explainable logic, she visited some of her displeasure upon those who had profited most, though passively, by her losses.

"I always feared something would happen to Mary," she said. "It seemed unnatural for her to be wearing herself out teaching little negroes who ought to have been working for her. But the world has hardly been a fit place to live in since the war, and when I follow her, as I must before long, I shall not be sorry to go."

She gave strict orders that no colored people should be admitted to the house. Some of her friends heard of this, and remonstrated. They knew the teacher was loved by the pupils, and felt that sincere respect from the humble would be a worthy tribute to the proudest. But Mrs. Myrover was obdurate.

"They had my daughter when she was alive," she said, "and they 've killed her. But she 's mine now, and I won't have them come near her. I don't want one of them at the funeral or anywhere around."

For a month before Miss Myrover's death Sophy had been watching her rosebush—the one that bore the yellow roses—for the first buds of spring, and, when these appeared, had awaited impatiently their gradual unfolding. But not until her teacher's death had they become full-blown roses. When Miss Myrover died, Sophy determined to pluck the roses and lay them on her coffin. Perhaps, she thought, they might even put them in her hand or on her breast. For Sophy remembered Miss Myrover's thanks and praise when she had brought her the yellow roses the spring before.

On the morning of the day set for the funeral, Sophy washed her face until it shone, combed and brushed her hair with painful conscientiousness, put on her best frock, plucked her yellow roses, and, tying them with the treasured ribbon her teacher had given her, set out for Miss Myrover's home.

She went round to the side gate—the house stood on a corner—and stole up the path to the kitchen. A colored woman, whom she did not know, came to the door.

"W'at yer want, chile?" she inquired.

"Kin I see Miss Ma'y?" asked Sophy timidly.

"I don't know, honey. Ole Miss Myrover say she don't want no cullud folks roun' de house endyoin' dis fun'al. I 'll look an' see if she 's roun' de front room, whar de co'pse is. You sed down heah an' keep still, an' ef she 's upstairs maybe I kin git yer in dere a minute. Ef I can't, I kin put yo' bokay 'mongs' de res', whar she won't know nuthin' erbout it."

A moment after she had gone, there was a step in the hall, and old Mrs. Myrover came into the kitchen.

"Dinah!" she said in a peevish tone; "Dinah!"

Receiving no answer, Mrs. Myrover peered around the kitchen, and caught sight of Sophy.

"What are you doing here?" she demanded.

"I—I 'm-m waitin' ter see de cook, ma'am," stammered Sophy.

"The cook is n't here now. I don't know where she is. Besides, my daughter is to be buried to-day, and I won't have any one visiting the servants until the funeral is over. Come back some other day, or see the cook at her own home in the evening."

She stood waiting for the child to go, and under the keen glance of her eyes Sophy, feeling as though she had been caught in some disgraceful act, hurried down the walk and out of the gate, with her bouquet in her hand.

"Dinah," said Mrs. Myrover, when the cook came back, "I don't want any strange people admitted here to-day. The house will be full of our friends, and we have no room for others."

"Yas 'm," said the cook. She understood perfectly what her mistress meant; and what the cook thought about her mistress was a matter of no consequence.

The funeral services were held at St. Paul's Episcopal Church, where the Myrovers had always worshiped. Quite a number of Miss Myrover's pupils went to the church to attend the services. The building was not a large one. There was a small gallery at the rear, to which colored people were admitted, if they chose to come, at ordinary services; and those who wished to be present at the funeral supposed that the usual custom would prevail. They were therefore surprised, when they went to the side entrance, by which colored people gained access to the gallery stairs, to be met by an usher who barred their passage.

"I 'm sorry," he said, "but I have had orders to admit no one until the friends of the family have all been seated. If you wish to wait until the white people have all gone in, and there 's any room left, you may be able to get into the back part of the gallery. Of course I can't tell yet whether there 'll be any room or not."

Now the statement of the usher was a very reasonable one; but, strange to say, none of the colored people chose to remain except Sophy. She still hoped to use her floral offering for its destined end, in some way, though she did not know just how. She waited in the yard until the church was filled with white people, and a number who could not gain admittance were standing about the doors. Then she went round to the side of the church, and, depositing her bouquet carefully on an old mossy gravestone, climbed up on the projecting sill of a window near the chancel. The window was of stained glass, of somewhat ancient make. The church was old, had indeed been built in colonial times, and the stained glass had been brought from England. The design of the window showed Jesus blessing little children. Time had dealt gently with the window, but just at the feet of the figure of Jesus a small triangular piece of glass had been broken out. To this aperture Sophy applied her eyes, and through it saw and heard what she could of the services within.

Before the chancel, on trestles draped in black, stood the sombre casket in which lay all that was mortal of her dear teacher. The top of the casket was covered with flowers; and lying stretched out underneath it she saw Miss Myrover's little white dog, Prince. He had followed the body to the church, and, slipping in unnoticed among the mourners, had taken his place, from which no one had the heart to remove him.

The white-robed rector read the solemn service for the dead, and then delivered a brief address, in which he dwelt upon the uncertainty of life, and, to the believer, the certain blessedness of eternity. He spoke of Miss Myrover's kindly spirit, and, as an illustration of her love and self-sacrifice for others, referred to her labors as a teacher of the poor ignorant negroes who had been placed in their midst by an all-wise Providence, and whom it was their duty to guide and direct in the station in which God had put them. Then the organ pealed, a prayer was said, and the long cortége moved from the church to the cemetery, about half a mile away, where the body was to be interred.

When the services were over, Sophy sprang down from her perch, and, taking her flowers, followed the procession. She did not walk with the rest, but at a proper and respectful distance from the last mourner. No one noticed the little black girl with the bunch of yellow flowers, or thought of her as interested in the funeral.

The cortége reached the cemetery and filed slowly through the gate; but Sophy stood outside, looking at a small sign in white letters on a black background:

"*Notice.* This cemetery is for white people only. Others please keep out."

Sophy, thanks to Miss Myrover's painstaking instruction, could read this sign very distinctly. In fact, she had often read it before. For Sophy was a child who loved beauty, in a blind, groping sort of way, and had sometimes stood by the fence of the cemetery and looked through at the green mounds and shaded walks and blooming flowers within, and wished that she might walk among them. She knew, too, that the little sign on the gate, though so courteously worded, was no mere formality; for she had heard how a colored man, who had wandered into the cemetery on a hot night and fallen asleep on the flat top of a tomb, had been arrested as a vagrant and fined five dollars, which he had worked out on the streets, with a ball-and-chain attachment, at twenty-five cents a day. Since that time the cemetery gate had been locked at night.

So Sophy stayed outside, and looked through the fence. Her poor bouquet had begun to droop by this time, and the yellow ribbon had lost some of its freshness. Sophy could see the rector standing by the grave, the mourners gathered round; she could faintly distinguish the solemn words with which ashes were committed to ashes, and dust to dust. She heard the hollow thud of the earth falling on the coffin; and she leaned against the iron fence, sobbing softly, until the grave was filled and rounded off, and the wreaths and other floral pieces were disposed upon it. When the mourners began to move toward the gate, Sophy walked slowly down the street, in a direction opposite to that taken by most of the people who came out.

When they had all gone away, and the sexton had come out and locked the gate behind him, Sophy crept back. Her roses were faded now, and from some of them the petals had fallen. She stood there irresolute, loath to leave with her heart's desire unsatisfied, when, as her eyes sought again the teacher's last resting-place, she saw lying beside the new-made grave what looked like a small bundle of white wool. Sophy's eyes lighted up with a sudden glow.

"Prince! Here, Prince!" she called.

The little dog rose, and trotted down to the gate. Sophy pushed the poor bouquet between the iron bars. "Take that ter Miss Ma'y, Prince," she said, "that's a good doggie."

The dog wagged his tail intelligently, took the bouquet carefully in his mouth, carried it to his mistress's grave, and laid it among the other flowers. The bunch of roses was so small that from where she stood Sophy could see only a dash of yellow against the white background of the mass of flowers.

When Prince had performed his mission he turned his eyes toward Sophy inquiringly, and when she gave him a nod of approval lay down and resumed his watch by the graveside. Sophy looked at him a moment with a feeling very much like envy, and then turned and moved slowly away.

THE WEB OF CIRCUMSTANCE

I

Within a low clapboarded hut, with an open front, a forge was glowing. In front a blacksmith was shoeing a horse, a sleek, well-kept animal with the signs of good blood and breeding. A young mulatto stood by and handed the blacksmith such tools as he needed from time to time. A group of negroes were sitting around, some in the shadow of the shop, one in the full glare of the sunlight. A gentleman was seated in a buggy a few yards away, in the shade of a spreading elm. The horse had loosened a shoe, and Colonel Thornton, who was a lover of fine horseflesh, and careful of it, had stopped at Ben Davis's blacksmith shop, as soon as he discovered the loose shoe, to have it fastened on.

"All right, Kunnel," the blacksmith called out. "Tom," he said, addressing the young man, "he'p me hitch up."

Colonel Thornton alighted from the buggy, looked at the shoe, signified his approval of the job, and stood looking on while the blacksmith and his assistant harnessed the horse to the buggy.

"Dat's a mighty fine whip yer got dere, Kunnel," said Ben, while the young man was tightening the straps of the harness on the opposite side of the horse. "I wush I had one like it. Where kin yer git dem whips?"

"My brother brought me this from New York," said the Colonel. "You can't buy them down here."

The whip in question was a handsome one. The handle was wrapped with interlacing threads of variegated colors, forming an elaborate pattern, the lash being dark green. An octagonal ornament of glass was set in the end of the handle. "It cert'n'y is fine," said Ben; "I wish I had one like it." He looked at the whip longingly as Colonel Thornton drove away.

"'Pears ter me Ben gittin' mighty blooded," said one of the bystanders, "drivin' a hoss an' buggy, an' wantin' a whip like Colonel Thornton's."

"What 's de reason I can't hab a hoss an' buggy an' a whip like Kunnel Tho'nton's, ef I pay fer 'em?" asked Ben. "We colored folks never had no chance ter git nothin' befo' de wah, but ef eve'y nigger in dis town had a tuck keer er his money sence de wah, like I has, an' bought as much lan' as I has, de niggers might 'a' got half de lan' by dis time," he went on, giving a finishing blow to a horseshoe, and throwing it on the ground to cool.

Carried away by his own eloquence, he did not notice the approach of two white men who came up the street from behind him.

"An' ef you niggers," he continued, raking the coals together over a fresh bar of iron, "would stop wastin' yo' money on 'scursions to put money in w'ite folks' pockets, an' stop buildin' fine chu'ches, an' buil' houses fer yo'se'ves, you 'd git along much faster."

"You 're talkin' sense, Ben," said one of the white men. "Yo'r people will never be respected till they 've got property."

The conversation took another turn. The white men transacted their business and went away. The whistle of a neighboring steam sawmill blew a raucous blast for the hour of noon, and the loafers shuffled away in different directions.

"You kin go ter dinner, Tom," said the blacksmith. "An' stop at de gate w'en yer go by my house, and tell Nancy I 'll be dere in 'bout twenty minutes. I got ter finish dis yer plough p'int fus'."

The young man walked away. One would have supposed, from the rapidity with which he walked, that he was very hungry. A quarter of an hour later the blacksmith dropped his hammer, pulled off his leather apron, shut the front door of the shop, and went home to dinner. He came into the house out of the fervent heat, and, throwing off his straw hat, wiped his brow vigorously with a red cotton handkerchief.

"Dem collards smells good," he said, sniffing the odor that came in through the kitchen door, as his good-looking yellow wife opened it to enter the room where he was. "I 've got a monst'us good appetite ter-day. I feels good, too. I paid Majah Ransom de intrus' on de mortgage dis mawnin' an' a hund'ed dollahs besides, an' I spec's ter hab de balance ready by de fust of nex' Jiniwary; an' den we won't owe nobody a cent. I tell yer dere ain' nothin' like propputy ter make a pusson feel like a man. But w'at 's de matter wid yer, Nancy? Is sump'n' skeered yer?"

The woman did seem excited and ill at ease. There was a heaving of the full bust, a quickened breathing, that betokened suppressed excitement. "I—I—jes' seen a rattlesnake out in de gyahden," she stammered. The blacksmith ran to the door. "Which way? Whar wuz he?" he cried.

He heard a rustling in the bushes at one side of the garden, and the sound of a breaking twig, and, seizing a hoe which stood by the door, he sprang toward the point from which the sound came.

"No, no," said the woman hurriedly, "it wuz over here," and she directed her husband's attention to the other side of the garden.

The blacksmith, with the uplifted hoe, its sharp blade gleaming in the sunlight, peered cautiously among the collards and tomato plants, listening all the while for the ominous rattle, but found nothing.

"I reckon he 's got away," he said, as he set the hoe up again by the door. "Whar 's de chillen?" he asked with some anxiety. "Is dey playin' in de woods?"

"No," answered his wife, "dey 've gone ter de spring."

The spring was on the opposite side of the garden from that on which the snake was said to have been seen, so the blacksmith sat down and fanned himself with a palm-leaf fan until the dinner was served.

"Yer ain't quite on time ter-day, Nancy," he said, glancing up at the clock on the mantel, after the edge of his appetite had been taken off. "Got ter make time ef yer wanter make money. Did n't Tom tell yer I 'd be heah in twenty minutes?"

"No," she said; "I seen him goin' pas'; he did n' say nothin'."

"I dunno w'at 's de matter wid dat boy," mused the blacksmith over his apple dumpling. "He 's gittin' mighty keerless heah lately; mus' hab sump'n' on 'is min'—some gal, I reckon."

The children had come in while he was speaking—a slender, shapely boy, yellow like his mother, a girl several years younger, dark like her father: both bright-looking children and neatly dressed.

"I seen cousin Tom down by de spring," said the little girl, as she lifted off the pail of water that had been balanced on her head. "He come out er de woods jest ez we wuz fillin' our buckets."

"Yas," insisted the blacksmith, "he 's got some gal on his min'."

II

The case of the State of North Carolina vs. Ben Davis was called. The accused was led into court, and took his seat in the prisoner's dock.

"Prisoner at the bar, stand up."

The prisoner, pale and anxious, stood up. The clerk read the indictment, in which it was charged that the defendant by force and arms had entered the barn of one G. W. Thornton, and feloniously taken therefrom one whip, of the value of fifteen dollars.

"Are you guilty or not guilty?" asked the judge.

"Not guilty, yo' Honah; not guilty, Jedge. I never tuck de whip."

The State's attorney opened the case. He was young and zealous. Recently elected to the office, this was his first batch of cases, and he was anxious to make as good a record as possible. He had no doubt of the prisoner's guilt. There had been a great deal of petty thieving in the county, and several gentlemen had suggested to him the necessity for greater severity in punishing it. The jury were all white men. The prosecuting attorney stated the case.

"We expect to show, gentlemen of the jury, the facts set out in the indictment—not altogether by direct proof, but by a chain of circumstantial evidence which is stronger even than the testimony of eyewitnesses. Men might lie, but circumstances cannot. We expect to show that the defendant is a man of dangerous character, a surly, impudent fellow; a man whose views of property are prejudicial to the welfare of society, and who has been heard to assert that half the property which is owned in this county has been stolen, and that, if justice were done, the white people ought to divide up the land with the negroes; in other words, a negro nihilist, a communist, a secret devotee of Tom Paine and Voltaire, a pupil of the anarchist propaganda, which, if not checked by the stern hand of the law, will fasten its insidious fangs on our social system, and drag it down to ruin."

"We object, may it please your Honor," said the defendant's attorney. "The prosecutor should defer his argument until the testimony is in."

"Confine yourself to the facts, Major," said the court mildly.

The prisoner sat with half-open mouth, overwhelmed by this flood of eloquence. He had never heard of Tom Paine or Voltaire. He had no conception of what a nihilist or an anarchist might be, and could not have told the difference between a propaganda and a potato.

"We expect to show, may it please the court, that the prisoner had been employed by Colonel Thornton to shoe a horse; that the horse was taken to the prisoner's blacksmith shop by a servant of Colonel Thornton's; that, this servant expressing a desire to go somewhere on an errand before the horse had been shod, the prisoner volunteered to return the horse to Colonel Thornton's stable; that he did so, and the following morning the whip in question was missing; that, from circumstances, suspicion naturally fell upon the prisoner, and a search was made of his shop, where the whip was found secreted; that the prisoner denied that the whip was there, but when confronted with the evidence of his crime, showed by his confusion that he was guilty beyond a peradventure."

The prisoner looked more anxious; so much eloquence could not but be effective with the jury.

The attorney for the defendant answered briefly, denying the defendant's guilt, dwelling upon his previous good character for honesty, and begging the jury not to prejudge the case, but to remember that the law is merciful, and that the benefit of the doubt should be given to the prisoner.

The prisoner glanced nervously at the jury. There was nothing in their faces to indicate the effect upon them of the opening statements. It seemed to the disinterested listeners as if the defendant's attorney had little confidence in his client's cause.

Colonel Thornton took the stand and testified to his ownership of the whip, the place where it was kept, its value, and the fact that it had disappeared. The whip was produced in court and identified by the witness. He also testified to the conversation at the blacksmith shop in the course of which the prisoner had expressed a desire to possess a similar whip. The cross-examination was brief, and no attempt was made to shake the Colonel's testimony.

The next witness was the constable who had gone with a warrant to search Ben's shop. He testified to the circumstances under which the whip was found.

"He wuz brazen as a mule at fust, an' wanted ter git mad about it. But when we begun ter turn over that pile er truck in the cawner, he kinder begun ter trimble; when the whip-handle stuck out, his eyes commenced ter grow big, an' when we hauled the whip out he turned pale ez ashes, an' begun to swear he did n' take the whip an' did n' know how it got thar."

"You may cross-examine," said the prosecuting attorney triumphantly.

The prisoner felt the weight of the testimony, and glanced furtively at the jury, and then appealingly at his lawyer.

"You say that Ben denied that he had stolen the whip," said the prisoner's attorney, on cross-examination. "Did it not occur to you that what you took for brazen impudence might have been but the evidence of conscious innocence?"

The witness grinned incredulously, revealing thereby a few blackened fragments of teeth.

"I 've tuck up more 'n a hundred niggers fer stealin', Kurnel, an' I never seed one yit that did n' 'ny it ter the las'."

"Answer my question. Might not the witness's indignation have been a manifestation of conscious innocence? Yes or no?"

"Yes, it mought, an' the moon mought fall—but it don't."

Further cross-examination did not weaken the witness's testimony, which was very damaging, and every one in the court room felt instinctively that a strong defense would be required to break down the State's case.

"The State rests," said the prosecuting attorney, with a ring in his voice which spoke of certain victory.

There was a temporary lull in the proceedings, during which a bailiff passed a pitcher of water and a glass along the line of jurymen. The defense was then begun.

The law in its wisdom did not permit the defendant to testify in his own behalf. There were no witnesses to the facts, but several were called to testify to Ben's good character. The colored witnesses made him out possessed of all the virtues. One or two white men testified that they had never known anything against his reputation for honesty.

The defendant rested his case, and the State called its witnesses in rebuttal. They were entirely on the point of character. One testified that he had heard the prisoner say that, if the negroes had their rights, they would own at least half the property. Another testified that he had heard the defendant say that the negroes spent too much money on churches, and that they cared a good deal more for God than God had ever seemed to care for them.

Ben Davis listened to this testimony with half-open mouth and staring eyes. Now and then he would lean forward and speak perhaps a word, when his attorney would shake a warning finger at him, and he would fall back helplessly, as if abandoning himself to fate; but for a moment only, when he would resume his puzzled look.

The arguments followed. The prosecuting attorney briefly summed up the evidence, and characterized it as almost a mathematical proof of the prisoner's guilt. He reserved his eloquence for the closing argument.

The defendant's attorney had a headache, and secretly believed his client guilty. His address sounded more like an appeal for mercy than a demand for justice. Then the State's attorney delivered the maiden argument of his office, the speech that made his reputation as an orator, and opened up to him a successful political career.

The judge's charge to the jury was a plain, simple statement of the law as applied to circumstantial evidence, and the mere statement of the law foreshadowed the verdict.

The eyes of the prisoner were glued to the jury-box, and he looked more and more like a hunted animal. In the rear of the crowd of blacks who filled the back part of the room, partly concealed by the projecting angle of the fireplace, stood Tom, the blacksmith's assistant. If the face is the mirror of the soul, then this man's soul, taken off its guard in this moment of excitement, was full of lust and envy and all evil passions.

The jury filed out of their box, and into the jury room behind the judge's stand. There was a moment of relaxation in the court room. The lawyers fell into conversation across the table. The judge beckoned to Colonel Thornton, who stepped forward, and they conversed together a few moments. The prisoner was all eyes and ears in this moment of waiting, and from an involuntary gesture on the part of the judge he divined that they were speaking of him. It is a pity he could not hear what was said.

"How do you feel about the case, Colonel?" asked the judge.

"Let him off easy," replied Colonel Thornton. "He 's the best blacksmith in the county."

The business of the court seemed to have halted by tacit consent, in anticipation of a quick verdict. The suspense did not last long. Scarcely ten minutes had elapsed when there was a rap on the door, the officer opened it, and the jury came out.

The prisoner, his soul in his eyes, sought their faces, but met no reassuring glance; they were all looking away from him.

"Gentlemen of the jury, have you agreed upon a verdict?"

"We have," responded the foreman. The clerk of the court stepped forward and took the fateful slip from the foreman's hand.

The clerk read the verdict: "We, the jury impaneled and sworn to try the issues in this cause, do find the prisoner guilty as charged in the indictment."

There was a moment of breathless silence. Then a wild burst of grief from the prisoner's wife, to which his two children, not understanding it all, but vaguely conscious of some calamity, added their voices in two long, discordant wails, which would have been ludicrous had they not been heart-rending.

The face of the young man in the back of the room expressed relief and badly concealed satisfaction. The prisoner fell back upon the seat from which he had half risen in his anxiety, and his dark face assumed an ashen hue. What he thought could only be surmised. Perhaps, knowing his innocence, he had not believed conviction possible; perhaps, conscious of guilt, he dreaded the punishment, the extent of which was optional with the judge, within very wide limits. Only one other person present knew whether or not he was guilty, and that other had slunk furtively from the court room.

Some of the spectators wondered why there should be so much ado about convicting a negro of stealing a buggy-whip. They had forgotten their own interest of the moment before. They did not realize out of what trifles grow the tragedies of life.

It was four o'clock in the afternoon, the hour for adjournment, when the verdict was returned. The judge nodded to the bailiff.

"Oyez, oyez! this court is now adjourned until ten o'clock to-morrow morning," cried the bailiff in a singsong voice. The judge left the bench, the jury filed out of the box, and a buzz of conversation filled the court room.

"Brace up, Ben, brace up, my boy," said the defendant's lawyer, half apologetically. "I did what I could for you, but you can never tell what a jury will do. You won't be sentenced till to-morrow morning. In the meantime I 'll speak to the judge and try to get him to be easy with you. He may let you off with a light fine."

The negro pulled himself together, and by an effort listened.

"Thanky, Majah," was all he said. He seemed to be thinking of something far away.

He barely spoke to his wife when she frantically threw herself on him, and clung to his neck, as he passed through the side room on his way to jail. He kissed his children mechanically, and did not reply to the soothing remarks made by the jailer.

III

There was a good deal of excitement in town the next morning. Two white men stood by the post office talking.

"Did yer hear the news?"

"No, what wuz it?"

"Ben Davis tried ter break jail las' night."

"You don't say so! What a fool! He ain't be'n sentenced yit."

"Well, now," said the other, "I 've knowed Ben a long time, an' he wuz a right good nigger. I kinder found it hard ter b'lieve he did steal that whip. But what 's a man's feelin's ag'in' the proof?"

They spoke on awhile, using the past tense as if they were speaking of a dead man.

"Ef I know Jedge Hart, Ben 'll wish he had slep' las' night, 'stidder tryin' ter break out'n jail."

At ten o'clock the prisoner was brought into court. He walked with shambling gait, bent at the shoulders, hopelessly, with downcast eyes, and took his seat with several other prisoners who had been brought in for sentence. His wife, accompanied by the children, waited behind him, and a number of his friends were gathered in the court room.

The first prisoner sentenced was a young white man, convicted several days before of manslaughter. The deed was done in the heat of passion, under circumstances of great provocation, during a quarrel about a woman. The prisoner was admonished of the sanctity of human life, and sentenced to one year in the penitentiary.

The next case was that of a young clerk, eighteen or nineteen years of age, who had committed a forgery in order to procure the means to buy lottery tickets. He was well connected, and the case would not have been prosecuted if the judge had not refused to allow it to be nolled, and, once brought to trial, a conviction could not have been avoided.

"You are a young man," said the judge gravely, yet not unkindly, "and your life is yet before you. I regret that you should have been led into evil courses by the lust for speculation, so dangerous in its tendencies, so fruitful of crime and misery. I am led to believe that you are sincerely penitent, and that, after such punishment as the law cannot remit without bringing itself into contempt, you will see the error of your ways and follow the strict path of rectitude. Your fault has entailed distress not only upon yourself, but upon your relatives, people of good name and good family, who suffer as keenly from your disgrace as you yourself. Partly out of consideration for their feelings, and partly because I feel that, under the circumstances, the law will be satisfied by the penalty I shall inflict, I sentence you to imprisonment in the county jail for six months, and a fine of one hundred dollars and the costs of this action."

"The jedge talks well, don't he?" whispered one spectator to another. "Yes, and kinder likes ter hear hisse'f talk," answered the other.

"Ben Davis, stand up," ordered the judge.

He might have said "Ben Davis, wake up," for the jailer had to touch the prisoner on the shoulder to rouse him from his stupor. He stood up, and something of the hunted look came again into his eyes, which shifted under the stern glance of the judge.

"Ben Davis, you have been convicted of larceny, after a fair trial before twelve good men of this county. Under the testimony, there can be no doubt of your guilt. The case is an aggravated one. You are not an ignorant, shiftless fellow, but a man of more than ordinary intelligence among your people, and one who ought to know better. You have not even the poor excuse of having stolen to satisfy hunger or a physical appetite. Your conduct is wholly without excuse, and I can only regard your crime as the result of a tendency to offenses of this nature, a tendency which is only too common among your people; a tendency which is a menace to civilization, a menace to society itself, for society rests upon the sacred right of property. Your opinions, too, have been given a wrong turn; you have been heard to utter sentiments which, if disseminated among an ignorant people, would breed discontent, and give rise to strained relations between them and their best friends, their old masters, who understand their real nature and their real needs, and to whose justice and enlightened guidance they can safely trust. Have you anything to say why sentence should not be passed upon you?"

"Nothin', suh, cep'n dat I did n' take de whip."

"The law, largely, I think, in view of the peculiar circumstances of your unfortunate race, has vested a large discretion in courts as to the extent of the punishment for offenses of this kind. Taking your case as a whole, I am convinced that it is one which, for the sake of the example, deserves a severe punishment. Nevertheless, I do not feel disposed to give you the full extent of the law, which would be twenty years in the penitentiary,[1] but, considering the fact that you have a family, and have heretofore borne a good reputation in the community, I will impose upon you the light sentence of imprisonment for five years in the penitentiary at hard labor. And I hope that this will be a warning to you and others who may be similarly disposed, and that after your sentence has expired you may lead the life of a law-abiding citizen."

"O Ben! O my husband! O God!" moaned the poor wife, and tried to press forward to her husband's side.

"Keep back, Nancy, keep back," said the jailer. "You can see him in jail."

Several people were looking at Ben's face. There was one flash of despair, and then nothing but a stony blank, behind which he masked his real feelings, whatever they were.

Human character is a compound of tendencies inherited and habits acquired. In the anxiety, the fear of disgrace, spoke the nineteenth century civilization with which Ben Davis had been more or less closely in touch during twenty years of slavery and fifteen years of freedom. In the stolidity with which he received this sentence for a crime which he had not committed, spoke who knows what trait of inherited savagery? For stoicism is a savage virtue.

IV

One morning in June, five years later, a black man limped slowly along the old Lumberton plank road; a tall man, whose bowed shoulders made him seem shorter than he was, and a face from which it was difficult to guess his years, for in it the wrinkles and flabbiness of age were found side by side with firm white teeth, and eyes not sunken—eyes bloodshot, and burning with something, either fever or passion. Though he limped painfully with one foot, the other hit the ground impatiently, like the good horse in a poorly matched team. As he walked along, he was talking to himself:

---

[1] There are no degrees of larceny in North Carolina, and the penalty for any offense lies in the discretion of the judge, to the limit of twenty years. [Original publisher's note.]

"I wonder what dey 'll do w'en I git back? I wonder how Nancy 's s'ported the fambly all dese years? Tuck in washin', I s'ppose—she was a monst'us good washer an' ironer. I wonder ef de chillun 'll be too proud ter reco'nize deir daddy come back f'um de penetenchy? I 'spec' Billy must be a big boy by dis time. He won' b'lieve his daddy ever stole anything. I 'm gwine ter slip roun' an' s'prise 'em."

Five minutes later a face peered cautiously into the window of what had once been Ben Davis's cabin—at first an eager face, its coarseness lit up with the fire of hope; a moment later a puzzled face; then an anxious, fearful face as the man stepped away from the window and rapped at the door.

"Is Mis' Davis home?" he asked of the woman who opened the door.

"Mis' Davis don' live here. You er mistook in de house."

"Whose house is dis?"

"It b'longs ter my husban', Mr. Smith—Primus Smith."

"'Scuse me, but I knowed de house some years ago w'en I wuz here oncet on a visit, an' it b'longed ter a man name' Ben Davis."

"Ben Davis—Ben Davis?—oh yes, I 'member now. Dat wuz de gen'-man w'at wuz sent ter de penitenchy fer sump'n er nuther—sheep-stealin', I b'lieve. Primus," she called, "w'at wuz Ben Davis, w'at useter own dis yer house, sent ter de penitenchy fer?"

"Hoss-stealin'," came back the reply in sleepy accents, from the man seated by the fireplace.

The traveler went on to the next house. A neat-looking yellow woman came to the door when he rattled the gate, and stood looking suspiciously at him.

"W'at you want?" she asked.

"Please, ma'am, will you tell me whether a man name' Ben Davis useter live in dis neighborhood?"

"Useter live in de nex' house; wuz sent ter de penitenchy fer killin' a man."

"Kin yer tell me w'at went wid Mis' Davis?"

"Umph! I 's a 'spectable 'oman, I is, en don' mix wid dem kind er people. She wuz 'n' no better 'n her husban'. She tuk up wid a man dat useter wuk fer Ben, an' dey 're livin' down by de ole wagon-ya'd, where no 'spectable 'oman ever puts her foot."

"An' de chillen?"

"De gal 's dead. Wuz 'n' no better 'n she oughter be'n. She fell in de crick an' got drown'; some folks say she wuz 'n' sober w'en it happen'. De boy tuck atter his pappy. He wuz 'rested las' week fer shootin' a w'ite man, an' wuz lynch' de same night. Dey wa'n't none of 'em no 'count after deir pappy went ter de penitenchy."

"What went wid de proputty?"

"Hit wuz sol' fer de mortgage, er de taxes, er de lawyer, er sump'n—
I don' know w'at. A w'ite man got it."

The man with the bundle went on until he came to a creek that crossed
the road. He descended the sloping bank, and, sitting on a stone in the
shade of a water-oak, took off his coarse brogans, unwound the rags that
served him in lieu of stockings, and laved in the cool water the feet that
were chafed with many a weary mile of travel.

After five years of unrequited toil, and unspeakable hardship in convict camps—five years of slaving by the side of human brutes, and of nightly
herding with them in vermin-haunted huts—Ben Davis had become like
them. For a while he had received occasional letters from home, but in the
shifting life of the convict camp they had long since ceased to reach him, if
indeed they had been written. For a year or two, the consciousness of his
innocence had helped to make him resist the debasing influences that surrounded him. The hope of shortening his sentence by good behavior, too,
had worked a similar end. But the transfer from one contractor to another,
each interested in keeping as long as possible a good worker, had speedily
dissipated any such hope. When hope took flight, its place was not long vacant. Despair followed, and black hatred of all mankind, hatred especially
of the man to whom he attributed all his misfortunes. One who is suffering
unjustly is not apt to indulge in fine abstractions, nor to balance probabil-
ities. By long brooding over his wrongs, his mind became, if not unsettled,
at least warped, and he imagined that Colonel Thornton had deliberately
set a trap into which he had fallen. The Colonel, he convinced himself, had
disapproved of his prosperity, and had schemed to destroy it. He reasoned
himself into the belief that he represented in his person the accumulated
wrongs of a whole race, and Colonel Thornton the race who had oppressed
them. A burning desire for revenge sprang up in him, and he nursed it until his sentence expired and he was set at liberty. What he had learned since
reaching home had changed his desire into a deadly purpose.

When he had again bandaged his feet and slipped them into his shoes,
he looked around him, and selected a stout sapling from among the undergrowth that covered the bank of the stream. Taking from his pocket a huge
clasp-knife, he cut off the length of an ordinary walking stick and trimmed
it. The result was an ugly-looking bludgeon, a dangerous weapon when in
the grasp of a strong man.

With the stick in his hand, he went on down the road until he approached a large white house standing some distance back from the street.
The grounds were filled with a profusion of shrubbery. The negro entered
the gate and secreted himself in the bushes, at a point where he could hear
any one that might approach.

It was near midday, and he had not eaten. He had walked all night, and had not slept. The hope of meeting his loved ones had been meat and drink and rest for him. But as he sat waiting, outraged nature asserted itself, and he fell asleep, with his head on the rising root of a tree, and his face upturned.

And as he slept, he dreamed of his childhood; of an old black mammy taking care of him in the daytime, and of a younger face, with soft eyes, which bent over him sometimes at night, and a pair of arms which clasped him closely. He dreamed of his past—of his young wife, of his bright children. Somehow his dreams all ran to pleasant themes for a while.

Then they changed again. He dreamed that he was in the convict camp, and, by an easy transition, that he was in hell, consumed with hunger, burning with thirst. Suddenly the grinning devil who stood over him with a barbed whip faded away, and a little white angel came and handed him a drink of water. As he raised it to his lips the glass slipped, and he struggled back to consciousness.

"Poo' man! Poo' man sick, an' sleepy. Dolly b'ing f'owers to cover poo' man up. Poo' man mus' be hungry. W'en Dolly get him covered up, she go b'ing poo' man some cake."

A sweet little child, as beautiful as a cherub escaped from Paradise, was standing over him. At first he scarcely comprehended the words the baby babbled out. But as they became clear to him, a novel feeling crept slowly over his heart. It had been so long since he had heard anything but curses and stern words of command, or the ribald songs of obscene merriment, that the clear tones of this voice from heaven cooled his calloused heart as the water of the brook had soothed his blistered feet. It was so strange, so unwonted a thing, that he lay there with half-closed eyes while the child brought leaves and flowers and laid them on his face and on his breast, and arranged them with little caressing taps.

She moved away, and plucked a flower. And then she spied another farther on, and then another, and, as she gathered them, kept increasing the distance between herself and the man lying there, until she was several rods away.

Ben Davis watched her through eyes over which had come an unfamiliar softness. Under the lingering spell of his dream, her golden hair, which fell in rippling curls, seemed like a halo of purity and innocence and peace, irradiating the atmosphere around her. It is true the thought occurred to Ben, vaguely, that through harm to her he might inflict the greatest punishment upon her father; but the idea came like a dark shape that faded away and vanished into nothingness as soon as it came within the nimbus that surrounded the child's person.

The child was moving on to pluck still another flower, when there came a sound of hoof-beats, and Ben was aware that a horseman, visible through the shrubbery, was coming along the curved path that led from the gate to the house. It must be the man he was waiting for, and now was the time to wreak his vengeance. He sprang to his feet, grasped his club, and stood for a moment irresolute. But either the instinct of the convict, beaten, driven, and debased, or the influence of the child, which was still strong upon him, impelled him, after the first momentary pause, to flee as though seeking safety.

His flight led him toward the little girl, whom he must pass in order to make his escape, and as Colonel Thornton turned the corner of the path he saw a desperate-looking negro, clad in filthy rags, and carrying in his hand a murderous bludgeon, running toward the child, who, startled by the sound of footsteps, had turned and was looking toward the approaching man with wondering eyes. A sickening fear came over the father's heart, and drawing the ever-ready revolver, which according to the Southern custom he carried always upon his person, he fired with unerring aim. Ben Davis ran a few yards farther, faltered, threw out his hands, and fell dead at the child's feet.

Some time, we are told, when the cycle of years has rolled around, there is to be another golden age, when all men will dwell together in love and harmony, and when peace and righteousness shall prevail for a thousand years. God speed the day, and let not the shining thread of hope become so enmeshed in the web of circumstance that we lose sight of it; but give us here and there, and now and then, some little foretaste of this golden age, that we may the more patiently and hopefully await its coming!

Another Color-Line Story

BAXTER'S PROCRUSTES

Baxter's Procrustes is one of the publications of the Bodleian Club. The Bodleian Club is composed of gentlemen of culture, who are interested in books and book-collecting. It was named, very obviously, after the famous library of the same name, and not only became in our city a sort of shrine for local worshipers of fine bindings and rare editions, but was visited occasionally by pilgrims from afar. The Bodleian has entertained Mark Twain, Joseph Jefferson, and other literary and histrionic celebrities. It possesses quite a collection of personal mementos of distinguished authors, among them a paperweight which once belonged to Goethe, a lead pencil used by Emerson, an autograph letter of Matthew Arnold, and a chip from a tree felled by Mr. Gladstone. Its library contains a number of rare books, including a fine collection on chess, of which game several of the members are enthusiastic devotees.

The activities of the club are not, however, confined entirely to books. We have a very handsome clubhouse, and much taste and discrimination have been exercised in its adornment. There are many good paintings, including portraits of the various presidents of the club, which adorn the entrance hall. After books, perhaps the most distinctive feature of the club is our collection of pipes. In a large rack in the smoking-room—really a superfluity, since smoking is permitted all over the house—is as complete an assortment of pipes as perhaps exists in the civilized world. Indeed, it is an unwritten rule of the club that no one is eligible for membership who cannot produce a new variety of pipe, which is filed with his application for membership, and, if he passes, deposited with the club collection, he, however, retaining the title in himself. Once a year, upon the anniversary of the death of Sir Walter Raleigh, who, it will be remembered, first introduced

Atlantic Monthly 92 (June 1904).

tobacco into England, the full membership of the club, as a rule, turns out. A large supply of the very best smoking mixture is laid in. At nine o'clock sharp each member takes his pipe from the rack, fills it with tobacco, and then the whole club, with the president at the head, all smoking furiously, march in solemn procession from room to room, upstairs and downstairs, making the tour of the clubhouse and returning to the smoking-room. The president then delivers an address, and each member is called upon to say something, either by way of a quotation or an original sentiment, in praise of the virtues of nicotine. This ceremony—facetiously known as "hitting the pipe"—being thus concluded, the membership pipes are carefully cleaned out and replaced in the club rack.

As I have said, however, the *raison d'être* of the club, and the feature upon which its fame chiefly rests, is its collection of rare books, and of these by far the most interesting are its own publications. Even its catalogues are works of art, published in numbered editions, and sought by libraries and book-collectors. Early in its history it began the occasional publication of books which should meet the club standard—books in which emphasis should be laid upon the qualities that make a book valuable in the eyes of collectors. Of these, age could not, of course, be imparted, but in the matter of fine and curious bindings, of hand-made linen papers, of uncut or deckle edges, of wide margins and limited editions, the club could control its own publications. The matter of contents was, it must be confessed, a less important consideration. At first it was felt by the publishing committee that nothing but the finest products of the human mind should be selected for enshrinement in the beautiful volumes which the club should issue. The length of the work was an important consideration—long things were not compatible with wide margins and graceful slenderness. For instance, we brought out Coleridge's Ancient Mariner, an essay by Emerson, and another by Thoreau. Our Rubáiyát of Omar Khayyám was Heron-Allen's translation of the original ms. in the Bodleian Library at Oxford, which, though less poetical than FitzGerald's, was not so common. Several years ago we began to publish the works of our own members. Bascom's Essay on Pipes was a very creditable performance. It was published in a limited edition of one hundred copies, and since it had not previously appeared elsewhere and was copyrighted by the club, it was sufficiently rare to be valuable for that reason. The second publication of local origin was Baxter's Procrustes.

I have omitted to say that once or twice a year, at a meeting of which notice has been given, an auction is held at the Bodleian. The members of the club send in their duplicate copies, or books they for any reason wish to dispose of, which are auctioned off to the highest bidder. At these sales, which are well attended, the club's publications have of recent years formed the leading feature. Three years ago, number three of Bascom's Essay on Pipes sold for fifteen dollars—the original cost of publication was one dollar and seventy-five cents. Later in the evening an uncut copy of the same brought thirty dollars. At the next auction the price of the cut copy was run up to twenty-five dollars, while the uncut copy was knocked down at seventy-five dollars. The club had always appreciated the value of uncut copies, but this financial indorsement enhanced their desirability immensely. This rise in the Essay on Pipes was not without a sympathetic effect upon all the club publications. The Emerson essay rose from three dollars to seventeen, and the Thoreau, being by an author less widely read, and by his own confession commercially unsuccessful, brought a somewhat higher figure. The prices, thus inflated, were not permitted to come down appreciably. Since every member of the club possessed one or more of these valuable editions, they were all manifestly interested in keeping up the price. The publication, however, which brought the highest prices, and, but for the sober second thought, might have wrecked the whole system, was Baxter's Procrustes.

Baxter was, perhaps, the most scholarly member of the club. A graduate of Harvard, he had traveled extensively, had read widely, and while not so enthusiastic a collector as some of us, possessed as fine a private library as any man of his age in the city. He was about thirty-five when he joined the club, and apparently some bitter experience—some disappointment in love or ambition—had left its mark upon his character. With light, curly hair, fair complexion, and gray eyes, one would have expected Baxter to be genial of temper, with a tendency toward wordiness of speech. But though he had occasional flashes of humor, his ordinary demeanor was characterized by a mild cynicism, which, with his gloomy pessimistic philosophy, so foreign to the temperament that should accompany his physical type, could only be accounted for upon the hypothesis of some secret sorrow such as I have suggested. What it might be no one knew. He had means and social position, and was an uncommonly handsome man. The fact that he remained unmarried at thirty-five furnished some support for the theory of a disappointment in love, though this the several intimates of Baxter who belonged to the club were not able to verify.

It had occurred to me, in a vague way, that perhaps Baxter might be an unsuccessful author. That he was a poet we knew very well, and typewritten copies of his verses had occasionally circulated among us. But Baxter had always expressed such a profound contempt for modern literature, had always spoken in terms of such unmeasured pity for the slaves of the pen, who were dependent upon the whim of an undiscriminating public for recognition and a livelihood, that no one of us had ever suspected him of aspirations toward publication, until, as I have said, it occurred to me one day that Baxter's attitude with regard to publication might be viewed in the light of effect as well as of cause—that his scorn of publicity might as easily arise from failure to achieve it, as his never having published might be due to his preconceived disdain of the vulgar popularity which one must share with the pugilist or balloonist of the hour.

The notion of publishing Baxter's Procrustes did not emanate from Baxter—I must do him the justice to say this. But he had spoken to several of the fellows about the theme of his poem, until the notion that Baxter was at work upon something fine had become pretty well disseminated throughout our membership. He would occasionally read brief passages to a small coterie of friends in the sitting-room or library—never more than ten lines at once, or to more than five people at a time—and these excerpts gave at least a few of us a pretty fair idea of the motive and scope of the poem. As I, for one, gathered, it was quite along the line of Baxter's philosophy. Society was the Procrustes which, like the Greek bandit of old, caught every man born into the world, and endeavored to fit him to some preconceived standard, generally to the one for which he was least adapted. The world was full of men and women who were merely square pegs in round holes, and vice versa. Most marriages were unhappy because the contracting parties were not properly mated. Religion was mostly superstition, science for the most part sciolism, popular education merely a means of forcing the stupid and repressing the bright, so that all the youth of the rising generation might conform to the same dull, dead level of democratic mediocrity. Life would soon become so monotonously uniform and so uniformly monotonous as to be scarce worth the living.

It was Smith, I think, who first proposed that the club publish Baxter's Procrustes. The poet himself did not seem enthusiastic when the subject was broached; he demurred for some little time, protesting that the poem was not worthy of publication. But when it was proposed that the edition be limited to fifty copies he agreed to consider the proposition. When I suggested, having in mind my secret theory of Baxter's failure in authorship, that the edition would at least be in the hands of friends, that it would be difficult for a hostile critic to secure a copy, and that if it should not achieve success from a literary point of view, the extent of the failure would be limited to the size of the edition, Baxter was visibly impressed. When the literary committee at length decided to request formally of Baxter the privilege of publishing his Procrustes, he consented, with evident reluctance, upon condition that he should supervise the printing, binding, and delivery of the books, merely submitting to the committee, in advance, the manuscript, and taking their views in regard to the bookmaking.

The manuscript was duly presented to the literary committee. Baxter having expressed the desire that the poem be not read aloud at a meeting of the club, as was the custom, since he wished it to be given to the world clad in suitable garb, the committee went even farther. Having entire confidence in Baxter's taste and scholarship, they, with great delicacy, refrained from even reading the manuscript, contenting themselves with Baxter's statement of the general theme and the topics grouped under it. The details of the bookmaking, however, were gone into thoroughly. The paper was to be of hand-made linen, from the Kelmscott Mills; the type black-letter, with rubricated initials. The cover, which was Baxter's own selection, was to be of dark green morocco, with a cap-and-bells border in red inlays, and doublures of maroon morocco with a blind-tooled design. Baxter was authorized to contract with the printer and superintend the publication. The whole edition of fifty numbered copies was to be disposed of at auction, in advance, to the highest bidder, only one copy to each, the proceeds to be devoted to paying for the printing and binding, the remainder, if any, to go into the club treasury, and Baxter himself to receive one copy by way of remuneration. Baxter was inclined to protest at this, on the ground that his copy would probably be worth more than the royalties on the edition, at the usual ten per cent, would amount to, but was finally prevailed upon to accept an author's copy.

While the Procrustes was under consideration, some one read, at one of our meetings, a note from some magazine, which stated that a sealed copy of a new translation of Campanella's Sonnets, published by the Grolier Club, had been sold for three hundred dollars. This impressed the members greatly. It was a novel idea. A new work might thus be enshrined in a sort of holy of holies, which, if the collector so desired, could be forever sacred from the profanation of any vulgar or unappreciative eye. The possessor of such a treasure could enjoy it by the eye of imagination, having at the same time the exaltation of grasping what was for others the unattainable. The literary committee were so impressed with this idea that they presented it to Baxter in regard to the Procrustes. Baxter making no objection, the subscribers who might wish their copies delivered sealed were directed to notify the author. I sent in my name. A fine book, after all, was an investment, and if there was any way of enhancing its rarity, and therefore its value, I was quite willing to enjoy such an advantage.

When the Procrustes was ready for distribution, each subscriber received his copy by mail, in a neat pasteboard box. Each number was wrapped in a thin and transparent but very strong paper, through which the cover design and tooling were clearly visible. The number of the copy was indorsed upon the wrapper, the folds of which were securely fastened at each end with sealing-wax, upon which was impressed, as a guaranty of its inviolateness, the monogram of the club.

At the next meeting of the Bodleian a great deal was said about the Procrustes, and it was unanimously agreed that no finer specimen of bookmaking had ever been published by the club. By a curious coincidence, no one had brought his copy with him, and the two club copies had not yet been received from the binder, who, Baxter had reported, was retaining them for some extra fine work. Upon resolution, offered by a member who had not subscribed for the volume, a committee of three was appointed to review the Procrustes at the next literary meeting of the club. Of this committee it was my doubtful fortune to constitute one.

In pursuance of my duty in the premises, it of course became necessary for me to read the Procrustes. In all probability I should have cut my own copy for this purpose, had not one of the club auctions intervened between my appointment and the date set for the discussion of the Procrustes. At this meeting a copy of the book, still sealed, was offered for sale, and bought by a non-subscriber for the unprecedented price of one hundred and fifty dollars. After this a proper regard for my own interests would not permit me to spoil my copy by opening it, and I was therefore compelled to procure my information concerning the poem from some other source. As I had no desire to appear mercenary, I said nothing about my own copy, and made no attempt to borrow. I did, however, casually remark to Baxter that I should like to look at his copy of the proof sheets, since I wished to make some extended quotations for my review, and would rather not trust my copy to a typist for that purpose. Baxter assured me, with every evidence of regret, that he had considered them of so little importance that he had thrown them into the fire. This indifference of Baxter to literary values struck me as just a little overdone. The proof sheets of Hamlet, corrected in Shakespeare's own hand, would be well-nigh priceless.

At the next meeting of the club I observed that Thompson and Davis, who were with me on the reviewing committee, very soon brought up the question of the Procrustes in conversation in the smoking-room, and seemed anxious to get from the members their views concerning Baxter's production, I supposed upon the theory that the appreciation of any book review would depend more or less upon the degree to which it reflected the opinion of those to whom the review should be presented. I presumed, of course, that Thompson and Davis had each read the book—they were among the subscribers—and I was desirous of getting their point of view.

"What do you think," I inquired, "of the passage on Social Systems?" I have forgotten to say that the poem was in blank verse, and divided into parts, each with an appropriate title.

"Well," replied Davis, it seemed to me a little cautiously, "it is not exactly Spencerian, although it squints at the Spencerian view, with a slight deflection toward Hegelianism. I should consider it an harmonious fusion of the best views of all the modern philosophers, with a strong Baxterian flavor."

"Yes," said Thompson, "the charm of the chapter lies in this very quality. The style is an emanation from Baxter's own intellect—he has written himself into the poem. By knowing Baxter we are able to appreciate the book, and after having read the book we feel that we are so much the more intimately acquainted with Baxter—the real Baxter."

Baxter had come in during this colloquy, and was standing by the fireplace smoking a pipe. I was not exactly sure whether the faint smile which marked his face was a token of pleasure or cynicism; it was Baxterian, however, and I had already learned that Baxter's opinions upon any subject were not to be gathered always from his facial expression. For instance, when the club porter's crippled child died Baxter remarked, it seemed to me unfeelingly, that the poor little devil was doubtless better off, and that the porter himself had certainly been relieved of a burden; and only a week later the porter told me in confidence that Baxter had paid for an expensive operation, undertaken in the hope of prolonging the child's life. I therefore drew no conclusions from Baxter's somewhat enigmatical smile. He left the room at this point in the conversation, somewhat to my relief.

"By the way, Jones," said Davis, addressing me, "are you impressed by Baxter's views on Degeneration?"

Having often heard Baxter express himself upon the general downward tendency of modern civilization, I felt safe in discussing his views in a broad and general manner.

"I think," I replied, "that they are in harmony with those of Schopenhauer, without his bitterness; with those of Nordau, without his flippancy. His materialism is Haeckel's, presented with something of the charm of Omar Khayyám."

"Yes," chimed in Davis, "it answers the strenuous demand of our day—dissatisfaction with an unjustified optimism—and voices for us the courage of human philosophy facing the unknown."

I had a vague recollection of having read something like this somewhere, but so much has been written, that one can scarcely discuss any subject of importance without unconsciously borrowing, now and then, the thoughts or the language of others. Quotation, like imitation, is a superior grade of flattery.

"The Procrustes," said Thompson, to whom the metrical review had been apportioned, "is couched in sonorous lines, of haunting melody and charm; and yet so closely inter-related as to be scarcely quotable with justice to the author. To be appreciated the poem should be read as a whole— I shall say as much in my review. What shall you say of the letter-press?"

he concluded, addressing me. I was supposed to discuss the technical excellence of the volume from the connoisseur's viewpoint.

"The setting," I replied judicially, "is worthy of the gem. The dark
green cover, elaborately tooled, the old English lettering, the heavy linen
paper, mark this as one of our very choicest publications. The letter-press
is of course De Vinne's best—there is nothing better on this side of the
Atlantic. The text is a beautiful, slender stream, meandering gracefully
through a wide meadow of margin."

For some reason I left the room for a minute. As I stepped into the
hall, I almost ran into Baxter, who was standing near the door, facing a
hunting print of a somewhat humorous character, hung upon the wall, and
smiling with an immensely pleased expression.

"What a ridiculous scene!" he remarked. "Look at that fat old squire
on that tall hunter! I 'll wager dollars to doughnuts that he won't get over
the first fence!"

It was a very good bluff, but did not deceive me. Under his mask of
unconcern, Baxter was anxious to learn what we thought of his poem, and
had stationed himself in the hall that he might overhear our discussion
without embarrassing us by his presence. He had covered up his delight at
our appreciation by this simulated interest in the hunting print.

When the night came for the review of the Procrustes there was a large
attendance of members, and several visitors, among them a young English
cousin of one of the members, on his first visit to the United States; some
of us had met him at other clubs, and in society, and had found him a very
jolly boy, with a youthful exuberance of spirits and a naïve ignorance of
things American, that made his views refreshing and, at times, amusing.

The critical essays were well considered, if a trifle vague. Baxter received credit for poetic skill of a high order.

"Our brother Baxter," said Thompson, "should no longer bury his
talent in a napkin. This gem, of course, belongs to the club, but the same
brain from which issued this exquisite emanation can produce others to
inspire and charm an appreciative world."

"The author's view of life," said Davis, "as expressed in these beautiful lines, will help us to fit our shoulders for the heavy burden of life, by
bringing to our realization those profound truths of philosophy which find
hope in despair and pleasure in pain. When he shall see fit to give to the
wider world, in fuller form, the thoughts of which we have been vouch-
safed this foretaste, let us hope that some little ray of his fame may rest
upon the Bodleian, from which can never be taken away the proud privilege of saying that he was one of its members."

I then pointed out the beauties of the volume as a piece of bookmaking. I knew, from conversation with the publication committee, the style of type and rubrication, and could see the cover through the wrapper of my sealed copy. The dark green morocco, I said, in summing up, typified the author's serious view of life, as a thing to be endured as patiently as might be. The cap-and-bells border was significant of the shams by which the optimist sought to delude himself into the view that life was a desirable thing. The intricate blind-tooling of the doublure shadowed forth the blind fate which left us in ignorance of our future and our past, or of even what the day itself might bring forth. The black-letter type, with rubricated initials, signified a philosophic pessimism enlightened by the conviction that in duty one might find, after all, an excuse for life and a hope for humanity. Applying this test to the club, this work, which might be said to represent all that the Bodleian stood for, was in itself sufficient to justify the club's existence. If the Bodleian had done nothing else, if it should do nothing more, it had produced a masterpiece.

There was a sealed copy of the Procrustes, belonging, I believe, to one of the committee, lying on the table by which I stood, and I had picked it up and held it in my hand for a moment, to emphasize one of my periods, but had laid it down immediately. I noted, as I sat down, that young Hunkin, our English visitor, who sat on the other side of the table, had picked up the volume and was examining it with interest. When the last review was read, and the generous applause had subsided, there were cries for Baxter.

"Baxter! Baxter! Author! Author!"

Baxter had been sitting over in a corner during the reading of the reviews, and had succeeded remarkably well, it seemed to me, in concealing, under his mask of cynical indifference, the exultation which I was sure he must feel. But this outburst of enthusiasm was too much even for Baxter, and it was clear that he was struggling with strong emotion when he rose to speak.

"Gentlemen, and fellow members of the Bodleian, it gives me unaffected pleasure—sincere pleasure—some day you may know how much pleasure—I cannot trust myself to say it now—to see the evident care with which your committee have read my poor verses, and the responsive sympathy with which my friends have entered into my views of life and conduct. I thank you again, and again, and when I say that I am too full for utterance—I 'm sure you will excuse me from saying any more."

Baxter took his seat, and the applause had begun again when it was broken by a sudden exclamation.

"By Jove!" exclaimed our English visitor, who still sat behind the table, "what an extraordinary book!"

Every one gathered around him.

"You see," he exclaimed, holding up the volume, "you fellows said so much about the bally book that I wanted to see what it was like; so I untied the ribbon, and cut the leaves with the paper knife lying here, and found—and found that there was n't a single line in it, don't you know!"

Blank consternation followed this announcement, which proved only too true. Every one knew instinctively, without further investigation, that the club had been badly sold. In the resulting confusion Baxter escaped, but later was waited upon by a committee, to whom he made the rather lame excuse that he had always regarded uncut and sealed books as tommy-rot, and that he had merely been curious to see how far the thing could go; and that the result had justified his belief that a book with nothing in it was just as useful to a book-collector as one embodying a work of genius. He offered to pay all the bills for the sham Procrustes, or to replace the blank copies with the real thing, as we might choose. Of course, after such an insult, the club did not care for the poem. He was permitted to pay the expense, however, and it was more than hinted to him that his resignation from the club would be favorably acted upon. He never sent it in, and, as he went to Europe shortly afterwards, the affair had time to blow over.

In our first disgust at Baxter's duplicity, most of us cut our copies of the Procrustes, some of us mailed them to Baxter with cutting notes, and others threw them into the fire. A few wiser spirits held on to theirs, and this fact leaking out, it began to dawn upon the minds of the real collectors among us that the volume was something unique in the way of a publication.

"Baxter," said our president one evening to a select few of us who sat around the fireplace, "was wiser than we knew, or than he perhaps appreciated. His Procrustes, from the collector's point of view, is entirely logical, and might be considered as the acme of bookmaking. To the true collector, a book is a work of art, of which the contents are no more important than the words of an opera. Fine binding is a desideratum, and, for its cost, that of the Procrustes could not be improved upon. The paper is above criticism. The true collector loves wide margins, and the Procrustes, being all margin, merely touches the vanishing point of the perspective. The smaller the edition, the greater the collector's eagerness to acquire a copy. There are but six uncut copies left, I am told, of the Procrustes, and three sealed copies, of one of which I am the fortunate possessor."

After this deliverance, it is not surprising that, at our next auction, a sealed copy of Baxter's Procrustes was knocked down, after spirited bidding, for two hundred and fifty dollars, the highest price ever brought by a single volume published by the club.

PART THREE

Selected Critical Perspectives

MR. CHESNUTT AT WORK: A TALK
WITH AN AUTHOR ON HIS METHODS

Max Bennett Thrasher

I recently met Mr. Charles W. Chesnutt, the well-known writer of Southern stories, in Alabama, and enjoyed the opportunity which I had there to learn something of his methods of work.

Mr. Chesnutt told me, when I asked him about his literary work, that his stories, as a general thing, develop gradually in his mind, sometimes taking a long time in the process, and that even then they are usually written out slowly. "'The March of Progress,' which was printed in the Century, was an exception to this, though," Mr. Chesnutt said. "I wrote the whole of that out one forenoon, copied it on the typewriter in the afternoon, and sent it off that same evening.

"Sometimes I write a story out complete, as I think at the time, and yet, after it is completed I have a feeling that it lacks something. Perhaps the story may lie around for months before I am able to tell just what there is about it that does not satisfy me. It was that way with 'The Wife of His Youth,' probably the most widely read story I have written—my best story, some people say. I wrote that story, complete, as I thought, and then it lay in my desk for a year because I was not satisfied with it. As the story was written then I made the little old black wife appear to her prosperous and cultured husband as he was getting ready to entertain a company of guests, before whom he eventually acknowledged her.

"There was something lacking in the story, though, and I knew it. One evening after dinner, when the manuscript was more than a year old, I picked it up and read it through, and at once there came to me a knowledge of what was wanting. The story lacked the element of conflicting interest. I saw that there ought to be another woman in it, by contrast with whom the little old black wife should be made more striking. I wrote the story over, and wrote into it the second woman—the young, educated, attractive woman whom the man was to have married if 'the wife of his youth' had not returned. Then the story was complete.

"I have been greatly interested," Mr. Chesnutt continued, "to see how women feel about the way in which I made that story end—whether they think that the man ought to have acknowledged the unattractive old

Boston Evening Transcript, September 4, 1901.

woman to whom he was bound by ties of sentiment and gratitude, rather than by legal bonds, or whether he did not owe it as a duty to himself to marry the other woman, the one who was a much more fitting mate for him, and who, with himself, was entitled to happiness. I have asked a good many women, cultivated, intelligent women, what they thought the man ought to have done—whether they thought he did right. The answer which I get almost invariably seems to depend on the age of the woman who gives it.

"Young women, those who are under twenty, reply promptly and enthusiastically, 'He did just right. He ought to have acknowledged the little old black wife whom he had loved years before, and who had loved and sought him through all those years.' Women between twenty and thirty stop to consider the question. They usually say, finally, in a deprecating sort of way, 'Ye-es, I think he did right. I suppose he ought to have married the woman he did.' When I ask the question of a woman over thirty, she does not take any more time for reflection than the very young woman did. She says promptly, 'He did not do right. He made a mistake. He ought to have married the other woman.'

"In all these cases I take it there is sympathy for both women in the story, but the woman under twenty, looking out upon life through the rose-colored glasses of youth, allows her sympathy for the older woman to predominate. She thinks the young woman in the story can afford to be generous, because she has life before her, and one chance to marry will not matter to her among the many she will have. The woman of twenty-five has had more experience with life. She has learned that chances to marry well are not frequent enough so that any ought to be passed over without careful consideration. The woman who is still older reasons that a good matrimonial opportunity should not be let slip for anything."

Mr. Chesnutt had been spending some time in the Southern States, getting impressions and collecting material which will doubtless find expression in future writings. "I was surprised," Mr. Chesnutt said, "after an absence of many years from the South, to note the fidelity with which my mind had retained the impressions received in youth. The old 'conjure woman' and 'conjure man' whom I have made it a point to unearth in my travels bear a faithful resemblance to old 'Aunt Peggy, the conjure woman,' and the roots and herbs still have, in the minds of at least a few surviving relics of the past, their ancient potency. I interviewed a conjure doctor who furnished mc with 'a hand,' a charm of mysterious significance which he guarantees will bring me good luck, and which he assured me would keep me 'from losing my job.' I also secured a genuine rabbit's foot, from a rabbit killed in a graveyard on a dark night. This is the 'real thing,' and not the spurious imitation which is marketed in Northern cities."

Mr. Chesnutt visited the neighborhood and the old house in which the scene of his recently published novel, "The House Behind the Cedars," was laid. He says that the house has fallen somewhat into disrepair, and of the cedar hedge which once surrounded it only one tree remains. He secured a photograph of the house, and brought away with him as a souvenir a twig from the sole surviving cedar.

Mr. Chesnutt says that he was deeply interested in the study of racial conditions during his Southern sojourn, and while he saw much to depress, he also found here and there, and especially in the educational work at Tuskegee and elsewhere, good grounds for hope that some time, in some way, a just and rational solution may be found for the many and vexed problems which have grown out of slavery and the contact of the two races which make up in so nearly equal numbers the population of the South.

I asked Mr. Chesnutt, one day, if it was because he had a vein of superstition in his nature that he wrote such weird stories. "No, indeed," he said. "I have not a bit of superstition. Sometimes I think that I have not even a proper amount of reverence. My first literary ventures were along the lines of short stories for newspaper syndicates, and squibs for Puck and such papers as that. I wrote about Southern themes because at that time I was comparatively fresh from the South, and was more familiar with things there than at the North. I soon found that there was a greater demand and a better market for writings along that line.

"I remembered a remarkable yarn which had been related to me by my father-in-law's gardener, old Uncle Henry, to the effect that the sap of a pruned grapevine rubbed on a bald head in the spring would produce a luxuriant growth of hair, which would, however, fall out when the sap in the vine went down in the fall. To the creative mind this was sufficient material for the story, 'The Goophered Grapevine.' That story resulted in several others involving the same idea, for instance, that of the man who was turned into a tree and by mistake chopped down, sawed into lumber and built into a house, which was ever afterwards haunted by the spirit of the unfortunate man. Those dialect stories, while written primarily to amuse, have each of them a moral, which, while not forced upon the reader, is none the less apparent to those who read thoughtfully. For instance, the story of the cruel master, who, through the arts of the conjure woman, was transformed into a slave and given for several weeks a dose of his own medicine, resulting in his reformation when he is restored to his normal condition of life, teaches its own story."

Mr. Chesnutt is an attorney by profession, and has been connected with the Ohio bar and the courts of the State for fifteen years. He lives at Cleveland. He has two daughters who graduated from Smith College last June, and two younger children. He spent ten years of his youth and early manhood as a teacher in North Carolina, and his daughters have fitted themselves for the work of teaching. Mr. Chesnutt's works have a deserved popularity, it seems to me, from the strength and delicacy with which they treat certain phases of the race question which are often avoided or neglected by other writers from lack of knowledge or want of courage. He writes frankly, and at the same time in a manner which commands attention and respect. He represents a new field in fiction. From his special knowledge, sympathy, and personal interest in his subjects, he is perhaps better qualified to discuss them than any other writer now before the American public.

THE ART OF *THE CONJURE WOMAN*

Richard E. Baldwin

In *The Conjure Woman* Charles Chesnutt analyzes with balance and subtlety the paradoxes and tensions of American racial life. The penetrating insights of these stories he never matched in his realistic fiction. Here Chesnutt avoids stifling stereotypes while criticizing the myths of white supremacy and demonstrating the range and quality of black experience. Other early black writers sought to do the same, but not until *Uncle Tom's Children* did any succeed as fully as did Chesnutt, for in *The Conjure Woman* he developed and exploited a finely balanced technique which solved the major artistic problems faced by early black writers.

The central problem was the audience. The reading public was predominantly white, and the audience that most early black writers cared most to reach was white, for it was to whites that they needed to tell the truth about the black experience in America. The need and the difficulty were one, for the problem of the black in America arose from the refusal of whites to perceive black experience accurately, and the artist's task was not simply to present the truth to white minds but to change those minds so that they could perceive the humanity of the black and the inhumanities which he suffered in America. The sentiments of white Americans could easily enough be touched, but the important and difficult task was changing their perceptions. Whites had to be trained to perceive black experience from the black point of view, for until the white man was so

American Literature, November 1971.

changed no serious black literature could receive a hearing because it would not be understood. The situation held dangers for the artist, since the task of reeducating America could not be completed quickly and the pressure of circumstances easily led writers to hasten the process by recourse to the melodramatic moral simplicity of propaganda.

Chesnutt began his career with a clear understanding of the problem and of the necessary response of the artist. In 1880, before he began writing fiction, he noted in his journal that "if I do write, I shall write for a purpose, a high, holy purpose. . . . The object of my writings would be not so much the elevation of the colored people as the elevation of the whites." A little later in the same entry, in an observation basic to the strategy of *The Conjure Woman,* he noted that in the struggle of the Negro to win "recognition and equality" it was "the province of literature to open the way for him to get it—to accustom the public mind to the idea [of Negro equality]; to lead people out, imperceptibly, unconsciously, step by step, to the desired state of feeling"[1] toward Negroes.

Chesnutt aimed to modify white minds to feel the equality of the black man, and with the conjure tales he developed a perfect vehicle for his artistic needs. Chesnutt's genius shows in the certainty of touch involved in the choice of Uncle Julius as his central character. Choosing a character so close to widely current pejorative stereotypes was a stroke as significant as Wright's choice of Bigger Thomas, for only by confronting and thus destroying the stereotypes could the black artist hope to alter the public mind. Further, Uncle Julius resolves for Chesnutt the black artist's problem of creating a black character in a situation in which significant dramatic incident is possible. To demonstrate the equality of blacks and whites, a black character must be presented in dramatic conflict with whites in a situation which allows the black not only to survive but to succeed with dignity. The difficulty of imagining such situations was clearly formulated by William Couch, Jr., in an essay on "The Problem of Negro Character and Dramatic Incident": "Serious dramatic situation necessitates consequential action committed by a protagonist with whom we can sympathize and admire. The assumptions of American culture, on the other hand, are not congenial to emphatic and uncompromising action on the part of a Negro. This is especially true when white interests are involved. Therefore, a dramatic situation, capable of producing a powerful effect, will usually suffer a distortion of that effect when the agent of action is a Negro character."[2]

---

[1] Helen Chesnutt, *Charles Waddell Chesnutt: Pioneer of the Color Line* (Chapel Hill, N.C., 1954), p. 21. [Baldwin's note.]

[2] *Phylon,* XI (Second Quar., 1950), p. 128. [Baldwin's note.]

In the face of this dilemma black artists have frequently relied on a conflict of virtuous blacks against vicious whites, thus accentuating the dilemma rather than resolving it.

Chesnutt's conjure stories, on the other hand, resolve this basic problem. The tales which Uncle Julius tells stand in the tradition of subterfuge, indirection, and subtle manipulation of whites developed by the slaves as a strategy for surviving in the face of oppression. Chesnutt's conjure stories turn the strategy of "puttin' on ol' massa" into effective dramatic action through parallels and tensions between the frames established by the white narrator and the tales told by Uncle Julius. In "The Goophered Grapevine," Chesnutt's first conjure story, Julius's attempt to use the tale of the goophered grapevine to place a new "goopher" on the vineyard in order to keep the white man from depriving him of his livelihood provides the most obvious parallel between frame and tale. Julius emerges from this dramatic conflict with a qualified success, for while he loses the vineyard he gains a more stable livelihood in the white man's employment.

The limitations of his success are illuminated by another parallel between frame and tale, however. An important part of the tale centers on the experiences of Henry, a slave of Dugald McAdoo, antebellum owner of the vineyard. McAdoo purchased Henry after the success of the fatal conjure Aunt Peggy had placed on his vineyards had so increased his crop that he needed more help. Henry ate some of the grapes before he could be warned of the conjure, and his life was saved by an antidote which involved his anointing himself with sap from one of the vines. From that time on Henry's life followed the rhythms of the growing season; he became strong and supple in the spring and summer, then withered up during the winter months. McAdoo made a great deal of money exploiting Henry by selling him when he was strong and buying him back cheap when he weakened in the fall. During the winter months McAdoo coddled Henry to protect the valuable chattel. Although Henry enjoyed this comfortable life, he was more than ever at McAdoo's mercy, for his life depended on the life of the vineyards. When McAdoo's greed led him to follow foolish advice which killed the vines, Henry paid with his life for his master's folly.

Henry was about Uncle Julius's age when McAdoo purchased him, and the narrator's hiring of Julius ominously parallels that transaction. Julius had been a free entrepreneur, and although his new job may pay more than the vineyard could yield to him, it represents a new form of slavery in which Julius loses a significant measure of his freedom in return for security; Julius's love of grapes, like Henry's, places him in the power of the white man. Yet this judgment must in turn be qualified by the implied parallel between the narrator and McAdoo, for it is obvious that the narrator is in some ways a wiser man than his slave-owning predecessor, a fact which mutes the threatening potential of his hiring of Julius while the mutual service of each to the other emphasizes the ways in which the story demonstrates the inescapable connections between the lives of black and white, a central theme in much of Chesnutt's work.

"The Goophered Grapevine" gains additional richness through the complicated nature of Julius's motivation. While he wants very much to preserve his vineyard, he simultaneously wants to strike out at the racial superiority assumed by the narrator. The tale which he tells consistently presents white men bested by blacks or acting in ways whose folly is clearly perceived by the blacks. Both in the broad outline of his tale of the goophered grapevine and in numerous minor points, such as the inability of the best white doctors to cure the goopher that Aunt Peggy has placed on Henry, Uncle Julius asserts the humanity of the black and his equality with, or superiority to, whites. Julius thus has the pleasure of effectively calling the white man a fool to his face, yet he fails to make any impression because the narrator is too blinded by racism to be able to perceive what Julius is up to. Ironically, that failure, while it underscores the truth in Julius's point, is vital to his success at preserving his livelihood, since the narrator would not likely have hired Julius had he perceived the insults. The concluding frame thus generates multiple ironies which illuminate the complex tension between the black's need to deny and attack white supremacy and the hard fact that while whites are not superior beings they nevertheless have very real power.

Chesnutt's success in dealing with this tension in *The Conjure Woman* depends not only on the complex motivation of Uncle Julius but also on the two white characters of the frame, the Northern narrator and his wife Annie. The two white people are crucial to Chesnutt's rhetorical strategy for leading white America "imperceptibly, unconsciously, step by step, to the desired state of feeling" toward blacks. The narrator, a basically decent sort of man, takes a typical paternalistic attitude towards Uncle Julius and his tales. He accepts Julius's attempts at manipulating him yet remains blinded by his own sense of superiority. His understanding of black life has been molded more by Uncle Remus and the plantation school than by Uncle Julius. As Julius begins the tale of the goophered grapevine, for instance, the narrator observes that "As he became more and more absorbed in the narrative, his eyes assumed a dreamy expression, and he seemed to lose sight of his auditors, and to be living over again in monologue his life on the old plantation."[3] This evocation of the plantation tradition reveals the

---

[3] Charles W. Chesnutt, *The Conjure Woman* (Ann Arbor, Mich., 1969), pp. 12–13 [page 121 of this volume]. Subsequent references to this work will appear in the text.

narrator's blindness to Julius's revelations about slavery, for life on the McAdoo plantation had nothing of the dreamy quality of the idyls of Harris. The statement becomes richly ironic when the conclusion shows that Uncle Julius has had his eyes very much on his auditors and the demands of the present moment. It is the narrator whose eyes are closed, and in an adumbration of the Invisible Man motif he is "beaten" by a man he never sees.

The narrator's posture has immense rhetorical value for Chesnutt, for it enables him to present his stories with detachment from the point of view of any of his characters. The framing narrative voice is that of a typical white American liberal, an unconscious racist who seems free of bigotry. In his reactions to Julius's tale the narrator is not so dull as to miss all that the black is up to, yet he misses enough that he can report the tale of slavery with no sense of the range of its meaning, especially those portions directed against him. The narrator thus appears as a mixture of sensitivity and callousness, and he can be treated sympathetically while his blindness to Uncle Julius's character and to the implications of his tales provides ironic commentary on his own character and on America's racial absurdities.

Chesnutt's technique relies heavily on irony, and like any ironic technique it runs the risk that readers will miss the point. Annie, the narrator's wife, is developed as a contrasting character in order to reduce this danger. Her permanent convalescent state underscores the feminine sensibility which leads her to respond more deeply to Uncle Julius than does her husband. When Julius announces that the vineyard is goophered, for instance, the narrator observes that "He imparted this information with such solemn earnestness, and with such an air of confidential mystery, that I felt somewhat interested, while Annie was evidently much impressed, and drew closer to me" (pp. 11–12 [p. 121]). The narrator's attitude toward his wife frequently is as condescending as his attitude toward Julius, and after the tale is finished he notes that she "doubtfully, but seriously" asked, "'Is that story true?'" (p. 33 [p. 127]). His own reaction to the tale appears only in his assertion that he bought the vineyard in spite of the purported goopher. Annie's question, however, allows Chesnutt to imply the presence of metaphoric meanings through the absurd literalness of Uncle Julius's response that he can prove its truth by showing her Henry's grave. At such levels the tale obviously is not true, but the nature of the question and answer implies that other levels of meaning can be discovered by any who care to look for them.

[Baldwin's note. Baldwin's parenthetical references to *The Conjure Woman* will be immediately followed by bracketed references to the present volume.]

Chesnutt seems not to have fully grasped the value of his white characters when he first wrote "The Goophered Grapevine," for his second
conjure story openly exploits the contrast, and when he prepared the first
story for book publication he added to the opening frame several long sections which develop the narrator more fully. The opening frame of the second story, "Po' Sandy," points out the difference between the narrator and
Annie. When she rises eagerly to Julius's hint of a story, her husband comments that "some of these stories are quaintly humorous; others wildly extravagant, revealing the Oriental cast of the negro's imagination; while
others, poured freely into the sympathetic ear of a Northern-bred woman,
disclose many a tragic incident of the darker side of slavery" (pp. 40–41
[pp. 129–30]). While the narrator has sufficient curiosity to listen to the
tales with pleasure he has no patience for discovering meanings in them;
rather than revelations about American life he sees only an "Oriental cast
of the negro's imagination." Annie, on the other hand, instinctively leaps to
at least some meanings. The resulting contrast helps Chesnutt bring a white
audience to perceive events from the black point of view, for while the narrator reacts with a typical white obtuseness, Annie, by seeing through the
surface of fantastic and supernatural machinery, points the reader to the
vital human life behind.

Chesnutt uses this contrast most effectively in "Po' Sandy." Uncle
Julius's tale tells of Sandy, a young slave devoted to his wife Tenie, a conjure woman. Mars Marrabo continually sends Sandy, an exceptionally
good worker, to help out relatives on distant plantations, and when Sandy
tires of this Tenie turns him into a tree to keep him near her. When Sandy
disappears, the dogs track him to the tree, where they lose the trail. After
the excitement of his disappearance passes, Tenie nightly returns Sandy to
human form. But then Marrabo sends Tenie to nurse his daughter-in-law,
and during her absence Sandy is cut down, and Tenie returns just in time
to watch her husband sawn into lumber to build a new kitchen on the
plantation. The kitchen remains haunted by Sandy's ghost, so it is eventually torn down and the lumber used to build a schoolhouse. The narrator
now plans to tear down the school and use the lumber to build Annie a
new kitchen.

After Julius finishes his tale, the following exchange between Annie
and the narrator occurs:

> "What a system it was," she exclaimed, when Julius had finished, "under
> which such things were possible!"
> "What things?" I asked, in amazement. "Are you seriously consider-
> ing the possibility of a man's being turned into a tree?"

"Oh, no," she replied quickly, "not that"; and then she murmured absently, and with a dim look in her fine eyes, "Poor Tenie!" (pp. 60–61 [p. 135])

The narrator as usual sees nothing but the surface of the tale, but with his insensitivity as a contrast Chesnutt needs no more than Annie's murmured "Poor Tenie" to alert us to the story of the pain caused by the inhuman violations of personal life and the brutalities endured by slaves. The narrator believes in the beauty of the Old South and the quaintness of Negro folktales, but through Annie we see the horrors of slavery.

Had Annie's role ended with "Poor Tenie!" the story would have verged on the sentimentality which so quickly destroys the effect of tales of pathos. But the sentimentality of the "dim look in her fine eyes" and the quiet murmur are the narrator's, not Chesnutt's. Annie has a sentimental streak, but Chesnutt nevertheless uses her to help effect a most unsentimental change of tone from the pathos and horror of the tale to the grotesquely incongruous, anticlimactic humor of the concluding frame. Through Annie's agency Chesnutt modulates the story from the grim brutalities of a man sawn into lumber to end on a note of gentle, ironic humor.

The humor of the conclusion is vital to the overall effect of the story, avoiding sentimentality and creating an impact more tautly complex than pathos. The humor of the frame relieves the pain of the tale itself, emphasizing the similar effect created by the incongruity between the horror experienced by the characters of the tales and the improbability of the conjure elements. The final effect has the complexity described by Ralph Ellison as the blues, the transcendence of pain "not by the consolation of philosophy, but by squeezing from it a near-tragic, near-comic lyricism."[4] At their best, Chesnutt's conjure stories require a response which sustains that type of tension between the tragic and the comic. The tension is most striking in "Po' Sandy," yet Chesnutt's third conjure story, "The Conjurer's Revenge," exploits it in an equally effective and perhaps more sophisticated way. In "The Conjurer's Revenge" the narrator needs a draught animal, and Julius hopes it will not be a mule; he hates to drive a mule for fear it may be a human being, and thereby hangs a tale. The tale tells how Primus, a slave, stole a shote from a conjure man who revenged the theft by turning him into a mule. A large portion of the tale deals with Primus's escapades as a mule—eating tobacco in the field, guzzling a huge quantity of wine, attacking the man who had taken over his woman. When the con-

---

[4] Ralph Ellison, "Richard Wright's Blues," in *Shadow and Act* (New York, 1964), p. 90. [Baldwin's note.]

jure man neared death he got religion, and feeling guilty about Primus summoned him in order to return him to human form. He lived long enough to turn back all of Primus except for one foot, which remained clubbed. When Uncle Julius finishes the tale it appears that he knows a man with a horse to sell. Shortly after the narrator buys the horse Uncle Julius sports a flashy new suit, apparently purchased with his share of the money paid for the horse. Within three months, the animal dies of diseases brought on by old age, and while the entire affair makes fine comedy, the comedy has a harsh, vindictive quality unknown in the two earlier tales. The tale itself is a disconcerting mixture of the comic escapades of a man turned into a mule and the story of a slave who, to take the view of Primus's master, "'had runned erway, en stay' 'tel he got ti'ed er de swamps, en den come back on him ter be fed. He tried ter 'count fer de shape er Primus' foot by sayin' Primus got his foot smash', er snake-bit, er sump'n, w'iles he wuz erway, en den stayed out in de woods whar he couldn' git it kyoed up straight, 'stidder comin' long home whar a doctor could 'a' 'tended ter it'" (pp. 126–127 [p. 156]). Either way this tale lacks the compelling quality of the tale of Po' Sandy, and Annie's reaction to it is negative: "'That story does not appeal to me, Uncle Julius, and is not up to your usual mark. It isn't pathetic, it has no moral that I can discover, and I can't see why you should tell it. In fact, it seems to me like nonsense'" (p. 127 [p. 156]).

There is a moral, although not the sort that would dim Annie's fine eyes. The moral is enunciated by the narrator when, after discovering that the fine looking animal he bought is half blind and thoroughly broken down, he exclaims, "But alas for the deceitfulness of appearances" (p. 130 [p. 157]). The story underscores this point. Julius's tale is pointless by comparison with the earlier two, but his telling of the pointless tale was a deceitful appearance intentionally used to cover his own motives and set up the narrator for the sales pitch made at the end.

Chesnutt's concern reaches beyond the sales of horses and mules, though, and "The Conjurer's Revenge" provides a broad commentary on the American racial situation. The title suggests that Uncle Julius's intentional swindling of his employer amounts to revenge. As in the tale Primus felt the wrath of the conjure man because he stole a shote, so in Chesnutt's story the narrator is bilked because Julius has had a valuable possession stolen—the dignity, freedom, and equality which are the components of his humanity—and works a goopher on the white man in revenge. The story focuses on "the deceitfulness of appearances" which lies at the heart of race relations, and in part on the deceitfulness of appearances in Chesnutt's earlier two stories. The earlier stories had glossed the moral turpitude of race relations by implicitly justifying Uncle Julius's behavior—in "The Goophered Grapevine" on grounds of practical necessity, in "Po'

Sandy" on grounds of service to a communal group. "The Conjurer's Revenge" strips all romantic gloss from Southern life and presents the hard core of racial conflict, that mutual dehumanization which eliminates all moral compunctions from the black man's dealing with whites and which enables the white man to hide from himself the fact that the black man is a human being. If the white man becomes vulnerable to the deceitfulness of appearances, the appearances are his own creation, the self-delusions spawned by his denial of the black man's humanity. In this situation the black man quite naturally becomes a conjure man, using his wits to exploit and encourage the deceitful appearances which the white man has created. There is nothing moral or pathetic here, just a bald power struggle which is comically, tragically human, the deepest reality of American racial conflict.

II

Nearly ten years intervened between the publication of "The Conjurer's Revenge" and the appearance of *The Conjure Woman* in 1898 [sic]. None of the additional four stories appeared previously in periodicals; so the sequence in which they were written is unknown. Each of these later stories, while it follows the original frame-tale pattern, reveals Chesnutt reaching the limits of the form's usefulness. The later four stories lack the complex balance of the earlier three. In "Sis' Becky's Pickaninny," for instance, the tight relation between frame and tale is lacking. By itself the tale fails to develop significant dramatic action, and unlike the tale in "The Conjurer's Revenge" it is not an integral part of a larger conception. "Hot-Foot Hannibal," on the other hand, has a frame and a tale technically well matched. Here, however, Julius has no significant role in either tale or frame. The parallels between tale and frame thus remain mechanical, and Chesnutt's point seems to be simply to demonstrate by the parallel that blacks feel the same pains, joys, and sorrows as whites. "Hot-Foot Hannibal" comes closer than any other conjure tale to the special group pleading of the propagandist.
    The weakness of "Hot-Foot Hannibal" appears clearly when it is compared with "The Gray Wolf's Ha'nt." Nothing in *The Conjure Woman* surpasses Uncle Julius's tale of the gray wolf's ha'nt. This story of love, jealousy, and murder among the slaves achieves tragic stature and has no taint of propaganda. The tale is perfect in itself, but it is badly marred by being forced into a trite and irrelevant frame. The tale deals with conflict within the slave community and lacks the interracial conflict on which vital parallels between tale and frame depended in the three earlier stories.

The tale does not need a frame, and its strength indicates that the conjure story could have been developed into a vehicle for exploring black culture. Interracial conflict was essential to the vitality of the form as Chesnutt initially conceived it, however, and his willingness to place this magnificent story in an unsuitable frame suggests that he was uninterested in forms which did not deal with such conflict.

The remaining conjure story, "Mars Jeems's Nightmare," suggests in fact that Chesnutt had reached the limits of the form even as a vehicle for exploring racial conflict. "Mars Jeems's Nightmare," which focuses on racial conflict with the unrelenting rigor of "The Conjurer's Revenge," is the only one of the later stories that creates something like the balanced tone, the intellectual strength, and the imaginative integrity of the early stories. The frame drama centers around Uncle Julius's grandson Tom, formerly employed by the narrator but fired for laziness and carelessness; Julius's aim in telling this tale is to get his grandson rehired. The tale tells how a vicious master is turned into a Negro and delivered into the hands of his own sadistic poor-white overseer until he is beaten into sympathy for his slaves. Moved by this tale Annie effects the desired change (in the concluding frame) by taking the boy back. Her act angers the narrator, but he lets the boy stay. Implicit in his acquiescence are the effects on him of the story of Mars Jeems's being turned into a slave. At the end of the tale the narrator acknowledges that the changing of a white man into a Negro was "powerful goopher," an ironic admission of the power of the tale on him and Annie, for it has in effect put them through the experience of Mars Jeems and has acted as a "powerful goopher" on them.

More than any other story, "Mars Jeems's Nightmare" examines the psychology which gives Uncle Julius power over the narrator. At the beginning of the story Chesnutt has the narrator characterize Uncle Julius at length in a passage which reveals more about the narrator than about Uncle Julius:

> Toward my tract of land and the things that were on it—the creeks, the swamps, the hills, the meadows, the stones, the trees—he maintained a peculiar personal attitude, that might be called predial rather than proprietary. He had been accustomed, until long after middle life, to look upon himself as the property of another. When this relation was no longer possible, owing to the war, and to his master's death and the dispersion of the family, he had been unable to break off entirely the mental habits of a lifetime, but had attached himself to the old plantation, of which he seemed to consider himself an appurtenance. We found him useful in many ways and entertaining in others, and my wife and I took quite a fancy to him. (pp. 64–65 [p. 137])

As an analysis of Uncle Julius this passage is accurate only in its assumption that the mental habits of a lifetime could not be cast off. It is dead wrong on the nature of those habits, however. The other stories in *The Conjure Woman* reveal how little Uncle Julius sees himself as another's property, while the tales reveal how little the slaves themselves had thought that way. The narrator's error reveals the patronizing attitude which blinds him to the reality of Uncle Julius's activities and which amounts to a wish to consign the freed slave to a new subservience.

The passage also reveals how the guilt created by this attempt to create a new slavery manifests itself in a sense of responsibility for blacks. Uncle Julius understands this psychological complex thoroughly enough to be able to exploit it cynically. At the conclusion of his tale about Mars Jeems he points the moral of the tale: "Dis yer tale goes ter show ... dat w'ite folks w'at is so ha'd en stric', en doan make no 'lowance fer po' ign'ant niggers w'at ain' had no chanst ter l'arn, is li'ble ter hab bad dreams, ter say de leas', en dat dem w'at is kin' en good ter po' people is sho' ter prosper en git 'long in de worl'" (p. 100 [pp. 147–148]). This sententious moralizing reveals Uncle Julius's awareness of the white man's guilt and his willingness to exploit that sense of guilt unscrupulously. Uncle Julius has no interest in having his grandson educated; he asks only that allowance be made for him. Uncle Julius wants the patronizing whites to pay for their sense of superiority by supporting the blacks whose shiftlessness they have created by their attitudes and actions. In this story Uncle Julius emerges as an opportunist like Ellison's Bledsoe, and his relation to the narrator in many ways resembles that of Bledsoe to Norton. The situation Chesnutt draws is virtually hopeless, a vicious circle of mutual exploitation with no will on either side to break the cycle.

Although the situation "Mars Jeems's Nightmare" exposes is nightmarish, the story avoids pessimism and bitterness. While it does not achieve that lyrical tension between tragedy and comedy which made "Po' Sandy" a prose blues, "Mars Jeems's Nightmare" nevertheless does balance the hopelessness of the situation with the humor of Uncle Julius's manipulation of the whites and Annie's active complicity in his success. The balance vital to the conjure stories is also threatened from another quarter, however. From the beginning Chesnutt has been the ultimate conjure man, hoping that by "wukking de roots" of black culture he might be able to work a powerful goopher on white America and lead it to accept the equality of the black. The indirection of the conjure stories enabled him to pursue his goal with consummate artistry but without sufficient power to save America from bad dreams.

His desire to deal more directly with racial problems shows in "Mars Jeems's Nightmare" in its concern with an issue with broad social implications, the questions of employment and education for blacks and of white responsibilities therefor. The indirection of the conjure story was ill adapted to such concerns, and "Mars Jeems's Nightmare" inevitably raises questions which the limits of the form prevent it from dealing with. The crucial relation of the drama—the relation between the narrator as employer and Tom as employee —is peripheral rather than central. We can never learn about Tom, the nature of his purported laziness and carelessness, the possible causes, or the possible ways of dealing with the situation. The point of the story, of course, is that the situation precludes either party from dealing directly with these issues, and the story quite properly does not attempt to examine them. Nevertheless, such questions arise simply because the frame drama and the point of Uncle Julius's tale both enter the realm of practical social problems where these questions exist and demand attention. The grim vision of "Mars Jeems's Nightmare" registers the hopelessness of America's racial life and reveals the limitations of the indirect approach to racism which the conjure story provided. On the one hand, the conjure story provided a subtle instrument which could portray with a terrifying accuracy and clarity the functioning of American racial life, but it offered no imaginative way out for either author or audience. The lesson of the white narrator—that whites are too blind to perceive the truth about race—may have suggested to Chesnutt that it was not enough to show race relations in action but that what was needed was an art which would outline explicitly the white misconceptions about blacks and the forces responsible for their formation and perpetuation. In any event, Chesnutt's concern shifted from working a subtle goopher on white minds to attacking specific social problems and clearly laying bare the mechanics and consequences of racism, and the conjure story ceased to be a useful vehicle. After *The Conjure Woman* was published Chesnutt gave full attention to the realistic fiction he had been working with throughout the 1890's.

If Americans were too blind for subtle methods, they were no more amenable to direct confrontation. White Americans would not allow themselves to perceive life from a black perspective, and Chesnutt's turn from the complex art of the conjure story was unavailing. Realism did give Chesnutt room to explore additional dimensions of racial life in America, but the ultimate irony is that his realistic fiction never achieved sharper insights than those of "Mars Jeems's Nightmare" and the early conjure stories, while losing their balance, control, and clarity. It is through the marvelously subtle conjure fiction, which transcends the nightmare of American racism in a near-tragic, near-comic lyricism, that Chesnutt works his most powerful goopher.

CHESNUTT'S CONJURE TALES:
WHAT YOU SEE IS WHAT YOU GET

David D. Britt

When Charles Chesnutt submitted a group of twenty stories for publication in book form, the editors of Houghton Mifflin were impressed equally with his promise as a writer and the uneven quality of the various works. The three stories that most interested the editorial staff were "The Goophered Grapevine," "The Conjurer's Revenge," and "Po' Sandy," and Chesnutt was asked to write more stories along the same lines for publication as a collection of conjure tales. He obliged, and *The Conjure Woman* has delighted readers since its publication in 1899. But the stories have also "goophered" the readers in that more is going on in them than the critics have yet described.

A journal entry of 1880 reveals Chesnutt's strategy as a writer that is most perfectly achieved in *The Conjure Woman;* he says, "The subtle almost indefinable feeling of repulsion toward the Negro, which is common to most Americans—cannot be stormed and taken by assault; the garrison will not capitulate, so their position must be mined, and we will find ourselves in their midst before they think it. This work is of a two-fold character. The Negro's part is to prepare himself for recognition and equality, and it is the province of literature to open the way for him to get it—to accustom the public mind to the idea; to lead people out, imperceptibly, unconsciously, step by step, to the desired state of feeling." [1] The artistry with which Chesnutt sought to expand the awareness of white Americans constitutes one of the significant achievements in Afro-American writing. Indeed, William Dean Howells likened the skill of the conjure tales to the works of Maupassant, Tourguenief, and Henry James.[2] Howells's comparison of these stories to those of the white writers—even so Olympian a group—reveals, however, the false scent that Chesnutt's contemporary readers followed in approaching *The Conjure Woman.* A reviewer in the New York *Times* expressed a common understanding when he likened the

---

CLA Journal, March 1972.

[1] Helen M. Chesnutt, *Charles Waddell Chesnutt* (Chapel Hill: University of North Carolina Press, 1952), p. 21. [Britt's note.]
[2] William Dean Howells, "Mr. Charles W. Chesnutt's Stories," *The Atlantic Monthly,* 85 (May, 1900), 700. [Britt's note.]

stories to Joel Chandler Harris' Uncle Remus narratives,[3] while *The Nation* observed that these tales ". . . told by an old plantation darky, are delightfully frank in their supernaturalism and lose effectiveness only by the deep policy imputed to their relator."[4] Nor have more recent critics fared much better in approaching *The Conjure Woman*. Vernon Loggins says in 1931, for example, that the stories ". . . proved Mr. Chesnutt's power to follow with remarkable skill and originality a passing fashion in literature."[5] Morehouse President Hugh Gloster observes (1948) that the tales ". . . have their raison d'etre [sic] in Uncle Julius' shrewd maneuvers to promote his own welfare and that of his friends."[6] And Ruth Miller (1971) dismisses ". . . the wistful, the amiable buffoonery of the 'conjore' stories. . . ."[7] But these tales are neither in the tradition of James and Maupassant nor are they parallel to the obsequious fantasies of Harris; this is not ". . . a collection of quaint tales, with an admirable Southern setting. . . ."[8] On the contrary, *The Conjure Woman* is primarily a study in duplicity that masks or reveals its meaning according to the predisposition of the reader. All the elements of fiction—structure, characterization, language, and theme—interlock in a subtle portrayal of a black writer "wu'kin' his roots" on an unperceiving audience.

The stories are deliberately structured to allow the reader to be deceived about the more significant levels of meaning if he chooses, or needs, to be deceived. The device that initially permits misunderstanding comes through the double narrative structure: both a black and white man participate in relating each story. In each story, John, the white narrator, introduces a practical business problem to a former slave, Julius. The problems range from whether John ought to buy a particular vineyard, clear a certain tract of land, or buy a horse instead of a mule. Julius then delivers himself of a conjure tale from slavery times that serves as a parable for how John should or should not proceed. Julius's tale depicts magical transformations in nature through the "goophering" of a conjurer—men turned

---

[3] New York *Times* (anonymous, untitled review) April 15, 1899, p. 246. [Britt's note.]
[4] "Recent Novels" (anonymous review) *The Nation*, 72 (February 28, 1901), 182. [Britt's note.]
[5] Vernon Loggins, *The Negro Author* (New York: Columbia University Press, 1931), p. 326. [Britt's note.]
[6] Hugh Gloster, *Negro Voices in American Fiction* (Chapel Hill: University of North Carolina Press, 1948), p. 35. [Britt's note.]
[7] Ruth Miller, *Blackamerican Literature* (Beverly Hills: Glencoe Press, 1971), p. 287. [Britt's note.]
[8] Florence A. H. Morgan, (untitled review) *The Bookman*, 9 (June, 1899), 373. [Britt's note.]

into wolves or trees, whites changed into slaves, boys turned into birds. The final section of each story shows the bemused John learning that Julius has some vested interest in the business venture. He owns a share in the horse, makes wine from the wild grapes in that particular vineyard, or sells honey from a tree in the land to be cleared. By sandwiching Julius's narrative in between John's sections, Chesnutt gives the first and final word to the white man, implying that the white man is the "official" interpreter of Julius's yarn. Through this structural device, Chesnutt creates a surface level of meaning that leaves the Southern caste system undisturbed.

The apparent vindication of Southern mores is furthered through the characterization of the white narrator. John comes to Patesville, North Carolina from northern Ohio, and can therefore be trusted as a disinterested observer of life in the South. He has nothing but the most effusive praise for the hospitality and generosity of the people. The mild climate, moreover, proves ideal for his wife's health and for the profitable growing of grapes. Minor things like the nine o'clock curfew in no way interfere with the social amenities; the unstated implication here, of course, is that the curfew pertains only to black people. This insensitivity to the living conditions of black people—which constitutes a dominant theme in Julius's tales—represents a central ingredient in John's characterization. From snatches of conversation in various stories it becomes apparent that his good humored condescension to black people serves as only one indicator of a thoroughgoing racist attitude. He says of Julius, for example, that "He was not entirely black, and this fact, together with the quality of his hair, which was about six inches long and very bushy, except on the top of his head, where he was quite bald, suggested a slight strain of other than negro blood. There was a shrewdness in his eyes, too, which was not altogether African, and which, as we afterward learned from experience, was indicative of a corresponding shrewdness in his character."[9] The underlying premise of this observation rests on the notion that a black man's shrewdness derives from what is euphemistically called the benevolent infusion of white blood. On another occasion he remarks that Julius ". . . was a marvelous hand in the management of horses and dogs, with whose mental processes he manifested a greater familiarity than mere use would seem to account for, though it was doubtless due to the simplicity of a life that had

---

[9] Charles W. Chesnutt, *The Conjure Woman* (Ann Arbor: University of Michigan Press), pp. 9–10 [page 120 in this volume]. All further references to this text are included parenthetically in the body of the paper. [Britt's note. Britt's parenthetical references to *The Conjure Woman* will be immediately followed by bracketed references to the present volume.]

kept him close to nature" (p. 64 [pp. 136–137]). John not only thinks of
Julius's intellectual powers as more congruent with dogs and horses than
men, he also believes Julius's spirit to be shackled with an abiding servil-
ity. In trying to articulate Julius's reasons for remaining on the plantation
where he had formerly been a slave, John contends that Julius ". . . had
been accustomed, until long after middle life, to look upon himself as the
property of another. When this relation was no longer possible, owing to
the war, and to his master's death and the dispersion of the family, he had
been unable to break off entirely the mental habits of a lifetime, but had
attached himself to the old plantation, of which he seemed to consider
himself an appurtenance" (p. 65 [p. 137]). There is a tone of lament in
John's phrase, "When this relation was no longer possible," that indicates
he thinks slavery, for Julius, was desirable. When these three statements
are brought together—in *The Conjure Woman* they are scattered—it becomes clear that John perceives of [sic] Julius as crafty but of low intelligence and essentially servile in spirit. In other words, he subscribes to the
racial biases common to most Americans. What Chesnutt does, therefore,
through the characterization of John and through the structural pattern of
the book is to make *The Conjure Woman* an apparently "safe" work, a reassuring collection of tales that depicts a contented, entertaining black
man working within the unchallenged framework of American social and
intellectual mores. One early critic even remarks on ". . . that peace of
mind and contentment of spirit which follow hard upon these entertaining
narratives of witchcraft." [10] Arna Bontemps articulates the rationale behind Chesnutt's deceptive manipulation of his material when he says in another context that "What annoys some readers of fiction, it seems, is not
so much that characters in a book are Negro or white or both as the *attitude of the writer* toward these characters. Does he accept the status quo
with respect to the races? If so, any character or racial situation can be
taken in stride, not excluding miscegenation. But rejection of traditional
status, however reflected, tends to alienate these readers." [11] With the pa-
rameters set by John—ostensibly—who could be offended?

Chesnutt's own powers as a conjurer, though, become obvious when
one sees that Julius's appearance does not correspond to his reality. Flip
Wilson, that Thursday night trickster, says it well: "What you see is what

---

[10] "Recent Fiction" (anonymous review) *The Critic*, 35 (July, 1899), 646. [Britt's note.]
[11] Arna Bontemps, "The Negro Renaissance: Jean Toomer and the Harlem Writers of the
1920's," *Anger and Beyond,* ed. by Herbert Hill (New York: Harper & Row, 1966),
p. 35. [Britt's note.]

you get." The most obvious technique for deception comes through Julius's language. Dialect—always quaint and humorous to the outsider—prevents the white narrator from taking Julius seriously. And operating safely from behind this language buffer, Julius is able to work on John with a considerable degree of impunity. The hustles that Julius works on John apparently revolve around picayune amounts of cash. And, given Julius's economic status, these small financial victories are not to be dismissed out of hand. But it is a mistake to view a few jugs of wine or a crock of honey as the prime objectives of Julius's maneuverings. In fact, Julius moves out of a solid economic base through being employed by John, a matter that John recognizes at the end of the first story but subsequently forgets. If this were not the case, Julius would be in terrible straits financially, for in only one of the stories, "The Conjurer's Revenge," is he successful in achieving something of personal material benefit. In "The Conjurer's Revenge" Julius persuades John to buy a horse instead of a mule, and Julius owns part interest in the horse. He is successful in two other stories, but the gain is not strictly of personal benefit. The outcome of "Mars Jeems's Nightmare" secures a job for Julius's grandson, while "Po' Sandy" results in a meeting place for Julius's secessionist church group. Following "The Goophered Grapevine" and "The Gray Wolf's Ha'nt," Julius has lost the income from grapes and honey. Two of the stories, moreover, "Sis' Becky's Pickaninny" and "Hot-Foot Hannibal" express not a trace of self-interest. Since in only one of the seven stories is Julius able to gain something of value to himself personally, he is either singularly unsuccessful as a hustler, or presented by Chesnutt as a "darky entertainer" in the minstrel tradition, or the stories are not about financial matters at all. My contention is that Julius's tales are not aimed at manipulating John in the way the surface narrative implies. They should be seen as elaborate metaphors, allegories really, in which the supernatural elements point toward those dread realities of the slave's life that lie beyond the comprehension of the ruling class. The black man is laying bare the nature of the slave experience, exploding myths about both masters and slaves, and showing the limitations of the white man's moral and imaginative faculties.

An extended analysis of one story, "Po' Sandy," will illustrate the tension between the outside and inside narratives, establish the thematic patterns, and serve as a model for interpreting the other works. The inside narrative of "Po' Sandy" shows Julius telling a tall tale about the hainted character of the wood in an old school house in order to prevent John from using the lumber to build his wife a new kitchen. In the coda, Julius receives the wife's permission to use the old school house for a meeting place, temporarily. Julius's narrative, however, expresses an extended metaphor that reveals the dehumanization of the slave, the brutality of treatment afforded the slave, and the intense love that a black man and woman have for one another. Julius tells about Sandy, who is such an exceptional worker that each of Mars Marrabo McSwayne's married children asks the father to deed Sandy to him as a gift. In order to prevent family friction, however, McSwayne lends Sandy to each of them for about a month at a time. This way each gets his services without denying the others of their "rights." McSwayne, a generous man who doesn't want to give offense to anyone (white), even lends Sandy to the neighbors on occasion. During one such work trip Sandy's wife is sold to a speculator.

The recurring metaphor associated with Sandy is homelessness. His forced wandering prevents him from establishing those basic roots that nurture a sense of belonging, order, and stability. With profound understatement he says, " 'I'm gettin' monst'us ti'ed er dish yer gwine roun' so much.' " Given the dehumanized state in which he lives, Sandy wishes for liberation through a magical transformation that, ironically, objectifies the dehumanization, but at the same time provides a stable existence. If he were ". . . a tree, er a stump, er a rock . . ." he tells his second wife, at least he ". . . could stay on the plantation fer a w'ile." Tenie wrestles momentarily with the conflict between the white man's religion (Christianity) and the powers available to her through African magic (conjuring). She has not goophered anyone for fifteen years, not since she got "religion." But now she decides that ". . . dey is some things I doan b'lieve it's no sin fer ter do." The preservation of the race—exemplified here in the well-being of her husband—justifies the use of whatever means are available. She conjures Sandy into a tree, after which he undergoes a series of natural disasters: a woodpecker gouges a hole in his arm and a slave, unwittingly, skins his leg while tapping the tree for turpentine. Tenie then decides to turn herself and Sandy into foxes, ". . . so dey could run away en go some'rs whar dey could be free en lib lack w'ite folks." The characteristics of white folks expressed in this metaphor are freedom laced with the cunning of a predator.

The brutalization of the slaves controls the next segment of the story. While Tenie is sent away to nurse a white woman, the owner decides to build a new kitchen, the lumber from which is later used to build the school house mentioned in the outside narrative. The tree into which Sandy has been transmogrified is selected for the construction. The tree, with much difficulty and groaning, is felled and hauled to the sawmill. Tenie arrives at the mill just as the saw is about to bite into the log. Her hysterical ravings prompt the mill hands to think her insane. They tie her to a post, and she is forced to watch as the log, Sandy, is cut into pieces. Thus, not only homelessness but dehumanization, mutilation, impotence, and love that drives a woman to distraction characterize the slave's experience.

This story further explodes the myth of casualness in the slaves' family structure. The fact that the slave did not have the power to keep his family together in no way diminished the intensity of love between a man and woman. When Sandy is turned into a tree, his owner cannot track him any farther than the tree itself. He questions all the slaves except Tenie about his whereabouts; not Tenie, because ". . . eve'ybody knowed Tenie sot too much sto' by Sandy fer ter he'p 'im run away whar she could n' nebber see 'im no mo'." She is, moreover, driven mad after watching him cut to pieces.

And what is one to make of the supernatural elements in the story? The identification of Sandy with the tree can be viewed as a comment on the status of slaves. They were simply natural resources to be used, not essentially different from cattle or timber. And the slave women's superstition that his ghost haunts the kitchen makes it possible for them to refuse, as they did, to work in the kitchen after dark. While the McSwaynes might rail against the ignorance implied in the belief in ghosts, they would not be able to force a terrified woman to work after sundown. One further suggestion arises from the belief that Sandy's spirit still inhabits the kitchen. Whether he was used as the lumber itself or was simply directed to build the kitchen, Sandy invested himself in the building process. A number of contemporary phrases come to mind at this point: "I have invested my life in that company," or "I really put myself into that—whatever." Perhaps the slave's spirit does reside in what he built. We are certainly haunted by his ghost.

The other stories in *The Conjure Woman* admit to a similar line of interpretation. The theme that unites all of Julius's narratives is the contrasting relationship of blacks and whites to the natural order, with nature serving throughout as a metaphor for the natural, moral order of the universe. The white men seek to exploit nature (cotton, vineyards, and especially other men), with a resulting atrophy of their capacity for human emotion. On the other hand, a close alliance exists between the blacks and nature. The acts of goophering show birds, animals, and even the growing seasons working in concert with black resistance against inhumane treatment. The tales accent the injustices suffered by the blacks because of enslavement and at the same time reveal their harmonious relationship with the natural order: witness, for example, their access to the powers of the conjurer, which stems directly from a compatibility with the natural order.

The themes of white dissonance and black harmony with the natural order predominate in "The Goophered Grapevine." Julius's tale turns, in effect, on a critique of the economics of the slaveholding system. The action begins when Mars Dugal' McAdoo has Aun' Peggy put a deadly goopher on his vineyard to keep the slaves from eating the grapes, a move designed to deny the blacks a share of what they produce while increasing his profits. A new slave, Henry, arrives on the plantation while the white folks are in the swamp with their guns and dogs looking for a slave who has broken for freedom. The other slaves on the place are too "flusterated" to tell Henry about the goopher, and he eats some conjured grapes. But because his action is inadvertent (and because he brings her a ham), Aun' Peggy puts a special goopher on Henry that cancels the original spell and allows him to eat the grapes with impunity, provided he rubs his head with first sap of the vines each year. An amazing transformation comes over Henry; he undergoes an annual rejuvenation: in the spring his hair grows long, his rheumatism leaves, his youth returns, and he chases the girls. In the fall, however, the process reverses, and the signs of age return. McAdoo, recognizing the economic potential here, begins selling Henry each spring for $1,500 and buying him back later for $500. With the profits from Henry's rejuvenation, McAdoo buys a second tract of land. His prospects for wealth increase further when a Yankee drummer promises to double the wine production through a new method of cultivation. According to Julius, Mars' Dugal' "'. . . des drunk it all in, des 'peared ter be *bewitch*' wid dat Yankee" (pp. 28–29, emphasis added [p. 126]). The language here indicates that whites, too, are subject to a form of conjuring through their greed. The new cultivation methods, however, prove disastrous; both the vines and Henry shrivel and die. McAdoo, now ruined financially, later dies in the Civil War. Julius's tale implies that the slaveholder's exploitative greed contains the seeds of its own destruction, while the attempt to defend the slaveholding system results in death. Henry, conversely, flourishes like a plant in the regenerative cycle of nature. He possesses an immunity to the destructive goophers that the white man works on the land. He—the black man—dies a natural death, not on a battlefield defending slavery. A further oblique comment on white America emerges from this tale. "The Goophered Grapevine," the first story in *The Conjure Woman*, attempts to dissuade John from perpetuating the plantation system. Hoping for profit, as did Mars McAdoo, John, however, buys the property and, as the subsequent stories make clear, remains locked into the racial and economic patterns engendered by the slaveholding system.

The themes of conflict and harmony seen in "The Goophered Grapevine" recur in "Sis' Becky's Pickaninny," but the emphasis shifts from the acquisitiveness of the whites to their failure of human sympathy. The whites' perception of black people as objects is dramatized here through the separation of a mother from her son. Becky, the mother, is traded by her owner for a horse, indicating the interchangeability of people for animals. This identification is completed by the horse's owner when he refuses to keep the mother and son together even though the son will cost him nothing. He says that ". . . I doan raise niggers; I raise hosses" (pp. 141–142 [p.160]). The son's owner becomes upset when the child falls ill following the separation from his mother, and calls a physician to look at him, not out of compassion but because ". . . he wuz a lackly little nigger en wu'th raisn'" (p. 145 [p. 161]). Julius avoids offending the white sensibilities by speaking of Kurnel Pen'leton's moral weakness only in terms of his relationship with race horses; he speculates in horses, not slaves. But the tale makes clear that the horses and slaves are interchangeable. Julius also speaks of the Colonel in the most favorable terms. The Colonel had wanted to buy Becky's husband when the neighboring plantation on which he lived was disbanded, but the Colonel was broke at the time. The Colonel, says Julius, does not like to separate children from their mothers—not, at least, "w'iles de chillun wuz little" (p. 141 [p. 160])—but he does. And this ". . . kin'-hea'ted man" lies to Becky about selling her in order to make the separation from the child easier. Julius's protestations of the Colonel's generosity must, however, be interpreted in light of the man's actions.

The slaves in the story find recourse against the vagaries of white sentimentality and empty pocketbooks through the ministry of the conjurer. Becky's grief following the separation from her baby, Mose, is made bearable through the singing of two birds. These birds, through conjuration, are really her transformed son, sent to her by the plantation nurse. But the visitations prove ineffectual in relieving the ache of separation. And the nurse asks Aun' Peggy to reunite Becky with Mose. Aun' Peggy directs a hornet to sting the legs of the race horse that has been traded for Becky. The horse's lameness and Becky's pining make each of the traders dissatisfied with the bargain, and they swap back. Thus, nature conspires with the slaves first to bring relief then reunion.

The disruption of slave families also controls the action in another story, "Hot-Foot Hannibal." The actions in the outside and inside narratives parallel one another, but the lines of action move in opposite directions. Both sections of the story deal with a recurring problem in human experience: a spat between lovers. Both sections turn on jealousy toward another woman. But the consequences of the quarrels prove antithetical; the white woman achieves a reconciliation, while the black woman loses both her man and her life. Black women are not allowed the same latitude in fighting with their men. Parallels and counterpoints are also established between the male characters. Both are involved in a journey: Jeff, the slave, is sold down the river and Malcolm Murchison contemplates a trip to New York. The directions, of course, are symbolic—the North representing freedom, the South, hell—and one trip is voluntary while the other is imposed. The effect of status on emotional depth constitutes one further counterpoint in the narratives. The white woman—spoiled, petulant, confident—shows no disposition toward experiencing painful emotions; indeed, she exhibits an almost brazen insensitivity to any emotion other than fits of pique. Chloe, on the other hand, commits suicide after learning that Jeff has died on the trip South. This contrast in emotional intensity highlights the inequities implicit in the slaveholding system, and, at the same time, reiterates the crippling effect that slavery has on the white masters and their descendants.

The disparity between the black experience and the white perception of that experience is explored in "Mars Jeems's Nightmare," the least original of Julius's tales in terms of basic metaphor. Here a cruel slave master is temporarily changed into a slave on his own plantation and subsequently lightens the misery of his slaves after learning from the receiving end about the brutality. The interest in "Mars Jeems's Nightmare" comes, therefore, not from Julius's section but from the comment it makes on the outside narrative. Julius has secured a job for his grandson even though John had "not liked his looks." John's suspicions prove correct; the grandson is trifling and inept, so John fires him. Julius's tale, however, underscores the difficulty a man has in accommodating himself to a dead-end job. Mars Jeems could not seem to get the hang of the hoe, "en could n' 'pear ter git it th'oo his min' dat he wuz a slabe en had ter wuk en min' de w'ite folks, spite er de fac' dat Ole Nick [the overseer] gun 'im a lesson eve'y day" (p. 84 [p. 142]). The point is that both work habits and caste training are hard to come by. And the obvious implication of Julius's tale is the difficulty white employers have in appreciating the conditions under which black workers are supposed to learn. It seems necessary for whites to undergo the black experience (the slave experience) to appreciate the perspective that blacks bring to a menial job.

Finally, two stories, "The Conjurer's Revenge" and "The Gray Wolf's Ha'nt," present the slaves in a totally black context, a situation designed to explode a number of stereotypes about black people. Obsequiousness, for example, drops away when no whites are present. Indeed, the black protagonists are presented as men feared by both whites and blacks. So much, then, for the notion that the slaves' retaliation against the system was limited to passive resistance (work slowdowns, broken tools), violent rebellion (Nat Turner, Denmark Vesey), or flight. Primus, the slave in "Revenge," ". . . did n' min' de rules, en went w'en he felt lack it; en de w'ite folks purten' lack dey did n' know it, fer Primus was dange'ous w'en he got in dem stubborn spells, en dey'd ruther not fool wid 'im" (p. 109 [p. 150]). Another myth, though—the lack of ethics among blacks—lies closer to the heart of these tales. The other stories are filled with instances of petty thefts of hams, scarves, and the like, things stolen from the whites to elicit the favors of the conjurer. These acts are presented as a matter of course by Julius, though he is careful to say that he never saw any of the slaves near the smokehouse. But "Revenge" and "Gray Wolf" deal with crimes of blacks against other blacks. Primus steals a pig that belongs to a black man and is turned into a mule, an appropriate punishment for such an action. "The Gray Wolf's Ha'nt" presents a more serious offense, murder, and the blood bath that follows is almost Orestian in its consequences. The point here is that internal crimes against the group are viewed as serious breaches of the norm and are dealt with accordingly. It is one thing to steal from a white man, quite another to rob a black. The ethical frames of reference are different for slaves and masters; but then who would expect the slave whose very person has been stolen to view the owner's property as the owner would? The elemental passion loosed in "Gray Wolf" attests to a reverence for both the marriage relationship and kinship that transcends the categories of black and white and reveals the incorruptible humanity that the slaves maintain despite their captivity. This statement of the slaves' enduring humanity despite the exploitive propensities of the whites brings the argument of the tales full cycle. The whites and blacks work from radically different moral bases, with many of the ethical premises deriving from social status.

Although the whites control the social and political realities of the world, the blacks are free to place their own interpretations on their experiences and to exert some degree of control through conjuration. Chesnutt drops conflicting clues about the approach one should take in interpreting the conjuring episodes in the stories. The African origins of goophering are explicitly stated in "The Conjurer's Revenge," in which the conjurer from Guinea says, according to Julius, that "'. . . his daddy wuz a king, er a guv'ner, er some sorter w'at-you-may-call-'er 'way ober yander in Affiky whar de niggers come fum, befo' he was stoled erway en sol' ter de spekilaters'" (pp. 120–121 [p 154]). But while the African influences on *The Conjure Woman* deserve serious attention, such a study is beyond my competence. Another (more western) line of interpretation, however, is provided by John's wife, Annie, who consistently demonstrates more sensitivity to Julius's tales than her husband. She views the supernatural elements as "'. . . mere ornamental details and not at all essential. The [conjure] story is true to nature, and might have happened half a hundred times, and no doubt did happen, in those horrid days before the war'" (p. 159 [pp. 165–166]). And Julius's tales do lend themselves to metaphoric interpretation. "The Conjurer's Revenge" and "The Gray Wolf's Ha'nt" exemplify appropiate punishments for crimes within the black community, while "Mars Jeems's Nightmare" contains not only an appropriate punishment but a method of illumination as well. An idea fundamental to all the tales—the slaves' harmonious relationship to nature—emerges through the seasonal rejuvenation of Henry in "The Goophered Grapevine." Sandy's vicissitudes constitute a veiled statement of the brutality to which slaves were subjected, and Hot-Foot Hannibal's troubles result from black resistance to white domination. Julius's narrative in "Sis' Becky's Pickaninny," while not essentially metaphoric, can nonetheless be seen as a specialized interpretation of natural events. In each of the stories the access to the power of the conjurer gives the slaves a sense of control over their environment, a control no more and no less efficacious than the Christian's seeking aid through prayer or interpreting events as the will of God.

If these observations about the importance of Julius to the structure and meaning of *The Conjure Woman* are sound, then the collection deserves renewed critical attention. The work should no longer be dismissed as a belated example of a minor Reconstruction genre, and similarly need not be approached as a tepid first effort in Chesnutt's increasingly militant literary career. Rather, the artistry of the tales suggests a studied control of the material that elicits multiple levels of interpretation. One begins with the literal, surface meaning suggested by the outside narratives. Julius is a hustler, and he hustles John for money. But he also, and more importantly, hustles both John and the reader by presenting the beauty and pain of his people. Thus Chesnutt becomes an artist of heightened stature, and Julius, a signifier ahead of his time, an excellent guide to the study of Afro-American Literature.

CHARLES W. CHESNUTT

Hiram Haydn

When I was living with my parents in a suburb of Cleveland in the 1920s, a new neighbor moved onto our street. My memory of him is very clear. I was then in my early teens, and frequently in the afternoon, when various men who lived in the neighborhood came home from work, I would be playing ball in the street with friends. The different thing about this new neighbor was that he seemed to have time to stop and say a pleasant word or two to us, or perhaps to watch us for a short time. What did not seem unusual to me was the color of his skin. It was a pale coffee color, but it never occurred to me that that in any way set him apart. What did set him apart, in addition to his afternoon ritual, were the clarity and serenity of his eyes and his spontaneous smile.

American Scholar, Winter 1972–73.

This gentleman had lived on our street for some four or five months before a delegation of neighbors waited on my father one afternoon. My father, Howell Haydn, who was professor of Biblical Literature at Western Reserve University, was badly crippled, and the combination tended to make the neighbors think of him with deference, and yet at the same time, of course, as not quite one of "the fellows." As a result, they had decided that he was the man on our street best fitted to fulfill a mission that they found imperative.

I overheard the ensuing discussion from a hidden spot in the dining room. I was intensely curious as to why a dozen neighbors would all come formally together to call on my father, and so I stayed throughout their conference.

The gist of their request was that my father, being a very kind and gentle man, go to our new neighbor and advise him in the most courteous possible way that he really was not wanted on this street, and that therefore they hoped indeed that he would sell his house and move elsewhere. It was with not only pride but a kind of joy that I watched my father struggle to his feet and literally brandish his cane in the faces of his guests. "Get out of my house, you whited sepulchres," he said (I shall never forget the words), "and if one of you dares to approach that fine man with the purpose you have just described to me, I shall personally thrash you."

This from the gentlest of men. They literally scurried out. And Mr. Charles W. Chesnutt, for that is who the man in question was, so far as I know lived in his house on our street for the rest of his life. At least, he was still there when I moved away. . . .

THE SIGNIFICANCE
OF CHARLES W. CHESNUTT'S
"CONJURE STORIES"

William L. Andrews

In August, 1887, *The Atlantic Monthly* published "The Goophered Grapevine," a local color story set in North Carolina and written by a literary unknown named Charles W. Chesnutt. The acceptance of this story

The Southern Literary Journal, Fall 1974.

initiated the rise of its author from literary obscurity to a position as the most widely read Afro-American fiction writer of his time. What made this story and others like it successful, however, was not the knowledge that their creator was black. As late as 1889 Chesnutt's publishers, including Houghton, Mifflin, who brought out his first collection of "conjure stories," chose to delete any mention of the new author's racial identity. Although such a deliberate omission of such a significant fact might indicate racist motives to a modern reader, in Chesnutt's case the omission of his racial background constituted a significant though left-handed compliment to him as a writer of fiction. For, as William Dean Howells pointed out in a review of *The Conjure Woman* and a subsequent collection of Chesnutt short stories, "It is not from their racial interest that we could wish to speak of them [i.e., Chesnutt's short stories]. . . . It is much more simply and directly, as works of art, that they make their appeal." [1]

Twentieth century critics have found several features of *The Conjure Woman* praiseworthy. In describing Chesnutt's collection as "a study in duplicity," David D. Britt has concentrated on the unity of the stories, a unity which combines "structure, characterization, language, and theme" in a successful effort to deceive "the unperceiving audience." [2] Donald M. Winkleman has studied Chesnutt's use of folk elements in the conjure stories and has evaluated Chesnutt as a "folk artist." [3] The "artistic objectivity" of Chesnutt in *The Conjure Woman* has been singled out by Saunders Redding as the principal source of the collection's success, especially among white readers. [4] But an accompanying comment by Redding in his examination of *The Conjure Woman* sheds more light on the subject of why Chesnutt's stories were popular among white readers and why they were accepted by the most important literary magazines of the day. "The book's reception as the work of a white writer . . . signifies that [Chesnutt] was judged by the standards of his white contemporaries. By these standards *The Conjure Woman* is successful." [5]

Redding's remarks point toward a truth about Chesnutt as a short story writer that often has been underplayed. Unlike almost every black

---

[1] William Dean Howells, "Mr. Charles W. Chesnutt's Stories," *Atlantic Monthly,* LXXXV (1900), 700. [Andrews's note.]

[2] David D. Britt, "Chesnutt's Conjure Tales," *CLA Journal,* XV (1972), 271. [Andrews's note.]

[3] Donald M. Winkleman, "Three American Authors as Semi-Folk Artists," *Journal of American Folklore,* LXXVIII (1965), 130–35. [Andrews's note.]

[4] J. Saunders Redding, *To Make a Poet Black* (Chapel Hill: Univ. of North Carolina Press, 1939), p. 68. [Andrews's note.]

[5] *Ibid.* [Andrews's note.]

writer before or contemporary with him, Chesnutt achieved his initial fame without reference to either his own racial identity or to the current racial issues of his time. He did not present himself as a "race author." He presented himself as a literary craftsman, and he won recognition because he met the standards for fiction by which his white contemporaries were judged. Thus Chesnutt's familiarity with and mastery of the accepted modes and traditions of the American short story in the 1880s and '90s should be recognized as the basis for his popular success and his place in American literary history. But Chesnutt was not merely an assimilator and imitator of prevalent trends. Though he attempted no innovations in either style or structure, he did widen the perspective of the conventional short story to include his peculiar subject matter and his individual thematic concerns. In this respect Chesnutt's conjure stories take on additional historical significance, for they reflect both his understanding of literary tradition and his ability to use the tradition as a means of approaching his readers with untraditional themes. An accurate assessment of the significance of Chesnutt's conjure stories in both American and Afro-American literature depends on two realizations: that Chesnutt achieved popularity in his own day through his adherence to tradition, and that he maintains his distinction today because of his expansion and occasional transcendence of tradition.

The literary tradition that Chesnutt followed when he wrote his conjure stories was the local color tradition, the predominant mode of the American short story during the period in which Chesnutt was primarily a writer of short stories. The 1880s in America were a "period of dialect stories, of small peculiar groups isolated and analyzed, of unique local 'characters' presented primarily for exhibition."[6] Local colorists offered American readers essentially sympathetic descriptions of unfamiliar people whose quaint and often out-dated mode of living had survived only in out-of-the-way places and cultural backwaters of America, or in the memories of American writers. Readers of local color and regional fiction expected a realistic treatment of subject from their favorite authors, but the type of realism they preferred did not take long looks at tragic or pessimistic features of American life. Local colorists satisfied their readers with superficial renditions of the life, manners, and environment of people whose day-to-day experience seemed simpler and less trying than that of the reader or the writer himself.

---

[6] Fred Lewis Pattee, *The Development of the American Short Story* (1923; reprinted, New York: Bilbo and Tannen, 1966), p. 268. [Andrews's note.]

For this sort of reader the subject, the central characters, the tone, and the style of *The Conjure Woman* were designed. A reviewer of the book when it first appeared sums up the nature of its appeal in this way, "You are not only listening to an old negro reciting his stories of folks being 'conjured,' but it is being conveyed to you just what kind of a country North Carolina is and the character of the people and the negroes [sic] who live there. You can gather more information from this story book in regard to grape-culture and farming generally in the South than you can from many extensive works on the subject." [7] These comments indicate several aspects of local color writing that are plainly evident in Chesnutt's conjure stories. By setting the stories in the sandhills region of central North Carolina, the author gave his reader a view of one part of the South that rarely found its way into belles-lettres. Through the comments of the white Northern businessman from Ohio, who functions as narrator of the stories, the physical appearance of the countryside and the manners and attitudes of the people of the region, especially the blacks of the region, are brought out.

This use of an outsider to report on life in an unfamiliar region was a standard convention in local color writing. The narrator from Ohio does not present an extensive study of his new North Carolina residence, but he gives his reader the kind of surface details and superficial realism that local color writing usually provided. "The Goophered Grapevine," the first story in *The Conjure Woman,* pays particular attention to grape-farming before and after the Civil War in sandhills North Carolina. Incidental details in other stories in the collection furnish information on Southern behavior and habits of speech, the condition of the sandhills soil, Sunday customs in the region, and the general climate of central North Carolina. Among the uncollected conjure stories, "Lonesome Ben" offers a brief characterization of the poor whites of the sandhills and introduces the reader to the custom of "clay-eating." [8] These details, presented by a detached but interested observer, contribute much to the success of the conjure stories as local color stories.

More central to the success of the conjure stories, however, was Chesnutt's use of the ex-slave Julius as a delineator of life on the ante-bellum "plantations" of the sandhills region. To tell a story in the words of an old

---

[7] From the St. Paul, Minnesota *Dispatch* for 29 April 1899. This review of *The Conjure Woman* appears in a scrapbook of press clippings on *The Conjure Woman* held in the Chesnutt Collection of the Fisk University Library, Nashville, Tennessee. [Andrews's note.]

[8] Charles W. Chesnutt, "Lonesome Ben," *The Southern Workman,* XXIX (1900), 137–45. [Andrews's note.]

black man was not a guarantee of literary success in the 1890s; by the time Chesnutt's stories appeared in book form, the novelty of writing in so-called "Negro dialect" was wearing thin. But, as one reviewer stated, "Un-like many books with negro characters, 'The Conjure Woman' was not written expressly to display its author's knowledge of dialect." The "chief aim" of the author is "to make vivid some of the superstitions current in slavery times."[9] Insofar as this view is accurate, it helps to explain once again the success of Chesnutt's conjure stories in the local color market. The ex-slave's testimonies to the power of a "goopher" or a rabbit's foot augment the quaintness of his character and the interest of his tales. More-over, through Julius's descriptions of the activities of various slave conjur-ers in the affairs of blacks and whites on the plantation, the ex-slave's memories of ante-bellum days receive a distinctly local color cast. The transformation of the peculiar customs of an isolated group of people into the materials for fiction was a familiar method of local color writers. It was also the method Chesnutt used to provide his stories of plantation life with a background and a principle of action that stemmed directly from the little-known, but fascinating culture of the slave.

Both Chesnutt and his publisher, Houghton Mifflin, realized that in choosing the rural South as a setting for his stories and an old ex-slave named "Uncle" Julius as a teller of what might be called "folk tales," Chesnutt was following the lead of a particular local colorist, the highly successful Joel Chandler Harris. The cover design of the first edition of *The Conjure Woman* featured pictures of a balding, white-haired old Negro and a rather mischievous-looking white rabbit over the title of the book. Vernon Loggins and Hugh M. Gloster have noted similarities between *The Conjure Woman* and *Uncle Remus, His Songs and Sayings,* but each has insisted on the individuality of Chesnutt's Uncle Julius and on the singu-larity of his tales.[10]

The second of these assertions may be proved more easily than the first. In an essay written not long before his death,[11] Chesnutt acknowl-edged several superficial similarities between his first book and Harris's

---

[9] From "Literature," New York, New York, 19 May 1899. This review also appears in the scrapbook of press clippings on *The Conjure Woman* held in the Chesnutt collection of the Fisk University Library. [Andrews's note.]

[10] See Vernon Loggins, *The Negro Author, His Development in America to 1900* (New York: Columbia Univ. Press, 1939), p. 311 and Hugh M. Gloster, *Negro Voices in Amer-ican Fiction* (Chapel Hill: Univ. of North Carolina Press, 1948), p. 35. [Andrews's note.]

[11] Charles W. Chesnutt, "Post-Bellum—Pre-Harlem," *The Colophon,* II, No. 5 (1931), no page. [Andrews's note, p. 100 in this volume.]

Uncle Remus. But, as he pointed out, the tales of Uncle Julius, while "sometimes referred to as folk tales," were, with the exception of "The Goophered Grapevine," [12] "the fruit of [his] own imagination." In this crucial respect, Chesnutt went on, "they differ from the *Uncle Remus* stories which are avowedly folk tales." This observation indicated the fundamental difference between the source and materials of Chesnutt's and Harris's so-called "folk tales." Chesnutt was not, and did not consider himself, a writer of "folk tales." He wrote short stories in which folklore played an important role in the development of the plot and the description of the culture with which he was dealing. But his conjure stories do not admit the sort of allegorical reading which Harris suggested and later critics have made of the Uncle Remus tales. [13] While Harris drew entire tales directly from folk tradition, Chesnutt used folk tradition as a basis and unifying principle for stories whose plots, characters, and themes were largely products of his own imagination.

Although the tales of Uncle Julius have their origins in the imagination of Charles Chesnutt, the character and role of the old ex-slave attest once again to the influence of literary tradition on his creator. Uncle Julius appeared at a time when the stock of the Afro-American was beginning to rise in the local color market. In the hands of early local colorists like the poet Irwin Russell and Sherwood Bonner, the Southern short story writer, "Negro dialect" was molded into a literary medium, and unfamiliar and picturesque aspects of Afro-American life before and after the war were treated with a mixture of sentiment and humor to produce a popular new subject for fiction. [14] The successors of writers like Russell and Bonner, realizing the popularity of dialect stories, used their talents to create black personae through whose mouths an author could not only tell a story but also speak his mind on other matters. In many of the early Uncle Remus sketches, Harris used his ex-slave persona as a means of making humorous but pointed comments on contemporary affairs in post-war Atlanta. [15] Thomas Nelson Page achieved his fame by telling romantic tales of antebellum Virginia through the dialect and point of view of aging ex-retainers

---

[12] The "norm" for "The Goophered Grapevine" was "a folk tale." [Andrews's note.]
[13] See, for instance, Jay Martin's allegorical reading in *Harvests of Change* (Englewood Cliffs, N. J.: Prentice-Hall, 1967), p. 99. [Andrews's note.]
[14] See the minor classic "Christmas Night in the Quarters" in Russell's *Poems* (New York: Century, 1888). For a representative selection of Sherwood Bonner's work see her *Suwanee River Tales* (Boston: Roberts Brothers, 1884). [Andrews's note.]
[15] Paul M. Cousins, *Joel Chandler Harris* (Baton Rouge: Louisiana State Univ. Press, 1968), pp. 96–106. [Andrews's note.]

to whom he gave different names but essentially the same nature.[16] Page's "Sam" and "Billy" and "Edinburg" reappeared in the works of people like F. Hopkinson Smith, Harry Stillwell Edwards, and James Lane Allen.[17] These writers renamed and added other whimsical or sentimental characteristics to the prototypes introduced by Page. But essentially the figure of the ex-slave and family retainer who usually has a story to tell and observations to make about pre-war life and post-war developments remained a picturesque but unrealized character in Southern local color fiction.

In the eyes of several reviewers of Chesnutt's day, Uncle Julius was a skillfully drawn successor to the prototypes created by Page and Harris. "Shrewd, wily, picturesque, ingratiating, deprecatory in manner, rich in imaginative lore, and withal kindly and simple at heart, the story teller [Julius] is a distinct addition to American literature. . . ."[18] This opinion of a Washington, D.C., reviewer accurately summarizes the main characteristics of Julius in almost all the conjure stories. These characteristics are not unique in Julius; they are standard features of the ex-slave narrator in a number of other Southern local colorists. Julius's often remarked technique of adapting a story to prevent his employer's intentions from clashing with his own interests does constitute one individualizing trait in him.[19] But this rather transparent cunning does not do violence to those qualities in Julius—loquacity, imagination, ingeniousness, and superstition—which were likely to stimulate the same kind of reader fascination and sympathy that made other ex-slave raconteurs so popular in the 1880s and '90s.

---

[16] Page's *In Ole Virginia* (New York: Scribner's, 1887) contains his most famous dialect tales of ante-bellum Virginia. [Andrews's note.]

[17] Page's prototypes reappear in Smith's *Colonel Carter of Cartersville* (Boston: Houghton Mifflin, 1891) in the person of Chad, in Edwards's "Two Runaways," *Two Runaways and Other Stories* (New York: Century, 1889), pp. 1–32, in the person of Isam, and in Allen's "Two Gentlemen of Kentucky," *Flute and Violin and Other Kentucky Tales and Romances* (New York: Harper's, 1891), pp. 97–134, in the person of Peter Cotton. [Andrews's note.]

[18] See the Washington, D.C. *Times*, 9 April, 1899, in the scrapbook of press clippings on *The Conjure Woman* held in the Chesnutt Collection of the Fisk University Library. [Andrews's note.]

[19] More often than not the motive behind Julius's storytelling is not nostalgia for the old times (as is the case in Page's stories) or a delight in entertainment (as is the case in the Uncle Remus tales), but rather the economic self-interest of old Julius himself who, as the businessman gradually learns in *The Conjure Woman,* has no intention of allowing the white man's economic encroachment on his holdings to go unchallenged. [Andrews's note.]

In his conjure stories Chesnutt did not attempt to expand Julius into a fully-rounded character. To a significant extent, the possibility of Julius's development is limited by the role he plays in the frame story in which his tales are placed. Popularized first by Thomas Nelson Page and later employed by his imitators in plantation fiction, the narrative structure which Chesnutt used in his conjure stories was not designed to delineate the ex-slave's character except insofar as his storytelling talents were concerned. The Page formula required only one thing of the ex-slave raconteur—that he recount his memories of ante-bellum times in an affecting and authentic manner to a curious and appreciative white outsider who would, in turn, record the story and the situation in which it was told. Chesnutt altered the conventional Page frame story by adding to it an ironic conclusion which grows out of the unusual presence of ulterior motives in Julius. But the repeated incidence of the ironic conclusion in Chesnutt's conjure stories, derived consistently from the same source, Julius's hidden economic motives, serves only to heighten the formulaic quality of those stories. Within that formula Julius remains a stable and familiar quantity, the black storytelling functionary of some charm and interest, but essentially a static character whose major purpose is to reaffirm his ingenuity in tale after tale.

J. Saunders Redding has also stressed the fact that Chesnutt did not break the traditional rules of local color characterization of the black man when he created Uncle Julius. While Chesnutt veered away from the view of the Afro-American as a "minstrel Sambo," he adhered to the Harris picture of the black man as "kind" and "childish," generous and loyal, "ignorant" and "dependent." [20] This assessment of Julius is accurate insofar as it describes the Julius of *The Conjure Woman,* but other conjure stories which were not included in the collection suggest a different view of Julius. In "Dave's Neckliss," [21] Chesnutt delves into the deeper nature of the old man not as storyteller but as human being, not as medium through which the old days may be viewed but as representative of the slave himself. Instead of ignoring the fact of Julius's slave background, the businessman narrator focuses directly on the effect of the old man's past on his present nature. The result is a drastic alteration of the standard type of the ex-slave narrator. The simple child of nature in *The Conjure Woman* [22] becomes in

---

[20] Redding, p. 69. [Andrews's note.]

[21] Charles W. Chesnutt, "Dave's Neckliss," *Atlantic Monthly,* LXIV (1899), 500–08. [Andrews's note, pp. 188–198 in this volume.]

[22] "Mars Jeems's Nightmare," *The Conjure Woman* (1899; reprinted Ann Arbor: Univ. of Michigan Press, 1969), p. 64. All further references to *The Conjure Woman* are from this edition. [Andrews's note.]

"Dave's Neckliss" a somewhat "chilling psychological spectacle of a mind enslaved long after the shackles had been struck off." [23] In *The Conjure Woman* the tales and behavior of Julius are cited by the white businessman as evidence of the "quaintly humorous" or "wildly extravagant" cast of "the negro's imagination." [24] But they are identified in "Dave's Neckliss" as "the legitimate fruit" of "centuries of repression." [25] The narrator of "Dave's Neckliss" realizes that a void exists in the central being of Julius, a void which his unconscious artistry and shrewdness of mind cannot fill. The businessman doubts whether Julius "had more than the most elementary ideas of love, friendship, patriotism, religion"; he doubts that the old man "even realized, except in a vague, uncertain way, his own degradation." In the businessman's doubts Chesnutt revealed the deficiencies of Julius as a character and the limitations of the popular literary stereotype of the "old-time Negro."

Charles Chesnutt's conjure stories do not break with the local color tradition in their depiction of Julius in a typecast role with familiar manners and traits of character. But "Dave's Neckliss" indicates what is sacrificed when the black man is treated as merely a local color vehicle. He becomes half a man despite his impressive credentials. The product of the slave system has paid a price for the idiosyncrasies and oddities which the local colorist celebrates, the price of a fully rounded, complex identity awakened to a world beyond his own locale. Thus in "Dave's Neckliss" Chesnutt, without attacking the local color presentation of the "old-time Negro," which was the model he followed in creating Uncle Julius, pointed out the particular conditions under which his remnant of pre-war days developed. He asked his reader to recognize the ex-slave as a partially blighted figure whose very picturesqueness and value as a local color figure were dependent on the stultifying effect of slavery on his innate endowments and capabilities.

The hints in "Dave's Neckliss" concerning the tragedy of Uncle Julius indicate Chesnutt's willingness, at least on one occasion, to question or offer alternative responses to local color conventions. While local color writers of the South found the black man a convenient comic type, Chesnutt pointed to his obvious limitations as a serious character and implied that slavery was to blame for his failure to develop. This realm of speculation was entered rarely if ever by other regional writers of Chesnutt's day. In the work of those local colorists who dealt most explicitly with the slave sys-

---

[23] "Dave's Neckliss," p. 501. [Andrews's note, page 189 in this volume.]
[24] *The Conjure Woman*, p. 41. [Andrews's note, pages 129–130 in this volume.]
[25] "Dave's Neckliss," p. 501. [Andrews's note, page 189 in this volume.]

tem in the South, the "plantation school" of writers, a view of slavery as cruel or stultifying was contradicted most often by an ex-slave narrator who eulogized the days "befo' de wah'" as carefree, happy, and harmonious for blacks and whites alike. The nostalgic utterances of Uncle Billy, Edinburg, and the other ex-slaves prominent in Page's *In Ole Virginia* attest to a close, almost familial bond between the slave and his master.[26] Such a relationship is celebrated in the works of other plantationists, particularly those of Harry Stillwell Edwards, F. Hopkinson Smith, and Joel Chandler Harris. But it should be noted that the typical relationship which appeared in plantation fiction was that of the aristocrat and his household servant. Page's Uncle Billy and Edinburg, Smith's Chad, Allen's Peter Cotton, and Harris's Uncle Remus, while they differ in personal characteristics and development in their stories, share at least one thing in common— they all enjoyed privileged positions as personal valets, house servants, or overseers while they were slaves. For these characters whose lives revolved around the plantation "big house," the claim made by Uncle Billy that "'niggers didn't hed nothin' 'tall to do'" before emancipation seems fairly accurate.[27]

But significantly, the ex-slave narrators of the popular plantation writers do not reminisce about life in the slave quarters or about the work the ordinary slave had to do. The careers of old "marster" and "mistis" and their children dominate the recollections of Page's narrators and those of his successors. Of their lives apart from the lives of their masters these old ex-slaves say little if anything, so completely has their self-concept depended on their intimate connection to the white world. Uncle Remus, it is true, assumes a degree of independence in his stories which the typical ex-slave narrator in plantation fiction does not possess.[28] But when Harris allowed Remus to voice his views about the Old South, as he did in "A Story of the War," Remus speaks "from the standpoint of a Southerner," as the standard ex-slave does in plantation fiction.[29] His admission of his automatic fidelity to his master, which earned for him the responsibility of overseer to the slaves and protector of his owner's family and estate during the war, affirms Remus's essential similarity to the plantation writers'

---

[26] Francis Pendleton Gaines, *The Southern Plantation* (New York: Columbia Univ. Press, 1925), p. 78. [Andrews's note.]

[27] The quotation is from Page's *In Ole Virginia* (1887; reprinted, Chapel Hill: Univ. of North Carolina Press, 1969), p. 10. [Andrews's note.]

[28] Cousins, p. 132. [Andrews's note.]

[29] See Harris's "A Story of the War" in *Uncle Remus, His Songs and Sayings* (1880; reprinted, New York: Appleton, 1920), pp. 201–202. [Andrews's note.]

favorite Negro type—the old and faithful retainer, the black adjunct to a white aristocracy.

Charles Chesnutt's first conjure story offered an alternative to the pre-occupation of Southern regional writing with the faithful retainer stereo-type as the major black figure of interest and significance on the old plantation. "The Goophered Grapevine" introduced a strange, new figure, Aunt Peggy, an enterprising black voodooist, whose powers and influence in the story opened up an untouched area of Southern custom and folk be-lief to a curious readership. The story also described the fate of Henry, an ordinary black field hand representative of the black laborer whose life and lot had been excluded from the pages of plantation fiction up to that time. The focus of "The Goophered Grapevine" on the experience of the slave who did the work rather than on the aristocrat who enjoyed the benefits of that work signaled Chesnutt's crucial reorientation of point of view in his stories of ante-bellum plantation life. The businessman narrator of "Dave's Neckliss," the second Chesnutt story in which Julius appears, defines this reorientation when he remarks that Julius "never indulged in any regrets for the Arcadian joyousness and irresponsibility which was a somewhat popular conception of slavery; his had not been the lot of the houseservant, but that of the toiling field hand." [30] By locating the point of view of his conjure stories in Julius, a field hand, Chesnutt was able to take a new look at the whites and blacks who were committed to the South's "peculiar institution," a look unbiased by the sort of affection and nostal-gia Uncle Remus and Page's uncles displayed for their erstwhile masters and their former positions. The possibility lay open to examine the mun-dane, everyday life of the slave, the relationship of the master to the ordi-nary slave, and the attitudes of such a slave to both his daily experience and his seldom-seen master.

The slave-master relationship in Chesnutt's conjure stories differs markedly from the typical relationship of benevolent aristocrat and loyal retainer which dominated Southern plantation fiction at the time. Accurate depiction of ante-bellum life in the sandhills region of North Carolina de-manded a departure from the plantation norm. The conventional picture of plantation life, epitomized in the writings of Page, the descendant of the Virginia aristocracy, held little in common with the realities of life in cen-tral North Carolina before the war. This region possessed neither the rich soil which supported vast plantations in the Deep South nor the old es-tablished families who maintained great holdings of land and slaves in the

---

[30] "Dave's Neckliss," p. 501. [Andrews's note, page 189 in this volume.]

Virginia Tidewater region. Thus the predominant class in central North Carolina was the middle class, chiefly represented by the small farmer who often worked in the fields beside the few slaves he owned, trying by "thrift and energy" to "get ahead in life." [31]

The desire to "get ahead" is what distinguishes the Mars Dugals, Mars Marrabos, and other slaveholders of Julius's tales from the stereotypical aristocrats of Page and Smith and Edwards. While the aristocrats in Page's stories duel and dance, court and politic and go off to war, the parsimonious Scots in Chesnutt's stories cheat each other, indulge their gambling vices, hunt down their runaways, argue with their wives, curse their slaves, and worry over their bankbooks. The salient characteristics of most of the masters Julius remembers are not cruelty and inhumanity but meanness and selfishness. [32] For these are the descendants of those hard-bitten small farmers, merchants, and ruffians who enliven the work of early Southwestern humorists like Johnson Jones Hooper and Augustus Baldwin Longstreet. They have become a bit more genteel; they can afford some of the vices of a gentleman. But they are still money-hungry, and their treatment of their slaves displays a fundamental regard for profit at the expense of the physical and emotional welfare of the slave. Even when these whites exhibit a qualified liberality toward their slaves, [33] their kindness is engendered by hard headed business sense, not humanitarianism.

Nevertheless, the slaveowners of Chesnutt's conjure tales, though only sketched in the recollections of Uncle Julius, do offer a more balanced, untinted portrait of the representative slaveowner in the South than the picturesque or eccentric aristocrats of Page, Allen, Smith, and Edwards. Through the bland commentary of an old ex-slave, Chesnutt joined early local color depicters of the Southern middle and lower classes like Joel Chandler Harris and Richard Malcolm Johnston [34] in their efforts to render an accurate impression of those regions of the South which did not

---

[31] Guion G. Johnson, *Ante-Bellum North Carolina* (Chapel Hill: Univ. of North Carolina Press, 1973), p. 59. [Andrews's note.]

[32] See, for example, Mars Dugal' McAdoo in "The Goophered Grapevine," a man who cheats his fellow slaveowners in order to make a quick buck off a peculiar slave who can work tirelessly in the spring but almost dies in the winter. [Andrews's note.]

[33] In "Mars Jeems's Nightmare" a previously cruel white man changes his treatment of his slaves, with the result that he earns more from his plantation than ever before. [Andrews's note.]

[34] Though often similar in tone and subject to the plantation writers, Harris in books like *Mingo and Other Sketches in Black and White* (Boston: James R. Osgood, 1884) did achieve a certain distinction as a depictor of lower and more representative classes of

support the kind of social and economic system exemplified in most plantation writing. Chesnutt did not focus on the Southern middle and lower
classes with the thoroughness and breadth of a Harris or a Johnston, but
his efforts do represent an introduction to a seldom-discussed people in a
region largely ignored by the best writers of his day.

If Julius's tales derive some historical significance from the fact that
they introduce a new class of slaveholder, they deserve even greater attention for their treatment of a class of slave unfamiliar to readers of Southern local color. Within the confines of the local color tradition, Chesnutt
depicted the situation of the average slave on an average plantation with
greater care and sympathy than any of his white fiction-writing contemporaries. This does not mean that Chesnutt created rounded, complex
black characters in his conjure stories; the brevity of his genre prevented
this. Nor does it claim for Chesnutt an early realistic examination of the
everyday experience of those who suffered most under slavery. The perva-
sive use of conjuration and supernatural events in the tales of Uncle Julius
removes Chesnutt's characters from the mundane world and places them
at varying distances from the reader's powers of sympathetic identification.[35] But the reason for resorting to conjuration by the slave heroes and
heroines in Julius's stories points back to the chief distinction of these tales
vis-á-vis the slave.

If the central black characters of Julius's tales do not possess a complex human identity, they usually evidence rather early in their stories some
quality or trait or obsession which motivates them and brings them eventually into conflict with the white slaveholding institutions. Tenie and Sandy
in "Po' Sandy"[36] are hardly individualized at all until their marital love
and devotion moves them to defy the plans of their master. Then Tenie re-
sorts to her conjure powers as a means of preserving their relationship. In

---

whites in rural middle Georgia. Johnston's *Dukesborough Tales,* 2nd ed. (New York:
Harper's, 1883) are similarly distinctive because of their attention to the life of the
middle class farmer of central Georgia. [Andrews's note.]

[35] An inordinate or capricious use of conjuring destroys the effectiveness of such stories
as "Tobe's Tribulations," *The Southern Workman,* XXIX (1900), 656–64, and "A Victim of Heredity," *Self-Culture,* XI, No. 5 (1900), 404–09. Great restraint in the use of
conjuring is a major factor contributing to the success of such tales as "The Goophered
Grapevine" and "Po' Sandy." This might explain why "The Goophered Grapevine" and
"Po' Sandy" were included in *The Conjure Woman* while "Tobe's Tribulations" and "A
Victim of Heredity" were excluded. [Andrews's note.]

[36] "Po' Sandy," *The Conjure Woman,* pp. 36–63. [Andrews's note, pages 128–136 in
this volume.]

the case of Becky and her child Mose,[37] mother and son lack vitality as characters until they are faced with the prospect of separation as a result of the master's decision to exchange Becky for a horse. But when the familial bond is threatened by the exigencies of the slave system, the love of child and parent manifests itself in the lengths to which both will go to circumvent the master's control. As a result Becky and Mose are vitalized and individualized in their story by the intensity of their feeling for each other.

While not every story told by Uncle Julius pits slave ingenuity and voodoo against the established power of the slaveholder,[38] almost all the stories portray conjuring as a means by which a slave expresses and attempts to preserve his most deeply felt emotions, human relationships, or identity. Lacking the space in his Uncle Julius tales to create complex human figures, Chesnutt concentrated on depicting slaves whose motives— love, hate, jealousy, envy, and pride—and pathetic or even tragic actions gave incontrovertible evidence of their humanity. By de-emphasizing physical descriptions and personal idiosyncrasies of his characters, Chesnutt avoided the dangers of local color caricature of blacks. He portrayed the slave's essential humanity beneath the accidents of his peculiar ethnic background and social status. To reveal the black man as a representative and sympathetic human figure, Chesnutt made his condition in slavery a kind of crucible which revealed authentic and profound human emotions and desires once its particularly restrictive, dehumanizing effects were applied to him specifically. Within the crucible the slave suffers from the abuses of slavery, but he or she does not become merely a victim, an object of pity. In Chesnutt's conjure stories the most disturbing aspect of slavery is not the possibilities of physical abuse, which occurs very rarely, but the likelihood of a more profound threat to the slave's dignity, his capacity to feel, his human identity. In response to this threat, Chesnutt's heroes and heroines need not perform superhuman acts of rebellion or express their superiority through a daring escape to freedom in order to confirm their human worth.[39] Neither Tenie nor Becky nor the other main characters in The Conjure Woman ever permanently escape her or his physical bondage, but the actions of each attest to a freedom from the enslavement

---

[37] "Sis' Becky's Pickaninny," The Conjure Woman, pp. 132–161. [Andrews's note, pages 157–166 in this volume.]
[38] "The Conjurer's Revenge," a seldom discussed story in The Conjure Woman, describes the use of voodoo by a conjure man against another slave. In "The Goophered Grapevine" Aunt Peggy sells her conjure powers to the white slaveowner. [Andrews's note.]
[39] Only rarely is permanent flight from slavery attempted in Julius's stories; only twice is it achieved. In both cases ("Lonesome Ben" and "Tobe's Tribulations"), the slave who

of the spirit. Within the restrictions of the slave condition, each illustrates a realistic standard of heroism. It is not the dog-like loyalty of the family servants and retainers too often celebrated by plantation writers. Nor is it the open militancy and defiance of slave insurrectionists and fugitives who were special favorites of the abolitionist writers.[40] Time after time in Uncle Julius's stories the exigencies of the slave condition force a particular slave into a desperate situation which elicits from him or her some kind of action. But whether or not this action is successful is less important than the fact that the action itself confirms the slave's identity in the story as a serious figure who deserves the reader's respect, concern, and empathy. At times the slave's action may constitute a direct challenge to the authority of the master. But what is at stake in Chesnutt's conjure stories is not the black man's triumph over the institution of slavery but something even more important to his progress in post-war America—his triumph over the view of Afro-Americans that the institution and its celebrators had perpetrated.

When Charles Chesnutt first began publishing his Uncle Julius stories, the writers of the plantation tradition had largely won the sympathy of Northern reading audiences for an ideal and a social system which an earlier generation of Yankees had fought in the Civil War. The aristocratic ideal revered by Page and his followers was not merely the nostalgic memory of a confirmed reactionary; it was proposed as a viable means of leading the South out of the chaos of Reconstruction.[41] Page spoke most explicitly of the need of the erstwhile slave for the guidance and correction of the "natural" leaders of the South.[42] Viewing the black man as happiest in slavery, Page and many of his followers frequently presented in their work ex-slaves unfitted for life outside its confines because they lack either the ambition or the ability to deal maturely and intelligently with the kinds of problems faced every day by whites.[43] The existence of these characters

---

escapes from his master eventually returns to the plantation with ironic and tragic results. [Andrews's note.]

[40] See Sterling Brown, *The Negro in American Fiction* (Washington, D.C.: Associates in Negro Folk Education, 1937), pp. 45–46. [Andrews's note.]

[41] The response of the Southern aristocrat to the problems of the post-war South is a central theme in two Page novels, *Red Rock* (1899) and *Gordon Keith* (1903). [Andrews's note.]

[42] Theodore L. Gross, *Thomas Nelson Page* (New York: Twayne, 1967), pp. 105–12. [Andrews's note.]

[43] Examples of this type of ex-slave are plentiful in the fiction of Thomas Nelson Page. Free Joe in Harris's "Free Joe and the Rest of the World," *Free Joe and Other Georgian Sketches* (New York: Scribner's, 1898), pp. 1–20 also illustrated the failure of the freed black to provide for himself. Such sentimental pairs as Isam and Major Washington in Edwards's fiction, Chad and Colonel Carter in Smith's popular novels, and Peter Cotton

reinforced the idea of "The Wretched Freedman," the childlike, undeveloped, incompetent black man of the Reconstruction.[44] But Chesnutt's picture of blacks in slavery, by concentrating on their tenacity of purpose, their depth of feeling, their resourcefulness, strength of character, and practicality, denied this view of the slave's disqualification for the responsibilities of a free person. By showing slavery not as a protected, sheltered condition of existence tailored to meet an inferior race's ample needs but as a difficult and fortuitous way of life in which great determination, courage, and quick-wittedness were needed in order to survive, Chesnutt proved his essential theme in the Uncle Julius stories—that in the midst of his degradation the black man had affirmed his human dignity and purpose. Chesnutt also left little doubt that having endured the crucible of slavery, the black man and woman could overcome the problems of a free status.

To William Dean Howells and J. Saunders Redding, the objectivity with which Chesnutt treated Uncle Julius and his memories of ante-bellum days stands as Chesnutt's most noteworthy achievement in his conjure stories.[45] But the significance of the stories should be divided between their excellence as local color fiction and their value as realistic, and at times unconventional, assessments of slavery and the Afro-American who lived under its domination. Reaction to the stories during Chesnutt's day reflects this divided significance. Most reviewers, struck by the new author's original materials and technical skill, received Chesnutt as a promising new regionalist who had mined a new vein and deserved credit for the literary ore he had discovered. However, several reviewers called attention to the pathos of Julius's stories and found in the stories an unromanticized picture of "a tragic period in our national life" whose "sorrowful legacy" still remained.[46] That both kinds of response to the conjure stories are possible, and in fact are suggested by Chesnutt, is a further tribute to the art and sophistication of this writer.

By having Julius narrate his tales to two listeners, the white businessman and his wife, Chesnutt opened up the possibility of two contrasting

---

and Colonel Fields in Allen's "Two Gentlemen of Kentucky" indicate the bonds which many Southern writers considered basic to the black-white relationship after the Civil War. [Andrews's note.]

[44] Sterling Brown, "Negro Character as Seen by White Authors," *Journal of Negro Education,* II (1933), 187. [Andrews's note.]

[45] Howells, "Mr. Charles W. Chesnutt's Stories," p. 700; Saunders Redding, *To Make a Poet Black,* p. 69. [Andrews's note.]

[46] See the Boston *Evening Transcript,* 22 March, 1899. This review may be found in the scrapbook of press clippings on *The Conjure Woman* held in the Chesnutt Collection of the Fisk University Library. [Andrews's note.]

ways of reading the conjure stories.[47] One could join the businessman in
regarding Julius's stories as "'ingenious fairy tale[s]'" and "'absurdly impossible yarn[s]'" concocted to entertain and subtly manipulate his
employers.[48] Or one could respond to the stories as absorbing and moving
narratives in themselves, as the businessman's wife does. At the end of "Sis'
Becky's Pickaninny," the wife, who has been moved to "sympathy, indignation, pity" and "satisfaction" by the story, chastises her husband for his
bemused skepticism in terming the story a "'fairy tale.'" "'[T]he story
bears the stamp of truth, if ever one did,'" she announces. When her husband objects to the credibility of "'the humming-bird episode'" and "'the
mocking-bird digression,'" she dismisses his criticism by insisting that,
"'those are mere ornamental details and not at all essential. The story is
true to nature, and might have happened half a hundred times, and no
doubt did happen, in those horrid days before the war.'"[49]

While the businessman-narrator has closed his literalistic mind to
Julius's story because some aspects of it are frankly imaginative, his wife
weighs the relative importance of the folk elements and potentially tragic
theme of the story and comes to a significant conclusion. She realizes that
the transformation of a child into a humming bird is fantastic, but she also
understands it to be a peripheral element in the story. What is essential to
the story, the misery of separation and joy of reunion as depicted in the example of the slave-mother and her son, she regards as being "'true to nature.'" She suspends her disbelief in the case of the conjure motifs so that
she may receive the emotional impact of Julius's stories, which depends not
on an adherence to narrow standards of literal reality but on an attention
to essential, representative, universal truths of "nature" reflected in the
lives of a group that had rarely been accorded such attention, black people
in slavery.

By dramatizing the distinctive reactions of the businessman and his
wife to Julius's tales, Charles Chesnutt suggested to his readers and critics
two essentially complementary approaches to his conjure stories. The
businessman views the stories as amusing and fascinating imaginative

---

[47] Richard E. Baldwin in "The Art of *The Conjure Woman*," *American Literature*, XLIII
(1971), 385–98, has also noted the importance of the frame story and the contrast between the businessman and his wife to the message of *The Conjure Woman*. [Andrews's
note.]
[48] At the conclusion to "Sis' Becky's Pickaninny," the businessman's view of the story as
a "fairy tale" is given. At the conclusion to "Po' Sandy" the businessman calls Julius's
tale "that absurdly impossible yarn." [Andrews's note.]
[49] "Sis' Becky's Pickaninny," p. 159. [Andrews's note, pages 165–166 in this volume.]

pieces enlivened by the presence of Julius's secret motives and his knowledge of Afro-American folklore. The quaintness of the ex-slave and the information in his stories that shed light on the history of the region or the way the black man's mind works are what interest the businessman. They are also what would and did interest the average reader of local color in Chesnutt's day. The businessman's repeated skepticism toward Julius's tales confirms the validity of a similar response from a local color reader who prefers verifiable reality to fantasy and speculation. For this type of reader, the white man's response to Julius's tales as "'ingenious fairy tales'" helps to pigeonhole the stories along with other popular and diverting collections of Negro humor and folk literature, headed, no doubt, by the Uncle Remus stories. The businessman's response represents and invites the traditional local color response to the stories of Uncle Julius.

But if the husband's view affirms the possibility of a traditional interpretation of Julius's stories, the view of the wife suggests the inadequacy of the traditional local color attitude toward such stories. Instead of responding to the unusual, picturesque, and highly imaginative details of slave life in North Carolina, the woman is moved by the reactions of Julius's characters to recognize their individual predicaments. Julius's adherence to or departure from the conventions of local color realism means less to her than his sometimes tragic revelations of the humanity of black people as reflected through their experiences as slaves. Through the inclusion of the wife's response, Chesnutt deepened the emotional channels of his conjure stories and transcended some of the limitations of the local color story. He called attention to the tragic or near-tragic elements of his stories, while avoiding what Saunders Redding has called "the weak pseudo-tragedy of propaganda."[50] The wife's sensitivity to the joys and sorrows of black mothers and children, black husbands and wives, argues the possibility of a new, untraditional response to blacks as representative human beings, not as "uncles" and "mammies," "pickaninnies" and "sambos." Chesnutt as author does not demand such a response from his readers; he merely dramatizes it in a few stories with a reticence that has been praised as his most significant achievement in the conjure stories. But reticence and objectivity alone do not summarize Chesnutt's achievement in the tales of Uncle Julius. The significance of these early stories by the first important black American writer of fiction lies in the objective balance that Chesnutt maintained in them between the demands of popular local color realism and the obligation of the artist to reveal "truth to nature" despite the traditions, conventions, and prejudices of the literature of his own day.

---

[50] Redding, p. 69. [Andrews's note.]

FROM *THE SHORT FICTION OF CHARLES W. CHESNUTT*

Sylvia Lyons Render

Public Reception

As has been the case with many other writers of distinction, [Charles] Chesnutt was not properly appreciated by his generation. Although he realized that he was ahead of his time, this awareness could not have altogether relieved the pain of rejection for writing works that promoted American ideals, according to acceptable contemporary literary standards, in popular American forms, published by the most reputable firms. Ironically, the contemporary Paul Laurence Dunbar, a poetic prodigy and able fictionist, became almost universally known in Negro communities across the country while the name of Chesnutt still has no significance for most blacks. Both writers had enthusiastic white readers, but Chesnutt's popularity — which never had a chance to develop among his people — diminished while Dunbar's increased. That relatively few blacks had read any of Chesnutt's works initially or were made aware of them later may account for this paradoxical trend. The main reason is that Dunbar focused largely on an idealized past cherished by whites while Chesnutt exposed the hypocritical nature of race relations in the United States and suggested remedies within the framework of the Constitution.

For a few years, beginning in 1899, Chesnutt's work received widespread attention both from the leading critics of the day and from the general public. Initially the reactions were overwhelmingly favorable; however, as Chesnutt began to explore aspects of race relations usually avoided by established writers, he stirred up lively debates about his fiction. *The Conjure Woman* tales were warmly received as unique, enlightening, "of entrancing interest and of finished literary execution." A reader who had known Frederick Douglass wrote that Chesnutt's biography gave him "a fuller and closer estimate of the man than ever before." The "finished style" and "interpretive" nature of this volume led Vernon Loggins to declare that its general excellence was sufficient to win for Chesnutt "a place of importance in Negro literature."[1]

Sylvia Lyons Render, ed., *The Short Fiction of Charles W. Chesnutt.*

[1] Vernon Loggins, *The Negro Author: His Development in America to 1900* (Port Washington, N.Y.: Kennikat Press, Inc.), p. 270. [Render's note.]

The author's "great delicacy and sympathy" in exploring some of the unacknowledged dilemmas of "the educated and well-to-do of the race" aroused strong feelings, often dictated by the personal or sectional bias of the reviewers. The Bridgeport, Connecticut, *Standard* found Chesnutt's disclosures of the underlying facts and inevitable conditions of the race situation in the color-line stories helpful to the reader's understanding, but Nancy Huston Banks in *The Bookman* (February, 1900) found only "The Wife of His Youth" wholly acceptable. While admitting that both "Uncle Wellington's Wives" and "The Sheriff's Children" were believable, she declared that Chesnutt showed "a lamentable lack of tact and reckless disregard of matters respected by more experienced writers in publishing the stories."[2] (She was doubtless referring to Chesnutt's frank discussion of race-mixing, with and without the benefit of clergy. The traditional treatment of this subject by both blacks and whites was less realistic than Chesnutt's; some aspects of it were carefully avoided.) A similar dichotomy of opinion was expressed about some of his novels. *The House Behind the Cedars* (1900) was a bold treatment of "passing" and miscegenation, and unusual in its sympathetic treatment of the major Negro characters.

Chesnutt's unusually forthright treatment of personal race relations from the Afro-American point of view prompted William Dean Howells, dean of American literary critics, to acknowledge in the May, 1900, *Atlantic Monthly*:

> We had known the nethermost world of the grotesque and comical Negro and the terrible and tragic Negro through the white observer on the outside . . . but it had remained with Mr. Chesnutt to acquaint us with those regions where the paler shades dwell.[3]

This appraisal is objective. However, after reading *The Marrow of Tradition* (1901), Chesnutt's most fiery and controversial novel, Howells let Chesnutt's race color his reaction in part by declaring in the December, 1901, issue of the *North American Review* that

> At his worst, he [Chesnutt] is no worse than the higher average of the ordinary novelist, but he ought always to be very much better, for he began better, and he is of that race which has, first of all, to get rid of the cakewalk. . . .[4]

---

[2] "Novel Notes," *The Bookman*, X (February, 1900), 597–8. [Render's note.]
[3] "Mr. Charles W. Chesnutt's Stories," *Atlantic Monthly*, LXXXV (May, 1900), 701. [Render's note.]
[4] "A Psychological Counter Current in Recent Fiction," *North American Review*, CLXXII (December, 1901) p. 882. [Render's note.]

The critic redeemed himself somewhat later in the review of the same novel. Though Howells found the novel too bitter, he could find no fault with Chesnutt's aesthetics or ethics. In essence he forecast the inevitable dissolution of the color bars which Chesnutt sought vainly to remove.[5]

The Colonel's Dream (1905) was anticlimactic. Though clearly conciliatory in tone and lacking the confrontations between blacks and whites which had especially aroused the public ire against the other novels, this book found few readers. Critics received it more kindly; its truth was generally conceded and a few rated it as Chesnutt's best work. However, most of the reading public, who were predominantly white, obviously reflected the general attitude of a nation setting out to become a world power based upon a doctrine of white supremacy and manifest destiny. They therefore rejected Chesnutt's increasingly explicit appeals for implementation of the principles of democracy on which this country had ostensibly been founded.

Because Chesnutt did not receive the recognition his artistry merited, he reopened his legal stenography firm in 1901. At that time too few black people, regardless of their views or their financial ability, bought enough books to support any writer. Moreover, the majority of the white reading public were either too censorious of or indifferent to Chesnutt's position on race relations to buy enough of his works to make authorship even supportive. Inevitably discouraged by the poor market, the publishers ceased more than routine promotion of Chesnutt's books. Invited to address a literary association in Boston, in 1902, Chesnutt wrote Monroe Trotter:

> If I were making any considerable sums out of these race problem books,
> I would cheerfully spend it in such ways (taking trips and making speeches
> gratis or for partial expenses); but books in sympathy with the higher as-
> pirations of the Negro do not sell by the tens of thousands, and mine have
> cost me more to write, in time spent, than I have got out of them.[6]

Chesnutt could recoup financial losses incurred while writing full time, but apparently he would not have a second chance to achieve his "high and holy purpose." As a writer whose works would not sell, he no longer had at his disposal the only practicable means of reaching the people he wanted to influence. He was too realistic to expect any publisher

---

[5] *Ibid.*, p. 882. [Render's note.]
[6] Letter from Chesnutt to Trotter, December 17, 1902, Correspondence, CC [Chesnutt Collection, Fisk University]. [Render's note.]

to handle writings promoting unpopular causes and too honest to assume a stance contrary to his convictions.

Ironically, Chesnutt was more successful in breaking down racial barriers in the United States by his own life than through any movement actuated by his writings. He became one of Cleveland's first citizens. Modest and proud, shy and witty, unassuming and outspoken, and more at home with individuals than with crowds, Chesnutt was wise to bypass the political career for which his legal training and skill as a public speaker would have been assets. Instead, he used his knowledge of the law and a perennial interest in politics to secure and protect the rights of the black minority in the community and in the courts. Politically active as a private citizen, he came to urge his people to abandon blind party loyalties and to support responsive candidates regardless of their political affiliations. He was a participating member of many local and national groups, including the Cleveland Chamber of Commerce, the Cleveland Bar Association, the Cleveland Council on Sociology (as its first secretary and later as president), the Playhouse Settlement, now famous as Karamu House (also as the presiding officer), Booker T. Washington's Committee of Twelve, and the General Committee of the National Association for the Advancement of Colored People, hereafter referred to as NAACP, which he supported from its inception as the National Negro Committee in 1909 until his death.

Chesnutt enjoyed a warm friendship with Washington, dating from the time of his visit to Tuskegee during his tour of black Southern schools in 1901 and lasting until the educator's death in 1915. Chesnutt and Du Bois seemed to have mutual respect and admiration. Recognizing that both these great leaders had the same ultimate goals and that one great need of Afro-Americans was unity, Chesnutt championed neither man publicly during the years of the Washington-Du Bois debates. Instead, he supported to some extent and constructively criticized the philosophies of both. Chesnutt was also adamant in his refusal to participate in the personal vilification of either by partisans of the other.

Many letters in the voluminous correspondence between Chesnutt and Washington constitute a debate on the black man's use of the ballot. Chesnutt once wrote to Washington:

> I am squarely opposed to any restriction of the franchise in the South on any basis now proposed. It is wholly and solely an effort in my opinion to deprive the Negro of every vestige of power and every particle of representation. How completely this leaves him in the power of the whites and exposes him to their cruelty and contempt, is indicated in the disclosure of the peonage investigation now in progress in your State. I have no

faith in the Southern people's sense of justice as far as the Negro's rights are concerned.[7]

Within two months Chesnutt addressed another long letter to Washington in which he announced that he had expressed in print his disagreement with his friend on voting, but at the same time recognized his "valuable services to the country."[8] Chesnutt also treated the educational biases of Washington and Du Bois, which he considered irrelevant in connection with the ballot:

> You Southern educators are all bound up with some cause or other, devotion to which sometimes unconsciously warps your opinions as to what is best for the general welfare of the race. You are conducting an industrial school, and naturally you place stress upon that sort of education, with perfect honesty and sincerity, but with the zeal of the advocate, before whose eyes his client's case always looms up so as to dwarf the other side. Unfortunately, those who would discourage the higher education of the Negro, use your words for that purpose. Du Bois is in much the same situation. He is connected with Atlanta [University] and it is hard for him to discuss the abstract rights of the Negro without ringing in the higher education. Neither sort of education has anything directly to do with the civil and political rights of the Negro—these would be just as vital and fundamental as if there were not a single school of any kind in the Southern States. . . .[9]

When, in 1910, asked by Du Bois to sign a protest, "Race Relations in the United States," which repudiated statements made by Washington during an interview published in the London *Morning Post,* Chesnutt responded with a reasoned refusal.[10] Through the years he had consistently avoided attacking Washington in the columns of *The* (Boston) *Guardian,* though invited to do so constantly by its courageous and impetuous editor, William Monroe Trotter, a Harvard college mate and partisan of Du Bois

---

[7] Letter from Chesnutt to Washington, June 27, 1903, Correspondence, CC. [Render's note.]

[8] Letter from Chesnutt to Washington, August 11, 1903, Correspondence, CC. [Render's note.]

[9] CWC, "The Disfranchisement of the Negro," *The Negro Problem: A Series of Articles by Representative Negroes of To-Day* (New York: James Pott & Company, 1903), 74–124. [Render's note. This quotation is *not* from this source but from *Charles Waddell Chesnutt* by Helen M. Chesnutt, pp. 195–196.]

[10] Letter from Chesnutt to Du Bois, November 21, 1910, quoted in Helen M. Chesnutt, *op. cit.,* pp. 240–44. [Render's note.]

who served a short jail sentence for heckling Washington when he spoke in Boston in July, 1903.

On the other hand, however, Chesnutt spoke out unequivocally against any misrepresentation of facts about blacks, regardless of the race of the perpetrator. Largely through his efforts, the Macmillan Company withdrew from sale the libelous *The American Negro* (1901) by a Negro, William Hannibal Thomas. Chesnutt gathered evidence to show that the author was a fraud, presented it to the publishers, and scathed the scoundrel.[11]

Chesnutt also served continuously as a source of information on Afro-American life and culture. He condemned the Supreme Court for increasingly depriving blacks of their rights. He expressed his views concerning contemporary or perennial problems on pending legislation to local, state, and national lawmakers as well as to other influential people on all these levels. He lobbied locally against an anti-intermarriage bill (later defeated with the help of the Cleveland delegation) before the Ohio Legislature in 1913 and another in the United States House of Representatives in 1914. In 1915, Chesnutt prodded the governor of Ohio into action which forbade the showing of *The Birth of a Nation* to about one thousand Ohio teen-agers who were visiting Philadelphia. During the First World War he protested the treatment of Negro soldiers, and in the Senate Judiciary Committee hearings of 1928 opposed the Shipstead Anti-Injunction Bill because of the anti-Negro practices of labor unions.

Chesnutt spoke on many other occasions and also published articles on various aspects of Negro life and art in this country and abroad. He always emphasized the accomplishments of his fellow-blacks; he did not "think it the part of policy to be always dwelling upon the weakness of the Negro race." Moreover, he insisted on their inherent right to all the privileges of American citizenship and strongly criticized all obstructing forces.

Signal recognition came to Chesnutt in many ways. He was among the literary figures (the only Clevelander) invited to attend Mark Twain's seventieth birthday party at Delmonico's in New York City in 1905. He was twice chosen to serve as president of the Ohio State Stenographers' Association. Besides being a member of the bibliophile Rowfant Club from 1910 until his death, he was elected to membership in the National Arts Club in 1917. Wilberforce University conferred the LL.D. degree upon Chesnutt when he spoke there in 1913, and he was awarded the NAACP

---

[11] See Chesnutt's letter to Robert C. Ogden, May 27, 1904, in which he enclosed copies of communications on this matter, Correspondence, CC. See also CWC, "A Defamer of His Race," *The Critic,* XXXVIII (April, 1901), 350–51. [Render's note.]

Spingarn Medal in 1928 as the black person who that year had rendered
"the most distinguished service in some field of honorable endeavor." . . .

"BAXTER'S PROCRUSTES":
IRONY AND PROTEST

Robert Hemenway

Black American writers have traditionally suffered the critical injunc-
tion to avoid "protest" and write "universally," the implication being that
a Black author who creates imaginative truth about Black people in the
United States will necessarily produce a limited art. Louis Simpson, for example, has felt compelled to remind Gwendolyn Brooks that "if being a
Negro" is her "only subject," then "the writing is not important."[1] Such
instruction supposes that a Black author who writes successfully of white
people will automatically validate his talent, a supposition the artist accepts at great peril, since it suggests that Black experience is not universal.
    Charles Chesnutt responded to the presumptions of a white subject
matter in one of his most subtle short stories, "Baxter's Procrustes," published in *The Atlantic Monthly* in 1904. Although it has not been previously acknowledged, "Baxter's Procrustes" is probably a "protest story,"
the protest directed towards a specific act of discrimination: the refusal of
the Rowfant Club, a Cleveland literary society, to grant Chesnutt membership. A story with exclusively white characters, it is also one of the few successes of white subject–Black artist fiction.[2] Chesnutt's story explores habits of mind which distort reality into the shape of preconceptions, and in the
process exposes the inherent ironies in a literary philosophy which equates
truth with subject matter, confuses whiteness with art. The author's "pro-

---

[1] Louis Simpson in *The New York Herald Tribune Book Week,* October, 1963. Quoted
by Hoyt Fuller, "Towards a Black Aesthetic," in *The Black Aesthetic,* ed. Addison Gayle,
Jr. (New York, 1972), p. 4. [Hemenway's note.]
[2] There is a long list of Black novelists for example, who have written of a white subject
matter, usually without much success: Dunbar (*Love of Landry*), Wright (*Savage Holiday*), Motley (*Open* [sic] *Any Door*), Petry (*Country Place*), Hurston (*Seraph on the
Suwanee*), Baldwin (*Giovanni's Room*), Toomer (*York Beach*), Frank Yerby (novels too
numerous to mention). [Hemenway's note.]

test" becomes "universal," not because his subject is a white book club, but because the fictional club's intellectual assumptions deny literature any possibility of universal reference.

The Rowfant Club was a nationally known book club, a well established bastion of Cleveland aristocracy, and it has long been identified as the source for "Baxter's Procrustes." What has not been stressed, perhaps because Helen Chesnutt's biography did not give a date for her father's abortive attempt at Rowfant membership, is the story's relation to the membership denial.[3] Chesnutt had been invited to meetings as a guest apparently as early as 1899,[4] but it was in 1902 that his nomination for membership was refused. As a member of the club reported the incident in 1966:

> Around 1902 some of his friends, whose Saturday night guest he had frequently been, proposed him for membership in the Rowfant Club . . . There is not a clear record, as there should not be, of this first nomination to the club. It is enough to say that the time was not ripe at the turn of the century for a gentleman of his race to be proposed.[5]

Helen Chesnutt was only a bit more explicit; in her account Chesnutt was denied membership because, in the words of the membership committee, "one or two members thought the time hadn't come."[6]

A book club presuming to deal in the universal expressions of the human condition risks obvious irony when it refuses to acknowledge a writer's humanity, and the act reveals the same deficiency of intellect that calls for the Black author to "universalize" his efforts by dropping Black subject matter. In both instances the reality of Black people is distorted so that the perceiver's illusion is not endangered. Chesnutt wished to explore

---

[3] Helen Chesnutt, *Charles Waddell Chesnutt* (Chapel Hill, 1952). The unpublished Ph. D. dissertation of Sylvia Lyons-Render, "Eagle with Clipped Wings: Form and Feeling in the Fiction of Charles Waddell Chesnutt," (Nashville: George Peabody College for Teachers, 1962) discusses briefly the association between the story and the Rowfant Club. This is an extremely useful study, one that all Chesnutt students are particularly indebted to for ideas and information. [Hemenway's note.]

[4] Chesnutt's first book, *The Conjure Woman* had been issued in a special pre-trade edition by Houghton Mifflin in 1899, most copies of which were subscribed for by Rowfant members. See Charles Chesnutt, "Post-Bellum—Pre-Harlem" in *Breaking into Print,* ed. Elmer Adler (New York, 1937) pp. 48–49. (This article originally appeared in the *Colophon,* February, 1931.) [Hemenway's note, pp. 100–105 in this volume.]

[5] John B. Nicholson, Jr., "A Biographical Essay" in *Baxter's Procrustes* (Cleveland, 1966), p. 51. This is a superbly appointed re-issue of Chesnutt's story, published by the Rowfant Club, and limited to 180 numbered copies. [Hemenway's note.]

[6] Helen Chesnutt, p. 244. [Hemenway's note.]

this distorting faculty, this willful preference for illusion over reality, and it made the Rowfant Club the perfect subject for his effort. The club was willingly white, awaiting the ripeness of time to universalize its membership; it was also, as we shall see, a literary fraternity with blatantly nonliterary values, a book club without a commitment to literature. Chesnutt's skill in exposing such ironies was so subtle that even the Rowfant members have traditionally taken the story as an example of how Chesnutt "was a philosopher incapable of bitterness." [7] It may be that Chesnutt was more forgiving than most, since he did join the club in 1910 and apparently enjoyed its activities, but a close examination of the story reveals a serious indictment of the club's principles. To understand the full dimension of that indictment it is necessary to know exactly what portions of the Rowfant experience Chesnutt selected for his satire, since his strategy in the story was to undermine the narrator's explanation of the club's system.

The Rowfant was one of the most exclusive of Cleveland's adult male fraternities, made up largely of the monied aristocracy that tended to rule the Cleveland bar. Founded in 1892, it soon became famous for its limited editions in superb bindings, and its club rooms were among the city's most privileged confines. [8] In "Baxter's Procrustes" this Cleveland fraternity becomes the Bodleian Club, "Composed of gentlemen of culture who are interested in books and book collecting." [9] The accent is decidedly on the latter activity, as illustrated by the club's collection of "personal momentos of distinguished authors," including "a paperweight which once belonged to Goethe, a lead pencil used by Emerson, an autograph letter of Matthew Arnold and a chip from a tree felled by Mr. Gladstone." This collection is comic, but such relics were only slight exaggerations of the Rowfant's own shrine of artifacts which included autograph letters from various 19th century authors and "a receipt for compensation from the Salem customhouse" signed by Hawthorne. [10] The emphasis is upon possession, upon

---

[7] Nicholson, p. 51. [Hemenway's note.]
[8] The Rowfant took its name from Frederick Locker-Lampson's English country home. Lampson's library was legendary among 19th century collectors. See Russell Anderson, *The Rowfant Club* (Cleveland, 1955), and A. Growell, *American Book Clubs* (New York, 1907), 310–312. The Rowfant Club still exists, but I have generally referred to it in the past tense, because I am speaking of it only in Chesnutt's time. [Hemenway's note.]
[9] *Atlantic Monthly*, XCIII (June, 1904), 823. All quotations from "Baxter's Procrustes" will refer to this text (pp. 823–830 of the June, 1904 issue) but since quotation is frequent, specific pagination will not be given for each citation. The story has been reprinted in Abraham Chapman's, *Black Voices* (New York, 1968), pp. 52–62. [Hemenway's note, page 331 in this volume.]
[10] Anderson, *The Rowfant Club*, p. 58. [Hemenway's note.]

defining an author's career through the objects that touched him, rather than on the art he shaped. The most obvious symbol of the Bodleian's possessiveness is its extensive collection of pipes ("as complete an assortment of pipes as perhaps exists in the civilized world"), and no one is eligible for membership unless he can produce a new variety. The Bodleian pipes are not a pure creation of Chesnutt's imagination, but simply a fusing of the Rowfant's puffing proclivities with its famous collection of candlesticks. The Rowfant began as a "pipe and book club" in an atmosphere "highly flavored with tobacco smoke,"[11] and the original organizers suggested an annual meeting on Candlemas (Ground Hog Day) during which all members would appear bearing a unique candlestick with his name attached.[12] This yearly festival consisted of a lighting of each member's special candlestick and a solemn procession into dinner, a ritual imitated by the Bodleians when they commemorate the death of Sir Walter Raleigh, introducer of tobacco into England, by lighting their special pipes and touring their quarters as a body, "all smoking furiously."

It was the Rowfant Club's obsessive, eccentric commitment to fine books and book collecting, a commitment apparently executed without much concern for literary achievement, that provided the major vehicle for Chesnutt's satire. The Rowfanters from the very first had been a society of dedicated bibliophiles, counting among their early members a man who bought only books on angling, another who had the world's largest collection of valentines, and still another who reportedly could see no value in a book unless it was large and flat.[13] The Club had begun issuing its own editions the year after its founding, and they periodically would hold book auctions for members and select visitors in their clubrooms.[14] Perhaps the nature of the club's interest was best expressed by Chesnutt's friend, President Frank Ginn, in 1911: "In no place is the line of distinction more clearly drawn between 'literature' and 'books' than in the Rowfant Club . . . Literature is primarily learning, and only in its secondary sense does it relate

---

[11] Anderson, p. 50. See also *Code of the Regulations of the Rowfant Club* (Cleveland, 1892). [Hemenway's note.]

[12] John Calder Pearson, *The Rowfant Candelsticks* (Cleveland, 1959), p. xviii. [Hemenway's note.]

[13] Anderson, p. 12. [Hemenway's note.]

[14] Commentators stress the Rowfant's desire to enhance rarity by printing only the number of books subscribed for. Auctions were held almost from the first, although apparently more than books were included in the early years, as attested to by the following headline of the *Cleveland Leader* of Dec. 13, 1896: "Auction! Auction! Rowfant Club members bid high for furniture, books, and a live shoat." [Hemenway's note.]

to printed books, and we do not pretend to learning." [15] This essentially anti-literary philosophy is shared by the Bodleians; they also publish their own editions, emphasizing "the qualities that make a book valuable in the eyes of collectors . . . fine and curious bindings . . . hand made linen papers, uncut or deckle edges . . . wide margins and limited editions . . . The matter of content [is], it must be confessed, a less important consideration."

It is not known if Chesnutt had a specific Rowfanter in mind when he created Baxter, but it is not impossible. Baxter is a Bodleian member who reads more than collects, a "mild" cynic with a "gloomy, pessimistic philosophy" who is "perhaps the most scholarly member of the club"; a Harvard graduate and a poet, Baxter has labored long on a poem entitled "Procrustes," expressive of his social philosophy. When the club proposes to publish this work Baxter demurs for some time, but eventually agrees to a limited edition of 50 copies, provided he personally can supervise the printing, binding, and delivery of the book, merely submitting the manuscript to the club's publication committee in advance. That committee is so circumspect that they refrain from even reading the manuscript, "having entire confidence in Baxter's taste and scholarship," but they thoroughly consider the details of the book making, deciding on Kelmscott Mills "hand-made linen," black letter type with rubricated initials, and a cover of "dark green morocco with a cap-and-bells border in red inlays and doublures of maroon morocco with a blind-tooled design." It is also decided to seal all 50 copies, with catastrophic results. After publishing the edition, and after a club meeting in which the literary contents of the Procrustes are reviewed, discussed, and praised, it is discovered by chance that the pages are blank: the club members are exposed as so disinterested in literature that they have not even broken the seals on their copies. Outraged, many members destroy the volume, but it eventually dawns upon a few that the book is the ultimate collector's item. It has fine binding, type, and paper, and the margins are the widest ever; only 6 uncut copies and 3 sealed survive. At the next auction a sealed copy brings "the highest price ever brought by a single volume published by the club."

What makes "Baxter's Procrustes" more than a banal homily—"don't judge a book by its cover"—is that last irony of the book at auction, and it is an irony carefully woven into the story's narrative design. The tale is told in retrospect by a club member, Jones, a victim of the ruse, and Chesnutt manipulates his narration to expose personal defects symptomatic of the deficiencies in the Bodleian itself. Neither Jones nor the other club members, with the exception of Baxter, are able to make meaningful distinctions be-

---

[15] Anderson, p. 13. [Hemenway's note.]

tween form and substance, books and literature, container and content, illusion and reality. Their ability to distinguish is crippled by the cash bias of
their collecting activities, which causes them to concentrate on ownership,
both for its narcissistic pleasures and capitalistic gains. Like the lawyer in
Melville's "Bartleby," the narrator always tells more than he knows, so that
in addition to describing how the club was rooked, he unwittingly explains
why the trickery was appropriate and why it could work so well. The ultimate irony of the story is not Baxter's manipulation of the club, but the narrator's unrecognized exposure of himself and his bibliophilic society; the
ultimate moral has less to do with books and covers than with the illusions
imposed on reality by self-serving materialism, the deficiencies of an intellect which can worship books but ignore the human truths they contain.

Chesnutt's narrative technique depends on the principle of dramatic
irony, of the reader coming to a more comprehensive understanding of
events than the narrator. Jones begins matter-of-factly, showing himself to
be a gentleman of culture who shares the members' passion for bookmaking. His diction is proper; he has a legal mien. His vocabulary and syntax
are excessively literate: notions "emanate," the "finest products of the human mind" are supposedly selected for "enshrinement" in the club's volumes, and when elected to review the Procrustes it is done "in pursuance
of my duties in the premises." The impression created is that of a brahmin
clubman at his leisure, sitting over brandy and cigars in an overstuffed
chair, telling his story to a friend similarly ensconced. The style of his narration is slightly pretentious, but then so is the Bodleian Club. As represented by the superficial qualities of the narrator, the club is only eccentric,
a New Yorker cartoon. It is easy to overlook both Chesnutt's hand in this
performance and the more serious implications of the narration. They are
both there, however, and a good example is in the story's fourth paragraph, here quoted in full:

> I have omitted to say that once or twice a year, at a meeting of which no-
> tice has been given, an auction is held at the Bodleian. The members of
> the club send their duplicate copies, or books they for any reason wish to
> dispose of, which are auctioned off to the highest bidder. At these sales,
> which are well attended, the club's publications have of recent years
> formed the leading feature. Three years ago, number three of Bascom's
> Essay on Pipes sold for fifteen dollars—the original cost of publication
> was one dollar and seventy-five cents. Later in the evening an uncut copy
> of the same brought thirty dollars. At the next auction the price of the cut
> copy was run up to twenty-five dollars, while the uncut copy was knocked
> down at seventy-five dollars. The club had always appreciated the value of
> uncut copies, but this financial endorsement enhanced their desirability
> immensely. This rise in the Essay on Pipes was not without a sympathetic

effect upon all the club publications. The Emerson essay rose from three dollars to seventeen, and the Thoreau, being an author less widely read, and by his own confession commercially unsuccessful, brought a somewhat higher figure. The prices, thus inflated, were not permitted to come down appreciably. Since every member of the club possessed one or more of these valuable editions, they were all manifestly interested in keeping up the price. The publication, however which brought the highest prices, and, but for the sober second thought, might have wrecked the whole system, was Baxter's Procrustes.

The casual beginning—"I have omitted to say"—ambushes the reader, leaving the impression that Jones considers the information relatively unimportant, as perhaps he does at one level of his thought. But what follows is the narrator's unconscious confession to the singleminded commercialism which will lead to the debacle. The inflation in Bascom's essay from $1.75 to $75.00, the commercial attraction of uncut copies, the members' interest in "keeping up the price," all unmask the club's "system." The irony of Emerson and Thoreau prices rising in smaller increments than Bascom discloses an absence of the powers of discrimination. Baxter will eventually manipulate the "appreciation" (a pun?) for uncut pages, thereby comically validating the absurd praise for the Procrustes as the highest priced book of all. It is a remarkably economical, well written paragraph accomplishing several purposes simultaneously. It establishes the narrator's control of his facts—note the precision of his memory, the frequency of qualifying phrases in his attempt to be exact—while exposing his ignorance of their meaning; it reveals the club's cash nexus and superficial interest in esthetic values; it suggests the narrator's acceptance of the Bodleian's principles. Above all, it exposes the ominous power of the club's "system," its rigid objectification of reality. The life of art is only a bound object to the narrator; it has no vital force, no existence beyond the letterpress and binding. Finally, with the phrase, "but for the sober second thought," the paragraph predicts the ultimate absurdity this system will demand: the auctioning off of a book which is without use or function, without literature, a book which only has value in an artificial market.

The craft displayed in this paragraph is manifest throughout the story. Chesnutt burdens Jones with a hopelessly commercial diction but one entirely appropriate to a man who believes that "a fine book, after all, was an investment." Jones consistently converts fine books into economic terms, admitting that "if there was any way of enhancing its rarity, and therefore its value, I was quite willing to enjoy such an advantage." The original idea of sealed copies came after New York's Grolier Club had seen such a book go for $300, and when an unsealed copy of the Procrustes sells for $150, Jones's "proper regard for my own interests" prohibits him from opening his copy even though he is scheduled to review it. Disclaiming monetary interest, he is appalled that Baxter has thrown away his proof sheets in a "total indifference to *literary values*"—after all, "the proof sheets of Hamlet, corrected in Shakespeare's own hand would be well nigh *priceless.*" (My italics.) After he and others are discovered to be talking about a book they haven't read, Jones is still enmeshed in a mercantile vocabulary. He can only remark that "the club had been badly sold."

The absence of self-consciousness in Jones's choice of language reveals Chesnutt's constant, ironic manipulation of his narration. His personality is represented by Baxter's Procrustes itself: he is without awareness, blank, and his mind is sealed, a closed book. He is not open to alternative truths derived from experience; though he is telling the story *a posteriori*, Jones has learned little from events. As a result, his reportage becomes increasingly ironic; despite all his commercial rhetoric, he reports that he "had no desire to appear mercenary." His absurd metaphor to describe the wordless book—"The text is a beautiful slender stream, meandering gracefully through a wide meadow of margin"—is one with the double meaning of his report to the club about the Procrustes: "this work, which might be said to represent all that the Bodleian stood for, was in itself sufficient to justify the club's existence." There is no evidence that the narrator finds the episode personally revealing; he remains in the club and still subscribes to its values. There is much evidence that Chesnutt has designed his narration to expose Jones's preoccupied superiority to the meaning of events. It is precisely this quality that makes him appear more harmless than he is, a bemused eccentric instead of a deluded, inadequate human being.

Jones fails to grasp the significance of his words because he has never been able to distinguish between form and substance, good and bad, great and small. These are general failures of the club members and they remain oblivious to their defects because their commercial perspective always transforms literary reality. In their system one *does* judge a book by its cover, for it is the cover that defines the book's value; one finds nothing incongruous about comparing Bascom to Emerson, or Baxter to Shakespeare, since the author's imagination is irrelevant to the book. As the club's president expresses it, the contents are no more important "than the words of an opera"—and thus he saves the club from disaster in *l'affaire Baxter*. He might as well be describing the dilemma of the Black artist facing the universality argument: the words are not important, only the subject determines how one will be judged as an artist.

This acceptance of appearance as reality is so pervading a pattern that it even affects personal relationships. Jones unveils a curious process of thought when he tries to deal with the substantive character of Baxter. "With light, curly hair, fair complexion and gray eyes, *one would have ex-*

pected Baxter to be genial of temper, with a tendency towards wordiness of speech"; yet he has a gloomy, pessimistic philosophy "foreign to the temperament that *should accompany* his physical type" (My italics). Chesnutt knows gray eyes do not indicate genial verbosity and that the physical types of morosity or heartiness are myriad. His narrator, however, lives his whole life on the premise that appearances are conclusive, that exterior features do make the man, that certain behavior can automatically be expected of certain physical types. It is his compensation for the absence of those discriminatory powers which produce value judgements, the same type of refuge from thought which might harbor a belief that certain literary subjects automatically produce limited results. The pattern is so encompassing that even when he senses its inadequacy, Jones is incapable of a different perspective. He discovers that Baxter had paid for an expensive operation for the child of the club's porter, even though he had disdained interest in the porter's subsequent report of his death. Jones decides that "Baxter's opinions upon any subject were not always to be gathered from his facial expression," but he can not translate this observation into knowledge, into an awareness that Baxter is laughing at the way Jones and others discuss the non-existent poetry of the Procrustes. Significantly, the remarks the club members make about the poetry are all related to their assumed knowledge of Baxter's Procrustean philosophies. Not only do they judge a book by its cover, but also by its assumed subject: "Having often heard Baxter express himself upon the general downward tendency of modern civilization, I felt safe in discussing his views in a broad and general manner."

Chesnutt uses the Procrustean motif to gloss such Bodleian inadequacies, and the reader almost forgets the explicit violence of the myth. Procrustes was a Greek bandit who captured wayfarers and tied them to an iron bed, making them conform to the bed's length by stretching those who were too short and cutting off those who were too tall. The nominal use of the myth in Chesnutt's story is to express Baxter's pessimistic philosophy about modern society: "Society was the Procrustes which, like the Greek bandit of old, caught every man born into the world and endeavored to fit him to some preconceived standard, generally to the one for which he was least adapted." The violence imposed on reality in "Baxter's Procrustes" is the "business," literally, of a small, specialized society called the Bodleian Club. Their Procrustean activities range from the harmlessly comic (their reviews of Baxter's poem are tailored to the pretension of the edition: Jones says soberly that Baxter's "materialism is Haeckel's, presented with something of the charm of Omar Khayyam,") to the metaphysically absurd (positing value in a phenomenological void). Procrustes was compelled to shape reality to his own perception of it; he could not assimilate human lengths which did not fit his standard, his one dimensional value system quantifying discrimination. In a similar way the club members' perception of literature is so much the product of their one dimensional commercial impulse that they can not accommodate any esthetic definition of literary value, any achievement of the artist himself, and they too quantify discrimination. Baxter's Procrustes should serve as an object lesson disclosing the inadequacy of myths the Bodleian members live by, yet their imposed values are so unyielding they survive the joke and even transform the blank pages into their definition of a literary artifact: their illusion becomes the reality.

It is here that Chesnutt's skill is best realized. He has fixed his story to its source, known to him if not to his reader, and only slightly exaggerated the actual fact. He has represented the club's eccentricities in the figure of his narrator, then subtly undermined the narration so that we finally realize the narrator has no capacity for value judgments, no capability to deal with men as men, no conception of literature as the representation of the universal experience of man. Although these are ominous revelations, on the surface of the story they are only vaguely disturbing, or apparently harmless, since the narrator operates within a world which honors artificial value and respects illusion more than reality: his eccentric environment defuses the danger of his inadequate self, apparently leaving the reader with a story of good-willed comic satire—Horatian if you wish. It is not surprising that at least one Rowfant member wrote to Chesnutt to praise the gentle comedy of this story, admitting that its sourse was well known to sophisticated Cleveland readers.[16] Yet, as David Britt warns us about Chesnutt, *what you see is what you get*.[17] The implications of living an illusion are ominous, the dangers of imposing on reality an artificial system of Procrustean preconceptions are considerable. Chesnutt's satire is ultimately from Juvenal rather than Horace. The Rowfant-Bodleian life eventually manifests no values at all, or values so perverse they have no reference outside their own artificial matrix, no "universal" reference in the family of man.

Chesnutt was a sensitive Black artist who knew a good deal about the way illusions come to govern men's lives, about the way judgements come to refer to a single "preconceived standard," about the way Black men are sized to accommodate illusion, about how Black writers are frequently judged less by what they write than by what they have written about. As a rejected Rowfant applicant he knew how men could accept illusion as the definition of the man; he also knew how men could so objectify reality that

---

[16] Helen Chesnutt, p. 208. [Hemenway's note.]

[17] David Britt, "Chesnutt's Conjure Tales: What You See Is What You Get," *College Language Association Journal*, XV (March, 1972), 269–283. [Hemenway's note, pp. 358–369 in this volume.]

the depositories of art become only bound volumes. Such knowledge always entered into his fiction, most prominently in *The Conjure Woman* where his Black narrator, Uncle Julius, consistently manipulates white preconceptions of Blacks, and offers a humanistic alternative to the single-minded commercialism of the white narrator, John. Britt has explained that book by brilliantly arguing that Chesnutt's method becomes "a study in duplicity that masks or reveals its meaning according to the predisposition of the reader."[18] Applied to "Baxter's Procrustes," this means that the reader's definition of reality, of literature, of books, becomes central to understanding the tale. One perceives the extended meaning of the story only if he grasps the full irony of a book club caring so little about literature that it can traffic in blank pages, a male fraternity so lacking in human values or the capacity to assess human qualities that they must impose illusions on each other. The narrator is fundamentally incapable of perceiving such ironies and his unwitting self-exposure becomes the measure of Chesnutt's craft. That craft itself, moreover, should be understood in the context of the white universality—Black artistry argument.

Critics without the predisposition necessary to explore the nature of Chesnutt's skill have consistently made critically absurd value judgements about his art, have consistently "gotten" less than is there because they couldn't visualize a shape too large for their own critical bed. Edward Margolies has called Chesnutt's novels "melodramatic, propagandistic and overwritten," adding that his "stories are on a level not much higher than his novels."[19] David Littlejohn has called him "very small beer. As with the lesser lady poets, it would be ungracious and inappropriate to press criticism too hard."[20] Julian D. Mason believes that "Chesnutt's fiction is usually too straightforward to suggest a need for more acute or sophisticated critical attention than has already been given it."[21] Behind each of these judgements is a suggestion of Chesnutt's lack of universal appeal, a belief that Chesnutt's "propaganda" need not receive detailed analysis. On the other hand, Black critics like Saunders Redding and Blyden Jackson long ago examined Chesnutt closely and come away enriched,[22] and both Jules Chametzky and Richard Baldwin have recently renewed this earlier ef-

---

[18] Britt, p. 269. [Hemenway's note.]
[19] Edward Margolies, *Native Sons* (Philadelphia, 1968), p. 24. [Hemenway's note.]
[20] David Littlejohn, *Black on White* (New York, 1966), p. 27. [Hemenway's note.]
[21] Julian D. Mason, "Charles Waddell Chesnutt as Southern Author," *Mississippi Quarterly*, XX (1967), 77. [Hemenway's note.]
[22] J. Saunders Redding, *To Make a Poet Black* (Chapel Hill, 1939); Blyden Jackson, "The Negro's Image of the Universe as Reflected in His Fiction," *College Language Association Journal*, IV (Sept., 1960), 22–31. [Hemenway's note.]

fort,[23] Baldwin's conclusion perhaps saying it best: "Chesnutt's technique relies heavily on irony, and like any ironic technique it runs the risk that readers will miss the point."[24]

Historically, irony has been more than just a literary device to Black people, for saying one thing and meaning another has often meant psychological survival in a racist society. It should not be surprising that Chesnutt had mastered the technique so well, or that it has been so frequently overlooked by his readers, or that Chesnutt was sophisticated enough to utilize the pleas for a "universal," "white" subject in order to protest the Rowfant's prejudice. This "non-racial" story about a white book club of Chesnutt's acquaintance serves to illustrate the nature of his talent, for it displays many of the same techniques that are so often missed in those "stories of the color line," which make up the bulk of the Chesnutt canon. One wonders if he wrote "Baxter Procrustes" to showcase talents which were being ignored in his stories about Blacks; and if perhaps his readers still overlooked his skill in the same way the Rowfant Club may have failed to note the gentle sarcasm of his acceptance letter in 1910, 6 years after "Baxter's Procrustes," 8 years after his first nomination. He anticipated considerable pleasure, Chesnutt said, from the company of gentlemen "with whom I am at last found worthy to associate."[25]

A LITERARY LOVE: RENA AND
THE HOUSE BEHIND THE CEDARS

Frances Richardson Keller

. . . Chesnutt composed the character Rena of dreams and despairs, of knowledge of complexities, and of strictures that he and the society exacted. By revealing the hostility this gentle girl encountered he hoped to

---

[23] Jules Chametzky, "Regional Literature and Ethnic Realities," *The Antioch Review*, XXXI (Fall, 1971), 385–396; Richard Baldwin, "The Art of *The Conjure Woman*," *American Literature*, XLIII (Nov., 1971), 385–399. [Hemenway's note.]
[24] Baldwin, p. 389. [Hemenway's note.]
[25] Chesnutt to F. H. Goff, Dec. 10, 1910, A. L. S., Fisk University, Charles Waddell Chesnutt Collection. [Hemenway's note.]

Frances Richardson Keller, *An American Crusade: The Life of Charles Waddell Chesnutt.*

reach depths where fears abide and cruelties originate. He hoped to arouse feelings of concern that must precede change. When finally the novel was published, Chesnutt hoped that Rena would touch the sympathies of a wide public as the characters Jean Valjean and Cosette, David Copperfield and Oliver Twist, Liza and Little Eva had found their ways into the fabric of their cultures.[1] Rena's story epitomized the anguish attendant on blameless disadvantage.

The records of Fayetteville, in Cumberland County, reveal that Chesnutt's concern with the situation of the part-Negro woman arose from parallels in his family and in situations he knew. Helen Chesnutt wrote that "Chloe Sampson" and her daughter Ann Maria—who was Chesnutt's mother—left Fayetteville in 1856.[2] Yet census records of Cumberland County, Fayetteville District, show no entries under the name Sampson for the census of 1850, and none for the census of 1840. The census of 1830, however, includes two interesting entries. Families are listed under the head of each household, and persons are listed with notations of age, sex, and color. The entries are:

1830
> Jacob Harris, Head of Household   age between 24 and 35 — 6
> free colored persons:
> > 2 male under 10
> > 3 male between 10 and 24 [possibly Moses Harris]
> > 4 female between 24 and 35
> > 5 female under 10
> > 6 female under 10

and

> Henry E. Sampson, Head of Household—3 white persons and
> 3 slaves
> > 2 wife
> > 3 child
> > 4 female slave 24-35 [possibly Chloe]
> > 5 female slave under 10 [possibly Ann Maria]
> > 6 male slave under 10 [this person disappeared][3]

---

[1] Chesnutt to Walter Hines Page, June 29, 1904. [Chesnutt Collection.] CC, Fisk. [Keller's note.]
[2] H. Chesnutt, *Pioneer*, p. 1. [Keller's note.]
[3] *Fifth Census of the United States, Cumberland County, North Carolina, Fayetteville District*, 1830. North Carolina Archives, Raleigh. [Keller's note.]

Since Henry E. Sampson does not appear in the census of 1840 or that of 1850, he could have moved or died and a will might have been probated; yet there is no record of a will of Henry E. Sampson in Cumberland County. Nor is there a record of his having received or given property deeds. There could have been a record of manumission of the Sampson slaves, yet among the twenty or so manumission records preserved in Cumberland County there is no mention of Henry E. Sampson's having manumitted any slaves.[4] Nor did a check of records of the General Assembly of North Carolina from 1827 through 1857 yield evidence of a Sampson manumission;[5] likewise, minutes of the Cumberland County Superior Court for 1831–1839 failed to show any reference to a Sampson manumission.[6] There were no birth certificates or records of death in North Carolina until 1913; there is no record of any Sampson marriage. Henry E. Sampson appears as a shadowy presence through the listing in the census of 1830 and through Helen Chesnutt's use of the name Sampson.[7] Apart from Sampson's slaves, his estate and the disposition of it remain a mystery.

An item in the 1840 census, however, appears related to the Sampson and Harris entries of the 1830 census. The item lists the family of Moses Harris as follows:

> *1840*   Moses Harris—age 24–36, Head of Household.
> 3 free colored persons:
> 2 female 24–36 [possibly Chloe, who would have been 34]
> 3 female under 10 [possibly Ann Maria]

A further item of the 1850 census appears thus:

> *1850*   Moses Harris, 45, Black Male, carpenter, unable to read
> and write

---

[4] Records of manumission. North Carolina Archives, Raleigh. [Keller's note.]
[5] Records of the General Assembly of North Carolina. North Carolina Archives, Raleigh. [Keller's note.]
[6] Minutes of the Cumberland County Superior Court, 1831–39. North Carolina Archives, Raleigh. [Keller's note.]
[7] Chesnutt made one reference to the name "Sampson." See Chesnutt to Victor K. Chesnut, Aug. 4, 1924, CC, WRHS [Western Reserve Historical Society]: "My ancestors, somewhat prior to 1775, lived in Sampson County, North Carolina, and my great-grandfather was at one time sheriff of that county." If Chesnutt was correct that prior to 1775 some of his ancestors lived in Sampson County, Henry E. Sampson—if descended from Sampsons of Sampson County—could have migrated to Fayetteville, there to have been counted in the census of 1830. Chesnutt does not say his ancestors living in Sampson County bore the name Sampson, however. [Keller's note.]

2 Chloe 40 Mulatto female, literate [Chloe would have been 44]
3 Anne M. Sampson, 18, Mulatto female, unable to read and
write.[8]

The next pertinent census is that of 1870, since the Chesnutts, Sampsons, and Harrises had migrated to Cleveland and were unlisted in Cumberland County in 1860. After these families had returned to Fayetteville,
we find them listed in the 1870 census:

1870
Entry No. 20, June 28: [entries were by then numbered in the order
of visitation by the census-taker]
    Jackson Chesnutt, Head of Household, 37, mulatto ret Grocer,
    Value of real estate, $500. Personal estate, $200. Literate.
    U.S. citizen.
    2 Ann Maria Chesnutt mulatto, literate, 35 [but Ann Maria
        would have been 38] born in North Carolina
    3 Charles 12, in school [this is Charles Waddell Chesnutt]
    4 minor in school [this is Lewis]
    5 minor in school [this is Andrew]
    6 minor not of school age
    7 minor not of school age
    [All the Chesnutt children, including Charles, are typed "M" for
        mulatto.]
Entry No. 21
    Moses Harris, Head of Household, 60, Black carpenter able to
    read and write [but this age should be 65].
    2 Chloe, 50, Mulatto housekeeper able to read and write [but
    this age should be 64].[9]

These records show some age discrepancies, and this casts some question about the identity of persons. And they show that Chloe lived as the
wife of Moses Harris six years before she and her daughter left Fayetteville
(in 1856) although Helen Chesnutt implies that Chloe met Moses Harris
in Cleveland, and states that she married him there.[10] Whatever the facts

---

[8] *Sixth Census of the United States, Fayetteville District,* 1840, and *Seventh Census of
the United States, Fayetteville District,* 1850. [Keller's note.]
[9] *Ninth Census of the United States, Fayetteville District,* 1870. Harris is listed as literate, though a deed, April 25, 1871, says, "Moses Harris, his mark." Respondents often
concealed literacy or illiteracy, age, or illegitimacy. [Keller's note.]
[10] Helen Chesnutt, *Charles Waddell Chesnutt: Pioneer of the Color Line,* p. 6. [Keller's
note.]

it is at least possible that Charles Chesnutt's maternal grandmother Chloe was once the slave of Henry E. Sampson and that in some manner she gained her freedom.[11] It is unclear who was the father of Chloe's daughter Ann Maria; this child appears to be listed with Chloe on three occasions— once in the Sampson household in 1830, once in the Harris household in 1840, and again in the Harris household in 1850, but that year under the name of Ann Maria Sampson. Ann Maria, who became the mother of Charles Waddell Chesnutt, was then (in 1850) a girl of eighteen. It is easy to find parallels to Rena's story in the real-life situations of Chloe and Moses Harris and Chloe's daughter Ann Maria.

Evidence exists for inferring that an even more poignant parallel to Rena's story existed on the paternal side of Chesnutt's ancestry. A heading in the Cumberland County census of 1840 is "Name of Heads of Families." One of the entries is "Ann Chesnutt." At that time the census taker entered only the approximate age, number, sex, color, and status of persons:

> *1840*   Ann Chesnutt, Head of Household, age 24–36
> 6 free colored persons
> 2 male under 10 [this was George Washington Chesnutt]
> 3 male under 10 [this was Andrew Jackson Chesnutt, father of Charles Chesnutt]
> 4 male under 10 [this was Stephen]
> 5 female under 10 [probably Mary Ann or Abram]
> 6 female under 10 [Sophia]

The census showed no husband or means of livelihood for Ann Chesnutt.[12]

The same family appears in the 1850 census of Cumberland County, Fayetteville District, dated July 24, 1850. By that time more information was requested, and the entry records that "Anna M. Chestnut," age 37, female, mulatto, was born in North Carolina. The census shows no occupation and no real estate value and no husband. Beneath the heading "Persons over 20 years of age who cannot read or write," the box for her name is left vacant; apparently she was literate. Seven persons are listed:

> *1850*
> Entry No. 39. Anna M. Chestnut
> 2 George 19 mulatto barber $100 Real Estate Literate

---

[11] She is listed as a free person of color in the *Sixth Census of the United States, Cumberland County, North Carolina, Fayetteville District,* 1840. [Keller's note.]

[12] *Sixth Census of the United States, Fayetteville District,* 1840. [Keller's note.]

3 Jackson 17 mulatto laborer $100 Real Estate Literate, had not
been in school that year
4 Stephen $150 Real Estate
5 Mary Ann 7 $150 Real Estate
6 Sophia $150 Real Estate
7 Dallas 3 $250 Real Estate

No husband is mentioned and no means of livelihood is noted.[13]

Through other references, it becomes clear that "Jackson Chesnutt"
of this entry was Charles Chesnutt's father. The question of the identity of
(Andrew) Jackson Chesnutt's father, who was the father of the children of
"Anna M. Chestnut" (Or "Ann Chesnutt," as it is spelled in the 1840 census) is interesting because it contributed to Charles Chesnutt's writing and
thinking.

Andrew Jackson Chesnutt's will mentions a "house & lot on C Street
which was given me by my father."[14] The list of taxable persons in Cumberland County covers only the years 1824–29, 1837–49, and some of the
years from 1857 to 1884.[15] The records from 1837 to 1849 reveal that
from the year 1829 the name of W. Cade, for Waddle Cade, is frequently
connected with the names of the "Chestnut" children. Though there is no
record of Waddle Cade's having left a will, and though there are no Cumberland County Estate papers in his name, the index of deeds shows that
Waddle Cade often bought or sold land. He started acquiring land in 1805;
twenty-five recorded deeds show that he is the grantee. The earliest date is
1821; in that year he got a "Lot Russell St. Fay" from Thos. D. Burgh. In
1836 Cade deeded to Andrew Jackson Chesnutt a "lot Morgan-Russell Sts.
Fayetteville."[16]

Surveying the list of taxable persons for the district of Fayetteville from
the year 1849 and working backward reveals the following information:

FOR THE YEAR 1849	PROPERTY LISTED	VALUATION
Ann Chesnut	"Russell Street Improved"	200
Stephen Chesnutt	"Wilmington Road Improved"	150
Sophia Chesnutt	"Wilmington Road Improved"	
Mary Chesnutt	"Wilmington Road Improved"	

---

[13] *Seventh Census of the United States, Fayetteville District,* 1850. [Keller's note.]
[14] Probate Records of Cumberland County, North Carolina Archives, Raleigh. Andrew
Jackson Chesnutt's will is dated June 21, 1920. [Keller's note.]
[15] North Carolina Archives, Raleigh. [Keller's note.]
[16] Cumberland County Index of Deeds, North Carolina Archives, Raleigh. [Keller's note.]

FOR THE YEAR 1848
"Chesnutte Washington
　by Ann Chesnutte"　Russell Street improved　　200
for Stephen Chesnutte　Wilmington Road improved　　150
for Mary Chesnutte　Wilmington Road improved　　150

[In this year Andrew Jackson Chesnutt was not mentioned, nor was Sophia. "Chesnutte Washington" was George Washington Chesnutt, Andrew Jackson Chesnutt's older brother; see the census of 1850.]

FOR THE YEAR 1847	PROPERTY LISTED	VALUATION
Chestnutt Ann for G. W. and A. J. Chestnutt [father of Charles]	improved Russell Street	200
Chestnutt Ann for Mary Chesnutt	improved Wilmington Road	150
Chestnutt Ann for Sophia Chesnutt	improved Wilmington Road	150
Chestnutt Ann for Stephen Chesnutt	improved Wilmington Road	150

For the year 1846 Ann Chesnutt's name does not appear in the list of taxable persons for the district of Fayetteville. The following year, 1847, is the first year in which the list includes her name. Though her name may appear elsewhere, it is unlisted in 1844, for example, in any North Carolina district. The Chesnutt name occurs, however, as follows:[17]

FOR THE YEAR 1846	PROPERTY LISTED	VALUATION
Cade, Waddill for James W. Cade	60 acres on Wilmington Road	1200
Cade, Waddill for William Cade	on Wilmington Road, Campbelton	200
Cade, Waddill for Sarah Cade	Campbelton	150
Cade, Waddill for Washington and Jackson Chesnutt	in Campbelton on Russell St.	150

---

[17] List of Taxable Persons, Fayetteville District, Cumberland County, North Carolina Archives, Raleigh. These tax books cover 1824–29, 1837–49. From 1857 to 1884 only miscellaneous tax lists have been preserved. [Keller's note.]

| Cade, Waddill for Sophia and Abram Chesnutt | on Wilmington Road | 100 |
| Cade, Waddill for Stephen Chesnutt | on Wilmington Road | 100 |

Although there is no reference to Ann Chesnutt for the year 1846, her children appear, and they are connected with the family of Waddill Cade. For whatever reason, he deeded these properties to the children of Ann Chesnutt. These children also appear connected with the land that Helen Chesnutt's book mentions[18] and which, in the case of "Washington and Jackson Chesnutt," appears to be the land spoken of in Andrew Jackson Chesnutt's will. When Ann Chesnutt appears as a taxable person in the list of 1847, Waddill Cade ceased listing the Chesnutt children under his name. Thus in 1847 Cade (whose first name had variously appeared as Waddell, Waddle, Waddill, Waddel, or just W) listed only the 60-acre lot on the Wilmington Road for James W. Cade, and the land "in campbelton" valued at $300 for William Cade. And in 1848 and 1849 Cade listed only one piece of property for "Wm." It was an "old Thames store" in "lower Fayetteville," valued at $300. This could have been the store turned over to Andrew Jackson Chesnutt on his return to Fayetteville after the Civil War.

It appears that 1846 was a crucial year; apparently Ann Chesnutt went on her own that year. It is possible to trace the listings for Waddle Cade further.[19]

FOR THE YEAR 1845	PROPERTY LISTED	VALUATION
Cade, Waddle for James Cade	60 acres on Wilmington Road, improved	1200
Cade, Waddle for William Cade	Campbelton	300
Cade, Waddle for Sarah Cade	Campbelton	150
Cade, Waddle for W. & J. Chesnutt	Russell Street	150
Cade, Waddle for S. & A. Chesnutt	Wilmington Road	100

---

[18] H. Chesnutt, *Pioneer,* pp. 4, 8. [Keller's note.]
[19] List of Taxable Persons, Fayetteville District, Cumberland County, North Carolina Archives, Raleigh. [Keller's note.]

FOR THE YEAR 1844

The list of taxable persons is almost identical for "Cade, Waddell" with James, William, and Sarah Cade listed for the properties as they appear above. Sarah and William are listed so that ditto marks are used, creating an ambiguity when the Chesnutt listings appear below. Thus William Cade's property shows:[20]

Cade, Waddle

for William Cade	Houses & Lots Campbelton	
for Sarah Cade	Houses & Lots	
for W. & Jackson Chesnutt	Houses & Lots Russell St.	150
for Sophia and Abram Chesnutt	Houses & Lots Wilmington Road & known as the Lot Stephens Lot & 1 other lot	100

It is difficult to tell whether there was more than one house and lot on Russell Street or whether the recorder used ditto marks carelessly. But the valuations remain the same.

FOR THE YEAR 1843

The list of taxable persons under "Cade, Waddel" shows the same properties for the Cade children and for "Washington and Jackson Chesnutt": "house and lot on Russell St." at the same valuation of $150. This is the first year in which "Sophia" and "Abram" are not mentioned, although the 1840 census shows that they had been born. It appears that Cade waited for a time before ceding land to these children.

FOR THE YEARS 1842 BACK THROUGH 1837

Washington and Jackson are mentioned in each of these years under a listing of Waddle Cade as owning this "House and Lot in Campbelton"; the valuation is always $150.[21] In the year 1836 Cade deeded to Andrew Jackson Chesnutt a "Lot Morgan-Russell Sts. Fayetteville."

---

[20] Ibid. A better description of the property owned on Wilmington Road, though still inconclusive. [Keller's note.]
[21] Workers of the WPA Writers' Program of the Work Projects Administration, North Carolina, *How They Began—The Story of North Carolina County, Town and Other*

For the year 1829 the following entry occurs: "Cade, Ino for W. Cade 'vacant [property] Russell Street, joins Davis,' Valuation $20." Since this is the only reference to Waddle Cade in 1829, this probably refers to the original deed to W. Cade of the land that he eventually improved and gave to Andrew Jackson Chesnutt, as stated in the Chesnutt will of 1920.[22]

According to these many instruments and the clause in Andrew Jackson Chesnutt's will identifying his father as the person who gave him his property, it seems clear that Waddell Cade was that father and that Ann M. Chesnutt was his mother. Though Cade was never legally connected with this family, he remained for many years interested to some extent in them, and he provided property for each of the children, as well as for his children bearing the Cade name. It is neither surprising nor coincidental that Charles Chesnutt, the first child of Andrew Jackson Chesnutt, was given the middle name "Waddell."

Most of the people involved in this dramatic situation lived in or near Fayetteville for most of their lives. Both of Charles Chesnutt's grandmothers found themselves in the situation Rena struggled to escape in *The House Behind the Cedars.* To all appearances both of Chesnutt's grandfathers were white men of property married to white women who bore them children and not married to the "other" women who bore their mulatto children. The sanctity of marriage was a pillar of the white caste structure; it is easy to imagine the pain and the embarrassment that must have been the life of the nameless white wives of Henry E. Sampson and Waddell Cade[23] and the humiliation, the insecurity, and the sense of futility that must have been the lot of Chloe (Sampson) Harris and Ann M. Chesnutt and their many children and grandchildren.[24]

Such census figures attest that this situation was typical of Southern communities, as do observations of travelers like Frederick Law Olmsted; in 1855 he wrote of the many "nearly white colored persons" he saw.[25] Property laws excluding women indicate how far the governing elite sanc-

---

Place Names (New York: Harian Publications, 1941), p. 33. The entry explains "Campbelton" in the tax records. [Keller's note.]

[22] Cumberland County Index of Deeds, North Carolina Archives, Raleigh. [Keller's note.]

[23] Ray Stannard Baker, *Following the Colour Line* (New York: Harper & Row, 1964), p. 166. [Keller's note.]

[24] See Cooper, *A Voice from the South,* pp. 90, 111. June Sochen, ed., *The Black Man and the American Dream* (Chicago: Quadrangle Books, 1971), p. 213; anonymous article, "The Race Problem—An Autobiography" by a Southern Colored Woman (Repr. from the *Independent,* March 17, 1904). [Keller's note.]

[25] Frederick Law Olmsted, *A Journey in the Seaboard Slave States* (New York, 1856), p. 18. [Keller's note.]

tioned these practices; even more convincingly tradition defined for all women a role supremely submissive to all indignities.[26] The situation of Charles Chesnutt's forebears worked to the deprivation of men as well as to that of women. Charles Chesnutt—and his white male relatives as well as his mulatto male relatives of several generations—never escaped the consequences of these partially covert relationships.

The records also reveal parallels to situations in other Chesnutt works. Living in and near Fayetteville were sisters and brothers whose relationship was unacknowledged. Sometimes they resembled one another; it is likely that, like characters in *The Marrow of Tradition,* they became entangled in financial difficulties.[27] As the character Frank Fowler remained loving and reliable in the novel about Rena, it appears that the real Moses Harris remained faithful to the real Chloe through many trials. Several persons disappeared from the records. Like the fictional John and Rena Walden, these real victims moved away and lived as white persons. Chesnutt noted that close relatives took this path in efforts to escape consequences.[28]

Chesnutt's ancestral background documents a sexual situation of black and white and mulatto women which was characteristic of Southern tradition. Nor is the experience of his forebears unrelated to Chesnutt's conclusion that only intermarriage and open assimilation will finally solve American racial dilemmas. Chesnutt wrote about Southern civilization from the point of view of the many who suffered from it rather than from that of the few who maintained it.[29]

---

[26] Women could not own property separate from that of their husbands, nor enter into transactions concerning property they owned prior to marriage, nor sue nor be sued in their own names. [Keller's note.]

[27] A subplot turns upon lost papers determining the property inheritance of unacknowledged sisters. [Keller's note.]

[28] Chesnutt to Dr. Park, Dec. 19, 1908, CC, WRHS, p. 3: "Several of my own near relatives, as nearly related to me as uncles, and aunts, have taken this course [passing as white persons]. Some I have kept track of, others have been swallowed up in the great majority. I hope they have won distinction. I am sure that their children will have a better opportunity in life, other things being equal, than had they taken a different course." [Keller's note.]

[29] Alfred H. Benners, *Slavery and Its Results* (Macon: J. W. Burke Co., 1923). p. 36; Chesnutt, "Age of Problems," November, 1906, CC, Fisk, MS, address delivered before the Cleveland Council of Sociology: "All of which leads to the serious question, 'Is there really in the South any such exaggerated respect for white womanhood before which all other laws must give way, or is it founded purely upon race and caste hatred?' I yield to no one in my respect for womanhood (and I don't judge it by its color either), but I have never yet been able to see why the virtue of a woman is more valuable than the life of a man." [Keller's note.]

Several legends have arisen about Chesnutt and Rena. One is that Rowena Bryant, daughter of the free Negro farmer David Bryant, lived in the house that Chesnutt described, and that she was the prototype for the character Rena.[30] Another is that Chesnutt's concern with Rena's situation is related to an earlier, dimmer era. In an autobiography titled *Fact Stranger than Fiction*, Chesnutt's cousin, John P. Green, disclosed another tale. In grammar more convoluted than his usual style, Green traced his mother's family, through whom he was related to the Chesnutts. Though they cannot conceal the human tolls, Green's commas, asides, and intricate subordinate clauses almost conceal the last statement:

> *In the latter part of the eighteenth century, 1792, to be specific, there resided near the town of Clinton, in Sampson county, North Carolina, about thirty miles from the city (then town) of Fayetteville, in the same state, a family, containing two beautiful daughters, of which a man, Chesnut (or Chestnutt) by name, was the head. This pater familias was known and respected far and wide, by persons of his class; moreover, since his daughters were young and comely, they were, frequently favored by the calls of young gentlemen, in the vicinage, who, socially and financially, deemed themselves their superiors.*
>
> *In the course of time, the young ladies became greatly enamored of two of these young men; but since they did not hasten to make to them proposals of marriage, they had recourse to the advice and services of a "likely" young colored man (the slave of their father), who advised them, in the premises, with the result that, ere long, each became the mother of a little colored girl. . . .*
>
> *A glance will suggest that these two babies, being the offspring of one father by two sisters, were, at once, sisters and cousins!! This condition during the womanhood of these two colored girls was doubly complicated, when each girl presented to two white brothers, severally, a child, one of whom was my mother.*
>
> *Bede 96 when died, Alice almost 90. Both left behind them a numerous progeny thus proving the fallacy of that "scientific" dogma—that mulattoes cannot reproduce their species; for both were mulattoes, having white mothers and a Negro father.*[31]

---

[30] Suggested by Sylvia Lyons Render, "Tar Heelia in Chesnutt," *College Language Association Journal,* 9 (September, 1965). [Keller's note.]

[31] John P. Green, *Fact Stranger Than Fiction, Seventy-Five Years of a Busy Life with Reminiscences of Many Great and Good Men and Women* (Cleveland: Riehl Printing Co., 1920), pp. 6–7, 69, 147. Green shows that the relationship to Chesnutt was on his mother's side: "Was my spirit broken? Had the Stanley-Chesnutt blood ever quailed be-

Whatever ancient and contemporary racial complexities influenced Chesnutt, and there were many, he could never have escaped a knowledge of his immediate family, nor a deep concern for their welfare. He had too many opportunities to observe their dilemmas. From them he provided in *The House Behind the Cedars* an impressive historical-cultural study. Chesnutt's literary love for Rena began with a profound comprehension of his personal situation.[32] It progressed to an understanding that the situation was meaningful to the future of the American nation.

Nor did the novel about Rena spring forth in a burst of creative fulfillment. Chesnutt first composed a short story; then *Rena Walden* became a "novelette," then again a short story, and finally a novel. Five manuscripts of 39, 91, 55, 51, and 231 pages respectively still exist.[33] Chesnutt showed an early manuscript to George W. Cable. Then Richard Watson Gilder of the *Century* criticized *Rena* and returned it. Cable had felt that the story stood "in a very important relation to the interests of a whole great nation," that Chesnutt could "become an apostle of a new emancipation to millions."[34] Chesnutt sent the novel more than once to Houghton Mifflin, whose readers more than once decided against publication.[35] Again and again Chesnutt reworked it; it was the story that would accomplish his life time goals.

Chesnutt even tested responses by reading it aloud. He considered bearing publication expenses.[36] More than once he sent the story to Walter Hines Page: "I have not slept with that story for ten years without falling in love with it and believing in it," he wrote.[37] Page answered:

---

fore that of another? Never!" (Green's parental grandfather was John Stanley, a lawyer, Speaker of the North Carolina House for seven sessions; pp. 2–4.) Chesnutt and Green exchanged many letters; see Chesnutt to Green, Feb. 13, 1899, John P. Green Papers, Container 5, Folder 4, Western Reserve Historical Society, Cleveland. This is written in French, evidently for the pleasure of the exercise. [Keller's note.]

[32] Chesnutt to John Chamberlin, June 16, 1930. CC, WRHS. Late in life Chesnutt wrote Chamberlin, critic of *The Bookman:* "With reference to 'The House Behind the Cedars,' it is, in a way, my favorite child, for Rena was of 'mine own people.' Like myself, she was a white person with an attenuated streak of dark blood, from the disadvantages of which she tried in vain to escape, while I never did." [Keller's note.]

[33] Freeney and Henry, *A List of Manuscripts,* p. 13. [Keller's note.]

[34] George W. Cable to Chesnutt, May 3, 1899. George W. Cable Collection, Tulane University, New Orleans. [Keller's note.]

[35] See Walter Hines Page to Chesnutt, March 31, 1899. CC, Fisk. [Keller's note.]

[36] Chesnutt to Houghton Mifflin & Company, probably early 1899. CC, Fisk. [Keller's note.]

[37] Chesnutt to Walter Hines Page, March, 1899. CC, Fisk. [Keller's note].

While I had a feeling that the story would probably succeed, I could not throw away another feeling that you had not by any means, even yet, done your best work on it, or had developed to the fullest extent the possibilities of the story. . . . I believe that a year hence if you read it over again you will agree with me that it is not even yet sufficiently elaborated and filled in with relieving incidents—not sufficiently mellowed—there is not sufficient atmosphere poured round it somehow—to make a full-fledged novel. . . . You had so long and so successfully accustomed yourself to the construction of short stories that you have not yet, so to speak, got away from the short story measurement and the short story habit.[38]

Chesnutt worked incessantly on writing and intermittently on structure. Professionally he grew from short-story-teller to novelist. "A novel," Page had said, "is . . . not simply a longer thing. It must also be a much more elaborate thing."

Chesnutt had known acclaim; but he experienced frustration over *Rena*. He felt tantalizingly close to convincing a first-rank editor that he had a superior novel; many times he received the answer that he almost did. Like a human love, this literary love became an anvil upon which quality would be defined and purpose tested. Chesnutt never abandoned *Rena*.

On January 24, 1900, Walter Page wrote to Chesnutt. Would Chesnutt care to have *Rena* brought out by Doubleday, Page? Three days later Chesnutt sat in Page's office. Outside interest turned the trick. Houghton Mifflin were considering another Chesnutt novel, *The Rainbow Chasers*. Though Bliss Perry and W. B. Parker liked the "homely sincerity," and the "freedom from affectation," they concluded that story was unsuitable as a serial.[39] Propitiously Chesnutt visited Boston, giving readings, dining with Joseph Edgar Chamberlin of the *Boston Transcript*, and with Professor Albert Bushnell Hart of Harvard.[40]

Surely Chesnutt informed Houghton Mifflin of the recently departed Page's offer. On March 24, Francis J. Garrison, son of William Lloyd Garrison, wrote Chesnutt: "We have decided to take *Rena* (under the title *The House Behind the Cedars*) in place of *The Rainbow Chasers*, and to publish it next fall."[41] On hearing all—especially on learning of Page's offer—

---

[38] Walter Hines Page to Chesnutt, March 31, 1899, CC, Fisk; Walter Hines Page to Chesnutt, Jan. 24, 1904. Walter Hines Page Papers, Houghton Library, Harvard. [Keller's note.]

[39] W. B. Parker to Chesnutt, Feb. 27, 1900. Quoted in H. Chesnutt, *Pioneer*, pp. 141–42. [Keller's note.]

[40] Albert Bushnell Hart to Chesnutt, March 13, 1899, CC, Fisk. [Keller's note.]

[41] "FJG" to Chesnutt, March 24, 1900. Quoted in H. Chesnutt, *Pioneer*, p. 146. [Keller's note.]

and though they had many times refused it, Houghton Mifflin asked "the privilege of reconsidering *Rena*."[42] So Chesnutt's tragic story entered the American literary-historical treasury. Except for critical praise and a negligible sale, there it has languished. People seldom bought the book because it was inopportune to entertain equitable solutions to racial problems. Like Americans at the drafting of the Constitution, and like their descendants, Americans of Chesnutt's time turned away. The reasons lie deep in the human psyche.

"THE FUTURE AMERICAN RACE": CHARLES W. CHESNUTT'S UTOPIAN ILLUSION

Arlene A. Elder

I am apt to suspect the negroes, and in general all the other species of men (for there are four or five different kinds) to be naturally inferior to the whites. There never was a civilized nation of any other complexion than white. . . .
— David Hume, "Of National Characters," *1748*

The colonial society . . . embodies a rejection of the colonizer by the colonized and vice versa. This opposition, however, is accompanied by an equally profound dependency, particularly on the part of the colonialist. For while he sees the native as the quintessence of evil and therefore avoids all contact because he fears contamination, he is at the same time absolutely dependent upon the colonized people not only for his privileged social and material status but also for his sense of moral superiority and, therefore, ultimately for his very identity.
— Abdul R. JanMohamed, Manichean Aesthetics, *1983*

At his execution [after being condemned as a witch in Salem in 1692, the Reverend George Burroughs] made a prayer and made an address

---

[42] Chesnutt to Daughters, March 24, 1900. Quoted in H. Chesnutt, *Pioneer*, p. 146. [Keller's note.]

MELUS (Fall 1988).

to the crowd of such ardent devotion that it seems to have shaken many.
But 'the accusers said the black man stood and dictated to him. . . .
Mr. Cotton Mather, being mounted upon a horse, addressed himself to
the people . . . to possess the people of [Mr. Burroughs'] guilt, saying
that the Devil had often been transformed into an angel of light; and
this somewhat appeased the people, and the execution went on.'
— *Charles Williams,* Witchcraft, *1958*

In both the social and psychological realms, Hume's view of the dichotomy of race and JanMohamed's insight into the colonial dependence
of the Self upon the Other reflect a society where, necessarily, one's skin
color, the determinant of power and powerlessness, must be easily perceived and one's intellectual and moral status, thereby, quickly ascertained.
Such a clear-cut perception was also assumed when the Puritans learned
New World agriculture from the Native Americans in order to plant the
New Jerusalem on this continent for the glorification of the Calvinist God
and the reward of his Elect.

Not only Puritans, of course, relied upon clear distinctions of good
and evil, symbolized by white and black, for their emotional security in
a dangerous New World. The settlers of Virginia, a more economically-
motivated group of adventurers than their original Massachusetts counter-
parts, also blanched at cultural confusion and expressed this discomfort in
strong racial and religious terms:

> As early as 1630, we find . . . in a Jamestown order that Hugh Davis, a
> white man, "be soundly whipped before an assemblage of Negroes and
> others for abusing himself to the dishonor of God and the shame of
> Christians by defiling his body in lying with a Negro, which fault he is to
> acknowledge next Sabboth [*sic*] day." (Kinney 5)

The union of John Rolfe and Pocahontas, then, should have been completely unacceptable but, possibly, was justified in white eyes as Pocahontas' second gesture testifying to their superiority. Without some such interpretation of her transference of cultural allegiance, her self-sacrificial
move to save John Smith would remain inexplicable for the daughter of
Powatan, the Chief ordering Smith's execution. "After her marriage to
John Rolfe, Pocahontas converted to Christianity, was renamed Lady Rebecca and led to England in triumph, her Indian selfhood apparently re-
nounced" (Dearborn 72). Such muddying of the racial waters, hence confusion of the semiotics of power, was not to be countenanced by the

authorities, however, if attempted by whites and blacks. The political validation and continuation of the official division of the races was to be guaranteed by a succession of restrictions against intermarriage of white and black that filled the law books of various States long after the theocracy declined, and Pocahontas became an American myth.[1]

Without denying the obvious economic benefits of racism for the imperialists, the slave-holders, and the non-slave population in general, turn-of-the-century racial restrictions, then, the large concern of Charles W. Chesnutt's three-part essay, "The Future American" (1900), usefully can be seen, as well, as rooted in western philosophical and religious assumptions and nurtured by the terror of the loss of identity, even of one's soul (rationality). Chesnutt's vision of a time when, through intermarriage, racial differences will fade and ultimately disappear, creating his "new American," strikes at much more than the commonly accepted segregationist policies of his day. Of profounder significance, he is heralding the erasure of the marker of color, the semiotic of skin, historically distinguishing between the civilized and uncivilized, the godly and the unregenerate. Such a *trompe d l'oeil* Cotton Mather warns is one of the hellish tricks of the Devil Himself. Because of the Devil's desire to corrupt the Elect (the civilized), Mather reminds the confused onlookers at the hanging that "[T]he black man" can appear "an angel of light." According to the Puritan Divine, one can believe neither eyes nor ears; with the people thus "appeased," "the executions went on." Is it any wonder, then, that "tragic mulattoes" expired nightly on the popular stage of nineteenth-century America, or that the threat of racial mixing was seen as ample justification for the rise of the Ku Klux Klan?

Chesnutt's interest in "The Future American" was two-fold. Most immediately, he was searching for a solution to the desperate straits in which black Americans found themselves at the beginning of the new century; more theoretically, he was speculating on the conditions necessary for social peace and stability. The resolution of both these issues he found in an inevitable "mingling" of the country's "three broad types—white, black, and Indian" (Article I). Interestingly, and possibly predictably, the mulatto Chesnutt largely accepted the concept of cultural dichotomies popular at his time. While viewing the amalgamation of the races as inevitable, he predicted that this development would be slowest with the Indians because of their isolation on the reservations. His egalitarian desire that they be

---

[1] An antimiscegenation law was still in place in Louisiana as recently as 1983 (Kinney, 20). [Elder's note.]

"given their rights once for all, and placed upon the footing of other citizens" belied his motive for such equality, which was that the "wilder Indians" be educated and brought into closer contact with civilization. . . ."
He demonstrated a similar distinction in regard to the blacks, speaking of the elimination of "the more objectionable Negro traits" as a to-be-hoped-for good that would come about with their increasing socialization in American society. Yet Chesnutt was democratic in assigning racial frailty, for he remarked in an understated way that the "white race [too] is still susceptible of some improvement" (Article III). Finally, though, the thrust of "The Future American" was to emphasize Chesnutt's awareness of the legal and social power inherent in assimilation rather than to suggest any value to ethnic diversity, an understandable, if unfortunate, position for a mulatto writer living during the racially-turbulent turn-of-the-century. What is incongruous, of course, was his advocacy of racial amalgamation as the ultimate solution to America's social ills when such a blending would result in an invisibility guaranteed to strike terror in more hearts than those consciously agreeing with the Reverend Thomas Dixon, Jr.'s white supremacist novels or with latter-day Fundamentalist prophecies of Armageddon.[2]

Charles Chesnutt's concern about the fate of those, like himself, of mixed blood, was expressed early and frequently in his career. On July 31, 1875, then seventeen years old, he confided to his journal, "Twice today, or oftener, I have been taken for white. . . . I believe I'll leave here and pass anyhow, for I am as white as any of them" (Helen Chesnutt, 15). By May 4, 1881, however, social conditions appeared to have improved enough to require no such racial disguise. His journal of that date stated optimistically that the Prohibition movement, among other occurrences, had had "the effect of partly breaking down the color line, and will bring the white and colored people nearer together, to their mutual benefit" (Helen Chesnutt 29). His article, "What Is a White Man?", published in the *Cleveland Independent* on May 30, 1899, pointed out the effect of discriminatory marriage laws in the South which declared unions between the races illegal, thereby branding a fair-skinned black, like himself, illegitimate. Chesnutt was born in Cleveland, Ohio in 1858, where his parents moved temporarily from North Carolina, presumably to avoid the legal insecurity of mulattoes in the South.

---

[2] On April 3, 1917, Chesnutt wrote to Munson R. Havens, Secretary of the Cleveland Chamber of Commerce, in an attempt to ban the showing of D.W. Griffith's "The Birth of a Nation," the film adaptation of Dixon's *The Clansman* (1905) (Chesnutt, Fisk University). [Elder's note.]

In the late summer and fall of 1900, "The Future American," Chesnutt's lengthiest non-fiction treatment of this subject, appeared in the Boston *Evening Transcript*. Then, in a letter of September 27, 1900 to Houghton, Mifflin, his publishers, Chesnutt mentioned a lengthy editorial, "The Yellow Peril in the United States," which appeared in the Washington, D.C. *Times* of August 18, 1900, in which the writer warned that "the white race was becoming insidiously and to a large extent unknowingly corrupted with negro blood . . ." (Chesnutt, Fisk University).

Chesnutt used some of this same language in Article II of "The Future American," where he noted, "how steadily, albeit slowly and insidiously, the stream of dark blood has insinuated itself into the veins of the dominant . . . race." The serpent-like movement of Chesnutt's own image of amalgamation suggests the power of cultural and, especially, religious symbolism; the recurrent sibilants, "steadily," "slowly," "stream," "insinuated itself," "veins," and "race" are auditory reminders of Mather's "black man" transforming Himself into the "angel of light" in an earlier Edenic manifestation. Chesnutt observed further to his publishers that the same topic was brought up at a conference of white leaders held a few months earlier in Montgomery, Alabama; "one of the solutions set forth involved the future amalgamation with the white race of at least a remnant of the black population" (Chesnutt, Fisk University). His belief that such amalgamation was the only viable solution for America's racial problems increased as his respect for Booker T. Washington's segregationist policies declined.

On June 25, 1905, Chesnutt presented what turned out to be an extremely controversial address, "Race Prejudice: Its Causes and Its Cure," before the Boston Literary and Historical Association in which he asserted the superiority of individual worth and common humanity over race. "We are told," he reflected,

> that we must glory in our color and zealously guard it as a priceless heritage. Frankly I take no stock in this doctrine. It seems to be a modern invention of the white people to perpetuate the color line. It is they who preach it, and it is their racial integrity which they wish to preserve—they have never been unduly careful of the purity of the black race. (Helen Chesnutt 210)

Chesnutt's position here is based upon more than his suspicion of the hypocrisy of such directives. He sincerely trusted in individual rather than racial worth: "Why should a man be proud any more than he should be ashamed of anything for which he is not responsible? Manly self-respect based upon one's humanity, a self-respect which claims nothing for color, every man should cherish" (Helen Chesnutt 210).

In a 1906 letter to Booker T. Washington, he expressed skepticism that blacks and whites could co-exist without intermingling: "experience has demonstrated this act and there will be more experience along that line" (Helen Chesnutt 199). As late as 1928, he was still involved with these issues. In an address before the Dunbar Forum in Oberlin, Ohio, "The Negro in Present Day Fiction," he opined that

> a better word to describe the modern American Negro would be the "New American." In my opinion, the American Negro, so called, or miscalled, is destined if his ultimate absorption in the composite American race is long deferred, to develop a type which is widely different from the West African type from which he has descended. (Sillen 14)

While a "composite American race" appears today not only possible, but probable, during Chesnutt's time, legal restrictions and distinguishing nomenclature were enforced to insure a racially distinct society:

> By 1915, 90 percent of all blacks still lived in the rural South, blacks and mulattoes were isolated from the white world, and their combined gene pool was twenty percent white. From this point on, no statistically significant miscegenation took place. . . . The dream of the assimilationists that blacks would marry lighter and lighter until they disappeared into the white world was over. Indeed, acceptance of the one-drop rule was so universal that the 1910 Census was the last to count mulattoes; after that all mulattoes were classified as "Negroes," officially creating a simplified biracial America. (Kinney 26–27).

These developments reflect a new and powerful source of segregationist thought that Chesnutt's "The Future American" was opposing, one supported for years by "scientific" research. Beginning with Dr. Samuel George Morton's *Crania Americania* (1839), a string of "scientific" arguments appeared and were popularly promulgated that suggested black inferiority and its probable natural sources. Racial theorists like Morton, and later, Thomas Drew, Samuel Cartwright, and Fredrick L. Hoffman influenced public opinion to such an extent that by Chesnutt's time, one drop of black blood was all that was necessary for a popular racial designation as "Negro." Chesnutt's awareness of this development is obvious in Article III, where he comments that it is "only a social fiction, indeed, which makes of a person seven-eighths white a negro. . . ." "Scientific racism," too, had its myths. The popular superstition was of an, apparently, white woman giving birth to a coal-black child by an, apparently, white father, a social

nightmare reflecting dormant fears of the unpredictable, even of the dia-
bolic, a racial Maul's curse imposed for ancient cultural transgressions.

However divergent were Chesnutt's and his society's views on racial
assimilation, his private and public statements present a consistent, lifelong concern with the personal and social plight of black Americans and
those of mixed blood. Of great importance for our understanding of him
as an artist was the literary potential he saw in his mixed heritage. When
he accepted the Spingarn Medal on July 3, 1928, an award given for outstanding contributions by an African-American, his thoughts were once
again with race:

> My physical makeup was such that I knew the psychology of people of
> mixed blood in so far as it differed from that of other people, and most
> of my writings ran along the color line, the vaguely defined line where the
> two major races of the country meet. It has more dramatic possibilities
> than life within clearly defined and widely differentiated groups. (Ches-
> nutt, Fisk University)

The writer's blackness, invisible to the eye, as the portrait on the dust-
jacket of William Andrew's *The Literary Career of Charles Chesnutt* attests, was at the core of his artistic impulse and political concerns. Ironically, his white appearance made him a vivid symbol of the blurring of "the
color line," the topic of so many of his works.

The effects of miscegenation serve as his topic in pieces as diverse in
length and complexity as the short stories in *The Wife of His Youth* (1899)
and the novel occasioned by the Wilmington race riots of 1898, *The Marrow of Tradition* (1901). His lengthiest treatment is *The House Behind the
Cedars*, a novel that appeared the same year as "The Future American,"
and one he worried with off and on for ten years. The contrast between the
two works suggests either the overwhelming influence upon Chesnutt of
the popular concept of the "tragic mulatto" who must be sacrificed when
her well-known tale has run its course, or his suspicion that neither "passing" nor assimilation would succeed at the beginning of the new American
century.

While James Kinney is correct in seeing gender stereotypes responsible
for much of the characterization of Chesnutt's protagonists, John and Rena
Walden (194–5), he discounts too readily the literary influence of popular
depictions of fated octoroons, with their coincidences of chance discoveries and meetings leading to revelation and death. More interesting than
these well-used devices and revelatory of Chesnutt's apparent ambivalence
by 1900, despite the confidence of "The Future American," are his repeated references in *The House Behind the Cedars* to "Time touch[ing] all

things with destroying hands" (3), "the sins of the fathers" (28), "the un-
pardonable sin" of racial mixing (116), and images of the Fates shuffling
the cards of Rena's fortune and weaving the fabric of her future.

It is significant that Chesnutt asked his publishers to keep his racial
identity secret in 1899, when *The Conjure Woman* was published, "first
because I do not know whether it would affect its reception favorably or
unfavorably, or at all; second, because I would not have the book judged
by any standard lower than that set for other writers" (Chesnutt, Fisk University). In truth, his second reason seems more genuine than his first. This
strategem failed, however, with subsequent publications because of the un-
popularity of his works' political views. None of his books after *The Conjure Woman* was a money-maker, leading to his retreat into the anonymity
and financial security of his business career.

Chesnutt's progress toward assimilation and away from the common
black experience can be traced easily in his business and social careers and,
most tellingly, in his art. Uncle Julius, the narrator of the stories in *The
Conjure Woman* (1899), stands at the opposite end of the racial spectrum
from Colonel French, the protagonist of Chesnutt's last published work,
The Colonel's Dream (1905). It is, perhaps, not completely coincidental
that the author's gradual movement from identification with the perspective of Julius, the black trickster artist, grounded in folklore and methods
of subversion, to that of the naive, liberal, northern white businessman co-
incides with Chesnutt's deepening pessimism about America's racism.
Julius assures himself a place in the post-war South through the magic of
black orature; French returns to the North, carrying his dead past and
dead future with him, his "fool's errand" emblematic of Chesnutt's own
disappointment with a society where "[W]hite men go their way, and
black men theirs, and those ways grow wider apart, and no one knows the
outcome" (*The Colonel's Dream*, 194).

While deliberate "passing" was commonplace throughout America's
history,[3] and as *The House Behind the Cedars* shows, Chesnutt was sympathetic to those it tempted, he and other Black novelists of his time, notably Sutton Elbert Griggs and James Weldon Johnson, rejected it on both
political and personal grounds. "If through the process of being made
White you attain your rights," one of Griggs's protagonists argues, "the
battle of the dark man will remain to be fought" (Griggs 198); Johnson's ex-
colored man is tortured by the suspicion "that, after all, I have chosen the
lesser part, that I have sold my birthright for a mess of pottage" (Johnson

---

[3] See James Kinney, *Amalgamation!* for a useful discussion of the history of this strategy
in the U.S. [Elder's note.]

511). As an individual, practical solution to barriers to the American Dream, however, Chesnutt realized that "lighten[ing] the breed" had strong appeal: "[T]he races will be quite as effectively amalgamated by lightening the Negroes as they would by darkening the whites" (Article III).

Of course, the mulatto who hides out as a white offers only a different kind of invisibility, albeit the most terrifying version to a Manichean society. As Ralph Ellison shows in *Invisible Man*, obviously black (red, yellow, brown) skin also signals a lack of understanding of a profoundly impenetrable sort, despite the self-deceptive, thus comforting, misperception of the racist viewer. "Passing," slowly assimilating, as Chesnutt sees the races inexorably doing, or decidedly remaining within the racial group, then, all constitute rocks and hard places pressing the person of color in a society dependent for its psychic, as well as economic, comfort on the maintenance of black and white dichotomies. "The Future American" and, indeed, Charles Waddell Chesnutt's generally out-spoken visibility throughout his life represent an honest, simple approach in an era when race relations were neither politically honest nor, if they ever have been or will be, psychologically simple.

Works Cited

Andrews, William. *The Literary Career of Charles W. Chesnutt.* Baton Rouge: Lousiana State U P, 1980.

Chesnutt, Charles Waddell. *The Colonel's Dream.* New York, 1905.

———. *The Conjure Woman.* New York, 1899.

———. "The Future American Race." *Boston Evening Transcript,* 18 August 1900, 25 August 1900, 1 September 1900.

———. *The House Behind the Cedars.* New York, 1900.

———. *The Marrow of Tradition.* New York, 1901.

———. *The Wife of His Youth and Other Stories of the Color Line.* New York, 1899.

Chesnutt, Helen. *Charles Waddell Chesnutt: Pioneer of the Color Line.* Chapel Hill, N.C., U of North Carolina P, 1952.

Dearborn, Mary V. *Pocahontas's Daughters, Gender and Ethnicity in American Culture.* New York: Oxford U P, 1986.

Griggs, Sutton Elbert. *The Hindered Hand.* Nashville, 1905.

Johnson, James Weldon. "The Autobiography of an Ex-Colored Man," in *Three Negro Classics.* New York: Avon, 1965.

Kinney, James. *Amalgamation! Race, Sex, and Rhetoric in the Nineteenth-Century American Novel.* Westport, Connecticut: Greenwood P, 1985.

Sillen, Samuel. "Charles W. Chesnutt: A Pioneer Negro Novelist," *Masses and Mainstream* 6 (February 1953): 8–14.

CHESNUTT'S GENUINE BLACKS AND FUTURE AMERICANS

SallyAnn H. Ferguson

Scholarship on novelist and short story writer Charles W. Chesnutt has stagnated in recent years because his critics have failed to address substantively the controversial issues raised by his essays. Indeed, many scholars either minimize or ignore the fact that these writings complement his fiction and, more importantly, that they often reveal unflattering aspects of Chesnutt the social reformer and artist.[1] In a much-quoted journal entry of 16 March 1880 [pp. 19–23 in this volume], Chesnutt himself explicitly links his literary art with social reform, saying he would write for a "high, holy purpose," "not so much [for] the elevation of the colored people as the elevation of the whites." Using the most sophisticated artistic skills at his command, he ultimately hopes to expose the latter to a variety of positive and non-stereotypic images of the "colored people" and thereby mitigate white racism. As he remarks in a 29 May 1880 entry, "it is the province of literature to open the way for him [the colored person] to get it [equality]—to accustom the public mind to the idea; and while amusing them [whites], to lead people out, imperceptibly, unconsciously, step by step, to the desired state of feeling" [pp. 21–22 in this volume]. Throughout his entire literary career, Chesnutt never strays far from these basic reasons for writing, in fiction and nonfiction alike.

It is in his essays, however, that Chesnutt most clearly reveals the limited nature of his social and literary goals. Armed with such familiar journal passages as those cited above, scholars have incorrectly presumed that this writer seeks to use literature primarily as a means for alleviating white color prejudice against *all* black people in this country. But, while the critics romantically hail him as a black artist championing the cause of his people, Chesnutt, as his essays show, is essentially a social and literary ac-

MELUS, Fall 1988.

[1] In *Charles W. Chesnutt* (1980), Sylvia Lyons Render either fails to mention the author's most controversial essays on race, such as the "Future American" series and "What Is a White Man?," or stresses their least radical ideas, as in her discussion of "Race Prejudice: Its Causes and Its Cure," 93. William L. Andrews in *The Literary Career of Charles W. Chesnutt* (1980), Dickson D. Bruce, Jr. in *Black American Writing from the Nadir* (1989), and a few other critics discuss Chesnutt's essays as they relate to his fiction but only in a limited way.

commodationist who pointedly and repeatedly confines his reformist impulses to the "colored people"—a term that he almost always applies either to color-line blacks or those of mixed races. This self-imposed limitation probably stems from the fact that he wrote during a time of intense color hatred in America, when the masses of blacks, because of their dark skin, could not unobtrusively be assimilated into the mainstream culture. Chesnutt was well aware that the dismal plight of these "genuine Negro[es]" (as he calls dark-skinned blacks in a 30 May 1889 *New York Independent* essay entitled "What Is a White Man?" [pp. 24–32 in this volume]) was not amenable to his kind of artistic stealth and subtlety and required more aggression. In his "White Man" essay, therefore, the pacifist author stresses the futility of such a measure, arguing that force can have little effect in bringing about equal citizenship for black people of any hue. After discarding both force and non-violence as potential remedies for the predicament of "genuine Negroes" in America, Chesnutt must have viewed their plight as virtually insoluble. Thus, it is not surprising that the author deliberately limits his goals to that which he believed he could reasonably accomplish—to improving the lot of the "colored people," as he indicates very early in his career.

That focus on the social condition of light-skinned blacks is especially evident in Chesnutt's race writings. In his "White Man" newspaper article, the author specifically distinguishes between "genuine Negroes" and "a very large class of the population who are certainly not Negroes in an ethnological sense, and whose children will be no nearer Negroes than themselves" (6 [pages 24–25 in this volume]). He reinforces this division by eliminating dark-skinned blacks from his criticisms of American court cases that attempt a legal definition of "white": "This discussion would of course be of little interest to the genuine Negro, who is entirely outside the charmed circle [the American color mainstream], and must content themselves with the acquisition of wealth, the pursuit of learning and such other privileges as his 'best friends' may find it consistent with the welfare of the nation to allow him; to every other good citizen the inquiry ought to be a momentous one. What is a white man?" (6 [p. 25 in this volume]). Ironically, before eliminating the "genuine Negroes," he reproves Southern whites for not enforcing their own miscegenation laws, that would classify some "colored people" as "white," and thus ensure "that no man entitled to it . . . is robbed of a right so precious as that of free citizenship" (6 [p. 25 in this volume]).[2] For the "colored people," enforcement tended to mean

---

[2] Even though Chesnutt criticizes the inconsistencies in American miscegenation laws, he rejects none of them and is apparently willing to accept any system of classification that

equal access to material rewards, peacefully attained in an economically strong America. For Chesnutt, however, free citizenship for "genuine Negroes" is apparently unworthy of argument.

Oddly enough, however, these key intraracial distinctions—so crucial to and consistent with Chesnutt's literary theme and method—have generally been overlooked by critics. Perhaps, these scholars subscribe to the antiquated racial notion that one drop of Negroid blood makes a person black—a practice Chesnutt thoroughly ridicules in "What Is a White Man?" Or, perhaps they regard both light- and dark-skinned blacks as belonging to one undifferentiated racial group—another concept rejected by Chesnutt, who is willing to accept any racial classification that would enable "colored people" to become the social and political equals of whites. Although he does not begrudge darker-skinned blacks whatever residual gains may accrue to them from his advocacy of racial equality, his nonfiction makes quite clear that Chesnutt writes, above all, to prompt white acceptance of color-line blacks. As he remarks in the journal entry of 29 May 1880, "The subtle almost indefinable feeling of repulsion toward the Negro, which is common to most Americans—cannot be stormed and taken by assault . . . so their [whites'] position must be mined, and we [colored people] will find ourselves in their midst before they think it" [p. 21 in this volume].

Not surprising, then, racial passing is a major theme in Chesnutt's works; and, indeed, by the time he writes the "Future American," his definitive, three-article series on racial amalgamation, published from 18 August 1900 to 19 September 1900 in the *Boston Evening Transcript,* he has contrived an elaborate scheme for accomplishing this en masse. More significantly, the "Future American" articles indicate that Chesnutt's ultimate solution to the race problem is a wholesale racial assimilation achieved by the genetic dilution of the black race. Because this mechanistic plan callously discounts the element of human dignity—most especially in its treatment of "genuine Negroes," the *Transcript* series starkly reveals Chesnutt's racial myopia and its impact on his art. In the final analysis, it provides an indispensable tool for evaluating the strengths and weaknesses of his fiction and of his literary and social imagination.

When Chesnutt wrote his "Future American" articles, he was reacting to the ubiquitous question of what to do with the black man in post-Civil

---

would designate colored people as "white." For example, in "White Man," he notes that in the 1860s and 1870s, South Carolina law defined as "white" "generally a person of mixed white or European and Negro parentage, in whatever proportions the blood of the two races may be intermingled in the individual" or, alternatively, left the matter "for a jury to decide by reputation, by reception into society, and by their exercise of the privileges of the white man, as well as admixture of blood" (6 [page 28 in this volume]).

War America. This "problem" had plagued the country ever since the 1620s, when the Dutch ancestors of present-day South African Boers sold "twenty negars" into slavery here and wreaked havoc on American democratic ideals. Although related to an earlier xenophobia, which stemmed mainly from cultural and racial differences between Africans and Europeans, the nineteenth-century variety was compounded by a fear that vengeful ex-slaves would subvert the almost unlimited white control of the American republic. By this time, both overt and more subtle racist perceptions of blacks, reinforced by centuries of slavery, had helped create a virulent intolerance to the idea of a shared, egalitarian, multi-racial society. In "A Multitude of Counselors," an essay that appeared on 2 April 1891 in the *New York Independent* [pp. 32–40 in this volume], Chesnutt himself describes the result of this corrosive process: "All over the country they [the black race] are the victims of a cruel race prejudice, the strength and extent of which none but cultivated, self-respecting colored people can rightly apprehend. It pervades every department of life—politics, the schools, the churches, business, society—everywhere. . . . There is actually no single locality in the United States where a man avowedly connected by blood with the Negro race can hold up his head and feel that he is the recognized equal of other men . . or where he is not taught to feel every day that he is regarded as something inferior to those who were fortunate enough to be born entirely white" (p. 4 [p. 32 in this volume]). Indeed, in *The Black Image in the White Mind* (1971), historian George Fredrickson regards white intransigence during this period as "the tragic limitation of the racial imagination of the nineteenth-century" (xiii). When the concept of black inferiority became entangled with the dictates of the postbellum democracy decreed by the Emancipation Proclamation, the ex-slavemaster lived alongside his former hostage, while continuing to devise ways to suppress his new competitor for the economic, social, and political fruits of the land.

In keeping with the American racial tradition, even the most liberal and humane among prominent nineteenth-century whites again presumed the basic inferiority of blacks. Accordingly, they proclaimed the entire race unworthy of their association and revived two prominent techniques, established by their forefathers, for eliminating them from the American scene. First, white leaders again urged the emigration of blacks to Africa and other tropical lands outside the United States. Then, after the black exodus, they could save America for "purely white people," as Benjamin Franklin had written more than a century earlier in his treatise, *Observations Concerning the Increase of Mankind* (1751). As a mathematician, Franklin recognized that whites themselves were a racial minority in the population of the world and, ignoring the fact that miscegenation was already an American tradition, asked "Why increase the Sons of Africa, by

Planting them in America, where we have so fair an opportunity, by excluding blacks and Tawneys [Asians], of increasing the lovely white . . . ?"
(234). Thomas Jefferson endorsed a similar view in his *Notes on Virginia*
(1784) where, acting on no evidence other than "a suspicion only" that the
black race was inferior to the white, he suggested the West Indies, especially
San Domingo, as an appropriate place for black relocation. Eventually, the
Congress of the United States was persuaded to pay the American Colonization Society, a "benevolent" organization developed between 1803
and 1817, $50 each to transport nearly 18,000 blacks to Liberia before the
Civil War and about 2000 more during and after it. By the mid-nineteenth
century, perhaps the most direct and blunt of the liberal-American advo-
cates of black emigration was the Great Emancipator himself, Abraham
Lincoln, who on 14 August 1862 invited a delegation of blacks to discuss a
proposed Central American settlement. At this meeting, he told the group
that blacks and whites were so different that each suffered from contact
with the other, and that blacks should leave America because they would
never receive equal treatment here.[3] Although other liberal whites protested this approach, they failed to become the prevailing voice on race before and during the nineteenth century.

Chesnutt too rejects emigration as an answer to the American race
problem, while also spurning the second- or even third-class citizenship endorsed by his prominent, accommodationist friend Booker T. Washington.
In his "Multitude" essay, he argues that a wholesale emigration of blacks—
whether to South America, Mexico, or Africa or to an American state or
territory—would not be economically feasible because the expense of
transportation, lost time and lost labor would cost more than the Civil War.
With marked irony, he observes that "A more practicable emigration, that
of Southern whites, who are more able to go . . . does not seem to meet with
much favor in their eyes, and yet, if . . . it is impossible for the races to live
together on terms of equality, this is more likely to be the ultimate outcome"
(5 [p. 35 in this volume]). But as his "Future American" essays clearly illustrate, Chesnutt does embrace the second popular nineteenth-century approach to race relations—the use of "science," in his case genetics.

Already a part of the American consciousness, the notion of racial science burst again into full bloom after the scientific explorations of the
nineteenth century. As Ronald Takaki explains in his study *Iron Cages:*

---

[3] For the preceding historical discussion, I am heavily indebted to the following sources:
Walter L. Fleming's "Deportation and Colonization," 3–9; George M. Fredrickson's
The Black Image in the White Mind, 1–18; Ronald T. Takaki's *Iron Cages,* 1–40, and
William E. B. DuBois's *Black Reconstruction,* 145–150.

Race and Culture in 19th-Century America (1979), this idea had its genesis in the nationalistic fervor of the Revolutionary War and the Age of Enlightenment, which sought to create the perfect moral and rational union
(14). The first prominent American to adopt a "scientific" approach to
race was Dr. Benjamin Rush, the father of American psychiatry and a
product of the Enlightenment who, like Chesnutt later, believed that the
black race could remain in the United States, if it were divested of its skin
color and racial mannerisms. Indeed, Rush wrote in his *Address to the Inhabitants of the British Settlements in America upon Slave-keeping* (1773)
"that blacks were not inferior to whites in their intellectual ability and capacity for virtue. Slavery, their social environment, was the cause of their
inferiority" (Takaki 29). Such liberalism, however, did not prevent Rush
from diagnosing blackness as a disease. On 14 July 1792, he introduced
this idea before the American Philosophical Society in a paper entitled "Observations intended to favour a supposition that the black Color . . . of Negroes is derived from leprosy." Leprosy-induced blackness, he claimed,
was caused by a combination of unwholesome diet, hot climate, savage behavior and bilious fever. Its more visible symptoms were thick lips, woolly
hair, and of course black skin color. One cure prescribed by Rush involved
separating temporarily blacks, who did not infect each other, from the
whites, who could catch the disease, as allegedly happened in the case of a
North Carolina white woman turned colored after marrying a black man.
White men who cohabitated with black women were conveniently immune
to the disease. Other blackness cures prescribed by Rush included physical labor, bloodletting, purging, and abstinence. The worst cases—those
really coal-black people—might require hospitalization (Takaki 30–33).
     Like Rush, Chesnutt claims to be repulsed by racial discrimination. In
the essay "Race Prejudice: Its Causes and Its Cure," published in a 1905
issue of *Alexander's Magazine* [pp. 85–94 in this volume], he asserts that
such discrimination has its roots in racial differences, or physical "antagonisms" of color, form, and feature. More specifically, he argues: "They
[genuine blacks and whites] differ physically, the one being black and the
other white. The one constituted for poets and sculptors the ideal of beauty
and grace: the other was rude and unpolished in form and feature. The one
possessed the arts of civilization and the learning of the schools: the other,
at most, the simple speech and rude handicrafts of his native tribe, and no
written language at all. The one was Christian, the other heathen. The one
was master of the soil; the other frankly alien and himself the object of
ownership" (21 [p. 85 in this volume]). Because of black "deficiencies"
such as these, Chesnutt maintains in the "Future American" series that the
race needs to dilute itself through miscegenation with apparently superior
whites, and he even provides a genetic formula for fully accomplishing this

over three generations. Ultimately, the process would yield Chesnutt's racial ideal, an ethnic hybrid that has been formed from an admixture of the red, white and black races inhabiting America and that will look essentially white. If these hybrid "Future Americans" fight, they will do so over problems other than racial and ethnic differences. In other words, Chesnutt, like Rush, also diagnoses blackness as a disease needing a scientific cure. His preferred remedy, however, is a pseudo-genetic scheme the implementation of which would infuse curative white blood into a socially dysfunctional black race.

Chesnutt's naive scientism accounts for the jubilant tone of his first "Future American" article, published 18 August 1900 and subtitled "What the Race Is Likely to Become in the Process of Time: A Perfect Type Supposably to be Evolved—Some Old Theories of Race that Are Exploded—the Ethnic Elements on Which the Fusion Must Be Based." He hails the recent American publication of *The Races of Europe: A Sociological Study* (1900) by Boston scholar William Zenobia Ripley, a work that, in Chesnutt's view, provides the solid scientific evidence needed to support his argument in the "Future American" series. According to Chesnutt, Ripley's book gives irrefutable genetic and anthropological proof that the so-called white races of Europe—the ancestors of American whites— are themselves mixed breeds. He focuses especially on Chapter 17 of *The Races of Europe,* entitled "European Origins: Race and Language; the Aryan Question," where Ripley contends that the European white races are an "impure" fusion of African and other races. Chesnutt then applauds the Boston author's refutation of anthropological studies linking head size with intelligence and quotes approvingly: "language, so recently lauded as an infallible test of racial origin is of absolutely no value in this connection, its distribution dependent upon other conditions than race. Even color, upon which the social structure of the United States is so largely based, has been no test of race" (20 [pp. 47–48 in this volume]). In his first "Future American" essay, Chesnutt also quotes with evident enthusiasm several other passages from Ripley's book. Then, he flatly predicts that, since the different races of Europe eventually formed "new people," as Chesnutt's character John Walden calls white-looking racial hybrids in *The House Behind the Cedars* (1900), then a similar miscegenation will inevitably occur in America. In Chesnutt's opinion, all this prospective racial blending is eminently desirable because a homogeneous culture would rid the country of all its racial strife, since its people would "look substantially alike, and . . . [be] moulded by the same culture and dominated by the same ideals" (20 [p. 49 in this volume]).

In the second "Future American" essay, published 25 August 1900 and subtitled "A Stream of Dark Blood in the Veins of the Southern Whites,"

Chesnutt credits slavery with greatly advancing miscegenation in America and discusses prominent "white" Europeans such as Alexander Pushkin, Robert Browning and Alexandre Dumas as well as several unnamed Americans as its products. He deals with the greatest obstacle to amalgamation—the black race—in the third essay, published 1 September 1900 and subtitled "A Complete Race—Amalgamation Likely to Occur: The Indian Will Fade into the White Population as Soon as He Chooses—The Process Is Going On Rapidly." Here he claims that black people need to prepare themselves for equality by lightening their restrictive skin color through miscegenation and eliminating their social crudeness through education.

In other words, Chesnutt regards whiteness and literacy as the ultimate goals for African-Americans. According to William Andrews in *The Literary Career of Charles W. Chesnutt* (1980), attaining "Future American" color status is "the final outcome of black advancement on a variety of political, economic, and educational fronts. It would be in his [Chesnutt's] mind, the final proof of Afro-American equality" (142). Chesnutt justifies his position in pragmatic terms, saying in the third "Future American" article that "If it is *only* by becoming white that colored people and their children are to enjoy the rights and dignities of citizenship, they will have every incentive to 'lighten the breed'" (24). Throughout his entire analysis, he offers no formula for peaceful and equal racial coexistence within the United States, except black genetic dilution. Moreover, he ridicules any idea of intraracial pride in "Race Prejudice" by saying "I take no stock in this doctrine" (25). He adds: "I can scarcely restrain a smile when I hear a mulatto talking of race integrity or a quadroon dwelling upon race pride" (25).

Nevertheless, these high-minded sentiments sound profoundly hypocritical coming from Chesnutt, whose "Future American" theory implicitly celebrates white skin. More simply, he illogically attempts to establish a color-blind, racially harmonious society through extreme color consciousness. But the ends and means of his plan are utterly inconsistent and would leave black victims the perverse task of joining white racists in devaluing an aspect of themselves in order to win societal approval. Thus, Chesnutt reveals an almost total disregard for the psychological needs and human aspirations of "genuine Negroes" living in a racist society, to whom he offers only a cultural ideal from which they alone are effectively excluded. His preoccupation with the "Future American" ethnic type leaves him indifferent to the consequences for dark-skinned Americans who, as a practical matter, could not become "white," even if they wanted to do so. Moreover, he remains in sharp contrast to his contemporary, novelist Sutton Griggs, who, as Dickson Bruce notes in *Black American Writing from the Nadir* (1989), understood that "the real issue was the active role of racism in black life" (159). When Chesnutt relegates "genuine Negroes" to the racial status quo, he simultaneously ignores the immediate obstacle of racism as well as undercuts the self-esteem they need to combat it daily. When he advises such blacks to restrict themselves to materialistic pursuits, he, by implication, also urges them to accept the self-hatred this compromise inevitably brings.

Consequently, Chesnutt's racial theory leaves him virtually incapable of creating strong dark-skinned characters who seek to achieve equality within American culture and live to tell about it. Indeed, the novelist almost always portrays "genuine Negroes" in stereotypical terms. In *The House Behind the Cedars* (1900), for example, ebony-hued Frank Fowler is clearly the most decent and ethical character in the novel, yet Chesnutt keeps him unduly subservient to a white man's willing but lighter-skinned concubine, Molly Walden. Furthermore, through the omniscient narrator and other literary devices in *House,* the author plainly indicates that he regards black Frank as unfit to marry the quadroon heroine Rena Walden.[4] For these reasons, Trudier Harris has criticized Chesnutt for his characterization of dark-skinned blacks.[5] For these reasons also, Oscar Micheaux, to whom Chesnutt sold the film rights for *House,* changed the ending to allow the marriage of Frank and Rena, knowing that his black movie audience would not tolerate such negative portrayals of themselves. Nearly fifty years later, Micheaux entirely rewrote Chesnutt's novel and published his revision as *The Masquerade* (1947). Although it is not the artistic equal of *House,* Frank gets the girl here, too.

On the other hand, Chesnutt has little difficulty depicting characters who embody his "Future American" ideal. Often, however, these light-skinned creations upset the aesthetic balance of his fiction. In an essay entitled "Confronting the Shadow: Psycho-Political Repression in Chesnutt's *The Marrow of Tradition*" (1979), Marjorie George and Richard Pressman are but two of the latest scholars to explore the apparent "contradiction in the novel between psychic rationality and emotionality, social compliance and obedience [*sic*], cultural dependence and independence"

---

[4] See, for example, my essay "Rena Walden: Chesnutt's Failed 'Future American'," in which I argue that Rena's death in the novel is due less to white racism than her own failure to rid herself of black characteristics that prevent her total assimilation into the white mainstream. See also my article "Frank Fowler: A Chesnutt Racial Pun," in which I explain the relationship among the Fowler name, Chesnutt's theme in *House* and the "Future American" series.

[5] In "Chesnutt's Frank Fowler: A Failure of Purpose?" Harris notes that ". . . Chesnutt did not *want* Frank to accept his blackness because Chesnutt himself could not accept it" (216).

(287). They, too, are intrigued by the supposed conflict between the theme of nonviolence and the strong underlying, unconscious message of resistance and independence in *Marrow* expressed through the characterizations of coal-black Josh Green and near-white Janet Miller. George and Pressman apply Jungian psychology to the "conflict" and conclude with vague remarks about "nonresolution" and "unreconciled" messages in the novel. In fact, however, *Marrow's* thematic development remains quite consistent with Chesnutt's "Future American" ideology. During the novel, the author kills off the static, black, and violent Green but steadily develops Miller, who outgrows her yearning for acceptance by her white half-sister, Olivia Carteret, to emerge racially secure and emotionally independent, neither hating nor groveling. More significantly, educated and almost-white, she symbolizes Chesnutt's simplistic vision and illusory hope for a color-blind and racially harmonious world.

The "Future American" series and other essays by Chesnutt reveal how his self-imposed social and literary mission is essentially at odds with racial realities, a dilemma that accounts for his often contradictory views. For instance, in the "White Man" article discussed earlier, he is forced to criticize Southern whites for failing to enforce conflicting miscegenation laws, which he despises, in order to protect the rights of the "colored people" these laws might benefit. Perhaps his daughter Helen, who subtitled the first biography of her father *Pioneer of the Color Line* (1952), understood best the purpose of her father's life and work. Present-day scholars may attain similar understanding if we begin to re-examine Chesnutt's fiction in light of his nonfiction. It may be that after blackness came into vogue, we grew too content with merely celebrating black literary achievement. Nonetheless, before African-American literature gains a solid footing in academe, it must undergo the same kind of tough critical scrutiny to which other literatures have been subjected. Although disputed by others, Chesnutt's published essays indicate that he was among the first "African-American" literary artists to break ranks with the race and openly advocate miscegenation.[6] In his quest to bring racial peace and a taste of the good life to the light-skinned segment of the black population, he did not hesitate to sacrifice the

---

[6] For instance, in his foreword to the 1989 University of Georgia Press reprint of Chesnutt's novel *The House Behind the Cedars,* William Andrews still claims that Chesnutt "did not wish to identify himself as an advocate of passing for white, since the trend of white and much black American literature in the nineteenth century opposed racial assimilation in any way that increased the likelihood of miscegenation" (x). However, Chesnutt's treatment of the passing theme in both his fiction and nonfiction argues to the contrary.

interests of dark-skinned people. In this latter respect, Charles W. Chesnutt
is oddly callous for an otherwise sensitive man—and, ironically enough,
not very different from the white founding fathers of America.

Works Cited

Andrews, William L. Foreword. *The House Behind the Cedars.* By Charles
W. Chesnutt. Athens, Ga.: U of Georgia P, 1989. vii–xxii.
———. *The Literary Career of Charles W. Chesnutt.* Baton Rouge: Louisi-
ana State U P, 1980.
Bruce, Dickson D. Jr. *Black American Writing from the Nadir: The Evolu-
tion of a Literary Tradition, 1877–1915.* Baton Rouge: Louisiana State
U P, 1989.
Chesnutt, Charles. *The House Behind the Cedars.* 1900; rpt. New York:
Collier-MacMillan, 1969.
———. "The Future American: A Complete Race-Amalgamation Likely to
Occur." *Boston Evening Transcript* 1 September 1900, 24.
———. "The Future American: A Stream of Dark Blood in the Veins of the
Southern Whites." *Boston Evening Transcript* 25 August 1900, 15.
———. "The Future American: What the Race Is Likely to Become in the
Process of Time." *Boston Evening Transcript* 18 August 1900, 20.
———. Journals. 16 March 1880 and 29 May 1880. Charles Chesnutt Col-
lection, Fisk University Library.
———. *The Marrow of Tradition.* Boston: Houghton Mifflin, 1900.
———. "A Multitude of Counselors." *New York Independent* 30 May 1889,
5–6.
———. "Race Prejudice: Its Causes and Its Cure." *Alexander's Magazine* 1
(1905): 21–26.
———. "What Is a White Man?" *New York Independent* 30 May 1889, 5–6.
Chesnutt, Helen. *Charles Waddell Chesnutt: Pioneer of the Color Line.*
Chapel Hill, NC: U of North Carolina P, 1952.
DuBois, William E.B. *Black Reconstruction in America: An Essay Toward a
History of the Part Which Black Folk Played in the Attempt to Reconstruct
Democracy in America, 1860–1880.* New York: Russell & Russell, 1935.
Ferguson, SallyAnn H. "Rena Walden: Chesnutt's Failed 'Future American.'"
Southern Literary Journal 25 (1982): 74–82.
———. "'Frank Fowler': A Chesnutt Racial Pun." *South Atlantic Review* 50
(1985): 47–53.
Fleming, Walter L. "Deportation and Colonization." *Studies in Southern
History and Politics.* New York: Columbia U P, 1914.
Franklin, Benjamin. "Observations Concerning the Increase of Mankind."
The Papers of Benjamin Franklin. Vol. 4, ed. Leonard W. Labaree. New
Haven, CT.: Yale U P, 1959.

Fredrickson, George M. *The Black Image in the White Mind: The Debate on Afro-American Character and Destiny, 1817–1914.* New York: Harper, 1972.

George, Marjorie and Richard Pressman. "Confronting the Shadow: Psycho-Political Repression in Chesnutt's *The Marrow of Tradition.*" *Phylon* 45 (1979): 287–298.

Harris, Trudier. "Chesnutt's Frank Fowler: A Failure of Purpose." *CLA Journal* 22 (1979): 215–228.

Micheaux, Oscar. *The Masquerade.* New York: Book Supply Company, 1947.

Render, Sylvia Lyons. *Charles W. Chesnutt.* Boston: Twayne Publishers, 1980.

Ripley, William Z. *The Races of Europe: A Sociological Study.* London: Kegan Paul, Trench, Trubner & Company, 1900.

Takaki, Ronald T. *Iron Cages: Race and Culture in Nineteenth-Century America.* Seattle: U of Washington P, 1979.

FROM "CHARLES CHESNUTT'S CAKEWALK" [1]

Eric J. Sundquist

Word Shadows and Alternating Sounds: Folklore, Dialect, and Vernacular

Who knows but that, on the lower frequencies, I speak for you?
—*Ralph Ellison*, Invisible Man

In 1901 Chesnutt contributed to *Modern Culture* an essay, "Superstitions and Folklore of the South." [2] What is remarkable about it, especially

---

Eric J. Sundquist, *To Wake the Nations: Race in the Making of American Literature.*

[1] "According to the black musician and former slave Shephard Edmonds, the cakewalk was a Sunday dance performed for their own pleasure by slaves, who 'would dress up in hand-me-down finery to do a high-kicking, prancing walk-around.' They did a takeoff on the high manners of the folks in the 'big-house,' but their masters, who gathered around to watch the fun, 'missed the point.' The cake, Edmonds related, would be awarded by the master to the 'couple that did the proudest movement'" (Sundquist 278).

[2] Charles W. Chesnutt, "Superstitions and Folklore of the South," *Modern Culture* 13 (1901), 231–35; rpt. in Alan Dundes, ed., *Mother Wit from the Laughing Barrel:*

in light of Chesnutt's conjure tales, is his apparent degree of skepticism about black folk beliefs. In charting the background of his Uncle Julius stories, Chesnutt carefully records methods and instances of "conjuration" practiced by purported conjure doctors, both women and men. But the emphasis falls decidedly on the various rational explanations that can be put forward to account for the apparent success of any curse or cure. Old Aunt Harriet, who claimed to have extracted a snake from her own arm (inhabitation by reptiles is one of the most common signs of conjure in the folk records of the day), is represented by Chesnutt as "lying" or "merely self-deluded." Her religion is probably little more than "superstition," and her belief that a mystic voice brought her a cure for an ankle sprain appears to be written off by Chesnutt: "She is not the first person to hear spirit voices in his or her own vagrant imaginings." Old Uncle Jim, another informant, is but a "shrewd, hard old sinner, and a palpable fraud." As Chesnutt records it, conjure thrives on "delusion" and the "credulity of ignorance," signaling the "relics of ancestral barbarism" that have not yet been shaken off as African Americans become more civilized. In these animadversions Chesnutt seemed to be little different from the majority of ethnologists and folklorists who had begun in earnest to collect material about conjure at the end of the nineteenth century. The overwhelming reliance on theories of racial hierarchy and the progress of civilization, fueled by the twin engines of science and Christianity, made any response but skepticism unlikely. Most ethnography about conjure (or "hoodoo") stigmatized such elements of slave culture and its aftermath as superstition or delusion—of interest from an anthropological point of view but nonetheless irrational and regressive—and implicitly cooperated with sociological theory and legal proscription to identify the potential for "reversion" and "degeneration" to forms of primitivism among contemporary African Americans who did not aspire to a more assimilated American middle class.

Given his own precarious position straddling the color line, and given his clear aspirations to middle-class professional respectability, it is not surprising that Chesnutt would detach himself from the irrationality of conjure. For this reason alone, his characterizations of conjure would be central to any estimate of his role as a writer committed to the notice and preservation of distinct black American traditions at an especially difficult historical moment when the legislated "superstitions" of Jim Crow held full sway. If the conjure tales in particular are evidence of such a commitment, they are nevertheless tales in which Chesnutt's curt personal belief that con-

---

Readings in the Interpretation of Afro-American Folklore (1973; rpt. New York: Garland, 1981), pp. 369–76. [Sundquist's note.]

jure was "superstition" is marked and in which his own imaginative transformation of the folk material, not its original substance, is predominant.
Or so it seems: Chesnutt no doubt identified to some degree with the skepticism voiced in the white narrative frames of his own conjure stories; and
yet it is the black liminal voice of the trickster, immersed in the strategies
if not the actual secrets of conjure, whose historical memory and cultural
values are most at stake in these stories. Chesnutt, that is to say, may himself have been signifying in "Superstitions and Folklore of the South" (the
essay's several oblique allusions to the barbarity of segregation and the
fetish of race purity are one kind of evidence), adopting the isolating voice
of contemporary ethnography while working inside it in order to preserve
African American cultural forms and to make them instruments of his own
gain, much as his character Uncle Julius does in the tales. Chesnutt, one
could say, was doing a literary cakewalk that assumed ever grander and yet
more detailed, subtly argued forms over the course of his writing career.

Preservation and transformation exist in a taut balance in the nineteenth-century ethnographic record of black folktales, and Chesnutt's focus on his *literary* appropriation of folk forms exacerbates rather than di-
minishes that tension. Seeming to remove himself as far as possible from
the "original" tales of slave culture, Chesnutt pointed on several occasions
to the privilege of authorial license, most notably in his late essay "Post-
Bellum—Pre-Harlem" [pp. 100–105 in this volume] in which he remarked
that with one exception his conjure tales were "the fruit of my own imagination, in which respect they differ from the Uncle Remus stories which
are avowedly folktales." And other critics have followed his lead in differ-
entiating him from Joel Chandler Harris, who, as Chesnutt put it in the
1901 conjure essay, "with fine literary discrimination collected and put
into pleasing and enduring form, the plantation stories which dealt with
animals." [3] Chesnutt's relationship with Harris is complex and worthy of
extended discussion, which will follow. The difference between them,
however, here asserted by Chesnutt on the spurious basis of an opposition
between folklore and imagination, is no simple one but must instead be
read within the overarching problem of African American cultural origins
and African retentions. His account of the origins of his own versions of
conjure tales was extremely canny and was dedicated to the promotion of
his own career as a writer. But one must begin with the fact, as Robert

---

[3] Chesnutt, "Post-Bellum—Pre-Harlem," *Crisis* (1931), rpt. in *Breaking into Print*, ed.
Elmer Adler (1937; rpt. Freeport, N.Y.: Books for Libraries, 1968), p. 50 [page 101 in
this volume]; Chesnutt, "Superstitions and Folklore of the South," p. 371 [page 59 in
this volume].

Hemenway has demonstrated in his landmark essay on Chesnutt's folklore, that there are numerous sources—or, at any rate, analogues—for
many of the central features of his conjure tales. This fact alone places
Chesnutt in a strikingly complicated relation to the issue of African retentions, for whatever his ultimate assessment of the cultural value of African
American folk beliefs in the late nineteenth century, Chesnutt appears to
have followed Harris and others in their view that, though many black stories were part of the world's stock of wonder stories, appearing throughout racially distinct cultures or reflecting European origins, some of the
tales had specific African beginnings. Although they are related to animal
trickster tales and to other story paradigms such as the Master-John cycle,
conjure tales were constituted, for Chesnutt, by a relatively distinct body
of imaginative structures that were at once more amenable to narrative
transfiguration and more precisely traceable to the ancestry of slave culture. The belief in conjure, he observed, was rooted in "African fetishism,
which was brought over from the dark continent." Lacking the "sanctions
of religion and custom" that supported them in Africa, such beliefs became, "in the shadow of the white man's civilization, a pale reflection of
their former selves."[4]

This "pale reflection" that African beliefs became under the pressure
of enslavement and American acculturation corresponds, moreover, to the
explanation that Chesnutt offered of his own imaginative processes.
Whereas he first thought—or remembered—that only "The Goophered
Grapevine" came directly from black folklore, his interviews with elderly
blacks, including a conjure man, reminded him that some of his seemingly
imaginative innovations were "but dormant ideas, lodged in my childish
mind by old Aunt This and old Uncle That, and awaiting only the spur of
imagination to bring them again to the surface." Chesnutt's eminently
Hawthornian account of his creativity—a literary influence that is evident
in the tales themselves—puts a limit on the liberty exercised by the artist:
ideas must already exist "somewhere in his consciousness," ready to be
subjected to the "power of rearrangement."[5] Yet Chesnutt's admission (or
his recognition, as the case may be) about the sources of his tales is interesting not for what it takes away from his artistry but for what it adds. By
locating elements of his stories in the childhood tales told him by elders of

---

[4]Robert Hemenway, "The Functions of Folklore in Charles Chesnutt's *The Conjure
Woman,*" *Journal of the Folklore Institute* 13 (1976), 283–309; Chesnutt, "Superstitions and Folklore of the South," p. 371. [Sundquist's note. His reference to Chesnutt's
"Superstition" appears on page 59 in this volume.]
[5]Chesnutt, "Superstitions and Folklore of the South," p. 372. [Sundquist's note, page 59
in this volume.]

the generation of slavery, Chesnutt placed himself closer to those originating beliefs that had become only a pale reflection of their former African selves, and he made the remembrance of slave culture a foundation for modern African American culture. More pointedly than Harris or other white folklorists, Chesnutt found himself at a demanding double remove— separated from the generations of slavery as they were in turn separated from all but the most resilient elements of African culture. But he made of this distance a powerful instrument to demystify the positivist constructions of primary material by folklorists, blurring the line between redaction and creation in a most profound way. The literary category of the imagination, which at first appears to separate Chesnutt's work from the "folktales" of Harris and the conjure beliefs collected by professional ethnographers, circles back, by the path of personal and historical memory, to merge his narrative art with the stories of the black ancestors. Chesnutt's theory suggests, too, that the distinction between the rearranging power of the imagination and the bequest of folklore is a tenuous one. Just as Harris's Br'er Rabbit tales must be seen as the product of the transforming forces of folk storytelling, long before Harris set them in his own problematically imagined plantation frames, so Chesnutt's consciously fabricated tales contain materials that were far from stagnant but instead were structured according to particular cultural pressures and belief patterns that had evolved generation after generation, from Africa to the New World, absorbing new European American elements along the way.

    Chesnutt was resolutely middle class, and the majority of his published fiction, especially his color line stories and *The Marrow of Tradition*, reflects in some measure his genteel literary tastes. At the same time, however, his fiction also reflects his concern that the rise of a black middle class could jeopardize racial cohesiveness in the very act of uplifting the race and sacrifice a distinctive strain of African American art whose record lay in the oral narratives. Leroi Jones (Amiri Baraka) is thus widely off the mark in his claim that Chesnutt subscribed to the proposition, a sign of "slave mentality," that the Negro "must completely lose himself within the culture and social order of the ex-master," and counted himself part of that black middle class that "wanted no subculture, nothing that could connect them with the poor black man or the slave."[6] The black middle class often ignored or ridiculed the folk culture that survived in trickster stories and plantation tales, in minstrelsy, and on the black stage, or that was preserved in the spirituals and was beginning to flourish in jazz, but Chesnutt

---

[6]Leroi Jones [Amiri Baraka], *Blues People: Negro Music in White America* (New York: William Morrow, 1963), pp. 58–59, 131–32. [Sundquist's note.]

incorporated those folk voices into his writing in the most remarkable ways. Indeed, he made such a rift within African American culture the very subject of his writing because it was, in perfectly visible ways, the subject of his life as a man of mixed race light enough to pass for white. One could say that his exploration of class and color divisions produced in Chesnutt an uneasy adherence to a "subculture" that was part of, not separate from, the middle class; the lower class, the "folk," and the reminders of slavery itself were contained "somewhere in its consciousness," just as the folk beliefs of African origin were contained somewhere in Chesnutt's own imaginative reservoir. The tension between the two realms, and the signs of Chesnutt's honest recognition of his moral obligation to keep them united, appear throughout his fiction. Not the best, perhaps, but the most classic statement is found in his famous story "The Wife of His Youth" [pp. 199– 209 in this volume].

First appearing in the *Atlantic Monthly* in 1898, the story was collected the following year in *The Wife of His Youth and Other Stories of the Color Line*. The plot, of course, concerns the dilemma confronted by a northern, upper-middle-class mulatto, a member of the best "Blue Vein" society of Groveland (modeled on Chesnutt's own Cleveland), when he must decide whether or not to acknowledge the validity of his marriage during slavery to a dark-skinned, illiterate woman from whom he was separated but who reappears on the eve of his engagement to a beautiful light-skinned woman of his own class. The story has a place in the larger structure of concerns examined in the color line stories as a group; but one can notice here several aspects of the story that illuminate Chesnutt's relation to his conjure stories as part of the "subcultural" content that had to be similarly acknowledged in his own career. By her coincidental appearance upon the scene, Ryder's wife, Liza Jane, interrupts his idyllic visions of increased assimilation of European cultural standards and upward progress through a further lightening of his children's dark skin. Standing in stark contrast to his fantasy of a social world represented by Tennyson's poem "A Dream of Fair Women," Liza Jane, who is "very black—so black that her toothless gums, revealed when she opened her mouth to speak, were not red, but blue," looks "like a bit of the old plantation life, summoned up from the past by the wave of a magician's wand." She is undeterred by the slim chances of finding the husband of her youth and tells Ryder, apparently without knowing yet who he is, that "de signs an' de tokens" have guided her search.[7]

---

[7] Chesnutt, *The Wife of His Youth and Other Stories* (Ann Arbor: University of Michigan Press, 1968), pp. 8–10, 14. [Sundquist's note, pages 203–205 in this volume.]

In addition to its role in Chesnutt's critique of color consciousness and intraracial racism, "The Wife of His Youth," written at the same time he was organizing a collection of his conjure stories, represents a meditation upon the complexities of his own acknowledgment of a past—not the literal past of his youth (although that is part of it as well) but rather the symbolic past of his race. Liza Jane seems summoned up as though by conjure, a reminder of Ryder's as well as Chesnutt's obligation to confront and, as Ryder finally does, to embrace a painful past and the culture that is carried with it. The embrace is nothing if not ambivalent. As Alice Walker reminds us, Ryder's black wife is too old to bear children, and his declaration that "our fate lies between absorption by the white race and extinction in the black" (complete with its bitingly ironic allusion to Lincoln: "with malice towards none . . .") therefore does not present to him quite the moral dilemma that it appears to. But Ryder's choice operates on other levels as well. Included within his recognition of Liza Jane are several implicit indications of Chesnutt's own cultural obligations: to join with the lower classes in the struggle for rights; to put the good of the community before the advances of the few who are able to enter directly into the white social and cultural mainstream; and to take control of the popular conceptions of "the old plantation life" that are being generated by racist commentary and unscrupulous artistry. In an age dominated by literary accounts of sectional reunion symbolized by North-South romantic alliances, Chesnutt's stories of reunion were typically dedicated to the postbellum reunification of scattered or racially divided black families. Marriage was a sign of communal healing, just as it remained, in the color line plots, a sign of continuing racism. In either case it was for Chesnutt also a metaphor for his art and for his place within an American literary community that was at best only tolerant of, and usually antagonistic toward, any but the mildest portraits of racial conflict. When Ryder narrates the story of his wife to the gathered throng of his middle-class peers, he speaks "in the same soft dialect, which came readily to his lips," that his wife had used earlier. What they hear in his story and in his voice are those "wrongs and sufferings of this past generation" that they usually ignore but that all of them "still felt, in their darker moments," as a "shadow hanging over them."[8]

Werner Sollors has suggested that "The Wife of His Youth" is a story in which the conflict between cultural "consent" (choice of a culture defined outside inherited ethnic or racial boundaries) and cultural "descent"

---

[8] Alice Walker, *In Search of Our Mother's Gardens* (New York: Harcourt Brace Jovanovich), p. 300; Chesnutt, *The Wife of His Youth*, pp. 7, 20. [Sundquist's note. His reference to Chesnutt's *Wife* appears on page 207 of this volume.]

(acceptance of inherited categories based on race) is marked. One must add to this that it is not Ryder alone who is the storyteller here but Chesnutt too. Like Ryder, he speaks in a dialect that is not his own but that comes readily to his lips, and in doing so he instantly casts in a critical light the post-Reconstruction vogue of dialect plantation literature by authors such as Thomas Nelson Page and Joel Chandler Harris, who wrote from the other side of the color line.[9] Chesnutt's pun on "darker" is a reminder that color is a fluid category, a mask that can hide but cannot obliterate a cultural past—and a mask that, as the rise of "one-drop" segregation made evident, could easily be punctured. The story self-consciously adopts a kind of mask, however, for although we are told Ryder reproduces Liza Jane's dialect in retelling her story, the text itself does not do so. One of the era's favorite literary devices and a necessary focal point for any interpretation of Chesnutt's relation to race writing at the turn of the century, dialect remains a sign of difference, a part of the past that Ryder accepts, even imitates, but that Chesnutt does not actually reproduce. It is a sign, that is to say, of Chesnutt's own very subtle acknowledgement of his complex "blackness" alongside his own membership in the best mulatto society. Liza Jane, a bit of the old plantation conjured up in his middle-class imagination, speaks in an alien voice, but one that Chesnutt knows to be bound indissolubly to his own cultural life. "The Wife of His Youth," then, may be read in part as an emblem of Chesnutt's divided sensibilities. His recognition of his own "wife" lay in the tribute his first book of stories, *The Conjure Woman*, paid to a world that was at once hindered by degradation and ignorance according to the standards of white middle-class society, but at the same time alive with powerful knowledge and cultural meaning generated on hidden but distinguishable African American planes of discourse.

The metaphor of the shadow, as Chesnutt uses it in "The Wife of His Youth," is not unlike Melville's "shadow of the negro" in *Benito Cereno*: both suggest a haunting black (African) presence within the structure of Euro-American civilization. But the "shadow of the white man's civilization" which Chesnutt in his essay on conjure sees to have fallen over African beliefs reverses this signification, and his work devoted to the color line (which for Chesnutt is also a shifting language line) frequently alternates between these two forms of veiling in order to show the perspectival

---

[9] Werner Sollors, *Beyond Ethnicity: Consent and Descent in American Culture* (New York: Oxford University Press, 1986), pp. 160–66; William L. Andrews, *The Literary Career of Charles W. Chesnutt* (Baton Rouge: Louisiana State University Press, 1980), pp. 39–73. [Sundquist's note.]

character of cultural assumptions. The easy exchange of places between the "savage" and the "civilized" is a reiterated theme in *The Marrow of Tradition* and other stories devoted to race violence. But Chesnutt's fiction plays even more broadly with the possibility, not widely accepted in his day, that cultural values are relative, fundamentally a function of political control and economic superiority. The metaphor of the shadow is therefore alive with signs of threat to the established racial order (or, what may seem the same thing, aspirations to join the established order). More than that, the "shadow" represents an amorphous, liminal realm between two worlds, neither dark nor light, neither past nor present, in which the language of cultural assimilation and resistance are in combat. . . .

Works Cited

Introduction

Abrahams, Roger D. *Deep Down in the Jungle*. Hatboro: Folklore Associates, 1964.

Chesnutt, Charles W. "Baxter's Procrustes." *Atlantic Monthly* 93 (1904): 823–30.

———. *Charles W. Chesnutt: Essays and Speeches*. Ed. Joseph R. McElrath, Robert C. Leitz, III, and Jesse S. Crisler. Stanford: Stanford UP, 1999.

———. *The Conjure Woman*. Boston: Houghton Mifflin, 1899.

———. "Dave's Neckliss." *Atlantic Monthly* 64 (October 1899): 500–508.

———. "The Disfranchisement of the Negro." *The Negro Problem*. New York: James Pott and Company, 1903. New York: Arno P, Inc., 1969: 79–124.

———. *Frederick Douglass*. Boston: Small, Maynard & Company, 1899. London: Kegan Paul, 1899.

———. "The Future American: A Complete Race-Amalgamation Likely to Occur." *Boston Evening Transcript* 1 Sept. 1900:24.

———. "The Future American: A Stream of Dark Blood in the Veins of Southern Whites." *Boston Evening Transcript*. 25 Aug. 1900:15.

———. "The Future American: What the Race Is Likely to Become in the Process of Time." *Boston Evening Transcript* 18 Aug. 1900:20.

———. *The House Behind the Cedars*. Boston: Houghton Mifflin, 1900.

———. *The Journals of Charles W. Chesnutt*. Ed. Richard H. Brodhead. Durham, NC: Duke UP, 1993.

———. *Limiting Scope of Injunctions in Labor Disputes: Hearings before a Sub-Committee of the Committee of the Judiciary, United States Senate Seventieth Congress*. 13 Mar. 1928: Washington: U.S. Government Printing Office, 1928. 603–14.

———. *The Marrow of Tradition*. Boston: Houghton Mifflin, 1901.

———. "A Multitude of Counselors." *The Independent* 2 Apr. 1891:4–5.

———. "The Negro in Cleveland." *The Clevelander* 5 (Nov. 1930): 3–4, 24, 26–27.

————. "Obliterating the Color Line." *Cleveland World* 23 Oct. 1901:4.

————. "Peonage, or the New Slavery." *Voice of the Negro* 1 (Sept. 1904): 394–97.

————. "Race Prejudice: Its Causes and Its Cure." *Alexander's Magazine* 1 (15 Jul. 1905): 21–26.

————. ["Remarks of Charles Waddell Chesnutt, of Cleveland, in Accepting the Spingarn Medal at Los Angeles."] 3 Jul. 1928. Unpublished manuscript. Charles W. Chesnutt Collection, Fisk University Library, Nashville, TN.

————. "Self-Made Men." 10 Mar. 1882, Unpublished Manuscript. Charles W. Chesnutt Collection, Fisk University Library, Nashville, TN.

————. "Some Requisites of a Law Reporter." *Proceedings of the Eighth and Ninth Annual Conventions of the Ohio Stenographers' Association.* Cleveland: F. W. Roberts, [1891]: 64–70.

————. "What Is a White Man?" *The Independent* 41 (30 May 1889): 5–6.

————. *The Wife of His Youth and Other Stories of the Color Line.* Boston: Houghton Mifflin, 1899.

Chesnutt, Helen. *Charles Waddell Chesnutt: Pioneer of the Color Line.* Chapel Hill: U of North Carolina P, 1952.

Cose, Ellis. *The Rage of a Privileged Class.* New York: Harper Collins, 1993.

Douglass, Frederick. *The Frederick Douglass Papers: Series One: Speeches, Debates, and Interviews.* Ed. John W. Blassingame and John R. McKivigan. New Haven: Yale UP, 1992.

————. *Narrative of the Life of Frederick Douglass, An American Slave.* 1845. New York: New American Library, 1968.

DuBois, W. E. B. *The Souls of Black Folk.* 1903. Greenwich, CT: Fawcett, 1961.

Dunbar, Paul Laurence. *Lyrics of Lowly Life.* 1896. New York: Carol, 1993.

Duncan, Charles. *The Absent Man: The Narrative Craft of Charles W. Chesnutt.* Athens: Ohio UP, 1998.

Ellison, Ralph. *Shadow and Act.* New York: Random House, 1964.

Ferguson, SallyAnn H. "Chesnutt's Genuine Blacks and Future Americans." *MELUS* 15 (1988): 109–19.

————. "Christian Violence and the Slave Narrative." *American Literature* 68 (1996): 297–320.

————. "Rena Walden: Chesnutt's Failed 'Future American.'" *Southern Literary Journal* 15 (1982): 74–82.

Gates, Henry Louis, Jr. *The Signifying Monkey: A Theory of African American Literary Criticism.* New York: Oxford UP, 1988.

Gillman, Susan. "Micheaux's Chesnutt." *PMLA Journal* 114 (1999): 1080–88.

Keller, Frances Richardson. *An American Crusade: The Life of Charles Waddell Chesnutt.* Provo, UT: Brigham Young UP, 1978.

Lamar, Jake. *The Last Integrationist.* New York: Crown, 1993.

Logan, Rayford W. *The Betrayal of the Negro, from Rutherford B. Hayes to Woodrow Wilson*. New York: Macmillan, 1965.

McElrath, Joseph R., Jr. Ed. *Critical Essays on Charles W. Chesnutt*. New York: G. K. Hall, 1999.

Morrison, Toni. *Playing in the Dark. Whiteness and the Literary Imagination*. Cambridge: Harvard UP, 1992.

Patterson, Orlando. *The Ordeal of Integration: Progress and Resentment in America's "Racial" Crisis*. Washington: Civitas/Counterpoint, 1997.

Render, Sylvia Lyons. *The Short Fiction of Charles W. Chesnutt*. Washington, D.C.: Howard UP, 1974. (Revised 1981).

Socken, June. "Charles Waddell Chesnutt and the Solution to the Race Problem." *Negro American Literature Forum* 3 (1969): 52–56.

Thrasher, Max Bennett. "Mr. Chesnutt at Work: A Talk with an Author on His Methods." *Boston Evening Transcript* September 4, 1901, p. 3.

Watts, Jerry Gafio. *Heroism and the Black Intellectual: Ralph Ellison, Politics, and Afro-American Intellectual Life*. Chapel Hill: U of North Carolina P, 1994.

Webb, Bernice Larson. "Picking at 'The Goophered Grapevine.'" *Kentucky Folklore Record* 25 (1979): 64–67.

"Whatever Happened to Integration?" *The Nation.* 267 (14 Dec. 1998). 11–42.

Notes to Chesnutt's Essays

Adams, Myron. *The History of Atlanta University*. Atlanta: Atlanta UP, 1930.

The Annotated Code of the General Statute Laws of the State of Mississippi. Prepared by R. H. Thompson et al. Nashville, TN: Marshall and Bruce, 1892.

Bacote, Clarence A. *The Story of Atlanta University: A Century of Service, 1865–1965*. Atlanta: Atlanta UP, 1969.

Bardolph, Richard. Ed. *The Civil Rights Record: Black Americans and the Law, 1849–1970*.

Benton, Elbert Jay. *The Movement for Peace Without a Victory During the Civil War*. Cleveland: Western Reserve Historical Society, 1918.

Berger, Morroe. *Equality by Statute: The Revolution in Civil Rights*. Garden City, NY: Doubleday & Company, Inc., 1967.

Cable, George Washington. "What Shall the Negro Do?" *The Forum* 5 (August 1888): 627–39.

Campbell, J. A. P. Ed. *The Revised Code of the Statute Laws of the State of Mississippi*. Jackson: J. L. Power, 1880.

Cleveland Gazette. "Barnwell and Jessup Deaths." January 4, 1890, p. 2.

——. "The Colored Race." June 26, 1886, p. 1.

———. "Front Page." February 22, 1890.

———. "Southern Outrages." January 25, 1890.

Dann, Martin E. Ed. *The Black Press 1827–1890: The Quest for National Identity.* New York: G. P. Putnam's Sons, 1971.

Davis, Harold E. *Henry Grady's New South: Atlanta, a Brave and Beautiful City.* Tuscaloosa: Alabama UP, 1990.

Davis, Rebecca Harding. "A Word to Colored People." *The Independent.* September 12, 1889, p. 1.

DeQuincey, Thomas. "The Revolt of the Tartars; or Flight of the Kalmuck Khan and His People from the Russian Territories to the Frontiers of China." *Blackwood's Edinburgh Magazine* 42 (July 1837): 89–137.

Dictionary of American History, Vols. *1, 2, & 4.* New York: Charles Scribners' Sons, 1976.

DuBois, W. E. B. *Black Reconstruction in America, 1860–1880.* 1935. New York: Atheneum, 1992.

Edmonds, Helen G. *The Negro and Fusion Politics in North Carolina 1894–1901.* Chapel Hill: U of North Carolina P, 1951.

Franklin, John Hope. *From Slavery to Freedom: A History of Negro Americans.* 5th ed. New York: Knopf, 1980.

Gerber, David A. *Black Ohio and the Color Line 1860–1915.* Urbana: U of Illinois P, 1976.

Hamilton, Kenneth Marvin. *Black Towns and Profit: Promotion and Development in the Trans-Appalachian West, 1877–1915.* Urbana: U of Illinois P, 1991.

Harlan, Louis R. *Booker T. Washington: The Wizard of Tuskegee, 1901–1915.* New York: Oxford UP, 1983.

———. Ed. *Booker T. Washington Papers: Volume 4, 1895–98.* Urbana: U of Illinois P, 1975.

Harris, Joel Chandler. *Uncle Remus: His Songs and His Sayings.* New York: D. Appleton and Company, 1880.

Haskins, James. *Pinckney Benton Stewart Pinchback.* New York: Macmillan Publishing Co., Inc., 1973.

Hickey, D. J. and J. E. Doherty. *A Dictionary of Irish History Since 1800.* Totowa, NJ: Barnes & Noble Books, 1980.

Hicks, John D. *The Populist Revolt: A History of the Farmers' Alliance and the People's Party.* Lincoln, Nebraska: U of Nebraska P, 1961.

Howell, Andrew, Compiler. *The General Statutes of the State of Michigan in Force: Including the Acts of the Extra Session of 1882 with Notes and Digests of the Decision of the Supreme Court Relating Thereto.* Vol. 2. Chicago: Callaghan & Company, 1882.

Howells, William Dean. "Mr. Charles W. Chesnutt's Stories." *Atlantic Monthly* 85 (May 1900): 699–701.

Kusmer, Kenneth L. *A Ghetto Takes Shape: Black Cleveland, 1870–1930.* Urbana: U of Illinois P, 1976.

Laband, David N. and Deborah Hendry Heinbunch. *The History, Economics and Politics of Sunday-Closing Laws*. Lexington, MA: Lexington Books, 1987.

Lewis, David Levering. *W. E. B. Du Bois: Biography of a Race, 1868–1919*. New York: Henry Holt and Company, 1993.

Lexicon Webster's Dictionary of the English Language. New York: Lexicon Publications, Inc., 1989.

McEnery, Samuel D. *Race Problem in the South*. The Independent 55 (February 1903): 424–30.

McKay, Claude. *Home to Harlem*. New York: Harper & Brothers, 1928.

Meier, August. "The Negro and the Democratic Party, 1875–1915." *Phylon* 17 (1956): 173–191.

———. *Negro Thought in America 1880–1915: Racial Ideologies in the Age of Booker T. Washington*. 1963. Ann Arbor: U of Michigan P, 1970.

Mitchell, John R. "Another Decision." *Richmond* [Virginia] *Planet*, May 2, 1903, p. 4.

Nixon, Raymond B. *Henry W. Grady: Spokesman of the New South*. New York: Knopf, 1943.

Olivier, Sydney H. "White Man's Burden." *International Quarterly* 11 (April 1905): 2–23.

Quillin, Frank U. *The Color Line in Ohio: A History of Race Prejudice in a Typical Northern State*. Ann Arbor: George Wahr, 1913.

Reports of Cases Argued and Determined in the Supreme Court of South Carolina . . . Book 8, Containing a Verbatim Reprint of Vols. 1 & 2, Bailey's Law Reports. St. Paul: West, 1920.

Reports of Cases Argued and Determined in The Supreme Court of South Carolina . . . Book 9, Containing a Verbatim Reprint of Vols. 1 & 2, Hill's Law Reports. St. Paul: West, 1919.

Reuter, Edward Byron. *Race Mixture: Studies in Intermarriage and Miscegenation*. New York: McGraw-Hill Book Company, 1931.

The Revised Code of the Statute Laws of the State of Mississippi: Reported to and Amended and Adopted by the Legislature at Its Biennial Session, in 1880, With References to Decisions of the High Court of Errors and Appeals, and of the Supreme Court, Applicable to the Statutes. Prepared by J. A. P. Campbell. Jackson: J. L. Power, 1880.

The Revised Statutes of the State of Missouri: Revised and Digested by the Eighteenth General Assembly during the Sessions of 1854 and 1855: to Which Are Prefixed the Constitution of the United States and of the State of Missouri: with an Appendix, Including Certain Local Acts of This State, and Laws of Congress, and Form Book. Vol. 2. [Editor unlisted, although Charles H. Hardin was the Commissioner]. Jefferson City: James Lusk, State Printer, 1856.

Ripley, William Z. *The Races of Europe: A Sociological Study*. New York: D. Appleton and Company, 1899.

Selby, John. *Beyond Civil Rights*. Cleveland: The World Publishing Company, 1966.

"Studies in the South." *Atlantic Monthly* 49 (February 1882): 191–92.

Turner, Arlin. Ed. *The Negro Question: A Selection of Writings on Civil Rights in the South by George Washington Cable*. Garden City, NY: Doubleday & Company, Inc., 1958.

Voorhies, Albert. Ed. *The Revised Statute Laws of the State of Louisiana: from the Organization of the Territory to the Year 1869, Inclusive, with the Amendments Thereto, Enacted at the Sessions of the Legislature, up to and Including the Session of 1876, and References of the Civil Code of Practice, and the Decisions of the Supreme Court of the State of Louisiana*. New Orleans: B. Bloomfield & Company, 1876.

Woodward, C. Vann. *Origins of the New South*. Baton Rouge: Louisiana UP, 1951.

For Further Reading

Andrews, William L. *The Literary Career of Charles W. Chesnutt.* Baton Rouge: Louisiana State UP, 1980.

Babb, Valerie M. "Subversion and Repatriation in *The Conjure Woman.*" *The Southern Quarterly* 25 (1987): 66–75.

Bone, Robert A. *Down Home: A History of Afro-American Short Fiction from Its Beginnings to the End of the Harlem Renaissance.* New York: G. P. Putnam's Sons, 1975.

Chesnutt, Charles W. *To Be an Author: Letters of Charles W. Chesnutt, 1889–1905.* Ed. Joseph R. McElrath, Jr. Princeton: Princeton UP, 1997.

———. *Mandy Oxendine.* Ed. Charles Hackenberry. Urbana: U of Illinois P, 1997.

———. *Paul Marchand F. M. C.* Ed. Dean McWilliams. Princeton: Princeton UP, 1999.

———. *The Quarry.* Ed. Dean McWilliams. Princeton: Princeton UP, 1999.

Dixon, Melvin. "The Teller as Folk Trickster in Chesnutt's *The Conjure Woman.*" *CLA Journal* 18 (1974): 186–97.

Flusche, Michael. "On the Color Line: Charles Waddell Chesnutt." *North Carolina Historical Review* 53 (1976): 1–21.

Heermance, J. Noel. *Charles W. Chesnutt: America's First Great Black Novelist.* Hamden, CT: Archon Books, 1974.

Howells, William Dean. "Mr. Charles W. Chesnutt's Stories." *Atlantic Monthly* 85 (1900): 699–701.

———. "Psychological Counter-Current in Recent Fiction." *North American Review* 173 (1901): 872–88.

Price, Kenneth M. "Charles Chesnutt, the *Atlantic Monthly,* and the Intersection of African-American Fiction and Elite Culture." *Periodical Literature in Nineteenth-Century America.* Ed. Kenneth M. Price and Susan Belasco. Charlottesville: UP of Virginia, 1995.

Werner, Craig. "The Framing of Charles W. Chesnutt: Practical Deconstruction in Afro-American Tradition." Ed. Jefferson Humphries. *Southern Literature and Literary Theory*. Athens: U of Georgia P, 1990.

Wideman, John Edgar. "Charles Chesnutt and the WPA Narratives: The Oral and Literate Roots of Afro-American Literature." *The Slave's Narrative*. Ed. Charles T. Davis and Henry Louis Gates, Jr. New York: Oxford UP, 1985.

Recommended Sites
on the Internet

Documenting the American South. Online. Updated 21 September 1998. UNC–Chapel Hill, NC, Libraries. <<u>http://metalab.unc.edu/docsouth/ chesnuttconjure/conjure.html</u>> Electronic texts for *The Conjure Woman, The Wife of His Youth, The House Behind the Cedars,* and other works. 24 August 2000.

Electronic Text Center. Online. Updated 14 September 2000. U of Virginia. <<u>http://etext.lib.virginia.edu/modeng/modengC.browse.html</u>> Electronic texts for nine short stories, including "The Partners" and "The Bouquet," the novel *The House Behind the Cedars,* and the essay "The Free Colored People of North Carolina." 24 August 2000.

Credits

Text

Charles W. Chesnutt, "The Negro in Cleveland." *The Clevelander,* 5, November 1930, pages 3–4, 24, 26–27. Reprinted by permission of the Greater Cleveland Chamber of Commerce.

The Journals of Charles W. Chesnutt, ed. Richard C. Brodhead. Copyright 1993, Duke University Press. All rights reserved. Reprinted with permission.

Richard E. Baldwin, "The Art of the Conjure Woman," *American Literature* 43:3 (November 1971), pp. 385–398. Copyright 1971, Duke University Press. All rights reserved. Reprinted with permission.

David Britt, "Chesnutt's Conjure Tales: What You See is What You Get." *CLA Journal* 15 (1972): 269–283. Reprinted by permission of the College Language Association.

Hiram Haydn, "Charles W. Chesnutt" Reprinted from *The American Scholar,* Volume 42, Number 1, Winter 1972/73. Copyright © 1973 by the Phi Beta Kappa Society.

From *The Southern Literary Journal.* Volume 7 (1974). Copyright © 1974 by the University of North Carolina Department of English. Used by permission of the publisher.

Sylvia Lyons Render, "Introduction" from *The Short Fiction of Charles W. Chesnutt.* Copyright © 1974 by Sylvia Lyons Render. Reprinted with the permission of The Permissions Company, P.O. Box 243, High Bridge, NJ 08829, USA on behalf of Howard University Press.

Robert Hemenway, "'Baxter's Procrustes': Irony and Protest." *CLA Journal* 18 (1974): 172–85. Reprinted by permission of The College Language Association.

Frances Richardson Keller, "A Literary Love: Rena and the House Behind the Cedars" in *An American Crusade: The Life of Charles Waddell Chesnutt.*

459

Photos